Latin America
A Naval History
1810–1987

LATIN AMERICA

A Naval History
1810–1987

by
Robert L. Scheina

NAVAL INSTITUTE PRESS
Annapolis, Maryland

Copyright © 1987
by the U.S. Naval Institute
Annapolis, Maryland

All rights reserved. No part of this book may be reproduced without written permission from the publisher.

Library of Congress Cataloging in Publication Data

Scheina, Robert L.
  Latin America : a naval history, 1810–1987.

  Bibliography: p.
  Includes index.
  1. Latin America—History, Naval.   I. Title.
  F1410.S37   1988   980   87-7960
  ISBN 0-87021-295-8

Printed in the United States of America

To Carlos Hernández-González of Venezuela,
David Mahan of Chile,
Jürg Meister of Australia,
Eduardo Italo Pesce of Brazil,
Antonine Tibesar of the United States, and
Carlos E. Zartmann of Argentina,
six scholars who provided bountiful help
even when the author's interpretations
differed from their own

Table of Contents

Maps and Drawings	ix
Preface	xi
1. The Wars of Independence, 1810–24	1
2. Defining the New Nations	9
3. The Evolution of Two Major Latin American Navies	42
4. Political Intervention During the Era of Gun and Longboat	53
5. The Dreadnought Race	80
6. World War I	88
7. Mutinies	105
8. Riverine Wars in the Twentieth Century	117
9. The Era of Foreign Naval Missions	127
10. World War II	143
11. The Rise and Fall of U.S. Influence	171
12. Marine Corps and Naval Aviation	188

viii TABLE OF CONTENTS

13. POLITICAL INTERVENTION DURING THE ERA OF MARINE CORPS
    AND NAVAL AVIATION   202
14. THE MALVINAS CRISIS, MARCH–APRIL 1982   234
15. THE MALVINAS WAR, MAY–JUNE 1982   255

APPENDICES
1. Latin American Naval Ranks   293
2. Naval Participation in Political Revolts   294
3. Ships in the Argentine and Chilean Navies,
   1890–1902   297
4. The Chilean Congress's Request for Naval
   Intervention and Reply   300
5. Manifestoes Issued by Rebellious Brazilian Naval
   Leaders, 1893–94   302
6. Naval Activities in Latin America by Extraregional
   Nations   304
7. Latin American Dreadnoughts   321
8. Naval Assistance to Latin American Nations,
   1810–1987   323
9. Declarations of War by Latin American Nations
   During World War II   326
10. Brazilian Warships Under Construction in 1939   327
11. U.S. Warships Transferred to Brazil in World War II   328
12. Italian Tankers Commandeered by México,
    8 April 1941   330
13. Attack Aircraft Employed on Argentine Aircraft
    Carriers   331
14. The Service Lives of the Carriers *Independencia*,
    25 de Mayo, and *Minas Gerais*   332
15. Information Received by Argentine Naval
    Intelligence During the Malvinas War   333
16. Distances in Nautical Miles Between Strategic Sites
    During the Malvinas War   338
17. The Malvinas Naval Support Force   339
18. Operational Statistics for Argentine Naval Aviation
    During the Malvinas War   340
19. Weather Conditions in the South Atlantic, 1 May–
    14 June 1982   342

SOURCE NOTES   343
BIBLIOGRAPHY   387
INDEX   407

Maps and Drawings

Major Territorial Disputes Since Independence	10
Theater of Operations During the War of the Triple Alliance, 1865–70	21
Riverine Operations During the War of the Triple Alliance, 1865–70	24
Federico Blume's *Toro Submarino*	37
Patagonia and Territories West of the Andes	44
Argentine Theater of Naval Operations, 1890 and 1893	58
Rosario, Argentina: Battle Between the *Los Andes* and the *Independencia*, 29 September 1893	60
Chilean Theater of Naval Operations, 1891	63
Torpedoing of the *Blanco Encalada*, 22 April 1891	65
Brazilian Theater of Naval Operations, 1893–94	70
Torpedoing of the *Aquidabã*, 16 April 1894	75
South Atlantic Maritime Patrol Zone, July 1917	93
Brazilian Theater of Naval Operations, 1918	96
Cuban Navy Patrol Areas	99
The Acre Dispute Between Bolivia and Brazil, 1899–1903	120

The Leticia Dispute Between Colombia and Perú, 1932–35	123
The Chaco Dispute Between Bolivia and Paraguay, 1932–35	125
Western Hemisphere Neutrality Zone, 1939–41	149
The *Uruguay* Intercepts the *Admiral Graf Spee* on the Río de la Plata, 13 December 1939	154
Brazilian Theater of Operations, World War II	156
Brazilian Convoy System, World War II	158
Cuban Missile Crisis Quarantine	181
The Beagle Channel Dispute	186
Argentine Theater of Naval Operations, 1955	214
Venezuelan Theater of Naval Operations, 1958	219
Puerto Cabello, Venezuela	228
Puerto Cabello Naval Base	230
The Argentine Coast and the South Atlantic	237
Argentine Landing at Port Stanley (Puerto Argentino), 1 April 1982	240
Disposition of the Argentine Navy, April 1982	246
The Malvinas Islands (Falklands)	260
The Super Etendard Attack on the *Sheffield*, 4 May 1982	267
Argentine Supply Ships in the Malvinas	271
The Skyhawk Attack on San Carlos, 21 May 1982	275
The Super Etendard Attack on the *Atlantic Conveyor*, 25 May 1982	278
The Super Etendard Attack on the *Invincible*, 30 May 1982	281
Land-Based Exocet, June 1982	283
The Final Defense of Puerto Argentino, June 1982	286

Preface

A NAVY IS BUT ONE instrument of a nation's power, and its activities must be judged according to the resources it is allocated and the missions it is assigned. Tremendous disparity has always existed in the capabilities of Latin American navies. This should come as no surprise, given the vast differences in the wealth of the nations that own them. The navies of Argentina, Brazil, Chile, and Perú have regularly undertaken local bluewater operations, Venezuela's more recently. Others, such as the seagoing force of México, have traditionally been tied to their coasts, primarily providing logistical support for the army and aiding in economic development. The navies of Bolivia and Paraguay have served exclusively in a river environment, the Paraguayan seeing two major wars. And all Latin American navies, big and small, have functioned as coast guards.

Over the years, these navies have matured into forces worthy of the investments made in them by their nations. Some have evolved into respectable fighting forces, serious opponents to foreign and domestic rivals, or better still, valuable allies for a common defense. The aim of this book is to provide information on the major successes and failures of these navies during the past 175 years, taking into consideration their resources and assignments.

A common theme in Latin American naval history is intervention in national politics. The amount of documentation available on rebellions and coups varies greatly. Where the author had enough information to give an overview of some such event, the facts are presented in the text. Two chapters are devoted to the capacity of Latin American navies to intervene, two to the interventions themselves. Events about which the author was unable to uncover enough detail are summarized in appendix 2.

An increasing amount of detail is presented as the book progresses. Many fine works, principally in Portuguese and Spanish, have been written about Latin American navies in the nineteenth century. Today multi-volume histories are being written in Argentina, Brazil, Perú, and Chile, but with the exception of the last effort, it will probably be a decade or more before these works address the twentieth century. The author believes that he can best serve those interested in Latin American naval history by first presenting an overview of the nineteenth century and then focusing on the twentieth.

This is not a history of Latin American navies as seen through the eyes of English-speaking people. Therefore, the author has chosen to use geographical names as they commonly appear in Spanish. The use of Malvinas instead of Falklands is the most notable exception to what is common practice in English-language books.

Neither is this work a history of foreign naval activity in Latin America. The actions of extraregional navies are detailed in the text only when they directly influence a Latin American navy or a naval development within Latin America. Otherwise, those actions are briefly described in appendix 6 so that the reader may judge for himself the magnitude of their influence.

Many people have generously contributed to this work. Chapters were mailed to contributors and reviewers on four continents for over five years. Although the author is responsible for what appears, much of the credit belongs to those listed below.

Eduardo Luis Alimonda, captain in the Argentine navy, was a confidant during the author's trips to Argentina in 1982 and 1983. His frank insight and constructive criticism significantly improved the two chapters dealing with the Malvinas War.

Many suggestions made by A. D. Baker III, editor of the English edition of *Combat Fleets of the World*, were incorporated in the pages of this volume.

K. Jack Bauer, expert on the 1846–48 war between México and the United States and naval activity in Latin America, gave constructive criticism of a working draft of this book.

Enrique Cárdenes de la Peña, author of numerous books on the Mexican navy, reviewed sections dealing with that navy and made helpful comments.

José María Cohen, retired captain in the Argentine navy, reviewed and made significant improvements to the chapter on the rise and fall of U.S. influence.

Luis Francisco Chacón Peña, lieutenant in the Colombian navy, supplied documentation on Colombian naval history, in particular the operations of the *Almirante Padilla* off Korea in 1951 and 1952.

Ivan R. Dos Santos, student of naval history, provided materials related to the history of the Brazilian navy.

Adrian J. English, author of *Armed Forces of Latin America*, was a valuable source of information on the Chaco War.

Pedro Florido, retired Argentine navy commander and professor at the Argentine Naval War College, sent the author data concerning Argentine operations in the early part of World War II.

Ruben Franco, former commander in chief of the Argentine navy, graciously permitted access to key participants in the Malvinas War.

Arthur Saldanha da Gama, a retired vice admiral in the Brazilian navy and author of books on his country's navy in World Wars I and II, reviewed chapters dealing with these wars and made significant additions.

Michael Grubb, the artist who prepared each map, persevered through numerous changes inflicted upon him by the author.

Charles B. W. Haberlein, student of naval history, reviewed all the chapters in their early stage and made numerous suggestions. His extensive reading and original thinking in the field of naval affairs makes him one of those few individuals with the ability to define trends.

Paul Heine, student of world navies, made details available on Latin American dreadnoughts.

Carlos Hernández-González, a Venezuelan lawyer who specializes in international affairs, did most of the research for the account of the 1958 and 1962 Venezuelan revolutions.

The advice of Agnes Hoover, historian with the Naval History Division in Washington, D.C., and a knowledgeable professional, was frequently sought and freely given.

Alfredo Luzuriaga, captain in the Argentine navy, served as the author's confidant during a trip to Argentina in 1980. Señor Luzuriaga reviewed the two Malvinas chapters and provided corrections as well as insight into Argentine operations.

Barbara Lynch, reference librarian at the Navy Department library in Washington, D.C., helped the author track down many obscure books used in this work and gave freely of her encyclopedic knowledge of naval literature.

David Mahan, bibliographer of Chilean naval history, has aided the author since 1974 in finding materials related to this subject.

Significant contributions to all pre–World War II chapters of this work were made by Jürg Meister, dean of Latin American naval historians. In particular, the history of the War of the Triple Alliance and the War of the Pacific are based on his research.

Emilio Meneses C., associate professor of political science at the Catholic University of Chile, had valuable comments on late nineteenth- and twentieth-century events, particularly as they related to Chile.

Eduardo Italo Pesce, author of works related to the Brazilian navy, professor of English at Rio de Janeiro State University, and founding member of the Brazilian Center for Strategic Studies, supplied research that affected chapters on the Brazilian navy in the 1893 revolt, World Wars I and II, and the cold war era.

John C. Reilly, Jr., historian with the Naval History Division in Washington, D.C., proved to be a valuable source on the evolution of naval technology.

Julio Cesar Reyes Canal, retired captain in the Colombian navy, provided details concerning that navy's participation in the Korean War. Captain Reyes commanded the *Almirante Padilla* during the war.

Carlos D. Rojo, retired captain in the Argentine navy, came up with documentation on the history of that navy. In particular, the author is indebted to him for obtaining primary materials from Admiral Isaac F. Rojas, Argentine Navy (Ret.), who led the 1955 successful attempt to oust Juan Perón.

Hugo Santillán, lieutenant commander in the Argentine marine corps, was the author's confidant in trips to Argentina in 1980 and 1982. He illuminated the evolution and mission of the marine corps.

Philip Somervell, British historian of the Chilean navy, has contributed materials and reviewed those portions of the book dealing with the Chilean navy. The history of the British naval mission to Chile and of the Chilean navy in World War I are based on his work.

Andrew Smith, student of naval history, provided documentation and insight into the history of the Chilean dreadnought and the proposed acquisition of cruisers by Chile in the 1930s.

Antonine Tibesar, professor emeritus at Catholic University in Washington, D.C., had the patience to guide the author's dissertation, *Indigenous Latin American Sea Power, 1890–1974*, to completion. Many of the ideas and much of the research used in this book were based on efforts made by the author under his direction.

John Vajda, reference librarian at the Navy Department library, energetically assisted a researcher in need.

Luis Felipe Villena, retired commander in the Peruvian navy and executive secretary of the Instituto de Estudios Historico-Maritimos del Perú, came to the author's aid during a trip to Perú in 1976. Since then, he and the *instituto* have freely given of their resources to support the author's work.

Carlos E. Zartmann, retired captain in the Argentine navy and author and historian, reviewed all the chapters and generously supplied information from his vast fund of knowledge. The two chapters on the Malvinas War were markedly strengthened by his contributions.

And foremost is the author's wife, Linda, who sacrificed more than anyone to help create this book. She was the typist who labored through draft after draft after draft.

This book is but a beginning. The author would be pleased to hear from anyone who wishes to contribute toward the improvement of future editions.

Latin America
A Naval History
1810–1987

CHAPTER ONE

The Wars of Independence, 1810-24

FROM THE TIME of the discovery of Latin America by Europe, the creation and preservation of the nation dominated Latin American naval history. For centuries most of the colonies were islands, confined either by bodies of water or by almost insurmountable geographical barriers. The only practical avenues being the sea and the big river basins, the navies of colonial powers exercised substantial influence. As time passed, the fledgling nation states emulated their colonial predecessors and built navies of their own. In the early decades of the nineteenth century these young fleets struggled for their survival. And like the nations they defended, many were stillborn, later to be created again and sometimes again.

The Spanish South Atlantic
The Spanish-American wars of independence (1810–24) were fought between Spain and her former colonies. Spain, though she began the struggle with naval supremacy, was shackled by grave political and economic problems at home and overseas. In 1811 her navy was bankrupt, having fought first on one side then on the other during the Napoleonic wars (1800–1815). The navy boasted twenty-three ships of the line, eighteen frigates, nine corvettes, twenty-one brigantines, eleven schooners, and fourteen or fifteen minor craft, but of these only six or seven liners,

ten frigates, and a corresponding number of minor craft were fit for service, and the majority of them were in European waters.[1] Spain, which had battled with most major European powers and their corsairs and pirates throughout the New World for centuries, also boasted numerous fortified harbors, the principal ones being at San Juan de Ulúa off Veracruz, México; Habana, Cuba; San Lorenzo on the Chagres River in Panamá; Portobelo, Colombia; Cartagena de Indias, Colombia; Callao, Perú; Valdivia-Corral, Chile; San Felipe and Montevideo, Uruguay. But like the warships, the best men, guns, and powder from these harbors had been dissipated in the European wars.

Many of Spain's important American colonies declared their independence from the motherland while the Napoleonic wars raged in Europe. The revolutionary governments quickly opened their ports to international trade, which had previously been monopolized, at least in theory, by Spain. The first attempts of the newly created governments to establish navies were ineffective. In March 1811 the first Argentine squadron of three small ships, commanded by the Maltese Juan Bautista Azopardo, was destroyed by a small Spanish squadron under Captain Jacinto Romarate at San Nicolás on the Río de la Plata. Apparently in 1811, William Taber, a North American, submitted a plan to the Argentine Junta de Mayo to build a submarine that would attack royalist ships lying in Montevideo. The concept was approved, the building materials were gathered, and Taber was given permission to move them to a launching site. Few facts are known beyond this point. Taber died on 8 November 1813, and neither technical data nor plans for his submarine have been found.[2] In northern South America naval engagements took place on the Magdalena River; there, too, royalist forces won out in the end.

In 1814, with the defeat of Napoleon, Spain was able to direct her energies toward subjecting rebellious colonies. The state of the Spanish fleet was much the same as it had been in 1811.[3] Although the fleet did have many experienced officers who had been trained in the Spanish naval academies at Cádiz, Cartagena, and El Ferrol, almost two hundred of them were criollos—those of Spanish blood born in Latin America—some of whom chose to fight for the land of their birth. Native soil was not the only magnet drawing the loyalty of men toward Latin America. The end of the Napoleonic wars caused massive unemployment among European soldiers and sailors. Many chose to fight in Latin America, most on the side of the insurgents.[4]

The first significant patriotic squadron was created in Buenos Aires early in 1814. It was composed of one frigate, four corvettes, a brigantine, five schooners, and lesser craft, most of which were armed merchantmen.[5] The crews consisted of foreign merchant sailors, adventurers, and some locals. An Irish merchant captain, William "Guillermo" Brown, was put in command. After an initial failure the Argentine fleet captured the island of Martín García and bottled up a Spanish squadron on the River Uruguay. Between 14 and 17 May it defeated a Spanish force in the Battle of Montevideo.[6] Brown's victory permitted the blockade of the royalist stronghold of Montevideo, which had been unsuccessfully besieged by land for three years. Montevideo surrendered a month later, thus depriving Spain of her only South Atlantic base. With the threat of the Spanish navy gone, the various provinces vied for domination of South Atlantic waters. Local maritime activity turned to privateering and the creation of a fleet to operate in the Pacific, where the heart of Spanish power lay.

In 1815–16 an Argentine naval squadron of four ships commanded by Admiral Brown raided the Pacific coast. This ended in a temporary disaster for the admiral. His flagship, the *Santísima Trinidad*, was stranded while attacking Guayaquil in February 1816, and the Spanish took him prisoner. The admiral was set free when his brother Michael threatened to bombard the city. Brown returned to the Atlantic coast and was ultimately detained by the British, who claimed that his papers were not in order. When he finally returned to Buenos Aires he was court-martialed. Undaunted by this disaster, French-born Hipólito Bouchard circumnavigated the world in *La Argentina*, a frigate, attacking Spanish shipping in the Philippines and capturing Acapulco and Monterey among other places.[7]

The Caribbean

Throughout the early years of the independence struggle, the Spanish navy held dominion in the Caribbean, anchored by its strongly fortified harbors at Habana, Veracruz, Cartagena, and Puerto Cabello. On land the fortunes of war favored one side and then the other. At sea a royal squadron defeated a patriot fleet in the Bay of Lorondo on 25 March 1812 after two days of fighting. Between 1813 and 1815 a small rebel squadron operated from Margarita Island, but it did not pose a serious threat to Spanish control.

With the return of Fernando VII to the throne of Spain, halfhearted steps were taken to subjugate the rebellious colonies. A force of ten thousand veteran troops was made ready to sail from Spain, and plans were proposed to reconstruct the Spanish fleet. The latter, however, never materialized. Spain did not possess the funds to pay crews, let alone repair the ships and reequip the arsenals. Moreover, pretending to be a major world power, she had naval obligations to fulfill elsewhere.[8] In 1815 she did manage to send the ten-thousand-man army under Lieutenant General Pablo Morillo to the Costa Firme (Colombia and Venezuela) to begin the reconquest of lost colonies. Sixty transports were escorted by the seventy-four-gun ship of the line *San Pedro de Alcántara*, three frigates, and twenty lesser warships. Morillo's force recaptured Cartagena on 7 December 1815 and destroyed the rebel's maritime base at Margarita Island. In addition, twenty-five hundred Spanish troops landed at Veracruz, México. The intention was for these two forces to join hands, but they never did.[9]

In spite of the weaknesses of the Spanish navy, Spain held undisputed command of the sea in regions such as the Caribbean where adequate logistics could be provided to the fleet. Patriot ships ceased to work as a naval force and had to resort to commerce raiding. Simón Bolivar, the future liberator of northern South America, was driven from the continent, and by mid-1816 the revolution in the north seemed almost at an end.

On 9 February 1816 King Fernando VII, attempting to increase the maritime threat to the rebellious colonies, authorized the use of corsairs against the insurgents in the Americas. The next year Spain purchased eleven old warships from Russia out of desperation. On 27 February 1818 five seventy-four-gun ships of the line, three fifty-gun frigates, and three forty-gun frigates arrived in Spain in appalling condition. None served for more than a few years.[10]

Haití, France's most important colony in the New World, won her independence in 1804, well before any of her colonial Spanish neighbors. Civil wars ravaged the island throughout the early decades of independence. Inhabitants, most of them uneducated ex-slaves, were ill-prepared for self-government. The warring factions acquired merchant ships, primarily from Great Britain and the United States, and fitted them out as warships. In January 1812 the Haitian flagship *Heureuse Réunion*, commanded by Augustin Gaspard, encountered HMS *Southampton* (thirty-eight guns) off Miragoâne. A bloody battle ensued in which the Haitian warship lost over one hundred men before surrendering.

In late 1816 Spanish-American patriots renewed the naval war in the Caribbean with help from Haití. Bolivar, supported by a squadron of seven ships, slipped back to the mainland and sapped the enemy's strength in a series of battles, some of which he lost. On 7 August 1819 he triumphed in the Battle of Boyacá, the decisive victory for the independence movement in the north. Between 1816 and 1823 Admiral Luis Brión, Bolivar's principal naval lieutenant and commander of the patriot fleet, engaged Spanish ships off the Costa Firme and on the rivers. Once again, Margarita Island served as a base of operations for the rebels. General Morillo sent a second expedition composed of three corvettes, five brigantines, five schooners, and minor craft to retake the island, but this failed. At the end of 1819 Captain Antonio Díaz commanded a rebel naval force which, in support of Brigadier General José Antonio Páez, defeated a Spanish squadron on the Apure River. By the middle of 1821 the only Spanish enclaves remaining on the Caribbean coast of South America were

Cumaná, Puerto Cabello, and Cartagena. On 24 July 1823, a naval force commanded by Rear Admiral José Prudencio Padilla destroyed the Spanish squadron commanded by Captain Ángel Laborde in Lake Maracaibo. Finally, Puerto Cabello surrendered on 7 November 1823, ending the naval war in the Caribbean.

Off the gulf coast of México and northward to New Orleans, Mexican corsairs involved in the South American insurrections attacked Spanish shipping, but too frequently they paid little attention to the distinction between enemy and neutral ships. The Mexican patriots were not able to create a serious naval or privateering force before the issue of independence had been decided elsewhere.

The Pacific

As elsewhere, on the west coast of South America early attempts by patriots to create a navy failed. In 1813 Chilean patriots purchased the frigate *Perla* and the brigantine *Potrillo*, but loyalists bribed the crew of the former and both ships were taken by the Spaniards. General José de San Martín, an Argentine, believed that the Spanish had to be driven from their seat of power in Perú if independence were to be permanently won.[11] Three rebel attempts to fight all the way from Buenos Aires to Lima overland had ended in disaster, so he conceived the strategy of crossing into Chile and invading Perú from the sea. To that end he spent three years (1814–16) creating a small but efficient army at Mendoza, Argentina. After crossing the Andes Mountains, San Martín won the Battle of Chacabuco on 12 February 1817, then entered Santiago two days later. In the meantime Chilean patriots were organizing a naval force. In February they purchased the brigantine *Águila*, commanded by Raimundo Morris, an Irishman and former lieutenant of the British navy. The merchant ship *San Miguel* was soon captured and the *Perla* recaptured. Command of the new squadron was entrusted to Manuel Blanco Encalada.

Spain, from her strongly fortified harbor at Callao, projected power along the west coast of the Americas but continued to concentrate her fleet in the Caribbean, leaving the naval forces on the west coast to their own resources. The first Chilean squadron, composed of armed merchantmen, broke the Spanish blockade of Valparaíso on 26 April 1818. Meanwhile the Chileans were busy acquiring first-class warships from England and the United States. The arrival of the sixty-four-gun *San Martín*, forty-four-gun *Lautaro*, corvette *Chacabuco*, and smaller warships gave Chilean patriots naval superiority which they tenaciously held on to for the remainder of the war.

In 1818 Spain sent a force of two thousand men to reinforce the royalists at Talcahuano, Chile, and Lima, Perú. The eleven transports were escorted by the fifty-gun frigate *María Isabel*, one of the ships acquired from

Russia. During the passage the chief of the expedition and some of the officers in the transport *Trinidad* were killed by a mutinous crew, and the ship sailed to Buenos Aires under the command of Lieutenant Dionisio Capaz. The Argentines learned full details of the expedition from the mutineers and sent word to Chile, whose foreign-built squadron, made up of the *San Martín*, *Lautaro*, and *Chacabuco*, intercepted the enemy at Talcahuano. After a brief fight the *María Isabel* surrendered. Only three of the transports reached safety at Callao, Perú; the remainder were all captured.[12]

The following year, 1819, Spain again tried to send troops to Perú. The expedition, which left Cádiz in May, was composed of the seventy-four-gun *San Telmo*, seventy-four-gun *Alejandro I* (acquired from Russia), the frigate *Prueba*, and various merchant ships. The *Alejandro I* was taking on so much water that she had to turn back after reaching the equator. The *San Telmo* was lost in a storm in Antarctic waters on 2 September. The frigate *Prueba*, with some surviving transports, arrived off Callao only to find it blockaded by a Chilean squadron. Finally the shattered squadron found safe haven to the north at Paita, Perú.

Lord Cochrane, the British officer who had distinguished himself as a frigate captain during the Napoleonic wars, now took command of the Chilean fleet.[13] His first expedition against Callao did not accomplish anything significant and he returned to Valparaíso. In his second expedition he reconnoitered Callao, but then he turned south and on 3 February 1820 captured Valdivia.

Meanwhile, Spain made one last desperate attempt to reinforce her troops in the Americas. An army of twenty thousand men, to be escorted by four liners, three frigates, ten brigantines, plus numerous minor warships, was assembled. On 1 January 1820 the troops revolted and marched against the crown instead of for it. This ended any hope for the reconquest of the colonies.[14]

At Valparaíso the Argentine-Chilean patriots were now preparing an invasion force of their own known as the Liberation Expedition. On 20 August 1820 seventeen transports carrying 4,314 men were escorted north by the sixty-four-gun *San Martín*, fifty-gun *O'Higgins* (the captured *María Isabel*), forty-six-gun *Lautaro*, twenty-eight-gun *Independencia*, and fourteen smaller warships. The Spanish squadron was too weak to oppose the escorts. The patriot expedition first stopped at Pisco, Perú, where a smaller expedition was sent inland. The force then sailed north of Lima to blockade the capital's seaport, Callao. On 2 November 1820 Lord Cochrane captured the most powerful Spanish warship on the coast, the frigate *Esmeralda*, boldly taking her while she lay at anchor under the guns of Spanish forts at Callao.

San Martín and Cochrane quarreled frequently over strategy. San Martín, greatly outnumbered by royalist troops, refused to risk a general action in Perú, which the admiral advocated. In July 1821 the royalists evacuated Lima without a fight, and the port of Callao surrendered to the patriot force on 19 September 1821. The intensity of the quarreling between San Martín and Cochrane increased—the admiral's flamboyant character clashed with the general's austere one—and finally in October Cochrane quit the campaign. In May 1822 the remaining Spanish warships on the west coast surrendered.

By 1822 the Spanish navy had been reduced, more by accident and neglect than combat loss, to four liners (three of which were in need of repair), eight frigates, eleven brigantines, seven schooners, and thirty-five minor craft.[15] Yet the fighting was not over. The Spanish recaptured Callao in February 1824, forcing Bolivar, who had taken command of the revolutionary forces in Perú, to evacuate Lima. The Spanish, in turn, had to surrender Lima once again on 8 June 1824. The final call for royalist arms in South America came with Spain's defeat at the Battle of Ayacucho on 9 December 1824, although the end was not immediately perceived. Fighting continued both on land and at sea. Callao held out and surrendered on 22 January 1826, after a stubborn defense. The Peruvian admiral Martín Guise, commanding a fleet manned principally by English sailors, defeated a royalist fleet off Callao on 18 October 1825 in the last major naval action in the fight for South American independence.[16] Still, no formal peace treaty was signed. So for a few more years the new South American republics continued to issue letters of marque and harass Spanish ships while the Spanish fleet, in turn, periodically blockaded their ports. Bolivar observed in 1824 that privateers were South America's only offensive weapon against Spain.[17]

The Portuguese South Atlantic

In 1807 the Portuguese royal family fled the Napoleonic invasion of their country and went to Brazil, the colony that became the temporary seat of the Portuguese government. Accompanying the royal family was most of the small Portuguese navy and marine corps. Portugal, unlike Spain a longtime ally of Great Britain, had been able to maintain an uninterrupted sea connection with her South American colony, owing primarily to the protection of the British navy. Following the defeat of Napoleon, Dom João VI, king of Portugal and Brazil (which was elevated to the status of a kingdom in 1814), reluctantly sailed for Europe in April 1821, leaving his son, the prince regent, in charge. On 7 September 1822 Brazil declared her independence from Portugal, and the prince regent, Dom Pedro I, became emperor. On 21 March 1823 Lord Cochrane took command of the Brazilian navy. He immediately blockaded Portuguese ships at Bahia. On 2 July 1823 the Portuguese evacuated Bahia in some sixty transports convoyed by thirteen warships. Cochrane's two frigates were too weak to force a battle, but they did succeed in cutting out a number of transports and getting them to surrender. Guessing the convoy's destination, Cochrane sailed ahead and captured Maranhão. He permitted the garrison to embark for Portugal. When the convoy arrived at Maranhão it could not offload because Cochrane was there. Left with no option, it returned to Portugal, subject to harassment from Cochrane and the new Brazilian navy all the way across the Atlantic. In 1825 British mediation secured Portugal's recognition of Brazil as an independent kingdom. Gaining nationhood was far less traumatic for Brazil than for the former Spanish colonies.

Thus by the mid-1820s most of Latin America had won its independence, thanks partly to naval effort. Argentine independence, the result of the only rebellion in South America not temporarily crushed by Spain, was secured when Admiral Guillermo Brown's victories led to the capture of Montevideo. Independence would have been greatly jeopardized if General Pablo Morillo's expeditionary army, sent from Spain in 1815, had been able to land at Montevideo as originally planned. San Martín's final campaign in Chile would have been much hindered if the Chilean fleet had not destroyed the Spanish relief expedition in 1818. And control of the sea allowed the Liberation Expedition in Perú to employ hit-and-run tactics along the coast, which finally forced the numerically superior Spanish ground forces to abandon Callao and Lima. In Portuguese America, naval power prevented Portugal from sending troops to recapture Brazil after the almost bloodless rebellion there. The ease with which Brazilian independence was won gave that country an initial advantage during the coming decades in confrontations with her war-weary, Spanish-speaking neighbors. On the Spanish side, naval power preserved colonial rule in Cuba and Puerto Rico. This control was not lost until the end of the century, when the Spanish fleet was finally defeated by the U.S. Navy.

CHAPTER TWO

Defining the New Nations

DEFINING BOUNDARIES, preserving independence, and developing international economies were the issues dictating the activities of Latin American navies immediately followng independence. Colonial Latin America had been divided into five viceroyalties. Those of Spanish origin included a number of semiautonomous, administrative areas that were shuffled among the Spanish viceroyalties in an attempt to solve administrative problems. And Portugal and Spain won and lost territory from each other as various colonial disputes flared and subsided. Thus borders in colonial South America were ill-defined, and the primary question following independence was where to delineate them. Latin America, moreover, was not yet entirely safe from the clutches of Spain, which did not easily abandon the idea of reconquering her former colonies. They had to struggle to preserve their hard-won freedom. The small nations, particularly in the Caribbean, faced an added threat from filibusters—foreigners, mostly North Americans, who had grandiose designs for conquest and empire. Indeed, Latin American navies had their work cut out for them. And as if this were not enough, they often entered into conflict with major naval powers. The wars of independence had left most Latin American nations nearly bankrupt, and in an attempt to recover, they often made usurious agreements

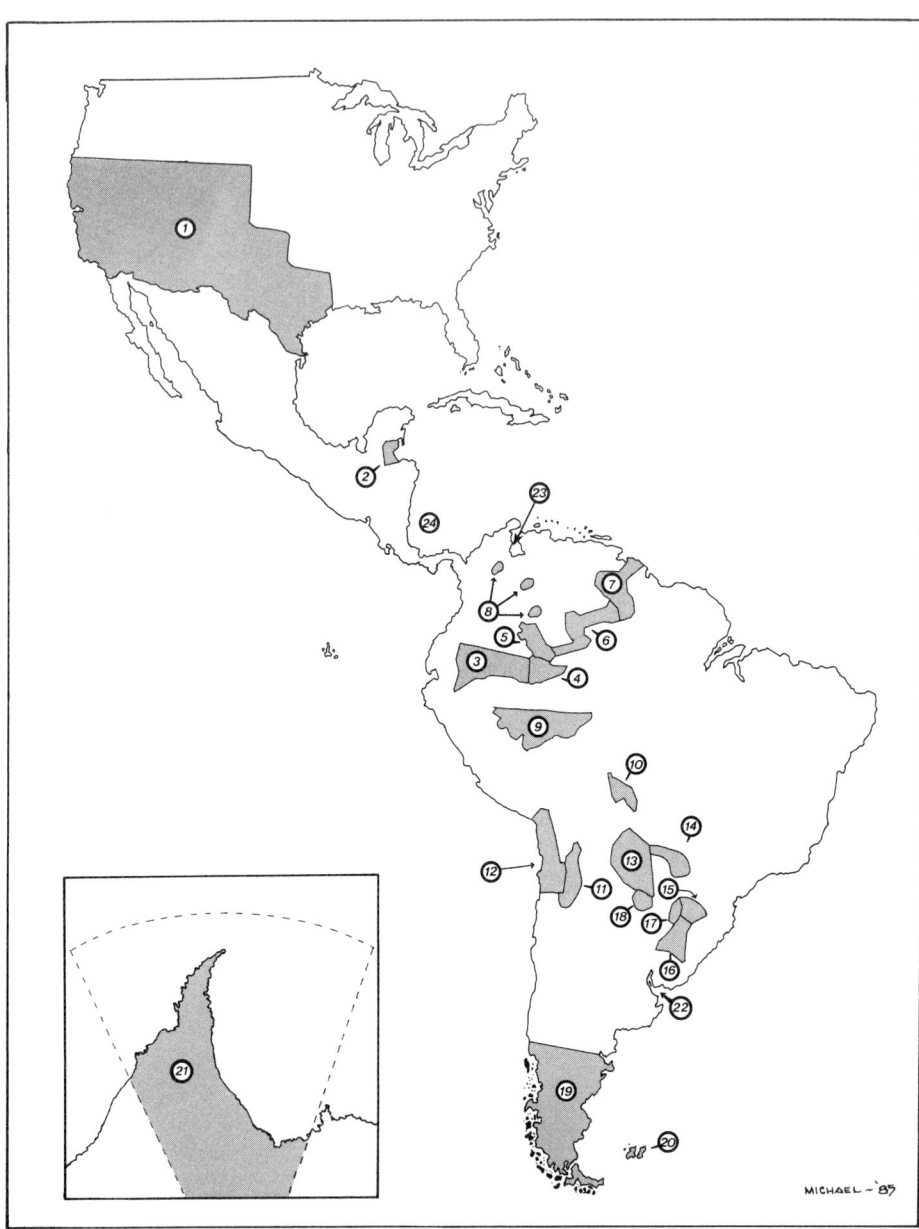

Major Territorial Disputes Since Independence

Key

1. Territories lost by México in wars with Texas and the United States, 1830s and 1840s
2. Dispute between Great Britain and Guatemala
3. Dispute among Colombia, Ecuador, and Perú

with European private concerns. The resulting trade frequently stirred the ire of naval powers, almost always to the detriment of a Latin American navy. A seemingly endless stream of wars created by poorly defined boundaries, the perceived threat of reconquest, and economic confrontation with naval giants helped forge the image within Latin America of the military as a nation builder.

As the nineteenth century wore on, technology had an increasing impact on Latin American navies. They searched for a weapon capable of deterring a vastly superior opponent. Although their primary rivals were their own neighbors, Latin American nations were particularly concerned about intervention by the world's naval powers. In 1822, even before independence had been assured, Simón Bolivar wrote, "When I look at Latin America I see her surrounded by the sea powers of Europe, . . . encircled by floating fortresses of foreigners who are therefore enemies."[1] In fact, throughout this era Latin American nations faced the warships of major powers in potential and actual combat many more times than they faced the fleets of their neighbors (see appendix 6).

Major powers used their fleets not only for outright intervention but also to play power politics in Latin America. Chile's relationship with the United States in the decades immediately following the War of the Pacific is an example. The United States feared that Chile might become a dominant Latin American nation and threaten U.S. ambitions, particularly in the isthmus of Panamá. But during the 1880s and into the 1890s the Chilean navy was superior to the U.S. fleet. In 1885 the Chilean armored

---

4. Dispute between Brazil and Ecuador
5. Dispute between Brazil and Colombia
6. Dispute between Brazil and Venezuela
7. Dispute between Great Britain and Venezuela
8. Dispute between Colombia and Venezuela
9–10. Dispute between Bolivia and Brazil
11. Dispute between Argentina and Chile
12. Territories won by Chile from Perú in the War of the Pacific
13. Dispute between Bolivia and Paraguay
14. Dispute between Brazil and Paraguay
15. Dispute between Argentina and Brazil
16. Dispute between Brazil and Uruguay
17–18. Dispute between Argentina and Paraguay
19. Dispute between Argentina and Chile
20. Dispute between Argentina and Great Britain
21. Dispute among numerous nations, including Argentina and Chile
22. Dispute between Argentina and Uruguay
23. Dispute between Colombia and Venezuela
24. Dispute between Colombia and Nicaragua

cruiser *Esmeralda* anchored in the presence of three U.S. warships on the Pacific coast of Panamá, apparently in an attempt to intimidate this weaker squadron. In another incident, the United States attempted to acquire Chimbote, Perú, as a naval base in order to block Chilean expansion. Evidence suggests that Chile agreed to support Colombia by staging a naval demonstration should the United States attempt to take control of the isthmus. By 1903, when the act did occur, Chile was no longer capable of intimidating the United States, but the latter nonetheless kept a watchful eye on Chile during the crisis.

Latin American navies, long aware of their vulnerability to powerful fleets, sought freedom from foreign military coercion by developing "forces in being." A force in being had to be able to inflict in its territorial waters unacceptable losses on a superior enemy. In an article in the *Revista de Marina* (1885), Chilean Captain Carlos Condell proposed that Valparaíso be fortified with floating batteries armed with Whitehead torpedoes in order to resist attack by European powers. During a procurement debate in the Chilean Chamber of Deputies in 1887, Enrique MacIver suggested the expenditure of one million dollars over six years to acquire two battleships and other warships. "We could not fight Brazil even with three *Esmeralda*s [the new Chilean armored cruiser]," he said, and in a war "with England, France, or Italy, our cruisers would be inadequate without one or two strong battleships."[2]

Mines and later automobile torpedoes became the hope of underdogs who wanted to reduce an opponent's naval superiority. Mines were cheap and technologically unsophisticated. Potentially, they could do great damage to an enemy. But mines lacked mobility and target discrimination; generally, the enemy had to come to you, and too frequently the victim proved to be a neutral. By the 1870s the automobile torpedo had been purchased by Latin American navies, but the problem remained of how to get close enough to attack the enemy. Even though the torpedo was self-propelled, it had a minimal range, and as the last decades of the century drew near the force in being that many Latin American navies sought seemed to have eluded their grasp.

North America

The large, independent nation of México now shared the North American continent with the United States and the British colony of Canada. They covered much vast, thinly populated territory, parts of which were claimed by several parties. México of 1821 was the largest, most populous, and richest nation to emerge from the Spanish empire. She stretched from the northern border of Panamá (then a province of Colombia) to the Oregon Territory and from the Pacific Ocean to the Sabine River, although her hold on these territories, centuries old, was admittedly tenuous.

Divergent political philosophies vied for ascendance following Mexico's independence. Liberals and conservatives, republicans and monarchists, federalists and centralists all competed, frequently outside the bounds of the law, for leadership of the nation. Such strife diverted Mexico's attention from outlying territories. Central America, which had joined the short-lived Mexican empire in 1821, broke away two years later. To add to her troubles, México was also subjected to a series of interventions, mainly from countries to whom she was in debt. In 1829 a Spanish expedition from Cuba seized Tampico in an effort to regain the mother country's lost colony, but it was forced to surrender to the Mexican army a month later. The Mexican navy played no role in this victory. Nine years later, a French expedition blockaded the Gulf coast of México and seized Veracruz on 16 April 1838. During the attack the French used shell guns for one of the first times in history, and the Mexican fleet was too weak to oppose such a formidable opponent. This conflict was known as the Pastry War because one of the allegedly offended parties was a baker. Almost a year later, when their claim had been satisfied, the French withdrew.

In addition to European powers, México struggled with rebellious provinces. The Yucatan, in particular, had preserved a high degree of independence for a number of decades due to its remoteness and international intrigues. It supported the federalist cause, as opposed to the centralist, during the frequent upheavals in México over the issue of whether power was to reside with the states or the national government.

México also fought with Texas, a province she had been unable to colonize effectively with her own people of Latin origin. By the 1830s U.S. citizens were freely passing across the international border with little regard for immigration regulations. Texas rebelled in late 1835 and seceded on 2 March 1836. War at sea was almost immediate. Texans on board two U.S. merchant ships, the *San Felipe* and steam tug *Laura*, captured a Mexican customs ship, the *Correo de Méjico*, at Brazoria on 1 September 1835. For three months the Mexican ship and crew were held by the U.S. district court in New Orleans. In late 1835 the Texas provisional congress issued six letters of marque and reprisal. The temporary detention of the *Correo de Méjico* plus the Mexican navy's search for privateers left the Texas coast unpatrolled. Men and munitions entered the territory from the United States. By late 1835 the Texans had driven the Mexican garrison across the Rio Grande, and in early 1836 a small Texan navy and privateers constantly harassed Santa Anna's supply lines. General Antonio López de Santa Anna, president of México, led an army north by land, captured the Alamo on 6 March 1836, but was defeated decisively at the Battle of San Jacinto on 21 April 1836. The victory at San Jacinto assured independence for Texas.

In early 1837 the Mexican navy blockaded the Texas coast with three brigs and two schooners. The USS *Natchez*, a sloop, was entering Matamoros, México, when the Mexican brig *General Urrea* was escorting in the captured U.S. merchantman *Louisiana*. An engagement took place between the *Natchez* and the *General Urrea*, *General Terán*, and *General Bravo*, supported by Mexican forts. The *Natchez* captured the *General Urrea* and recaptured two U.S. merchant ships, the *Louisiana* and the *Climax*. The *Geneal Urrea* was returned to México on orders from Washington.[3]

On 17 April 1837 the Mexican brigs *Vencedor del Alamo* and *Libertador*, under command of Commodore Francisco López, captured the Texan navy's *Independence* and renamed her the *Independencia*. In retaliation two warships, the *Brutus* and the *Invincible*, cruised the Mexican coast with Texan Secretary of the Navy S. Rhodes Fisher on board as a volunteer. In mid-1837 the force landed on Mujeres Island off the Yucatan and claimed it for Texas. The Texans then raided Mexico's stretch of the Gulf Coast, burning two villages. They tried to extract a twenty-five-thousand-dollar tribute from Campeche but were driven off after a three-hour gun duel. The Texan squadron seized one British and five Mexican merchant ships at sea. On 27 August it was caught by a Mexican squadron while entering Galveston harbor. The *Brutus* and the *Invincible* were driven ashore and later broken up in a storm. Thus the Texan navy lost its last ships. The loss was not crippling, however; México was too occupied at the time with the Pastry War and internal political problems to take advantage of her rebel territory's vulnerability.

Between mid-1839 and early 1840 Texas rebuilt its navy. In October, commanded by Commodore Edwin Moore, it blockaded the Mexican coast. On 20 November the Texas navy steamer *Zavala* towed the *Austin* and the *San Bernard* seventy-five miles up the Tabasco River, where in support of 150 rebellious Yucatecans they captured San Juan Bautista. Moore extracted a twenty-five-thousand-dollar ransom from the city. Following this expedition negotiations about the status of Texas and the boundary resumed between México and Texas, but nothing came of the talks.

Texas and the Yucatan then entered into an agreement whereby the former would provide a squadron to prevent the reconquest of the latter. The Yucatan would pay Texas eight thousand dollars a month for use of the ships. In early 1842 the Texan squadron patrolled the Mexican coast, concentrating off Veracruz where it blockaded the smaller Mexican navy and captured four merchant ships. In April the Yucatan came to terms with México and ended the subsidy. The Texan squadron returned home on 26 April 1842. During the cruise a serious mutiny took place on board the warship *San Antonio*, and the U.S. revenue cutter *Jackson* had to restore order. In September the *San Antonio* was lost with all hands in a storm. By now the fleet was in a sad state of repair.

México once more built her navy by capturing prizes and purchasing new warships in Great Britain and the United States. On 5 July 1842 Commander Tomás Marín of the Mexican navy led fifty-seven men in a surprise attack, capturing the Yucatecan brigantine *Yucateco*, which was laid up in ordinary. As the Mexican *Mexicano* she captured the Yucatecan brig *Iman* and the gunboats *Campecheano* and *Sisaleno* on 22 August. The Yucatan navy was thus eliminated.

Also at this time México purchased the large sidewheel steamers *Guadalupe* and *Moctezuma* from Great Britain. The former, built on speculation that the British navy would purchase her, was the first steam warship built of iron. She was divided into watertight compartments.

In April 1843 the *Austin* (eighteen guns) and the *Wharton* (fifteen guns) sailed under Commodore Moore for the Yucatan. Acting on intelligence, he hoped to catch the *Moctezuma* alone at sea but arrived too late. On 30 April the two Texan warships fought an indecisive battle with the Mexican squadron, composed of the *Guadalupe* (four guns), *Moctezuma* (eight guns), *Mexicano* (sixteen guns), *Águila* (seven guns), *Iman* (nine guns), *Campecheano* (three guns), and tug *Regenerador*. Yellow fever had ravaged the Mexican fleet, and in most of the ships there were barely enough men to get under way.[4]

In the decades following independence Mexico's relations with the United States deteriorated. The primary catalyst for this state of affairs was Texas. The United States declared war in June 1846 following a border clash. Early in the contest most of the small Mexican navy was either sold off or barricaded up the Alvarado River to prevent capture by the much more powerful U.S. Navy. This, plus the fact that the Mexicans did not encourage privateering, gave the U.S. Navy complete freedom to blockade ports and transport troops for amphibious assaults.[5]

While the U.S. Army won a series of battles in northern México, the U.S. Navy captured one port after another in the Gulf of México and in the Pacific. Despite both land and naval successes, the United States invaded Mexico's central valley in search of a decisive battle. The only practical route started at Veracruz, to which U.S. forces, between the ninth and twenty-ninth of March 1847, lay siege. Following the city's surrender, the U.S. Army pushed inland and the navy continued to blockade and capture ports. Some were held and others abandoned after the destruction of materials of potential value to the enemy. No decisive naval engagements took place during the war, but with the U.S. Navy's seizure of west coast population centers a de facto annexation of California took place. The navy's well-planned amphibious landing and capture of Veracruz enabled the U.S. Army to force its Mexican counterpart into a series of decisive battles in the central Mexican valley. México lost one-third of her national territory as a result.

The devastating war with the United States left México in turmoil. In

January 1858 she had two governments: that of President Félix Zuloaga, who presided in México City and was supported by the regular army, the church, and the Conservatives, and that of President Benito Juárez, whose weak grip on the outlying states was supported by a militia and remnants of a liberal congress. Juárez was chased across México to the northwest. At Manzanillo on the Pacific he embarked in the North American steamer *John L. Stephens*, which carried him to Panamá. His trek took him to Habana and on to New Orleans. He and a small following then sailed for Veracruz, where in May he set up his government. Veracruz held strategic significance. It was the beginning of the only practical land route between the Gulf of México and México City and, as the location of the country's most important customhouse, a prime source of revenue. The customhouse collected the revenues generated by the central valley of México, the nation's wealthiest region. To control the customhouse was to control a large part of Mexico's income.

Initially the Conservatives won most of the land battles, but they were unable to take Veracruz. In an attempt to blockade the port they assembled a small squadron in Habana. On 6 March 1860 the squadron, made up of the steamers *General Miramon* and *Marqués de la Habana* and commanded by Captain Tomás Marín, appeared off Veracruz. The senior U.S. naval officer present, Captain Joseph Jarvis, was under orders not to recognize any blockade of Mexican ports by the Conservative forces. Jarvis detailed an officer and about eighty men to each of the steamers *Indianola* and *Wave*, which were under charter to the Juárez government. As had been arranged, the officers took command of their respective steamers, which proceeded to tow the sloop *Saratoga* to where the Conservatives' steamers had anchored. A short action ensued and the *Saratoga* fired ninety shots. The *General Miramon*, trying to defend itself while escaping, went aground, and the *Marqués de la Habana* surrendered without a fight. The two prizes were sent to New Orleans along with Tomás Marín, at which point the U.S. district court declared the capture illegal and ordered the ships returned. The decision did not do much to help the Conservatives; they had been deprived of the services of the two warships and the munitions on board for some months at a critical time.[6]

In 1861 México was once again invaded by foreigners, this time the British, French, and Spanish, who were attempting to collect debts. On 8 April 1862, the British and Spanish withdrew, leaving behind the French, who were interested in regaining American territory. The United States, fighting her civil war, could not influence the situation. The French, soon drawn into a grueling land campaign, were forced to commit more and more troops. In 1862 an additional thirty thousand soldiers were sent. Although they captured most of Mexico's cities and drove many opposition leaders into the United States, they were unable to end the fighting. When her Civil War ended the United States demanded the withdrawal of French troops. They complied and left behind the French-supported regime of Emperor Maximilian, which collapsed.[7] México continued in a state of turmoil until 1877. Her lack of naval power had allowed the French to move men and supplies freely upon the seas.

South America's Atlantic Coast

A few in Spanish South America harbored a dream of a great nation confined only by the Isthmus of Panamá, Brazil, and the oceans, but the impracticality of this was brought home during the wars of independence when frequent quarrels broke out among the allied revolutionary leaders. Nor did postwar events rekindle the dream. In the aftermath of the independence struggles Argentina and Brazil fought to define their relationship. More often than not, control of Uruguay was the catalyst, as it had been in colonial times when Spain and Portugal fought several campaigns for the possession of this territory. Like most Latin American countries, Uruguay had numerous political factions that aligned themselves along two poles and warred. Inevitably one or the other side would seek help from Argentina or Brazil, and when in exile the "outs" would find a safe haven in one of those countries. Argentina and Brazil, each wanting to prevent the other from controlling the destiny of Uruguay, took advantage of these opportunities.

On 10 December 1825 Brazil declared war on Argentina, who was virtually without a navy. The Brazilian navy blockaded Buenos Aires with impunity and won a series of small encounters in 1826, but none were decisive. Argentina's attempts to expand her modest fleet were initially frustrated, and when eventually a purchase was made of a frigate and two corvettes from Chile, all veterans of the wars of independence, the ships failed to live up to expectations. The corvette *Independencia* (Chilean name retained) had to turn back to Valparaíso after four days at sea. She was in such poor condition that she sank in the harbor and was broken up. The frigate *Buenos Aires* (ex-Chilean *O'Higgins*, formerly of the Spanish and Russian navies) disappeared with all five hundred hands off Cape Horn. Only the corvette *Chacabuco* (ex-Chilean *Coquimbo*) made it to Buenos Aires. Argentina also sent envoys to Colombia in an attempt to forge a naval alliance. Although Simón Bolivar, the great patriarch, was receptive, the delegation failed to secure the services of the Colombian navy.[8]

Despite these setbacks Argentina, inspired by her naval hero Guillermo Brown, organized a squadron composed of four frigates, two corvettes, and lesser craft. It fought a series of battles against Brazil's navy and managed to wrest the initiative from Brazil, a success reinforced on 20 February 1827 when Argentina won the critical land battle of Ituzaingo. However, the Brazilian squadron held on tenaciously to a blockade of Buenos

Aires. By September 1827 the Brazilians had captured ten British merchant ships and one each from Germany, Holland, and the United States. This brought pressure from Great Britain to accept a mediated peace. It was agreed upon, and the resulting treaty stipulated that Uruguay be an independent nation.[9]

Between 1838 and 1853 the Río de la Plata area was once again embroiled in warfare, the principal catalysts being the warring factions in Argentina, the unresolved political status of Uruguay, and economic controversies, primarily between Argentina and foreign countries. It seemed that Argentina was at war with everyone—rebellious nationals, soldiers of fortune such as Giuseppe Garibaldi, and foreign fleets and troops. The Argentine navy was reduced to a small coastal force. Between March 1838 and October 1840 the French fleet blockaded the Río de la Plata and occupied the island of Martín García at the mouth of the Paraná River. Finally in 1840 France dispatched a six-thousand-man force that brought the Argentine ruler Manuel Rosas to terms.

An incident occurred on 28 September 1844 that revealed the frailty of the Argentine squadron. The one-gun Uruguayan schooner *Sancala*, allied with the Argentine blockading fleet, fired at a fishing craft close aboard the North American merchantman *Rosalba*. The U.S. ship was struck by musket fire, and as a result the commander of the U.S. squadron, Captain Philip F. Voorhees, seized the entire Argentine blockading squadron, a much weaker force than his own. Soon, however, he released the Argentine squadron.[10]

In September 1845 a combined English-French fleet blockaded Río de la Plata after Argentina attempted to control navigation on the Paraná River and again occupied Martín García. Actions took place between the British-French warships and Argentine shore batteries at Vuelta de Obligado on 21 November 1845 and near Quebrado in June 1846. In August 1847 Great Britain withdrew from the blockade, as did the French in June 1848. In exchange Argentina agreed to grant those countries free passage on the Paraná River.

Various factions in Argentina were still fighting to see whether Buenos Aires or the provinces would control the direction of the country. In 1853, when Justo José Urquiza defeated Manuel Rosas, the provinces won out. At this time Uruguay was finally recognized by Argentina and Brazil as an independent nation.

Paraguay remained aloof from regional wars during the decades immediately following independence, but during the 1850s this river-dominated nation became drawn into confrontations with her neighbors and with foreign naval powers. On 1 February 1855 the Paraguayan fort Itapiru fired on the stranded USS *Water Witch* while she was on a surveying expedition. Four years later the United States sent a squadron to the Río de la Plata and extracted an indemnity (see appendix 6). The Paraguayan navy was not directly involved in this affair.[11]

In early 1855 Brazil sent a squadron of twenty warships under Admiral Pedro Ferreira de Oliveira up the Paraguay River to intimidate the Paraguayans. The expedition was the result of Paraguay's tampering with Brazilian shipping on the river as well as her attack on the Brazilian frontier port at Salinas, above Fuerto Olimpio. The squadron stopped at Tres Bocas. The Brazilian admiral proceeded to Asunción on board the gunboat *Maracana* and negotiated and signed a treaty on 4 April 1855 that helped to resolve some of the disputes between the two nations.

The Paraguayan navy ran afoul of its British counterpart four years later. British policy was to forbid Paraguayan navigation outside the Paraná River until grievances against Paraguay had been settled, and in the enactment of this policy, HMS *Grappler* and *Buzzard* prevented the *Tacuari* from steaming from Buenos Aires to Montevideo on 29 November 1859. One shot was fired in the direction of the *Tacuari*, carrying the Paraguayan general (later president) Francisco S. López, to force her back to her moorings. The *Tacuari* was the only real warship of the Paraguayan navy. Apparently a sidewheeler, she had been built in 1854 by Blyth and Co., a British company, as a gunboat.[12] At issue was the arrest by Paraguay of Santiago Canstatt, a British and Uruguayan citizen, on 16 February 1859. After much diplomatic wrangling the British finally dropped most of their demands in 1862.[13]

The War of the Triple Alliance (1864–70) pitted Paraguay against Argentina, Brazil, and Uruguay. Although all fighting took place in the interior of the continent, navies played an important role because in most areas rivers were the only avenues of access.[14]

The Uruguayan government was being challenged by dissidents in exile who had the support of both Argentina and Brazil. In early June 1863 Uruguay captured the Argentine steamer *Salto*, which was carrying weapons. The crew and ship were released, but the suspected contraband was held at Montevideo. Uruguay asked the Argentine government to claim the property and prove that it was not intended for Uruguayan rebels. In response an Argentine warship seized the Uruguayan warship *General Artigas* and blockaded the mouth of the Uruguay River, an action allowing the dissidents to land troops and ammunition unmolested by the Uruguayan navy. Uruguay, whose relations with both Argentina and Brazil were strained, sought the aid of Paraguay's large military force as a counterbalance.

The Brazilians tried to redress grievances with Uruguay through diplomacy, but this failed. In 1864 a Brazilian army invaded Uruguay. The Uruguayan army retired and the Brazilians halted, hoping that their enemy now appreciated this display of resolve. They also sent three warships under Admiral Joaquim Tamandaré to blockade Montevideo. While ascending the Paraná River, the squadron met the Uruguayan warship *Villa del Salto*. A fight ensued. The warship was forced to seek refuge in Argentine waters, and later when the Uruguayans tried to run past the Brazilian ships she was run ashore and burned. This led to all-out war. The Brazilians captured the Uruguay River port of Paysandú in a combined land and amphibious assault on 2 January 1865. A small Brazilian naval brigade was landed from the fleet. The Brazilian squadron steamed down the river and landed the sick and wounded at Buenos Aires, then sailed to attack Montevideo.

Next Uruguay invaded the Brazilian province of Rio Grande do Sul, claimed by Paraguay, in hopes of drawing the support of that nation in war. Paraguay declined, and the Uruguayans were soon forced to retreat. In February 1865 Montevideo fell to the Uruguayan dissidents and their Brazilian allies. Before going into exile, the embittered Uruguayan government denounced Paraguay's lack of timely support.

Since independence Paraguay had been ruled by two successive long-lived dictators, Rodriguez de Francia (1811–41) and Carlos López (1841–62). Her third dictator, President Francisco S. López, built the largest army in South America and purchased a limited amount of the best European military hardware money could buy. Paraguay also had a naval squadron built around the steamer *Tacuari*. Too late to be of help to Uruguay, this warship captured the Brazilian mail steamer *Marqués de Olinda* on 11 December 1864 after she had sailed from Asunción and took her into the Paraguayan navy. There was no declaration of war; however, a Paraguayan diplomatic note formulated on 30 August 1864 contained a veiled threat of warlike actions if Brazil continued its military and diplomatic actions against Uruguay. In December 1864 a Paraguayan force invaded Brazil's Matto Grosso to the north. On 6 January 1865 the Paraguayans captured the Brazilian gunboat *Anjambahy* and the Argentine merchant steamer *Jacabina* on the San Lorenzo River. A Paraguayan riverine expedition successfully pushed its way up the Paraguay River, but Brazil had no regular forces in the region to defeat. The area was so isolated that it took three months for news of the invasion to reach the Brazilian capital.

Both Brazil and Paraguay sought permission to send their armies across the Argentine province of Misiones, which separated the two warring countries. Argentina refused both requests but stated that the Paraná and Uruguay rivers were open to both parties. With war threatening, the two warships *25 de Mayo* and *Gualeguay*, which constituted just about all of Argentine's navy at that time, were sent to Corrientes, the river port capital of the province by the same name. On 13 April 1865 a Paraguayan squadron of five warships attacked and took Corrientes and the two Argentine

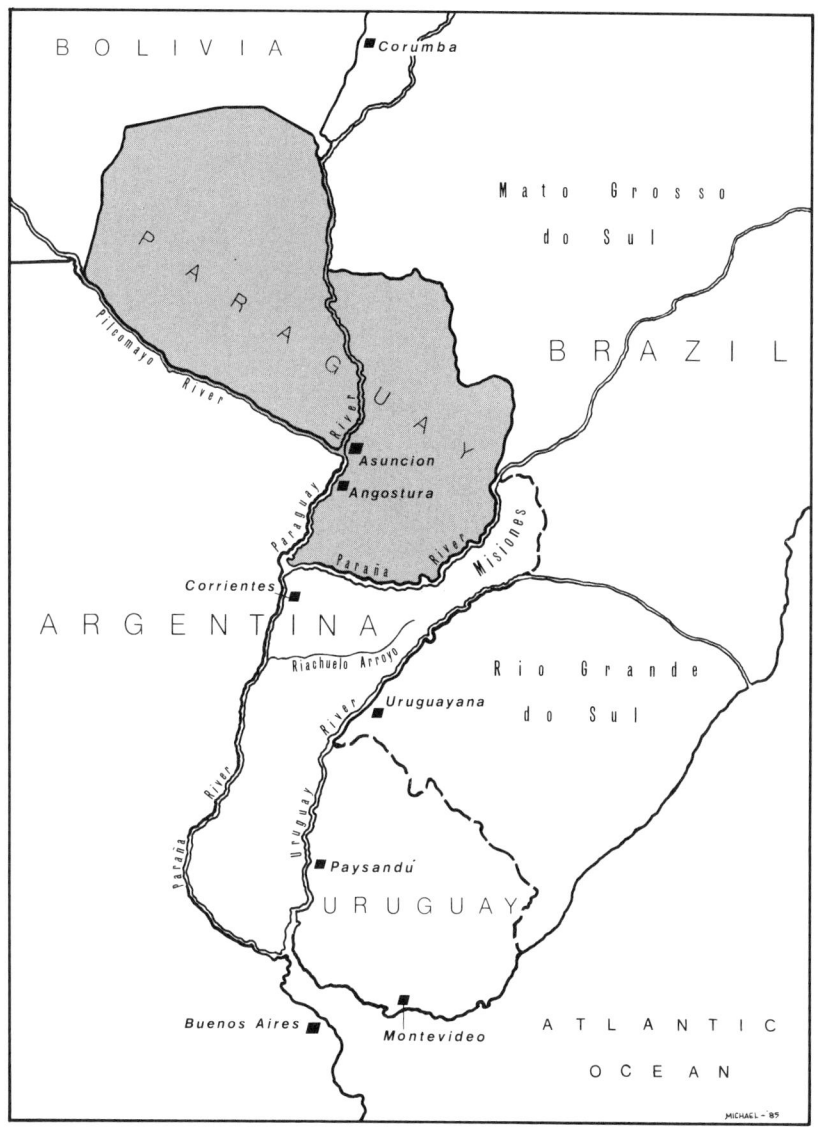

Theater of Operations During the War of the Triple Alliance, 1865–70

warships, one of which was then undergoing repairs. Both were commissioned in the Paraguayan navy. The Paraguayans then pushed down the Paraná River. On 1 May Argentina, Brazil, and Uruguay formed the Triple Alliance to oppose Paraguay. The three allies were ill-prepared for a great war and required more time. Each raised an army, and Brazilian Vice Admiral Viscount Tamandaré was given command of naval operations.

In the meantime an Argentine land force under General Wenceslao Paunero watched the enemy's advance. The general embarked his troops along with 250 Brazilians in the Brazilian squadron, proceeded up the Paraná River, and on 25 May recaptured Corrientes after heavy fighting. After the Paraguayans sent reinforcements against the town the allied raiding force withdrew, holding Corrientes for less than twenty-four hours. The allied victory, though short-lived, bought time, boosted morale, and changed the Paraguayan posture from an offensive to a defensive one.

During May 1866 six North Americans, probably ex-Confederates, proposed to the Paraguayan embassy in Paris that it purchase and arm six raiders, sail them under the Paraguayan flag, attack allied shipping and ports, and blockade the Río de la Plata. In exchange they asked for letters of marque, Paraguayan passports, and half the prize money. The chargé d'affaires was enthusiastic but told the North Americans that he did not have the authority to accept the offer. Apparently the Paraguayan government did not pursue it. Shortly afterward James Manlove, an ex-Confederate, arrived in Buenos Aires, where a number of newspaper articles speculated about his presence. Crossing the Paraguayan lines on 2 August, he traveled to Asunción and made a proposal to organize commerce raiders. It is not clear whether Manlove was associated with those who had made a similar offer to the Paraguayan ambassador in Paris. In any case López, not a trusting individual under the best of circumstances, had Manlove arrested. Perhaps Manlove had lingered too long in Buenos Aires and raised suspicions. He was handed over to the U.S. ambassador but his luck eventually ran out; he was later arrested by López and executed.

Paraguay now attempted to destroy the Brazilian squadron anchored off the mouth of the Riachuelo Arroyo. On 11 June 1865 a Paraguayan fleet of eight steamers and six guncraft attacked nine Brazilian warships. As it passed the Brazilian anchorage the fleet fired, then anchored under the twenty-two guns of the Second Paraguayan Horse Artillery Regiment. The Brazilians counterattacked, and the battle raged for several hours with victory seemingly within the grasp of the Paraguayans. At this point Brazil's frigate *Amazonas* successfully rammed four enemy ships and gave the Brazilians a total victory. The Paraguayans lost three steamers, six gunrafts, and several hundred men.[15] The *Tacuari*, severely damaged at the Battle of Riachuelo, was towed to Asunción and repaired. The Brazilians lost one ship and sustained heavy damage to a second ship. At the time of the naval attack, the Paraguayans invaded and attacked the Argentine province of Misiones, pushing southward down the Uruguay River. The invaders were stopped and surrounded at Uruguayana, Brazil, where they capitulated on 18 September. The allies then marched up north to the Paraná River and the Paraguayans withdrew before them.

The allies now decided on the strategy of pushing up the Paraguay River to Asunción with the armies moving up the left bank and the Brazilian navy controlling the river. Paraguay concentrated her forces in the peninsula between the Paraguay and Paraná rivers. At Humaitá on the Paraguay River they had constructed powerful fortifications. The allied army landed near Paso de la Patria. On 2 May 1866 the Paraguayans attacked the allied advanced guard at Estero Bellaco by surprise but were beaten back. The forces met at the first Battle of Tuyuty on 24 May. Paraguay was defeated, losing thirteen thousand men against the allies' four thousand. The Triple Alliance did not exploit its success.

Allied armies now confronted the strongly fortified position at Humaitá. In the meantime the allied fleet pushed up the Paraguay River to attack Curuzu, another fortified position. The allies hoped that a success there would force the Paraguayans to disperse their forces. In September 1866 six allied warships escorted nine thousand troops up river, and while sailing they were fired upon by undiscovered batteries. On the second a mine floated from the river banks exploded under the new Brazilian ironclad *Rio de Janeiro*, and she sank with most of her crew. The next day the allies landed below Curuzu and captured the position, a victory counteracted on 22 September when the allies suffered a crushing defeat at the Battle of Curupaití. Endeavoring to drive the Paraguayans out of the fortified position, they lost four thousand men, Paraguay less than one hundred. Brazilian gunfire from the fleet proved ineffective because the Paraguayan batteries were well camouflaged and relatively high above the water. However, Paraguay failed to take advantage of the success; her army, like that of the Triple Alliance, was being ravaged by cholera.

The Brazilian navy ran afoul of the U.S. Navy on 2 November 1866 when the U.S. ambassador to Paraguay, Charles A. Washburn, reached Tres Bocas, just above Corrientes, in the U.S. gunboat *Shamokin*. He was en route to Asunción after a fourteen-month absence. The Brazilian blockading warships refused to let the *Shamokin* pass. Washburn and Commander Peirce Crosby protested, telling Admiral Tamandaré that the United States did not recognize the allied blockade because an 1853 treaty guaranteed free navigation on the Río de la Plata. Tamandaré, who could easily have disposed of the North American warship, did not wish to risk war with the United States, so he permitted the *Shamokin* to pass under protest.

In May 1867 Brazil tried to open another front and launched an inva-

Riverine Operations During the War of the Triple Alliance, 1865–70

sion of northwest Paraguay. This met with mixed results. Some indecisive actions were fought on the way to Laguna, and the Brazilians were forced to retreat because their supply system broke down and cholera ravaged their force. Of 1,680 men, 980 died; still, the Brazilians managed to bring all four guns and their flags back in a thirty-five-day operation that took its place among the prouder pages of Brazilian military history. On 13 June 1867 the force landed 430 men north of Corumbá and captured the town by surprise. Subsequently the Paraguayan warships *Rio Apa*, *Anjambahy*, and *Salto de Guairaa* pursued the Brazilians, which evacuated Corumbá on the twenty-third. On 11 July the Paraguayan force caught up with the Brazilians at Point Rio San Lorenzo. It captured a barge carrying nine hundred carbines and later the Brazilian gunboat *Jaura*, which had damaged engines. Finally the Paraguayan ships were forced to retreat and the Brazilian gunboat *Antonio João* recaptured the *Jaura*, which had to be scuttled later because of the heavy damage she sustained. In this action the Paraguayans had forty-one men killed and some taken prisoner, the Brazilians nine killed and fifteen wounded.

With impatience increasing at home, the Triple Alliance sent new commanders to the field. Vice Admiral Joaquin José Ignacio replaced Admiral Tamandaré. Another revolution in Argentina diverted part of her forces. Even more than before the brunt of the fighting fell to the Brazilians, who successfully outflanked the Paraguayans and forced them to abandon the heavily fortified forward line that protected Humaitá. The allies concluded that forcing passage of the Humaitá fortification and threatening the Paraguayan capital were the keys to ending the war. The Paraguayans now resolved to block the passage of the Brazilian squadron. On 8 August 1867 the *Tacuari*, making her first appearance since sustaining heavy damage at the Battle of Riachuelo, sailed from Asunción to Humaitá, transporting 225 recruits. On 15 August the Brazilian squadron took up position below the fort. The way was blocked by three iron chains stretching across the river. Political crises in Argentina and Uruguay had divided the interest of these allies and again diverted troops, so the attack was delayed. On 2 November, when the allies encircled Humaitá by occupying Tayi, Brazilian army artillery destroyed the Paraguayan gunboats *25 de Mayo* and *Olimpo*. The *Igurey* escaped undamaged upriver.

Finally at 0300 on 19 February 1868 the Brazilian fleet, composed of forty-three warships mounting 223 guns and manned by over four thousand men, steamed toward the fortifications. It was the Brazilian intention to pass the fortress with only six ships, the three armored ones each towing a monitor alongside. Guns of the fleet concentrated on the two barges that supported the ends of the great chain. The fire was so effective that they sank immediately, allowing five of the six ships to pass the forts by night. The remainder of the fleet stayed below the fortifications. The cable with which the armored corvette *Bahia* towed the monitor *Alagoas* was shot away, and the latter drifted down below the batteries. The captain was signaled from the flagship not to attempt to force the batteries in daylight. The commanding officer nevertheless successfully ran the gauntlet, taking over two hundred hits in the hull and settling two inches each hour. The six ships, three monitors and three armored craft, had received 380 hits. The armored craft were so badly damaged that they could not proceed. The *Bahia*, along with another armored corvette, the *Barroso*, and the monitor *Rio Grande do Sul*, steamed to Asunción and shelled the capital on 20 February, firing some sixty rounds. Although they did little material damage, the bombardment had grave political consequences. López ordered the evacuation of Asunción, an action that drove a wedge between the dictator's supporters.

The Paraguayans tried again to eliminate the Brazilian fleet. They lashed canoes to floating water plants called *camalotes*, common in those waters, and rowed in disguise among the allied fleet. At daybreak on 2 March 1868 the first of the canoes fell on the *Lima Barros* while a guard boat sounded the alarm. The Paraguayans boarded the *Lima Barros* and killed some men on deck, but the crew remained in control. The fleet opened fire on the *camalotes* as they drifted by and few of the Paraguayans escaped.

Late in March the Paraguayan gunboats *Tacuari* and *Ygurey* were trapped. The first, scuttled while under the fire of the *Bahia* and the *Pará* in the Riacho Guyacuru, was nonetheless able to land her guns before being destroyed. The *Ygurey* was sunk by the Brazilian ironclad *Barroso* and monitors *Pará* and *Rio Grande do Sul*.

The allied siege on Humaitá tightened and for the next three months the fort was bombarded almost daily. On 9 July the Paraguayans tried unsuccessfully to capture the monitor *Rio Grande do Sul* by again disguising themselves as floating water plants. Impatient, the allies tried to storm Humaitá but failed. In late July the Paraguayans abandoned their fortifications, which had held the allies at bay for more than two years. After the fall of Humaitá the surviving Paraguayan warships were laid up in the Rio Manduvira, and all personnel, except for one officer and thirty men who remained on board as skeleton crews, were used to form a naval infantry battalion and several artillery batteries. Notwithstanding the loss of their steamers and the Brazilian domination of the river around Humaitá, the Paraguayans evacuated all defenders on the Chaco side of the river, where many escaped to the north, recrossing the river at Timbó. The last eighteen hundred men, blockaded on Poi Island, surrendered finally on 5 August 1868 after a tenacious defense. Humaitá was razed, the great chains cut in three pieces and delivered to the governments of Argentina, Brazil, and Uruguay.

The allied armies pushed up the banks of the Paraguay River escorted by their flotilla. The advance was stopped by heavy rains and the Angostura defenses south of Asunción. In December 1868 the allies won the battles of Ytororo (on the sixth), Avay (the eleventh), and Ita-Ybaté (the twenty-first through the twenty-seventh), destroying the Paraguayan army. On 30 December Angostura surrendered, and the first Brazilian troops entered Asunción on 1 January 1869.

López, having rebuilt his army with children, escaped prisoners of war, and invalids, remained in the field for another fourteen months, always outnumbered and defeated. What remained of the Paraguayan navy's manpower was defeated at the end of April 1869, near Garayo on the Ihaguay River, where they tried to fight it out with the Brazilian squadron. The six surviving Paraguayan warships were set ablaze on 18 August 1869, near Ihu on the Manduvira River, to prevent their capture by the Brazilians. López did not attempt guerrilla warfare for fear of losing personal control of his troops.

The war finally ended with the death of the Paraguayan dictator on 1 March 1870 at the Battle of Coro Cora. At least four Paraguayan naval officers were among the five-hundred-odd man force that supported the dictator in his last battle. The war had cost Paraguay four-fifths of her male population. Her navy had fought tenaciously against increasing odds and without much hope of adding to its inventory. Among its successes was the sinking of the new Brazilian ironclad *Rio de Janeiro* with a mine floated from a river bank. The mine was finding its way into the arsenal of the underdog.

The contribution of the Brazilian navy was essential to the allied effort. Several of the principal warships had been built in Brazil, including the ironclads *Rio de Janeiro, Barroso, Tamandaré*, six monitors, and numerous lesser craft. Admittedly these warships were of rather simple construction, similar to those used on western rivers in the United States during its Civil War, but they were effective. And their blockade forced European builders to sell warships under construction for Paraguay to other customers. Most of these warships, including the turret ships *Lima Barros, Bahia*, and *Silvado*, plus the central battery warships *Mariz e Barros* and *Herval*, were purchased by Brazil, swelling her navy.[16]

South America's Pacific Coast

The Pacific coast of South America was the last area on the continent to win its independence from Spain. It also was the region most influenced by naval power during the nineteenth century. Many of the newly created west coast countries had formerly been administrative entities within the viceroyalty of Perú. Following independence they fought one another, each hoping to become the dominant west coast nation. In other actions Chilean and Peruvian warships from time to time ran afoul of the British navy, sometimes at the invitation of their own governments.

Between 1827 and 1829 Perú invaded Bolivia and then Ecuador, the latter still part of Gran Colombia. A Peruvian naval squadron captured Guayaquil in January 1829, but Admiral Martín Guise, who had earlier fought for Perú's independence from Spain, lost his life in the attack. A combined Bolivian-Ecuadorian effort defeated the Peruvians at the land battle of Tarqui on 27 February. Guayaquil was retaken, and on 24 November an improvised Ecuadorian fleet of twelve gunboats forced the Peruvians to lift the blockade of the port. The status quo at the time of independence was restored.

In December 1828 crew members of the Chilean warship *Aquíles* mutinied when she lay at Valparaíso and many of the officers and some crew members were ashore. The mutineers left them behind, setting sail. The Chilean president, Ramón Vicuña, requested one Captain Bingham of the British navy to put to sea and capture the rebels. The British forty-six-gun frigate *Thetis* overtook the Chilean brigantine, captured her, and took the mutineers to Valparaíso, where they were delivered to the governing authorities. The Chilean public was outraged by the president's request for aid from a foreign nation to solve what they perceived to be an internal affair, and President Vicuña was forced to go into hiding.[17]

In 1835 Bolivia and Perú joined in union, an act both Argentina and Chile opposed, declaring war. As with most of the intracontinental struggles, exiles played a role in fostering this one. In 1836 a group of Chilean exiles sailed from Callao in two merchant ships, the *Monteagudo* and the *Orbregoso*, owned by the Peruvian government. The ships were separated by a storm. The *Obregoso* sailed into and captured San Carlos de Ancud, the principal port on the island of Chiloé. The crew of the *Monteagudo* mutinied, carried her into Valparaíso, and surrendered. The Chilean government then dispatched the *Monteagudo*, crewed by those loyal to the government, to Chiloé, where they surprised the rebels and crushed the uprising. As these events took place Chile sent the warships *Aquíles* and *Colocolo* under Commander Pedro Angulo to cruise off Perú with orders to capture Peruvian warships in reprisal for suspected Peruvian aid to the Chilean insurgents. During the night of 21 August 1836 Victorino Garrido surprised and captured three unarmed Peruvian warships and one merchant ship off Callao.

Chile demanded without success that the union between Bolivia and Perú be dissolved. On 11 November 1836 Chile declared war, and what ensued was the struggle known in history books as the War Against the Peruvian-Bolivian Confederation, or the Andean War. Having blockaded the Peruvian coast without the desired effect, Chile sent a three-thousand-man expedition by sea to Chilca, Perú, in October 1837. The force was surrounded and Admiral Blanco Encalada, commander of the expedition, negotiated a truce, the Treaty of Paucarpata, before returning to Chile with all of his personnel and armaments. Chile denounced the truce. In July 1838 a second and larger expedition was sent out under the command of General Manuel Bulnes. There were fifty-four hundred troops, including sixty Peruvian dissidents, carried in twenty-seven transports and escorted by eight warships. The force landed at Ancón, Perú, and captured Lima on 21 August after defeating a Peruvian army. It then lay siege to Callao and captured the seaport. Andrés Santa Cruz, president of the

Peruvian-Bolivian Confederation, retook Lima and Callao on 9 November, but nevertheless, the Chilean army decisively defeated the confederation at the Battle of Yungai on 20 January 1839. While these land operations were taking place the Chilean fleet blockaded Peruvian ports, preventing some privateers from getting to sea. On 12 January 1839 a Peruvian fleet attacked Chilean warships at Casma. The action, indecisive, was the last attempt of Peru's navy to challenge Chile's during this conflict. Chile found trouble from another quarter, however. Admiral Charles Baynes Hodgson Ross of the Royal Navy "arrested" the Chilean warships stationed off the Peruvian coast because of an alleged assault by a Chilean soldier against a British subject. After the intervention of the British consul in Lima the Chilean warships were released.[18]

The Bolivian-Peruvian Confederation collapsed, and two years later Perú invaded Bolivia in an attempt to annex disputed territory. On 20 November 1841 the Peruvians were defeated at the Battle of Ingavi, culminating in a war in which naval power did not play any role.

In 1851 Chilean rebels seized the *Arauco* and the *Firefly* after rebellions broke out in the north at Coquimbo and in the south at Concepción. The acquisition of the two merchant steamers gave the rebels the potential to open communications between their groups and take maritime action against those governing. At the time the Chilean navy had but one armed sailing ship ready for action. The Chilean government asked that the British squadron be used to arrest the two steamers. The paddle-wheel frigate *Gorgon* was dispatched, and she captured the rebel steamers. The rebellion collapsed.[19]

During the early 1860s Peru's relationship with Spain disintegrated. At issue were debts dating back to the colonial period and a confrontation between Spanish Basques and Peruvians in southern Perú. One member of each group was killed in a fight. Spain sent a naval squadron under Rear Admiral Luis H. Pinzón to the west coast of South America, ostensibly for scientific purposes and exploration. It arrived off Perú in 1863. When diplomacy crumbled the Spanish squadron seized the guano-rich Chincha Islands, twelve miles off the coast of Perú, on 14 April 1864.

Soon after the occupation of the islands Spain notified Perú that her representatives had exceeded their authority by seizing the islands. Admiral Pinzón was relieved by Admiral José Manuel Pareja. The Spanish warship *Triunfo* was accidentally destroyed by fire, thus reducing the force to the frigate *Resolución* and the gunboat *Covadonga*. The diplomats agreed to the terms of a treaty, but these were not well received in Lima and the Peruvian government revolted. In the meantime Pareja demanded an apology from Chile for her actions in support of Perú. It was not given. The Spanish admiral decided to declare a blockade of Chilean ports, to which the Chilean government responded by declaring war on 25 September.

Earlier it had ordered its only warships, the *Esmeralda* and the *Maipo*, to Chiloé to await the results of the negotiations. In early January the *Esmeralda*, commanded by Captain Juan Williams Rebolledo, captured the Spanish gunboat *Covadonga*, thus depriving the Spaniards of their only dispatch boat and providing the Chileans with the Spanish signal book. This disaster along with other setbacks so depressed the Spanish admiral that he committed suicide.

Perú did not declare war on Spain until 14 January 1866. She wanted to be sure that her newly built seagoing monitor *Huáscar* and armored ship *Independencia* had departed England first. These ships and the corvettes *Unión* and *América*, recently purchased by Perú as well, would give her a formidable squadron when added to the existing fleet.[20]

The west coast nations banded together. On 27 February Ecuador declared war on Spain and Bolivia did so on 4 April, though their participation was primarily symbolic. When joint actions were undertaken by the nations it was not with a spirit of great cooperation. After the Peruvian navy joined the Chilean warships at Chiloé, there was much discord between the two fleets. The Spanish squadron blockaded Valparaíso, inflicting considerable damage on commerce by capturing more than thirty merchantmen, but it did not have enough warships to extend the blockade beyond this port. On 6 February the Spanish squadron, now commanded by Captain Casto Méndez Nuñez, attacked Peruvian and Chilean ships off Abtao, Chiloé, in a two-hour battle that proved indecisive.

In an attempt to break the Spanish blockade of Valparaíso, Chilean President José Joaquin Pérez endorsed the construction and use of a submarine. Designed by a Mr. Flach (his given name is undiscovered), built at Duprat Shipyard in Valparaíso, and launched in 1866, the boat was less than forty-two feet six inches (thirteen meters) in length, spindle-shaped, and crewed by a maximum of six persons who provided propulsion. A small cannon was installed for firing above or below water. The president observed the launching of the craft. It submerged with the inventor and four of his friends, and was never heard from again.

Chile attempted to devise a spar torpedo to be used against the blockaders. The British minister in Santiago advised against this on the grounds that Valparaíso would no longer be entitled to claims that it was a defenseless port and, therefore, free from bombardment. In fact, Rear Admiral Méndez Nuñez (recently promoted) declared that any attempt to damage his ships would result in the bombardment of Valparaíso, and on 23 March he notified the neutrals that he had no choice but to bombard the city since he could not bring the enemy fleets into action. On 31 March 1866 four Spanish warships bombarded Valparaíso for three hours, their principal targets being customs warehouses filled with merchandise. Considerable damage was done.

The Spanish fleet next attempted to bombard Callao. Shortly after noon on 2 May 1866 Spanish warships entered the harbor there and a general melee ensued. The *Villa de Madrid* was so badly damaged that she had to be towed out of danger. The *Berenguela* briefly raised the distress signal. On shore, a shell exploded inside a tower and killed the minister of war, among others. At 1500 the Spanish fleet withdrew. Casualties were heavy on both sides, and all of the ships received serious damage. On 9 May 1866 Spain ceased hostilities, Admiral Méndez Nuñez's decision undoubtedly influenced by the anticipated arrival of the two new Peruvian ironclads *Huáscar* and *Independencia*. Actually, both Peruvian armored ships were then still far away on the east coast of South America, delayed by minor collisions, crew unrest, and all sorts of mechanical problems. They missed an opportunity to offer battle to several Spanish ships as they rounded Cape Horn, and they did not even arrive at Callao until several months after the battle at Callao. On 9 May, when the fighting ended, the United States mediated a peace agreement.

One long-term effect of the war was the decline of the Chilean merchant marine. Besides the direct losses to enemy action, the war induced many Chilean shipowners to register their vessels under foreign flags. As for her navy, Chile was forced to rebuild it. In 1872 the government ordered construction of the ironclads *Almirante Cochrane* and *Valparaíso* (later to be named the *Blanco Encalada*), the gunboat *Magallanes*, and the paddle steamer *Tolten*. Two corvettes, the *O'Higgins* and the *Chacabuco*, which had been seized by Great Britain while under final construction, were released in 1868 following the end of the fighting.

Perú, meanwhile, was absorbed by internal problems. In 1876 a group of rebels seized the Peruvian turret-ironclad *Huáscar* and set sail, whereupon the government declared them pirates. After the *Huáscar* stopped British merchant ships and removed provisions and coal from them, HMS *Shah* and *Amethyst* attempted to capture her. An indecisive battle took place off Pacocha, Perú, during which one of the British warships fired a self-propelled torpedo that missed. This was the first use of a mobile torpedo in combat. Those in the *Huáscar*, realizing the futility of their position, surrendered to the Peruvian navy.

The War of the Pacific (1879–83) was a struggle to control the guano- and nitrate-producing Atacama Desert. The area and control of its resources had long been disputed by Chile and Bolivia, the latter with the active support of Perú. Bolivia administered much of the disputed territory, while Chile had certain commercial rights guaranteed by treaty. Numerous confrontations took place, and relations became so strained in the mid-1870s that Chile ordered the *Almirante Cochrane* to sail from England even though her bottom had not yet been zinc lined.[21] Matters came to a head when Bolivia, contrary to an agreement with Chile, increased taxes on nitrate exports.

Contemporary analysts believed the navies of Chile and Perú to be about equal because each had two ironclads. However, a closer examination would have revealed the Chilean pair, the *Almirante Cochrane* and the *Blanco Encalada* (ex-*Valparaíso*), to be substantially superior to the Peruvian *Huáscar* and *Independencia*.[22] The Chilean ships were larger, faster, and more heavily armed and armored. The Peruvian navy, moreover, had lost a number of warships through accident since the war with Spain.[23] Bolivia herself had no navy, despite efforts the Bolivian president had made earlier toward that end. In 1873 he had proposed to the country's congress that two armored warships of the type purchased by Chile be bought. The congress replied that Bolivia was "a peaceful nation and La Paz [the capital of Bolivia] does not need nor will it ever need ships of war. . . ."[24] What Bolivia and Perú lacked in naval power they made up for in military muscle. Their armies were twice as large as Chile's. Based on this fact along with the erroneous conclusion that the navies were equal, many expected Chile to lose the war.

On 14 February 1879 a Chilean naval expedition seized the principal Bolivian nitrate port of Antofagasta. The nearby countryside was quickly occupied by the five-hundred-man landing force and Chile gained control of the Atacama Desert. On 1 March Bolivia declared war on Chile and asked for Peru's assistance under the terms of a secret 1873 defensive treaty against Chile. Peru granted the request, and Chile, aware of the provisions of the treaty, declared war on Perú.

The belligerents spent the next few months occupied with naval operations and preparations for the land campaign. The Chilean navy blockaded Iquique, Peru's principal port in the south, and used its anchorage as a base of operation. The navy also raided Peruvian ports, destroying the nation's economic and war potential. The Peruvian navy, by contrast, was not yet ready to fight. The *Huáscar* lay at Callao with her boilers removed for retubing, and it took more than a month to get her operational.

The Chilean navy sought a decisive engagement with the Peruvian fleet. On 16 May Chilean Admiral Juan Williams Rebolledo sailed north to reconnoiter Callao with the *Blanco Encalada* and the *O'Higgins*. The *Esmeralda* and the *Covadonga* maintained the blockade at Iquique. On the same day Peruvian Captain Miguel Grau sailed south with the *Huáscar* and the *Independencia*, escorting three transports that were carrying troops personally commanded by General Mariano Ignacio Prado, the president of Perú. The fleets did not sight each other; the Chileans steamed far out to sea to conceal their movements and the Peruvians hugged the coast. The Peruvian troops landed at Tacna. Captain Grau, learning of Admiral Williams' sailing when he arrived at Tacna, decided to attack the weakened blockade force at Iquique, sixty miles to the south. On 21 May 1879 the *Huáscar* and the *Independencia* fought it out with the Chilean warships *Esmeralda* and *Covadonga*. The *Huáscar* closed to within three hundred yards of the *Esmeralda*, which could only steam at four knots owing to the poor condition of her boilers, but the main battery of the seagoing monitor was ineffective. The *Huáscar* then rammed the Chilean warship three times, during which Commander Arturo Prat, commanding officer of the *Esmeralda*, attempted to carry the *Huáscar* by boarding. He was followed by First Sergeant Juan de Dios Aldea and a sailor named Arsenio Canave. All three were killed in the attempt. During the second ramming Lieutenant Ignacio Serrano and about a dozen men again tried to carry the *Huáscar* by boarding; a few escaped over the side of the Peruvian ironclad, but the majority were killed or taken prisoner. After a four-hour fight and a third ramming the *Esmeralda* sank. Of the two hundred crew members only fifty-four survived. One man in the *Huáscar* was killed, Lieutenant Jorge Velarde. While this action was taking place the *Covadonga* enticed the *Independencia* onto some rocks, where she became stranded. Her loss came as a severe blow to the Peruvians. Now they had but one ironclad—a seagoing monitor—which either of the Chilean warships *Blanco Encalada* and *Almirante Cochrane* outmatched.

Next the *Covadonga* made her escape to Antofagasta, and Captain Grau sailed north to Callao. On 3 June he encountered the *Blanco Encalada*, outmaneuvered her, and escaped after exchanging a few shots. The Chilean navy reinstituted the blockade of Iquique, which subsequent activities of the *Huáscar* forced it to abandon on 2 August. The ships were needed to protect Antofagasta, where the Chilean water supply was exposed to naval gunfire.

During the next few months the *Huáscar*, commanded by Grau, paralyzed the movements of the Chilean army. She cruised the coast, evading the Chilean squadron, and made sudden and unexpected appearances at Carrizal, Chañaral, Huasco, Antofagasta, Tocopilla, Taltal, and Caldera. On 23 July she captured the transport *Rimac*, carrying a Chilean cavalry unit, and a month later, on 17 August, she entered Antofagasta and attacked the Chilean warships *Magallanes* and *Abtao*. These ships were saved when they sought protection behind neutral merchant ships. Grau, for fear of intervention by warships of a foreign naval power, had the *Huáscar* fire only one torpedo, a Lay, against the *Abtao*. The weapon turned on the *Huáscar*, and Lieutenant Diez Canseco jumped overboard to deflect its course. This was the first torpedo fired in the conflict.

Grau's successes caused consternation in Chile. Captain Galvarino Riveros was ordered to replace Admiral Williams Rebolledo, who resigned because of "ill health." Chile overhauled her two ironclads to improve their ability to bring the *Huáscar* into action. All warships except those guarding Antofagasta were sent to Valparaíso to receive a thorough overhaul of their machinery and to have their bottoms cleaned. This was a major undertaking since Chile had no dry dock. Divers cleaned the bottoms an inch at a time. Eighteen hundred boiler tubes were made by hand in Santiago. When the work was completed, the *Almirante Cochrane* could make eleven knots—one more than the *Huáscar* at that time. On 1 October 1879 the Chilean fleet, built around her two ironclads, sailed north from Valparaíso, hunting for the *Huáscar*. After a visit to Arica the squadron split in two, one ironclad being assigned to each half.

On the morning of 8 October the Peruvian squadron, made up of the *Huáscar* and the *Unión*, was trapped between the Chilean forces, built around the ironclads *Cochrane* and *Blanco Encalada*. Grau, now a rear admiral, ordered the *Unión* to escape, a feat she accomplished owing to her superior speed. Grau, himself unable to flee, decided to fight against the overwhelming odds favoring the Chileans and make victory as costly as possible for them.[25] The Chileans captured the *Huáscar* following a battle that lasted an hour and a half. Admiral Grau, four succeeding commanding officers, and about thirty Peruvians were killed.[26] Of the 150 shots fired at the *Huáscar*, 76 hit the target. With her capture the Chilean navy won control of the sea, gaining unimpeded mobility and tying the Peruvians to defensive positions in a barren and mountainous terrain not easily traversed. The Chilean navy still had to overcome Peruvian fortifications, a task made easier by the length of Peru's coastline, which prevented the erection of defenses at every landing site.

On 2 November 1879 a Chilean expedition of ten thousand men carried in fifteen transports and escorted by four warships captured Pisagua.[27] A second landing took place simultaneously at Junin, six miles to the south. The *Blanco Encalada* captured the Peruvian corvette *Pilcomayo* on the seventeenth; the Chilean navy took her in and retained her name. On 19 November the Chileans won the land battle of Dolores. The Peruvian forces at Iquique now believed their position to be untenable and evacuated the city, giving the Chileans absolute control of the nitrate districts—an area that furnished Perú with a large part of her export revenues. The Chileans pursued the retreating Peruvians but suffered a rebuff at Tarapacá on 27 November, whereupon the Peruvians continued their retreat unmolested to Arica, the principal seaport in southern Perú.

Arica's defenses were strong: 1,858 Peruvians, nineteen rifled guns, the monitor *Manco Capac*, and a torpedo boat. The fortification, commanded by Colonel Francisco Bolognesi, had occasionally been bombarded by the Chilean blockading force beginning in late 1879. On 24 February 1880 fourteen thousand Chilean troops embarked at Pisagua in sixteen transports and warships; between the twenty-sixth and twenty-eighth they were landed at Ilo and Pacocha, two ports eighty and eighty-five miles northwest of Arica. On 17 March the wooden corvette *Unión*, one of the few surviving Peruvian warships, successfully ran the Chilean blockade. She escaped from Callao and then entered Arica, delivering munitions and supplies to the defenders before returning to Callao. The Chileans were attempting to cut off allied coastal positions from help from the interior. On 22 March they captured Torata and successfully isolated the allies. The opposing forces met at the Battle of Tacna on 26 May. After a bloody four-hour fight, one quarter of the twenty-two thousand combatants were killed or wounded. The Chileans won. Arica fell by storm on 7 June 1880, and the *Manco Capac* was scuttled. Chile, now in control of all of southern Perú, carried the war to the heart of that land.

On 10 April 1880 the Chilean fleet appeared off Callao, and its commander, Rear Admiral Riveros (promoted after the Battle of Angamos) declared a blockade of the port. Neutral ships were allowed eight days to leave, after which he would be at liberty to bombard. Callao was Peru's chief port, lying eight miles from Lima, the capital. Since colonial days it had been heavily fortified, with defenses strong enough in 1866 to dissuade the Spanish attack. In 1880 the port was defended by fourteen heavy guns, more than thirty thirty-two-pounders, the monitor *Atahualpa*, the *Unión*, one U.S.-built Herreshoff torpedo boat, steam launches, a torpedo brigade, mines, and a submarine. The Chilean blockade squadron was made up of the *Blanco Encalada*, *Huáscar*, *Angamos*, *Pilcomayo*, and *Matias Cousiño*. As the blockade dragged on for nine months most of the Chilean navy, including recently acquired torpedo boats, saw service there.

Over the next few months the two sides dueled with each other, inflicting damage. On 10 May the Chilean fleet sank a school ship and several barges and damaged docks and warehouses. In this same action the *Huáscar* sustained moderate injuries.

Both navies had difficult tasks. The Chileans had to maintain a tedious blockade against an enemy that showed no signs of giving up. The Peruvian navy, most of its major warships having been lost, had to attack the enemy with cunning. On 25 May the Chilean torpedo boat *Janequeo* was lost while patrolling in Callao harbor. Lieutenant José Gálvez of the Peruvian navy heaved a one-hundred-pound case of powder from a steam launch onto the torpedo boat and exploded it with a pistol shot.[28] Both launches went down. On 3 July the Chileans discovered an abandoned boat loaded with fresh vegetables at anchor sixteen miles north of Callao. The prize was towed into the Chilean anchorage and tied alongside the transport *Loa*. As the last of the cargo was being offloaded, a tremendous explosion ripped a fifteen-foot gash into the side of the *Loa*. She sank and over fifty of her crew perished. Speculation is that some type of explosive was hidden in the vegetable-filled ship. While blockading Chancay, the Chilean warship *Covadonga* discovered a launch with a fine gig astern. Her guns sank the launch, and the seemingly undamaged gig was brought alongside and hoisted on board. As it was being hauled up the davits, an explosion shattered the starboard side of the *Covadonga*. She sank and most of her crew was killed or taken prisoner. The Chileans retaliated for these losses by bombarding Chancay, Ancón, and Chorillos.

In September 1880 Captain Patricio Lynch of the Chilean navy led a three-thousand-man force that laid waste to the Peruvian coast between Callao and Payta. The expedition paralyzed the flow of commerce in northern Perú.

Peru's situation grew more desperate with each passing day. For the navy, an event of the previous year had offered a flicker of hope. On 12 October 1879, four days after the *Huáscar* had been captured, Federico Blume Othon launched his submarine, the *Toro Submarino* ("underwater bull").[29] Her general specifications are provided in the sketch on page 37. On the surface, she was powered by a small steam engine. Submerged, she ran on a compressed air motor. Blume took her under water for the first time on 14 October, along with his son and four mechanics from the railway workshop (she could accommodate up to ten). The craft submerged to twelve feet, navigated at three knots, and remained semisubmerged for thirty minutes. After eighteen more test dives the submarine and her inventor were taken to Callao, where, following much delay, Blume demonstrated his craft's submersible capability. President Nicolás de Piérola appointed a committee of naval officers and engineers to study the invention. They found it worth developing, and the government dedicated ten thousand soles to the work of building an improved craft. The construction began at Cristobal del Tren.

Before the new boat was ready the situation at Callao grew desperate. The blockade had been tightened, and Callao and Lima were threatened. The Peruvian government decided to modify and use the original boat constructed by Blume at Paita. The two viewing towers were replaced by one amidships, the two snorkels were removed, and four Lay torpedoes, each carrying ten pounds of dynamite, were fitted externally, rigged to detonate on impact. The Lay torpedo of 1870 was a semisubmerged automobile torpedo controlled remotely by an electric cable. Whether these torpedoes were launched, dropped, or attached to spars is unclear. After devising operational procedures, Midshipman Manuel Elías Bonnemaison tested the craft. The *Blanco Encalada* and the *Cochrane*, the backbone of the Chilean fleet, were chosen as targets. The attack was to be carried out at night, but before it could take place the Chilean warships retired, possibly alerted to the danger by a spy.

After a futile series of peace talks on board the USS *Lackawanna* in October 1880, Chile began to advance from Tacna to Lima. A force of twenty-two thousand disembarked at Pisco on 18 November 1880. The last naval engagement occurred on 6 December when Chilean torpedo boats attacked a Peruvian launch, sparking a general bombardment that lasted for an hour and a half. The Chilean torpedo boat *Fresia* was sunk but later raised and repaired, and the Peruvian corvette *Unión* was damaged.

Federico Blume's *Toro Submarino*

Within six weeks the Chilean army moved against Peruvian troops defending Lima. The Chilean fleet lay within range of the Peruvian positions, and guns of the fleet were used to support Chileans ashore. On 17 December, after the bloody battles of Chorrillos and Miraflores, the Chilean army occupied Lima, losing fifty-five hundred men to the Peruvian total of more than nine thousand. When the news of the fall of Lima reached Callao, the Peruvian navy destroyed its remaining ships, principally the corvette *Unión*, the monitor *Atahualpa*, the school ships *Apurimac*, *Meteoro*, and *Marañon*, and the transports *Rimac*, *Chalaco*, and *Talisman*. Blume, who probably participated in the defense of the capital, returned to Callao in hopes of finding a new target for his submarine. There he was surprised to learn that the boat had been scuttled to keep her from falling into the hands of the enemy.[30] On 17 January 1881 Callao surrendered, and though all organized resistance stopped, guerrilla warfare continued for over two years. The Treaty of Ancón (20 October 1883) ended the fighting, leaving Chile the dominant country on South America's west coast. Her victory in the War of the Pacific was complete.

The Caribbean

Added to the woes of the newly independent Caribbean nations following the wars of independence—civil wars, attacks by filibusters, and confrontations with European powers and the United States—was the nagging threat of reconquest by Spain, which maintained a strong military presence in Cuba and Puerto Rico.

Throughout the nineteenth century the island of Hispaniola was constantly in turmoil. Haití, independent since 1804, gained control of the entire island in 1822, taking over from the French and Spanish. In 1844 the eastern two-thirds of the island—the Dominican Republic, or as it was frequently called at that time, Santo Domingo, primarily inhabited by those of Spanish descent—declared its independence from Haití. Decades of fighting followed between the two nations, interrupted only by brief periods of exhaustion. More wars have been fought between the Dominican Republic and Haití than between any other two countries in the western hemisphere.

During their fight for independence, the Dominican schooners *General Santana*, *La Separación Dominicana*, and *La María Chica* drove off three Haitian warships near Azua and exchanged gunfire with shore batteries during the Battle of Tortuguera on 15 April 1844. Apparently the Haitians lost one ship through stranding. On 27 September 1845 they declared a blockade of all Dominican ports, and on the same day their navy attacked a Dominican squadron near Mari-Baru. On 21 December the Haitian schooners *Unión*, *Dieu Protège*, and *Guerrière* ran aground accidentally near Puerto Plata, and the Dominicans took 149 survivors prisoner.

A brief hiatus in the fighting ensued. Then, on 1 March 1849, the Dominican privateer *27 de Febrero* transported two hundred men to Azua. Dominican warships captured the schooner *Caridad* on 29 October and a number of minor craft off Aquin, Haití. Next the Dominican fleet bombarded the town of Petite Rivière. On 6 December the Haitian schooner *Picolet* engaged two Dominican warships, and a little later the Haitian schooner *Avant-Garde* and the Dominican corvette *Oliva* exchanged fire, but these actions were indecisive.

By 1854 the two countries were once again at war. During May the Dominican frigate *Cibao* and the schooner *Buenaventura*, commanded by General Juan Alejandro Acosta, cruised along the southern coast of Haití destroying commerce and raiding the coast. In November the Dominican brigantine *27 de Febrero* and the schooner *Constitución* captured the Haitian *Charité* and bombarded l'Anse à Pitre and Sale Trou. During the hurricane of 26–27 August 1855 the Dominicans lost the warships *Las Carreras*, *Buenaventura*, and *La Constitución* in Rio Ozama and the schooner *Merced* at Puerto Plata. The fighting ended in 1856.

Naval forces played a minor role in the Dominican civil war of 1857–58. Government warships bombarded Matanzas on 11 September 1857, and the rebel corvette *Desolación* captured a number of coastal schooners.

In 1859 the Haitian navy, supporting Haitian emperor Faustin I against rebels who wanted to bring democracy to their country, bombarded Saint Marc but was driven off by Fort Gergerac. Faustin lost to the republicans.

In 1865 another civil war broke out in Haití. The rebel steamer *Providence* tried to stop a British mail steamer, the *Jamaica Packet*, on 18 October.

HMS *Bulldog* intervened, sinking the *Providence* and another ship, then ran aground herself. With no other recourse, her crew blew up their own ship. The loyal Haitian corvette *22 de Decembre* rescued the British sailors, and the Royal Navy supported government troops in the destruction of rebel forts. His hopes shattered, the leader of the uprising left in a U.S. warship.

In yet another revolt in Haití in May 1868 the two warships *Libérté* and *Sylvain* defected to the rebel side. The government acquired the *Pétion* and crewed her with North American adventurers; J. Frederick Nickels, the commanding officer, was made a rear admiral. On 20 September 1868 she sank the *Sylvain* off Petit Goave, while the *Libérté* was beached by her crew. On 4 October the *Pétion*, with the help of a second gunboat, attacked rebel positions at Jérémie and Forts Télémaque and La Pointe to no avail. To deceive the rebels the crew of the *Pétion* (which had on board the U.S. Minister Gideon Hollister) suddenly lowered the U.S. flag and hoisted that of Haití. In its next action the government landed troops and captured Miragoâne on 29 November 1868. The Haitian navy bombarded Cayes off and on for nine months but gave up on 31 October. The rebels now acquired two former U.S. merchantmen and named them the *Mont Organisé* and the *République*.

On 14 September 1869 the two fleets met near Port de Paix in the Battle of Le Borgne. When the government ships *Salnave* and *Pétion* engaged the rebels' *Mont Organisé* and *République*, the *Salnave* was rammed and could only steam in circles. The *République* ruptured a steam line and was without power, while the *Mont Organisé* received twenty-six hits and was making water. The *Pétion* towed the *Salnave* into the Cap as the two rebel ships reached Acul. All four ships were put out of action for some time.

In the meantime, Haiti's government added to its fleet. The former USS *Pequot* was purchased and renamed the *Terreur*. And the old ironclad USS *Atlanta* was bought for $160,000 in gold only to be lost with all hands off Cape Hatteras in December 1869.

The *Pétion* defected to the rebel side and, along with the repaired *Mont Organisé* and *République*, attacked Port-au-Prince. There the rebel forces captured the *Terreur* at 0300 on 18 December without firing a shot. The *Terreur*'s gunnery officer, a North American, was forced at gunpoint to fire on the presidential palace, where two thousand barrels of gunpowder were stored. Within seconds the palace and much of Port-au-Prince blew up, and soon the president was captured and executed. The rebels had won.

On 18 April 1893 Presidents Ulises Heureaux of the Dominican Republic and Florville Hyppolite of Haití rendezvoused in their respective warships in Manzanillo Bay, ending decades of hostilities.[31]

Filibusters plagued the Caribbean also. Among these self-anointed, mostly North American revolutionaries who invaded México and Central American and Caribbean nations and brought chaos to weak governments, the most notorious was William Walker. In 1853 he led a small group to Baja California, where he declared an independent republic. The Mexican authorities captured him but he soon escaped. In 1855 he landed in Nicaragua and within a year gained control of the government. The other Central American governments banded together against him, and in 1857 he prudently surrendered to a U.S. naval officer. Walker, who attempted to invade Central America two more times, was finally captured in Honduras in 1860 and shot.

Walker was not the only filibuster. In 1883 ninety-two men debarked from the merchant ship *Tropic* near Source Salée, Haití. The government sent twelve hundred soldiers in the steamers *Bois de Chêne*, *L'Egalité*, and *L'Estère* to oppose them, but the merchant ship *Alvena* successfully ran the government blockade and carried supplies to the rebels. The rebels also purchased the royal mail steamer *Eider*, renamed her *La Patrie*, and used her as a corsair, in which role she was heavily damaged and driven into Jacmel by the Haitian gunboat *Dessalines*. The revolt was crushed by June 1883. In 1888 the Haitian *Dessalines* captured the U.S. merchant ship *Hayitian Republic*, which was carrying filibusters, and turned her over to a U.S. warship.

At one time or another most Caribbean nations were blockaded, bombarded, or invaded by navies of Europe and the United States. Panamá, a province of Colombia until 1903, suffered more interventions by foreign warships and marines than any other Latin American region. The area was a hotbed of revolution throughout the nineteenth century, and when upheaval threatened the political or economic status of a naval power on the isthmus, that power would intervene. Often interference was on behalf of the Colombian government, but on occasion it was intended to aid a rebel cause, and there was little the weak Colombian fleet could do to prevent this. Such was the state of that fleet that in 1903, when the U.S. Navy guaranteed the success of a rebellion leading to Panama's nationhood, Colombia's hands were tied. Shortly after the rebellion broke out the Colombian gunboat *Almirante Lezo* was dispatched to Panamá carrying five hundred troops. She arrived at Colon (formerly Aspinwall), the Caribbean terminus of the trans-Panamá railroad, on 2 November. The next day U.S. marines from the cruiser *Nashville* refused to allow the Colombian troops, who could not pay for the train fare on the U.S.-owned and -operated railroad, to proceed across the isthmus to the heart of the rebellion at Panamá City, the Pacific terminus of the railroad.[32] Meanwhile, on the Pacific side of Panamá, a Colombian gunboat fired the only six shells it carried at Panamá City, killing one Chinese and one dog. On 4 November Panamá declared her independence, which the United States recognized unofficially on the sixth and officially a week later.

On occasion Latin American warships were trapped into fighting vastly superior opponents. The German warships *Gazelle* and *Vineta* captured the Haitian warships *Mont Organisé* and *Unión* by surprise while they were at anchor off Port-au-Prince on 11 June 1872. They were returned after a three-thousand-pound debt was settled. Thirty years later, on 7 September 1902, the German gunboat *Panther* indirectly caused the destruction of the Haitian gunboat *Crête à Pierro* off Gonaires when Admiral Hamerton Killick chose to blow up himself and his ship to prevent capture.[33]

In northern South America the Republic of Gran Colombia, made up of Colombia, Ecuador, and Venezuela, dissolved in 1830. For the remainder of the century these republics were caught up in internal struggles in which naval power played almost no role.

Venezuela, like most Latin American nations, particularly those in the Caribbean, was subject to frequent threats by foreign fleets. On 9 December 1902 almost the entire Venezuelan navy was seized over the issue of debts she owed to European nations. British and German warships kidnaped the warships *Osún*, *Crespo*, and *Margarita* in Venezuelan waters, apparently without a fight. Two days later the foreign warships blockaded the Venezuelan coast, and on the thirteenth they bombarded forts at Puerto Bello. The German gunboat *Panther* attempted to enter Lake Maracaibo on the seventeenth but was driven off by Fort San Carlos, which guarded the entrance, and was forced to retire to Curaçao for repairs. Italy joined the blockade two days later, when President Theodore Roosevelt agreed to arbitrate claims. On 29 December the Argentine foreign minister, Luis M. Drago, publicly spoke out against the forceable collection of Venezuela's debt by foreign maritime powers, an act that Venezuela would repay when she supported Argentina through diplomacy and by supplying arms during the 1982 Malvinas War. The blockade ended on 17 February 1903.[34]

CHAPTER THREE

The Evolution of Two Major Latin American Navies

Tensions

AT THE END of the nineteenth century Argentina and Chile emerged as potential political leaders of Latin America, and the dispute over the poorly defined demarcation between the two countries threatened to plunge them into war. Each had a growing understanding not only of the need for delineated borders but also of the economic possibilities of the disputed area. One could only imagine what hidden resources were buried beneath the surface or, for that matter, lying on top to be scraped off. As we have seen, in the War of the Pacific Chile and Perú had recently fought over a nitrate-rich desert that not many would have considered worth contesting a few decades earlier. But now technology was changing the face of South America. More and more railroad lines were being completed, crisscrossing regions and drawing them together. A telegraph line between Buenos Aires and Santiago opened in 1872, accelerating the rate of diplomatic exchange. More land meant increased national wealth, for more land would make the task of attracting immigrants, many of whom were farmers, easier.

Argentina and Chile both laid claim to the area known as Patagonia, roughly the lower part of the continent. In 1855 each had recognized the boundaries of the other as they had existed in 1810, when independence from Spain was declared.[1] But this had little practical value, since neither the colonial viceroys of Buenos Aires nor the captains-general of Chile took a serious interest in Patagonia.

The next several decades revealed the economic potential of the region. Guano, rich in nitrates, was discovered in 1870. Two years later coal was found on its Atlantic coast.[2] Border clashes between Argentina and Chile ensued, becoming especially acute in 1873. Between 1876 and 1879 numerous conferences were convened to settle the dispute, but with little result. Just before the War of the Pacific Chile sought the mediation of the United States through the U.S. ministers at Buenos Aires and Santiago.[3] On 23 July 1881 a treaty was signed that outlined the frontier and set forth vague means of handling disagreements that might arise. In this vaguely worded document Chile was awarded the west coast of the Andes, half of the island of Tierra del Fuego, and the coasts of the Straits of Magellan, which were to remain unfortified. Argentina was awarded Patagonia east of the Andes. A protocol agreement in 1893 attempted to define the terms of the treaty, but many issues remained unresolved and negotiations for the actual demarcation dragged on and on. Finally in 1896 Great Britain, the foremost economic and military power in the world, was asked to arbitrate the boundary issue.

Each side had much to lose in a war. A decisive Argentine victory could mean the destruction of Chile's fleet, the loss of her southern Pacific coast, and her restoration to Perú and Bolivia of the territories they had lost in the 1879–82 war. A decisive Chilean victory would probably mean the loss of Argentina's claim to Patagonia east of the Andes and possibly a large indemnity payment to Chile. Clearly, the future of both countries was at stake.

Maritime Confrontation and the Naval Arms Race

During the years that diplomats struggled to resolve the dispute, soldiers and sailors prepared to fight. Argentina and Chile shared a border along the Andes Mountains, making movement by land very difficult. Thus, as in the War of the Pacific, whoever could gain control of the sea would at least stalemate the other and in all probability win the war. And the country most likely to gain control of the sea would be the one with seagoing warships that could transit the stormy tip of the continent and operate for a reasonable amount of time far from home with little logistic support. As the Argentine-Chilean naval arms race gained momentum, the reputation of the seagoing cruiser was enhanced by its successes in the Sino-Japanese War (1894–95).

At the beginning of the fourth quarter of the nineteenth century Chile was militarily superior to Argentina. Her navy was stronger, built around

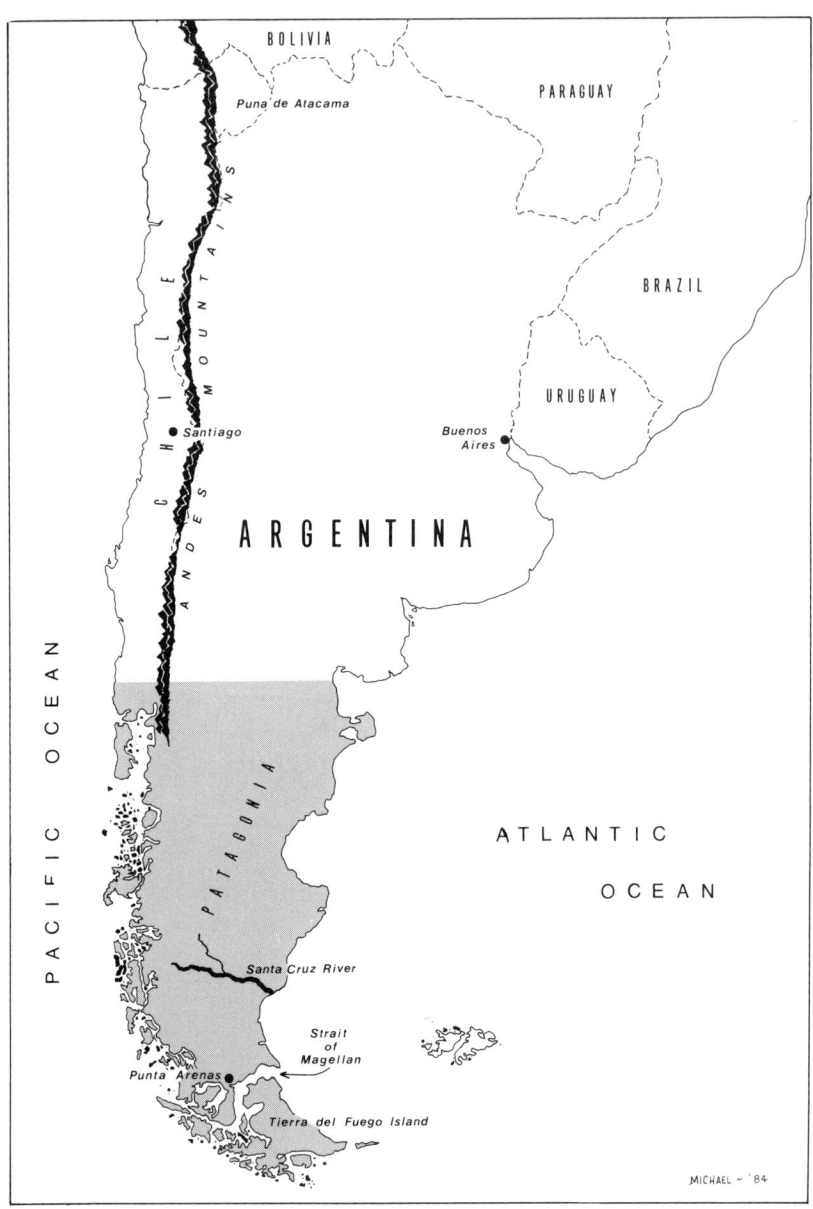

Patagonia and Territories West of the Andes

two new central-battery ironclads and two new gunboats acquired in the mid-1870s.[4] The Argentine navy had been reborn during the administration of President Domingo F. Sarmiento, but it was primarily a riverine fleet designed for use on the Paraná and Paraguay rivers in a possible war against Brazil.

During the 1870s Argentina and Chile came into direct confrontation over the control of Patagonia. In 1872 Chilean warships based at Punta Arenas curtailed the activities of the Argentine-licensed fishing enterprise owned by a Frenchman and operating out of Santa Cruz. Two years later the Argentine ship *Rosales* reported to Buenos Aires that she saw Chilean warships operating in the mouth of the Santa Cruz River.

In early 1878 at Santa Cruz the Chilean warship *Magallanes* seized the French merchantman *Jeanne Amélie*, in possession of an Argentine permit to collect guano, on the grounds that she was operating in Chilean territory without permission. The merchant ship was conducted to the Straits of Magellan, where she was accidentally lost on the rocks off Cape Dungeness. The two countries exchanged diplomatic notes over the incident. In October the *Magallanes* seized the U.S. merchant ship *Devonshire*, with another Argentine permit, off Patagonia just north of the mouth of the Santa Cruz River. There was a public outcry in Buenos Aires.[5]

In early November Argentina dispatched to the river a squadron under Commodore Luis Py made up of the monitor *Los Andes* (flagship), the gunboats *Constitución*, *República*, and *Uruguay* (officers' school ship), and the barkentine *Cabo de Hornos* (subofficers' school ship)—a heterogeneous collection of riverine and school ships. Chile replied by ordering her fleet, built around the ironclads *Almirante Cochrane* and *Blanco Encalada* (ex-*Santiago*, renamed on 15 December 1876), to prepare to sail. The Argentine squadron arrived at the mouth of the Santa Cruz River in late November after a stormy passage down the coast. The Chileans had already departed with the *Devonshire*. At first war seemed imminent, but cooler heads prevailed. On 6 December Argentina and Chile signed the Fierro-Sarratea Treaty, which provided for arbitration and, pending the settlement, stated that Chile was to "exercise jurisdiction over the waters and shores, canals, and adjacent islands of the Straits of Magellan," Argentina "the waters, shores, and adjacent islands of the Atlantic." Actually the treaty resolved nothing—it was simply in the best interest of the two countries to find a quick solution to patch up the immediate crisis.[6]

Tensions between Argentina and Chile over the southern regions subsided in 1879 and over the next few years primarily owing to the internal problems of each and external conflict elsewhere. Argentina, led by General Julio A. Roca, "conquered the desert," to use an Argentine phrase describing the war against the plains Indians in northern Patagonia, the ferocity of which equaled that between the plains Indians and the U.S.

government in the latter part of the nineteenth century. During the bloody confrontation the Argentine navy gained experience providing logistics to the army and exploring the Patagonian rivers and lakes.[7] In these same years Chile fought the War of the Pacific against Bolivia and Perú. Chile's annexation of Bolivian and Peruvian territories in that war, although it temporarily diverted her focus from Patagonia, increased Argentine anxieties that she might attempt to do the same in Patagonia.

By 1890 the two countries began to arm for war. At that time the Argentine navy had more seagoing modern warships, but the Chilean ships were generally larger and the Chilean navy was among the most experienced in the world.[8] Argentina financed the construction of her new fleet with revenues derived from cattle and grain exports, Chile with monies earned through the sale of nitrates.[9] Just who began the subsequent naval arms race is difficult to determine, for it is not known when the countries decided to build or purchase particular ships. Both began to acquire major warships as well as torpedo boats (see appendix 3). The automobile torpedo appeared in naval inventories in the second half of the nineteenth century. Shortly after the U.S. Civil War, Argentina employed a number of former Confederate sailors with torpedo experience. By 1888 Chile had over thirty officers and men in Europe, many of them training in the use of the torpedo at Whitehead's Fiume factory. The development of the torpedo boat, made possible by the creation of small, powerful steam engines and light but strong steel hulls, meant that, for the first time in naval history, major warships at sea could be seriously endangered by tiny opponents. For Argentina, Chile, and other minor navies, the new warship offered the hope of inflicting unacceptable damage on the blockading cruisers and battleships of major navies. The torpedo boat was perceived to be an equalizer.[10]

In 1887 Chile appropriated £3,129,500 to build a balanced fleet—perhaps the first naval program of such financial magnitude in Latin America. It called for the construction of the second-class battleship *Capitán Prat* (costing £391,000), the protected cruisers *Presidente Errázuriz* and *Presidente Pinto*, and the torpedo boats *Lynch* and *Condell*.[11] Within a year Argentina ordered two coastal defense battleships, the *Libertad* and the *Independencia*, but the Chilean battleship was much larger than either and a match for both. Some time after May 1890 Argentina also purchased the protected cruiser *25 de Mayo*, which was being built in England on speculation. Late the following year Argentina ordered an improved version, the cruiser *9 de Julio*.[12]

Significantly influencing the naval arms race between the two nations was the Chilean revolution of 1891, in which the congress and the navy warred against the president and the army. The outcome, a victory for the navy, greatly strengthened the seagoing service's prestige in national politics. The commander of the victorious fleet, Admiral Jorge Montt, held the Chilean presidency from 1891 to 1896 and exercised considerable power in the making of subsequent administrations. The enhancement of naval influence, however, introduced a new problem. Events during and immediately after the revolution brought Chile and the United States dangerously close to war. The Congresionalistas' "voluntary surrender" of the *Itata* to a North American cruiser and the killing of two U.S. sailors from the cruiser *Baltimore* by a mob in Valparaíso generated much ill feeling on both sides. In 1892 Argentina intimated that she would support the United States in a war against Chile if asked to do so.[13] Increasingly, then, Chile had to be concerned about the prospect of an Argentine-U.S. alliance, and in the meantime the arms race with Argentina continued. Chile purchased the protected cruiser *Blanco Encalada* in late 1892; this ship had been laid down by Elswick in England on the speculation that the South American country might buy the ship once construction had begun. Argentina's acquisitions were interrupted by her own civil wars in 1893 during which a few naval units supported the rebels. On 23 November 1893 the government purchased the protected cruiser *Buenos Aires*, laid down for the British navy. Part of the price was raised by public subscription. Then, in August 1895, Chile bought the protected cruiser *Ministro Zenteno* from Brazil while the ship was still under construction. Each of these protected cruisers was slightly larger than and outclassed its predecessor.[14]

During the decade of the nineties two vital ingredients of sea power, national wealth and population, increased in favor of Argentina. By 1895 the Argentine economy had grown to approximately twice that of Chile, yielding greater revenues for the government, and the population, primarily through immigration, had increased to almost four million, a growth of one million since the previous decade. Immigrants, however, only added to economic strength; they could not be drafted into the armed forces and therefore added little to the military. In 1895 the Chilean population was approximately 2.8 million.[15]

Chile toyed with the idea of a submarine for a second time within the century, but when she finally built a boat it ended up stranded on a beach. In 1895 a Bavarian watchmaker named José Huber successfully experimented with a scale model submarine at Apoquindo, Chile. Following a successful demonstration for Rear Admiral Luis Uribe, Huber was charged with building the boat at the foundry of Stricker and Küpfer in Santiago. The sixty-ton craft, constructed from sections that were transported by railway to Talchuano, was launched on 18 March 1896. She successfully navigated to the Belén lighthouse on the surface, then had trouble while submerged. The situation, apparently due to "fractures in essential pieces," was serious, for the boat remained on the beach.[16] Argentina's efforts to build a submarine fell far short of Chile's. In 1891 the Argentine navy approved and ordered the construction of a submarine designed by Dr. Jorge Bolthauser, a civil engineer, but it never materialized. Ten years later Dr. Tebaldo Ricaldoni designed another submersible that failed to make it beyond the planning stage.[17]

Both countries continued to raise their antes as they acquired larger and more powerful cruisers. Apparently to obtain foreign currency so that she could purchase an armored cruiser, Chile sold the protected cruiser *Esmeralda* in late 1894.[18] She ordered a new *Esmeralda* and four torpedo boats in May 1895,[19] and the Argentines purchased the armored cruiser *Garibaldi* on 14 July while she was under construction in Italy.[20] Once again it is difficult to determine who acted first. Initially, the Argentine negotiations for the Italian-built armored cruiser failed; presently the former Argentine president, Julio A. Roca, received a telegram from the builders, telling him that the first of a new class of these cruisers, the *Giuseppe Garibaldi*, being built for the Italian navy, would be available at a very favorable price on credit. The Argentine commission signed a contract in London on 14 July 1895, and the price, £750,000 sterling, was divided in four installments. The Argentines retained the original name to honor Garibaldi's participation in their recent civil wars. Remarkably, in less than four months after launching, the ship was delivered. Chile then ordered the armored cruiser *O'Higgins* and six 140-ton torpedo boats, and Argentina replied by ordering the armored cruiser *San Martín*, a near-sister to the *Garibaldi*.[21] This, at least, is the presumed sequence of events; the orders were placed at about the same time, April 1896, and it is difficult to determine who was reacting to whom, if indeed one side was reacting to the other at all. Argentina was purchasing a ship already under construction, whereas Chile was ordering one to be built. Regardless of this, the two ships arrived in their respective countries less than a month apart. The Argentines had agreed to purchase the *San Martín* on 25 April 1896, but the fall of the Crispi government in Italy delayed final approval. The Italian naval minister, Benedetto Brin, had to convince the new foreign minister that it was in Italy's best interest to sell the ship to the Argentines.[22]

In May 1898 Chile learned that Argentina was planning to purchase yet another Italian armored cruiser named *Giuseppe Garibaldi*, originally intended for the Italian navy, and protested that such an acquisition would be inappropriate while delicate boundary talks progressed. The Argentine president responded that the ship was but an answer to recent Chilean arms acquisitions. Chile's fears increased when it was learned that the armored cruiser *Varese*, also being built for the Italian navy, would be purchased by Argentina and that Argentina had placed a major ordnance contract with Krupp. On the brink of war, the two countries agreed to submit the southern boundary dispute to British arbitration.[23]

Argentina moved ahead to acquire the two new ships, buying the Italian *Giuseppe Garibaldi* and *Varese* and renaming them *Pueyrredón* and *General Belgrano*, respectively. The Chilean minister in Berlin, Carlos Concha, tried to prevent the sale of the ships to Argentina by expressing an interest in them on behalf of Chile, but the Chilean navy, preferring larger warships, did not support his position. The contract Argentina signed in 1897 for the *Pueyrredón* stipulated that the ship should be completed within *two* months of launch. The builders had initially insisted on six months, but the Argentines won the argument by offering £782,000 sterling, £30,000 more than the asking price. The *Pueyrredón* arrived in Argentina on 1 September 1898. The fourth unit, the *General Belgrano*, arrived two months later.[24]

Tension between the nations eased in November when they signed two pacts that in effect made the U.S. ambassador to Argentina the arbitrator of the Puna de Atacama boundary dispute. Late in the month the Argentine and Chilean ministers to London requested that the British government arbitrate the boundary dispute in the south. Although neither of these pacts provided solutions, they did create the potential for them.[25]

In celebration of this reconciliation, and possibly as a show of strength, the presidents of both nations were borne to the Straits of Magellan by their respective fleets on 12 February 1899. The Argentine squadron passed through the Beagle Channel from east to west to the meeting place at Punta Arenas. The Chileans, who thought the Argentines were ignorant of this passage and would come through the Straits of Magellan, must have been surprised when the Argentine force arrived at Punta Arenas from the south instead of the north.[26] The presidents embraced one another and officially pledged eternal peace. The Argentine squadron was made up of the armored cruiser *General Belgrano*, the torpedo gunboat *Patria*, and the school ship *Sarmiento*, carrying President Julio A. Roca. The Chilean squadron was composed of the armored cruiser *O'Higgins*, the protected cruiser *Ministro Zenteno*, and the transport *Angamos*, carrying President Federico Errázuriz and the former president and director general of the navy, Vice Admiral Jorge Montt.

Although the U.S. minister to Argentina, William P. Lord, successfully negotiated a solution to the Puna de Atacama question by dividing the territory between the two nations, the southern dispute remained unresolved, and once again Argentina and Chile began augmenting their fleets. Argentina ordered yet two more armored cruisers from Ansaldo, the *Bernardino Rivadavia* and the *Mariano Moreno*, and guaranteed a premium for delivery within the contract time.[27] Construction began in March 1902 and both ships were launched by February 1903. In late 1901 Chile purchased the protected cruiser *Chacabuco*, being built on speculation.[28]

Numerically, the Argentine navy continued to grow faster than the Chilean, a fact that Chile became increasingly concerned about. On 26 June 1901 the Chilean minister to the United States, Carlos Morla Vicuña, visited the acting chief of the Office of Naval Intelligence, Lieutenant Thomas Snowden, in Washington. According to Snowden, Morla asked "if the Government of the United States would consider a cash offer for those battleships [the *Indiana* class] equal in amount to the cost of a battleship of the latest type." This offer showed a degree of desperation. The price offered was excessive, particularly given the well-publicized shortcomings in the design of these coastal battleships. The minister was told that all such requests needed to be addressed to the State Department. Lieutenant Snowden did detail the conversation to the chief of the Bureau of Navigation, who forwarded it to the U.S. Navy's General Board. On 29 June the General Board wrote to the Office of Naval Intelligence, "In view of the fact that the United States Navy has but few battleships, the General Board has to recommend that none of them be sold as long as they are in serviceable condition."[29]

Apparently this decision was not passed along to the government in Chile. On 3 July 1901 the president-elect, Germán Riesco, invited the U.S. minister to Chile, Henry L. Wilson, to a private dinner and asked him if the United States would sell Chile two ten-thousand-ton battleships for immediate delivery. Wilson's 11 July telegram to Secretary of State John Hay describes the Chilean president's anxiety: "The President then informed me that he believed an addition of two first-class battleships to the Chilean Navy would be necessary to maintain peace with the Argentines; that at present the Argentine Navy was superior to that of Chile, and that this superiority had resulted in bringing about an aggressive policy on part of the Argentine Government, which, if persisted, is most certainly lead to an armed conflict."[30] Given the cool relations between Chile and the United States, it is surprising the offer was even made.

To offset growing Argentine naval superiority, Chile ordered two "lightweight" battleships from English yards to be delivered in eighteen months at a cost of about $4,800,000. By European standards these ships were second-class battleships, but their excellent speed of nineteen knots, which was exceeded on their trials, made them the ideal answer to Argentina's armored cruisers.[31] European bankers, anticipating war, would lend money only on excessively harsh terms, and in order to purchase these ships Chile had to divert to the navy funds that had been appropriated for the conversion of paper currency.[32] Not to be outclassed, in May 1901 Argentina requested that Ansaldo submit a proposed design for two twenty-two-knot, fifteen-thousand-ton battleships armed with 305-mm guns, to be built in a period not exceeding two and a half years. The design was to follow that of the Italian *Regina Margherita* class. Whether Argentina was serious about acquiring these two battleships or whether she made the inquiry to pressure Chile is unclear.[33]

Compromise

By now the hostility between Argentina and Chile, sparked by the boundary dispute, was aggravated by other factors. Luis Vicente Varela put the problem succinctly: "The only question that has agitated the two countries is that of the influence of each in the South American equilibrium."[34] In early 1902 Great Britain ordered her ministers in Argentina and Chile to offer their good offices in search of a solution, for war would endanger British citizens and economic interests in the two countries. Argentina and Chile imported British goods and supplied food, raw materials, and dividends to Great Britain. *The Times* of London estimated that "the total foreign capital already embarked in Argentina exclusive of the public debts is estimated at the enormous sum of nearly £123,000,000. The amount invested in Chile is not nearly so large, but it is still very considerable. . . ."[35] Negotiations proved to be extremely difficult. Meetings were held in Santiago between the British minister to Chile, Gerardo Lowther; the president of Chile, Germán Riesco; the Chilean foreign minister, José Francisco Vargara Donoso; and the Argentine minister to Chile, José Antonio Terry. Buenos Aires was in constant touch with the situation via telegraph. Finally on 28 May the Chilean foreign minister and the Argentine minister signed three agreements and exchanged several notes, known collectively as the Pacts of May.

The first pact was a preamble that stated the good intentions of both parties: neither would undertake territorial expansion. The second pact was a general treaty of arbitration. The third was an agreement to reduce naval armaments, the articles of which follow:

> Art. I. With the view of removing all motive for uneasiness or resentment in either country, the Governments of the Argentine Republic and of Chile desist from acquiring the vessels of war which they have in construction, and from henceforth making new acquisitions. Both Governments agree, moreover, to reduce their respective fleets, for which object they will continue to exert themselves until they arrive at an understanding which shall establish a just balance (of strength) between the said fleets.
>
> This reduction shall take place within one year, counting from the date of exchange of ratifications of the present Convention.
>
> II. The two Governments bind themselves not to increase, without previous notice, their naval armaments during five years; the one intending to increase them shall give the other eighteen months' notice. It is understood that all armaments for the fortification of the coasts and ports are excluded from this Agreement, and any floating

machine destined exclusively for the defence of these, such as submarines, etc., can be acquired.

III. The two Contracting Parties shall not be at liberty to part with any vessels, in consequence of this Convention, in favour of countries having questions pending with one or the other.

IV. In order to facilitate the transfer of pending contracts, both Governments bind themselves to prolong for two months the term stipulated for the delivery of the vessels in construction, for which purpose they will give the necessary instructions immediately this Convention has been signed.

V. The ratifications of this Convention shall be exchanged within the period of sixty days, or less if possible, and the exchange shall take place in this City of Santiago.[36]

The Pacts of May were ratified by the Argentine congress on 30 July and the Chilean congress on 11 August. The ratifications, exchanged in Santiago on 22 September 1902, stated that "both Governments retain the necessary squadrons, the one for the natural defense and the permanent presence of the Republic of Chile in the Pacific; and the other for the natural defense and permanent presence of the Argentine Republic in the Atlantic and Río de la Plata."[37] Argentina dropped her plans to build the fifteen-thousand-ton battleships (this may even have been done for economic reasons prior to the signing of the pact). Argentina sold her two seventy-eight-hundred-ton armored cruisers to Japan.[38] Chile sold her two twelve-thousand-ton battleships to Great Britain.[39] Argentina disarmed the armored cruisers *Garibaldi* and *Pueyrredón* and Chile the *Capitán Prat*.[40]

As with all such compromises, there were many on both sides that believed their nation had conceded too much to the other. But the Pacts of May managed to end the imminent threat of war between Argentina and Chile. Not for seventy-six years did another dispute erupt. And the treaty finally established the spheres of influence: Argentina would be an Atlantic nation and Chile a Pacific one. Still, the question over which nation owned what territory in the Antarctic remained unresolved and would prove troublesome for generations to come.

CHAPTER FOUR

Political Intervention During the Era of Gun and Longboat

LATIN AMERICA has a long history of military coups, but it was not until the late nineteenth century that naval leaders felt strong enough to challenge their army counterparts for political leadership. True, following independence, a few navy men had been politically active and Latin American sailors had shown their support or lack of the same through demonstrations. But so far there had been no significant attempt by any Latin American navy to overthrow those in power. This changed in the last decade of the nineteenth century, when major naval revolutions erupted in Argentina (1890), Chile (1891), and Brazil (1893–94).[1]

At this time the gun and longboat were the only two tools with which navies could directly oppose shore-based installations. The first and foremost weapon of the fleet was the gun. Although the destructive power of cannons had advanced markedly by the close of the century, their range was still very short in real terms, and their accuracy was limited. In 1890 a muzzle-loading twelve-inch gun had an absolute range of eight miles, about ten times greater than that of a thirty-two- or forty-two-pounder mounted on the lower deck of a ship of the line seventy years earlier. But like its predecessor the twelve-inch gun was still directly aimed by the eye, so its effective range was really not much increased. With a point-blank range of less than a mile still the rule, only the tidal area could be directly affected by the gun.[2]

To a certain extent the longboat made amends for the gun's shortcomings. At most it could carry about one-third of a warship's crew of four hundred, which was all that could be spared when the ship was not engaged with the enemy. Thus even a major warship could contribute the equivalent only of a lightly armed infantry company to activities ashore.[3] Throughout Latin America landing parties typically consisted of army troops—and in a few cases marines—hastily transported by warships to meet emergencies.[4]

Thus Latin American navies did not possess their own amphibious capability, nor could their guns reach far ashore. As a result, they did not have a reasonable possibility of enforcing their will on the land. Only the Chilean navy was successful in overthrowing a government, and its success was due in large measure to its ability to create an amphibious force. Throughout the rest of Latin America, navies remained secondary influences in the evolution of national politics until after World War II (see appendix 2).

Argentina

Since independence Argentina had been ruled by an aristocracy of landlords, merchants, and bankers. During the latter part of the nineteenth century, as European immigrants formed the beginning of a middle class that sought political participation, the power base, or the franchised population, began to broaden. The transition was not easy; beginning in the last decade of the nineteenth century, the upper and middle classes clashed in open warfare.

The government of President Juárez Celman (1886–90), noted for its economic disasters, fell victim to this confrontation. The Unión Cívica, a recently formed, popular political party, forged an alliance with junior and mid-level army and naval officers that conspired to overthrow the government. To buttress their support the rebellious forces, commanded by General Manuel J. Campos, told more and more officers of the revolt, and eventually the obvious happened: the government learned of the plans. General Campos was arrested and troops suspected of disloyalty were posted outside the capital. After this turn of events the civilian members of the conspiracy successfully convinced their military compatriots to delay the uprising. General Campos was freed after a brief period when the Tenth Infantry Regiment, his captor, shifted loyalty. Campos took command of the insurgent forces and decided to launch his attack on 26 July. The rebels gathered in Parque de Artillería (today's Lavalle Square in

Buenos Aires). The government's forces were centered at the Retiro, the railroad station.[5]

An elaborate plan was developed to commandeer the naval squadron lying in Buenos Aires harbor. Lieutenant Eduardo O'Connor was the ringleader of the rebellious sailors. On the night of 25 July 1890 he and five other naval officers crossed in a launch from the Boca del Riachuelo to the transport *Villarino*, whose commanding officer was already committed to the rebellion. Hoping to enlist the support of the captain of the division, the rebels crossed to the protected cruiser *Patagonia*, where he flew his flag. The squadron commander was absent, but the officer in charge, Lieutenant (j.g.) Enrique Martinez Quintana, agreed to join the rebels, and the *Patagonia* was placed under the command of Lieutenant Ramón Lira. Next the rebels summoned the officer of the day of the gunboat *Paraná*, Lieutenant (j.g.) Antonio Pérez, to the flagship and invited him to join the rebellion. He refused and was detained. The rebels then took two launches across to the *Paraná*, where the officer in charge, Lieutenant (j.g.) Alberto Encina, pledged to support the rebels. When the torpedo boat *Maipú*, commanded by Lieutenant Atilio S. Barilari, was boarded, he resisted and was wounded. The rebels failed to take the monitor *Los Andes*.[6]

The government, unaware of these events, ordered Rear Admiral Bartolomé Cordero to take command of the squadron and be ready to act on its behalf. The admiral attempted to board the *Paraná* but was refused permission. Shots were fired over his head, and he immediately changed course to the *Los Andes*. He boarded the monitor, went to the captain's cabin, and wrote a note informing the government that the squadron had rebelled. Junior officers who had by now gained control of the monitor arrested him, and the note was never delivered.

Meanwhile the insurgent fleet commander ordered his units to bombard the concentration of government forces in the Retiro and the Plaza de Mayo. The Parque de Artillería, where the rebel ground forces were located, was to send a signal: if two paper globes were released the fleet was to bombard Retiro, if three, the Plaza de Mayo. As it turned out, the signaling system didn't work. Moreover, the rebel ships prepared to battle the *Los Andes*, which they had not yet learned had already joined the rebellion. Precious time was lost. Throughout the day the rebels on land failed to act decisively, thus losing the element of surprise. Meanwhile government forces were being mobilized. They temporarily abandoned Retiro, possibly fearing a naval bombardment. Sporadic fighting broke out in the city, during which the marines proved to be among the stoutest defenders, suffering twenty-six casualties.[7]

On 27 July the rebel squadron began bombarding suspected troop concentrations at Retiro and the presidential palace, Casa Rosada. Ships maneuvered to within half a league of the shore, as close as they could get in the shallow water. In the afternoon the *Patagonia* captured a government transport after a short engagement while attempting to enter the Boca. Late in the day higher tides permitted the warship to move nearer to the city and the rebel warships renewed their bombardment, many of their rounds falling into parts of the city where foreign-owned businesses were located. Foreign warships in port intervened to stop the bombardment.[8]

At 1500 the Spanish *Infanta Isabel*, the Uruguayan *General Rivera*, and the British *Beagle* and *Bramble* steamed in column in pursuit of the *Patagonia* and a transport. The other rebel vessels escaped to the north.[9] The *Patagonia* and the transport were overhauled by the foreign squadron. Commanding officers of the foreign warships appealed to the commander of the insurgent squadron to stop the bombardment, Lieutenant O'Connor responding that he would only obey the orders of the provisional government.[10] What accommodations were made is unclear. Late that day heavy fighting took place between opposing ground forces around the Casa Rosada.

All the rebel warships returned to Buenos Aires. On the morning of 29 July they took up position near the city once again. At 1245 the *Los Andes*, joined by the *Maipú* and the *Patagonia*, opened fire on the city. Over one hundred shells were unleashed, most of which fell short and burst in the water. At the same time, heavy rifle fire opened in the city. At 1455 the international code signal CGL ("peace has been proclaimed") was hoisted in the city but went unnoticed by the rebel fleet.[11] An hour later a small steamer carrying a flag of truce made its way to the rebel fleet and the firing ceased.[12]

The insurgents' position was weak. Their land forces had not acted decisively on the twenty-sixth, and by the twenty-seventh government forces had been able to collect themselves and gain the upper hand. The rebel squadron resorted to the time-honored method of attempting to influence those ashore through naval bombardment, and this failed, in part because of the fire's lack of accuracy and in part because of the intervention of foreign powers. However, the fleet did remain an important card in the hand of the rebels. It represented a force in being. The terms of the capitulation demonstrate that the rebels still had some perceived military prowess. No reprisals were to be taken against those who participated in the rebellion; the insurgents were to be allowed to return to their barracks; the ships' crews were to be treated in the same manner as those ashore; and civilians were to disarm peacefully.[13] After signing the capitulation the rebels sailed to La Plata, where they disembarked.

The fact that the fleet remained an effective fighting force and that the government had little chance of effectively opposing it in the short term was important in winning acceptable cease-fire terms. Furthermore, the rebellion in the fleet was strong enough to lead to President Juarez Celman's resignation on 5 August. Senator Manuel D. Pizarro declared to the congress, "The revolution is crushed, but the government is dead."[14]

Predictably, unrest continued. Following the selection of Luis Sáenz Peña (1892–95) as president, the Radical Party, formerly the Unión Cívica, proclaimed one of its leaders provisional president. Argentina was again rocked by discord. By the late summer of 1893 two provinces, San Luis and Buenos Aires, were in open revolt. The rebels swept through the countryside. On 14 August 1893 the city of Corrientes fell, and by 7 September unrest had spread to Tucumán. On the twenty-fourth rebellion broke out in the city of Santa Fé, where the fighting was particularly bloody. But in this instance, the rebels were defeated by government reinforcements which had arrived in the steamers *Ceres* and *Quinto Misiones* from the province of Entre Ríos.[15]

The Paraná River ran through the heart of the troubled countryside, and whoever controlled it possessed a significant advantage. The river port of Rosario became the central stronghold for the rebels. Unlike sailors in the 1890 revolt, naval personnel were not among the first to declare for the rebellion. The torpedo gunboat *Thorne* had joined the rebels in early 1893, but this had been the only early defection by a ship. On 25 September Colonel Mariano Espina and Commander Santiago Danuzzio led sailors and civilians manning the torpedo boat base at Tigre to revolt. They seized two torpedo boats. Ensign Carlos Montaña was given command of the *Comodoro Murature* and Ensign Hilario A. Ibarra command of the *Numero 7*. The next day, while the coastal monitor *Los Andes* was steaming up the Paraná River, most of the officers and crew, led by Lieutenants (j.g.) Gerardo Valotta and Alberto Encina, took the *Numero 8* in the name of the rebellion.[16] The commanding officer, Commander Ramón Flores, was injured while resisting and later put ashore. The *Los Andes* joined the rebels at Rosario, bringing with her a valuable cargo of eighteen hundred Remingtons, two thousand carbines, four seventy-five-mm cannons, and six hundred thousand rounds of ammunition—arms and munitions that had been destined for government forces in Entre Ríos.[17] The rest of the navy remained loyal to the government, which had changed those in key positions prior to the general uprising to assure the loyalty of the bulk of the squadron.[18]

The government fleet reacted to the defections with great speed. On 26 September the torpedo boat base was surprised by a government squadron composed of the coastal defense battleships *Independencia* and *Libertad*, the central battery corvette *Almirante Brown*, and the protected cruisers *Nueve de Julio* and *Patagonia*. This overwhelming force crushed the rebels.

The government sent the torpedo gunboat *Espora* up the Paraná River to

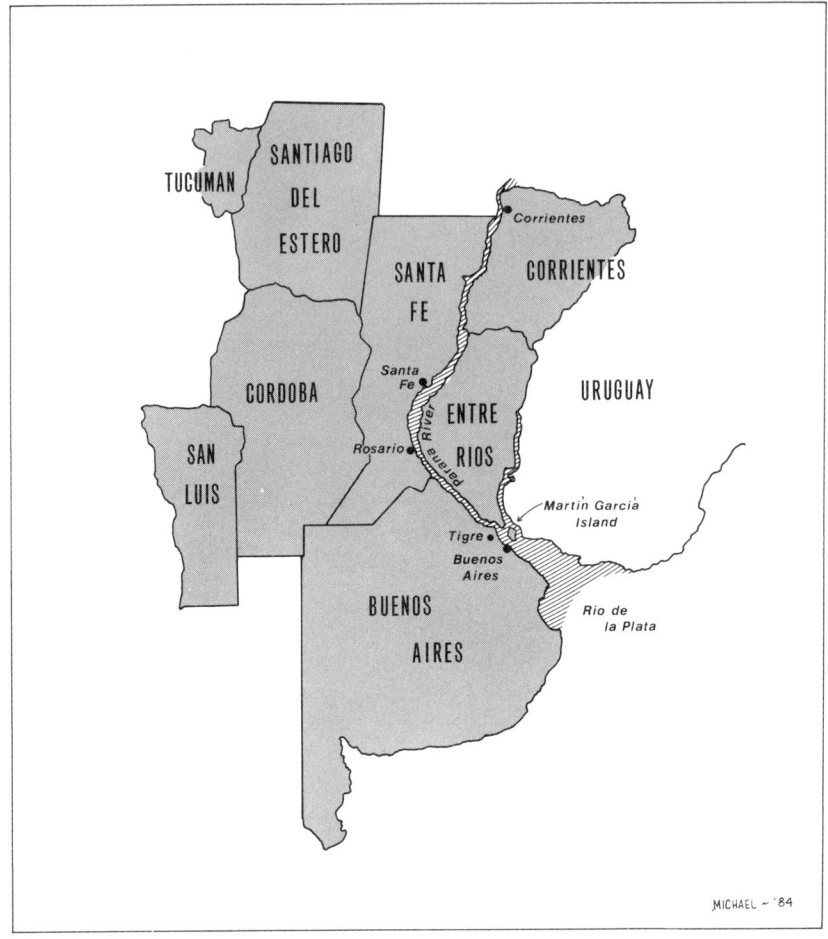

Argentine Theater of Naval Operations, 1890 and 1893

find the *Los Andes*. Earlier the rebels had seized the tug *Victoria R.*, and under the command of Cadet Héctor Contal she had been sent down river to reconnoiter. The *Victoria R.* discovered the government vessels near Martín García Island, evaded notice, and alerted the *Los Andes*.[19]

Early in the morning of 27 September the coastal defense battleship *Independencia* started up the Paraná River searching for the *Los Andes*. That night the *Independencia* anchored and the next morning was joined by the *Espora*. On the twenty-eighth they sailed together toward Rosario, the *Espora* in the van. At 1020 on the twenty-ninth the *Espora* sighted the *Los Andes* with the *Victoria R.* in front of Espinillo Island off Rosario. Shallow water prevented the *Independencia* from closing the enemy. At 1125 the *Los Andes* opened fire on the *Espora* with her two 9.45-inch guns at two thousand yards; the *Espora* returned the fire.[20] Partly because of poor gunpowder the *Los Andes* fired seventeen shots with little effect. The two government ships, now under fire from the *Los Andes* and rebel batteries ashore, continued to maneuver toward the rebel ship. At 1232 the *Independencia* opened fire, soon joined by the *Espora*. The government ships fired 356 shots of various calibers, scoring numerous hits. The battered *Los Andes*, no match for her opponents, sought refuge among river traffic that included some foreign ships. At 2130 the *Los Andes* raised the white flag, and at 0130 on 30 September she was boarded by government forces, which found her sinking. The *Independencia* was only slightly damaged. On that same day Rosario fell to government land forces and the rebellion was crushed.[21]

The Argentine navy's role in the 1893 revolution was not decisive, but it would have been less effective had the government, possibly reflecting upon the navy's role in the 1890 revolution, not taken the precaution early to assign important positions in the fleet to loyal officers. Though many in the navy sympathized with the new popular movement, the service was held in check.

Chile

The Chilean navy has long been said to be the best maritime force in Latin America, a reputation based in large part upon its victories in the War of the Pacific and its success against the army during the 1891 revolution. A constitutional crisis over presidential vice parliamentary rule split Chile in late 1890, with the president, José Manuel Balmaceda, supported by the majority of the army, the congress by most of the navy. The congress, realizing the need for a sword, had approached General Manuel Baquedano, conqueror of Perú during the War of the Pacific, for support. The general's prestige was substantial and might have carried the day, but he would not be drawn into the contest. The legislature then sought the aid of Captain Jorge Montt, who made his support conditional. The heads of both congressional chambers had to assume in writing the responsibility for a possible military action and thus give the navy a constitutional right to interpret the national political will (see appendix 4).[22]

The august body and its supporters embarked in the fleet that same day. The Congresionalistas, the name given to members of the congress, the navy, and their supporters, had substantial assets. Almost the entire navy was immediately available at Valparaíso—the battleship *Blanco Encalada*, the turret ironclad *Huáscar*, the corvette *O'Higgins*, and the gunboat *Magallanes*.[23] The only other major warship, the battleship *Almirante*

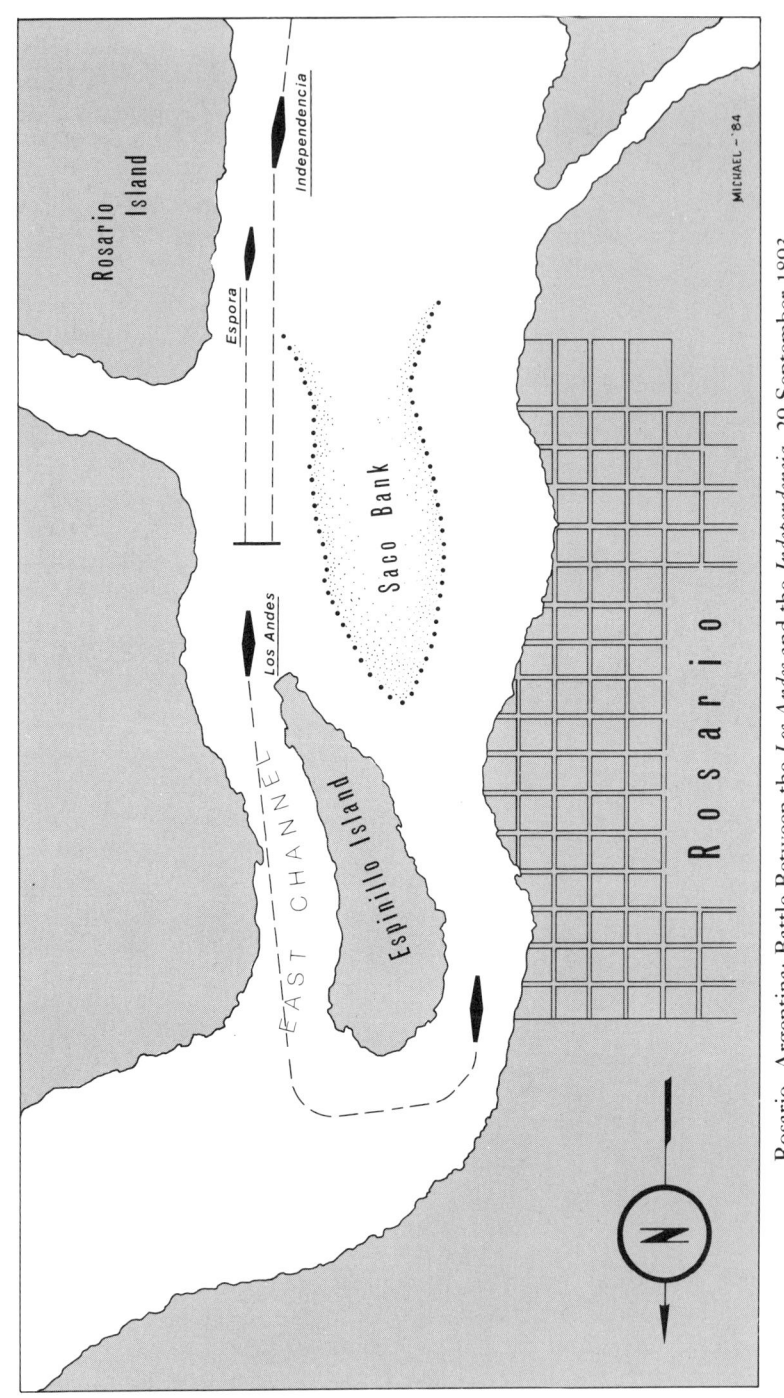

Rosario, Argentina: Battle Between the *Los Andes* and the *Independencia*, 29 September 1893

Cochrane, lay eighteen miles north in Quintero Bay. The Congresionalistas also had substantial sympathy from bankers and nitrate czars, a group from which the insurgents reaped money and people.[24]

Over the next week the Congresionalistas and the Gobiernistas—the president, the army, and their supporters—consolidated their positions. The navy was busy shepherding stray warships, seizing merchant ships, establishing a blockade of the northern ports, and seeking a base of operations. They succeeded in rounding up the entire navy, except for the new torpedo gunboats *Almirante Lynch* and *Almirante Condell*, in transit from England, and the gunboat *Pilcomayo*, on survey duties in the south. The fleet did not declare a general blockade. It was small and would have been hard pressed to enforce such a declaration, which might lead to a confrontation with a major naval power. Also, land routes over the Andes, still very rugged, made a total blockade impossible.

At first the insurgents set up a base of operations at Caldera. However, their ground forces being too weak to hold the port against the Gobiernistas, they had to establish their base to the north, protected by the vast Atacama Desert.

The Gobiernistas were likewise consolidating their land position by expanding infantry and cavalry battalions into regiments. They mobilized the national guard, which turned out to be a very unpopular move, and armed the new troops from government warehouses filled with trophies from the recent War of the Pacific.

While the Congresionalistas formed their army, the Gobiernistas attempted to create a navy. The Chilean foreign minister asked the British minister in Santiago to help the Balmaceda government purchase the British Pacific squadron's flagship, the armored cruiser *Warspite*. The request, dismissed, was only one of a series of aborted efforts made by the Gobiernistas to scratch a navy together. Another was the odyssey of cruiser *Presidente Pinto*. This unit was being constructed for the Chilean navy by Forges et Chantiers de la Mediterranée, at La Seyne, Toulon, when the revolution broke out. Rushed to completion, she sailed without official trials, crewed by a motley collection of nationalities including Chileans, English, Spanish, Italians, Greeks, Turks, and possibly others. Leaving Toulon, the luckless cruiser grounded and was refloated ten days later without injury. Then she sailed from one European port to another foraging for necessary fittings such as guns, which were not available at the time. Her trek took her to Genoa, Mahon, Southampton, and Kiel before events in Chile overtook her and she was returned to France for proper completion. Even if the *Presidente Pinto* had arrived in Chile before the Gobiernista cause had been lost, she would still have been outgunned by a number of units in the Congresionalista fleet.[25]

The Gobiernistas did succeed in acquiring the new torpedo gunboats *Almirante Lynch* and *Almirante Condell*. But by the time they reached Valparaíso their boilers needed to be retubed and the necessary steel stock was not available in Chile. Instead, brass tubes were removed from locomotives and used as an expedient.[26]

Chilean geography afforded special opportunities to the naval force, for in the 1890s, owing to the country's lack of adequate rail transportation, a large body of men could be transported by water about twenty times as fast as it could be moved on her land. Santiago, Valparaíso, and Coquimbo were joined by rail, as were the important population concentrations south of the capital, but in the north there were few lines, and these ran from east to west and serviced the mines. The sea, moreover, was a natural screen. Once the Congresionalista fleet was beyond sight of land, its destination could not be predicted, an advantage compounded by the fact that, regardless of the size of the Gobiernista forces, they had a strategic tendency to disperse to meet the enemy wherever he might strike. The navy, however, was faced with one enormous strategic problem. How could it exert pressure on the land forces? The ships had hesitated before Valparaíso, hoping that the mere view of the muzzle of the fleet's guns would cause the enemy to balk; as it turned out, they made no impression on the resolute opponent. Bombarding the nation's chief seaport, home of many of the sailors, was out of the question. And throwing a callow fleet landing party against the experienced army would be disastrous.

The Congresionalistas early concluded that a war of attrition would not bring victory. Their warships could close Chile to the outside world, a development not likely to enlist the sympathies of the population or to force the Gobiernistas to capitulate. Their defeat could only be realized ashore, and for this amphibious force was required. It would take time and money and manpower—an army of ten thousand. To round up this many troops from the fleet and the northern territories would have been a difficult task had the War of the Pacific not ended but seven years earlier, leaving most of the male population with valuable military experience in one of the branches of service.

Congresionalista strategy in the early days was to send the fleet north to capture lightly defended ports and collect booty that included nitrate revenues, volunteers for the naval brigade, and some arms. Not until 6 February, when they recaptured Pisagua, were the Congresionalistas able to gain their first permanent foothold. Two weeks later they succeeded in taking the key port of Iquique, which became their main base. By mid-April they occupied the northern third of the country and, controlling the sea, were able to import much-needed modern rifles. Ten thousand Mannlicher rifles were acquired from Europe. The steamer *Maipo* picked these up in Tierra del Fuego and, on her return run north, broke down forty

Chilean Theater of Naval Operations, 1891

miles outside Valparaíso. She remained in peril of detection by the enemy for almost forty-eight hours. Eventually she arrived safely at Iquique with her cargo of rifles, which gave the Congresionalista soldiers a decided advantage over their opponents ashore. Next, on 8 April, the steamer *Itata* was sent north to the United States to buy arms. She loaded a cargo of munitions outside the three-mile limit, then stopped on 5 May for coaling at San Diego, where she was seized and a marshall was placed on board. In a few days she slipped her cable and quietly sailed, depositing the marshall ten miles down the coast. This created a furor within the United States, which sent the cruiser *Charleston* to Iquique, the Congresionalistas' principal base. Arriving on 3 June, she sequestered the *Itata*, then had the Congresionalista ship escorted back to San Diego pending U.S. court proceedings. The incident strained relations between Chile and the United States, but it did not weaken the cause of the Congresionalistas.[27] Time was their ally; they would grow stronger through support from the outside world, while the Gobiernistas had little hope for similar aid. The friendly neutrality of two key world powers, Great Britain and Germany, was almost guaranteed, because of their close military ties with the rebels. The British navy had long regarded the Chilean navy as a favored grandchild. The embracing of the Congresionalistas' cause by Captain Emilio Körner assured the sympathies of Germany and brought to their side a brilliant tactician.[28]

On the morning of 22 April the Gobiernistas won an impressive sea battle when their two torpedo gunboats attacked the Congresionalista fleet at Caldera. A torpedo from the *Almirante Lynch* struck the *Blanco Encalada* amidships and she sank in less than ten minutes. Five or six torpedoes had been fired, one had hit. This was the first successful use of an automobile torpedo.[29] However, it was the Gobiernistas' only success at sea; they could but organize, train, and wait the time and place of attack chosen by the enemy. Typical of the tactical difficulties confronting the Gobiernistas was the experience of a one-thousand-man force sent to reinforce Antofagasta under Colonel Hermógenes Camus. These orders being countermanded, the force twice traversed seven hundred miles on foot in the winter, losing two hundred men to the elements without even sighting the enemy.

By July the Congresionalistas had assembled, equipped, and trained a naval brigade in the north at Caldera, Huasco, and Iquique. The Gobiernista forces had been busy strengthening fortifications and were scattered, their major concentrations located in Santiago, Valparaíso, Concepción, and Coquimbo. Descending from their harbor strongholds, the Congresionalistas carried out a well-executed amphibious landing north of Valparaíso in the afternoon of 20 August 1891. A U.S. intelligence report recounted the obsession with detail:

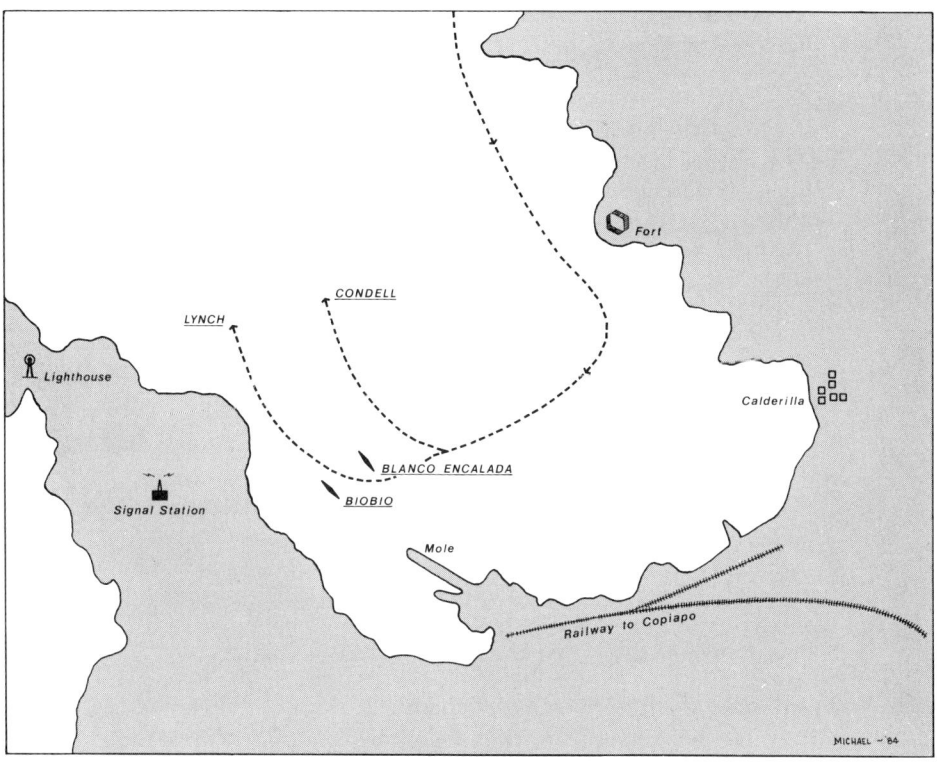

Torpedoing of the *Blanco Encalada*, 22 April 1891

Equally careful orders for disembarkation were issued on the trip down as those for embarkation. A great quantity of flat-bottomed bateaux had been made which were transported, lashed bottom out on the sides of the ships. They were each capable of landing 150 men in pleasant weather in one trip. They were not all completed on embarkation, but were finished on the way down. Ladders were also provided, one for each 150 men, and an officer detailed for each ladder at the upper end, with two seamen to receive the soldiers in the boats. Arrangements were made for buoys to be planted near the shore as guides, with lines running to the shore to haul out and in with. Each float was to be towed by a launch, and to go and return as quickly as possible. The cavalry were instructed to land with their saddles and bridles in one package, while the crews of the vessels looked out for disembarkation of the horses. The horses were to be directed in the water to a suitable place on the beach for landing, where the troopers were to assemble. The general officers and staff were to be landed in pulling boats.

It was provided also that each officer and soldier should have but one blanket roll. Every man was to carry two days' rations, consisting of preserved meat, bread, and packages of sugar and coffee. In case of being opposed on landing the commanders of transports and paymasters were to be responsible for landing the equipment as quickly as possible after the troops had secured a foothold. The men were to carry their pieces in the left hand at the height of the lower band on the ladders, and in case of landing through a surf the cartridge belts were to be worn around the neck. Commanders of transports were to provide an abundant warm meal to be given the men just before the formation for disembarkation.[30]

After eight days of stubborn fighting, Congresionalistas entered Valparaíso and victory was assured them.

H. W. Wilson, a well-known contemporary naval analyst, summarized the tactical significance of the war:

> The Chilean Civil War is important for two reasons. Firstly, because then the Whitehead Torpedo for the first time sank an ironclad; secondly, because of the admirable strategy of the insurgents. They used their fleet sparingly against fortifications, making no attempt to capture Valparaíso by bombardment from the sea. They recognized a truth which is sometimes forgotten, that fleets cannot act on land, though they do exercise a very marked influence on land actions.[31]

The tactical key to victory was the superb execution of amphibious warfare doctrine—not the nineteenth-century long-boat variety but rather a well-coordinated amphibious-assault doctrine that anticipated the future. The assault at Valparaíso is a classic when judged against other contemporary amphibious operations.[32] The Congresionalista plan allowed concentration of force when and where the attacker desired, rendering the Gobiernistas' numerical superiority of more than three-to-one in men and equipment useless. This is what won the war for the rebels, and this is what catapulted Admiral Jorge Montt to the presidency in 1891. He was the first naval officer to be elected president in Latin America.[33]

Brazil

A contrast to the Chilean navy's success at interpreting the national political will during the era of gun and long boat was the failure in 1893 of the Brazilian navy. It took on an active though little noticed political role early in the life of the republic, following the downfall of the monarchy in 1889. The first president, Marshal Manoel Deodoro da Fonseca, declared martial law and assumed dictatorial powers on 3 November 1891. Opposition was almost immediate; garrisons in the state of Rio Grande do Sul forced the governor there to resign, and the ex-minister of justice published a scathing attack against the militarists. On 23 November 1891 Rear Admiral Custódio José de Mello took command of the warships in Rio de Janeiro harbor and trained the guns on the city. Army units in the city soon declared their support of the fleet. Fonseca resigned, and the vice president, Marshal Floriano Vieira Peixoto, assumed the reigns of government. As a reward for his services Admiral Mello was appointed minister of marine. This was the Brazilian navy's first attempt to interpret the national political will, and because of general support from the army and populace, it succeeded.

A split soon developed between Acting President Floriano Peixoto and his minister of marine. Peixoto continued preferential treatment of the army. Sporadic uprisings occurred in Rio de Janeiro, Minas Gerais, Matto Grosso, São Paulo, Amazonas, and Maranhão. Several state governments had not yet organized themselves along federal lines; they were to have adopted a state constitution patterned after the constitution of the republic by the end of 1892. Civil war flared up again in the state of Rio Grande do Sul, and conditions were ripe throughout the nation for revolt. Peixoto retired thirteen generals and admirals who signed a political manifesto urging a presidential election. In April 1893 Rear Admiral Mello and Lieutenant Colonel Serzedello Corrêa, minister of finance, resigned their portfolios and publicly criticized Peixoto. On 23 May he was verbally attacked in the house by a congressman, J. J. Seabra, who accused him of unconstitutional acts.[34]

For a second time in less than two years the navy attempted to interpret the national political will and change the government by force. The first rebellious naval act, an isolated incident endorsed by the former minister of the navy, occurred on 6 July 1893 when Admiral Eduardo Wandenkolk seized the Brazilian merchantman *Júpiter* in Montevideo, Uruguay. The admiral embarked a makeshift army of a few hundred men and proceeded to the city of Rio Grande do Sul, arriving three days later. He then seized two gunboats and several merchantmen. The seaward batteries were ominous and the admiral's forces not strong enough to attack the city, so a hoped-for rebel land attack never materialized. The *Júpiter* and the rebellious admiral were soon captured by the Brazilian cruiser *República* off the coast of Santa Catharina State on 15 July. The rebels were taken to Rio de Janeiro and confined in Fort Santa Cruz, where Senator Ruy Barbosa attempted to obtain a writ of habeas corpus for Admiral Wandenkolk.[35]

On 4 September Peixoto vetoed a proposed law that would have prohibited him, a vice president acting as president, from participating in the next presidential election. On the evening of 5 September the naval battalion (marines) rebelled. On the sixth Admiral Mello rebelled for the second time and assumed the title of commander of the naval insurgent forces of the united states of Brazil. The admiral, supported by thirty to forty officers, seized the fleet. The flagship, the battleship *Aquidabã*, had been removed from dry dock two days earlier.[36] A small group of officers awaiting the revolt had taken the torpedo warheads from storage and kept them on board the gunboat *Orion*. A small number of prominent citizens, including six or seven members of congress, joined the admiral in the *Aquidabã*. If he envisioned a repeat of his 1891 effort with the army and populace rallying to his side, he was to be greatly disappointed.[37]

On 7 September (Brazilian independence day) Admiral Mello and his officers as well as the politicians on board the *Aquidabã* issued a manifesto making it clear that they intended to remove Peixoto, but their declaration left the fate of the republican government in doubt (see appendix 5).

The admiral's immediate military acquisitions were all the naval units at Rio de Janeiro, many of the most experienced naval officers, and about one fourth of the navy's active-duty enlisted men. The heart of the rebel fleet was the flagship *Aquidabã*, a second-class battleship completed in England in 1885. The protected cruiser *República*, also built in England in 1892, would provide yeoman service in the forthcoming struggle. To this force Admiral Mello was able to add numerous smaller warships and captured merchantmen, which he armed. As it turned out, the large number of ships was to little advantage: manpower was so limited that the protected cruiser *Almirante Tamandaré* had a crew of no more than thirty-seven men during the height of the gun duels against the harbor forts in the fall.[38]

Significantly absent among the warships commandeered by Admiral Mello were the second-class battleship *Riachuelo*, new cruiser *Tiradentes*, new training ship *Benjamin Constant*, and smaller vessels in Montevideo and Bahia. These scattered units loyal to President Peixoto gave him a potentially stronger fleet than that of the rebels, but it would take considerable time to pull together the loyalist force and there were not enough loyal officers remaining to staff the units. The *Riachuelo*, slightly more powerful than *Aquidabã*, was undergoing repairs in Europe, and the *Benjamin Constant*, being completed in France, would not be ready to join the loyal fleet for a long time.

Rear Admiral Luis Philipe de Saldanha da Gama, a monarchist sympathizer, was commander of Fort Villegaignon, strategically located on an island opposite Rio de Janeiro, and the superintendent of the naval academy. In a powerful position, he nevertheless declared neutrality in the revolution. For all practical purposes, rebellious Admiral Mello controlled the Brazilian ships in the harbor of Rio de Janeiro, Acting President Peixoto held the forts, and neutral Admiral Saldanha commanded Fort Villegaignon.

Admiral Mello's strategy was to reduce the harbor forts by gunfire, gain concessions through the threatened bombardment of Rio de Janeiro and Nictheroy, and establish a provisional government at Desterro (now Florianópolis), the principal seaport of Santa Catharina.

Rio was protected by some of the New World's most modern and powerful forts, soon to be the sites of long, ineffective duels that would virtually stop the movement of normal harbor traffic but never alter the status quo. At dawn on the first day of the revolt, the rebels captured ammunition dumps at Armação in Nictheroy (then capital of Rio de Janeiro State) on the east side of the bay, opposite the federal capital. Only seventy-four state militia troops were defending the city when it was attacked. Rio was bombarded for ten days in September, killing eighteen and wounding twenty-seven civilians. The population of Nictheroy, bombarded almost daily, was evacuated.

During the first day of the revolt the government's new minister of the navy sent the chief of naval staff to the French cruiser *Aréthuse*, British cruiser *Sirius*, Italian *Giovanni Basan*, and Portuguese gunboat *Mindello* to tell them that the fleet was rebelling and recommend that they take measures for their own protection. The Brazilian government also sent a letter to the Portuguese, British, French, German, U.S., and Italian diplomatic representatives (who were then in Petrópolis) inviting them to discuss the protection of their citizens. To Peixoto's surprise, all of them refused the invitation.

On 5 October the foreign powers finally intervened in an attempt to protect Rio de Janeiro and their commercial interests. Foreign naval commanders informed Admiral Mello that they would not permit another bombardment of Rio, and they asked the government to refrain from acts that would encourage the fleet to retaliate with a general bombardment. Thus Mello, while he lost the power to flex his arm with the threat of bombardment, unofficially gained recognition as a belligerent. But as the conflict spread, the major naval powers were unable to eliminate the threat to shipping by mines. The forces of President Peixoto sowed Rio de Janeiro's harbor with so many mines that crews from neutral warships attempted to clear the harbor of these devices out of self defense.

The city of Nictheroy was not spared under this arrangement. On the fifth the rebels exchanged fire with the battery on São Bento Hill while attempting to capture the steamer *São Diego*, tied up along the quay. A number of shells from the fleet fell into Nictheroy and inflicted heavy casualties on civilians.

Gunnery duels between the fleet and the gun emplacements added to the casualty list in October. Nictheroy took most of the punishment, being shelled by the *Aquidabã* and the *Guanabara* on 6 October. Two weeks later the monitor *Javary*, while bombarding Nictheroy, was sunk by shore batteries.

Despite setbacks, Admiral Mello seized Desterro (now Florianópolis), located on an island off Santa Catharina. The acting governor of Santa

Brazilian Theater of Naval Operations, 1893–94

Catharina, Christóvão Nunes Pires, surrendered on 28 September to a naval expedition composed of the cruiser *República*, the converted merchantman *Pallas*, and the torpedo boat *Marcílio Dias*, led by Captain Frederico Lorena. Lorena established a provisional government in Desterro on 14 October, unrealistically expecting world powers to recognize a government representing a population of twelve thousand when the government at Rio de Janeiro represented fourteen million.

President Peixoto realized that he needed a navy if he were to end the stalemate. He could not rely on the scattered loyal remnants of the Brazilian navy, the most important warships of which could not be made ready to sail for more than a year, and anyway he lacked experienced officers to staff them. True, the rebellious navy could be held at bay by the forts protecting Rio de Janeiro, especially with the benevolent support of the major powers, but the rebel fleet might be able to provide the margin of victory for secessionists in the south, thus shattering the central government's hold on the country.[39]

In mid-October Peixoto placed Admiral Jerônimo Gonçalves in charge of the government's sea forces. On 12 October Gonçalves left for the south in the *Thames* with his officers and loyal troops, planning to take possession of the coastal defense battleship *Bahia* and the cruiser *Tiradentes*, which lay in Montevideo.

In addition to pulling together the remaining loyal warships, Peixoto tasked his ambassadors in the United States and Europe to create naval forces. In North America they enlisted the services of Charles R. Flint, the flamboyant entrepreneur who once again charged headlong into the mission of creating a naval force for a Latin American nation. Funds were transferred and Flint went to work. He realized that to build a fleet within a few weeks he would have to purchase ships that were immediately available and crew them principally with North Americans, while those coming from Europe would have to be crewed by Europeans. Flint decided to buy ships with speed and the newly invented dynamite gun. The gun threw an aerial projectile to a distance of about three thousand yards with a launcher that had a fifty-foot-long cylinder and was fifteen inches in diameter. But the aerial torpedo, which contained fifty pounds of dynamite, could not be pointed; the ship had to change course to train it. The problem was hitting the target. The performance of the gun was erratic and the velocity of the projectile very slow, making it difficult at best to hit anything that was moving. Despite these shortcomings, Flint hoped to intimidate the rebels by aggressively publicizing the military capabilities of his new acquisitions. He set up a "literary bureau" to control information traveling between Brazil and the United States. For the consumption of the rebels, the material entering Brazil emphasized the ingenious character of "the dynamite fleet" and the destructive power of its new weapon. Dispatches released in the United States extolled the successes of the loyalists.[40]

Flint's fleet was composed of armed merchantmen and experimental craft. The flagship was the steamer *El Cid*, purchased from the Morgan Line. A fast merchantman, she was the only ship actually armed with the dynamite gun. The *Destroyer*, a creation of the famed John Ericsson, Flint bought more for her publicity value than her military prowess.[41] He also acquired the Norwegian *Midnight Sun*, a fast tourist ship. The units were armed with guns that Flint bought off the floor of the Columbian Exposition in Chicago. He selected a former clipper ship commander to head the fleet. The frivolity of the enterprise was exposed in a poem written by an American reporter:

> Mello, Mello, where are you, old fellow?
> A Yankee ship and a Yankee crew is out on
> The sea to look for you
> To knock you all to hell-o.
>
> We fly a flag of orange and green, Sir,
> The like of which we ne'er have seen, Sir,
> Our good ship's name, we cannot tell it,
> We haven't had time to learn to spell it.
>
> But what has a flag and a name to do
> With a Yankee ship and a Yankee crew
> That's out on the sea to look for you
> To knock you all to hell-o.[42]

Indeed, the dynamite fleet was more bravado than substance, whether those manning it knew so or not. President Peixoto's agents in Europe were much more practical and productive. Their primary acquisitions were one large torpedo gunboat from Armstrong in England and five small ones from Schichau in Germany.

Meanwhile, back in Rio de Janeiro, Admiral Mello finally extended his area of operations. On 1 December the transport *Esperança* and the battleship *Aquidabã* with the admiral embarked ran the gantlet of forts protecting the harbor entrance, receiving only slight damage. The departure of the admiral, going south in an attempt to aid the secessionists in Rio Grande do Sul, raised speculation that Admiral Saldanha was about to join the ranks of the rebels.[43] On the ninth Saldanha finally declared in favor of the revolution and took command of the units in the harbor. It was assumed that he wished to restore the monarchy. However, the revolt was supported by many ardent republicans, including Ruy Barbosa, then exiled in Argentina, and many of the congressmen who had embarked in the fleet back in September were avid republicans. The admiral's manifesto, dated two days earlier, contributed to the confusion over his political objectives. It condemned the administration and said that the nation should "solemnly choose" its form of government (see appendix 5). It was published by both sides in slightly but significantly different wording. The government claimed that the manifesto proved Saldanha wanted to restore the monarchy; the rebels argued that the admiral favored self-determination. Straddling sides as it did, the manifesto had a negative effect on pro-republican rebels and neutrals and failed to gain pro-monarchist support, so on 20 December Admiral Saldanha issued a second manifesto attempting to show his support for the republic (see appendix 5). However, the damage was already done; the new manifesto did not allay the suspicions of the republicans or win over the reluctant monarchists.

Devastating to the rebel cause was the refusal of the U.S. commander, Rear Admiral Andrew Benham, to recognize the zone in which Admiral Mello declared ships were not permitted to unload. Benham gave two U.S. ships permission to discharge their cargoes at wharves there and informed Mello that if he interfered they would open fire on the rebel fleet. The U.S. squadron, consisting of the armored cruiser *New York* and the protected cruisers *Charleston*, *Detroit*, *Newark*, and *San Francisco*, was far superior to the rebel fleet, and the threat went unchallenged. Because Admiral Benham refused to recognize the belligerent status of the rebellious navy, Admiral Saldanha loosened the grip on the harbor blockade. This was an irreversible action, as he soon realized.[44]

On 16 January 1894 the rebels in Rio received renewed confidence with the return of the battleship *Aquidabã*. She immediately justified their hopes, her big guns forcing government troops from prepared positions. Admiral Mello, having remained with the *República* in the south, was not on board.[45] On the night of 8 February Saldanha led an attack on Armação in Nictheroy in a desperate attempt to destroy or capture the batteries located there. He went ashore with the landing parties and was seriously wounded.

Meanwhile, in early 1894, the government's dynamite fleet and the torpedo gunboats arrived off the coast of Brazil from North America and Europe. Admiral Jeronimo Gonçalves, commander of the loyal forces afloat, sailed from Montevideo on 19 January to the rendezvous at Bahia, where he found some of the ships from North America and Europe on his arrival on the twenty-fifth. Over the next few days the remainder of the warships straggled into port.[46] On 1 March the government fleet sailed from Bahia for Rio de Janeiro and anchored outside that harbor ten days later after great difficulty. The government ships were ill equipped. They lacked boarding weapons—swords and cutlasses. No one knew how to operate the Sims-Edison torpedo that was on board some of the ships. There were only a few rounds for the dynamite gun. Many of the ships had been improperly loaded. And many in the crews were suspected of being rebel sympathizers. In fact, the only reliable element of the entire fleet was the European-built torpedo boats.

On 7 March the fleet arrived at Cabo Frio (north of Rio de Janeiro), where all divisions were assembled. The next day the tug *Audaz* brought orders from the president and took Minister of the Navy Coelho Neto, who had traveled in Admiral Gonçalves' flagship, the *Nictheroy*, ashore.[47] The fleet dropped anchor in Rio's harbor on 10 March.[48]

Admiral Saldanha did not, he judged, have sufficient force to meet a combined attack by fort and ship, nor could he force an exit. His most formidable ship, the protected cruiser *Almirante Tamandaré*, had only one engine room operational and could therefore make only six knots. In fact, for the last several months Admiral Saldanha's charisma and professionalism had been all that had kept the revolt alive in Rio. The immobility of the rebel fleet had doomed the revolution.[49]

On 11 March the admiral tried to negotiate terms, without success. He offered to surrender, provided that his officers were permitted to leave Brazil and that the lives of his men were spared. President Peixoto rejected the proposal on the grounds that a government could not accept terms offered by rebels. The next day the government announced that its forces would attack within forty-eight hours. Admiral Saldanha and his supporters sought and received asylum on board two Portuguese warships. The government, although aware that the ships and strongpoints had been abandoned, still carried out its bombardment, which started at noon on the thirteenth and lasted for an hour and a half. By nightfall the government's forces controlled the entire harbor.[50]

Admiral Saldanha had quit the fight. Whether Flint's propaganda about the dynamite fleet played a part in his decision is unclear. Probably the admiral just succumbed to a tenacious adversary. Luckily for the dynamite fleet, the admiral did not have enough strength left in Rio de Janeiro to confront it. The *Aquidabā* alone, had she been present, could have made it uncomfortable for the Yankee-manned fleet.

The naval rebellion was not yet extinguished, though. Admiral Mello was in Curitiba coordinating efforts with the southern rebels ashore, and he still had under his control the *Aquidabā, República, Íris, Meteoro, Uranus, Esperança*, two torpedo boats, and a few commandeered merchantmen. A half-hearted attempt to capture the state of Rio Grande do Sul failed. On 16 April the rebel cause received its coup de grace when Admiral Mello took his ships into Argentine waters and surrendered to local authorities. Under his command at the time were all rebel naval units except the *Aquidabā*. It was fitting that she, the rebel mainstay, held out to the last.

After gaining control of Rio's harbor, President Peixoto sent his expensive new navy south to deal with the remnants of the rebel fleet. A squadron of six ships and four torpedo craft found the *Aquidabā* in Santa Catharina Bay, near Desterro, the remaining rebel stronghold.[51] They kept a watchful eye on the battleship, protected by mines and lookouts stationed ashore. Apparently there were no small boats patrolling. On the night of 14–15 April boats from the squadron reconnoitered and found the battleship anchored under the lee of fortified Santa Cruz. The torpedo boats *Gustavo Sampaio, Pedro Afonso, Pedro Ivo*, and *Silvado* attempted to attack, but they were discovered entering the bay. The *Aquidabā* was alerted and the torpedo boats retired. The following evening the *São Salvador* entered

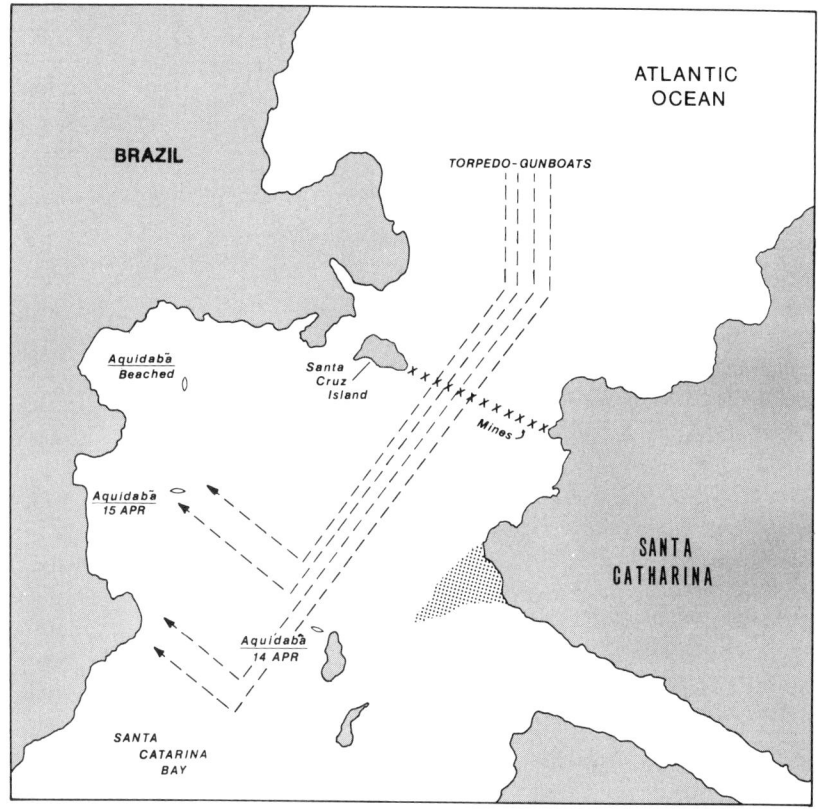

Torpedoing of the *Aquidabā*, 16 April 1894

the bay and destroyed the lookout station with machine-gun fire. After the moon set the torpedo boats started in a second time and passed through the mines without mishap.

The night was very dark. The torpedo boats entered the bay line abreast and, once in the harbor, turned in succession to starboard. They did not find the battleship where they believed her to be. Soon, however, the *Gustavo Sampaio* stumbled on the *Aquidabā* and drew her fire. The *Gustavo Sampaio* launched her first torpedo prematurely and without result. The second torpedo, fired at a distance of four hundred feet, struck the *Aquidabā* forward without seeming to damage her. The exchange of fire drew the other torpedo boats to the battleship. The *Pedro Ivo* had boiler problems and abandoned the attack; the *Silvado* was driven off by a launch coming from shore; and the *Pedro Afonso* fired two torpedoes but apparently neither hit. The torpedo craft withdrew without knowing the extent of their success. In fact, the torpedo from the *Gustavo Sampaio* had ripped a large hole in the bow of the *Aquidabā*. The battleship had gotten under way, beached in relatively shallow water, and been abandoned. She was boarded by government forces on 16 April, the same day Admiral Mello surrendered to Argentine authorities.

Admiral Saldanha, who had been granted asylum by the Portuguese fleet, escaped to Buenos Aires with a few of his supporters. They returned to Brazil and again were defeated in a battle with government troops. The admiral was killed.

A succession of blunders had doomed the Brazilian naval revolt. First, the navy did not gauge the national political will accurately. Although some of the enfranchised population was opposed to President Peixoto, he still enjoyed the loyalty of a majority of that group. And the heterogeneity of the navy's supporters compounded the fleet's problems. Second, a primary rule of sea power, eliminate the enemy's fleet, was ignored. The government's sea force slowly but surely gathered together, and it played a significant role in the defeat of the revolution because the rebel navy failed to take advantage of one great opportunity. If as they arrived piecemeal the ships of the government's dynamite fleet had been met at sea and defeated, all of Flint's propaganda would have worked against them. Given the poor track record of the dynamite gun, a rebel victory would not have been inconceivable. But the insurgents made other tactical errors. The blockade of Rio de Janeiro was inconsistently enforced, ultimately causing its collapse, and reliance on the gun to pressure the government was a failure. The presence of the *Aquidabā*'s big guns was often the margin of a local victory; however, it could not bring strategic success. Whether a meaningful union with rebellious land forces in the south was practical is open to conjecture, but it is clear that only through such a union could the fleet have acquired what was a decisive weapon, the amphibious force. The Brazilian navy failed to forge such a weapon.

Mello's actions were in sharp contrast with the strategy used by the Congresionalistas in Chile. The Chilean navy had recognized that bombardment of Valparaíso would be more detrimental than beneficial to its cause, and that ultimately the seat of government had to be captured by a land force. Having failed to obtain political support for a coup, Mello's insistence on concentrating his forces in Rio for nearly two months may have ultimately defeated him. He did not have the means to defeat the city's defenses and failed to find a way to exploit the mobility of sea power.

México

The Mexican navy, traditionally one of the weakest in Latin America, also raised the red flag of rebellion. In the chaotic years between 1910 and 1924, when liberal and conservative forces continuously clashed, the navy generally remained loyal to the central government, but after the expulsion of Victoriano Huerta in 1914 opposing naval units did confront one another. On 14 June 1914 the Mexican gunboat *Guerrero* fired three hundred rounds of 100-mm ammunition into the rebellious *Tampico* off Guayamas, sinking her and leaving sixteen dead, seventeen wounded. Before she sank, the *Tampico* fired 103 rounds of 101-mm shells, hitting the *Guerrero* three times and wounding three. Ten years later Secretary of the Treasury Adolfo de la Huerta revolted against the government when he did not receive the support of the president, Alvaro Obregón, in an election to determine the latter's predecessor. Huerta managed to entice the Gulf Fleet to his cause along with a small army, which together gave him substantial control of the Yucatan, Campeche, Tabasco, and Chiapas. The fate of the rebellion, though, had already been decided elsewhere, and the insurgent ships did no more than provide transportation to exile.[52]

Brazil

During the years between 1920 and 1930 revolutions divided Brazil, in part because of the dissatisfaction of young military officers with the social and economic conditions of their country. In 1922 army officers in the military academy and at Fort Copacabana revolted, an insurrection sparked by letters, falsely attributed to the president and printed in an important newspaper of Rio de Janeiro, that insulted the military hierarchy. The navy had no part in this insurrection. In 1924 the state of São Paulo once again unsuccessfully tried to separate itself from the nation, while the navy remained loyal to the central government. In an unrelated incident, three patrol craft on the Amazon River supported several rebellious army units, but this also was suppressed.

At about 0300 on 4 November 1924 Lieutenant (j.g.) Hercolino Cascardo and two other lieutenants (j.g.) arrested the senior officers in the dreadnought *São Paulo* and hoisted the red flag of rebellion against the government of Arthur da Silva Bernardes. The *São Paulo* was anchored in the harbor of Rio de Janeiro off the navy yard (*arsenal de marinha*), five hundred yards from her sister ship, the *Minas Gerais*, flying the flag of the commander in chief, Rear Admiral José Maria Penido. Some of those on board the *São Paulo* had been suspected rebels, and so many essential military items had already been removed. After some discussion, the revolutionaries on board the *São Paulo* were able to enlist the support of six junior officers and a number of enlisted men. At the time some five hundred were on board, with the remaining crew members ashore on liberty. Steam was immediately raised.[53]

The minister of marine, informed by phone of these events, hastened to the navy yard. He and Admiral Penido headed for the *São Paulo* in a launch. The battleship fired on the launch, so the two officials reversed course and boarded the *Minas Gerais* instead. In the meantime the *São Paulo*

78   POLITICAL INTERVENTION

signaled the shore to send off its liberty parties. Two six-pounders were fired in the general direction of the shore, and the liberty parties were hastily embarked. The launches carrying them arrived alongside the *Minas Gerais*, where all the sailors from both ships were taken on board. As this was taking place, the following radiogram was sent from the *São Paulo* to the *Minas Gerais:*

> The battleship *São Paulo*, hearing the just call of the people of Brazil, has resolved unanimously with other elements of the navy and a large part of the army to assume a repressive attitude against the irregularities of the actual Government. On account of this break, we invite the *Minas Gerais* to accompany us on our cruise. Reply must be given in 10 minutes after receipt of this. In the event it is affirmative, you must call together the officers and crew, and those who do not wish to adhere shall be disembarked immediately. The *São Paulo* has fires lighted and is ready for combat.[54]

Apparently, the *Minas Gerais* made no reply. The rest of the fleet remained loyal except for the old torpedo boat *Goiás*. She was being used as a school ship for midshipmen, and there were no officers on board her at the time. The *Goiás* hoisted the red flag and steamed up the harbor.

At 0900 the *São Paulo* got under way and circled slowly near the *Minas Gerais*. Thirty minutes later the *São Paulo* fired a six-pounder into her sister ship; the shot passed through the galley and severely wounded a cook. The battleship then continued to mill about the upper harbor, unchallenged by the *Minas Gerais* and evidently waiting to see if other ships would join the mutiny. At about 1030 the *São Paulo*, followed by the *Goiás*, headed very slowly down the harbor for the entrance. The harbor forts had hoisted the national flag but made no immediate attempt to stop the two rebel ships. But just as the *São Paulo* was clearing the entrance of the harbor, at 1116, Fort Santa Cruz opened fire. The dreadnought returned the fire with her 12-inch and 4.7-inch guns, at least one 12-inch striking the masonry of the fort. The *São Paulo*, free of hits, continued to fire. At about 1140 Fort Copacabana opened fire. This went unanswered by the *São Paulo*, possibly because a residential area lay directly behind the fort. No hits were scored on the battleship, and it may have been that the gunners were intentionally trying to miss it. At 1445 all firing ceased, and the *São Paulo* was barely visible sailing to the east.

When Fort Santa Cruz had opened fire, the *Goiás* had turned back. At first she headed toward Nictheroy, then steamed up the harbor and anchored half a mile from the *Minas Gerais*, hauling down her red flag and surrendering. At 1730 the *Minas Gerais* got under way and stood outside the harbor. She milled around off Copacabana and returned during the evening, anchoring opposite the presidential palace.[55]

The next day, 5 November, the destroyers and the *Minas Gerais* armed their torpedoes, the warheads being kept ashore. That night the *Minas Gerais* sailed with the minister of marine and the commander in chief on board, followed by one destroyer and one submarine that later returned to the harbor. On 7 November the cruiser *Barroso* and three destroyers left the harbor. Two of the destroyers took up station well off the entrance of the harbor and continued their picket duty until 10 November.

After departing Rio de Janeiro, the *São Paulo* headed south, short of water and provisions and with her condensers in poor repair. To aggravate matters there was much infighting among the rebels. On the evening of 4 November the ship was sighted about thirty-five miles south of Rio de Janeiro making about nine knots. She made no effort to enter any Brazilian port. Instead, at 0600 on 10 November she anchored at Punta del Este, Uruguay, requesting a pilot from Montevideo. The red flag was hauled down and the Brazilian flag hoisted. A pilot was sent and the ship anchored at Montevideo at 1300. Approximately six officers and two hundred crew remained on board and declared their loyalty to the Brazilian government. The revolutionaries went ashore and requested asylum, which was granted. The *Minas Gerais* arrived at Montevideo the next day, 11 November, whereupon the *São Paulo* was turned over. The socialist leader of the revolution, Hercolino Cascardo, was exiled until 1930, when he returned to Brazil under a general amnesty, regained his place in the navy, and served loyally. Cascardo became one of the founders of the National Liberation Alliance, a socialist party. Before his death in 1967 he had been promoted to the rank of fleet admiral in the naval reserve.[56]

During the 1930 revolution, which brought Getulio Vargas to power, the Brazilian navy remained loyal to the central government. In 1932 the navy blockaded Santos when the state of São Paulo struggled with the central government. On 11 May 1938 Brazilian fascists (the Brazilian Integralist Party) revolted, receiving some support from within the navy; the insurrection, however, was immediately suppressed.

CHAPTER FIVE

The Dreadnought Race

The Brazilian Navy

JUST BEFORE World War I a second naval arms race absorbed the energies of the major Latin American navies. It was initiated by Brazil and led by Baron de Rio Branco, a man who believed his nation was emerging as an international power.[1] To give credibility to this image a powerful fleet was needed.

There were two schools of thought within Brazil concerning the character of the new navy: those who favored a fleet built around a few heavily armored ships and those who wanted a larger number of small, fast warships. Initially, the latter group prevailed, and the minister of the navy, Admiral Julio Cesar de Noronha, asked for a shipbuilding program focused on small combatants. He intended, under the naval program of 1904, to buy three 13,000-ton battleships, three 9,700-ton cruisers, six 400-ton destroyers, six 130-ton torpedo boats, and six 50-ton torpedo boats. Law no. 1452 of 30 December 1905 provided the navy with £4,214,500 for new construction, of which £1,685,250 was to be spent in 1906, but many officers belonging to this school, including the minister's son, died in the accidental explosion of the second-class battleship *Aquidabā* on 27 January 1906. On 14 November Rear Admiral Alexandrino Faria de Alencar, who as a senator had supported the big-ship theory, became minister of the navy, and soon modified the 1904 naval program to include three dreadnought-type battleships of 19,250 tons, two scout cruisers of 3,150 tons, ten destroyers of 560 tons, and three submarines.[2] He used the money appropriated to 1905 to buy larger but fewer warships.[3]

Coinciding with the emergence of the large-ship school in the navy was the appearance of the revolutionary *Dreadnought*-type man-of-war, which gave the impression that in worldwide naval competition all fleets were starting anew and on an equal footing. The new ship-of-the-line design outclassed its predecessors so much that predreadnought battleships, no matter how new, were considered second-class warships. Suddenly Latin American navies, which had never maintained a first-class battleship, were given the opportunity to start over. And there was a small nation to emulate. In but a few short decades, Japan had created a modern navy that won the respect of world naval powers by defeating giant Russia. In this air of excitement and nervousness, Brazil leaped into the greatest naval arms race that the world had yet known by ordering two dreadnoughts.

The delivery of the *Minas Gerais* and the *São Paulo* in 1910 gave Brazil superiority over many major naval powers and over all her neighbors that would not be challenged for four years, and she had plans to increase it. In a press dispatch of 6 August 1910 Rear Admiral Duarte Huet de Bacellar Pinto Guedes, head of the Brazilian naval commission, "astonished the naval world" by announcing that a third dreadnought, the *Rio de Janeiro*, the largest and most powerful warship in the world, would be constructed for Brazil by Armstrong, Whitworth & Company.[4] He added that this would not be the end of Brazil's dreadnought acquisitions; there was a strong movement led by the country's navy league and supported by the press to obtain a fourth dreadnought.

These first South American dreadnoughts attracted attention throughout the nautical world. The voice of the powerful British navy league, *The Navy League Annual*, remarked: "Never has the Navy of a minor power loomed so large on the international horizon as that of Brazil during the past year. The reason is that this nation has had the audacity to order (not merely to 'project'; this is done monthly by insignificant powers) three warships equal in fighting value to anything afloat or building."[5]

Brazilian hopes for naval supremacy in Latin America and the respect that would come with it from major powers abroad were shattered on the night of 22 November 1910 when a serious fleet mutiny broke out, resulting in the deaths of a number of officers, including the captain of the *Minas Gerais*. Crew members of the recently delivered dreadnought played a prominent part in this uprising. Adding to his problems, newly elected President Hermes Rodrigues da Fonseca had a severely crippled economy on his hands. The price of coffee was falling and rubber faced strong competition from newly developed Asiatic plantations. Forced to reduce government expenditures, he shocked leading warship constructors on 3 May 1911 by implying that the *Rio de Janeiro*, then in the early stages of construction, was an unmanageable white elephant.[6] The navy's need of sound reform and additional shore installations were more pressing than any acquisition of dreadnoughts, he had decided. To answer these criticisms the builders revised the *Rio de Janeiro*'s plans, reducing her tonnage from thirty-two to twenty-eight thousand tons and her armament from twelve fourteen-inch to fourteen twelve-inch guns. This was totally inconsistent with contemporary decisions. Finally, in late 1913 Brazil sold the redesigned, uncompleted unit to Turkey, citing as the reason tactical incompatibility with the *Minas Gerais* class. *The Navy* (London) editorialized:

> It is strange that the excuse given for selling the *Rio* [*de Janeiro*] should be that she will not form a tactical unit with the *Minas Gerais* and *São Paulo*, because it is pretty obvious that a more modern ship would be still more unsuitable to manoeuvre in their company, while the *Rio* was especially designed so as to form a trio with Brazil's present Dreadnoughts.[7]

Brazil again altered her position and opened negotiations with Armstrong for the construction of an even larger dreadnought, the *Riachuelo*, to be thirty thousand tons and to mount fifteen-inch guns. Whether the decision to dispose of the *Rio de Janeiro* was based on tactical incompatibility, followed by a change in heart and the ordering of the *Riachuelo*, or whether Brazil sold the *Rio de Janeiro* to obtain a more powerful unit is not clear.[8] The fourth dreadnought was never laid down. Regardless, the initial advantage gained over rivals by leaping into the dreadnought race early on was lost to the swift progress of technology and the actions of other major South American powers.

The Argentine Navy

Argentina reacted to the Brazilian dreadnoughts by ordering some of her own. There was an internal argument initially over the wisdom of spending such a large sum on naval armaments, but contemporary border problems with Brazil, Chile, and Uruguay helped convince doubters.[9] The Argentine method for acquiring the best possible dreadnought design, which stirred controversy in competing nations, was to set up a naval commission in an office in London and request that all interested parties submit plans for the construction of two dreadnoughts (with an option to add a third).[10] In 1908 the office, headed by Rear Admiral Onofre Betbeder, opened and published dreadnought guidelines sufficiently sketchy to allow bidders to develop the best plans the state of the art would allow.

The proposal prescribed only trial displacement, the number of guns in the main battery, a secondary battery large enough to be adequate, the armor thickness, propulsion details, and a twenty-one-knot speed. Argentina was not disappointed in the response; fifteen companies submitted plans.[11] After reviewing the initial submissions and selecting the best features from each, the commission revised and reassigned the guidelines to competing firms. This process was then repeated a second time. It threw the competitors, who believed their trade secrets had been looted, into a fury. *The Navy* (London) observed:

> If the contract really goes to the United States, the feeling of soreness already present to the minds of the French, German, and British shipbuilders in regard to these ships will be greatly accentuated, for the *Moniteur de la Flotte* has mentioned that they have already been asked three times for their detailed plans, and alleges that the secret is not sufficiently kept as to the successive proposals presented by the tendering and foreign builders. It is even maintained that outside competitors have got knowledge of these details.[12]

Nevertheless, British firms assumed they had the inside track.[13]

The U.S. government was anxious to see these dreadnoughts built in its country. Secretary of the Navy George Meyer, responding to a Senate resolution requesting details of the government's involvement in this undertaking, made it quite clear that the U.S. Navy would provide any help necessary to the American builders or the Argentine navy for the construction of the ships. This even included a fire-control system and torpedo tubes. The secretary wrote:

> The plan for the fire-control system has not yet been furnished, but it is the intention of the department to supply the necessary information for use in the installation of fire-control systems. . . .
>
> The plans of these [torpedo tubes] were developed by the Bureau of Ordnance and it has not been deemed advisable to make these plans public. . . . These tubes could not be purchased from any private firm; . . . for this reason it was decided to permit their manufacture at the Washington Navy Yard.[14]

The U.S. firm of Fore River Company of Quincy, Massachusetts, offered an attractive price and was awarded the contract.[15] The maximum price was fixed at £2,200,000, a savings per ship of £224,000 over the nearest competitor. This was a shock to European builders, Great Britain in particular, for the United States lagged far behind in the dreadnought race and was not initially viewed as a serious contract competitor. After the contract was awarded, Professor John H. Biles, a noted English naval architect, strongly condemned Argentina's "unethical" methods:

No shipbuilder in this country can separate the knowledge which he acquires in the building of ships for the British Admiralty from the rest of his knowledge. We may assume that the British battleships embody good ideas and good practice—in all probability the very best. These cannot fail, in a greater or less degree, to become part of the designs which the British shipbuilder first submits to the Argentine Government. In the second inquiry it may be presumed that everything that was good in the first proposals had been seized upon by the Argentine authorities and asked for in the new design. This second request went not only to British builders but to all the builders of the world, and in this way it is exceedingly probable that a serious leakage of ideas and practice of our ships was disseminated through the world by the Argentine Government. The British builders, in replying to this second inquiry, would in all probability point out that some of the things are impracticable, or have been tried and found undesirable in the British Navy, and the Argentine authorities would be informed on additional matters which have come under the builders' knowledge by their acquaintance with British practice. The third inquiry that was issued showed to all the builders of the world what has been eliminated or modified in the second inquiry; and so the process of leakage went merrily on, and with it that of the education of foreign builders and the Argentine Government.[16]

The controversial dreadnoughts, the *Rivadavia* and *Moreno*, which Fore River Company delivered to Argentina, had numerous teething problems. Their coal consumption exceeded that specified in the contract and during trials the turbines in both ships failed and later had to be completely rebladed. Correcting this problem caused considerable delay in delivery.[17]

The Chilean Navy

Chile reacted to the Argentine acquisition by striving to obtain the most powerful dreadnoughts possible. She solicited tenders from European and U.S. firms. An American naval officer, Lieutenant Commander R. W. McNeely, visited Chile in the second half of 1911, ostensibly to observe the attempted extension of U.S. naval and commercial influence, actually to help the Chileans choose the right builder. The U.S. effort was too little, too late. The British navy already had a naval mission in Chile and a long tradition of cooperating with her navy. Commander McNeely observed:

In addition to a sense of distrust which the Chilean naval officer seems to have toward us, it appeared that there was being carried out in Chilean newspapers systematic propaganda against American naval materials while the battleship proposals were under consideration. In frequent editions of these newspapers, an attack on our powder, guns, or other material was given prominent place.[18]

Not surprisingly, the contract for the dreadnoughts was let to Vickers, Armstrong of Newcastle upon Tyne, England.

Both Chilean dreadnoughts were still under construction when World War I broke out, at which time the British Admiralty commandeered them. Also at this time Chile acquired her first submarine.[19]

After the war, on 1 August 1920, England returned one of the dreadnoughts, which was christened the *Almirante Latorre*. The second Chilean battleship had been converted into an aircraft carrier, HMS *Eagle*, so as a replacement the British navy offered two *I*-class battle cruisers. A debate developed within Chile between those favoring the big-gun warship and those advocating aircraft carriers and submarines. Apparently the state of the economy precluded the purchase of either, and the debate straggled along inconclusively, some in the Chilean navy persisting in their advocacy of the big-gun warship.[20]

The importance of the dreadnought to the rivalry among Latin American navies may be deduced from a conversation between Lieutenant Commander F. M. Beasley, RN, and Chilean naval Captain Carlos Torres at a luncheon in Valparaíso on 9 October 1937.[21] Torres explained that Chile wanted to acquire one or two heavily armored eight-inch-gun cruisers in case of war with Argentina. He speculated that in such an event a naval engagement between main fleets, each a long way from their bases, was plausible, and that the principal units of each fleet would be present. Chile would, therefore, face the problem of defeating two dreadnoughts with one. To succeed in such a situation, he stated, Chile would need one or two eight-inch-gun cruisers (eight to nine thousand tons) and six eight-inch guns, heavily armored, since there was no prospect of obtaining another dreadnought. The Chilean dreadnought would have to engage one Argentine battleship at extreme range, 21,900 yards (20,000 meters), using her superior ordnance to disable the opponent, and then engage the second Argentine dreadnought at decisive range, 15,300 yards (14,000 meters). The projected eight-inch-gun cruiser or cruisers would distract this second Argentine ship, keeping her engaged while the Chilean dreadnought dealt with the first Argentine battleship. Thus the Chilean navy, Torres said, had concluded that only the acquisition of eight-inch-gun cruisers would solve its tactical problem.[22]

When completed, the Argentine, Brazilian, and Chilean dreadnoughts took their place among the most powerful ships in the world and often excited the envy of other navies, including those of the builders. *The Navy* (Washington) published a detailed article comparing Argentine and U.S. battleships under construction in the United States and concluded that the South American design was superior:

It is to be noted particularly that while the displacement of these Argentine battleships [*Rivadavia* class] is greater than the American [*Arkansas* class], with 23 feet more length and something over 4 feet greater beam, the mean draft of the Argentine vessels is one foot less than that of the Americans. Careful attention is invited to the difference of 2 knots in speed and to the fact that the Argentine designs call for a bunker capacity of 4,000 tons as against 2,500 of the American, with a similar disparity in oil fuel stowage, namely, 660 tons as compared with 400; in other words, the Argentine ships carry 60 per cent more coal and 65 per cent more oil fuel than the American.

Just what, if anything, is sacrificed in the Argentine designs to get 39,500 horsepower as against the American 28,000 does not appear. It is certain that the secondary battery of the Argentine vessels outclasses that of the American, while their main batteries are identical. In fuel and ammunition endurance, the Argentine ships undoubtedly show a permissible maximum under the limiting conditions; and, even if it be assumed that the *protection* of the American vessels is on a par with the Argentine (which is open to question), it is patent that the Argentine designs—on the whole—are greatly superior to those of the latest vessels building for the United States Navy.

The Brazilian units received lavish praise as well: ". . . their new Brazilian ship [the *São Paulo*] is today the largest, most powerful warship that has ever been launched."[23] The noted German naval writer, Siegfried Breyer, comparing the British *Iron Duke* and the Chilean dreadnought, stated that the latter "was substantially greater and more powerful."[24]

The dreadnought race in Latin America came to an end because of its horrendous cost. The price of the three dreadnoughts ordered by Brazil was £6,110,100. Their maintenance for only five years would have cost £3,750,000, their ammunition, £605,520, and adequate docking facilities, another £832,000. A contemporary Brazilian newspaper calculated that the sum would have been sufficient to lay 3,125 miles of railroad track or to provide homesteads for 30,300 immigrant families.

Adding to the bill was the money needed to keep dreadnoughts operational. The funds were not always available. After their crews mutinied in 1910, the Brazilian ships *Minas Gerais* and *São Paulo* lay unused until the closing years of World War I. Argentina's dreadnoughts were inactive during the early 1920s because of a depressed economy. And for a few years after the 1930 naval mutiny the Chilean *Almirante Latorre* had nothing but a caretaker crew.

Thus the cost of acquiring a major warship was peanuts compared with the cost of maintenance over a number of decades. This was the first of three important lessons Latin American navies learned during the dreadnought race. The second was that, in the long run, the dreadnought could not serve as a force in being for small navies. The ship's primary opponent was another dreadnought. As long as the major powers possessed few such vessels, those in Latin America loomed large, both militarily and politically.[25] Once the giants had time to build them in large numbers, those in Latin America dwindled in significance. The third lesson was that the acquisition of dreadnoughts stimulated interest among nations outside Latin America for military alliances. This interest lasted only as long as the relative importance of Latin American dreadnoughts (see appendix 7).

CHAPTER SIX

World War I

WORLD WAR I, with the severe shortage of shipping it caused, wrought economic havoc in Latin America. Only Brazil possessed a merchant fleet of respectable size that could get her goods to market. But they were the wrong goods, at least as far as Great Britain was concerned, and Brittania ruled the waves. England greatly restricted the amount of coffee that could be sent to Allied and neutral Europe and placed it on the contraband list so that none could be shipped to the Central Powers. Argentine wheat and beef plus Chilean nitrates were in demand, but the shortage of ships' bottoms prevented these products from leaving port.

Also adversely affected were Latin American navies, which purchased all warships and most munitions abroad, primarily in Europe. When the war began, those ships under construction in European yards were commandeered. For Chile, and to a lesser degree Brazil, these seizures made the task of enforcing neutrality much more difficult.[1]

In this era warships were fueled by coal—for optimum performance, hard coal. Latin America, without hard coal reserves itself, had prior to the war been importing it mainly from Great Britain. After 1914 the United States became the principal supplier, and once she entered the war, in 1917, coal became even more difficult to obtain. This compounded the difficulties created by the commandeering of ships, restricting fleet operations even further.[2]

Latin America tried to enforce neutrality on belligerent ships. They illegally used their radios inside Latin American territorial waters; they coaled in these waters; and here they even captured enemy shipping. But for the most part Latin America failed in this task. Some countries, such as Colombia, Ecuador, México, and Venezuela, had substantial coastlines and few warships to patrol them. Even neutrals possessing moderate-sized navies, such as Argentina and Chile, had too few warships and too little coal to do the patrolling effectively. And occasionally individuals living in Latin America aided ships from belligerent countries whose cause they supported.

Brazil Once Forgotten

Brazil was the only major Latin American country to declare war on the Central Powers in World War I.[3] Before she did so, the war brought swift economic disaster to her shores. One of her chief exports, natural rubber, which the war machines did not need in huge quantities, fell sharply in price. So did her other major export, coffee. The British, after imposing a blockade on the Central Powers, terminated the importation of coffee, arguing that shipping tonnage was needed for essential items. Britain placed coffee on the contraband list so that shipments going to the Central Powers were subject to seizure, and she restricted coffee exports to European neutrals to prevent excess from flowing into Germany.[4] Numerous Brazilian firms were blacklisted by the British merely on suspicion of trading with the Germans. While belligerents were buying munitions and grain from neutral North America, Brazilian coffee and other agricultural goods sat in ports unsold. The value of the country's exports in 1914 was only half of what it had been the preceding year, even though the war was only five months old. Brazil, like most Latin American countries, derived a large part of her annual income from import taxes. When trade stagnated, revenues plummeted.[5]

Brazil declared neutrality on 4 August 1914, but from the start her sympathies lay with the Allies. She maintained strong cultural ties with France, economic ones with Great Britain, and she boasted of sharing a political heritage with her sister republic, the United States. A number of pragmatic considerations influenced the initial neutrality. Germany owed Brazil between six and seven million pounds for coffee seized at Hamburg at the outbreak of the war. If any action were taken against Germany, she might renounce this debt. There was also a large number of German immigrants in southern Brazil who were believed to retain loyalty to their mother country.

Friction between Brazil and Germany was inevitable. The war created a shortage of merchant ships. Ship construction, largely concentrated in the belligerent nations, could not keep up with the increased demand of war. Brazil possessed the largest merchant marine in Latin America and one of respectable size by world standards—377 steamers of 290,637 net tons in 1916.[6] As the war took its toll on the merchant ships of other countries, Brazilian vessels extended the scope of their operations to ports previously dominated by British merchantmen. Soon Brazilian merchant ships were regularly found in U-boat-infested European waters. Moreover, hundreds of German merchantmen lay interned in neutral ports throughout the world, forty-five of them in Brazilian ports. Commercial interests in Brazil argued for the requisition of these vessels, but for almost three years the government respected their sanctuary.

Brazilian merchant ships were sunk despite Brazil's neutral stance. The first loss came on 2 May 1916, when the steamer *Rio Branco* was torpedoed. This action solidified the pro-Allied attitude of Brazil, but not enough to draw the country into war. The *Rio Branco* had been leased to British subjects and no lives were lost in the torpedoing, facts that tempered Brazil's reaction.[7] It didn't remain tempered for long. On the night of 8–9 December 1916 the Brazilian steamer *Rio Pardo*, en route from England to Holland, was seized by German destroyers. On 31 January 1917 Germany announced a blockade of Allied coasts, to be enforced by unrestricted submarine warfare. Now a submarine might attack without warning, whether surfaced or submerged. The Brazilian government protested this action on 9 February and again on the thirteenth, but to no avail: on 4 April a Brazilian merchant ship was torpedoed without warning. Brazil sent the Germans the following notification:

> The *Paraná* was proceeding under reduced speed, was illuminated outside and inside, including the shield with the name "Brazil," and considering that the steamer received no warning to stop, according to the unanimous deposition of the crew, and further, that the steamer was torpedoed and was shelled five times, and that the submarine made no attempt to save life . . . the Brazilian Government severs relations with Germany.[8]

The German reply, that the ship had struck a British or a French mine, was received in Brazil as a cruel joke.

Brazil severed diplomatic relations with Germany on 10 April and three days later authorized the arming of merchant ships.[9] Although she reaffirmed her neutrality on 25 April, U.S. entry in the war earlier in the month had swayed her further to the Allied side. On 20 May a German U-boat sank the merchantman *Tijuca* off the coast of Brest, France. President Wenceslau Braz Pereira Gômes made Brazil's sympathies clear in a 22 May message to congress: "The Republic has thus recognized that one of the belligerents is an integral part of the American continent and that we are bound to this belligerent by a traditional friendship and by a similarity of political opinion in the defense of the vital interests of America and the principles accepted by international law."[10]

In the second half of 1917 Brazil moved closer to war. On 1 June she revoked her neutrality in the war between the United States and Germany, and President Gômes authorized the requisition of interned German merchant ships in accordance with the principles of the 1907 Hague Convention concerning the rights and duties of a neutral in naval warfare.[11] He declared "that the utilization of the German merchant ships anchored in Brazilian ports, without any notion of confiscation . . . is urgently necessary."[12] All forty-five German merchant ships were seized over the next day; thirty-three had been so badly neglected or sabotaged that foreign help would be needed to put them back in service.[13]

Both France and the United States wanted to acquire these ships, the latter offering to tow them to a North American port for repairs. Great Britain said she would allow some coffee to be shipped to England, provided it was carried in the requisitioned ships. Brazil turned down the North American and British offers, possibly fearing that their acceptance might weaken her claim to requisitioned merchantmen at the end of the war. On 3 December 1917 she leased thirty of the ships to France until 31 March 1919. They were to sail under the Brazilian flag but with British crews. In compensation, France paid one hundred million francs and purchased two million sacks of coffee plus one hundred million francs' worth of Brazilian goods. Despite all of this clamoring for their use, the ships were very slow entering service because of their poor condition at the time of seizure.[14]

Although Brazil was on the path to war, the visit of four American armored cruisers with Admiral William B. Caperton, commander in chief of the Pacific Fleet, on board probably sped up the timetable. Caperton went to spread U.S. influence and convince the South American nations to join the war on the Allied side, a mission his force, with its handsome armored cruisers and smart U.S. bluejackets contrasting with the heavily used British warships and the patrol-weary Royal Navy sailors who frequented Brazilian ports, was well suited to. Caperton also had experience in Latin American affairs to recommend him. In 1915 he had commanded naval forces that had intervened in Haití and the Dominican Republic, and a year later he had led a fleet in support of U.S. policies in Nicaragua.

On 14 June 1917 the armored cruisers *Pittsburgh*, *South Dakota*, *Pueblo*, and *Frederick* were officially received at Salvador, Bahia. Within a week the squadron had arrived in Rio de Janeiro, and on the fourth of July North American, Brazilian, British, and French sailors paraded in the capital city. The elite wined and dined the charming Admiral Caperton, and he reciprocated, asking Washington for five thousand dollars to pay for the affair. After two weeks in Brazil he tried his hand in Uruguay and then Argentina. The Uruguayans were duly impressed but would not move from their neutral position without a favorable sign from Argentina, and the Argentine president, Hipólito Irigoyen, remained steadfast in his commitment to neutrality.[15] After his trip south Admiral Caperton spent most of his time in Brazil's waters influencing that country's maritime policy and prosecuting his mission.[16]

On 28 June Brazil completed the more limited action of 1 June and revoked her neutrality in the war between the Allied and Central powers. This made her status—as a nonneutral, nonbelligerent—somewhat ambiguous but not without its advantage, for Brazilian merchantmen could now travel in convoys guarded by Allied and North American warships. The day after the end of neutrality the minister of foreign affairs asked to be told the areas patrolled by the Allied and U.S. squadrons "so that . . . Brazilian ships may derive, for their greater safety, the full benefits of these patrols."[17] On paper the small Brazilian navy included some decent warships acquired under the 1904 modernization program: the dreadnoughts *Minas Gerais* and *São Paulo*, the scout cruisers *Bahia* and *Rio Grande do Sul*, and ten *Para*-class destroyers, all completed between 1908 and 1910 in British yards. But all shared problems. Boilers and condensers were in poor condition, most of the power plants were unreliable, and none of the ships could come close to their designed speeds. Nor did any of them carry fire control equipment of the sort that had come into use during the war. Except for the three *F*-class submarines and the tender *Ceara*, the Brazilian navy was run-down or hopelessly obsolete.

The Brazilian minister of the navy, Vice Admiral Alexandrino Faria de Alencar, argued successfully that the task of patrolling the South Atlantic should be shared. The North American, Brazilian, British, and French navies were each assigned a sector of the ocean. In July the Brazilian navy established three divisions within their realm of responsibility. The Northern Division, responsible for the area from Amazonas to Sergipe, was commanded by Rear Admiral Joao Carlos Mourao dos Santos and included the predreadnought coastal defense battleships *Floriano* and *Deodoro*, the old cruisers *República* and *Tiradentes*, the destroyers *Piauhy* and *Santa Catharina*, and the ships of the Amazon flotilla, *Jurua*, *Acre*, *Missoes*, *Jutahy*, *Teffe*, and *Amapa*. The Center Division, commanded by Rear Admiral Francisco de Mattos, patrolled an area from Bahia to Rio de Janeiro. It included the battleships *Minas Gerais* and *São Paulo* and the destroyers *Amazonas*, *Para*, *Parahyba*, *Alagoas*, *Parana*, and *Mato Grosso*. The Southern Division, under Rear Admiral Pedro Max Fernando de Frontin, patrolled

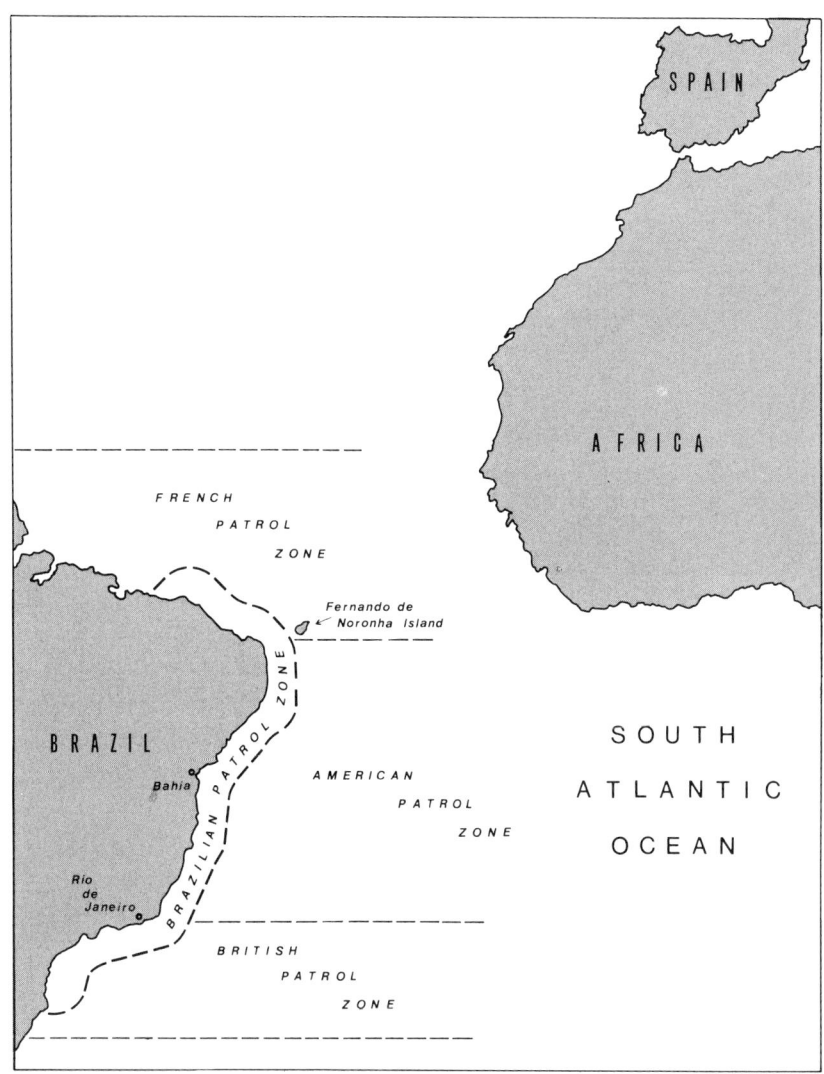

South Atlantic Maritime Patrol Zone, July 1917

the area from São Paulo to Rio Grande do Sul with the cruisers *Barroso*, *Bahia*, and *Rio Grande do Sul*, the destroyers *Rio Grande do Norte* and *Sergipe*, and the converted yacht *Jose Bonifacio*, among others.[18]

The Brazilian navy was in a somewhat awkward position. Of the patrolling navies it alone was not at war with the Central Powers, and thus it had no right to take action outside territorial waters. Although this limited the navy's usefulness, it could still, even as a nonbelligerent, contribute to the Allied cause. It could shadow and "tattletale" on suspected German ships, and it could patrol Brazil's coastline, where the large number of German immigrants who had settled in southern Brazil were suspected of supporting the German war effort. Moreover, with rumors of secret U-boat hideaways in northern rivers persistent, the Brazilian patrols were to begin as soon as the boiler and condenser tubes of the scout cruisers *Bahia* and *Rio Grande do Sul*—as well as those of a number of destroyers—were replaced.[19] Parts for the cruisers, which could make only eighteen knots in their current condition, and for the equally handicapped *Para*-class destroyers, without hydrophones or reliable depth charges, had been ordered from the United States. The patrols, scheduled for 1 September, had to be delayed a month because repairs had not yet been completed, coal was in short supply, and the Ministry of the Navy was waiting for an order of six seaplanes plus armament and range finders for the two dreadnoughts. On 8 August 1917 an antisubmarine net was installed in the port of Rio de Janeiro, and beginning that day a Brazilian destroyer regularly patrolled the entrance from sunrise to sunset. The port could be entered after dark only by a prearranged recognition signal.[20]

On 7 July the senior German diplomat in South America, Count Luxburg, wrote to the German Ministry of Foreign Affairs that "a submarine squadron with full powers" could "still save the situation" in Brazil, "where the people under thin veneer are Indians." A month later he was still trying to get his submarine squadron.

> I am convinced that we shall be able to carry through our principal *political aims* in South America, the maintenance of open market in Argentina and the *reorganization of South Brazil equally well whether with or against Argentina*. Please cultivate friendships with Chile. The announcement of the visit of a submarine squadron to salute the President [of Chile] would even now exercise decisive influence on the situation in South America.[21]

Unfortunately for Germany, Count Luxburg's dispatches were intercepted and published.

The next few months rode on tension. Brazilian merchant ships were sailing under the protection of Allied combatant ships. On 18 October the merchantman *Macao*, one of the German merchant ships requisitioned by Brazil on 2 June, was torpedoed off the Spanish coast, her captain taken prisoner. On 24 October the Brazilian president sent a message to congress declaring that a state of war had been forced on Brazil. Two days later the senate proclaimed "a state of war between Brazil and the German Empire, provoked by the latter. . . ." The senate passed the resolution by a unanimous vote, the Chamber of Deputies by 149 to 1.[22] U-boats immediately scored successes against the Brazilian merchant fleet; the *Acary, Cuyaba, Rio de Janeiro, Ceara,* and *Taquari* were sunk in November and December 1917.

Brazil's first belligerent act occurred on 26 October 1917 when her destroyers *Mato Grosso* and *Piauhy* attempted to seize the disarmed and interned German gunboat *Eber* at Bahia. The German crew scuttled her.[23] In late 1917 Rear Admiral Francisco de Mattos was sent to Europe to study Allied fleet operations and superintend any Brazilian naval operations that might take place in European waters.[24] On 21 December 1917 the British government requested a Brazilian force of light cruisers and destroyers in the war zone, to be placed under the British navy's operational control; the Admiralty offered to provide logistical support. On the last day of 1917 the Brazilian government replied, "The Federal Government . . . has ordered a fleet to make ready, composed of the scouts *Rio Grande do Sul* and *Bahia* and the destroyers *Parahyba, Rio Grande do Norte, Piauhy,* and *Santa Catharina.* . . ."[25] The squadron, designated the Naval Division in War Operations (Divisão Naval em Operações de Guerra, or DNOG), was put under the command of Rear Admiral Pedro Max Fernando de Frontin on 30 January 1918. The admiral insisted that all of the officers be volunteers.[26]

A herculean procurement effort began. Brazil had neither the industrial base nor the coal to support her war fleet. Nothing the DNOG used was indigenous to the country save the crews, and they were in part foreign trained. Even charts of the African coast had to be taken from interned German merchantmen. The most significant additions to the squadron were the tender *Belmonte,* armed as an auxiliary cruiser, and the high-seas tug *Laurindo Pitta.*[27]

On 31 July the DNOG sailed from Fernando de Noronha for Sierra Leone, a British colony on the west coast of Africa. The division was forced to stop several times so that coal and water could be transferred from the *Belmonte* to the cruiser and destroyers, and emergency repairs had to be made at sea, the tug *Laurindo Pitta* ferrying equipment from the tender to the other ships. These necessities were dangerous: whenever the force stopped, its ships became more vulnerable to U-boat attack, a problem the destroyers, having trouble maintaining a protective ASW screen, could not mitigate. In the end the DNOG managed to navigate this Scylla and Charybdis of repairs and U-boat threat, meeting Admiral Sheppard's British squadron off Sierra Leona at midnight, 8–9 August 1918. The Brazilian ships entered Freetown on 9 August, then left for Dakar on 23 August.

During the night of 25–26 August the division believed that it had been attacked by an enemy submarine when the *Belmonte* reported a torpedo

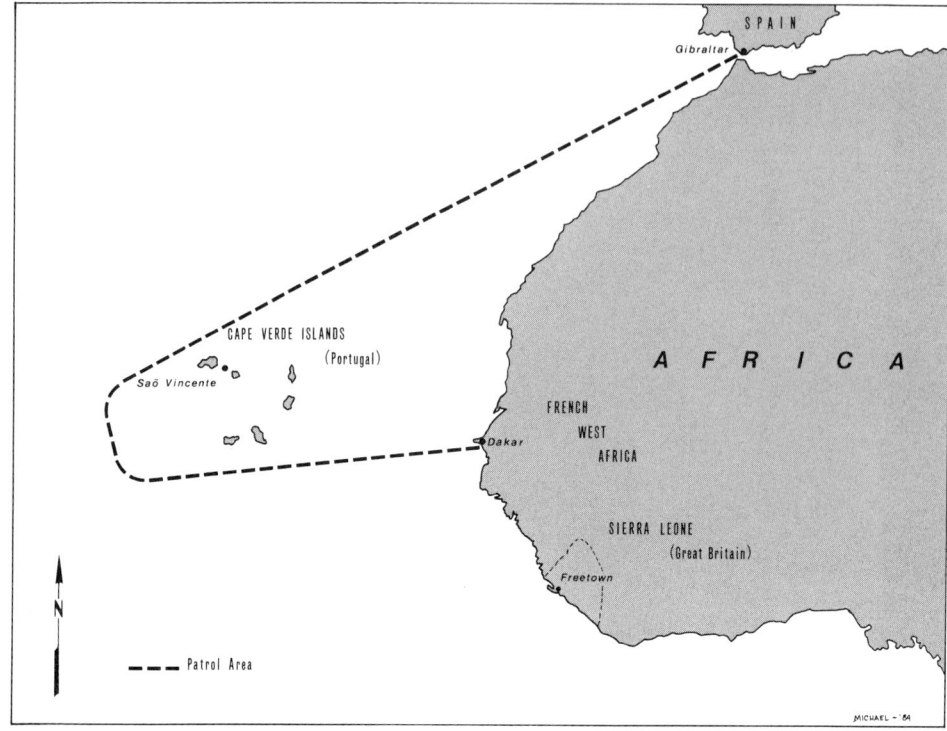

Brazilian Theater of Naval Operations, 1918

track. The suspected U-boat was depth-charged, fired at, and supposedly sunk by the destroyer *Rio Grande do Norte*—an action that was never confirmed.[28]

On 26 August the DNOG arrived at Dakar, its new base of operation. The force, with 134 officers and 1,361 enlisted men on board, was responsible for patrolling the Dakar–Cape Verde–Gibraltar triangle, an area believed to be frequented by U-boats lying in wait for Allied convoys. The Brazilian squadron was to guarantee the safe passage of convoys and sweep for mines. While in African waters both cruisers, whose new parts still had not arrived from the United States prior to sailing, experienced numerous problems with their condensers, a situation the excessively hot weather off the African coast exacerbated.

Meanwhile, after a confrontation in Rio de Janeiro between pro-U.S. and pro-British officers over their roles, Brazil's Ministry of the Navy decided to send both of its dreadnoughts to the United States to be completely refitted. The *São Paulo*, scheduled to go first, was to arrive in time to take part in the 1918 Fourth of July celebration. Before her departure people gave parties in her honor and the president, Wenceslau Gômes, held a farewell reception, but at the last minute he canceled the 6 June sailing date because U-boats had been reported off the coast. Admiral Caperton immediately offered the protected cruisers USS *Cincinnati* and *Raleigh* as escorts, a proposal the president vacillated for more than a week before accepting. The *Raleigh* was undergoing minor repairs, so the *São Paulo*'s departure was delayed a while longer. Finally on 17 June she and her escorts sailed. On the first day at sea fourteen of her eighteen boilers failed, and the Brazilian battleship had to put into Bahia. Ninety firemen, machinists, and boilermakers from USS *Nebraska*, which was in port, made emergency repairs. The *São Paulo*, now escorted by the *Nebraska*, arrived in New York forty-two days out of Rio. The period of her overhaul, two years, outlasted the war. The *Minas Gerais* underwent a similar refit following the return of her sister.[29]

On 6 September, while the fleet was lying in Dakar, Spanish influenza broke out among the crews of the Brazilian squadron. It started on board the *Bahia* and for seven weeks ravaged the ranks, at its peak incapacitating ninety-five percent of several ships' companies. One hundred and three Brazilian sailors were buried in the Dakar and St. Vicente cemeteries. Two hundred and fifty, disabled by the sickness, were sent back to Brazil where many later died.

On 3 November the DNOG sailed from Dakar for Gibraltar, leaving behind the cruiser *Rio Grande do Sul*, destroyer *Rio Grande do Norte*, and tender *Belmonte*. The squadron arrived at its destination on 10 November to begin operating in the Mediterranean. On entering the strait, it mistook three American subchasers for U-boats, but the error was realized before any damage ensued. World War I, "the war to end all wars," came to a close the following day.[30]

Brazil had earned the right to be represented at the Versailles Peace Conference. A major question for her was the disposition of the forty-three surviving vessels of the German merchant fleet requisitioned in 1917, thirty of which had been leased to France during the war and the remainder of which had been operated by the Brazilian merchant marine. The Brazilian representatives maintained that their country should be allowed to keep them. The conference's finance committee, however, was determined to distribute German merchant marine tonnage proportionately, based on the ratio of losses among the Allies, an arrangement the Brazilian merchant marine, which had suffered comparatively few casualties, would gain little from. The Brazilians argued that France had acknowledged Brazilian ownership when she leased a large number of requisitioned ships from Brazil, and that the United States had done the same when she attempted to buy them.[31] The Brazilians refused to budge. The head of their delegation, Senator Epitacio da Silva Pessôa, wrote directly to Prime Minister Lloyd George and President Woodrow Wilson pleading Brazil's case. In his letter to the prime minister, Pessoa stated that Brazil would refuse to sign the peace treaty if the position of the finance committee was not reversed. On 8 March 1919 the conference's Supreme Council adopted a protocol giving Allied and associated governments the full right of property and use of the ships "captured, seized, or retained during the war." Great Britain and the United States signed without reservation. Brazil still refused to back down, and on 2 May France fully recognized the claims of the Latin American country. On 28 June Brazil signed the Treaty of Versailles, which was ratified on 11 November. In addition to the forty-three merchant ships, it ceded to her the German torpedo boats V-105 and V-106 as war prizes.[32] Brazil sold the first to Poland and the second to Great Britain.

After the armistice the DNOG visited European ports, then returned to Rio de Janeiro on 9 June 1919. The squadron was disbanded on the twenty-fifth, its personnel having been reduced to eighty percent of their original strength by the ravages of war and disease.[33] In addition to these casualties Brazil lost seven merchant ships totaling 25,504 gross tons to U-boats.[34]

The historian Percy Martin's assertion "that the military contributions of the Latin American belligerents to the common cause did little to tip the balance of victory in favor of the Allies," though accurate, disregards Brazil's noble and extensive efforts to make what contribution she did.[35] It took five months to prepare a small antisubmarine group that would have required but a few weeks from a major naval power, but this should not overshadow the fact that the squadron materialized and served. After frequent German violations of the Declarations of Paris (1856) and London (1909) concerning freedom of the seas, Brazil went to war, in defense of her honor and for American solidarity.

Cuba: A North American Island

Cuba's participation on the side of the Allies came as no surprise. The country had been recently wrenched from Spanish control by North American arms, and the United States dominated her internal and external affairs. In 1916 the Cuban navy recruited Lieutenant Commander Carlton R. Kear, USN (Ret.), to teach gunnery at the Cuban Naval Academy with the knowledge and consent of the U.S. Navy.[36] On 7 April 1917 American marines had to be used to put down a revolt in Cuba; over two thousand "leathernecks" were stationed on the islands. Throughout the war U.S. warships used Cuban ports.

The small Cuban navy had two gunboats and about a dozen patrol boats, most built since the Spanish-American War and rather new compared with those of other small Latin American navies. The *Baire* and the

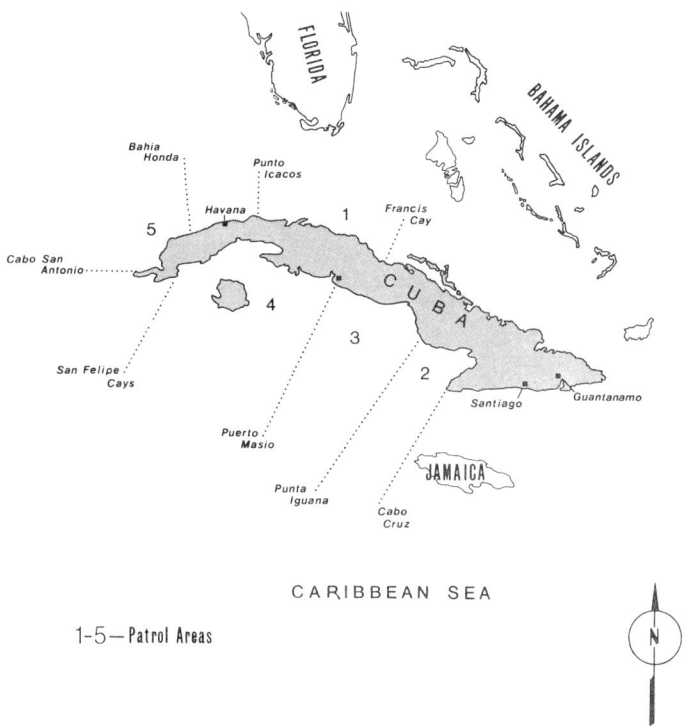

Cuban Naval Patrol Areas

Patria were sent to the United States to be overhauled and rearmed with U.S. ordnance. Allied naval leaders incorrectly believed that German U-boats had insufficient range to operate in the Caribbean and off South America from their bases in Europe. They were convinced that the U-boats in South American waters were operating from secret bases within the western hemisphere. The Cuban navy's campaign order no. 1 of 10 August 1917 reflected this misconception: ". . . submarines to operate successfully for any length of time must have bases for supplies and overhaul."[37] The Cuban navy was tasked with ferreting out these nonexistent bases. U.S. warships patrolled the heavily trafficked areas of the Cuban coast, such as Habana and Guantánamo. On 21 August Cuba transferred to the United States without cost four large German steamers she had seized after declaring war. She retained a fifth steamer as a transport.[38] Campaign order no. 2, of 19 June 1918, redistributed the Cuban navy, moving it from the remote areas to those frequented by merchant ships. A mobile force made up of the navy's largest ships—the *Cuba, Patria, Baire*, and four submarine chasers—was stationed at Habana. This force was to proceed to the location of any U-boat sighting, but as it turned out, the Cuban navy did not encounter any enemy ships during the war.[39]

Argentina's Neutrality Strained

Argentina, like Brazil, had attracted a large number of citizens of German descent. Most of them had immigrated a few decades earlier than their counterparts in Brazil, between the 1870s and 1890s, and many held positions of influence. Soon after the war began Argentina declared her neutrality and continued to maintain cordial relations with Germany.

She took a number of measures to enforce her neutrality. As early as 6 August 1914 the Ministry of the Navy issued a general order forbidding foreign merchantmen in Argentine waters to arm themselves as auxiliary cruisers. On three occasions German merchant ships were interned for violating Argentine neutrality. In mid-December 1914, following the Battle of the Falklands, the Argentine armored cruiser *Pueyrredón* intercepted the German steamer *Patagonia* off the coast for which the German ship had been named. The merchant ship was escorted into Puerto Madryn, a port on Golfo Nuevo, to await orders from the Navy Department. The navy minister sent the *Patagonia* to Puerto Militar (Puerto Belgrano). Rear Admiral M. J. Lagos, commander of Argentina's training squadron, assigned the *Pueyrredón* to escort the merchantman, ordering her cleared for combat so that she "will be prepared to defend our neutral rights."[40] The Argentine flag was to fly from the *Patagonia*. That ship was interned on 18 January 1915. Two other ships were interned, the *Seydlitz* on 23 January, the *Holger* on 26 February. The *Seydlitz* had been part of Vice Admiral Maximilian von Spee's squadron, which was operating off the South American coast, and the *Holger* had been a consort of the auxiliary cruiser *Kronprinz Wilhelm*. The Argentine navy was not always so successful at patrolling the waters it claimed to be national. On 27 November 1915 the British auxiliary cruiser *Orama* captured the Argentine steamer *Presidente Mitre* off Cape San Antonio in Argentine-claimed territorial waters at the mouth of the River Plate. Owned by Hamburg South American Line of Buenos Aires, the steamer was taken into Montevideo, Uruguay, then subsequently released.[41]

The Argentine navy, like most fleets in Latin America, depended upon Great Britain for its hard coal. The war interrupting this supply, the navy sent three naval auxiliaries to the United States in late 1915 to help transport coal home. This supply was augmented in mid-1917 when Argentina imported some soft Chilean coal that proved to be ill-suited to the fleet's needs.[42]

Argentina had a small merchant fleet, primarily engaged in coastal trade, that shrank as the war progressed and belligerents, particularly the

Allies, purchased these ships for use in the lucrative war trade. By the end of 1916 the 230,000-ton Argentine merchant fleet was reduced to 180,000 tons, principally owing to sales abroad.[43] With fewer merchant ships on the seas, foreign affairs were less affected by U-boat activities than Brazil's. However, by mid-1917 Argentina was almost embarrassed into war when the few U-boat sinkings she had suffered were magnified by German diplomatic blunders. On 4 April 1917 a U-boat sank the first Argentine merchantman, the sailing ship *Monte Protegido*. On 2 May Germany apologized for the incident and promised to salute the Argentine flag from the imperial squadron "at the first opportunity."[44] But in June, when the Argentine merchant ships *Oriana* and *Toro* were sunk by U-boats, the Argentine government demanded an apology and indemnity. The reply stated that Germany "in order to maintain friendly relations with Argentina is willing to modify her blockade of enemy coasts, allowing freedom of the seas to vessels under the Argentine flag carrying food."[45] The note also promised that an indemnity agreed to by Argentine and German appraisers would be paid. All seemed settled.

On 8 September U.S. Secretary of State Robert Lansing published three secret dispatches from the German minister at Buenos Aires to his government:

May 19, 1917, Number 32

This government has now released German and Austrian ships on which hitherto a guard had been placed. In consequence of the settlement of the Monte [Protegido] case there has been a great change in public feeling. Government will in future only clear Argentine ships as far as Las Palmas. I beg that the small steamers *Oran* and *Guazo*, 31st of January [sailing] 300 tons, which are nearing Bordeaux with a view to change the flag, may be spared if possible or else sunk without a trace being left.

LUXBURG

July 3, 1917, Number 59

I learn from a reliable source that the Acting Minister for Foreign Affairs, who is a notorious ass and Anglophile, declared in a secret session of the Senate that Argentina would demand from Berlin a promise not to sink more Argentine ships. If not agreed to, relations would be broken off. I recommend refusal and, if necessary, calling in the mediation of Spain.

LUXBURG

July 9, 1917, Number 64

Without showing any tendency to make concessions, postpone reply to Argentine note until receipt of further reports. A change of Ministry is probable. As regards Argentine steamers, I recommend either compelling them to turn back, sinking them without leaving any trace, or letting them through. They are all quite small.

LUXBURG

The Argentine reply was remarkably restrained.

The Argentine Government has recognized and valued highly the exalted manner in which the government of Germany has solved in ample terms all the Argentine claims, but must inform the German Government that, because of the texts of Minister von Luxburg's telegrams which have been published, he has ceased to be *persona grata*, and in consequence this government has delivered to him his passports.[46]

Many Argentines were outraged by von Luxburg's audacity. There was much talk of war. The navy was ordered to sea, ostensibly because of a general strike. Crew members from the destroyer *Corrientes* reinforced naval patrols on Buenos Aires' river front, preventing strikers from interfering with the strike-breaking naval stokers operating the city's electric power plant. On 28 September Argentina placed armed guards on board interned German merchant ships to prevent sabotage. In January 1918 the Argentine merchant marine's fourth and last ship was sunk by U-boats, amounting to a total merchant shipping loss of 4,275 gross tons.[47] Perhaps in a spirit of reconciliation, Germany sold the steamer *Bahía Blanca* lying at Buenos Aires to Argentina for twelve million marks; the price, though, was several million above the real value of the ship. Argentina remained neutral to the end, in spite of the growing public pressures caused by U-boat activities and von Luxburg's stupidity.

The Remaining Navies Defend Neutral Rights

The Chilean navy had a particularly difficult task enforcing the neutrality of Chile, whose long and irregular coastline traced by numerous islands offered havens for surface raiders. To protect the merchant shipping of belligerents the Chilean navy convoyed vessels while they transited territorial waters, but a shortage of coal made such escorts infrequent. On 31 October 1914 a Chilean gunboat had to go to the rescue of the British steamer *Colusa*, which the German auxiliary cruiser *Prinz Eitel Friedrich* was pursuing within the three-mile territorial limit. The merchant ship found safety in Valparaíso. In late 1914 Chile restricted the amount of coal belligerent warships and merchantmen could obtain in Chilean ports in an attempt to exclude belligerent warships from Chilean waters altogether and conserve a limited resource.[48]

British and German naval activities spanned the globe in the early days of the war, before the British were able to track down German warships that had been on foreign stations. On 1 November 1914 German Vice Admiral Graf von Spee's Asiatic Squadron, which had been forced to flee the Orient, defeated a British squadron off Chile in the Battle of Coronel. Beforehand, the British cruisers *Glasgow* and *Monmouth* had been operating from a secret base in the Chilean Chonos Archipelago, at 45° 24' South latitude, 74° 18' West longitude. The only surviving crew from the British cruisers *Good Hope* and *Monmouth* were observers who earlier had landed in Chile, violating her neutrality in an attempt to monitor German ship movements. On 4 November the victorious German ships entered Valparaíso. The Chilean authorities dispatched two ships to the scene to search for survivors, but none were found.[49]

The Juan Fernández Islands, lying hundreds of miles off the Chilean mainland, were a particularly difficult place to enforce neutrality. In November 1914 German warships sank the French barque *Valentine* off Mas Afuera Island, one of this group, an incident prompting the minister of foreign affairs to ask the navy to station a warship in the islands. An effective defense would have required two or three ships, which the navy could not spare. Instead it promised to send the training ship *Baquedano* to the islands at frequent intervals.[50]

Following the Battle of the Falklands, the Chilean navy destroyer *Almirante Condell* discovered the German cruiser *Dresden* in territorial waters and ordered her to leave within twenty-four hours. The cruiser ignored the command, sailing to Punta Arenas, Chile, where she coaled. Since she had coaled a month before in Valparaíso, she was in violation of the law limiting the supply of coal belligerent warships could obtain in Chile. But the Chilean official in charge at Punta Arenas sympathized with the German cause. The *Dresden* coaled with impunity and was permitted to send telegraph messages in code.

In March 1915 HMS *Glasgow* caught the cruiser *Dresden* in Cumberland Bay, Juan Fernández Island, and after a brief artillery exchange the Germans scuttled their vessel. Chile, invoking the Hague Convention clause that stated neutrals should safeguard their rights in territorial waters within "the means at their disposal," protested that the British action was a violation of her neutrality.[51] But she was not very successful in preventing warships of either side from committing future violations. Over Chile's objections, German cruisers and merchant ships operated in Chilean waters and sustained von Spee's squadron and later the *Dresden*.[52] Great Britain was the more willing to extend apologies—*ex post facto.*

Throughout much of the war Chile negotiated unsuccessfully with Germany for the use of interned merchant ships—thirty-two steamers and fifty-seven sailing vessels. On the night of 3 September 1918 German crews in three ports—Corral, Valparaíso, and Antofagasta—simultaneously sabotaged the machinery in seven steamers. Two days later Chile ordered troops on board to prevent further damage and to maintain order.[53] She lost no merchant ships in the war and remained neutral to the end. But the war was particularly devastating to Chile and ultimately her navy. First, the war pitted her major foreign supporters, Germany and Great Britain, against each other. Second, it forced Germany to develop a synthetic substitute for nitrates, which were Chile's prime source of hard currency. After the war, the synthetic technology became available for all. Adding to Chile's problems, in 1914 the Panamá Canal opened, a blessing to the world but a curse to Chile's maritime enterprise. Her ports were transformed from important stopping points on the way to the Pacific into backwater calls.

Perú, which like most of the producers of raw material in Latin America suffered severely from the initial economic repercussions of the European war, did not at first declare neutrality but dealt with problems on a case-by-case basis. On 10 December 1914 the German ship *Luxor*, considered an auxiliary warship because of her aid to von Spee's squadron, was ordered to leave Peruvian waters within twenty-four hours. Her captain refused—the British were waiting outside those waters—and the *Luxor* was interned. With the threatening presence of von Spee's ships on the coast, the Peruvian cruisers *Almirante Grau* and *Coronel Bolognesi* escorted merchant ships inside territorial waters. On 4 February 1917 a U-boat off northern Spain sank the Peruvian merchant ship *Lorton*, the only Peruvian maritime war casualty. On 29 September 1917 Perú placed armed guards on board the five German steamers and three sailing ships interned in Callao and ordered Peruvian warships to illuminate the bay with their searchlights. The government suspected that Germany was about to deliver an ultimatum and that at least some of the ships would try to escape. In October 1917 Perú broke diplomatic relations with Germany and on 14 June 1918 seized the eight German merchant ships in Callao. Several of the steamers were large passenger ships that had been used between San Francisco, South American ports, and Germany. Perú made these ships available to the United States.[54]

Uruguay lost more merchant ship tonnage to U-boats than any other Latin American nation except Brazil—three ships totaling 6,889 gross tons. In 1917 Uruguay protested the announced German policy of unrestricted submarine warfare, and shortly thereafter the merchantman *Rosario* was torpedoed. On 24 November 1918 Uruguay sought revenge, seizing eight German steamers for use by the government.[55] Throughout the war, however, she remained neutral.

CHAPTER SEVEN

Mutinies

SOCIAL UNREST influenced by international political movements affected Latin America navies during the early twentieth century, and as a result serious mutinies occurred.[1] In each case, the fleet unit involved had recently returned from a stay in foreign waters where crews were exposed to advocates of revolutionary social movements. The mutineers came mostly from the enlisted ranks. None of the mutinies sought the overthrow of a government; rather, they aimed to redress particular grievances. Insurgents discredited their respective navies at home, and in the case of the Chilean navy, were probably the reason it lost its most favored status among the nation's military.

Brazil, 1910, 1919

On 22 November 1910 crew members of the *Minas Gerais* mutinied, murdering the captain and a few officers, putting other officers ashore, and detaining British engineers who had accompanied the newly completed warship from the builders. The mutiny soon spread to the *São Paulo*, the old coastal defense ship *Deodoro*, and the newly completed scout cruiser *Bahia*. A number of shore units were in sympathy with the mutiny, including men at the barracks on Cobras Island. The crews of several torpedo boats remained loyal to the government. The mutineers fired on these small craft, but their superior speed enabled them to escape injury.[2]

The primary cause of the mutiny was the stern discipline code being enforced throughout the Brazilian navy. A few days earlier a sailor had been flogged—a punitive measure frequently inflicted for minor offenses. In addition to corporal punishment, the mutineers complained of overwork and poor pay. An incident that occurred during the *São Paulo*'s passage from England may have served as catalyst to the rebellion. En route she had stopped at Lisbon, Portugal, and taken on board the Brazilian president elect, Marshal Hermes da Fonseca. While she was in port a rebellion arose against Portugal's King Manuel. The rebels attempted to search the *São Paulo* for the king, who meanwhile had gone into hiding elsewhere. Though they didn't accomplish their immediate goal, in the course of their attempt the Portuguese insurgents may have exerted some influence on the crew of the dreadnought.[3]

Discipline among the Brazilian mutineers was surprisingly good. In addition to other measures, the leader, João Cândido, ordered all liquor thrown overboard. Moreover, the dreadnoughts performed their evolutions in an orderly fashion, as one eyewitness who had seen service in warships described:

> The handling of the Brazilian warships sans officers was a novel sight to us. I confess that I never saw evolutions performed in smarter style than those undergone by the mutinous warships. . . . All day long the mutinous ships performed evolutions in the bay and at night retired in perfect order to the anchorage grounds outside, signalling all the time. I doubt whether a flag officer of rank would have done any better.[4]

Rio de Janeiro was now the captive of two powerful warships whose crews were demonstrating their proficiency and which may have had the loyalty of the harbor forts. That was open to question. Thus in responding the government had few options. It offered the mutineers an amnesty and agreed to investigate their grievances, terms they accepted. The mutiny had far-reaching effects on the Brazilian navy. A new code for the punishment of crimes was issued and naval administration was reformed. In addition, the newly elected president reordered the navy's priorities. Instead of money continuing to be used for dreadnoughts, it was reallocated to improve shore facilities and living conditions for the sailors. But the mutineers did not get everything they wanted. More than one thousand were cashiered from the service.[5]

Nine years later the Brazilian navy was again ripe for mutiny. During the general state of turmoil that descended on Brazil in the latter part of 1919—the economy, based upon foreign loans compounded by postwar depression, was faltering, and secessionist movements arose in several states—the police broke up workers' meetings, the newspaper *Spartacus* was closed down for printing anarchistic writings, bombs were planted in various buildings, a riot erupted in a railroad station, and at least one political assassination was attempted. Unrest spread to the fleet, and in September 1919 the navy acted to prevent mutiny. The trouble started when police reported that some enlisted men in destroyers were attending Bolshevik meetings. The fleet sailed hastily for maneuvers off Ilha Grande before it had completed the necessary preparation for target practice. Twenty-two days at sea appeared to settle the political dyspepsia. But the day before the fleet left Ilha Grande, which lay south of Rio de Janeiro, an officer in the *Minas Gerais* found a message sent from a destroyer to a battleship inviting the crew of the latter to join a general strike the day the fleet arrived in Rio de Janeiro. The signalman who received the message had inadvertently failed to destroy it. Another officer found a letter confirming the information.[6]

When the fleet arrived in Rio de Janeiro, all officers and men were kept on board as the fleet's admiral went ashore to discuss the matter with the minister of marine. Only some of the officers were granted liberty that night, and at about 0100 they were recalled. Twenty-five crew members of the *Minas Gerais* were taken ashore and imprisoned and at least ten others subsequently arrested. As a precaution, all of the valves to the hydraulic mechanism for the turrets in the *Minas Gerais* were removed, and the guns were wedged so they could not recoil. All of the firing locks for the 4.7-inch guns were taken out, as were parts for the main engines, disabling them. The mutiny had been defused.[7]

Chile, 1931

In the early morning of 1 September 1931 enlisted personnel of the Chilean warships anchored at Coquimbo mutinied. Coquimbo, about two hundred miles north of Valparaíso, was used as the base for the fleet during winter maneuvers. Present there was the active squadron under Rear Admiral Abel Campos: the armored cruiser *O'Higgins* (flagship); the destroyers *Riquelme, Hyatt, Videla,* and *Aldea;* the submarines *Simpson* and *O'Brien;* and the division of school ships under Commodore Alberto Hozven, made up of the dreadnought *Almirante Latorre* (flagship), the destroyers *Lynch, Serrano,* and *Orella,* and a number of H-class submarines.[8]

The underlying cause was demoralization due to a sudden pay cut. On 31 August there had been a boxing competition in the dreadnought that brought together disgruntled sailors from throughout the fleet. That afternoon officers' staterooms were robbed of firearms, and shortly after midnight armed men arrested the officers in the *Almirante Latorre* and the armored cruiser *O'Higgins.* No one resisted in the battleship. On the cruiser a midshipman, the officer of the deck, obtained a pistol and wounded two of the mutineers before he himself was wounded. Another officer had to be overpowered. But, with these exceptions, the officers did not resist, and some may have condoned the mutiny. Armed parties were then sent from the *Almirante Latorre* and the *O'Higgins* to the other ships at Coquimbo. Half a dozen to a dozen armed mutineers boarded each ship and closed the hatches to the wardrooms, thus making captives of the officers. Again no resistance was met. Mutineers sent all small arms to the battleship and proceeded to board the small units to replace men of questionable loyalty.[9]

Shortly before midnight the rebels radioed a set of demands to the government:

1. Full pay for enlisted men;[10]
2. The millionaires of Chile loan 300 million pesos to the Government;
3. That all Government-owned uncultivated land be divided among the workmen;
4. That the Government continue all public works;
5. That employment be provided for the unemployed;
6. That sailors be given free clothing allowance;
7. That the ration be improved;
8. That the ration include more sugar;
9. That navy-yard watchmen be replaced by sailors;
10. That contract pilots be no longer employed;
11. That service trade [officer] schools be closed for two years;
12. That retirement for enlisted men be optional at 15 years but compulsory at 20 years of service.[11]

The insurgents formed the "Lower-Deck Committee"—a sailors' council made up of two members from each ship—and the mutinous warships each formed their own central committee of six men who commanded their respective warships. Ernesto González, a yeoman, was the ringleader. His principal confidants were Manuel Astica, an apprentice accountant, and Lautaro Silva, an apprentice pay clerk. Interestingly, reservists and apprentices exerted substantial influence in the lower-deck committee.

At 1655 on 1 September the Lower-Deck Committee radioed the minister of the navy, Rear Admiral Calixto Rogers, telling him it had control of the ships in Coquimbo and demanding the restoration of their full salaries. It also wanted those responsible for the prevailing economic chaos in the nation punished. The committee urged an end to the propaganda campaign which it perceived was being waged against the armed forces by the current administration in the wake of the ouster of General Ibáñez del Campo at the end of July. The sailors demanded a reply in forty-eight hours, adding that they would not use force to win their demands and that their actions had not been instigated by the Communists or any other political party.[12]

Rogers convened a conference of Inspector General of the Navy Vice Admiral Hipólito Marchant, Chief of Staff Rear Admiral Alejandro García Castelblanco, Director of Personnel Captain Julio Merino Benítez, and Director of Material Real Admiral Edgardo von Schroeders.

At 1900 on 1 September the cabinet also met to deal with the crisis. It was divided. The minister of the navy and the minister of war, General Enrique Bravo, were against the use of force and believed the rebels would come to terms. Civilian cabinet members wanted to use force immediately. Acting President Manuel Trucco decided to negotiate, whereupon his cabinet resigned.[13] A new cabinet was immediately formed that proved to be more hard-line. The new minister of the navy was Captain Enrique Spoerer, who had earlier been purged from the navy by Former President Carlos Ibáñez; the new minister of war was General Carlos Vergara Montero, reputed to be a strict disciplinarian; and the air force was headed by Ramón Vergara Montero, the general's brother.

The government decided to send Rear Admiral Edgardo von Schroeders north by plane to mediate. His instructions were not to concede anything to the mutineers. They did, however, have some leverage: The government feared that if the mutiny was prolonged it could develop into a nationwide uprising fueled by economic discontent.

On 2 September the mutiny spread to Talcahuano, the principal naval base, which lay 220 miles south of Valparaíso. The new mutineers invited the officers to join them but they refused. Crews seized control of the ships without meeting resistance. On the night of 3 September forces fired rifle shots at the submarine tender *Araucano* from ashore. The fire was returned, and apparently both sides sustained some casualties.[14] In an attempt to defuse the situation the base commander, Rear Admiral Roberto Chapuseaux, boarded the *Araucano* and, after a conference, ordered the officers ashore; but this act only delivered the ships, and eventually the entire base and other warships, into the hands of the mutineers. Early the next day those ships not undergoing repairs sailed in company with the cruiser *Blanco Encalada* to unite with the mutinous crews in the north.[15] Enlisted men at the Talcahuano Naval Base, the coastal defense forces there, and the communication school and naval station at Quintero also joined the mutiny. The personnel at the Naval Academy in Valparaíso remained loyal.[16] Three coast guard craft and two tugs accompanied the mutinous *Araucano* and some submarines after they fueled at Dichato. Two old cruisers and a few destroyers and submarines remained behind at Talcahuano for various reasons.[17]

On the morning of 2 September Admiral von Schroeders, along with Captain Luis Muñoz Artigas, had flown from Santiago to Coquimbo, where he arrived in the afternoon. At 1430 Chief Radioman Guillermo

Steembecker, accompanied by a few sailors, presented the admiral with a note from the Lower-Deck Committee, inviting him to a meeting on board the *Almirante Latorre*. They placed a steam launch at his disposal. The admiral, who had been instructed to meet with the mutineers on land but not at sea, radioed Santiago for instructions and was told that under no conditions could he meet with them in the *Almirante Latorre*.[18] He informed the mutineers of his instructions, but they held fast to their condition. After again cabling the government, he was left with the decision in his hands. Negotiations over the site of the proposed meeting dragged on, until finally von Schroeders agreed to meet with the mutineers in the *Almirante Latorre*. In the late morning of 3 September the admiral, who had been second in command of the dreadnought in 1926 and 1927, arrived amidst full honors. As soon as the talks got under way he perceived that a split was developing among the mutineers. Those from the *Almirante Latorre* argued for sweeping social change, while members of the Lower-Deck Committee from other ships were only concerned with the sailors' issues. Admiral von Schroeders tried to take advantage of this rift and get the fleet to surrender before the units from the south arrived. He promised that the government would study their demands and that no disciplinary action would be taken until the matter was fully investigated. The sailors, he added, would receive the same pay for work in August that they had received for work in July. The government believed that pay was the major issue and that the concession would help defuse the situation.[19] Though authorized to mention this issue, von Schroeders was not empowered to grant amnesty.

The talks continued through the fourth. Hindering settlement was the fact that the mutineers sensed growing public support for their actions; in radio messages the Talcahuano units urged their brethren to hold out until they arrived. The admiral's arguments did not prevail, nor did those of a delegation of students the government sent to parley with the rebels.[20]

The arrival of the southern units injected those at Coquimbo with renewed confidence. Several of these intercepted two small coastal steamers and brought them into Coquimbo. Some cargo was commandeered and the ships' logs were duly annotated by the boarding parties. Beneath the signature of Chief Orlando Robles Osses, a signalman, was the title Commander of the Southern Squadron.[21] One merchantman, the *Flora*, was transporting sheep; these were appropriated to feed the mutineers.

The Second Air Group, stationed at Quintero, mutinied on 4 September. Enlisted personnel led by two sergeants seized the air force base and imprisoned the officers. The rebels radioed the government their demands, which were similar to those listed by the fleet. The naval mutineers promised to send their air force compatriots the destroyer *Aldea* if she was needed for defense. In return they requested that the group sabotage its aircraft so they could not be used against the fleet. The request was honored.²²

On the morning of 5 September the government decided to force the mutineers to come to terms. Loyal ground forces attacked and captured the communication school at Las Salinas, and the Quintero Air Base surrendered when confronted by the Coraceros Regiment. But the mutiny was far from over, for the key naval strongholds at Coquimbo and Talcahuano remained in rebel hands. General Guillermo Novoa was ordered to retake Talcahuano. He commanded a force of five thousand men, which included a company of over one hundred naval officers under Captain Luis Muñoz Valdés. This force was to oppose about one thousand rebels, of whom about sixty percent were civilians, mostly navy veterans. The terrain greatly favored the defenders. The attackers had to advance along a narrow road that paralleled the ocean. The rebel advantage, however, was offset by an expectation of naval gunfire support from the destroyers *Riveros* and *Condell* that never materialized.²³

At 0800 the army demanded that the mutineers surrender. They refused, possibly comforted by an assumption that the army would not attack, and that if it did naval gunfire would win the day. At 1400 the army did attack, coming down the mountains at the back of the base. While the defenders were busy with this threat, other units stormed the main gate. Talcahuano surrendered within a few hours. In late afternoon that same day the destroyer *Riveros*, under the control of the mutineers, belatedly closed on the forts protecting the naval base. Seeing that they were manned by soldiers, she opened fire. The shore batteries returned the fire and drove her off. She sustained moderate damage, three of her crew were killed, and some others were wounded.

The loss of Talcahuano was a severe blow to the mutineers, it being their only possible support base. Coquimbo did not have the facilities to support the fleet, nor did the area around Valparaíso, where government forces subdued mutinous units with few casualties.²⁴

On 6 September General Carlos Vergara, on a visit to William S. Culbertson, U.S. ambassador to Chile, said that his country's problem was a continental and not an internal one. A recent trip to Europe had exposed Vergara to spreading communist fervor abroad, and he spoke of the imminent danger of civil war between communist and government forces in Chile. The general requested help from the United States, first in the form of war materials, particularly bombs and tear gas, second in the form of submarines. Actually, he wanted only to intimidate the rebels by announcing that Chile was negotiating with the United States for the immediate delivery of two or more submarines; the purchase was never intended to be made. General Vergara "emphasized that intervention was not being requested in any form." Culbertson told the general he would informally query his government.²⁵

Washington informed the ambassador that the sale or transfer of submarines was forbidden by the Washington Naval Armament Limitation Treaty of 1922. As for munitions, given the fact that it was the Labor Day weekend, the department could not immediately ascertain what was available in Panamá, the nearest U.S. ammunition depot. It did know, however, that no tear gas was there. In any case, delivery of available munitions would be slow, since they could not be shipped via commercial air.²⁶ The ambassador relayed this news to the Chilean government.

At this point the government had gathered some forty aircraft near Coquimbo, including rebel planes from the Second Air Group that had surrendered. Insurgent mechanics had been forced to repair the aircraft and, as a guarantee of their workmanship, were required to accompany the air crews in their attack against the fleet. Early in the morning, two aircraft were sent to reconnoiter the fleet. This was easily accomplished, but they attacked the *Araucano* without success.²⁷

In early afternoon of 6 September 1931 the government's air squadron took off from the Tuquí Airfield near Ovalle to attack the fleet. The force consisted of nine Curtiss Falcon observation planes armed with 25-pound bombs, two Vickers Vixen bombers armed with 110-pound bombs, two French Wibault pursuit planes with 25-pound bombs, and two Junkers bombers with one 660-pound bomb each. The maximum altitude the Junkers bombers could fly was five thousand feet, which curtailed the force's tactics.²⁸

The aircraft approached from the west, flying out of the sun at about five thousand feet. One Junkers flew a zigzag course over the anchored fleet and dropped its 660-pound bomb, which fell several hundred yards from any of the ships. Minutes later the second Junkers flew a straight course over the ships and dropped its lone bomb; it fell within fifty yards of the *Almirante Latorre*. Minutes passed. Then the remaining thirteen aircraft attacked, the nine Curtiss Falcons approaching in three V formations accompanied by the two Vickers and two Wibaults. The Falcons and Wibaults each dropped approximately four 25-pound bombs, the Vickers several 110-pound bombs. Some aircraft also used their machine guns. The ships returned the fire, but like most warships in 1931, they only had a few antiaircraft (AA) guns each. The *Almirante Latorre* carried four four-inch AA guns, mounted during her 1929–31 refit in England.²⁹ Six of the destroyers had one three-inch AA gun each. The only other AA guns were twenty-six machine guns scattered among the fleet. Some accounts state that officers, now released from bonds, took charge of the AA defenses.

Neither side received much damage. The submarine *H-4* was caught on the surface, unable to dive because of mechanical problems, and strafed. With two of her crew wounded, she proceeded to the dock at Coquimbo and surrendered. One of the disabled men died in a hospital ashore, the only casualty of the attack. Sources agree that damage sustained by the aircraft was slight, though they disagree about what precisely it was. Photographs do show one of the attack aircraft crashing on landing.[30]

The attack broke the spirit of the mutineers. The Lower-Deck Committee met with officers and agreed to send a delegation to Santiago to negotiate a settlement. But the government, fresh from victory, would have no part of that. A split developed among the committee over whether to continue the mutiny, and while they were arguing, the destroyers *Hyatt* and *Riquelme* slipped out of the bay and sailed to Valparaíso to surrender.[31]

In retaliation for the aerial bombing, the fleet threatened to bombard various coastal towns, some of which were evacuated in a state of panic. Fleet searchlights illuminated the clocktower of the cathedral at La Serena, but the guns remained silent. The threat did much to dissolve any lingering unity of the Lower-Deck Committee, and the remaining destroyers followed the defecting pair at night. At midday on 7 September the destroyers *Hyatt* and *Riquelme* arrived at Valparaíso under the control of their officers and declaring their loyalty to the government. They were followed by the *Videla*, *Orella*, *Aldea*, and *Serrano*.[32]

In the late morning of the seventh the ships that remained in Coquimbo weighed anchor and sailed south. The *Almirante Latorre* sent a radio message later in the day saying that the mutineers had surrendered and the officers and loyal crew members were in control of the dreadnought. The officer-less *Blanco Encalada*, it added, was in the company and also under the control of the dreadnought. Now the *O'Higgins* was the only remaining rebel, and by late afternoon she had also surrendered. When they ended their rebellion the ships were scattered along the coast. The destroyers were at Valparaíso, the *O'Higgins* and the *Araucano* at Coquimbo, the *Almirante Latorre* and the *Blanco Encalada* at the Bay of Tongoi, the submarines at or proceeding to Valparaíso, the *Riveros* without fuel at Mocha Island. Upon landing, the crews were put under arrest. After a preliminary investigation, the government ordered a small percentage back to their ships as caretakers. All commanding officers and executive officers were relieved and new ones assigned. The two flag officers afloat, Admiral Campos and Commodore Hozven, were also relieved.[33]

Courts-martial were held at a number of locations. Prosecutors sought the death penalty for all the ringleaders and long terms of imprisonment for others. The board at San Felipe, where the crew members of the *Almirante Latorre* were tried, deliberated for three days. Ernesto González and five others were sentenced to death; Manuel Astica and another officer received life sentences. Crew members of the *O'Higgins*, the destroyers, and the submarines were tried at La Serena and Valparaíso, leading to seven death sentences, ten sentences of life imprisonment, and other sentences ranging from one hundred days to fifteen years. The rebellious air force and army units were also tried, the defense lawyer for the former arguing that they had rebelled only to rejoin the navy. The severe punishments coming out of these trials caused a popular outcry. Telegrams of objection flooded into government offices. Some presidential candidates argued for the commutation of capital punishment, and most of the press favored a reduction of the other sentences. Large demonstrations testified to widespread public support for the mutineers.[34]

In early October a number of newspapers published evidence, provided by those convicted at San Felipe, that many officers had collaborated with the enlisted mutineers by signing documents supporting the mutiny while they were being held. The defense argued that there had been a cover-up; the prosecution argued that these documents had been disregarded since they were signed under duress. Regardless of the prosecution's stand, this public revelation gained additional support for the mutineers' cause. On 16 October Acting Vice President Manuel Trucco commuted the death sentences, and many prison terms were shortened. In fact, some of the ringleaders gained influential government positions within a few short years.[35]

The officers involved were brought to court at the Las Salinas Naval Base. Only two men were convicted: Roberto Valle, found guilty of signing the petitions (which, of course, many others officers had signed) and supporting the crews' actions, and Ramón Beytiá, convicted of collaboration. Both were discharged from the navy. Defense lawyers for the other officers successfully argued that they had been coerced into signing. A large number of officers went into forced retirement as a result, including the two flag officers afloat, Admiral Campos and Commodore Hozven. Admiral Chapuseaux, commander of the Talcahuano Naval Base, also retired. Others had to explain their actions.[36]

The mutiny had had many causes, paramount among them the economy. Like the rest of South America, Chile was staggering from the effects of the Great Depression. To eliminate unnecessary expense the government had planned to reduce naval pay, decommission a number of ships, and concentrate the fleet at Talcahuano. Operations were also to be greatly cut back, training terminated when possible. Prior to the mutiny Commodore Alberto Hozven, commander of the Division of Instruction, had refused to forward to the government a petition drafted by the sailors objecting to these changes. Instead, he assembled the crew of the *Almirante Latorre* as well as commanders and enlisted representatives from the other ships in his command and lectured them on the virtues of self-sacrifice. Another prod to rebellion may have been communist interference. At the time the Chilean government suggested that the mutiny was part of a

Marxist conspiracy. There is ample evidence of communist meddling; however, it would be overstating the case to say that this was the prime mover.

If the causes of the mutiny were many, its effects upon the Chilean navy were far-reaching and lingering. Above all, the service lost much of its former prestige and its preeminent political position among the nation's military. Since the mutiny, the navy has frequently had to settle for secondhand combatants. This compares poorly with the era following the 1891 revolution, when the navy purchased the best warships money could buy. Other economic and political factors have something to do with the navy's being forced to purchase hand-me-downs, but it was the mutiny that marked the beginning of that decline.[37]

Perú, 1932

At about 2130 on 7 May 1932 mutineers surprised and overpowered officers on watch in the Peruvian cruiser *Coronel Bolognesi*. The action may have been sparked by the arrest of Victor Raúl Haya de la Torre, a leader of the Apristas party, founded in 1924 and opposed to foreign influence, particularly that of the United States.[38] Apparently only the lowest grades supported the movement. The mutineers locked the officers in their cabins and moved on to the cruiser's sister ship, the *Almirante Grau*, where they proceeded again to overpower those on watch. The prisoners were then moved to the *Coronel Bolognesi*.[39]

While the insurgents were busy with the *Almirante Grau*, a loyal sailor slipped over the side and swam to the submarine flotilla, warning them of the uprising. In an attempt to gather more support for the mutiny, the mutineers sent emissaries to the submarines. The men were greeted and their leaders escorted below decks, expecting to read a manifesto to the crew. But the lights below were turned out and loyal submariners arrested the men. Then the submarine started to submerge, forcing the remaining mutineers on deck to retreat to their boats.[40]

The sailor who escaped from the *Almirante Grau* had been sent ashore to spread the warning of mutiny. He notified the port authority (capitanía de puerto), which called the commander in chief of the squadron, Captain Carlos Rotalbe, and the chief of staff, Captain Juan Althaus. They proceeded immediately to the waterfront and gathered loyal sailors, police, and soldiers to prevent a landing by the mutineers. The two senior officers then embarked on a submarine and moved the flotilla to the San Lorenzo Island Naval Base, four miles across the bay, where the boats were armed with torpedoes and munitions. The chief of staff set up a command post at the naval academy in Callao and was soon joined by the minister of the navy, Alfredo Benavides, along with numerous officers who had offered their services.

When the news of the mutiny reached the government palace, the president's naval aide and former commander of the *Coronel Bolognesi*, Commander Félix Vargas Prada, volunteered to go to Callao and resolve the crisis. It was agreed, but when Vargas tried to approach his old cruiser in a launch he met with rifle fire and one of his party was wounded.

At 0230 on 8 May President Sánchez Cerro told the minister of the navy to order the two cruisers to surrender at 0500. If they refused, they were to be attacked by aircraft and the submarine squadron. At 0400 the government issued the following communiqué:

> Last night at 11 P.M., a mutiny broke out on board the cruisers *Grau* and *Bolognesi*.
>
> The movement is of a Communist character and surely forms part of a revolutionary social plan prepared for execution yesterday. Similar acts ought to be occurring throughout South America. The government was informed of this plan some five days ago in a telegraph received from Europe.[41]

The communiqué went on to describe the events of the mutiny and warned all other units to remain loyal. The Council of Ministers declared a state of siege, claiming that "communists in the squadron had produced a mutiny that endangered the social order and peace of the Republic. . . ."[42]

At 0530 the mutineers were ordered by radio to surrender unconditionally. No answer came. A few minutes later three government aircraft attacked the cruisers. At the same time the submarine *R-4*, with Captain Rotalbe on board, opened fire with her deck gun. One shot passed through an oil tank on the cruiser and started a fire and a second shot hit her waterline, whereupon the white flag was hoisted and the mutineers surrendered. The officers and loyal enlisted crew members were immediately freed. They put out the fire and stopped the leak. By 0800 on a Sunday morning the mutiny, which had lasted ten and a half hours, was over.[43]

One hundred and sixty alleged mutineers were taken to San Lorenzo and held for immediate trial. Peruvian law required the court to meet in continuous session and the sentence to be executed within forty-eight hours of the verdict. After a fifteen-hour trial, eight ringleaders were condemned to be shot, fifteen others received ten to fourteen years' imprisonment, and the remainder were exonerated.[44]

The court testimony showed that on a recent visit to Balboa, Panamá, many of the crew of the two cruisers had been in contact with Apristas, who had been deported from Perú. A few of the defendants stated that they had acted "to better their conditions on board."[45] No communist involvement has ever been proven.

CHAPTER EIGHT

Riverine Wars in the Twentieth Century

THE STRUGGLE to control the interior of the continent helped to mold many South American navies during the late nineteenth and twentieth centuries. Numerous border conflicts involving riverine operations took place between nations sharing the Amazon and Río de la Plata tributaries. These clashes were usually sparked by incursions of government representatives into regions claimed by more than one nation.

The disputed areas in the heart of northern and central South America were almost inaccessible. The towering Andes created a formidable barrier separating them from the population centers of most nations of Spanish heritage. Rivers and streams provided the only access to much of the region. In each confrontation, the country holding the downstream position had a distinct advantage because it controlled the influx of practically all material and manpower. The Amazon and its tributaries provided the only access to the northern heartland of the continent; the main river was navigable by oceangoing ships for over three thousand miles. But the Amazon presented horrendous logistical obstacles, and Brazil had the advantage of downstream position. The conflicts she won primarily through negotiation, occasionally through small-scale warfare, gaining most of the disputed territory from her Spanish neighbors.

In the Río de la Plata basin, the central heartland, Paraguay had the downstream advantage over Bolivia in their fight for the Chaco Boreal, or northern Chaco. Unlike the confrontations in the Amazon basin, the Chaco War was no mere skirmish. Almost four hundred thousand combatants fought for three years, and nearly ninety thousand lives were lost. It was the first large-scale war of this century fought in a jungle environment.

Amazon Basin Conflicts

Maritime forces played key roles in the struggles of nations bordering the Amazon basin to define national boundaries. Between 1899 and 1903 Bolivia and Brazil clashed over the province of Acre, which lies in the heart of South America. Both countries laid claim to the region but neither effectively governed it. Its population was made up of Indians without a national identity, a few Bolivians, and almost eighteen thousand Brazilians. Very few roads existed, and canoes and rafts were the primary means of transportation. By the end of the nineteenth century Brazil was exporting rubber from the province without taxing it. On 2 January 1899 Bolivia opened a customhouse at Puerto Alonso (now Porto Acre), a move that angered Brazilian settlers, who wanted the Bolivian authorities to retire. When they refused, Dr. José de Carvalho led an unsuccessful revolt on 30 April 1899. A Spanish adventurer, Luis Galvez Rodriguez de Arias, who had served as the Bolivian consul at Belem, Brazil, led a second revolt. On 14 July 1899 he declared the independent republic of Acre at Empresa, near Puerto Alonso. The Bolivians reacted by dispatching a five-hundred-man force. In October Galvez was imprisoned by Antonio Sonza Braga, who declared himself president of Acre. Shortly, however, he reinstated Galvez to power. In March 1900 a Brazilian flotilla reached Puerto Alonso and put an end to the republic, returning the port to Bolivian control.

A force primarily composed of Brazilians organized another revolt in November 1900, its objective to wrestle control of Acre from Bolivia and create an independent republic. Known as the Expedition of the Poets, this quasi-Brazilian force was built around the river steamer *Solimoes*, outfitted with the aid of the governor of the Brazilian province of Amazonas, Silverio Neri. The *Solimoes* operated on the Purus River and captured the Bolivian launch *Alonso*, which was renamed the *Rui Barbosa*. Rodrigo de Carvalho was the newly declared president of Acre; his authority rested in one light cannon, a machine gun, and some two hundred men. Around Christmas 1900 this force attacked Puerto Alonso and was beaten back, losing the cannon and machine gun. On 29 December the Bolivian armed launch *Rio Afua* brought relief to the Puerto Alonso garrison.

José Placido de Castro, a gaucho and former professional soldier, now took charge of the quasi-Brazilian force. At 0500 on 6 August 1902 he and some thirty-three armed men landed from canoes and captured the river town of Xapuri on the Alto Acre River, whereupon Placido proclaimed a revolution and an independent republic. On 18 September a 180-man Bolivian battalion led by Colonel Rosendo Rojas surprised Placido's force, now numbering some seventy men. The Brazilians, armed only with Winchester rifles, short of munitions, and suffering from tropical diseases and desertion, lost twenty men. They were defeated.

Undaunted, Placido now recruited another force of about a thousand men. Part of this group laid siege to Puerto Alonso on 10 May 1902. On 14 October the force captured some outer defenses along with the Bolivian armed launch *Río Afua*, which had been stranded during the fighting. The river craft was renamed the *Independencia* and used against her former owners. In spite of this setback, the Bolivians stubbornly held on to Puerto Alonso.

Elsewhere, the Brazilians laid siege to Empresa, which surrendered on the fifteenth. Other engagements, most of them victories for Placido's quasi-Brazilian force, took place at Bom Destino, Santa Rosa, and various river towns. On 15 January 1903 the force assaulted and captured some of the Bolivian positions outside Puerto Alonso. The *Independencia*, which lay upstream from the Bolivians loaded with thirty tons of high-quality rubber, forced her way past Bolivian river batteries to carry the rubber downstream where it could be sold. Placido's force was to use the money to buy weapons and munitions. On 24 January the Bolivians at Puerto Alonso surrendered.

The besieging force, now seven hundred strong, occupied the port and advanced to where the Chipamanu (Manuripe) and Tauamanu rivers meet to form the Orton River. Soon a Bolivian force under General José Manuel Pando, president of Bolivia, occupied the opposite bank. At this time the Brazilian government formally stepped in, sending troops into the disrupted area then held by the quasi-Brazilian force. Bolivia, after losing at least two river steamers to the enemy, reluctantly agreed to sell the province of Acre, a concession formalized in the Treaty of Petropolis and signed on 17 November 1903.[1]

In 1901 Ecuador established outposts on the Napo and Aguarico rivers in an area also claimed by Perú. When Peruvian troops, ravaged by illness, had to be withdrawn from the immediate area, Ecuadorian troops worked their way down the Napo River to the trading post at Angoteros. The Peruvians reacted. The launch *Cahuapanas*, commanded by Midshipman Oscar Mavila, carried twenty soldiers from the Peruvian river port of Iquitos to Angoteros, secretly landing them below the Ecuadorian position. The launch then moved up river. When it took position opposite Angoteros, a discussion ensued between representatives of the two countries. On 26 July 1903 shots were fired, and the Peruvians, who had been offloaded,

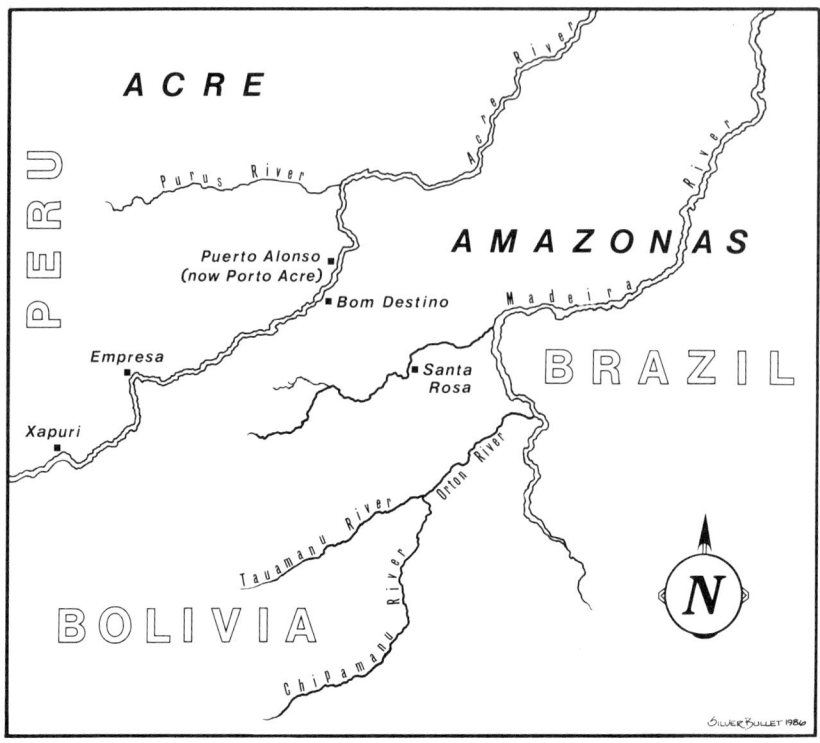

The Acre Dispute Between Bolivia and Brazil, 1899–1903

attacked and successfully drove the Ecuadorians from Angoteros. A year later a Peruvian force repeated these tactics and captured the trading post of Torres Causano from the Ecuadorians. This time the launch *Veloz*, commanded by Midshipman Mavila, was used. The attacking Peruvian force was seventy strong and there were forty defenders. The issue, temporarily defused while under arbitration by the king of Spain, was not resolved.[2]

Fighting also erupted between Bolivia and Perú as a consequence of the Argentine arbitration of 9 July 1909, when Bolivian Captain Lino Echeverría decided to maintain himself with sixteen men at the small fort of Avaroa on the Manuripi River. On 21 June 1910 the Bolivians repulsed an attack by twenty-five Peruvians and both sides suffered losses. The Peruvians landed 180 men of Infantry Regiment No. 5 with two machine guns from twenty canoes at the confluences of the Manuripi and Mejahuira rivers on 22 July. The Bolivians evacuated Fortin Health as the Peruvians approached. On 4 September a Bolivian raiding force led by Captain Echeverría crossed the Manuripi River by boat and attacked the Peruvians. After an initial success Echeverría and three others were killed, a few were taken prisoner, and the remainder, perhaps five, escaped. Both sides had been totally dependent upon the river system for transportation. Ultimately the issue was resolved by negotiations.

A conflict in the Amazon basin took place between Colombia and Perú in 1911. The point of confrontation was La Pedrera, an outpost that a Colombian military force had occupied. The Peruvians reacted by sending the gunboat *América*, commanded by Lieutenant Manual Clavero and escorting the troop-laden launch *Loreto*. The *América*, built in Great Britain in 1905 specifically for use in the Amazon region, was the dominant warship there. The Peruvian force arrived off La Pedrera at midday on 10 July 1911. An ultimatum was presented to the Colombians demanding that they abandon their position, which they did not. Fighting began at 1620. The *América* and the *Loreto* steamed towards the enemy, bypassing some makeshift mines the Colombians had planted. Apparently demoralized by this failure and considerably outnumbered, the Colombians surrendered on the twelfth. On the fifteenth, representatives of Colombia and Perú signed an agreement at Manaos, Brazil, and four days later a convention in Bogotá, Colombia, ended the fighting.[3] But this was only a respite.

The renewal of the Colombian-Peruvian dispute extended operations into deep water. On 1 September 1932 three hundred armed Peruvian civilians seized public buildings in the Colombia river port of Leticia to protest a transfer of territory to Colombia under a 1922 treaty settlement. The Peruvian government in Lima disavowed the action, but Peruvian authorities at Loreto provided military support to the disaffected. In response, the Colombian government prepared to send a fifteen-hundred-man expedition around the Atlantic coast and up the Amazon River, a measure the Peruvian public viewed as punitive. They demanded action. Both countries prepared for war.

At first glance, it would appear that Peru's navy was vastly superior to Colombia's and therefore equipped with the sort of decisive advantage it had had in 1903 and 1911. This was not the case, however. The major warships of the Peruvian navy—the two scout cruisers *Almirante Grau* and *Coronel Bolognesi*, the old cruiser-school ship *Lima*, the torpedo-boat *Teniente Rodriguez*, and four modern *R*-class submarines—had been designed for ocean operations and were of little use in a riverine environment.[4] Perú did have a naval seaplane base at Iquitos, but there were only five aircraft, and those were commercial types that had all long surpassed their recommended number of flying hours. Colombia did not have any first-class oceangoing warships, but her riverine forces were clearly superior.[5]

Acting quickly, Colombia brought together the scattered elements of her riverine force. The gunboats *Cartagena*, *Santa María*, and *Barranquilla*, just completed in Great Britain, crossed the Atlantic in twenty-four days, stopping only at São Vicente in the Cape Verde Islands.[6] These new gunboats rendezvoused in the Amazon with the river stern-wheeler *Presidente Mosquera* and two launches carrying some one thousand troops in January 1933. After a riverine bombardment, Colombian forces captured Tarapacá on the lower Putumayo River on 15 February. Moving up river, they captured Güepi on 26 March after a series of skirmishes with Peruvian forces fighting from fortified positions along the river.

Perú attempted to use her blue-water navy to influence the outcome of the conflict—a burdensome task, for she was beset by an internal crisis that resulted in the assassination, on 30 April, of President Sánchez Cerro. Oscar R. Benavides succeeded him.[7] On 3 May the cruiser *Almirante Grau* and two *R*-class submarines passed through the Panamá Canal. Four days later Perú replied to an inquiry from the advisory committee of the League of Nations that the warships were bound for the upper Amazon. On 8 May they reached Willemstad, Curaçao, took on supplies, then sailed for Port of Spain, Trinidad, and Pará, Brazil, near the mouth of the Amazon River. In all probability they had been dispatched to intercept any Colombian efforts to transport reinforcements up the river. For the defense of Iquitos, Perú ordered the old gunboat *Lima* and the old torpedo boat *Teniente Rodríguez* from Callao through the Panamá Canal and up the Amazon River to Iquitos. Although these two warships were ill-suited to operate in a riverine environment, they would be valuable floating batteries.

To augment her naval forces Perú purchased two destroyers from Estonia and hurried them to the mouth of the Amazon. These ships, renamed the *Almirante Guise* and the *Almirante Villar*, had been built in Russia, captured by Great Britain in 1918 during the Russian civil war, and turned over to Estonia. A few Estonians accompanied them from the Baltic. The *Almirante Guise* proved troublesome at first, but both units reached South America safely. Colombia, in turn, purchased two new destroyers from Portugal, the *Antiquois* (ex-*Douro*) and the *Caldas* (ex-*Tejo*). The *Almirante Guise* and the *Almirante Villar* were dispatched to the Caribbean to intercept the Colombian warships, a vigil that kept them there for two months, using Martinique and Trinidad as supply bases. Despite their efforts, the two Colombian destroyers arrived without incident.

In May 1933 Colombia and Perú accepted the League of Nations proposals for settlement of the quarrel. This was the first time that the league assumed direct control in a territory dispute and that it involved itself in the affairs of the western hemisphere. The Protocol of Rio de Janeiro, signed on 27 September 1935, ended the disagreement, awarding most of the contested territory to Colombia.[8]

The Chaco War, 1932–35

The Chaco Boreal, or northern Chaco, is a swampy, wooded triangle bordered on the west by the Pilcomayo River, on the east by the Paraguay

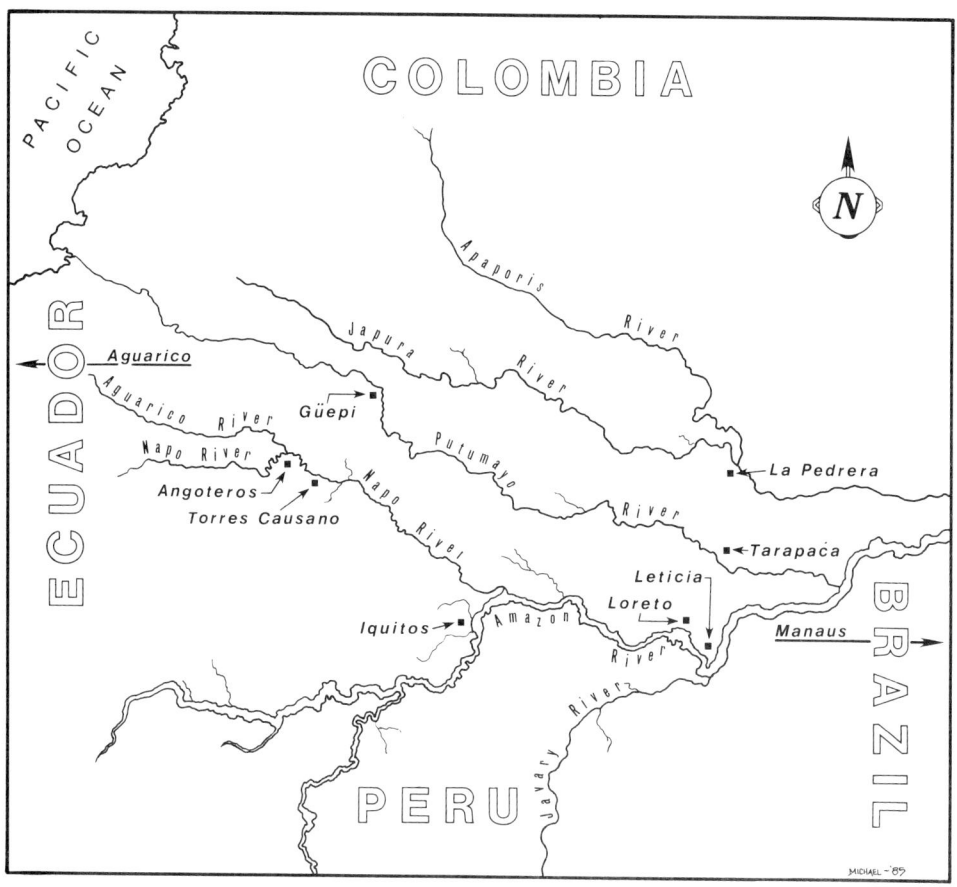

The Leticia Dispute Between Colombia and Perú, 1932–35

River, and on the north by the foothills of the Andes Mountains. It is approximately a hundred thousand square miles in size—about a fifth of the total area of Bolivia and as large as Paraguay—and lies between these two countries, which from the time of independence disputed the ownership of the sparsely inhabited region in numerous border skirmishes. In January 1930 the frequency of border clashes increased. The following year Bolivia discovered a large fresh-water lake in the central Chaco that made for the possibility of large-scale military operations in an area previously thought to be without adequate fresh water for such undertakings. A series of incidents led to war in 1932.[9]

Although both countries were landlocked, Paraguay's location down river from the disputed territory and from Bolivia gave her a geographical advantage. She could control all movement up the Paraguay River system, thereby acquiring aid, including naval forces, from the outside world while denying the same to Bolivia. On the other hand, Bolivia could obtain aid only over land, at best a torturous alternative.

Bolivia, despite an attempt to increase her naval strength during an earlier crisis, still had no navy. Her sole "warship" was the *Tahuamanu*, a German-built craft acquired sometime during the early part of the twentieth century and so obscure that she escaped notice in all of the naval annuals of the era. And the country's sole naval dockyard was a small one built on the Madeira River at Cobija in 1897. The Madeira, part of the Amazon River complex, not that of Río de la Plata, could be used to transport material and personnel to the northern Chaco, but strategically it was not as important to the war effort as the Paraguay River. Small river craft were built at Cabija and along with *Tahuamanu* used to transport war materials during the Chaco conflict. In January 1927 a grey-painted river steamer named the *Presidente Saavedra*, crewed in part by "blonde gringos" went up the Paraguay River, took on wood at Bahia Negra, and reached Porto Suarez in the Chaco after great difficulty. Soon afterward the ship sailed down the Paraguay River, joining a sister ship, the *Presidente Siles*, which never did brave the trip up river. Apparently Bolivia sold these ships as the crisis abated. How they were to function without a base of operations is unclear.[10]

In contrast, Paraguay was able to use her navy to good advantage. In July 1932 her merchant marine was incorporated into the navy, resulting in a formidable fleet with which to provide logistical support to the army.[11] All troops and supplies destined for the war zone were shipped by river from Asunción to Puerto Casado and other ports along the river, and from there by narrow-gauge railway and trucks to the interior. Older Paraguayan naval guns were concentrated in a river battery at Fortin Olimpo, while the modern *Paraguay*-class gunboats, one stationed at Asunción, the other at Puerto Casado, acted as floating AA batteries when not being used as transports. The *Paraguay* and the *Humaitá* alone could each transport over one thousand troops on each trip. During the war the *Paraguay* transported 1,234 officers and 51,373 soldiers to and from the combat area. Naval craft provided AA protection for the river convoys against a relatively strong Bolivian air force, which launched at least one air strike on a Paraguayan warship. It came on 22 December 1932 when three Bolivian aircraft attacked the *Tacuary* at Puerto Suarez. The warship may have shot down one of the planes. The surviving aircraft then attacked the *Humaitá* some thirty kilometers to the south, near Puerto Leda, but neither side did damage. Among other air attacks, there were incidents of Bolivian aircraft pestering Paraguayan merchant craft.[12] While bringing cattle to the front, the steamer *Jorge I* was attacked on both the Negro and Verde rivers but never hit.

Paraguay deployed naval personnel on land. Early in the conflict they garrisoned the upper Paraguay River, thus freeing army troops for the war

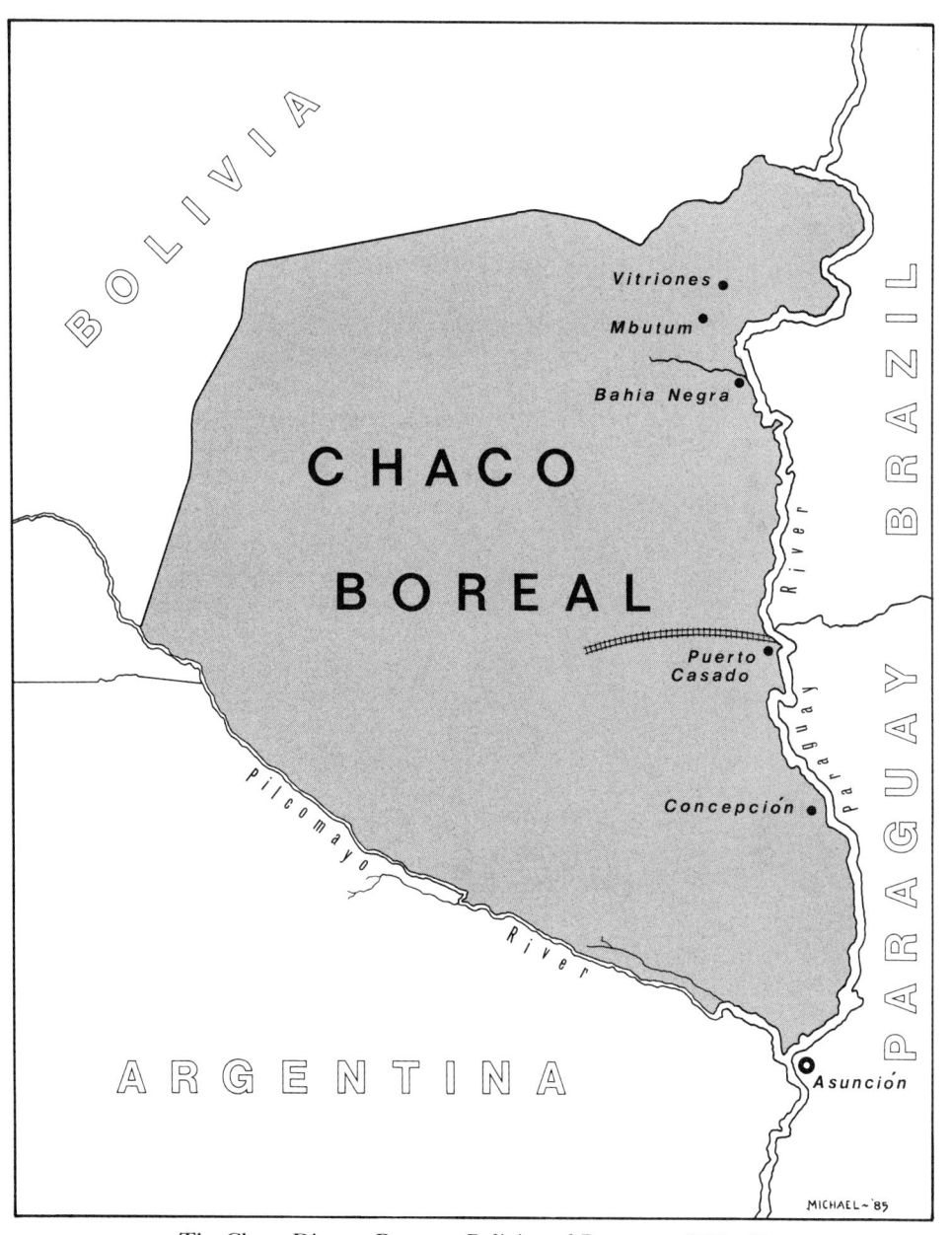

The Chaco Dispute Between Bolivia and Paraguay, 1932–35

zone. Naval officers staffed part of the Paraguayan Second Army Corps, and the marines manned some of the forts along the Pilcomayo River captured from the Bolivians. Most importantly, the navy administered the complex of arsenals and workshops around Asunción. The workshops produced truck bodies, munitions, and modified small arms and adapted naval munitions to fit artillery pieces of a slightly larger caliber.[13] Later in the war, naval personnel formed the naval infantry regiment Riachuelo, composed of three battalions and a sapper battalion that took over a forty-kilometer stretch of the frontier. In 1935 the Paraguayan navy planned to dismantle a twin 120-mm turret from an Italian-built gunboat and tow it overland to the front near Villa Montes, where it was to destroy a bridge over the Pilcomayo River used by the Bolivians to transport supplies.[14] The war ended before this could be carried out.

The Paraguayan naval aviation arm, although small, played an important role in the war. When it began the service had three aircraft, a Savoia 59 bis (R-1) seaplane, a CANT 10 Ter (R-2?) seaplane, and a SALM land plane (R-4?), which served on the ground as a trainer. In 1933 two more seaplanes, Macchi 18s (R-3 and R-5), were added to the force and used for transport (principally between Asunción and ports along the Paraguay River), reconnaissance, aerial photography, and bombing (primarily in the north and northwest of Bahia Negra). On the night of 28 December 1934 the R-5 bombed Vitriones and Mbutum with ten 880-pound (400-kg) bombs. This was the first nocturnal bombing in South America. When the war ended three aircraft, R-1, R-3, and R-5, which had flown 1,039 hours in 145 sorties, remained operational.[15]

After three years of fighting the Paraguayan army had reached the Andean foothills, having won most of its battles and proven itself superior to the enemy in the tropical region. The Paraguayan navy had lost only two officers and eighteen men, a low casualty count that belies the important logistical role it played. Nonetheless, by mid-1935 Paraguay had exhausted her resources. Bolivia, a nation mostly of high plateaus and mountains, had not been able to overcome the problems of jungle warfare. Her advantage of size and resources failed to offset the Paraguayans' advantage of fighting in their native environment. The Peace Protocol, signed on 12 June 1935, took effect two days later. A treaty delineating the border was signed on 21 July 1938. Paraguay was awarded eighty percent of the disputed territory, although she had captured much more.[16]

CHAPTER NINE

The Era of Foreign Naval Missions

DURING THE NINETEENTH CENTURY Latin American navies contracted foreign sailors to work in their fleets, particularly in engineer ratings. Beginning at the turn of the century these men were replaced by foreign naval missions, which would become a dominant influence on practically all Latin American navies from the 1920s until well after World War II.[1]

Circumstance determined when and for what specific purpose Latin American countries sought naval missions. For example, Perú agreed to a U.S. naval mission in 1920 to strengthen itself militarily and politically against Chile. The Chilean navy obtained a mission from Great Britain in 1911 ostensibly to modernize itself but also to strengthen its position vis-à-vis the U.S. Navy and the Chilean army. The call for a mission, moreover, did not always come from senior officers; it could come from junior officers as well. This happened in Chile in 1925. In the midst of a political upheaval, junior- and middle-level officers took the initiative and wrested from the navy a promise to request a mission from Great Britain.

Nations supplied missions for pragmatic reasons. Commander W. O. Spears, a member of the five-man U.S. commission to Brazil between 1917 and 1927 and chief of the U.S. naval mission to Perú between 1929 and 1932, wrote, "The success of these missions has not only been a great value to our political and economical expansion in South America in the past but will probably be of more value as time goes on."[2] One benefit of sending naval missions to Latin America was that it significantly influenced the purchasing habits of the host navy. This is borne out by contemporary testimony and a survey of acquisitions. Frederick E. Chapin, a representative of the Electric Boat Company, wrote the U.S. ambassador in Brazil:

> I have no doubt if the members of the mission were asked to give opinion as to the merits of the submarine boat built by the Electric Boat Company as compared with the submarine boat built by the Italian firm, it would unhesitatingly speak in favor of the American manufacturer. Possibly they may be called upon for such an opinion, in which case awarding of the contract to our Company would follow as a matter of course.[3]

Other gains for benefactor nations—which included, in addition to the United States and Britain, Austria, Belgium, France, Germany, Italy, and Spain, and sister republics Argentina, Brazil, Chile, and Perú—generally were a favorable treaty, either economic or military, and continued presence within the recipient country.[4] The political harvest of a few men, usually numbering less than a dozen and in some cases only one, could be almost immediate.

The advantages sought by the client nation were military proficiency and modern war equipment, and in many cases that is what it got. The only true measure of military prowess is success against an enemy. The Brazilian navy fought in World War I and World War II. At the beginning of the first war, its principal warships were in such poor condition that they had difficulty just putting to sea, but at the start of the second they were able immediately to go on patrol. The pre–World War II Brazilian navy was not maintained to the standards of a major naval power; it lacked base facilities and modern ships. Still, it was in far better condition than it had been before World War I, an improvement that in part can be attributed to the work of the U.S. naval mission.[5]

No one can deny the immediate rewards of foreign naval missions. However, it is not clear whether missions fostered or hindered the long-range development of recipient navies. For better or worse, what evolved was a symbiotic relationship between recipient and supplier. The former obtained, in addition to the mission itself, benefits such as unique training opportunities, for example, on board the warships of the host country; access to facilities like naval yards and arsenals; and exclusive information on the design of secret weapons. In all cases, modern military equipment tied the recipient to the supplier for a considerable time. A major piece of hardware such as a ship or aircraft could have a life cycle of twenty or more years, and the supplier was often the only source of spare parts and training. Many contracts legally tied the purchaser to the supplier for repair work.

As the world moved closer to World War II, the United States increased her efforts to dominate military affairs in Latin America, and ultimately she beat Great Britain at the game of influence in all the significant navies there except those of Argentina and Chile. In 1936 Secretary of State Cordell Hull articulated America's position: "If the governments of other countries in this hemisphere find it necessary to turn to foreign governments for assistance in matters of this character [military aid] it would be preferable for obvious reasons, that such assistance be extended by the United States rather than some other foreign government."[6]

Foreigners in the Fleet

In the nineteenth century Latin American navies depended heavily on outsiders to man their fleets. The Chilean navy in 1816 had thirty-one officers; seven were Chileans and the remainder foreigners, mostly English. Lord Cochrane's first naval division was composed of 1,006 men. Eight hundred and twenty-eight were Chileans (7 officers, 331 seamen, 137 landsmen, 128 gunners, and 225 soldiers) and 278 foreigners (24 officers and 254 seamen). During the fight for independence the number of mercenary seamen gradually diminished in the major warships of Cochrane's squadron, while the officers remained predominantly foreigners.[7]

From the time steam was first introduced into ships Latin American navies contracted for engine-room personnel from other countries. This practice became common in the second half of the nineteenth century. Usually pensioned foreign sailors were hired, often from private shipyards that built warships for the Latin American country. The first Paraguayan naval steamer, the *Tacuari*, sailed from Bordeaux on 11 November 1854 with a crew of seventy, composed of twenty-eight Paraguayan, sixteen British, and six French men, and citizens of numerous other countries. The *Tacuari* was commanded by a former Royal Navy officer, Captain George Francis Morice, who served as a technical advisor to the Paraguayan navy between 1854 and 1859. President Francisco Solano López, the man that led his nation into the disastrous War of the Triple Alliance, designated a special cemetery in Asunción for British engineers who died in the service of his navy. Chile, following the War of the Pacific, terminated her contracts with foreign engineers only to discover problems developing due to the lack of adequately trained nationals. In the 1890s, for example, the *Esmeralda* sustained costly boiler and engine damage after being in the hands of native engineers for less than six weeks.[8] So once again the nation recruited her senior fleet engineers from Great Britain. At the Battle of Angamos the Peruvian *Huáscar* was crewed by 151 Peruvians, 30 Englishmen, and 12 other foreigners.[9] México contracted the services of former British naval officers for her naval academy and training ship in 1891.

While these individuals did not directly involve their mother governments in Latin American naval affairs, their services gave foreign navies, particularly the Royal Navy, a window into naval activities in the region.

Perú

Since independence Perú, like other Latin American countries, had hired foreign naval instructors and on occasion sent cadets to foreign warships for schooling. In 1903 Peruvian naval cadets, after completing their training at Callao, served on board U.S. warships. In 1905 the secretary of foreign relations, Javier Prado y Ugarteche, reported to the Peruvian congress that "with much good will the Government of the United States has admitted new Peruvian midshipmen into its navy. . . . "[10] Peru's navy was the first in Latin America to obtain a foreign naval mission.

On 25 May 1905 the nation hired Commander Paúl de Marguerye of the French navy to direct the Peruvian Naval Academy. Why an officer from France? Since 16 September 1896 Perú had had a French army mission whose members probably influenced the decision. Moreover, the Chilean navy's close ties with the British navy probably made British personnel an unlikely choice, and U.S. naval personnel had not yet served in such a capacity. In April 1908 the Peruvian president requested that the function of the French naval officer be expanded to include reorganization of the Peruvian navy and that he exercise the responsibility as commander of the navy and commander of the squadron. Under his direction Marguerye improved the education of Peruvian officers. In 1909 the naval academy was moved from the training ship *Iquitos* to its present site at Callao, and the curriculum was improved. In 1907–1908 five Peruvian cadets were admitted to the French school ship *Duguay-Trouin*. Other Peruvian cadets joined the Spanish school ship *Nautilus*. A Lieutenant Guette replaced Marguerye in 1910. By 1912 the size of the French naval mission had increased to three officers. Captain José A. Therón arrived in 1911 and a naval engineer came the following year.

The French naval mission attempted to rebuild the Peruvian fleet, which had two modern cruisers, the *Almirante Grau* and the *Coronel Bolognesi*, built by Vickers in 1906. It also possessed assorted relics that had been collected after the War of the Pacific. The Chilean navy, Peru's most serious potential opponent, was overwhelmingly superior, and given the resources available there was no way possible for the Peruvian fleet to match its strength. Evidence suggests that Guette believed the only possible short-term defense improvement was the submarine. The French naval mission turned to its mother country for material, and two French-built submarines, the *Ferré* and the *Palacios*, were purchased. Their crews were trained in France. In 1912 the *Ferré* was carried to Perú in the *Kangaroo*, specifically built for such work; the *Palacios* followed by the same means of transportation a year later. The submarines were active during their early years in the Peruvian navy, so much so that the loss of torpedoes during practice proved to be an expensive problem. Inactive during World War I because of a scarcity of batteries, both boats were decommissioned in 1921.[11]

Perú also bought the French destroyer *Actée*, a relatively new warship. Renamed the *Teniente Rodríguez*, she was detained in Brazil during passage because of diplomatic complications. On 18 August 1914 she passed through the Panamá Canal, the very first warship to do so.

Peru's purchase of the French armored cruiser *Dupuy de Lôme* proved to be the undoing of the French naval mission, although it did not conceive the idea. Unlike the other warships Perú purchased from France, this cruiser, completed in 1895, was obsolete. Renamed the *Comandante Aguirre*, she was to cost three million gold francs, fifteen percent of the cost of a new ship of comparable size. The French viewed this as a bargain, but many Peruvians believed they were getting a relic, a ship that would not improve the balance of power vis-à-vis the Chilean navy. After being taken out of the French reserve fleet, the ship was reactivated and modified. When a Peruvian crew arrived in France on board the *Lima*, apparently only some of the payment had been made. The crew took possession of the ship, and she lay in Lorient while controversy raged at home. Adequate funds were not sent to allow the ship to sail to her new country. Such was the state of affairs when World War I broke out. The war severely depleted the world supply of merchant ships, and in 1920 a Belgian firm offered to buy the *Comandante Aguirre* for conversion to merchant service. This was accepted by the Peruvian government, whereupon the old armored cruiser became the cargo ship *Peruvier*.[12] This conclusion did not keep the French naval mission from falling out of favor in Perú. Its contracts were canceled just prior to World War I and it collapsed. Despite this outcome the mission left an important legacy. It had found a permanent home for the Peruvian Naval Academy, and it had renewed the Peruvian navy's interest in the submarine.[13]

In a letter of 1919 Admiral William B. Caperton of the U.S. Navy informed the U.S. Navy Department that the success of the North American naval commission to Brazil had influenced Peru's decision to ask for a similar arrangement. On 8 January 1920 the U.S. State Department received a cablegram from the North American legation in Lima stating that President Augusto B. Leguía y Salcedo, an ardent admirer of American technology, wanted U.S. naval commissioners. Commander Luis Aubry, the Peruvian naval attaché in Washington and a close supporter of his president, was instrumental in requesting the American mission.[14] The U.S. secretaries of state and navy exchanged views and a bill was prepared, the passage of which would permit officers of the U.S. Navy to accept employment by the South American republics. Congress passed the bill, which was signed by President Wilson on 5 June 1920. It laid the foundation for all future naval missions to Latin America until World War II.[15]

The chief of the U.S. naval mission to Perú had extensive power; he was "not [to] be subject to the orders of the Commanding Officers of the Peruvian Navy and will be subject and will comply only to the orders he would receive from the President of Perú and from the Ministry of the Navy. . . . "[16]

Five U.S. officers arrived in Lima on 6 September 1920. Work undertaken by them included the administration of education and testing, the supervision of repairs to ships, and the direction of base construction. On 14 August 1924, when Captain Sherwoode Taffinder, USN, returned from supervising the repair of a Peruvian cruiser in the Canal Zone, he "took command of [Peruvian] forces afloat, relieving Captain Loayza [of the Peruvian navy] as Comandante General."[17]

The U.S. mission judged the Peruvian navy to be in poor condition. Ships were old and morale was low. Thus the mission emphasized training, readiness, and organization, a campaign that sparked disagreements between the North Americans and Peruvian officers and required the arbitration of the Peruvian president. He directed the chief of the mission to come up with a building program for the navy, and the latter recommended the purchase of six submarines, six destroyers, and twenty-five seaplanes, as well as the building of a training station, a submarine base, a repair shop, a marine railway, support facilities, and improvements at the naval academy. The plan would require an additional one thousand enlisted men.[18] On 11 January 1924 the Peruvian congress created a national defense fund for new acquisitions. Subsequently, Perú contracted the Electric Boat Company to build two R-class submarines, twenty-four torpedoes, and a submarine base, including a power plant, repair shop, and marine elevator capable of lifting a 1,500-ton boat. The bill was $3,285,987.[19] In 1926 an officer was added to the U.S. naval mission to serve as an advisor for submarines and torpedoes. In 1928 two more R-class submarines were ordered.[20]

The size of the U.S. mission fluctuated according to the funds available. Its members held key positions such as commander of the squadron, director of the naval academy, commander of the naval station, chief of staff of the naval squadron, director of administration, and other prominent ones usually associated with aviation and submarines. Most importantly, U.S. naval officers actually commanded the Peruvian fleet from August 1923 through April 1929.

Possessing command authority, mission members found their position difficult and ultimately impossible to maintain. According to the terms of their contracts they were not to engage in wars or revolutions, but at times it was hard to draw the line between legality and reality. During a U.S. Senate investigation of the munitions industry, it was disclosed that mission members had prepared a war problem calling for the capture of the Colombian town of Leticia, which "could not possibly involve anything except conflict between Perú and Colombia. . . ."[21] In August 1930 the mission chief temporarily removed his personnel from command authority to avoid getting embroiled in a revolt against President Augusto B. Leguía. The president ordered Commander H. B. Grow, chief of the naval aviation service, to fly a mission carrying propaganda leaflets.[22] This was done, and Grow was arrested by the successful insurgents. The chief of the mission arranged for his release and reprimanded him.

Between 1930 and 1933 Perú descended into political turmoil and the government's support for the mission waned. In 1931 it was reduced to three members who were retained as advisors.[23] The navy's budget shrank drastically, and frequently the fleet went unpaid. In July 1932 the chief of the naval mission was asked to provide bombs to be used against insurrectionists. Interestingly, although Peruvian naval aviation had been amalgamated in the new national air force two years earlier, the mission's influence in aviation matters remained substantial. In part this was due to the impact of the movie "Hell Divers," which had premiered in Lima in May of 1932. The request for bombs was unsuccessfully referred to the U.S. State Department. In March 1933 the mission was dismantled.

In 1937 Perú requested that it be reestablished, a proposal that the U.S. chargé in Lima endorsed, viewing it as an opportunity to enhance North American prestige and restrain growing Italian influence. A three-year contract, based on the agreement of 1920, was signed between the Peruvian government and eight U.S. naval personnel.[24] Once again the North Americans held prominent positions and were invested with substantial authority. A new bilateral agreement between Perú and the United States issued on 31 July 1940 replaced the Peruvian contracts with individual North American officers.[25] U.S. naval officers with aviation background joined the mission. By the eve of World War II the U.S. naval mission had regained most of its influence within the Peruvian navy.

Brazil

In 1914 Brazil requested that two active-duty U.S. naval officers serve as instructors at the newly established Brazilian Naval War College. This being a first for the U.S. Navy, congressional authority was needed and obtained, but the two officers were never sent.[26] The only North American instruction came from the naval attaché to Brazil, Commander Phillip Williams, who taught at the naval war college as an extra duty. The congressional action did, however, have some impact: along with similar actions relating to requests from Cuba, the Dominican Republic, and Haití, it laid the foundation for later North American naval missions in Latin America.

Brazil received her first formal naval mission in 1917 when she declared war on Germany and signed a contract with five members of the British navy, one commander and four gunnery instructors. This aid was far from sufficient. Rear Admiral William Caperton, USN, persuaded the Brazilians to obtain North American instructors as well. In December the Ministry of Marine requested five U.S. officers, two to serve as instructors at the naval war college and three to teach fire control. In late March 1918 four naval officers arrived, assigned to the U.S. ambassador for duty with the Brazilian navy.[27]

An extensive refitting of the dreadnought *São Paulo* was carried out at the New York Navy Yard with all labor and material being furnished at cost. Once the *São Paulo* was complete, the *Minas Gerais*, a sister ship, underwent a similar overhaul. Brazil and the United States mutually benefitted from the overhaul of these ships—the former obtained two modernized dreadnoughts and the latter, among other rewards, had the opportunity to evaluate British equipment. Thus the overhaul work smoothed the waters for the U.S. mission.[28]

In February 1920 the *São Paulo* detoured from her return trip to Brazil and underwent extensive ordnance tests at Guacanaybo Bay, Cuba.[29] A target practice in 1922 proved the success of the modernization, as a North American observer noted:

> I cannot speak too highly of the . . . efficiency of this link in the chain [station in the plotting room]. There was no excitement, no unnecessary moving around, no nervousness, and the practice went off just as smoothly as if it were only a drill. This especially impressed me. . . .[30]

With two naval missions, the Brazilian government was in an awkward position in the spring of 1918. Pro-American and pro-British factions had developed within the Brazilian navy, and both foreign naval powers tried to increase their influence at the expense of the other. The government reached a verbal agreement with Captain C. T. Vogelgesang, head of the U.S. unit, concerning the division of responsibility. The North Americans would be known as the U.S. commission to Brazil. Vogelgesang was assigned to head the Brazilian War College, another American, Commander W. O. Spears, was assigned to the battleships, and the two junior American officers worked on aviation problems.[31] But the agreement did not solve matters. The U.S. naval commission was withdrawn soon after the war ended, and the British commander, possibly dissatisfied with his position, left Brazil in 1920. The British chief petty officers stayed on until 1922, in February of that year taking part in the Brazilian dreadnought's first long-range target practice.[32]

After the war Great Britain and the United States competed intensely for Brazil's attention. In 1920 President Epitacio da Silva Pessôa visited the United States and returned to Brazil in the battleship USS *Idaho*, a relatively new dreadnought commanded by Captain Vogelgesang. In 1921 Great Britain offered to sell Brazil the dreadnought *Agincourt* [ex-*Rio de Janeiro*] at the attractive price of one million pounds. Although the leading Rio de Janeiro newspaper, *O Jornal*, compared the advantages of future naval missions from Great Britain and the United States, the choice had obviously already been made by the government.[33] Upon the expiration of the British naval mission in 1922, it asked the United States for assistance under the direction of Vogelgesang. The request was granted on 9 November of that year, and the two nations signed a bilateral agreement. The mission, sixteen officers and nineteen noncommissioned officers strong, arrived in the steamer *Pan America* on 21 December 1922.[34] Vogelgesang, now a rear admiral, served on the Brazilian General Staff as technical assistant. The influence of the mission was substantial. Its chief military successes were remodeling the war college after that of the United States, overhauling the second Brazilian dreadnought at the New York Navy Yard, sending Brazilian officers to North American schools, and reorganizing the routine in the Brazilian battleships along lines established in the USS *North Dakota*. In addition, Brazil purchased considerable amounts of equipment from her northern neighbor.[35]

The Brazilian navy had been in deplorable condition when it joined the Allies and North Americans in World War I. By 1923 it had partially pulled itself together. According to one U.S. naval intelligence report,

> During its recent cruise the Brazilian Fleet revealed itself as being in bad condition. However, there were signs of improvement over its state in 1917. The engines of most of the ships appear to be in good condition and reasonable care is taken of them. . . . The morale of the Brazilian Navy is higher than one would expect, due largely to the fact that the enlisted personnel [are] a body of remarkably good men considering the country, the climate, and the conditions prevailing in the Navy.[36]

Such mildly positive observations, in large part a result of the U.S. and British missions, could not have been made in 1917.

In 1924 the U.S. naval mission submitted a ten year rearmament proposal to the minister of marine calling for seventy thousand tons for battleships, sixty thousand tons for cruisers, fifteen thousand tons for destroyers, and six thousand tons for submarines. The cost of the program would be high, even by prewar standards, and the ships would certainly have to be built in foreign yards, probably the United States. Why not a shipbuilding program designed to provide a reasonable number of smaller, locally built ships at a more moderate cost? The U.S. State Department was flabbergasted by the magnitude of the naval mission's proposal. If carried out, it would spawn new problems for Latin America. Purchase of a new battle fleet by the Brazilian navy would begin another dreadnought race on the continent. Secretary of State Charles Evans Hughes conveyed to the naval mission that the State Department "would rather recall [it] than assume the responsibility for a naval program that the Mission had proposed."[37] The plan was withdrawn, but the mission was not discouraged. On 22 June 1927 Commander L. M. Atkins, a member of the mission, wrote to the U.S. Navy's Bureau of Construction and Repair requesting a preliminary design for a fifteen-thousand-ton battleship to mount four fifteen-inch guns (the choice of armament is puzzling, since the U.S. Navy did not even have a fifteen-inch gun). Rear Admiral J. D. Beuret, chief of the bureau, forwarded a sketch design on 9 July. On 6 February of the following year Commander Atkins revised his request and increased the size of the proposed battleship to twenty thousand tons. This preliminary design was sent on 31 March, but it never came to fruition.[38]

Probably under the influence of the U.S. mission, the Brazilians did pursue the acquisition of submarines. In the mid-1920s Brazil's president announced to congress that he wanted to purchase ten additional submarines. In 1924 Brazil had sold the coastal defense monitor *Deodoro* to México for eight thousand contos, money set aside for submarine construction. Additional funds could not be found, so only one boat was to be built. A board of eight Brazilian naval officers and three advisors from the U.S. naval mission reviewed proposals from two North American, two British, and two Italian firms. In that order, the bids ranged in price from high to low. Although the U.S. advisors argued in favor of the craft being built in their country, they could not argue against the attractiveness of the Italian prices. An additional reason to take up the Italian offer was that, if built in Italy, the boat would be compatible with those already serving in the Brazilian navy. Thus Ansaldo San Giorgio of Spezia constructed a minelaying submarine, the *Humaitá*, a large boat for her day that reached a depth of 344 feet on her trials. She was added to the fleet in 1927.[39] Brazil's 1934 naval construction program also provided for three boats, the *Tamoio*, *Timbira*, and *Tupi*, to replace the recently discarded F-class units.

In 1926 Brazil and the United States renewed the agreement concerning the naval mission for an additional four years. At the end of 1930 Brazil temporarily terminated the mission, ostensibly for reasons of cost, actually because of a U.S. arms embargo during the revolution of 1930.[40] On 25 June 1932 a mission of two officers and a petty officer was requested and supplied. It later grew in number.

By the 1930s, when the Chaco War created a sense of urgency about the state of the fleet, Brazil's navy was antiquated.[41] With the exception of the Italian-built submarine *Humaitá*, it did not possess a single modern warship. Although the submarines *Tupi, Tamoio,* and *Timbira* were purchased from Italy, the North American naval mission persuaded Brazil to turn to the United States for other help. In 1931 and 1936 Brazil tried to buy cruisers from the United States, but provisions in the Washington Naval Treaty of 1922 and the London Naval Treaty of 1936 prevented the sale. In 1936 Brazil tried to contract U.S. yards to build her warships; this too was unsuccessful. After ordering six H-class destroyers from Britain in 1936, Brazil embarked on an indigenous building program. As a stopgap measure she tried to lease six old U.S. destroyers, to have been used to train crews for the new construction.[42] The request for the destroyers was an outgrowth of a conversation between President Franklin Roosevelt and the Brazilian ambassador, Oswaldo Aranha, which led to a U.S. Senate resolution supported by the president, the State Department, and the Navy Department. It was entitled "A joint resolution authorizing the President to lease, upon application from the foreign Governments concerned, and whenever in his discretion the public interests render such a course advisable, to lease destroyers to the Governments of the American republics under such terms and conditions as he may prescribe."[43]

The discussions between Brazil and the United States were a secret whose revelation came as a shock to many. There could be no escaping the close military tie legislation resulting from the resolution would create between Brazil and the United States. Argentina vocally opposed the transfer, primarily on the grounds that it would upset the regional naval balance. In mid-August the proposed lease filled front page after front page of Buenos Aires' newspaper *La Prensa* and was the subject of numerous editorials. Great Britain opposed the lease because it would violate the London Naval Treaty and hurt British arms sales to Latin America. The U.S. Navy League opposed it, arguing that the transfer would reduce U.S. naval power at a time when that power should be augmented. And North American pacifists opposed it because they believed the proposed transfer would foster an arms race in Latin America. In an editorial, "Leasing Naval Vessels," the *New York Times* questioned whether it was "really a neighborly policy to encourage the American republics, to enlarge their naval armaments, or to risk kindly naval rivalries among them." Discretion being the better part of valor, on 20 August the Brazilian and U.S. governments renounced the proposed lease.[44]

By the outbreak of World War II the U.S. naval mission had regained its extensive influence over the Brazilian navy, which was better prepared for war in 1941 than it had been in 1917, a situation brought about through hard work and spartan conditions. In the years preceding the war the fleet was at sea from the fifth to the twenty-fifth of each month. Two months of every year were spent at short-range battle practice, three months at long-range practice, and the remaining months at combined fleet exercises. The fleet was put in dry dock and repaired during annual leave periods at the end of December, January, and March. Despite this increased efficiency, the fleet was not prepared for ASW, amphibious warfare, or shore bombardment, but neither was the U.S. Navy.[45]

Chile

As we have seen, Chile's sea service has traditionally had strong ties with the British navy. During the wars for independence the Chilean navy employed English sailors and confirmed their military prowess, most notably that of Lord Cochrane. Beginning in 1839 Chilean junior officers frequently sailed in British warships for training and experience. Midshipman (later Vice Admiral) Patricio Lynch sailed in a Royal Navy ship that became embroiled in the Opium Wars off China. In 1909 Lieutenant Vicente Merino Bielich (later an admiral and the commander in chief of the Chilean navy) served in the British battle cruiser *Invincible*. Other Chilean junior officers who later reached influential positions in their navies also underwent training in the British navy. Favor such as Great Britain showed Chile found no parallel in the world's other important navies.[46] The French, German, Italian, Spanish, and U.S. fleets took a few Latin Americans in for training between 1850 and 1930, but these were modest efforts compared to those of Great Britain. The Royal Navy also trained a few Argentines and Brazilians.[47]

The special relationship between the British and Chilean navies can be seen in the reaction of the former to a Chilean request to have ten midshipmen train with the British navy in 1912. The Admiralty had a committee to formulate a policy regarding the training of foreigners which had concluded that requests were to be denied unless "special political reasons" existed. But in reference to the Chilean request, an unsigned Foreign Office internal minute to the Admiralty stated that "it might be urged that the question of Chileans stands on a different footing from the general question of foreigners in the Navy."[48] The request was granted.

In 1911 Chile contracted for a British naval mission, her first. The mission was made up of three officers and some ten petty and warrant officers, the noncommissioned group on pension from the British navy. The British Admiralty approved the appointments, made by the head of the Chilean naval commission, Vice Admiral L. A. Goñi. One officer was employed as instructor in strategy and tactics, another as inspector of gunnery, the third as inspector of torpedoes. They wore Chilean naval uniforms. Captain Charles Burne, founder of the Chilean Naval War College, brought with him from Britain the Royal Navy's latest war games, with models and textbooks. His contract stipulated that he was to return to England periodically to keep abreast of the latest developments. The mission ended in 1914 with the outbreak of World War I. Captain Burne, in fact, was in

England when the war started, the Admiralty appointing him naval attaché for the whole west coast of South America.[49]

Chilean engineers and artisans continued to visit England's private shipyards and to attend her universities. Between 1920 and 1923 Lieutenant Commander A. C. W. Domville, a member of the 1912–14 mission, returned to Chile as a gunnery advisor. In 1922 Captain George N. Tomlin, commanding officer of the Royal Navy dreadnought *Canada*, went back to Chile as the director of the naval war college. Close relations were reinforced when Great Britain sold the commandeered *Canada* (the future *Almirante Latorre*) to Chile for one million pounds, less than half of her construction cost. Minor craft were also sold at a significant savings to the Latin American country. In 1922, however, the British presence in Chile shrank because of economic stringencies resulting from World War I. At the same time the Chilean treasury was cutting back on expenditures.[50]

A new mission was sent to Chile in 1926 and remained until 1932. The mission, which was established by the navy hierarchy at the insistence of mid-level officers, operated under difficult circumstances, but by 1927 the air had cleared. With Commander Carlos Frödden serving as the Chilean navy minister, significant educational and organizational reforms were made in the navy with the help of British advice and consultation.[51] The mission planned to play a role promoting fleet preparedness. A North American observer wrote, "Before the ships depart from Puerto Aldea for the 1926 maneuvers, the British naval technicians will go aboard for the purpose of making such observations and criticisms as they may have gleaned from the lessons learned during the World War."[52] The naval mission also influenced the purchase of hardware. In 1927 the British firm of Armstrong, Vickers and Company competed with the Swedish company of Bofors for a contract to arm six destroyers under construction for Chile in Great Britain. According to a U.S. intelligence source, the contract was awarded to Armstrong, Vickers because "the British minister in Santiago, Sir Thomas Hohler, had objected [to the awarding of the contract to Bofors] on the ground that, as the destroyers were being built in England, to order their armaments from a foreign firm would be construed as an unfriendly act." The editor of the U.S. *Monthly Information Bulletin* stated that, "as in the case of the Argentine program, no bids were asked or received from the United States. Chile is also inflicted with a certain amount of anti-American virus which the British turn to their advantage. . . ."[53] By 1945 Chile, like most of Latin America, had accepted a U.S. naval mission.[54]

Argentina

Argentina has always remained outside the formal mission system, thus leaving her navy relatively free from foreign influence and permitting it to fill its hardware needs by competitive bidding. From time to time the navy has contracted with foreign specialists, for example, when it purchased the *La Plata* and the *Los Andes* from Great Britain in 1876 and English sailors were hired to indoctrinate the new Argentine crews in seamanship and gunnery.[55] In 1898 it employed retired English gunners as instructors.

During World War I the U.S. Navy invited officers from various Latin American fleets to train in its facilities. Seven Argentine naval officers underwent submarine warfare training at New London, Connecticut, and seven aviators received their wings at Pensacola, Florida, between 1917 and 1921. More officers trained in the United States after the war. (Argentine officers were also sent to France for postgraduate training in the use of radio.) The construction of the Argentine dreadnoughts *Moreno* and *Rivadavia* in the United States between 1910 and 1915, plus their refits in the mid-1920s, generated the transfer of technology and cultural ties. But in 1921 the Argentine navy prohibited the training of additional officers in the U.S. Navy. In 1934 Argentina hired two North American naval officers to serve as advisors at the Argentine Naval War College. Eventually three officers were assigned to this task, and in 1937 a fourth was assigned to naval aviation. The officers had one-year contracts, not renewed in 1941 but subsequently reinstated during the war.

Today the Argentines are proud of the fact that, strictly speaking, they have had no mission. It is possible that the navy has not accepted a formal mission because it does not want any foreign nation looking into its private affairs.[56]

Argentina has kept a "naval commission in Europe" from the end of the nineteenth century to the present. For many years it was seated in London, but as a result of the 1982 Malvinas War and because most of the Argentine navy's new ships are of German construction or design, the commission was moved to Hamburg, Germany. Today Argentine naval officers regularly attend the French and U.S. naval war colleges and take courses in gunnery, engineering, optics, electronics, and other specialties in those countries as well as in Germany, Italy, Holland, and Spain. The Argentines, it seems, would rather send officers and petty officers abroad to be trained than have foreigners teaching in Argentine naval schools.

Colombia

North American naval aid to Colombia commenced on a bizarre note. In 1932 the U.S. Navy "loaned" the country an officer, Commander James H. Strong, to act as an advisor. At the time Colombia and Perú were engaged in a border dispute in the Amazon basin, and North American naval officers found themselves supporting opposed forces. Strong drew up plans for the defense of Colombian ports and advised the government concerning arms purchases. In February 1934 he resigned from the U.S. Navy and continued for a while in the services of Colombia.

Between 1936 and 1938 Colombia contracted for three British officers to serve as instructors at her naval academy. On 23 November 1938 she signed a contract for a U.S. naval mission.[57]

Other Latin American Navies

Foreign naval missions have influenced the remaining significant Latin American navies. Ecuador had a military mission from Italy for twenty years until the eve of the Ethiopian War. In 1936 two retired U.S. naval officers began teaching at the Ecuadorian Naval Academy. Four years later their efforts were expanded into a formal mission of two officers and twenty men.

Italian influence also extended to Venezuela. In 1939 that country requested a naval officer from the U.S. naval construction corps. The North American attaché questioned whether his work might conflict with that of the Italian naval mission. The minister of war replied that the Italians were there merely as instructors and had no command authority. Thus the United States filled the void and established a formal mission in 1940 by executive agreement.

Just before World War II the United States initiated a program to displace German and Italian military influence in Latin America. Training programs for military services increased, U.S. naval units made visits more frequently and demonstrated their hardware, and high-ranking military officials were encouraged to go to Latin America on good-will missions. War in Europe caused the remaining Latin American navies previously outside the sphere of U.S. influence to fall into orbit, and by the close of the war Latin American naval policy was almost completely shaped by the United States (see appendix 8).[58]

Naval Missions from Latin American Countries

Every leading Latin American maritime nation has practiced the statecraft of dispatching naval missions to woo countries sharing interests with it. Argentina has persistently aided the Paraguayan navy over the decades. In 1926 several Paraguayan naval officers received scholarships to train in Argentine naval schools. At that time, one officer and two cadets were already taking courses at the Argentine Naval Academy, and fifteen apprentices were undergoing instruction at the chief petty officers' school. In 1943 Argentina sent a naval mission to Paraguay; it was deactivated in 1951 and reestablished two years later. The two Paraguayan gunboats *Humaitá* and *Paraguay* were overhauled and refitted several times in Buenos Aires. In a ceremony on 17 January 1927, attended by President Alfredo Stroessner, Argentina donated the converted medium landing ship *Corrientes*, formerly of the U.S. Navy, to the Paraguayan navy. This was but one of many such donations. In 1937 and again in 1941 Peruvian midshipmen sailed in the Argentine ship *Sarmiento* during her annual training cruise. Since the 1960s Argentina has maintained a naval mission in Bolivia and has made similar donations to that country's navy.[59]

Perú and Brazil became unlikely bedfellows in 1920 when midshipmen of the former sailed in the Brazilian school ship *Benjamin Constant*. The catalyst may have been the U.S. naval missions in the two countries.[60]

After the War of the Pacific the Chilean navy dominated the west coast of South America and maintained a close relationship with the military in Ecuador. In 1895 Chile sold the cruiser *Esmeralda* to Japan, and she crossed the Pacific flying the flag of Ecuador, an official of that nation playing a diplomatic role. From 1896 through 1920 there was a Chilean naval mission in Ecuador. Between May 1905 and January 1908 the Chilean *Casma* was chartered to Ecuador as the *Marañón*. Part or all of her crew may have remained Chilean. In 1907 the *Almirante Lynch*, *Almirante Condell*, and *Almirante Simpson* were offered for sale to Ecuador, which acquired only the best (the *Almirante Simpson*) and renamed her *Libertador Bolivar*. On 18 September 1910, commanded by Capitán de Fragata C. B. Heli Nuñez, she represented Ecuador at Chile's Centennial Naval Review. Chile has traditionally trained Ecuadorian naval officers.

Chilean naval aid also went to Colombia at the turn of the century. In 1902 Chile ceded to that country a "second-class cruiser" in exchange for guaranteed passage of military goods across present-day Panamá. A Chilean naval officer, Lieutenant Alberto Asmussen, was the first director of the Colombian Naval Academy, serving between 1907 and 1910.

In 1931 Chile sent a naval mission of two officers to Paraguay whose arrival coincided with the delivery of the Paraguayan gunboats *Paraguay* and *Humaitá* from Italian yards.

Chile has received Colombians, Ecuadorians, Paraguayans, and Uruguayans into her naval schools.[61]

CHAPTER TEN

World War II

TWO LATIN AMERICAN NAVIES dramatically increased their combat potential and strength vis-à-vis their neighbors between the two world wars. It is notable that neither was the recipient of a foreign naval mission. Most significant turned out to be the burgeoning of the Argentine navy in the 1920s. At the start of the decade it was an obsolete fleet of ships—with the exception of the dreadnoughts *Moreno* and *Rivadavia* and a squadron of German-built torpedo boats. To remedy this state of affairs Argentina launched a massive revitalization program, and between 1924 and 1926 her two battleships were refitted. In 1926 the government authorized an expenditure of seventy-five million gold pesos to be apportioned over ten years for a naval program. With considerable national sacrifice it was carried through almost in its entirety. Argentina purchased two small heavy cruisers (the *Almirante Brown* and the *25 de Mayo*), a light cruiser-training ship (*La Argentina*), twelve destroyers, and three submarines. With her naval power waxing, she regarded herself as the rival of the United States for the political leadership of the western hemisphere.

In 1936 and 1937, during the Spanish civil war, the *25 de Mayo* and the destroyer *Tucumán* were sent to Spain to protect Argentine interests, which were extensive because of the number of Argentines living there. The warships remained on station for almost a year, becoming more and more involved in the evacuation of refugees from Republican-held ports. In all, 1,825 displaced persons were transported to Marseille and Genoa. This is the only time Latin American warships were sent to Europe to exercise their influence—exactly the reverse of what had been taking place on the South American continent for centuries (see appendix 6).[1]

Between world wars the Mexican navy also began to recover from years of neglect resulting from economic and political turmoil. The gunboats *Guanajuato*, *Potosí*, and *Querétaro*, the gunboat-transport *Durango*, and ten large patrol boats were purchased in the mid-1930s. Such additions would hardly have been noticed in a moderate-sized navy, but for México, this was a phoenix rising from the ashes. Mexican sailors now had the opportunity to gain substantial experience at sea.

For the most part, though, Latin American navies slipped farther behind world standards between the wars. Brazil's was still on the building ways. Chile attempted to rebuild her fleet but could only afford to modernize her dreadnought and acquire six destroyers and three submarines. What she wanted most—cruisers—were beyond her means.

When global war mushroomed for the second time within the century, it profoundly influenced the development of Latin American navies. On 1 September 1939 the western hemisphere was politically divided. Strict diplomatic neutrality was championed by Argentina, favoring neither Allies nor Axis, whereas the United States jockeyed for a noncombatant position that favored the Allies. Events preceding the attack on Pearl Harbor upset the traditional alignment of the four South American naval powers. Argentina contested the United States for the political leadership of the western hemisphere. Perú, Argentina's long-time de facto ally, supported the United States. Brazil was soon to become the most important hemispheric ally of the United States. And Brazil's traditional de facto ally, Chile, remained neutral.

War in Europe was a critical concern to the United States and many Latin American nations supporting her position, principally Brazil, Uruguay, and the Caribbean nations. Three weeks after the invasion of Poland the United States called a foreign ministers' meeting. It was held in Panamá in September 1939. The issues of neutrality, protection of peace in the western hemisphere, and economic cooperation made up the agenda. The conference adopted a general declaration of neutrality establishing a neutrality zone around all of North and South America except for Canada, which was at war (see the map on page 149).[2] Most Latin American countries did not possess the naval power to enforce the zone, though some modest attempts would be made.[3]

The second wartime meeting of American foreign ministers was held in Habana in July 1940, following the fall of France. A primary concern for the United States was the danger to American colonies belonging to European countries occupied by German forces. A joint resolution of the U.S.

Congress, dated 17–18 June 1940, had stated "that the United States would not recognize any transfer, and would not acquiesce in any attempt to transfer, any geographic region of this hemisphere from one non-American power to another non-American power. . . ."[4] Argentina led the opposition to the U.S. position, arguing that such provocative action threatened neutrality and if the matter of colonies was addressed, the goal should be to end colonialism in the Americas altogether, not to protect the status quo.[5] The United States won on this point, and the conference issued the following statement: "An attack on one American state is considered as an attack on all American states."[6] This was the most significant result of the conference, which provided the diplomatic basis for bilateral defense commissions.

Between August and October 1940 representatives of the U.S. Navy met with their counterparts in all of Latin America except Bolivia, which had no navy or coastline, and Panamá, which was already part of U.S. defenses of the Panamá Canal. The United States made bilateral agreements with most of her southern neighbors, but not Argentina and Ecuador. The former reserved the right to remain neutral and to trade with both the Allies and Axis.[7] And at the time Ecuador was engaged in fighting with Perú and wanted the agreement to include a guarantee of national territories. An understanding between Ecuador and the United States was reached in February 1942 without such an arrangement.[8]

During 1941 Uruguay, one of the closest supporters of the United States, proposed that "any American nation engaged in a defensive war against a non-hemispheric power should be treated as a non-belligerent by the other American republics."[9] This meant that if the United States was provoked into a defensive war, the Latin American nations endorsing this proposal would still accord the United States all the privileges due to neutrals. By September 1941 sixteen nations had accepted the proposal; four (Argentina, Chile, Colombia, and Perú) had not.

Following the Japanese attack on Pearl Harbor, the United States requested a third foreign ministers' conference of Latin American nations. This was held at Rio de Janeiro in January 1942.[10] The United States sought the adoption of a resolution whereby all the American republics would break diplomatic relations with the Axis powers.[11] The response of the American republics was divided geographically. By the time of the conference, nine Central American and Caribbean nations—Costa Rica, Cuba, the Dominican Republic, Guatemala, Haití, Honduras, Nicaragua, Panamá, and El Salvador—had already declared war on the Axis powers, and three countries in the same region—Colombia, México, and Venezuela—had severed diplomatic relations. The eleven remaining nations had proclaimed their status as nonbelligerents. At the conference Chile asked for guarantees of economic and military aid from the United States as a condition for breaking relations, but this could not be arranged. Argentina held to her traditional position of neutrality. Thus by the end of the meeting all the Latin American republics except Argentina and Chile had broken diplomatic relations with the Axis powers (see appendix 9).[12]

Another outcome of the meeting at Rio was the establishment of the Inter-American Defense Board to coordinate military and technical matters throughout the hemisphere. Militarily, the United States bore the brunt of hemispheric defense throughout the war. More than a hundred thousand U.S. soldiers were stationed throughout Latin America, and U.S. ships and aircraft were primarily responsible for protecting its sea routes. Over $475 million in lend-lease aid was provided to Latin America. More than seventy percent of this went to Brazil. And of the South American nations, only Brazil and México sent military forces overseas. Other Latin American military contributions to the war effort were small. In fact, the United States discouraged a number of nations from participating directly in the fighting, considering such military contributions to be more trouble than they were worth. The United States preferred that the Latin American participants provide raw materials to the war effort.[13]

The greatest impact World War II had on inter-American relations was the solidification of U.S. influence in much of Latin America, especially Brazil. The United States looked to her southern neighbors as a source of raw material, and they in turn looked to the United States for manufactured goods. But U.S. influence was not pervasive. Argentine and Chilean reluctance to enter a war they did not regard as their own kept their relations with the United States cool. With only brief periods of modest improvement, this has been the state of affairs ever since.

World War II changed the balance of naval power in Latin America. During the first decades of the century Argentina had tried to maintain a navy equal to the combined fleets of her two strongest neighbors, Brazil and Chile, and in the thirties she made a quantitative leap that almost accomplished that goal. But the extensive aid given by the United States to Brazil in the war greatly increased her fleet's strength in relation to that of Argentina and Chile.

The war also significantly shifted foreign military influences in Latin America. Beforehand, no one foreign nation had dominant sway over any country on the continent. Great Britain and the United States had been the most consequential presences, but Germany, Italy, and France also made themselves felt in the name of their strong interests in the region. After the war the United States emerged as the predominant foreign power, establishing naval missions in every major Latin American nation except Argentina (see appendix 8).[14]

With one exception, Brazil's fleet, Latin American navies did not do much fighting during the war. But they received training in the latest techniques and equipment on small warships such as submarine chasers and patrol craft, and they were introduced to radar and sonar. The smaller navies received fire-control equipment for the first time as well.

Uruguay Takes on the Admiral Graf Spee

The neutrality zone declared by the American foreign ministers when World War II broke out was soon tested. On the morning of 13 December 1939 Uruguay's military authorities learned that a naval battle was raging two hundred miles southeast of Punta del Este, already inside the neutrality zone. They radioed this information to the training ship *Uruguay*, on an exercise with naval academy students, whereupon she weighed anchor from Maldonado Harbor and sailed to the southeast.[15] At 1814 she found the German pocket battleship *Admiral Graf Spee* at 35°06' South latitude, 50°51' West longitude, where the heavy fighting with British cruisers later referred to as the Battle of the River Plate had ended. At 1844 the German ship fired two shots at smoke on the horizon to keep the British cruisers at a respectable distance. The combatants had been navigating toward the South American coast at eighteen knots, and by this time they were approximately ten miles from it. The *Uruguay* took up position within the three-mile limit, which forced her to cross between the *Admiral Graf Spee* and the *Ajax*. Fernando J. Fuentes, her commander, noted, "I took this decision in spite of the danger in steering a course between the enemy vessels, and also in spite of the supposed warning of danger given by the German battleship, thus carrying out my duty of enforcing respect for our territorial waters."[16] He reported to the Uruguayan Admiralty, "I must state categorically that the whole of the action, with the exception of the first few minutes, took place within territorial waters. . . ."[17]

The crippled *Admiral Graf Spee* entered Montevideo, Uruguay's chief seaport. By international law, hostile warships may remain in a neutral port for twenty-four hours; if they are unseaworthy this period may be extended by the host country. A committee visiting the ship on behalf of the Uruguayan government estimated that fourteen days would be necessary for essential repairs. The government initially wanted to grant only forty-eight hours, in part because of diplomatic pressure brought to bear by the British ambassador, Millington Drake; the period was extended to seventy-two hours in response to a protest by the German ambassador.[18] Uruguayan officials ordered the German ship to leave port on 17 December or face internment. Seriously wounded crew members had already disembarked at Montevideo. At the appointed hour the *Admiral Graf Spee* sailed out of Montevideo.

Uruguayan warships were standing by to ensure that the German warship left territorial waters and to rescue survivors from any sea battle that might erupt. None did, and the *Admiral Graf Spee* was scuttled. Remaining crew members—over one thousand men—were brought in Argentine ships to Buenos Aires, where they were interned in various camps. All of the officers escaped and returned to Germany to continue fighting the war.

Earlier, during the battle, the Argentine high command had ordered light cruiser *La Argentina* to the Montevideo area to reinforce the obsolete *Independencia*-class coastal defense battleship on patrol off Rio de la Plata (Plate River). *La Argentina*, recently constructed in Great Britain for the Argentine navy and similar in appearance to the British cruisers *Ajax* and *Achilles*, had been ordered to intervene between the *Admiral Graf Spee* and the British cruisers should any fighting break out in Argentine waters. Accordingly, the Argentine authorities gave orders for the national ensign to be painted on her sides and for the flag to be illuminated during the night. When the battle had ended, Argentine President Ramón S. Castillo personally ordered Minister of the Navy Admiral León L. Scasso to intensify patrols so that Argentine neutrality would be respected. When an Argentine naval air patrol discovered HMS *Exeter* sailing slowly toward the Malvinas and listing, the government said the ship could enter Puerto Belgrano Naval Base for emergency repairs. The offer, however, was declined.

The Battle of the River Plate affected all the countries of South America, which felt as if the war had trespassed their borders. On 23 December they issued a joint resolution formally protesting actions that had taken place then and in earlier times by belligerents within the neutrality zone. The resolution went to the governments of Great Britain, France, and Germany. Great Britain replied "that the proposal, involving as it does abandonment by belligerents of certain legitimate rights, is not one which, on any basis of international law, can be imposed upon them by unrelated actions...."[19] France and Germany sent similar answers.

Brazil Twice Forgotten

In the early days of World War II Brazil's geographical location held strategic importance. Jutting far into the Atlantic Ocean, the country lay just eighteen hundred nautical miles from the African coast. All ships transiting between the North and South Atlantic had to pass through these waters, and thus they were ideal hunting grounds for the U-boat. But for the Axis they were also a bottleneck, being the only practical route for blockade runners and raiders traveling to and from the South Atlantic, Indian, and Pacific oceans.

The naval war came early to the vicinity of Brazil. On 3 September 1939 the British cruiser *Ajax* forced the German freighters *Olinda* and *Carl Fritzen* to scuttle themselves south of Rio Grande do Sul. The *Admiral Graf Spee* began her attack on Allied shipping off the Brazilian coast on the thirtieth when she sank the British merchantman *Clement* in the vicinity of Pernambuco. (It was only ten weeks later that the German battleship's short career ended at Montevideo.) On 12 February 1940 the German

WORLD WAR II 149

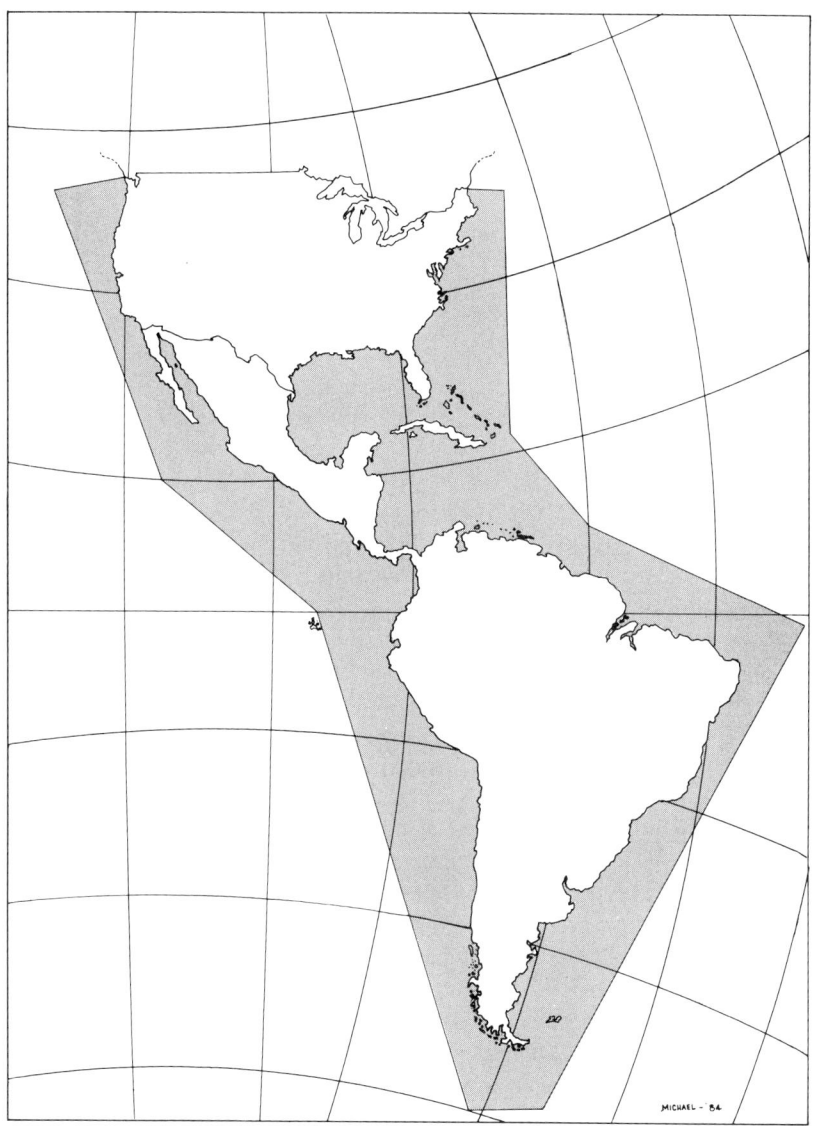

Western Hemisphere Neutrality Zone, 1939–41

freighter *Wakama*, caught by the British cruiser *Dorsetshire* off Cape Frio, scuttled herself. She had sailed from Rio de Janeiro two days earlier. During the first weeks of July the German auxiliary cruiser *Schiff 10* (*Thor*) sank five Allied merchantmen and captured one in the South Atlantic.[20]

Across the ocean from Brazil lay French West Africa, controlled by the Vichy government after the fall of France in May–June 1940. There, in the port of Dakar, were important French naval units, including a nearly completed but damaged battleship,[21] two light cruisers, four destroyers, three submarines, and numerous smaller warships. Between 23 and 25 September Free French and British forces attempted unsuccessfully to capture the port by amphibious assault. This failure further increased Brazil's strategic importance.

Brazil's attitude toward the world conflict was not readily apparent. Brazilians greatly admired French culture, and the years of service performed by the U.S. naval mission had resulted in many friendships between North American and Brazilian seamen. But relations between Brazil and Great Britain were strained. As in World War I, Great Britain had commandeered warships under construction for Brazil in British yards. And British warships frequently violated the Pan American security zone, leading to diplomatic conflict. Early in the war seventeen of thirty-two German merchantmen caught in Brazilian waters attempted to run a British blockade and return to Germany. A number of them were intercepted inside the security zone by British warships and destroyed.[22]

On 11 October 1940 a British warship caught the Brazilian merchantman *Siqueira Campos*, which had sailed from Lisbon, Portugal, for Rio de Janeiro carrying a cargo of German manufactured arms destined for the Brazilian army. The ship was taken to Gibraltar and detained. This infuriated Brazilians. It took the intercession of the United States before the ship was allowed to proceed. In another incident the merchantman *Buarque*, en route to the United States from Brazil, both neutral, was boarded by a British inspection party and commandeered for allegedly carrying contraband. On 1 December a more serious event occurred. The British auxiliary cruiser *Calvin Castle* stopped the Brazilian merchantman *Itape* off the São Tomé lighthouse and removed twenty-five Germans and two Italians. And on 18 January 1941 a British party from the auxiliary cruiser *Asturias* boarded the French merchant ship *Mendoza* in Brazilian territorial waters.[23]

Germany violated Brazilian neutrality, less frequently at first because, in hopes of keeping the Latin American countries out of the war, she tried hard not to antagonize them. She also had fewer opportunities to do so. On 22 March 1941 German aircraft attacked the Brazilian merchant ship *Taubaté* while she was transiting between Cyprus and Alexandria; one crew member was killed. The ship had been tempting fate, transiting between two British-controlled ports in a combat zone.[24]

If Brazil was to join the Allies, it would take courage. A prime concern, which had caused national leaders worry during World War I, were first- and second-generation immigrants from Axis countries living in Brazil. Their numbers had increased dramatically. Germany in particular was making a special effort to win the loyalty of these individuals in cultural clubs, in schools, and by covert means. Although fears of the possibility of a German invasion of Brazil in 1941 may seem incredible today, they did not appear unreasonable at the time.

Moreover, if Brazil entered the war her domestic transportation system would be very vulnerable to attack. Almost all goods traveled by sea. The rail system was only regional, most of it narrow-gauge, and train engines burned wood. Air France, the German Condor, and Italy's Lati airlines controlled air traffic, internal and external. The Axis powers were using the air to support their activities, which Air France, after the fall of France, could not prevent. Brazil needed the Axis airlines and could not suppress their activity without replacing them. Brazil made a secret agreement with the United States government and Airport Development Project, a subsidiary of Pan American Airlines, to displace the influential Axis companies, but this took time.

The Brazilian navy prepared itself for the inevitable conflict. In October 1941 the minelayer *Camaquã* patrolled the northeast coast, being relieved by the *Camocim* at the time of the Pearl Harbor attack. On 27 January 1942 Brazil broke diplomatic relations with Germany as a result of the declaration of war by the United States.[25]

Between February and April U-boats torpedoed five Brazilian merchant ships, causing 109 deaths.[26] On 16 May the German high command issued orders that all armed ships belonging to South American nations, except those of Argentina and Chile, could be attacked without warning.[27] Two days later, off Cape São Roque, the Italian submarine *Barbarigo* torpedoed the Lloyd Brasileiro ship *Comandante Lira* and attacked her with gunfire. The cruiser USS *Omaha* picked up survivors from two lifeboats; the third reached the coast. Two lives were lost. The USS *Thrush* and the Brazilian naval tug *Heitor Perdigão* towed the damaged ship into Fortaleza. In retaliation the Brazilian Ministry of Aeronautics announced that aircraft would attack any U-boats sighted.[28]

Following these incidents, Rear Admiral Jonas H. Ingram, USN, brought to Brazilian waters elements of his Task Force 3, which consisted of four old cruisers and five destroyers. Its patrol area was a triangle formed by Trinidad, Cape São Roque, and the Cape Verde Islands. Admiral Ingram met with President Getúlio Vargas, who said that his naval advisors recommended the closing of all ports until the United States could provide convoy protection. The admiral explained that adequate protection would be impossible for some time, but that together the Brazilian and U.S.

navies would allow merchant ships to move without undue loss. Vargas asked Ingram "to assume informal unity of command over Brazilian naval forces. . . ." The president also opened all ports and facilities to the North Americans. In return, Ingram promised to expedite the training of Brazilian personnel and the delivery of naval materiel.[29]

Admiral Ingram developed a force operating plan dividing responsibilities between the Brazilian and U.S. forces. The Orange Force (U.S. planes) would patrol offshore shipping lanes from Belém to Rio de Janeiro; the Blue Force (Brazilian planes, under Brigadier Eduardo Gômes) would patrol inshore waters. The Brazilian Admiral Jorge Dodsworth Martins would help to organize two task groups of Brazilian cruisers and destroyers. The joint operations began before the end of April 1942.

In response to the announcement that Brazil's air force would attack U-boats on sight, and to an encounter between the armed merchant ship *Gonçalves Dias* and the *U-502* on 24 May, Adolf Hitler ordered his submarine command to prepare the plan for a concentrated attack off the Brazilian coast. Initially he approved the resulting plan, but fear that the attack would drive not only Brazil but Argentina and Chile to war as well drove him to cancel it. He changed his mind again, and on 29 June U-boats were diverted from other areas to attack ships in Brazilian waters.[30] A blitzkrieg launched by the *U-507* off the coast shocked the Brazilian public. On 14 August the U-boat sank the *Baependi*, carrying pilgrims to the São Paulo Eucharistic Congress, off the mouth of the Rio Real, between Recife and Bahia; 270 lives were lost. The *U-507* torpedoed the *Araraquara* the same day, causing another 131 deaths. The following day it sank the *Aníbal Benévolo*, killing 150 people, including 120 soldiers. On the seventeenth it sank the *Itagiba* and the *Arará*, on the nineteenth the small coaster *Jacira*. Over six hundred lives were lost to the *U-507*'s activities alone.[31] President Vargas, outraged, ordered the withdrawal of all Brazilian merchant ships from the seas, a move that paralyzed coastal and international trade and played into the hands of the German war effort.

As in World War I, the German U-boat offensive drove Brazil to action. On 21 August 1942 she made a declaration of war on Germany and Italy to take effect on the thirty-first. Admiral Karl Dönitz, the German U-boat commander, appraised the situation: "Although this [the declaration] altered nothing in our existing relationship with Brazil, which had already taken part in hostile acts against us, it was undoubtedly a mistake to have driven Brazil to an official declaration. . . ."[32]

Militarily, Brazil's greatest contribution to the Allies was the use of her territory for air bases. On 18 August 1941 President Franklin Roosevelt announced that the United States was ferrying warplanes to the British in Africa via Brazil.[33] On 1 October Brazil and the United States concluded a secret agreement for the close defense of the continent, which was later modified. On 14 November Brazil granted permission for U.S. aircraft and warships to operate from Natal and Maceio; the aircraft could use the facilities formerly owned by Air France.[34] From this beginning the system expanded greatly. The United States built air bases at Belem, Fortaleza, Recife, Natal, and Bahia.

The Brazilian merchant marine was another important asset. In 1939 it had 485,000 gross registered tons of shipping. It was the fourth largest in the Americas behind the merchant marines of the United States (11,362,000 tons), Canada (1,224,000 tons), and Panamá (717,500 tons). By 1940 there were 276 ships in the fleet, including some small river types.[35]

When Brazil entered the war, she had few warships of value. The two battleships *São Paulo* and *Minas Gerais* (somewhat modernized in 1934–37) were long out of their prime, their only real value being to function as harbor defense ships.[36] The two light cruisers *Bahia* and *Rio Grande do Sul*, workhorses of the earlier world war, had been extensively refitted in 1925–26, when Thornycroft installed new engines and boilers, but they were thirty years old and "nothing more than over-grown and not particularly fast destroyers."[37] The Brazilian navy owned four modern submarines—the *Tupi*, *Tamoio*, and *Timbira*, completed in 1937, and the minelaying submarine *Humaitá*, completed a decade earlier—of limited operational value. Being Italian-built, however, and nearly identical to some submarines used against Brazil, these craft were valuable for antisubmarine training. Pre–World War I relics, including six of the old *Pará*-class destroyers and the destroyer *Maranhão*, made up the remainder of the deep-water fleet. The auxiliaries were equally obsolete. The heart of the Brazilian navy was as yet on the building ways. Brazil had nine destroyers and six minelayers (later converted to corvettes) under construction (see appendix 10), perfect ships for the pending conflict.

Once again at the eleventh hour Brazil learned the dangers of purchasing warships from abroad. Following the World War I pattern, Great Britain appropriated Brazil's six *Juruena*-class destroyers for her own needs in late 1939.[38] The war also delayed completion of the *Marcílio Dias*–class destroyers and the *Carioca*-class minelayers, which were being built in Brazil and depended upon foreign assistance.

As for natural resources, in May 1938 Brazil possessed enough petroleum reserves to fight no more than an eight-day war.[39] She was, however, a possible source for the Allies of important raw materials, particularly rubber and quinine.

When Brazil declared war, her fleet was reorganized into two forces: the Northeast Naval Force, *Força Naval do Nordeste*, Rear Admiral Alfredo Soares Dutra commanding, and the Southern Naval Group, Commander Ernest de Araujo commanding. Both were administratively subordinate to

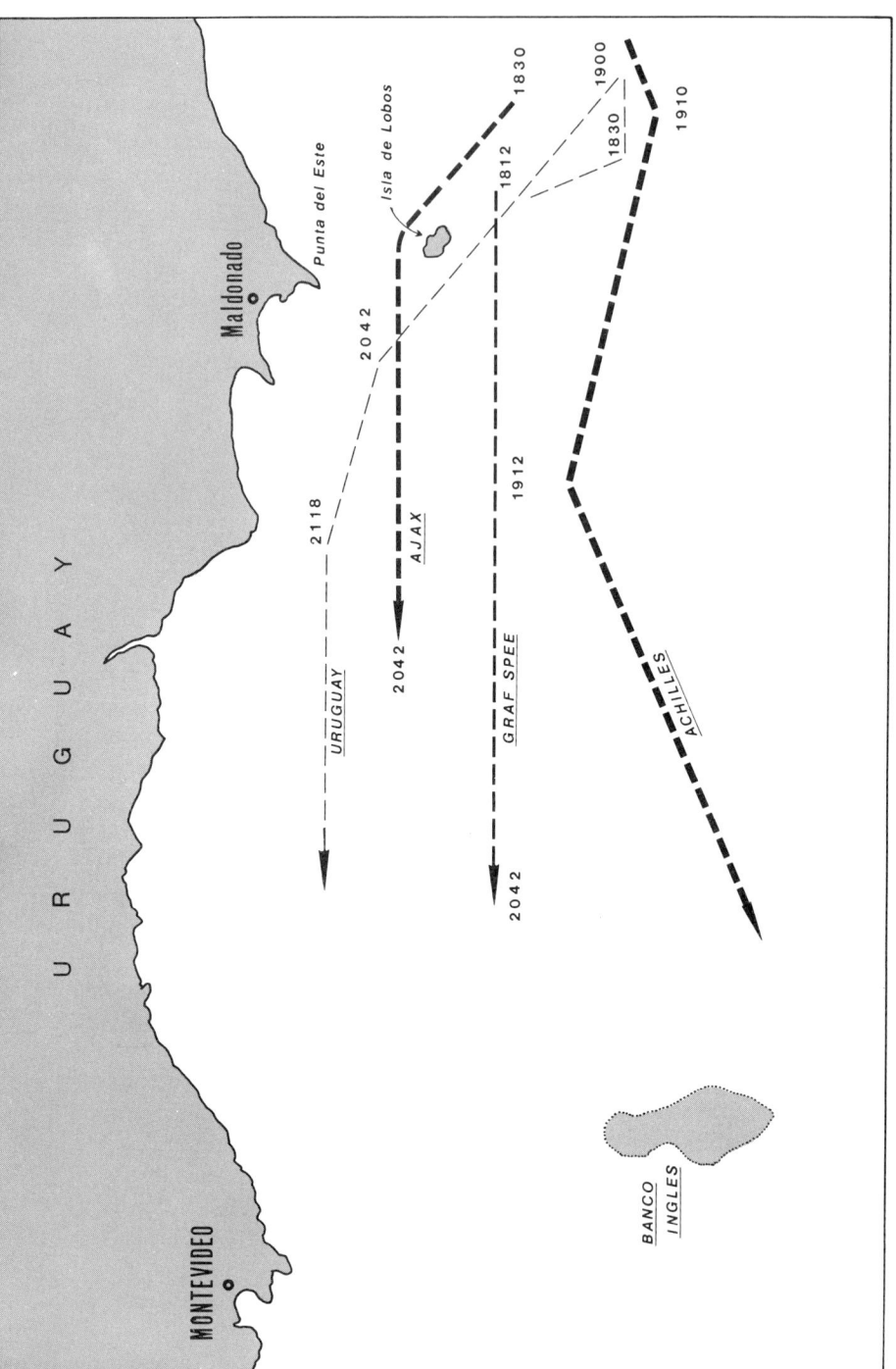

The *Uruguay* Intercepts the *Admiral Graf Spee* on the Río de la Plata, 13 December 1939

the naval chief of staff. Operationally, the Northeast Naval Force belonged to Admiral Ingram's command, the Southern Naval Group to the chief of staff's.

The navy's task would not be an easy one. It was called on to perform ASW, which required the most technologically advanced equipment available. The Allies could not spare from the North Atlantic the amount of assistance needed. The poor sound conditions that prevailed off the Orinoco and Amazon rivers further complicated the task. The large amount of fresh water flowing into the ocean created temperature layers that reflected sound and made submarine detection difficult.[40]

On 12 September 1942 Admiral Ingram assumed operational command of a new unit, the Northwestern Naval Force. Two old light cruisers and four (later six) modern minelayers of the *Carioca* class, which doubled as antisubmarine escorts, comprised the Brazilian component. On the fifteenth Ingram's title was changed from commander, Task Force 23, to commander, South Atlantic Force, to increase his control over air as well as sea forces.[41] Despite these increased efforts the U-boats kept up their onslaught. Two more merchant ships were sunk in the area on 27 September.

As the war progressed the combined Brazilian-U.S. force grew. Additional North American destroyers and destroyer escorts were assigned to the South Atlantic, and patrol vessels were turned over to Brazil on lend-lease. By the end of 1943 sixteen submarine chasers (eight 173-foot PCs and eight 110-foot SCs) had been turned over to Brazil (see appendix 11). The Brazilians also wanted to obtain two battleships, two carriers, four cruisers, fifteen destroyers, nine submarines, and numerous auxiliaries, but the United States could not spare more ships.[42]

As elsewhere, a convoy system was created to counter the U-boat threat. Initially, it operated between Trinidad and Bahia. Brazilian warships escorted merchant ships between Bahia and Recife, and U.S. warships took them from Recife to Trinidad. The first southbound convoy (TB-1) sailed on 15 December 1942, the first northbound (BT-1) on 6 January. On 3 July the convoy system was extended to Rio de Janeiro (TJ-1), increasing the range of protection for Brazilian warships. South Atlantic convoys sailed every ten days until December 1944, then every five days beginning with JT-54 and TJ-54. The convoys' normal speed was eight knots. Strong westward currents across the north coast of Brazil usually affected speed by two knots.

The U.S. area of responsibility between Trinidad and Recife was the more dangerous, being closer to U-boat bases in Europe. The *U-124* attacked the first southbound convoy, TB-1, on 9 January 1943, sinking five ships. On 9 March the *U-510* attacked BT-6; eight ships were lost. The *U-154* attacked BT-14 on 27 May 1943 and destroyed five ships. The

Brazilian Theater of Operations, World War II

U-185 attacked BT-18 on 7 July; five ships were lost. When TJ-1 was attacked on 8 July by *U-510* three ships were sunk. None of these incidents occurred while Brazilian warships were serving as escorts.[43]

Brazil's navy also had its trial by fire. The merchant ship *Brasilóide*, en route to join BT-6, was sunk on 18 February 1943 by the *U-518* off Bahia. This U-boat then sank the American Liberty Ship *Fitz-John Porter*, being escorted by the *Carioca*, *Caravelas*, and *Rio Branco*, part of BT-6. On 31 July 1943 the *U-185* torpedoed and sank the merchant ship *Bagé* between Recife and Bahia, shortly after she had been expelled from convoy BJ-2 for making excessive smoke. At 2355 on 19 July 1944 the *U-861* torpedoed the naval auxiliary *Vital de Oliveira*, under the escort of the *Javari*. The auxiliary sank on the twentieth. The next day the Brazilian corvette *Camaquã* capsized in heavy seas off Recife after her group had been relieved by U.S. warships escorting a JT convoy.[44]

Brazil's geographical position, lying between neutral Argentina and Spain, forced the navy to deal with the problem of neutral merchant ships, captained by Axis sympathizers, radioing information concerning convoys and stragglers to the enemy. The Brazilian navy believed this practice to be common among Spanish captains. One particularly annoying incident occurred in early July 1943 when the Argentine ship *Río de Carapaña* continued to shadow a convoy being escorted by the Brazilian cruiser *Rio Grande do Sul*. Finally the cruiser fired on the merchant ship, forcing it to turn away. As a result, the Brazilian chief of naval staff issued the following order on 8 July:

> So far, when moving convoys through areas in which neutral or Spanish ships can be found, the procedure of the Naval Staff has been to keep those ships in harbor until their scheduled courses cannot coincide with that of the convoys.
>
> In case an Argentine or Spanish ship is in sight of the formation, even innocently, the procedure must be to keep her away from the convoy so that, when she returns to her original course, the ship cannot follow it.
>
> On applying this rule it can be understood, from the dispatch sent by the Senior Officer of Escort, that the *Rio Grande do Sul* ordered the suspect ship to sail eastward for a number of hours, enough to keep her away from the convoy.
>
> If there is evidence that the neutral ship is supporting the enemy, the procedure to be adopted by our ships must be to order the neutral to change her course completely, so as to keep distance from the convoy.
>
> This order will be implemented in two ways: (1st) by putting a prize crew on board, so as to force the ship to sail under supervision from our personnel; (2nd) by putting a prize crew on board, so as to force her to enter a convenient harbor.[45]

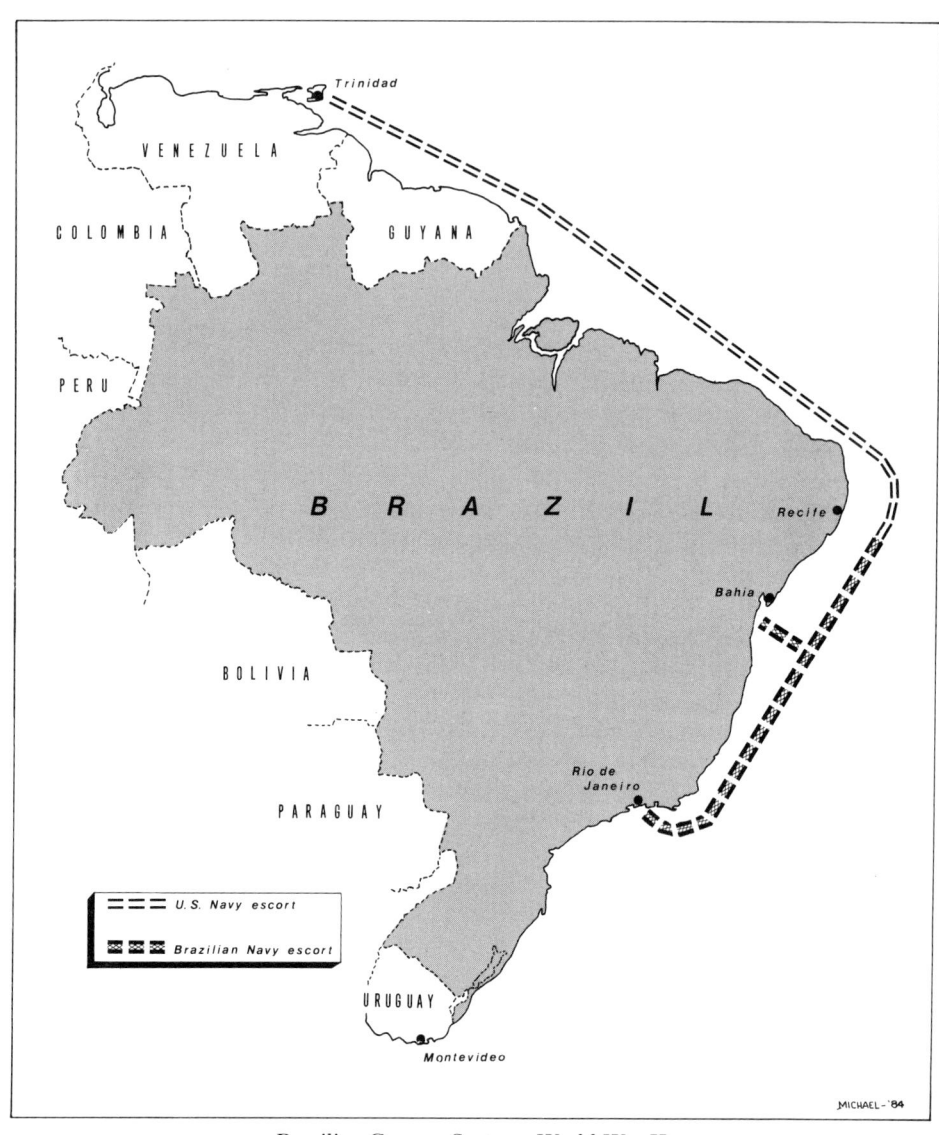
Brazilian Convoy System, World War II

After the incident with the Argentine merchant ship, the Brazilian minister of the navy wrote to President Vargas on 14 July summarizing the suspected activities of Argentine and Spanish merchant ships:

> The suspect attitude of Argentine merchant ships has been observed for a long time. Before the declaration of war against the Axis powers, ships of that nationality sought to create confusion, by sending distress signals near our coast, using their own signal calls or those of our ships. As a consequence, rescue aid was mobilized, information was sought from ships at sea, and a certain confusion was established, exposing the authorities to ridicule, which was probably the aim of those transmissions.
>
> It is known that recently an Argentine ship, chasing the tail of a convoy escorted by Brazilian warships, under the excuse of asking the Olinda radio station about any messages for her, was caught radioing her coordinates at sea.
>
> On the 3rd of this month an aircraft of the Brazilian Air Force spotted near Campeche (Santa Catarina) an Argentine ship, *Glorioso*, that had left Paranagua with a lighter alongside; then the ship sailed to Ganchos (Santa Catarina), where she laid anchor without the lighter she should have had. Her Captain did not agree to a search on board, and left harbor shortly after.
>
> A few days ago, the Argentine ship *Río de Carapaña* followed a convoy under our responsibility for twenty-four hours; sent away by the Convoy Commodore, who prescribed her a different course for three hours, she was again seen in the proximities of the convoy, on the following morning.
>
> So as to get rid of the annoying and indiscreet presence of such ship, the Captain of the *Rio Grande do Sul* had to lead her away, breaking contact at last.
>
> The deception used by such ships to give away the position of the convoy they follow and watch is to send radio messages, often giving their fuel consumption in 24 hours, their available engine power, etc., everything followed by their position at the moment.
>
> It is very difficult to admit the good faith of the Captains of such ships, but, even if that is so, their approaching our convoys leads to espionage from other members of the crew, such as radiomen, whose signals cannot be completely controlled, as has been verified, especially on ships of Spanish nationality.
>
> The frequency of attacks to ships along our coast, lately, and even attacks to convoys, leads us to face the issue with the necessary prudence and energy.[46]

Incidents involving neutral merchant ships continued. On 5 January 1945 Captain Edmundo Jordão Amorim do Vale, commanding the *Rio Grande do Sul*, radioed Admiral Soares Dutra that Argentine ships had crossed Brazilian formations, illuminating the ships and exchanging messages. The skipper of the destroyer *Marcílio Dias*, Commander Olavo de Araujo, complained that the Argentine tanker *Juncal* sent suspect signals. Captain Euclides de Souza Braga, in the cruiser *Bahia*, had to intimidate a neutral that had crossed through convoy JT-64.[47]

As the war progressed the Brazilian navy developed antisubmarine training facilities. In August 1943 it transferred the Brazilian submarine *Tupi* from Rio de Janeiro to Recife to act as a practice target. The navy established the submarine sanctuary "Zebra" off Recife and on 23 October 1943 created the Brazilian school for ASW tactics. The first regular class started on 28 April 1944 with Commander Ernesto Mello Baptista, a graduate of the U.S. Navy's Key West sound school, in command. Prior to the establishment of the school, North American officers had taught ASW courses at Recife. On 26 May a second submarine sanctuary, "Yoke," was established off Rio de Janeiro.

Brazilians remember with justifiable pride that their troops fought in southern Europe. On 2 July 1944 the first contingent of the Brazilian Expeditionary Force sailed from Rio de Janeiro in the transport USS *General W. H. Mann*, escorted by Brazilian destroyers and U.S. Fourth Fleet ships. On 22 September the largest contingent of Brazilian troops during the war embarked in two transports at Rio de Janeiro.

On 6 June 1945 Brazil declared war on Japan. Brazilian and other Allied warships were stationed in the Atlantic as potential rescue craft for U.S. Army transport planes carrying personnel from the European to the Pacific theaters. The Brazilian light cruiser *Bahia* operated on station 13, located on the equator at 30' West longitude. On 4 July the *Bahia* was conducting antiaircraft exercises, firing her 20-mm guns against a kite streamed abaft. A gunner shot the kite down and, in the course of firing, unintentionally hit a rack of depth charges stowed on the stern, which exploded. The *Bahia*'s guns had not been fitted with protective guide rails that would have prevented their barrels from firing at dangerous angles. In a matter of minutes the ship lost all power and 367 men took to the boats. Less than half of the crew survived; four U.S. Navy radiomen were also lost. The disaster was not discovered until 8 July, when the Brazilian cruiser *Rio Grande do Sul* arrived on the scene to relieve the *Bahia*. One lifeboat reached the Brazilian coast.

During World War II the Brazilian navy escorted 3,164 merchant ships totaling over sixteen million gross tons. Only three ships were lost on convoy—the *Fitz-John Porter*, *Pelotaslóide*, and *Vital del Oliveira*. This amounted to 14,141 gross registered tons.[48]

What Brazil did for the Allied war effort was not the difference between winning and losing, but it shortened the war and saved lives. And it was timely: in the bleak summer of 1942, with U-boats ravaging the seas, Brazil's entry into the war heartened the Allies.

As we have seen, her most important contribution was territory for air bases. Aircraft flying from them sank eleven Axis submarines.[49] Her sacrifices, moreover, were substantial. The navy lost the old cruiser *Bahia*, the corvette *Camaquã*, and the auxiliary *Vital de Oliveira*. Four hundred and ninety-two naval men died, including the commanding officers of the corvette and cruiser. Thirty-two Brazilian merchant ships sank during the war; 470 crew members and 502 passengers went down with their ships.[50] For Brazil, World War II was fought primarily at sea.

The importance of Brazil's effort must be evaluated within the context of her national development. During the war she was making the transition from a rural agrarian society to the early stages of industrialization. In a country without a significant industrial base, dependent upon imports for military equipment, nothing short of strenuous measures could meet a commitment to the Allied cause. Although U.S. aid was indispensable, it only temporarily answered Brazil's problem of defending herself in time of war.

The Southern Cone

During the early days of World War II the issue of fortifying the Straits of Magellan influenced diplomatic and military relations between Argentina, Chile, and the United States. Argentina and Chile's border dispute in the area to the south, a volatile international problem, touched on the question of the straits. They lay entirely within Chilean territory, but by the terms of the Argentine-Chilean Treaty of 1881 were to remain neutral and open to free navigation. No defenses were permitted. In 1941 the United States, recognizing the vulnerability of the Panamá Canal to possible Japanese attack, "was ready to approve fortification of the Straits [by Chile] for the duration of the war."[51] Chile favored the undertaking; however, Argentine agreement could not be obtained, and the matter was dropped.[52]

At the outbreak of war Argentina continued her diplomatic path of neutrality, which meant selling to both the Allies and the Axis. Buenos Aires pressured Uruguay not to grant base facilities to the United States, and on 13 May 1941 Argentina barred submarines of belligerent nations from her ports and waters.

The economies of Argentina and Chile were initially stunned by the war. Both nations exported meats and grains and imported finished goods. Argentina in particular had depended on foreign merchant fleets to carry the goods. These fleets were now in perpetual danger: German U-boats torpedoed British and Dutch merchant ships on the high seas, and the British navy hunted down and blockaded German and Italian merchantmen. Moreover, Great Britain declared a blockade of Axis-controlled Europe, while Germany blockaded Great Britain and, later, parts of the coast of the United States.[53] Thus in the early part of the war Argentine and

Chilean goods were difficult to get to market. Exports to Great Britain flourished and there was uninterrupted traffic with neutral Spain. The problem eased in 1942 when Argentina purchased sixteen Italian merchant ships that had been blockaded in her ports.[54] After the sinking of the tanker *Victoria* and steamer *Río Tercero* off the northeast coast of the United States during the first half of 1942, Argentina would not permit her state-owned merchant ships to enter blockaded areas.[55] In July 1942 the ships were told to use the port of New Orleans because of an announced German blockade of New York and the U-boats' successes.[56] In September 1943, with Allied successes against Axis submarines growing, Argentina ordered her merchant fleet to use the port of New York once again.

In January 1942 a flight of three Argentine navy Consolidated P2Y-3As flew to the Malvinas and, on the twenty-second, landed off the Salvajes islands in the northwest part of the archipelago, apparently undetected by the British. This flight demonstrated the feasibility of such an operation; it was kept a secret.

Also in 1942 the transport *1 de Mayo* went to the Antarctic on an exploratory expedition, the first Argentine naval visit to that area in almost two decades. The *1 de Mayo* sailed from Buenos Aires on 19 January. On her way south she visited Decepción, Melchior, and Inverno, three islands in the South Shetland group. At each landfall an Argentine flag was raised, a ceremony held, and a bronze plaque deposited, claiming the lands south of 60° South latitude, between longitudes 25°00' and 68°34' West, for Argentina. The *1 de Mayo* returned to Buenos Aires in late February. Two years later she revisited the Antarctic, stopping at Decepción. There the landing party found that the bronze plaque had been replaced by a note from an auxiliary cruiser, HMS *Carnavon Castle*, claiming the territory for the British crown. The *1 de Mayo* removed the note and replaced it with another bronze plaque.[57]

Argentina and Chile were the only major Latin American nations that still maintained diplomatic relations with the Tripartite Powers (Germany, Italy, and Japan) in late 1942. As a result they became the last significant fascist refuge in the New World. The Argentine merchant marine had a number of Axis sympathizers who from time to time attempted to aid U-boats and confound the Allies. Diplomatic relations between Argentina and the United States continued to deteriorate. On 4 June 1943 a coup brought to power a government that continued to advocate neutrality but teemed with blatant admirers of the Axis. Out of political necessity Argentina broke off diplomatic relations with the Axis on 26 January 1944, and on 27 March 1945 she finally declared war on Germany and Japan.

The Argentine navy was informed that U-boats hoping to reach Japan might try to use the Drake Passage to cross from the Atlantic to the Pacific. Argentine naval aircraft and *Buenos Aires*–class destroyers were ordered to patrol the area to the east of the Cape Horn meridian. Warships stationed at Ushuaia intensified their patrols of the Lemaire Strait and Isla de los Estados areas to prevent U-boats from taking haven in the natural harbors there.

At the close of the war two German U-boats, the *U-530* and the *U-977*, surrendered to Argentina. Captain Heinz Schäfer, commanding officer of the *U-977*, explained his decision:

> The [Argentine] Flotilla Commander went on to ask why exactly we should pick on the Argentine for our surrender. That question wasn't hard to answer. The rules of war provide that all war material belonging to a defeated power shall become the property of the victors, and so the Soviet Union must now be in possession of all our improvements in technique. I had therefore taken care to carry out Admiral Dönitz's order to surrender—as soon as I had verified it—in such a way as to ensure that it should be advantageous to a nation which had already displayed such chivalry towards the German Navy in the matter of the pocket battleship *Graf Spee*. I had also to consider the welfare of my crew. There was no other enemy country from which they could expect such good treatment. There had never been any hatred between Germany and Argentina, only a condition of honourable belligerency, and that for a relatively short time only.[58]

The United States paid back Argentina's reluctance to enter the war in kind by demanding the two U-boats and their crews, even though they were technically the Latin American country's spoils. U.S. intelligence wanted to question the prisoners and inspect the U-boats to see if they had been used to carry Adolf Hitler and other high-ranking Nazis, as well as treasure, to Argentina.[59] The demand, which was met, aggravated already badly strained relations between Argentina and the United States.

As war approached, relations between Chile and the United States began to improve. A few Chilean naval aviators had been trained in the United States during the late 1930s, and in the early 1940s Chile, perceiving a possible threat from Japan, wanted to modernize her fleet. At the very least the United States wanted a friendly neutral nation bordering the Straits of Magellan. The two countries began to discuss military matters of mutual concern in late 1940. It was known publicly that the Chilean navy was in the market for cruisers, for Argentina owned three modern units and Chile had none.[60] Given the lengthy coast the Chilean navy patrolled, a cruiser would have been a very practical ship as well. During conferences held between representatives of the Chilean and U.S. navies in the fall of 1940, Chile outlined her needs: two cruisers, two destroyer leaders, three submarines, two minesweepers, one minelayer, ten torpedo boats, and one tanker. The United States was not in a position to extend much aid, either through new construction or transfers, and she herself turned to Chile to acquire warships following the Pearl Harbor attack. Commander L. R. McDowell, USN, from the Office of the Chief of Naval Operations, wrote to the chief of the British Naval Staff in Washington on 16 January 1942 regarding the U.S. request: "The question of our taking over these ships, 'the Chilean Battleship and Destroyers,' has been discussed unofficially with the Chilean Naval Attaché and with the Vice Admiral in charge of the Chilean Naval Commission now in Washington. The results were not favorable."[61]

México at War

In 1910 a great revolution erupted in México that would eventually alter all her national institutions. At its outbreak relations with the United States deteriorated and they remained bad, particularly in the mid and late 1930s. In 1914 U.S. troops, to extract a salute to their flag, forcefully landed at Veracruz, México, and in 1916 a U.S. Army expeditionary force was sent across the border to search for Francisco "Pancho" Villa, who had previously raided a town in New Mexico. On more than one occasion during this era U.S. warships intervened in México to protect national interests. On 18 March 1938 President Lázaro Cárdenas nationalized Mexico's petroleum industry, thereby sparking a new crisis with Great Britain and the United States. Relations between México and Great Britain were so bad that in May 1938 both countries recalled their ambassadors.

By expropriating the petroleum industry, México alienated a number of the major shipping nations and found it necessary to create her own tanker fleet to carry petroleum to world markets. México began building the fleet with the assets of San Cristóbal: one tanker, five tugs, one dredge, twenty lighters, and twenty launches.[62] On 1 January 1939 the Mexican merchant marine academy, Fernando Siliceo, reopened its doors.[63] On 22 March México ordered three tankers from Ansaldo Shipbuilders in Genoa, Italy. The demand for tanker tonnage at the start of the war in Europe further reduced the number of foreign tankers available to México. On 4 September she declared her neutrality. The same day the Italian government took title to the three tankers under construction at Genoa. To offset this loss, the Mexican government purchased the Norwegian tankers *Binta* and *Bisca*.[64] And on 22 April 1940 it bought the German tanker *Tine Asmussen*, renaming her the *Juan Casiano*.[65]

México had not remained aloof from events in Europe. When the Republicans in Spain were waging civil war against General Francisco Franco's Nationalists, she was one of the most ardent supporters of the former. Mexicans contributed to the purchase of war materials for the Republicans in Europe and the Americas, probably with Spanish money, and helped transport them to Spain. Items purchased in Europe were loaded in merchant ships carrying papers for disembarkation in Veracruz. At least seven of these ships attempted to run the Nationalist blockade and enter Spanish ports held by the Republicans. Six of them succeeded. In late 1937 the Nationalists captured one ship, the *Sylvia*, whose cargo included sixteen field pieces, mortars, ammunition, forty thousand Lebel rifles, and fifteen hundred machine guns. She had been sailing from Gdynia for Veracruz.

Some of the activities of the ships, most of which flew the Spanish flag and used México as a base of operations, have come to light. The *Mar Cantabrico*, which had sailed from Veracruz, was captured by the Nationalist cruiser *Canarias* on 8 March 1936 while trying to run the blockade. The *Mar Cantabrico* was carrying seven aircraft, fifty field pieces, five hundred machine guns, and four million cartridges.[66] In September of that year the *Magallanes* hauled seventeen thousand rifles purchased from México to Spain. On 12 January 1937 the *Sil* reached Santander, Spain, from Veracruz with a cargo of two thousand rifles, twenty-four field pieces, fifteen thousand shells, one hundred machine guns, and eight million cartridges. The *Yolande*, flying the French flag, was seized by the Nationalist destroyer *Velasco* on 27 December 1937 and taken into Palma de Mallorca, Spain. She was released when the French destroyer *Vanquelin* intervened. In February 1938 the *Yolande* carried ammunition from Marseille to Barcelona, where she was sunk by Nationalist aircraft the next year. The cargo transported to Spain in the Spanish ship *Motomar* included at least fifteen aircraft—four Orions, one Vultee, one Spartan, two Consolidateds, six twin-engine Curtiss-Cyclones, and one bimotor Electra. The Spanish *Ibai* carried seventeen aircraft and twenty-three spare engines; on one occasion she served as a raider for the Spanish Republican navy and made at least one trip to Buenos Aires.[67]

México also supported the activities of the Republican ambassador from Spain. He chartered merchant ships to collect war materials in México and ship them to Spain. One such ship, the Japanese *Florida Maru*, carried arms purchased in Bolivia to Manzanillo on Mexico's Pacific coast. These were then transported by rail across México to Veracruz. It is unclear whether the shipment ultimately reached Spain. The ambassador also chartered the British flag vessels *Cydonia* and *Essex David* to carry food to Republican Spain.

Sources concerning the possible involvement of the Mexican navy in the Spanish civil war are contradictory. Some credit the Mexican gunboat *Durango* with two or three trips in July 1936 from Valencia, Spain, where she was fitting out, to Marseille, France, and back. There may also have been plans to officer and possibly crew the merchantman *Manuel Arñus* with Mexican naval personnel. This ill-fated merchant ship, declared stateless on 25 October 1936, had to remain in Habana for some time. Finally, on 27 May 1938, she arrived in Veracruz, where she was supposed to take on board twenty-two U.S.-built aircraft. She never sailed on this mission.

México provided the largest number of Latin American volunteers to fight for Republican Spain. At least 464 Mexicans fought in the International Brigade and some 200 others served with additional units.[68] México also became one of the most important havens for Spanish refugees, the first of whom arrived on 20 April 1939. On 27 July alone, twenty-one hundred refugees arrived at Veracruz in the French steamer *Mexique*. Spanish refugees, who had initially received sanctuary in other countries, continued to flock to México throughout World War II.

Although relations with Great Britain and the United States remained uncertain, Mexico's position vis-à-vis developments in Europe was quite clear. On 12 May 1940 the country sent a note to Germany protesting the invasions of France and the Netherlands. Mexican president Cárdenas denounced the Italian declaration of war against France on 11 June, one day after the event. And, on the following day, the head of the German legation was asked to leave México. Recently elected president Manuel Avila Camacho condemned German aggression in Greece and Yugoslavia on 7 April 1941.[69]

In early June 1940 México and the United States held a series of meetings that addressed the problems of hemispheric defense. President Cárdenas assured the North Americans of Mexico's readiness to collaborate with them in the development of plans for the common defense. México needed equipment and munitions, the United States air and naval bases. Cárdenas intimated that his country was prepared to develop the latter "at places to be chosen strategically, not only from the purely national point of view but from the broader point of view of hemisphere defense."[70] Thereafter the government in México had to move cautiously. Avila Camacho was elected president, and followers of the losing candidate threatened revolt. Any rapprochement with the United States would probably be denounced by the opposition as a sellout to the gringos. Complicating matters was a controversy over the expropriation of the petroleum industry, an issue that had plagued relations between the two countries for some time.

The day following the attack on Pearl Harbor México broke off relations with Japan, freezing her assets, and on 11 December severed all relations with Germany and Italy. A month later the Latin American country declared that ships and aircraft of American republics at war would not be treated as belligerents. This meant that their stays in México would be immune to the provisions of international treaties limiting the activities of belligerents.[71]

When the war broke out numerous German and Italian merchant ships took refuge in Mexican ports. On 15 November 1940 the German merchantmen *Orinoco, Idarwall, Rhein,* and *Phrigia* tried to depart, but Mexico, now more embroiled in the issues, would not let them go. The *Phrigia* was scuttled by her crew, the others returned to port. On 8 April 1941 México commandeered the remaining interned merchantmen for the good of the state, adding the Italian tankers to the Mexican-owned fleet of seven tankers (42,980 gross tons total, 425,000 barrels capacity) and more than doubling its capacity (see appendix 12).[72] Also commandeered were three German merchant ships.[73] Petróleos Mexicanos took control of the tankers; the cargo and passenger ships became the responsibility of Mexicana de Navegación S. de R. L. y C. V. Three days later the Mexican tanker fleet acquired the yacht *Vita*, anchored at Acapulco. Spanish Republicans had used her to transport valuables to Mexico.

During these trying times cooperation between México and the United States improved. On 18 July the latter published a black list of German and Italian commercial interests in México that would not be permitted to do business with the United States. On 19 November the two nations signed agreements relating to compensation, petroleum, finance, and commerce. As the American Cordell Hull noted, this was "a large factor in having our neighbor to the south in full accord with us at the moment of Pearl Harbor."[74]

Commanded by Mexican naval officers and manned by Mexican merchant seamen, Mexico's newly created tanker fleet proved to be easy prey during the 1942 U-boat blitz off the coast of North America. On 9 April and again on 16 April 1942 the tanker *Faja de Oro* reported that a submarine had attempted to attack her. On 11 April the *U-552* torpedoed and sank the U.S. flag tanker *Tamaulipas*, owned by a subsidiary of Petróleos Mexicanos, off Cape Hatteras. Five minutes before midnight on 13 May the tanker *Potrero del Llano* was torpedoed by *U-564* off the Fowey Rock Lighthouse in the Florida Keys, resulting in fourteen lives lost. The USS *PC-536* rescued surviving crew members. Seven days later the *U-106* sank the tanker *Faja de Oro*, also late at night and in the Florida Keys; ten lives were lost. The U.S. Coast Guard cutter *Nemesis* picked up survivors.

The sinkings had a tremendous impact on Mexican public opinion. On 1 June 1942 President Avila Camacho signed a decree declaring war against Germany, Italy, and Japan and stating that México could be considered as having been a belligerent since the twenty-second of May. On 26 June at 2315 the tanker *Tuxpan* was sunk by torpedo and gunfire from the *U-129* near the Tecolutla Bar; four men died. The next day the same U-boat sank the tanker *Las Choapas* between Tecolutla and Tuxpan, killing three men, and the *U-171* torpedoed the steamer *Oaxaca* near Matagorda, Texas, killing six.[75] As a result of the U-boat successes México authorized the use of Cozumel Airfield by U.S. aircraft for antisubmarine operations—an extraordinary concession, considering the animosity that had divided the two nations a few years earlier. At this time the United States was also establishing a convoy system on the western side of the Atlantic, thus ending the extreme vulnerability of the Mexican merchant marine to U-boats. The Mexican navy had no antisubmarine capability, so up to this point merchant ships had had to trust to their own skills and luck.

The merchant marine acquired additional ships as U-boat successes began to abate. Mexico's government seized the French tanker *Merope*, interned in Tampico, and renamed her the *Potrero del Llano II* on 21 August 1942. At 2300 on 4 September the tanker *Amatlán* became the last Mexican merchant ship to fall victim to a U-boat. The *U-171* torpedoed and sank her off Tordo Bar, resulting in five deaths.[76]

From mid-1942 to early 1943 México permitted the United States to use Cozumel Airfield and two other airfields in the Yucatan, plus a bomber base at Tehuantepec, for operational flights. With the decline of U-boat activity in the waters off the Americas, U.S. use of the airfields wound down at the request of México.[77] On 2 October 1942 México and Cuba signed a covenant for the joint surveillance of the Gulf of México.

Mexico's maritime contributions and sacrifices were not confined to the merchant marine. On 24 December 1942 the Mexican naval aviation school was established, and on 1 September 1943 the first naval air squadron was formed. On 29 March 1944 the patrol craft *G-28* was lost in a hurricane at Veracruz. The tanker *Juan Casiano* broke in two off the Georgia coast when a storm hit on 19 October 1944; twenty-one lives were lost.[78]

When measured against the war losses other nations suffered, Mexico's were small. She lost six tankers, one merchant ship, and sixty-three naval and merchant marine personnel.[79] By comparison, the United States lost over six hundred merchant ships and thousands of merchant sailors. Yet the Mexican government chose to give close support to the United States and the Allies when a neutral stance, particularly in 1942, would have been much less risky.

The Caribbean

Cuba, closely tied to the United States economically and politically, declared war on the Axis powers on 11 December 1941. Her navy had six old gunboats and no antisubmarine capability, but she wanted to increase her naval strength, a wish matched by the United States' interest in obtaining operating bases in the Caribbean.[80]

On 7 September 1942 the two countries signed a military and naval agreement. The United States established an American-manned Cuban flotilla made up of twelve small coast guard craft stationed at Habana.[81] Its duties were convoying, patrolling, investigating contacts, and training Cuban personnel. Initially, because of the small size of the craft, this training had to be limited to officers. On 1 February 1943 Cuba and the United

States signed an agreement further defining their military cooperation and establishing a North American naval mission to Cuba. Under this agreement the U.S. Navy directed the operations of Cuban warships, providing logistics ships and establishing depots to support them. In return the Cuban navy was to receive warships under lend-lease. Later in February the first U.S. Coast Guard–designed eighty-three-foot patrol craft arrived and joined the Cuban flotilla, thus making it possible to extend training to enlisted personnel.[82] Cubans gradually replaced the North American crews.[83]

The United States turned over ten eighty-three-foot patrol craft to the Cuban navy on 22 March 1943 at Habana. She delivered two more five days later. On 18 April four fifty-six-foot craft arrived. These developments allowed the United States to disband the Cuban flotilla in June.

The Cuban navy had its modest victories and defeats. On 15 May 1943 the subchaser *SC-13*, Ensign Mario Ramirez Delgado commanding, joined U.S. aircraft flying from Cuban airfields to 23°21′ North latitude, 80°17′ West longitude, where they put an end to the *U-176*, which had sunk a Cuban freighter two days earlier. On 4 December the *U-129* torpedoed the Cuban auxiliary *Libertad* off the U.S. coast. By mid-1943 the war against the U-boat had moved far out into the North Atlantic, and the newly acquired Cuban naval craft, though they had no further contact with the enemy, escorted local convoys. By May 1944 U.S. naval airfields had been opened in San Julian, La Fe, Santa Fe, Cayo Frances, and Camaguey; the North Americans had numerous other facilities throughout the island as well. In 1945 the United States, hoping to make the Cuban navy more self-sufficient, intensified its training and established additional logistic facilities, among them an engine overhaul school. The war, however, ended before most of these new programs could be put into effect.

Five Cuban merchant ships were sunk during the war; seventy-nine men were killed or missing. Ship losses totaled 10,296 gross tons and represented seventeen percent of the national merchant marine. In all, the Cuban navy escorted 528 ships with 2,768,680 gross registered tons, of which less than one percent were lost. The escorts rescued 221 people.[84]

The Colombian navy joined the Allied war effort in late 1943 and had its trial by fire. It lost two schooners transporting cargo between Cartagena and the Colombian islands to U-boats. The *U-505* sank the sail ship *Roamar* on 22 July 1942, and the *U-516* destroyed the sail ship *Ruby* on 17 November 1943. On 23 July 1943 the Colombian warship *Carabobo* rescued the seven-man crew of a North American B-17 bomber that had ditched off Guajira. The Colombian destroyer *Caldas*, while escorting the naval tanker *Cabimas* from Colon to Cartagena, observed the surfaced *U-154* on 29 March 1944 and fired one shell from gun no. 2 at one thousand meters, which fell short. The submarine dove and the *Caldas* then dropped six depth charges in a tight circle, the first of which produced a column of completely black water. The commanding officer concluded that the submarine had been sunk and was awarded the Cruz de Boyacá; in fact, the boat had slipped away. On 20 October 1944 the Colombian subchaser *Carabobo* succumbed to a storm off Cuba; her crew was rescued by the Colombian patrol craft *Ayacucho*.[85]

The Dominican Republic, among other Caribbean nations, declared war on the Axis powers in December 1941. Though her navy saw no action against enemy ships, her tiny merchant marine suffered losses. On 21 May 1942 the *U-156* torpedoed the merchantman *Presidente Trujillo*. On 13 June the *U-166* sank the schooner *Carmen*. And three days later the *U-126* put an end to the schooner *Nueva Altagracia*.

Venezuela, a critical source of oil throughout the war, strongly supported the Allies from the outset of the fighting. She participated in the action briefly in February 1942. On the sixteenth a German U-boat shelled the Standard Oil Refinery on Aruba, in the Dutch Antilles, and attacked merchant ships near the entrance to Lake Maracaibo. Among those sunk was the Venezuelan tanker *Monagas*, which lost eleven crew members. The gunboat *General Urbaneta*, on patrol in the area, aided in the rescue operations. Neither this warship nor any in the Venezuelan navy was equipped with ASW sensors or weapons at the time.[86]

CHAPTER ELEVEN

The Rise and Fall of U.S. Influence

WITH THE EMERGENCE of the United States as the preeminent power in the western hemisphere, Latin American navies subordinated their regional concerns to the consideration of their projected roles in a possible East-West conflict. They studied these new roles in a number of new North American schools and during exercises with the U.S. fleet. One result was a notable increase in professionalism in many Latin American navies.

U.S. naval dominance in Latin America began to diminish in the late 1960s, a trend that accelerated in the next decade as North American political influence in the area waned. Some in Latin America viewed their northern neighbor's outspokenness on human rights as sanctimonious meddling in their internal affairs, and when the United States placed restrictions on the use of military hardware traveling south, it was considered an offensive infringement upon Latin American sovereignty. The U.S. Congress ended grant aid. Interest on credit sales piled up year after year, and spares could only be acquired by cash purchase. On 5 March 1977 Brazil, the United States' most important Latin American ally, refused sixty million dollars in U.S. military aid because it was tied to the human rights issue. Six days later she denounced the Interamerican Treaty of Mutual Assistance on the grounds that Washington was meddling in matters that were the responsibility of Brazil. The United States also barred assistance in nuclear technology. For all these reasons, Brazil sent the U.S. naval mission packing. This came at a time when thirty-two hundred Brazilian military personnel were being trained in the United States.[1]

The United States was also losing influence among Latin American navies because her supply of surplus warships was almost exhausted, progressing from nearly new and obsolescent to well used and obsolete. U.S. rivals—Great Britain, Germany, France, and Italy—had recovered and could once again compete in the Latin American market by offering custom-made ships. And the more powerful Latin American nations were developing indigenous shipbuilding, although this still remained a fledgling industry. By the mid-1970s South American navies had reached the limit of the possibilities offered by inexpensive, used hardware from the north, and they recoiled, at the same time, from the heavy emphasis the United States wanted them to put on antisubmarine warfare. This, they felt, was turning them into single-mission navies.

In the 1980s many Latin American navies once again changed their emphasis from ASW, which had been promoted by the United States to aid in a potential East-West conflict, to the support of traditional national goals by fending off regional threats, whether internal or external.

The decline of U.S. military missions was drastic, as the situation in Paraguay suggests. In that country only three U.S. military personnel remained by 1985. By comparison, it had a combined Argentine-Brazilian representation of fifty-five.

The era ended with mutual disenchantment between the United States and Latin America. The former, having spent a half billion dollars on military assistance for regional armed forces, expected to see lasting results and did not. The latter, for their part, felt used on occasion, as in 1962 when the United States solved the Soviet Missile Crisis with the use of a blockade that included Latin American warships. To a number of Latin American countries, Cuba presented more of a threat as an exporter of subversion than as a missile base. Years later they had to fight Cuban-trained terrorists in their cities. The United States objected to their inhumane methods of antiterrorist warfare, but many in the Latin American services believed the United States had allowed the situation to develop through her neglect of the Cuban problem.

Reshaping Latin American Navies

The United States emerged from World War II with a surplus of obsolete and obsolescent yet relatively new warships along with an excess of modern amphibians and auxiliaries.[2] Latin American nations lacked a significant shipbuilding industry, and they had not been able to fill the vacuum by purchasing warships during the conflict. None of these countries had acquired a large warship since 1939. In Europe the war destroyed many shipyards that had traditionally supplied Latin American navies. Thus the United States—and to a lesser extent Great Britain—had an excessive supply of ships while Latin America had an increasing demand.

In 1944 the U.S. Congress passed the Surplus Property Act permitting friendly nations to purchase at a modest price warships scheduled for mothballing or scrapping at the end of the war. Surplus warships and auxiliaries of all ages were put up for sale. Though some Latin American nations took advantage of the act, it did not make major combatants and newer units available.[3] Moreover, the Lend-Lease Act, the legal apparatus for ship transfers during World War II, had expired, and Congress had rejected a Truman administration proposal in 1946 for continued military cooperation with Latin America outside of the naval mission system. As a result, many Latin American navies purchased British and Canadian *Flower*- and *River*-class escorts to meet their immediate needs. One member of a Venezuelan buying commission stated that the reason his country purchased corvettes from Canada and not the United States was to avoid red tape.[4] But these sales left Latin American desires for cruisers, destroyers, and submarines unfulfilled.

The immediate post–World War II era was one of worldwide communist expansion. Eastern Europe and China fell under communist control and the Berlin Blockade heightened tensions. To buttress democracy against the onslaught of a rival ideology, the United States began to dispense military aid throughout the world. The U.S. Mutual Defense Assistance Act of 1949 provided military grants to NATO members and authorized sales of military equipment to countries in other regions, including Latin America. To be eligible, a Latin American nation had to have ratified the Inter-American Reciprocal Assistance Treaty of 1947, commonly known as the Rio Treaty, and had to pay the original cost of the item, in cash, prior to delivery.[5] While more than ninety percent of the aid provided under this act went to European and Asian countries, the United States, now the dominant foreign power in Latin America, used surplus ships as a tool to further mutual interests. The most significant transfers took place when two prewar cruisers each went to Argentina, Brazil, and Chile by bilateral agreements reached in January 1951.[6] The warships cost four million dollars apiece, which included ammunition, spare parts, and rehabilitation—a bargain if one wanted obsolescent cruisers. The United States used the cruisers and other warships to reshape the Latin American naval panorama. Thus Argentina's pre–World War II formula that she had to possess a fleet equal in strength to the combined fleets of Brazil and Chile changed in one stroke to $1A = 1B = 1C$.[7]

In October 1951 the U.S. Congress passed the Mutual Security Act providing grant assistance to Latin America. To be eligible a nation had to agree to participate in the defense of the western hemisphere and had to have a bilateral defense agreement with the United States. By 1956 every Latin American country with a U.S. naval mission except Venezuela had signed such an agreement. As we have seen, Argentina had no formal U.S. naval mission or agreement.[8]

The U.S. strategy for the defense of the free world assigned Latin American navies the mission of ASW by the late 1950s. In 1959 the U.S. chief of naval operations wrote to the Joint Chiefs of Staff, "Hemispheric defense requires an ASW contribution by Latin American Navies. This is a complicated type of naval warfare in which Latin America has little experience and in which they [sic] need U.S. guidance and the United States needs their help."[9] The political basis for military cooperation was the Rio Treaty, article 3 of which stated that an armed attack by any state against an American state would be considered an attack against all American states. The U.S. naval missions, which by now held extensive influence in almost all countries, disseminated the antisubmarine doctrine to Latin American navies. The Mutual Security Act of 1951 and subsequent bilateral agreements provided material support for the task. ASW tactics were taught through training supplied by the U.S. Navy and combined exercises.

Joint ASW exercises began a few years after World War II. In 1950 the Brazilian and U.S. navies trained together. An intelligence report stated, "The first submarine diving operations in three years were conducted by the Brazilian Navy on April 28, 1950, and since that date the O.S.S. *Tamoio*, together with DEs and PBY patrol aircraft, has been engaging in actual ASW at-sea training." The report also noted the establishment of a navy–air force ASW course and ASW tactical program.[10] In the summer of 1953 three destroyer escorts and one frigate, approximately fifty percent of the combat strength of the Peruvian navy, spent five weeks in intensive training with the U.S. Navy at San Diego, California. Perú, which had signed a mutual defense assistance agreement with the United States in February 1952, also established a new training center at Callao with a curriculum based on instructional materials from the United States. The courses included basic electronics, ASW, and gunnery.[11] During the late 1950s the United States and Chile held a series of ASW exercises known as Panamex. The first large multinational exercise involving Latin American navies took place in the beginning of 1959. Participating in the unnamed exercise were the United States, Argentina, Brazil, Uruguay, and Venezuela.

In 1959 the chiefs of U.S. naval missions in Latin America, accompanied by a senior naval officer from each host nation, gathered in Panamá for an annual conference. The Latin American officers recommended that their respective navies hold exercises with the U.S. Navy on a regular basis. Undoubtedly the serious quarrels that most Latin American nations had with their neighbors (see the map on page 10) prevented them from suggesting a multinational exercise.[12] The result of this conference was UNITAS, a term that has become shrouded in myth. A recent news release from the U.S. Atlantic Command said that it "is a Latin word meaning unity." Older releases claim that it is an acronym for United Interamerican Antisubmarine Warfare [Exercise]. Whatever its meaning, UNITAS refers to the annual circumnavigation of the South American continent by a U.S. task force composed of a few destroyers, a submarine or two, and some ASW aircraft. Along the way the task force participates in fleet exercises that have been dominated by ASW training, particularly in the 1960s and most of the 1970s. In port, activity has centered around social events, frequently featuring the U.S. task force's band.

UNITAS has been the object of both praise and criticism. Joint exercises have promoted good will between fleets that were previously rivals, notably those of Argentina and Brazil, but they have failed to bring together the navies of Argentina and Chile. Among its achievements, UNITAS has unified methods and doctrines used by navies, established English as the common operational language, and made NATO tactical manuals the rule books for exercises. Thus it has contributed to the ability of American navies to operate together.

Complicating the UNITAS mission was the fact that in the 1960s and 1970s Latin American navies did not possess the modern warships or technology to conduct modern ASW, the primary focus of UNITAS. Tactically, the success of such warfare is dependent on a superior number of advanced aircraft and warships plus sophisticated sensor networks to overwhelm the subsurface opponent. An Argentine officer recalled:

> I still remember, I was on board ARA *Entre Ríos* (D-7) that year [1965] and we participated in Unitas VI. The ship was built in 1939. I can still hear the USS *Van Voorhis* on the radio saying, "One Lima [sonar contact] 050/340 [bearing 050 at 34,000 yards]." My ships' crew would have been happy if we would have had a 2,000-yard contact. The difference in capabilities between U.S. ships and ours was as wide as the ocean.[13]

By the mid-1970s Latin American navies were still ill equipped against the modern submarine. The premier antisubmarine weapon available to the free world in 1974 was the ASROC system, and only two Latin American warships were armed with it, the Brazilian destroyers *Marcílio Dias* and *Mariz e Barros*.[14] And, while the U.S. Navy ascribed to Latin American navies a task requiring the most modern military hardware, North American politicians opposed the transfer of sophisticated systems. As Secretary of Defense Robert McNamara testified before Congress in 1965, "We have absolutely opposed the acquisition of what I call sophisticated weapons [by Latin America]. . . ."[15]

Additionally, some Latin American naval officers did not believe that the dominant mission of these navies should be ASW. Captain José María Cohen of the Argentine navy wrote:

> The Argentine Navy after WW II, mainly because of USN material and publications, was evolving to become an ASW force only. But this "model" never was very attractive to us, even if we had no chance but to play the game as it was. The first important departure from this model was made in 1959 with the acquisition of our first aircraft carrier (the *Independencia*) and our efforts (not very successful at the beginning) to get attack planes for it. I can't say how this fact was perceived by the USN or the US Government, but I think I'm not very far from the truth saying that they were not very happy, as it meant a clear departure from the role assigned in the "Interamerican" plans to our navy.[16]

In the last few years UNITAS has given Latin American navies their only chance to train against nuclear submarines. But the exercises, frequently conducted at the level of proficiency of the worst-trained or -equipped participant, have not been especially profitable. To the United States they have brought ambiguous results, providing intelligence on the equipment and training levels of Latin American navies while at the same time affording Latin American leftists opportunities to demonstrate against their giant northern neighbor. Some in the Argentine navy believe that the advantage UNITAS gives to U.S. intelligence worked against them during the 1982 Malvinas War.

UNITAS, in its stress on ASW training, neglected surface, air, and amphibious operations for years until the major Latin American navies expressed these concerns to the U.S. Navy. Only recently has such training been emphasized. UNITAS held its first amphibious exercise in 1981.

A great deal of attention has been lavished on the social and political roles of UNITAS. Press conferences, cocktail parties, and courtesy exchanges are numerous. The UNITAS band makes its appearances with the fanfare of a Broadway show. These events have allowed many Latin American governments to show North American support of their regimes.

In its attempt to reshape navies through warship transfers and exercises, the United States has offered educational opportunities to hundreds of Latin American officers at U.S. naval facilities. By 1983, 185 had graduated from the command course at the Naval War College in Newport, Rhode Island. Of these, ninety-five have reached flag rank, twenty have become commanders in chief of their respective navies, and one has been a head of state.[17]

Latin American Navies in the Cold War

The only Latin American country ever to contend with the United States for predominance in South America was Argentina. Juan Perón's national and Pan-American popularity was in part based on his pronouncements against the United States. Between 29 October and 22 December 1946 the Argentine battleship *Rivadavia* carried Senator Diego Luis Molinari on a good-will mission to México, Cuba, the Dominican Republic, Venezuela, Panamá, and Colombia.[18] But Argentina was hardly in an economic, military, or diplomatic position to challenge the United States for hemispheric leadership.

At the outbreak of the Korean War in 1950 the Truman administration sought Latin American military participation and closer military cooperation between the American republics to help the United States meet the threat of communist expansion. Recipients of aid provided under the Mutual Security Act of 1951 had reaffirmed their intention "to give their full cooperation to the efforts to provide the United Nations with armed forces as contemplated by the charter," but Latin America's contributions to the Korean War effort proved modest. Only Colombia sent military force; other nations made token contributions of food, medicines, and miscellaneous materials.[19]

On 18 September 1950 Colombia announced that she was offering her only frigate, the *Almirante Padilla*, to the United Nations for service in Korea. On 2 October the offer was accepted, and on 1 November the frigate sailed for Long Beach under the command of Lieutenant Commander Julio Cesar Reyes Canal, who had served a year in the old U.S. destroyer *Roper* as an exchange officer. After an extensive overhaul the *Almirante Padilla* sailed from San Diego, California, on 14 March 1951, for Hawaiian waters. Joint Colombian–United States exercises were held there to indoctrinate the Colombian crew in American methods and procedures. On 8 May the *Almirante Padilla* arrived in Sasebo, Japan, to join Task Force 95. On 20 May, newly assigned to South Korea's West Coast Support Group, she started operating in Korean waters. Between mid-May and mid-June the frigate, whose presence was particularly important due to the shortage of shallow-draft warships, operated off the west coast in various patrolling, escorting, and bombarding missions.[20] She then shifted her operational area to the east coast and was placed under the command of Korea's East Coast Support Group. Between mid-June and September 9 she operated off Wonsan and Songjin, being used extensively for bombardment and inshore patrols and, on a number of occasions, for landing special agents behind enemy lines. On 19 January 1952 the *Almirante Padilla* completed her tour of duty and sailed for Yokosuka, Japan, then to Cartagena, Colombia.[21] She arrived there on 21 March, having steamed forty-eight thousand nautical miles.

Colombia acquired a second frigate that was to rotate with the *Almirante Padilla* in the war zone. In February 1952 the nation agreed to buy the USS *Bisbee*, which was already in Korean waters. Lieutenant Commander Hernando Beron Victoria, together with 7 officers and 114 enlisted men, sailed to Korea, where they took over the newly acquired ship, renamed the *Capitán Tono*, on 22 February. The entire crew of the *Almirante Padilla* volunteered to join the *Capitán Tono;* of them, four officers and sixty-two men were chosen to remain in the war zone.[22] The frigate trained extensively until 19 April, when she was ordered to Pusan. For two months she patrolled the east coast, on 23 May participating in the bombardment of Wonsan. There she shelled road and rail communications day and night, an activity that frequently provoked duels with shore batteries. This lasted until the end of August. After a brief rest she escorted major U.S. units, then departed Korean waters on 12 November and sailed for home from Japan on 27 January 1953. In all, the *Capitán Tono* steamed fifty thousand nautical miles.[23]

Colombia began negotiations for a third frigate to relieve the *Capitán Tono* of her duties. On 26 June 1953 the nation took over the USS *Burlington* at Yokosuka Naval Base and renamed her the *Almirante Brion*. Lieutenant Commander Carlos Prieto Silva commanded a crew composed primarily of veterans from the *Capitán Tono*. The *Almirante Brion* was only in Korean waters a few days before the armistice was signed on 27 July, but she remained there as part of a contingency force. On 22 April 1954 she sailed for Colombia, relieved by the *Capitán Tono*, which was now commanded by Lieutenant Commander Jorge Taua Suarez. This frigate patrolled chiefly along the west coast and on 11 March 1955 was relieved by the *Almirante Padilla*, now under the command of Lieutenant Commander Dario Ferero Gonalez. On 11 October the last Colombian frigate left Korean waters.[24]

The three Colombian frigates had served five tours of duty in support of UN forces in Korea, a contribution from which the Colombian navy benefitted. At a time when the United States was anxious to obtain the support of as many UN members as possible, Colombia stepped forward, receiving in return ships, training, and equipment that would not otherwise have been available.

In 1956–57 the Brazilian navy participated in the activities of the UN Suez Force. The transport *Custodio de Melo* carried some eight hundred Brazilian soldiers to the Middle East.[25]

The Argentine and Venezuelan navies took part in the 1962 quarantine of Cuba. Following the discovery of Soviet missile bases in that country, the United States requested a meeting of the Organization of American

States (OAS), which recommended that its members "take all measures, individually and collectively, including the use of armed force . . . to insure that . . . Cuba cannot continue to receive from the Sino-Soviet powers military materials. . . ."[26] The stipulation was that Latin American forces would operate under an OAS command headed by a U.S. officer. Accordingly, Task Force 137 was created and placed under Rear Admiral John A. Tyree, commander in chief of the South Atlantic Fleet. Tyree would report directly to the commander in chief of the Atlantic Fleet, Admiral Robert L. Dennison, a set-up intended to increase the stature of the force and render it "more political than military."[27]

Once the OAS resolution appeared, all the Caribbean nations except México, longtime champion of nonintervention, offered assistance.[28] So did Argentina and Ecuador. Most of these countries made their ports and airfields available. Argentina contributed substantially more. Her army formed the Libres del Sud brigade; her air force offered aircraft squadrons; and her navy volunteered a marine battalion, Neptune ASW aircraft, the carrier *Independencia* (carrying F4U Corsair and S-2 Tracker aircraft), and two of its three newly acquired *Fletcher*-class destroyers. Of the navy's offer, only the *Fletchers*—the *Espora* and the *Rosales*—were accepted. These two twenty-year-old World War II veterans dashed from Puerto Belgrano to the U.S.-controlled Chaguaramas Naval Base on Trinidad Island in nine days, refueling in Rio de Janeiro and Recife. Having achieved an average speed of well over twenty knots for the 4,500-nautical-mile distance, they arrived on 8 November. Their first load of fuel they purchased on arrival at Argentine expense, making a point of being fully combat ready without U.S. support.

The Dominican Republic sent two frigates, the *Capitán Pedro Santana*, Commander Augusto Bienvenido Lara commanding, and the *Gregorio Luperon*, Lieutenant Commander Jose Altagarcia Modesto commanding. They arrived at San Juan, Puerto Rico, in need of extensive repairs before they could be incorporated into the task force. Guatemala offered the corvette *José Francisco Burrunda*, which, because she was undergoing an overhaul at Miami, Florida, would not be available until early December. Uruguay promised a destroyer escort; however, this could not be made available until after the national elections scheduled for 25 November. Venezuela offered the destroyers *Nueva Esparta* and *Zulia* plus the submarine *Carite*. The former were sent to Chaguaramas while the latter remained at Puerto Cabello.[29]

On 7 November Task Force 137 was ordered to "conduct naval quarantine operations in the Lesser Antilles passes into the Caribbean Sea in order to intercept designated shipping and prevent the importation of prohibited material into Cuba."[30] A string of patrol stations was established in the Lesser Antilles, and the Venezuelan destroyers *Zulia*, Captain Miguel

Benatuil Guastini commanding, and *Nueva Esparta*, Commander Luis J. Ramirez commanding, patrolled between the South American mainland and Grenada. The *Rosales*, in the hands of Commander Carlos F. Peralta, covered the area between Dominica and Guadaloupe. The other Argentine destroyer, the *Espora*, commanded by Commander Julio A. O. Vazquez, watched the Guadaloupe Passage and the waters off Monserrat Island. The northernmost station in the Anegada Passage was guarded by the U.S. destroyer *Mullinix*.

Task Force 137 had been on station for nine days when, on 20 November, President John F. Kennedy ordered an end to the quarantine. During this time 153 ships were observed and reported—21 by the *Espora*, 55 by the *Mullinix*, 31 by the *Nueva Esparta*, 6 by the *Rosales*, and 40 by the *Zulia*. Task Force 137 was not officially dissolved until 24 December, just as the two Dominican ships completed their repairs.[31]

The Latin American ships had been assigned to an area through which few if any Soviet ships were likely to pass. Obviously, their contribution was more political than military. In Admiral Dennison's words, Latin American military participation "didn't mean a damn thing."[32] Interestingly, of the nine Latin American warships offered for use in the quarantine, seven were former U.S. warships of World War II vintage.[33]

Military forces from Brazil, Costa Rica, Honduras, and Nicaragua participated in the 1965 Dominican Republic operation. Although many of these contributions were small when measured against the total effort, the participation of Latin American warships allowed the United States to show hemispheric support for her political position.

Cuba: A Communist Victory

The United States had long regarded Cuba's geographical location as strategic to her interests. Throughout the nineteenth century the island was the choke point between the northern and southern hemispheres, for prevailing winds forced sailing ships to pass near Cuban shores. The opening of the Panamá Canal in 1914 guaranteed that the island's location would now hold strategic significance not only for the western hemisphere but for the entire maritime world as well.

Shortly after coming to power, Fidel Castro disbanded the old Cuban navy because its loyalty came under question. In 1962 he created a new navy with different objectives, personnel, and equipment. Its immediate goal was to prevent landings or raids on the island, activities being carried out by Cuban dissidents using U.S. ports as safe havens. The raids ended with the Cuban Missile Crisis, after which the United States refused to harbor the counterinsurgents.

Outfitted with Soviet equipment, Communist Cuba built up an efficient gunboat navy. It consisted of three elements: large patrol boats, which

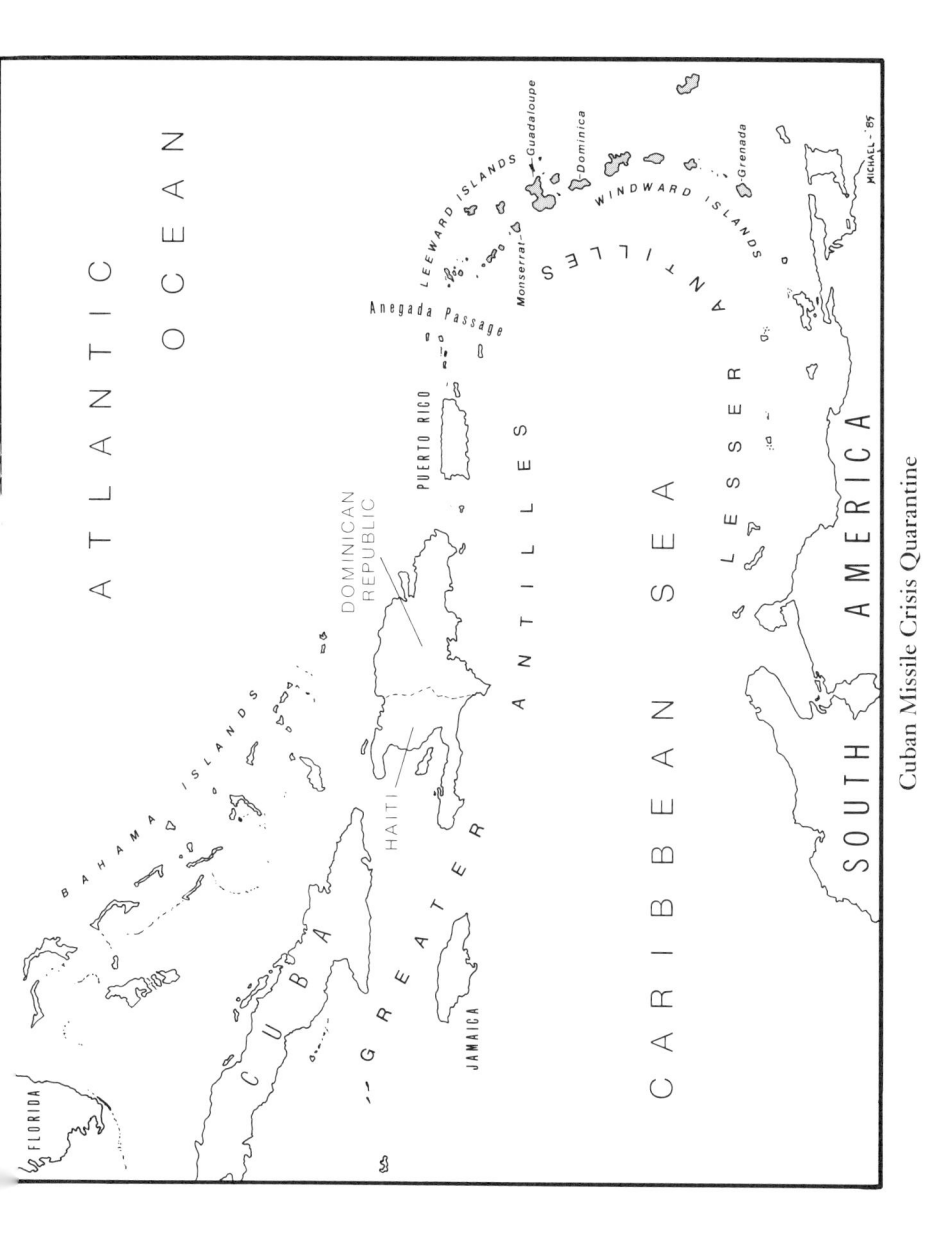

Cuban Missile Crisis Quarantine

cruised territorial waters; fast patrol craft, which darted out from Mariel and other bases on randomly scheduled patrols; and missile attack boats, which remained on alert in base, ready to attack any surface threat. The missile boats were well maintained, the elite of the new navy. The Soviet-built "Komar"s, introduced into Cuba in 1962, were the first missile-armed antiship warships in the western hemisphere. Over the past two decades the Cuban navy has modernized itself by replacing older Soviet-built warships with vessels of newer design. By the mid-1980s it had matured from a single-purpose counterinsurgency force to a multimission navy, as the acquisition of three "Foxtrot"-class submarines and two "Koni"-class frigates suggests. The navy has not been used directly to export revolution. This aim can be better accomplished by less risky means, using ships, for example, from the merchant marine and the fishing fleet or employing third-world merchantmen.

The Two-Hundred-Mile Limit

West-coast Latin American nations began talks on a two-hundred-mile maritime zone in the 1940s. The idea of a zone ran contrary to the interests of those countries possessing powerful navies, merchant marines, and fishing fleets—Great Britain, Japan, the Soviet Union, and the United States, for example. As North American political influence waned in Latin America, more of the regional countries supported the two-hundred-mile territorial limit.

A number of Latin American navies have either used or threatened to use force to protect their maritime zones. In one of the first attempts to enforce the zone, on 16 November 1954 Peruvian warships captured five Panamanian whalers operating within two hundred miles of Peru's coast. In early 1963 Brazilian warships seized three French lobster boats some sixty miles off the Brazilian coast, in response to which France dispatched the destroyer *Tartu*. The Brazilians countered with a cruiser, five destroyers, and two corvettes, the French ship withdrew, and a compromise was reached.[34] In 1966 the Argentine destroyer *Santa Cruz* fired on and holed a Russian trawler that refused to obey instructions to enter Mar del Plata.

A decade later a larger confrontation took place. On 21 September 1977 the Argentine destroyers *Py*, *Rosales*, and *Seguí* intercepted nine Soviet fishing vessels about 130 nautical miles off Cape Dos Bahías. A naval patrol aircraft had discovered the fishing fleet. The Soviet vessels were ordered to heave to; when they refused, warning shots were fired. Continued intransigence forced the Argentines to board the Soviet boats, a difficult task due to rough seas and lack of cooperation on the part of the Soviets. The Argentines tried to board with small boats but ultimately had to board gunwale to gunwale. Five trawlers escaped by dispersing, four were seized by the Argentines and escorted into Puerto Madryn. Five days later the *Rosa-*

les corralled the new Soviet factory ship *Herey*. On 1 October the Argentine cruiser *General Belgrano* and the destroyers *Piedrabuena*, *Py*, and *Seguí* trapped four more factory trawlers, two Soviet and two Bulgarian, approximately 170 nautical miles east of Comodore Rivadavia. When the two Bulgarian vessels refused to stop, the Argentine ships fired at them with five-inch guns, hitting one three times and critically wounding a crew member. The vessel was crippled and had to be taken in tow by its captors. During the boarding, conducted at night in choppy seas, a small boat overturned and one Argentine sailor was drowned. Eventually all four vessels were escorted to Argentine ports. The operations against the trawlers were directed by Rear Admiral Jorge Anaya, commander of the fleet, and later the key player in the Malvinas War.

Between 11 and 16 January 1971 Ecuadorian warships seized eight U.S. fishing craft alleged to be poaching within the two-hundred-mile zone. They were released after paying a large fine.

The Southern Cone: Old Disputes Resurface

Seven nations claim territory in the Antarctic, including Argentina and Chile, and many others claim certain rights without sovereignty.[35] Among the most contested land is that which lies between longitudes 20° West and 90° West; Argentina, Chile, and Great Britain all assert their right to various areas there, many of them overlapping. Following World War II, Argentina and Chile intensified their exploration of the region and set up permanent bases. At the end of 1947 an Argentine naval DC-4 aircraft flew along the west coast of the Antarctic Peninsula, passing over the Antarctic Circle and returning to the Piedra Buena Naval Air Station in Santa Cruz. In response to Argentine and Chilean activity in the Antarctic, Great Britain sent the cruiser *Nigeria* and frigate *Snipe* to Melchoir Island in the South Shetlands. Argentina responded by sending the cruisers *25 de Mayo* and *Almirante Brown* and the destroyers *Cervantes*, *Entre Ríos*, *Mendoza*, *Misiones*, *San Luis*, and *Santa Cruz* to Decepción Island in the South Shetlands. Each of the countries protested the activities of the others. In 1949 the three parties signed an agreement whereby no naval demonstrations would take place south of 60° South latitude. In January 1953 the Argentine navy again landed and erected buildings on Decepción. On 16 February a police squad from the Malvinas, backed by a platoon of heavily armed marines from the British frigate *Snipe*, demolished the buildings and expelled the Argentines.

On 23 June 1961 twelve nations signed the Antarctic Treaty maintaining the status quo of 1959. Article 12 allows any of the signatories to call for a review conference thirty years after the effective date of the treaty and offer amendments. If an amendment is not approved by unanimous consent, the nation presenting it may withdraw from the treaty. In effect, this means that any signatory can withdraw from the treaty after 23 June 1991.

Despite these problems, the harsh Antarctic environment has frequently brought the navies of the disputing nations to each other's support. In 1971, in one of the most hazardous undertakings, an Argentine navy PC-6 evacuated a British scientist from Fossil Bluff who had taken ill. Due to appalling meteorological conditions the flight took over two months to complete. When their mission was accomplished the crew was decorated by the British government.

The Antarctic issue bears on two other controversies, that between Argentina and Britain over the Malvina islands and between Argentina and Chile over the eastern entrance to the Beagle Channel. Argentina and Great Britain have each used naval force to support their claims to the disputed islands. In September 1966 Great Britain sent HMS *Puma* from Capetown, South Africa, to Port Stanley following an invasion of the islands by a group of Peronists who hijacked a DC-4 aircraft over Patagonia, flew to Port Stanley, and landed on the race track, the airport not yet having been built. On 4 February 1976, a time of particularly strained relations, the Argentine destroyer *Almirante Storni*, guided to the scene by a P-2 Neptune, fired across the bow of the unarmed British research ship *Shackleton*, possibly in the belief that Lord Shackleton was on board. The British frigate *Chichester* made a detour to Port Stanley on her way to Great Britain from Hong Kong. The controversy led to war in 1982.[36]

Probably no Latin American imbroglio has posed a greater threat of war than the Beagle Channel dispute between Argentina and Chile. The disagreement centers around three small islands at the eastern entrance to the channel—Picton, Nueva, and Lennox. None was specifically mentioned in the Boundary Treaty of 1881 or in subsequent agreements, and both nations have interpreted the implied meaning of these documents differently. One underlying question is whether Beagle Channel runs to the north or to the west of the islands or ends before reaching the western tip of Picton. There is also a question whether the islands are in the Atlantic or Pacific Ocean. Chile argues that the Pacific includes the submerged Antillean loop formed by an immense crescent to the east and bordered by Shag Rocks, South Georgia, the South Sandwich islands, the South Orkneys, and the Antarctic Peninsula.[37] Argentina maintains that Cape Horn separates the Atlantic from the Pacific.

In 1958, following an incident on Snipe Island, both nations rushed naval forces south and conducted blackout exercises in their cities. In May 1977 an arbitration court awarded the disputed islands to Chile. In January 1978 Argentina declared the ruling null, arguing that the court had exceeded the authority to which both countries agreed prior to entering negotiations. The bilateral negotiations that followed broke down late in the year.³⁸ Argentine and Chilean forces concentrated in their respective southern areas, and blackout exercises were conducted in numerous Argentine and Chilean cities. In October 1978 the presidents of Argentina and Bolivia ratified their solidarity by issuing a communiqué linking Bolivia's claim for an outlet to the Pacific (which it had lost to Chile in the War of the Pacific) with the question of Argentine sovereignty in the South Atlantic, including the Beagle Channel and Malvinas.³⁹

Chilean troops have held the disputed islands since 1915. Apparently Chile stationed only a small force at first to act as a trip wire.⁴⁰ If the Argentines chose to seize the islands, this force would make a show of opposition. It seems that Chile then changed her mind and on the main islands based a substantial force whose task was one of stout defense. The force may have consisted of two army regiments and two naval infantry battalions. The new strategy was to tie the Argentine fleet to protection of its landing force and thereby render it more vulnerable to attack by the Chilean fleet. The Argentine strategy was to seize the islands with a substantial force supported by the fleet. If the Chileans reacted militarily, then Tierra del Fuego Island would be taken by the Argentine marines. They were to be supported by almost one hundred naval aircraft operating from the Ushuaia and Rio Grande naval air stations as well as more than half a dozen campaign airfields that had been hastily completed for the operation. Both countries mobilized their reserves in late 1978, and on the Argentine side alone an army of about a quarter million men was stationed along the frontier ready to defend the few mountain passes across the Andes. This was probably the largest concentration of troops on the South American continent since the Chaco War.

Chilean surface warships, probably in November of 1978, anchored at a hideaway near Channel O'Brien, approximately one hundred miles west of Cape Horn. The Chilean fleet was commanded by Vice Admiral Raúl López, a naval aviator specifically selected to confront the Argentines. (Normally a rear admiral held the post.) In order to position itself for neutralization of the Argentine aircraft carrier *25 de Mayo* if war broke out, a Chilean submarine, possibly the *Simpson*, transited Drake Passage around 21 December and likely entered a free fire zone in the Atlantic Ocean.

The Argentine fleet, built around its light attack carrier, sailed from Puerto Belgrano in early December for the south. The *25 de Mayo*'s defenses had been modified with antitorpedo nets hung from the flight deck for missile defense. The nets, almost seventy years old, had been salvaged from the Argentine dreadnoughts. This, it was hoped, would cause an attacking missile to explode outside the hull. The Argentine fleet, commanded by Rear Admiral Humberto J. Barbuzzi, took up position east of Cape Horn in the shallow waters of Burdwood Bank to minimize the submarine threat. While cruising in these waters the fleet made an underwater

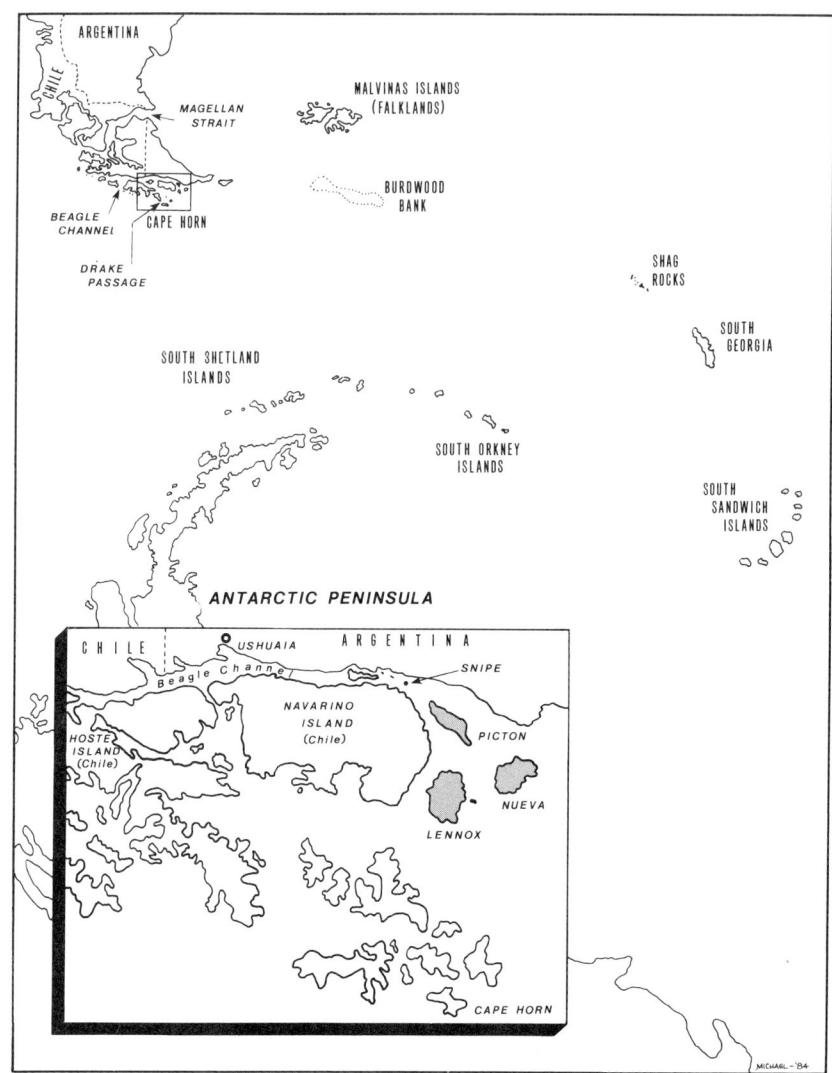

The Beagle Channel Dispute

contact, which it classified as a probable submarine and may have attacked, unsuccessfully, with planes, helicopters, and destroyers. It is possible that, meanwhile, a naval Tracker aircraft dropped a live ASW torpedo. In another incident, naval A-Q Skyhawks armed with Sidewinder B missiles flying from the *25 de Mayo* intercepted a Chilean Casa 212 Aviocar naval patrol aircraft near the fleet, but the pilots were ordered not to fire first.

The Argentine force, apparently the Fourth Marine Corps Battalion, was scheduled to land on the disputed islands at 0400 on 22 December. Air force, army, and navy helicopters were to deliver the marines, but four hours before this happened Pope John Paul II defused the situation by agreeing to mediate the dispute. The Argentine decision to accept the papal offer may have been influenced by U.S. pressure for a peaceful solution and the fact that the Argentine fleet had already spent twenty stormy days at sea far from its base of operation. In late 1984 the Vatican announced that Argentina and Chile had reached a "total coincidence of points of view" concerning the Beagle Channel dispute, and both countries signed a treaty delineating Argentine and Chilean territory. The boundary line stopped a few miles south of Cape Horn, and thus disputes in the Antarctic were avoided.

One lesson the Argentine fleet learned during the tensions was its need for greater logistics capability. The fleet had been supplied with fuel by a commercial oiler from Yacimientos Petroliferos Fiscales, but this could only be transferred to the naval tanker *Punta Medanos* and not directly to any of the combatants. In addition, the transfer could only be conducted over the stern of the merchant tankers in very calm water. The awkwardness of the procedure prompted the navy to contribute to the purchase of two commercial tankers and their outfitting with underway refueling systems. During hostile situations the civilian crews were to be augmented by naval specialists. This scheme worked well during the Malvinas War.

The Ecuadorian-Peruvian Dispute

In 1981 Ecuador and Perú clashed in a border dispute during which naval forces were used. The latter launched an attack against Ecuadorian forces that allegedly had occupied three abandoned Peruvian outposts in the Condor Mountains. Air, land, and sea units arrived at the border to pin down Ecuadorian units. On 28 January 1981 Peru's Soviet-built Mi-8 "Hip" helicopters overwhelmed Ecuadorian outposts. Then three Peruvian amphibious warfare ships, supported by surface combatants, landed one hundred vehicles—tanks, armored cars, and trucks—north of Talara, near the border. A cease-fire went into effect after Perú had gained her objectives.

CHAPTER TWELVE

Marine Corps and Naval Aviation

TECHNOLOGIES AND DOCTRINES developed during World War II gave Latin American navies the capability to project their power ashore more effectively. This had national as well as international implications, because now fleets could be more influential in interpreting the national political will. The two naval arms that gained the most strength were amphibious forces and aviation.

A number of nineteenth-century Latin American leaders recognized the potential of an amphibious force. San Martín, in his campaign to liberate Perú from Spain, showed a clear understanding of what amphibious warfare could achieve. During the War of the Triple Alliance the Brazilian navy landed the allied armies of Argentina, Brazil, and Uruguay at Paso de la Patria after one of the largest and best executed river crossings in Latin American military history. Among the most clairvoyant advocates of an amphibious capability was Domingo F. Sarmiento, president of Argentina from 1868 to 1874. In his four-pronged program for developing a modern sea force, Sarmiento had advocated the acquisition of modern ships and believed "it would not be possible to conceive of our navy without a squadron of transports."[1] In 1891 the Chilean navy carried out numerous amphibious landings to assist the revolution, on one occasion landing 10,500 men after a twelve-hundred-mile passage. Still, the state of South

American technology severely limited the probability of a successful opposed amphibious assault until the middle of the twentieth century.

A strong, highly trained marine corps is the backbone of any effective inland projection of amphibious power. Eleven Latin American navies have had marine corps, many of them patterned after the colonial Spanish model of a marine corps engaged in coastal defense and security, and six—those of Argentina, Brazil, Chile, Cuba, Perú, and Venezuela—took new directions as amphibious warfare became increasingly important to them.[2] For Argentina and Brazil this change took place shortly after World War II. The others waited a few decades for change. Their orientation toward amphibious warfare enables these services to function as fast-reaction intervention forces.

The full value of the amphibious modus operandi was not realized until World War II, at which time the campaigns of U.S. marines in the Pacific left a lasting impression upon students of strategy. The magnitude of the lesson is suggested by a 1946 Argentine law calling for a corps "with a landing force similar to that of the United States Marine Corps."[3] Nineteenth-century practices were discarded. Attack transports designed for specific missions replaced the transport fleet of chartered merchantmen and warships crowded with troops. A fleet of specialized amphibious craft and vehicles that could handle even large equipment supplanted ships' boats, which had been used in moving men ashore. And specialized assault groups rendered the old landing party composed of sailors and a few ships' marines obsolete.

Despite these advances, the lack of amphibious fleet capability has been a problem for Latin American marine corps. After World War II they had to turn to foreign suppliers, principally the United States, for their large and small amphibians. Beginning in the 1970s navies struggled to reduce their reliance upon other nations. Binational shipbuilding agreements and the expansion of indigenous capability have started to reduce this dependency. The Argentine tank landing ship *Cabo San Antonio*, a modified U.S. *DeSoto County*–class design, was the first major amphibian built in Latin America. She was commissioned on 11 February 1978, and in April 1982 she landed the Argentine Second Marine Battalion on the Malvina islands. Brazil, which already had four attack transports built in Japan (one of which is used as a training ship), acquired two ex-U.S. tank landing ships and built four utility landing craft with U.S. assistance. Chile has constructed four medium landing ships, two with U.S. help and three with French.

Too much can be made of this shortage of large specialized amphibians. Most Latin American countries have a government-owned coastal freight-passenger fleet. These ships, though they lack over-the-beach capabilities, have transport potential. Modern merchantmen and auxiliaries equipped with helicopter facilities can be useful in an amphibious assault. During the Malvinas War the Argentine icebreaker *Almirante Irizar* and polar support ship *Bahía Paraíso* were used to good advantage in amphibious operations. And new merchant-ship types such as the Ro/Ro (roll on/roll off) and Baco (barge container) have some potential for use as amphibians.

Tracked amphibious vehicles have been the exclusive domain of foreign manufacturers. In 1970 Brazil implemented a program to equip her marine corps through domestic manufacture. The most significant development was the design and production of the "Urutu" armored amphibious vehicles and similar light amphibians.[4] The first unit was turned over to the marine corps on 20 July 1973 at the training facility on Ilha do Governador. The EE-11 Urutu can carry a rifle squad. The Brazilian marine corps also operates the EE-9 "Cascavel," an armored personnel reconnaissance vehicle armed with a 90-mm gun. Yet a critical need—an amphibious craft that can bring a marine corps company ashore from a tank landing ship while under fire—has not been met within Latin American borders. To date the demand has been too small to make indigenous production economically feasible, so to fill the need Latin America still depends on the United States and Europe. Argentina in particular has been adversely affected. She has wanted to replace her twenty aging tracked landing vehicles, but replacements have been embargoed by the United States.

As for naval air power, in the years preceding World War II many countries developed a land-based capability, but until 1987 only one country, Argentina, had acquired an aircraft carrier equipped with attack aircraft. Brazil's *Minas Gerais* was equipped to operate attack aircraft but never received any. The Chilean navy has hoped to establish such a force, but it has not yet been able to do so. Aviation that carried political significance in the mid-twentieth century was carrier based.

Marine Corps

The oldest and currently largest marine corps in Latin America is that of Brazil. It descended without a break from Portugal's Royal Brigade of Marines, which arrived in Brazil in its entirety, twenty-five-hundred artillery- and infantrymen strong, with the royal family in 1808.[5] When Dom João VI and his entourage departed for Portugal thirteen years later the corps remained, establishing a nucleus of loyal troops for the new emperor. During the fifteen decades of its existence the corps has been employed in activities that include modest amphibious exercises. Its nomenclature has changed over the years from the corps of naval riflemen in 1847, the naval regiment in 1924, to the marine corps in 1932. The Brazilian marine corps has always been subordinate to the navy, and before a permanent officer corps was established officers were obtained through a rotation system from the fleet.[6]

The mission of the marine corps was defined in 1940: "to effect landing operations, to provide garrisons for naval bases and fortifications, provide ships' detachments, orderlies, guards, prisoner escorts and to provide bands and drummers for ships and naval establishments and organizations." But these tasks exceeded the capabilities of the corps' manpower and training, and moreover, its amphibious capabilities were constantly sapped by secondary missions. A fleet marine force existed on paper only, and amphibious exercises were modest. The successful example of the U.S. Marine Corps in World War II plus the presence of marine corps officers in U.S. naval missions influenced the Brazilian corps to model itself after its northern neighbor. A decree of 4 April 1950 removed the marine corps from the control of the Naval Staff and once again made it directly subordinate to the minister of the navy. But lack of personnel still prevented the corps from carrying out its primary mission of amphibious operations.

Another serious handicap was a lack of training facilities. Construction of a marine training center began in 1948 on Ilha do Governador in Guanabara Bay. Training was provided by U.S. Marine Corps personnel and Brazilian officers who had attended the U.S. Marine Corps junior and senior amphibious course given yearly in Quantico, Virginia. The first practice exercise took place in March 1948, when after a limited bombardment three companies of marines stormed Marambaia Beach from destroyers.[7]

The present organization of the Brazilian marine corps includes a fleet marine force with a brigade-sized amphibious division and force troops. The fleet marine force consists of infantry, artillery, light armor, combat support, and service units. The corps also has a support command, a training center, and several regional groups for security duty.

The roots of the Argentine marine corps go back more than a century. To capture the island of Martín García from the Spanish in 1814 Admiral Guillermo Brown used Argentine marines who went ashore to the tune of "St. Patrick's March." A number of times over the next century the corps was recreated and abolished (sometimes it was a de facto organization).[8] It took permanent hold in 1905 with the creation of a corps of coastal artillery.

Amphibious assault responsibilities rested with the sailors manning ships' boats. Using longboat-style tactics, Argentine naval landing parties fought against bandits in the southern regions in 1921. On 17 December 1921 soldiers and crew from the gunnery training ship *Almirante Brown* landed and routed a party of 250 bandits at Mata Tapera. In 1934 the coastal artillery corps was reorganized to include the new specialties of infantry and coastal and antiaircraft artillery. In 1935 a provisional marine infantry battalion was created and embarked with the fleet for maneuvers. Two additional battalions appeared in 1936, one in 1937, and another the next year. Still the marines relied on the longboats of the fleet for their transportation ashore.[9]

An amphibious marine corps was created in 1946. As in the case of the Brazilian service, U.S. Marine Corps advisors played a significant role in the shaping of the new force. Great Britain also contributed to its making. According to the U.S. intelligence publication, the *ONI Review*, the Argentine marine corps was "well on the way to becoming the best trained and most effective landing force in Latin America" by early 1950. That year saw the establishment of a marine command school, an important step toward increased amphibious capability. In 1955, after participating in an unsuccessful attempt to oust Juan Perón, the marine corps was ordered cut in half. But before the order could be executed the corps took part in another, successful stab at Perón, thereby proving its capabilities. Its full amphibious capabilities were exhibited in November 1952 during Operation Corso, when a full brigade carried out an amphibious landing in the wake of air and naval bombardment. In 1964 a combined army-navy force carried out Operation Caiman. Two marine battalions conducted an amphibious landing after air and naval bombardment of the objective. Both operations took place in the area of the Valdes Peninsula. In 1981 Argentine and U.S. marines landed together on the Patagonian coast.[10]

The Chilean marine corps has its origins in the sixteenth century. Ever since colonial times Chile, exposed to coastal raids by freebooters, has been compelled to organize coastal defense units to oppose the threat. In 1818 she formed a company of marines as well as a brigade of naval artillery. During the Wars of Independence Chilean marines acquired more amphibious experience than any corps in the western hemisphere, at the close of fighting assuming garrison duty. In the War with Spain and the War of the Pacific the marines served as infantry and artillery units. In 1887 the force became subordinate to the army and was renamed the coastal artillery. In 1912 coastal defense fortifications and a reduced regiment were again placed under navy command. The corps' weakness was decentralization: it was under the supervision but not the command of the inspector of coastal artillery, and the regiments were delegated specific functions such as communication, the operation of coastal batteries, searchlights, and mine, smoke, and gas units, and air and submarine detection. Personnel shortages kept the amphibious element, the battalion of marines, nothing more than a paper unit. In 1947 a temporary battalion formed from garrison troops conducted landing exercises. On 5 March 1964 the force was officially designated the marine corps. Like its counterparts in Argentina and Brazil, the Chilean marine corps emulated the

American marines after World War II. Its most notable activity of recent years was involvement in the overthrow of the Allende government in 1973.[11]

The Peruvian marine corps traces its origins to the independence era. It was disbanded after the War of the Pacific but reestablished in 1920 as a marine battalion. On 14 June 1930 the Peruvian minister of the navy, A. Loayza, ordered the "Marine Corps landing force to conform to the [tactical] instructions of April 22 for an Army Infantry Regiment. . . ." In 1943 Perú established a small commando unit, and four years later one hundred men took part in maneuvers. By 1955 the amphibious strength of the Peruvian marine corps had expanded to that of a brigade.[12]

The beginning of the Paraguayan marine corps goes back to the War of the Triple Alliance, when Infantry Battalion No. 1 was made up of *bogavantes* ("oarsmen"). Infantry Battalion No. 6, armed with boarding knives seized from the captured Argentine warships at Corrientes, served in Paraguayan warships during the Battle of Riachuelo. Since World War II Paraguay has developed, with the assistance of the Argentine marines, a small marine corps that conducts riverine amphibious operations on the Paraña and Paraguay rivers in joint maneuvers with the Argentine navy.

Fidel Castro gave the Cuban navy permission to establish a marine corps in 1959, but perceiving that this force might be used against him, he abolished it shortly thereafter. In the late 1970s the Cuban marine corps was reestablished in keeping with the redefinition of the Cuban navy—formerly assigned the single mission of interdiction—as a multimission service.

The Venezuelan marine corps, established in 1943, followed the Spanish pattern of coastal defense and guard duty for a few decades. In the 1970s, with increased pressure from subversive groups based primarily in the Caribbean and Central America, it began to develop an amphibious capability.[13]

The remaining Latin American marine corps have no amphibious experience and currently lack potential for it, their traditional activities having been coastal defense and guard duty. Most have been plagued by limited manpower and rapid turnover of personnel, lack of equipment, inadequate training, and poor pay.

Naval Aviation

The seeds of Argentine naval aviation were planted during the second decade of the twentieth century. In 1920 the naval aviation division was established and funds were allocated for the naval aviation school, which opened two years later.[14] The new naval arm flexed its muscle for national leaders and the public on 21 May 1923 when three naval aircraft flew from Puerto

Militar (Puerto Belgrano) to Buenos Aires via Mar del Plata. The planes, one Curtiss bomber and two Curtiss scouts fitted with wartime equipment, took the coastal route for a distance of just under five hundred miles.[15]

Naval aviation conducted aerial defense of the coast in its first decade, when both the United States and Britain influenced the development of the service. Great Britain supplied it with many aircraft.[16] About half of the pilots and all of the instructors graduated from the U.S. naval aviation school at Pensacola. The Argentine navy placed much emphasis on aviation development, and as a result a U.S. naval intelligence publication reported that future advancement in the navy would depend heavily on service within the air arm.[17] During the early 1930s the national financial situation did not permit much naval air activity or the purchase of new equipment. In 1936 the position of director general of naval aviation was created to give naval aviation new impetus, and by the late 1930s the arm had two fighter squadrons, a patrol squadron, and a transport group, in addition to spotter aircraft on the cruisers *Almirante Brown*, *25 de Mayo*, and *La Argentina*. By 1940 the naval air arm had become a substantial force with fifty-four aircraft and one hundred pilots. By comparison, the army air corps had two hundred planes and 325 pilots. Still Argentina was dependent on the United States and Europe for aircraft. The outbreak of World War II led to the stagnation of all aviation development.[18]

In the post–World War II era Argentina, in a race with Brazil, showed interest in acquiring an aircraft carrier. In a study initiated in 1953 to determine the practicality of an in-country carrier conversion program, two alternatives were studied. The first called for the reconversion of a C3-S-A1 cargo vessel, a type that had served as an escort carrier in the British and U.S. navies during World War II. The second called for the conversion of an *Almirante Brown*–class cruiser. Neither idea materialized.[19] Instead Argentina obtained a carrier. In early 1957 Great Britain offered to sell her either an *Illustrious*- or a *Majestic*-class carrier. The former was considerably larger and faster than Brazil's recent acquisition, the *Minas Gerais*, but the ship offered, HMS *Indefatigable*, was in poor material condition and would have cost considerably more to purchase, refit, operate, and maintain than the smaller Brazilian unit. Argentina turned down the offer for this ship and for a second, the *Magnificent*, which had originally been a sister to the recently acquired Brazilian carrier.[20]

In 1958 Argentina purchased the British *Colossus*-class aircraft carrier *Warrior*. She had been modernized in 1955–56, while still in the Royal Navy, putting her on an operational par with the Brazilian carrier. The cost of purchase Argentina covered with money obtained by selling the dreadnoughts *Moreno* and *Rivadavia* and the old armored cruiser *Pueyrredón* for scrap. So, very aptly, the old backbone of the fleet paid for the new one. The carrier, renamed the *Independencia*, saw extensive service during her ten-year tour with the Argentine navy and by the mid-1960s was in need of overhaul or replacement. Fortunately for Argentina, the Dutch in 1968 were disposing of their carrier, the *Karel Doorman*. Argentina bought this ship, which also belonged to the *Colossus* class, and renamed her the *25 de Mayo*. A refitting at Rotterdam in 1969 mended damage sustained during two major engine-room fires in 1967 and 1968.[21]

Following World War II the Argentine navy created the most potent naval flying corps in Latin America, but during the Perón years it was almost liquidated because of prevailing antigovernment sentiment amongst personnel. As we shall see in chapter 13, the value of naval aviation in interpreting the national political will was demonstrated during the 1955 overthrow of Juan Perón.

The possession of attack aircraft has frequently brought the Argentine navy into disagreement with the air force, as it has everywhere else in the world. During an interservice disagreement in 1960 the navy reportedly collaborated with the U.S. embassy, attempting unsuccessfully to block the sale of U.S. aircraft to the Argentine air force.[22]

The strength of Argentine naval aviation today is its carrier-borne attack aircraft force. In a training exercise on 4 November 1968 the Argentine carrier, operating near the coast, guided four F9F Panthers against her mock opponent, the new French carrier *Clemenceau*. Aircraft, which could not fly from the *Independencia* because of her weak catapult, had to be based at a naval air station for simulated carrier launching. Making a four-point attack, two Panthers broke through the *Clemenceau*'s air screen. This success, along with the inability of a small, old carrier to accommodate adequate numbers of modern attack aircraft, presented a problem—one that resurfaced during the Malvinas War (see appendix 13).

The military and political significance of naval aviation had not gone unnoticed in Brazil, which established her naval air arm on 23 August 1916 with the creation of a naval aviation school. The school was equipped with American-built Curtiss model F flying boats. Other aircraft were very difficult to obtain because of the world war.

The first use of Latin American naval aircraft in combat came during a military revolt in 1922 when two planes bombed the rebellious Fort Copacabana in Rio de Janeiro. Earlier in the day the fort had been fired upon by the dreadnought *Minas Gerais*, then-reigning naval champion. By 1924 the Brazilian naval aviation arm had established nine scheduled logistics transport routes and operated over fifty aircraft.[23] In November of that year twenty-two of the thirty-nine naval pilots were arrested for antigovernment activity.[24] After a revolt in 1924 the Naval Aviation Directorate was suspended and aviation units were placed under the control of the General Staff.[25] On 3 October 1931 the naval air arm was reorganized and a naval aviation corps established.

The 1932 revolution helped restore the potential of naval aviation and revealed the inadequacies of the big ships whose deployments were restricted owing to a lack of antiaircraft guns. The loyal naval air arm was increased by about sixty planes to be used against the rebels. This more than doubled its size.[26]

By 1935 Brazilian naval aviation was organized into two fighter divisions and one training division. By the end of the decade the arm operated about a hundred sea and land planes of assorted types. But the navy had no carriers then, nor did its battleships and cruisers operate seaplanes, so naval aircraft had to be based ashore. In the late 1930s there was a campaign for the establishment of an air ministry to control military and civil aviation in Brazil, a movement inspired by Giulio Douhet, Alexander P. Seversky, and other aviation theoreticians whose doctrines were practiced by the Italian *Reggia Aeronautica* and the newer German *Luftwaffe*. But the Brazilian navy did not have a Rear Admiral William Moffett to campaign for development of naval aviation as a weapon for achieving victory at sea. On 20 January 1941 the aviation branches of the navy and the army were amalgamated to form the Brazilian air force under control of the new Ministry of Aeronautics.[27]

The air force arrived before the value of tactical air power, in combination with naval and land forces, had been demonstrated. In early 1941 the aircraft carrier had not yet proved itself as a weapon in the Pacific. The lessons of Taranto in November 1940 had not yet been fully realized, except by the Japanese, and recent successes of the *Luftwaffe* and the *Reggia Aeronautica* against British carriers (equipped with obsolescent aircraft) seemed to corroborate the opinion of the air power enthusiasts that land-based aircraft were superior to carrier-borne planes. Although the U.S. Fleet was the most carrier-minded navy of the time, its views on the use of air power at sea had not been assimilated by the Brazilian navy, probably because the latter lacked experience with shipboard aviation.

The 1950s saw further developments in the Brazilian navy. Its reorganization in 1950 resulted in the establishment of a directorate of aeronautics in the Ministry of the Navy. In 1958 the navy bought two Bell 47-J helicopters to operate from the survey ships *Sirius* and *Canopus*. It also purchased three Westland Widgeon helicopters from Great Britain. An air-naval training center was set up near Rio de Janeiro, construction was begun on a naval air station near Cabo Frio in the state of Rio de Janeiro, and a naval air transportation service came into being.[28] Despite these developments, Brazilian naval aviation, like its Chilean counterpart, has still not acquired the attack aircraft that would lift it out of political impotence and extend its military value.

Regarding warship acquisitions, the Brazilian navy has been the Latin American trend setter. It was the first to build a submarine force and to obtain a dreadnought and aircraft carrier. In 1922 it played with the idea of converting the former German merchant ships *Aracaju* (ex-*Monte Penedo*) and *Sabara* (ex-*Persia*) to carriers.[29] But it was not until 1956, when Brazil purchased the *Colossus*-class aircraft carrier *Vengeance* from the British Admiralty for nine million dollars, that she acquired her first carrier. Threefold the purchase price was then spent to modernize and adapt her to Brazilian needs. From the summer of 1957 to December 1960 the ship, renamed *Minas Gerais*, was extensively reconstructed by Verolme Rhine-Schelde of Rotterdam. Afterwards she was able to operate modern, light attack aircraft.[30]

The acquisition of the *Minas Gerais* caused a major struggle between Brazilian services. At issue was the control of aircraft flown from the carrier. From the completion of her modernization until 1963 the carrier was planeless, and neither President Juscelino Kubitschek nor his two successors, Jânio Quadros and João Goulart, was able to resolve the problem.[31] The carrier was jokingly called Bel-Antonio, after a film in which Marcello Mastroianni played a handsome but impotent man.

In early 1959 the government decided that all aircraft operating from the carrier would belong to the air force. However, the navy was intent on flying from the carrier. Naval personnel trained with the U.S. Navy in the hope of taking possession of American-built S-2A Trackers and Sikorsky SH-34J Seabat helicopters in the air force inventory. In early 1963 the navy created the naval air force, which included the First Shipboard Air Group. Although nothing more than a paper force, it caused quite a stir.[32]

In 1963 the navy purchased six North American T-28 trainers and four helicopters. The T-28s were smuggled into the country in Brazilian warships, then driven under cover of darkness to the new naval air base at São Pedro d'Aldeia, where they were assembled. A similar modus operandi was used to obtain six Pilatus P3 trainers, one Fairchild PT-26, and one Taylorcraft L-2K. A number of low-level reconnaissance missions flown by air force T-6s discovered the new naval air force. The naval T-28s began operating from the *Minas Gerais*, which entered Rio de Janeiro's Guanabara Bay with four of the aircraft on her deck on 22 January 1964.[33] The air force, responsible for all military aircraft, refused to permit the planes to be assigned to the carrier. President Humberto Castello Branco forbade the navy to operate the T-28s from the carrier during the annual UNITAS exercise. In December 1964 he ended the impasse and gave the navy permission to operate the planes from the *Minas Gerais*. Possibly in protest, air force personnel machine-gunned a naval helicopter on the ground at Porto Alegre. The air minister, Lieutenant Brigadier Nelson Freire Laveriere-Wanderley, resigned rather than investigate the incident. His successor, Brigadier Marcio de Souza e Mello, argued violently over the issue with President Castello Branco and was removed from the post, which was then filled by the much-respected air marshal Eduardo Gômes. The president decided that fixed-wing planes would be operated by the air force and that seagoing rotary aircraft would be flown by the navy. This decision, announced on 26 January 1965, caused the resignation of key Brazilian naval figures.[34] Thus the navy today has no control over fixed-wing aircraft, and even the antisubmarine squadron of S-2 Trackers is an air force unit, not subject to the commanding officer of the carrier.[35]

Following the presidential decision, the Brazilian navy's fixed-wing air units, ASW/Attack Squadron 1 and Training Squadron 1, were disbanded. Helicopter Utility Squadron 1 and Helicopter Training Squadron 1 remained intact, and Helicopter ASW Squadron 1 (Esqd HS-1) was formed with six Sikorsky SH-34J Seabat ASW helicopters from the air force. All naval air units were to be based at the naval air station at Sao Pedro d'Aldeia, near Rio de Janeiro, when not at sea. The Brazilian air force's only shipboard unit, *1° Grupo de Aviação* Embarcada, based at Santa Cruz Air Force Base in Rio de Janeiro, continued to operate its fourteen Grumman S-2A Tracker ASW aircraft. An air force liaison-observation light unit was attached to the naval air force and moved to the naval air station São Pedro d'Aldeia, receiving ex-navy fixed-wing aircraft.

With stronger U.S. influence the Brazilian navy became an ASW-oriented navy, and the *Minas Gerais* was fitted as a small CVS, in 1983–84 operating an air group of twelve to fourteen ASW aircraft and helicopters (a typical mix was six Grumman S-2E Tracker ASW aircraft with four Sikorsky SH-3D Sea King ASW helicopters and three Aerospatiale/HELIBRAS HB-350 Esquilo utility helicopters).

In late 1983 the Ministry of Defense announced that the *Minas Gerais* was to be fitted with McDonnell-Douglas A-4 Skyhawks, which would give her a limited surface strike and air defense capability in addition to her primary ASW role. Twelve refurbished aircraft were sought, possibly from Australia, Israel, Singapore, and the United States. By 1985 the plan to purchase the Skyhawks had been canceled in favor of developing the Brazilian-Italian AM-X (EMB-330) light strike fighter, a cooperative design by Aeritalia and Aermacchi in Italy and Embraer in Brazil.

The *Minas Gerais* is scheduled for decommissioning by the end of the 1980s with no firm replacement in view. The fact that shipboard fixed-wing aircraft are now under control of the Brazilian air force complicates the problem of replacement. The navy certainly will not begin a carrier project before the economic situation in Brazil improves, and perhaps not before the future of shipboard fixed-wing aircraft is settled once and for all. Continued opposition from the air force might even drive the navy out of the carrier business completely.

The Latin American country with the oldest naval aviation tradition is Chile. In 1916 army and navy officers received flying instructions in country, and at the end of 1918 the naval air arm, as a branch of the army air corps, received its first planes—three Sopwith "Babies," five Short seaplanes, and one Vickers P2A seaplane. A Sopwith "Baby" was attached to a cruiser in 1919, becoming the first shipborne aircraft in Latin America. The other aircraft types became operational in 1920. During these years the Chilean naval organ *Revista de Marina* aired the controversy over an old navy based on the big-gun ship and a new one founded on naval air power and the submarine. On 30 August 1921 three Short planes flying from Valparaíso carried out a mock raid against Coquimbo. The success of this exercise influenced the decision to separate naval aviation units from the air corps. During the following year the naval force moved to Quintero and construction was begun on a permanent naval air facility. Commander Eduardo von Schroeders, who had championed naval aviation against the blue-water sailors, was appointed commandant, and because of his accomplishments he was called the founder of Chilean naval aviation.[36] In January 1923 two English-built Supermarine "Channel"-type Mk II seaplanes equipped with radio telegraph and telephone system arrived to augment the naval aviation arm, which President Arturo Alessandri Palma made a separate entity two months later. The force grew in significance, and new bases were constructed at Chamezor in Puerto Montt and Bahia Catalina in Punta Arenas. As national finances permitted, aircraft were added and joint exercises with the fleet were held, including a raid on the Channel Zone at the tip of South America.[37] In 1930, during the presidency of Carlos Ibañez del Campo, naval aviation suffered a severe blow: it was absorbed by the existing military air arm to create a national air force such as Great Britain had. Thus for twenty-three years Chilean naval aviation was nonexistent.

During the 1929–31 refit of the battleship *Almirante Latorre* at Devonport, England, a platform and a structure for a catapult were installed, but apparently the English catapult was too expensive so the battleship returned to Chile without one. In February 1923 an air-impulse catapult designed by the Italian air force and manufactured in La Spezia, Italy, arrived in Chile on board a merchantman. In mid-March the catapult was tested and installed. Meanwhile the Chilean navy had acquired a British Fairey IIIM Mk IIIB floatplane, strengthened for catapult launching. The catapult was removed during the 1937 refit at Talcahuano, Chile.

In the late 1930s six Chilean naval aviation pilots went to Pensacola for training. In 1942 and 1943 Chile received a number of Catalina and Vought-Sikorsky patrol aircraft through lend-lease. In 1943, wishing to comply with U.S. requests for collaboration on maritime patrols, the Chilean navy prepared to send five more pilots for instruction, but the air force objected and the program had to be cancelled.

During World War II naval aviation regained a semi-official status. The navy controlled the operation of a few aircraft, but they were still administered by the air force. After the war agitation for a separate naval air arm continued. In 1953 Undersecretary of the Navy Captain Angel Custodio Lira took up the battle, supported by Vice Admiral Juan Agustin Rodriguez's crusading pen. Brigade General Jorge Gaña championed the air corps cause. The fleet met with some success, for in July 1953 President Carlos Ibañez del Campo gave the navy authority to operate transports and helicopters. Eleven years later President Jorge Alessandri Rodriguez authorized a naval air force without restrictions.[38]

The navy has campaigned long and hard for an aircraft carrier capable of handling attack aircraft. During the late 1940s and 1950s retired naval officers authored numerous newspaper and magazine articles expounding the need for a carrier. The principal proponent, Rear Admiral Juan Agustín Rodriguez Sepulveda, wrote that while Chile did not have a carrier it "ought to compensate for the lack of this type with [land-based] naval aviation. . . ."[39] In an interview in 1982 Vice Admiral Maurice Poisson, chief of the Naval Staff, stated, "I think every sailor has in the back of his mind the idea of . . . a carrier-based task group. It is for the service to try to make ends meet with the present size of resources allocated, so . . . we are trying to see if we can."[40] In August 1983 the navy inspected the British carrier *Hermes* with a view toward buying her, but while the cost was reasonable, it would have been prohibitive to add an air group, so the purchase never materialized. Today Chilean naval aviation continues to operate a variety of aircraft, but it has failed to regain the attack aircraft that were once its teeth.

Naval aviation was introduced into the Peruvian navy in 1920. By 1925 the Navy Department ordered each naval academy graduating class to receive flying instruction at the naval aviation school in Ancon. In the mid-1920s the navy toyed with plans to convert the submarine depot ship *Lima* into an aircraft carrier, which called for a landing deck the full length of the ship, a hangar deck, and workshops.[41] The decision not to carry out this proposal was undoubtedly influenced by the unsuitability of a two-thousand-ton, fourteen-knot ship. During its first decade the naval aviation arm extensively explored and mapped the Selva region. At its peak during the late 1920s it consisted of thirty aircraft and about 180 personnel.[42] In 1930, following the worldwide trend, the navy air force and army air arm were fused into a national air force. In the 1960s naval aviation was reinstated throughout South America, due in part to the increasing usefulness of the helicopter. Its introduction into the fleet gave added dimension to the navy's capabilities, particularly in the area of ASW. Perú reestablished her naval air arm in 1963 with some help from Argentine naval aviators, and toward the end of the 1960s the *Chimbote* and the *Paita*, formerly U.S. Navy LSTs, were modified to handle helicopters on their main decks.

In 1975–76 the four units of the Peruvian destroyer force had landing platforms added to their fantails, the work being done at Callao Naval Yard. In 1976 the navy purchased the Dutch cruiser *De Zeven Provincien* and converted her into a helicopter ship. She joined the fleet in 1978. The Peruvian naval air arm does not include attack aircraft.

Cuban naval aviation was established in 1937 with the acquisition of four aircraft. The force acquired a number of support aircraft during World War II but never numbered as many as a dozen planes. It was to have played a role in the failed revolt of 5 September 1957 against Fulgencio Batista y Zaldívar. After Fidel Castro's rise to power in 1959 all aviation elements were consolidated in the air force.[43]

México formally established her naval air arm in 1940 and began a naval aviation school on 24 December 1943, three years before the first operational unit was formed.[44] Mexican naval aviation currently operates about fifty aircraft and has about 350 personnel.

In 1929 Paraguay gained a naval air arm which played an important role in the Chaco War. In 1972 a converted LSM given to Paraguay by Argentina as part of an aid program was outfitted with a helicopter landing pad and two Bell 47 helicopters.

Uruguayan naval aviation was officially established in 1925, but it did not acquire its first three aircraft until 1930 or a permanent air base until 1934. During the late 1940s and 1950s the Uruguayan navy had the second largest naval air arm in Latin America. It included Grumman Avenger torpedo bombers, Hellcat fighters, and Martin Mariner amphibians—a wealth of resources awarded to Uruguay for her strong support of U.S. policies in World War II. Currently her naval aviation has a very modest ASW and search and rescue capability.

Venezuela established a naval air service in 1922 that eventually merged with her air force. Naval aviation was reestablished in the late 1970s. Today it flies support aircraft and helicopters.[45]

Even Bolivia, which does not have a sea coast, possesses a navy with an air arm—two ex-Argentine AT-6 trainers and one Cessna U206G utility aircraft.

The Colombian naval air arm was created in the 1920s and absorbed into the newly created air force in 1943. The Tactical Naval Air Support Group of the air force now provides air support to the navy.

In 1967 the Ecuadorian fleet established an air component when it acquired a Cessna 320E. Since then the navy has acquired additional support aircraft and Alouette III helicopters.

CHAPTER THIRTEEN

Political Intervention During the Era of Marine Corps and Naval Aviation

Since World War II elements of at least seven Latin American navies have used force in attempts to precipitate changes in their respective governments: the Argentine navy in 1945, 1951, 1955, and 1963; the Brazilian in 1955 and 1964; the Chilean in 1973; the Cuban in 1952 and 1957; the Haitian in 1970; the Paraguayan in 1947; and the Venezuelan in 1958 and 1962. Although naval aviation and amphibious forces gave some of these navies added power, these arms could not guarantee victory to the rebels. In fact, only in Argentina did a Latin American navy (aided by only a few army troops) successfully oppose the combined efforts of the air force and the majority of the army; in the confrontation, which occurred in 1955, the marine corps and naval aviation played critical roles in defeating the opposition. In 1947 the Paraguayan navy created an impromptu amphibious force that almost wrestled victory from a numerically superior government force; but an inability to neutralize the air force significantly contributed to the navy's defeat. In the remaining contests, Latin American navies employed old-fashioned gun- and longboat tactics or acted in consort with superior elements of sister services.

Paraguay

In 1947 the Paraguayan navy played an important role in a revolt of elements of the army led by junior officers against the government of Higinio Morinigo. Morinigo had come to power in 1940 when the president, José Felix Estigarribia, was killed in a plane crash. Opposed to Moringo's iron rule, the conspirators rose up on 7 March and were taken prisoner; during the fighting six people were killed and four wounded, including some bystanders. Two days later the Second Infantry Division in Concepción revolted and was joined by other army units, including most of the troops garrisoning the Chaco. On 23 March four rebel aircraft bombed Asunción but caused little damage and no casualties. Apparently the Paraguayan navy protected some fugitive rebels and stole a transmitter from the offices of the Union Oil Company of California in Asunción. The radio was flown to Concepción for rebel use. When the president asked the commander in chief of the navy, Captain Sindulfo Gill, to surrender the conspirators, the latter replied, "You may come look for them." At 1900 on 26 April the navy joined the rebellion.

The next day loyal army units attacked the navy in the Asunción-Sajonia region. After a few hours of fighting the commanding officer of the loyalists, Colonel Federico W. Smith, joined the rebels under the pretext of negotiating an armistice and then chose to go into exile in Argentina. In spite of this modest success the navy and its supporters were badly outnumbered. Some naval personnel fled to Argentina in a steamer, while others, supported by the communist workers at the naval arsenal, fought on. The army overwhelmed the defenders on 29 April. A few days later two government aircraft attacked the steamer *Pratt Gill*, fleeing the country with naval fugitives on board. She was forced to beach near the mouth of the Pilcomayo River, and the fugitives were interned in Argentina. The contest, quiet now in the south, continued in the north. The loyalists needed oil, so on 5 May they dispatched the *Mariscal Estigarribia* with twenty armed sailors to Argentina. The ship returned on the thirteenth with the cargo.

During the early months of fighting, the gunboats *Paraguay* and *Humaitá*, Paraguay's two most formidable ships, lay in Buenos Aires undergoing repair. On 6 May crewmembers of the two ships called a political meeting to air a number of grievances. Some wanted a more democratic government at home, some wished to show support for their rebellious naval comrades, and a few were communists who supported world revolution. The officers, for the most part, remained loyal to the Morinigo government. The rift between officers and crew ended in a fight in which four men were wounded and ten officers arrested. On 7 May part of their crews took over the *Paraguay* and the *Humaitá* and joined the revolution. Two days later the gunboats sailed from Buenos Aires, leaving behind their machine guns, ammunition, and fuses, which had been put ashore when the ships entered dry dock. Some ten officers who remained loyal to the government were also left behind. The two ships sailed up the Paraña River and between 9 May and 5 July anchored in the Guazu Canal, opposite the Uruguayan port of Carmelo. Those on board discovered that most of their rifles were unserviceable and that they had only fifteen hundred pesos with which to pay the ships' expenses. On 1 July, with the help of Captain José A. Bozzano, who was then living in Uruguay, they acquired rifles and ammunition: eight shells for the 4.7-inch main battery, seven machine guns, three heavy and four light, and more than two hundred rifles, some in very bad condition. Not one centavo of money remained, and there was only enough food and fuel for eight to ten days.

At 0745 on 10 July the gunboats, accompanied by three steamers, passed Paso de la Patria and entered Paraguayan waters. Lieutenant Colonel Alfredo Stroessner, commanding loyalist forces in the south, asked the air force to take action. In the ensuing attack at least one bomb hit the *Humaitá* in the fire control center. On the twelfth aerial reconnaissance revealed that one gunboat was beached some three miles above Ituraingo. Four sorties flew that afternoon, and at least one seventy-five-kg bomb scored a hit. Stroessner moved troops and ordnance down river in the steamers *Tirador, Hellen Gunther,* and *Mariscal Estigarribia* and the armed tug *Capitán Cabral*. On 18 July he landed 180 men and five guns on Cerrito Island, where his ordnance fired on the beached gunboat. The rebel ships were also attacked from the air between the fifteenth and the twenty-first of July. On the twenty-fourth and twenty-fifth Stroessner's forces captured the Coratei islands from the rebels.

The rebels were faring poorly in the north as well. On 29 July they decided to evacuate Concepción, their principal stronghold. In twenty-four hours Lieutenant Commander Nestor Martínez Fretes organized a flotilla capable of transporting three thousand men. He armed three ships, ten large river boats, and twenty-four lesser craft with field pieces, heavy and light machine guns, and mortars. All rebel troops were embarked by 1430 on the thirty-first.

The rebels' plan called for Infantry Regiment No. 1 to attack Puerto Milagro at 1300 and then march upon Ybapobó. Meanwhile the flotilla would force passage through La Caida and, while steaming to Ybapobó, sink or capture en route the loyal gunboat *Coronel Martinez* and the armed tug *Neembucu*, lying between La Caida and Puerto Milagro. Overcoming the resistance, the flotilla would then make the best possible speed toward Asunción.

The initial assault went well. Infantry Regiment No. 1 successfully attacked La Caida and the flotilla reached Puerto Milagro on 1 August, dispersing government forces there. After heavy fighting at Puerto Milagro the rebels captured the *Coronel Martinez* and the *Neembucu* as well as two shore-based guns. The flotilla then continued down the Paraguay River and was attacked by loyal aircraft. While passing Ybapobó, the large river boat, carrying many of the rebel provisions, was hit and exploded. Later the flotilla lost much time landing small attachments in villages without military significance.

On 2 August the rebels landed and took Puerto Ybapobó after the garrison there fled. Fire from a river battery hit at least one of the ships. On the third the flotilla joined forces with a rebellious cavalry unit at San Pédro and Rosario but halted its push toward Asunción.

In the south the rebel gunboats *Paraguay* and *Humaitá* tried once again to force passage up the river on 4 August. One of the gunboats received several hits in heavy fighting with Stroessner's guns, whereupon both boats retired. On the same day the rebel flotilla disembarked twenty-seven hundred men at Arecutacua, some thirty-two miles north of Asunción. At first the rebels successfully rolled back the army that opposed them, but soon they were running short of munitions and supplies. A Sikorsky S-44 seaplane belonging to the Uruguayan TAG II Society crashed while attempting to fly munitions from Uruguay to the rebels. The rebellion began to fall apart.

Stroessner's guns beat back the *Paraguay* and the *Humaitá* at Punta Jacquet Island. They retreated down river and asked Argentine authorities at Ita Ibaté for internment on 15 August. In the north government troops captured Cuatro Mojones from the rebels. On the eighteenth the rebels abandoned the thirty-six surviving ships and craft of the flotilla at Puerto Copacar. They were immediately taken over by loyal naval personnel under the command of Captain Pedro Meyer and brought to Asunción on 19 August. The next day the revolution collapsed. Rebellious officers and political leaders fled by plane and boat to Argentina while soldiers and marines surrendered.

No figures have ever emerged as to the number of losses, but it must have been substantial. Much of the fighting was fierce, in particular the bloody boarding of the *Coronel Martinez* and the *Neembucu*. The idea of a riverine assault from Concepción to Asunción was brilliant and well organized but poorly executed, and the force was too easily diverted from its primary goal, the capture of Asunción. Moreover, the loyal air force helped halt the up-river progress of the *Paraguay* and the *Humaitá* and slow down the Concepción river flotilla with air attacks that the rebels had no effective means of opposing.[1]

Cuba

Since the early 1930s, during the regime of Fulgencio Batista, the Cuban navy has actively suppressed armed uprisings. Batista was an opportunist of the first order. He favored those elements of society that held political influence, and as they changed, so did his patronage. In particular, he cultivated the labor movement. His assumption and resumption of power brought purges of the officer corps of all services and a resulting loyalty to the regime—as well as poor leadership and a lack of military professionalism. Twice during Batista's early years naval guns shelled rebel strongholds. In September 1933 the gunboat *Cuba* attempted to bombard the Hotel Nacional in Habana and because of poor marksmanship devastated the surrounding neighborhood. Two months later the gunboats *Patria* and *Cuba* engaged rebels in Ataris Castle and supported the bloody repression of rebel forces.[2]

On 10 March 1952 the Cuban navy helped reinstate Batista as chief executive. Unlike earlier actions, this one turned out to be almost bloodless. The navy's part in the coup d'état was executed by eleven men led by then-retired Commander José Rodriguez Calderón, who entered naval headquarters and took control of the duty room and daily operations. The plan, simple and well executed, met with no opposition and, together with the efforts of Batista supporters in other services, put the former strongman in control of Habana in one hour and seventeen minutes. Eight months later, in December 1952, a group of retired naval officers including the former chief of the navy, Captain José Aguilar Ruiz, was arrested for alleged conspiracy and put under house arrest.[3]

The navy remained politically inactive until the closing days of Batista's reign. In the years immediately preceding Castro's emergence it became increasingly restless and was accordingly harassed by Batista forces. Arrests, investigations, and involuntary retirements "for the good of the service" increased. Among those singled out were many officers who had graduated from the Cuban Naval Academy in the summer of 1952.

The navy struck back by planning a revolt. Lieutenant Miguel Pons Goizueta intended to take the first step. His plan was to get the patrol ship *Baire* under way from Casablanca Naval Yard on 5 September 1957 and open fire on naval headquarters at 0645. The warships *Caribe*, *Siboney*, *José Martí*, and *Antonio Maceo*—equipped with three-inch guns, formidable weapons considering the opposition—were then to join the *Baire*. After a token shelling of the presidential palace, the ships would proceed to Campo Colombia and bombard army headquarters. The plan to this stage relied on the seldom successful tactics of the gun and longboat era, although an attack by the naval air arm was to have accompanied the bombardment. Naval aircraft would fly over Campo Colombia at the time of the attack and, joined by rebellious air force planes, ensure the surrender of this key ground installation.

The plan was postponed when two pro-Batista officers assumed important watch posts, but the conspirators at Cienfuegos did not receive news of the change. On 5 September, as originally scheduled, they revolted. Their local tactical attempt was successful, but due to the lack of external support they failed. The Batista government isolated the dissident elements and eliminated them. The rebellion was crushed and between fifty and one hundred naval officers were arrested, among them officers holding key positions.[4] Despite this purge Batista, for good reasons, never again trusted the sea service, and in 1958 the fleet was constantly engaged in anti-invasion patrols, seeking to halt the flow of supplies to Castro's revolutionary forces.[5] This action had little consequence since Castro's men obtained most of their arms and recruits from within Cuba.

Like most Latin American navies, Batista's fleet was a conservative organization led by officers who came from the middle and upper classes, and it was inevitable that these men would come to odds with Fidel Castro. Following the fall of the Batista regime, naval leadership devolved to the naval academy class of 1952, who for the most part had been dismissed by Batista in 1956 and 1957. In July 1959 Raul Castro, commander in chief of the armed forces, assigned to the navy thirty-six army officers who had been indoctrinated in communist ideology. In September he ordered the marine corps dissolved. Raul, now minister of the revolutionary armed forces, moved into the Navy Department building, along with the chiefs of the army, air force, and police in November. Naval personnel, including ships' crews, were given various construction projects, primarily the improvement of transit facilities, which diluted the cohesiveness of the navy. The Castro government assigned commanding officers additional duties within government bureaus, in particular the Agricultural Reform Institute. This impaired military efficiency and eliminated the navy as a political force.

In July 1960 Fidel Castro dissolved the naval air arm and ordered the chief of the Oriente Naval District at Santiago to Habana, a move that deactivated the station for all practical purposes. Meanwhile the Cuban naval attachés in Caracas, Washington, and México City defected, a turn of events that must have stunned the Castro government, for they had all been supporters of the revolution.

At about 0100 on 16 August a large contingent of troops led by Fidel and Raul encircled the Casablanca Naval Base, across the bay from Habana, forced entry, and assumed control of the facilities and ships at anchor. Only the duty officer in the frigate *Antonio Maceo* refused to obey, so the ship's commanding officer had to be rousted out of bed to set him straight. A few hours later Castro forces assumed control of the southern naval district headquarters at Cienfuegos and took over two hundred naval personnel into custody for questioning. The old gunboat *Cuba*, permitted to continue a midshipman training cruise around the island, was not deactivated until 31 August.

Naval personnel joined cooperative farms and the merchant marine, for all practical purposes reducing the navy's strength by mid-October to about one thousand. But Cuba had a real need for a navy, and the dismemberment of the existing one necessitated the creation of a new one. In a speech of 15 October Premier Castro outlined the future of the seagoing service, saying that it would be reconstituted with reliable personnel. A month later Raul's former aide, Lieutenant Commander Jorge Cainas Sriva, was appointed deputy administrator of the revolutionary armed forces and assigned the task of rearranging the navy.[6]

Brazil

Since World War II elements of the Brazilian navy have actively participated in two attempts to interpret the national political will. In November 1955 General Henrique Lott seized control of the Brazilian government. The primary reason for the coup was to secure the constitutional inauguration of Juscelino Kubitschek, who had recently been elected president. Acting President Carlos Luz and a number of his supporters fled in the recently acquired cruiser *Tamandaré*. Forts in Rio de Janeiro opened fire on her as she put to sea, but when a freighter came into the line of fire the guns ceased. The *Tamandaré* sailed to Santos. Supporters of General Lott seized the forts at Santos and Kubitschek's presidency was assured.[7]

The next time the navy engaged in political activity it brought about a change in the presidency. On 25 March 1964 the Brazilian navy minister, Admiral Sylvio Borges de Souza Motta, ordered the arrest of a seaman who had been organizing a left-wing sailors' association. In protest over one thousand sailors and marines barricaded themselves in the headquarters of the metallurgical workers' union. Rear Admiral Candido de Costa Aragão, commander of the marine corps, joined the mutineers.[8]

President João Goulart, courting the left, dismissed Admiral Motta and chose to replace him with Rear Admiral Paulo Mario da Cunha Rodrigues, who had been among those suggested by the leaders of a communist-influenced labor union. The new minister, given a free hand, immediately granted full amnesty to the mutineers. The naval leadership was outraged. An ad hoc group of admirals denounced the action as an attack on the principles of military discipline and bitterly condemned the president for giving a labor union the privilege of nominating the head of the navy. This was the last in a series of confrontations between the military and the president. On 1 April he fled from Rio de Janeiro and the senate declared the presidency vacant.[9]

Argentina

In Latin America the most significant naval interpretation of a national political will during the era of airplane and amphibian was the action the Argentine navy took against the Juan Perón regime. Perón was an army man whose chief support came from organized labor, which he patronized at the expense of other elements in his country. Four times the navy tried to oust him from power. After the first attempt on 17 October 1945, which failed, the navy suppressed its sentiments to avoid suffering more economic and political reprisals than had already been imposed by Perón. The relationship between the service and the government was manifestly cool at public gatherings. Rarely did a naval official sit in the place of honor next to the president and seldom did Perón receive an enthusiastic reception at a naval-sponsored event.

On 28 September 1951 the navy revolted with a very narrow base of army support—one or two units led by General Benjamín Menéndez. Captain Vicente M. V. Baroja, commandant of the naval air unit at Punta Indio, led a squadron of fourteen fighter planes in a show of strength, to have been supplemented by the rebellious army units. The Peronists, well organized and able to isolate these few dissidents within a day, implemented an emergency law after the outbreak of the revolt that empowered the president to transfer, promote, or retire any armed forces personnel at his discretion. A wholesale reorganization of the navy ensued. The minister of the navy, the undersecretary of the navy, the chief of naval operations, and the director of naval intelligence, along with numerous ranking naval officers, were replaced. And the Prefectura, the Argentine coast guard, was removed from naval control and placed under the minister of the interior.[10]

The navy's third try came on 16 June 1955. The principal backer of the revolt was Commander Antonio H. Rivolta, part of the navy's General Staff. Among others, he had won supporters from the school for noncommissioned officers, the largest naval unit within the city of Buenos Aires. On the evening of 15 September Rivolta informed his colleagues at the school that the revolt would begin at 1000 the next day. The plan called for the seizure of public broadcasting stations and the bombing of the government house by naval aircraft. Those at the school were to commandeer transport and proceed with the troops—the naval students at the school—to the navy building, which was only two blocks from government house. There they were to join forces with Commander Juan C. Argerich of the marine corps, with whom they would move against the government house and take Perón prisoner.

At 0700 on 16 June the conspirators cancelled daily classes at the school, sent civilians home, and called naval personnel to general quarters. Then they proceeded to confiscate local buses passing in front of the complex. The weather was foul and rainy. By 1000 no radio stations had been taken and there was no incidence of bombing. At this point the superintendent of the school reacted. He countermanded the orders given by the conspirators, put them under arrest, and tried to contact the Navy Department. Passersby witnessed all of this activity.

Perón reacted at 1100 with typical bravado: he announced that he was going to the school to investigate but never went. At about noon pandemonium broke loose. Naval aircraft started to bomb the government house in spite of a ceiling of less than one hundred feet. The Fourth Marine Battalion seized the navy building and then moved against the government house. En route they met army troops loyal to Perón and fierce fighting broke out. Perón had already taken refuge in a sub-basement of the army building; from there General Franklin Lucero directed his forces. Within a short time they were reinforced by tanks, which turned the tide against the marines.

Naval aircraft and a few rebel air force planes dominated the air space to little avail. Bad weather lessened their effectiveness, and many of the bombs dropped did not explode because of the limited ceiling. A force of Martin A-26 bombers and Douglas C-47s flew low over the center of Buenos Aires in hopes of intimidating the opposition, but the populace had expected to see a scheduled air show on this day and the demonstration did not produce the desired effect. (The sixteenth of June was the date that the naval aviation arm paid homage to "the Liberator," General José San Martín, the Argentine who had freed the southern half of the continent from Spanish colonial rule.) The logistics detachment at Punta Indio Naval Air Station, some sixty miles from Buenos Aires, found its location untenable as army troops approached, so naval transport aircraft airlifted it to Ezeiza, on the outskirts of Buenos Aires. There the detachment was fueling and arming aircraft within the hour. A wave of naval planes had already landed marines at the airfield, and they captured it without a struggle. The air base at Moron also fell to marine assault, allowing the installation of a service group there. Fifteen minutes after the base changed hands, it began refueling and rearming naval aircraft.[11]

A few retired officers and civilians seized a radio broadcasting station at around 1200 and broadcast a few revolutionary communiqués before being cut off.

The ill-coordinated rebellion collapsed and by 1800 the rebels had surrendered. Many of the sixty-eight officers assigned to the Punta Indio Naval Air Station fled to Uruguay. Photographs of some of them were published in the 18 August issue of *Democracia*, the Peronist party's newspaper, along with the caption, "They Massacred the Defenseless Population and Ran Cowardly to Uruguay."[12] One hundred and six officers were charged with conspiracy, eighty-one from the navy. The Perón-controlled press tried to reassure the populace that "the fleet and naval forces at Puerto Belgrano, Río Santiago, Mar del Plata, and Ushuaia . . . maintained total loyalty to the government." In fact, the fleet had been awaiting the successful completion of the first phase before acting.[13]

The revolt failed principally because of poor coordination. The burden of fighting had fallen on the naval aviation arm and the marine corps, though some support had come from army, air force, and regular navy units. Junior commanders and officers of lower rank had led the revolt, which proved extremely difficult to conduct without the direction of admirals and captains. Many of the senior officers either were pro-Peronist or held positions of little value to the movement. Rear Admiral Toranzo Calderón, chief of staff of the marine corps, was an exception, but he did not take an active part in the revolt. Rear Admiral Benjamín Gargiulo, director of the marines on the Naval Staff, learned of the coup a few hours before the attempt and did nothing to stop it. Rear Admiral Anibal Osvaldo Olivieri, minister of the navy, had been taken to the naval hospital with chest pains on the fifteenth. When the coup started he returned to the navy building to take charge. The three admirals were arrested by army troops, and on the morning of the seventeenth were advised by the commanding officer of the troops occupying the navy building to commit suicide. Admiral Gargiulo did so.

Naval personnel were singled out for punishment. Even though he had not been a conspirator, Admiral Olivieri claimed responsibility for everything done by his subordinates and received eighteen months of minimum-security imprisonment and destitution. (Rear Admiral Isaac F. Rojas, soon to lead the successful overthrow of Juan Perón, was defense counsel for Admiral Oliviero.) Admiral Toranzo Calderón was sentenced to indefinite confinement and public degradation. Many other admirals and captains, although they had had no connection with the event, were retired because Perón lacked confidence in them.[14] And numerous officers of lower rank received punishment.[15] But many others implicated in the action were not indicted, possibly because Perón did not want to reveal the weakness of his military support. In fact, the inquiries brought together the old conspirators and gave them the opportunity to win new ones to their cause. Legal proceedings, which took place at the First Army Headquarters, persuaded many young army officers to defect to the rebel side, and the fate of the accused gave the movement martyrs.

A heavy and predictable price was extracted from the navy. On 19 June the government issued a decree of the executive power, the purpose of which was to eliminate the navy's ability to interpret the national political will. Article 1 removed naval aviation and the marine corps from the Ministry of the Navy, article 2 placed the dispersed units of these two bodies under the authority of various naval zone commanders, and article 3 distributed field service activities to the naval zones. Instructions for the implementation of the new system were listed in article 4. A senate resolution of the same date gave the chief executive power to promote or retire any military officer without complying with established regulations.[16] Additional steps attempted to render the navy impotent. All bomb fuses in naval custody were collected and consigned to Davy Jones's locker, and loyalists confiscated ordnance that had been gathered at Ezeiza Airfield for the revolt. Most naval aircraft were grounded and made inoperable. At the marine corps school, ammunition was closely guarded and issued sparingly, and manpower was slashed in half, to twenty-five hundred men.[17] The school was later abolished.

Thus the Perón scalpel cut deeply into the navy following the ill-fated revolt. But as we have seen, some conspirators went unpunished, and several powerful officers kept their positions. Rear Admiral Isaac F. Rojas, director of the naval academy, emerged as the chief of the anti-Perón naval forces, which, with the additional leadership of Captain Arturo H. Rial, Captain Mario Robbio Pacheco, Commander Jorge Julio Alejandro Palma, and Commander Alberto Sánchez Sañudo, forged a plan to rearm. Trusted junior officers were charged with the replacement of necessary hardware and munitions by whatever means necessary—stealing, bribery, or manufacture. Ingenuity was the order of the day. Ordnance experts provided drawings for fuses and disseminated them to the various machine shops at Puerto Belgrano Naval Base for manufacture. The dental laboratory, manned after regular work hours by junior officers and their wives, was used to work over the small pieces with dental drills and to assemble the fuses one by one. By 16 September they had reached a capacity of five hundred fuses a day. Bombs were rigged from torpedo warheads and depth charges, and naval air strength was reinforced. The rebels obtained ten air force Gloster Meteor jets and three Avro Lincoln bombers at Córdoba Air Force Base, forty naval AT-6 trainers at Comandante Espora Naval Air Base, and ten miscellaneous aircraft at El Plumerillo Air Force Base.

The fourth attempt to remove Perón began on 16 September 1955 with a broad base of support from the navy and its high-ranking leadership. On the eighth of September the Argentine navy's major fleet element, the High Seas Fleet, had sailed for its yearly exercises. On the fifteenth, five senior captains presented themselves to the fleet with fictitious orders, allegedly from Secretary of the Navy Luis J. Cornes. Agustin P. Lariño assumed the position of commander in chief of the fleet; Carlos M. Bruzzone took command of the cruiser *17 de Octubre;* Bernardo F. Benesch took command of the cruiser *9 de Julio;* Luis Mallea took command of the destroyers; and Mario Robbio assumed the position of chief of staff. Ostensibly they were replacing officers of questionable loyalty, but after securing command, the new arrivals informed Vice Admiral Juan B. Basso, commander in chief, and Rear Admiral Nestor P. Gabrielli, commander of cruisers, that a revolution was imminent and gave them fifteen minutes to state their position. Both declared their loyalty to Perón and were placed under arrest. Other key Perón supporters arrested were Vice Admiral Ignacio C. Chamorro, the commander of the maritime zone, and Rear Admiral Hector W. Fidanza, the commandant of Puerto Belgrano. The ships' crews, when mustered and given the same choice, overwhelmingly gave their support to the revolution. The same plan was executed at Puerto Belgrano Naval Base and Comandante Espora Air Station. Of approximately four thousand naval personnel asked to join the revolution, only ninety-three refused to cooperate.[18] By the close of the fifteenth the rebels controlled key sea- and shore-based elements.

Meanwhile, at the naval academy, third- and fourth-year cadets were assigned to the destroyers *Cervantes* and *La Rioja* to complete their complements and get them ready for sea. The remainder of the cadets prepared to defend the academy. They were armed with rifles and supported by the forty-mm guns from the small frigates *King* and *Murature*. The *King*'s turbines were being repaired, so she could not get under way.

At midnight on 16 September Admiral Rojas announced the revolt. Army General Eduardo Lonardi joined the cause. At 0800 the destroyers *Cervantes* and *La Rioja* sailed from Rio Santiago with orders to blockade accesses to the ports of La Plata, Buenos Aires, and the interior rivers. At about 1000 air force Gloster Meteor aircraft loyal to Perón attacked the destroyers, which sustained numerous casualties. At about midday their commanding officers requested permission to retire to the mouth of the river owing to insufficient antiaircraft protection. The *Cervantes* offloaded her dead and wounded at Montevideo and was interned. Sister ship *La Rioja* avoided the same fate by transferring her casualties to tugs.

At 2100 Admiral Rojas and most of his supporters embarked on the *B.D. I* and *II*, two personnel landing craft. Knowing that the school would be occupied by the Second Division, the admiral left a note for its commanding officer on his desk.

> General [Heraclio] Ferrazzano, you will assuredly be in charge of the naval academy and base. Remember that both establishments are the property of the Argentine nation and that there ought not to be a repeat of the shamefulness that occurred on 16 June when army forces occupied the navy building as if it were war bounty.[19]

The admiral transferred to the *Murature* at about midnight. The next day, the seventeenth, he declared a blockade of Rio de la Plata and its tributaries but stopped short of declaring a total blockade. He was aware that, as yet, he did not have the ships to enforce it.[20] The cruisers *17 de Octubre*

Argentine Theater of Naval Operations, 1955

and *La Argentina* joined the admiral's forces near the Pontón lighthouse at midday on Sunday the eighteenth, whereupon he declared a total blockade.

The *9 de Julio* was the only commissioned major unit not with the High Seas Fleet when it was taken over. At the time repairs to her turbines were being made at Puerto Belgrano Naval Base. Her crew, when they heard news of the revolt, worked around the clock to prepare her for sea. Forty-eight hours after the fleet had been commandeered she sailed to join her sister units off Río de la Plata.

The quick action the crew of the *9 de Julio* took indicates the degree of solidarity within the navy. Even the naval attaché to Washington, Vice Admiral Jorge P. Ibarborde, acted on instructions from the rebels when he requested that the United States recognize a state of belligerency. The United States did not comply.[21]

On the eighteenth Admiral Rojas received a message from General Lonardi saying that his position in Córdoba was precarious and requesting a show of force to secure it. At the same time the admiral learned that elements of a Peronist armored column were proceeding from the center of Buenos Aires province to attack Puerto Belgrano Naval Base. In order to refuel, the column had to pass through Mar del Plata. If it successfully captured the naval base, the fleet would be without an adequate base of operations and the principal naval air base nearby, Comandante Espora, would be lost. The admiral ordered naval aircraft to attack the column, which was brought to a halt. Next he ordered the cruiser *9 de Julio* to destroy the tank farm at Mar del Plata with naval gunfire. This would keep the armored column from getting fuel and serve as a show of strength to take pressure off General Lonardi.

In the meantime an intensive propaganda war was being waged between the opposing forces. Over radio the rebels wanted to convince the populace that the entire navy had revolted and that it had the support of substantial elements of the army and air force. The rebels also used the radio to direct efforts to keep workers off the streets. Appeals to pray for freedom, liberty, and justice alternated with hymns. On Saturday evening, 17 September, the rebel radio said the Fifth Regiment in Bahia Blanca had surrendered and troops in Mendoza and San Luis defected. The navy announced the blockade, adding that any attempt to leave or enter would be considered an attempt to run it and dealt with accordingly. Juan Perón was ordered to resign by 0600 Sunday, a deadline later postponed to noon; failure to comply would result in the bombardment of Buenos Aires. The radio described in full detail the capabilities of the fleet's guns. They were, in fact, substantial: the ordnance of the cruisers *17 de Octubre*, *9 de Julio*, and *La Argentina* could have devastated Buenos Aires.

The government radio declared Buenos Aires an open city and requested that no bombardment be made. This implicit admission that the rebels could actually execute their threat contrasted with the boastful broadcasts the government had made earlier, declaring that only a small portion of the fleet was discontent and that the air force could defend the city. Weather conditions, which had helped foil the navy's third attempt to oust Perón, now worked against the air force. There was a thousand-foot ceiling and one mile or less visibility.

Sunday the eighteenth was quiet. Monday morning at 0700 the cruiser *9 de Julio*, commanded by Commander Alberto de Marotte and escorted by two destroyers, bombarded the oil storage tanks near the submarine base at Mar del Plata, which the navy had been forced to evacuate earlier.[22] The first salvo fell near the tank farm and the second hit the target.

Three frigates then landed a force of about 350 marines and naval personnel that captured Mar del Plata after meeting only light resistance. The three major warships shifted fire to the antiaircraft school, which surrendered and joined the revolt after only a few rounds had been fired. Various ground forces coming under fire either surrendered or retreated. The ease with which the attack was accomplished lent credence to the navy's statement that it could bombard Buenos Aires at will.[23]

Juan Perón renounced the presidency of Argentina on the morning of 19 September. Possibly contributing to his downfall was a lack of confidence following the death of his wife Evita. In a communiqué issued at 1300 General Franklin Lucero, the minister of defense, announced the resignation and stated that the government was in the hands of a military junta. Immediately afterwards Admiral Rojas received a dispatch inviting the revolutionary chiefs to Buenos Aires to negotiate. The admiral immediately responded: "Your invitation to travel to Buenos Aires is an imposition; the meeting will take place on board the flagship of the operational fleet, the cruiser *17 de Octubre*, Tuesday the twentieth, at 1700 hours. I will be anchored in La Plata. . . ."[24] The admiral gave the military junta a few hours to respond favorably, which they did.

The junta delegates arrived at the appointed hour and after an all-night session tentatively agreed to the terms of Act No. 1:

1. The President, Vice President, and all the cabinet will resign.
2. The Chief of the Revolution, Division General Eduardo A. Lonardi, will head a provisional government, Thursday, 22 September, at 1200.
3. All necessary steps will be taken immediately to implement conditions 1 and 2.
4. All military units will be ordered immediately to return to their normal peacetime duties and status with the exception of those

assigned to the Capital which will be evacuated before 1200 on the 22nd.
5. All military aircraft will be ordered immediately to fly to the Comandante Espora Naval Air Base and will remain at the orders of the Revolutionary Government.[25]

According to the members of the junta delegation, they were not empowered to accept the terms but had to report back to Buenos Aires. They departed.

At 0800 on 21 September Admiral Rojas received a dispatch from the head of the junta asking whether he would allow one or two tankers to enter Buenos Aires because the city was running out of oil.[26] This request proved to Rojas the effectiveness of his blockade, and he responded, "When you accept the terms of Act No. 1 signed yesterday the blockade will be lifted and all the necessary ships may enter."[27] At 0930 the admiral received a dispatch accepting the terms.

Perón, either informed of the terms or fearful of his fate, fled to the Paraguayan embassy and thence to the gunboat *Paraguay*. On 2 October he flew to Asunción.[28] The navy had won. To symbolize the victory it renamed the *17 de Octubre* the *General Belgrano*. The name *17 de Octubre* had commemorated Perón's coming to power.[29]

On 23 September General Eduardo Lonardi was sworn in as provisional president, Rear Admiral Isaac F. Rojas as provisional vice president.[30] A few days later the president publicly greeted Rear Admirals Olivieri and Toranzo Calderón, who had been imprisoned in the penitentiary for common criminals at Santa Rosa following the 16 June coup attempt. Olivieri was appointed a delegate to the UN, and Calderón became ambassador to Spain. The naval air arm and the marine corps were returned to their former strengths. In Buenos Aires the school for noncommissioned officers, which had been closed for its part in the revolt of 16 June, was reinstated at its former site.[31]

The success of the Argentine navy in 1955 must be ranked with that of the Chilean navy in 1891. In each case a fleet provided the might to uproot those holding the reins of power. During the course of events in Argentina the navy graduated from the era of gun and longboat to that of aircraft and amphibian. Naval aviation and the marine corps dominated the third attempt to remove Perón. In his successful coup Admiral Rojas combined these two elements with the firepower of the fleet's guns.

Venezuela

The Venezuelan navy has also played an important role in interpreting the national political will. Prior to the mid-1950s it was nothing more than a modest coastal force, but the post–World War II prosperity of the country

218 POLITICAL INTERVENTION

and dictator Marcos Pérez Jiménez's courtship of the military increased its strength to an unprecedented level. In 1950 Vickers-Armstrong of Barrow-in-Furness, England, contracted for three destroyers of the *Nueva Esparta* class. Several years later three frigates of the *Almirante Clemente* class were ordered from the Italian firm of Ansaldo. An additional three units of this class were ordered in 1954. Unlike Venezuela's acquisitions in previous decades, the ships were by world standards thoroughly modern, first-class units, not a major power's discards. They gave Venezuela more power than she had ever had. Still, in spite of its significant increase in size during the 1950s, the navy took back seat to the army and abstained from political activity.[32]

Pérez Jiménez had come to power in 1950 as the head of a military triumvirate. He ruled for eight years by generously patronizing the military with the revenues provided by Venezuela's blossoming petroleum industry. Toward the end of the decade a grass roots reaction against his authoritarian rule developed. In October 1957 a group called the Civilian-Military Committee was created from the Patriotic Junta—composed of businessmen, intellectuals, students, priests, and journalists—and the young officers assigned to the military and the armed forces academies.[33] Two naval officers belonged to the movement, Lieutenant (j.g.) Tulio Márquez Planas and Ensign Andrés Brito Martínez.[34]

On 15 December 1957, election day, Pérez Jiménez declared that he had won another five-year term. On the last day of the year he was informed that an army officer by the name of Hugo was heading a conspiracy. Assuming that his source was referring to the commander in chief of the army, Brigade General Hugo Fuentes, Pérez Jiménez ordered his arrest. In fact, the head of the conspiracy was army Lieutenant Colonel Hugo Trejo, who had no association with the general at all.[35]

At five minutes past midnight on New Year's Day air force and army units stationed around Maracay, 120 kilometers west of Caracas, staged a revolt headed by mid-level officers.[36] The rebels captured the area in their vicinity. Rebel air force Major Edgar Suárez Mier y Terán, commander of Fighter Squadron 35, overflew Caracas in a Vampire jet fighter to assure those rebels below that the revolt in Maracay had succeeded. An hour and a half later rebel planes began reconnaissance flights over the capital and were met by antiaircraft fire. At 1305 rebel Vampire, Venom, and Sabre jets attacked Miraflores Palace, where the president had his office, the defense ministry, and other military targets in the Caracas area. Although the attacks continued throughout the day, they produced no results.[37]

In late afternoon navy Captain Ricardo Sosa Ríos, director of the naval education center at Catia La Mar and chief of La Guaira Zone Joint Garrison, called a meeting of his senior and some junior officers to analyze the situation.[38] They decided to support the rebellion and ordered the war-

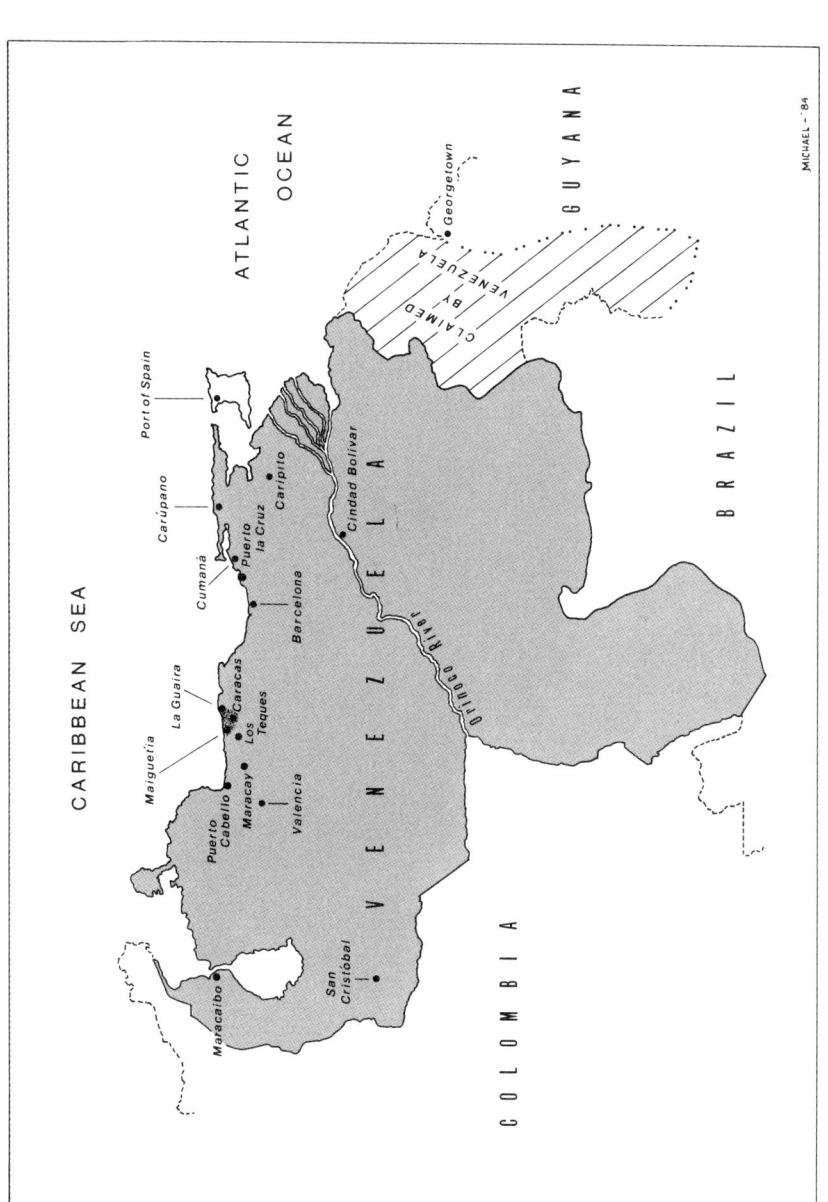

Venezuelan Theater of Naval Operations, 1958

ships anchored near La Guaira to put to sea without the normal authorization from Caracas.[39]

In the meantime the government organized four powerful columns to recapture Maracay and its vicinity. Three columns consisted of loyal army troops, and the fourth, which would come from the north, were marines. The naval tug *Felipe Larrazabal* transported a company of marine Battalion No. 2, commanded by Lieutenant Victor Hugo Morales Monasterios, from Puerto Cabello to Turiamo Auxiliary Naval Base.[40] A company from marine Battalion No. 1, commanded by Lieutenant Commander Oscar Paredes López, was carried from La Guaira to Turiamo in the transport *Dos de Diciembre*.

On 1 January 1958 army lieutenant Colonel Hugo Trejo—the officer who had been confused with the commander in chief of the army on 31 December—declared for the rebellion at the Urdaneta barracks west of Caracas, winning over Armored Battalion No. 8 and Artillery Group No. 1.[41] In early evening of the same day Trejo led his force, bringing ten M-18 tanks and two 155 field pieces, against Miraflores Palace, where Pérez Jiménez was conferring with his supporters. While the forces defending the palace prepared to resist the attack, the president, a former artillery officer, expressed pessimism concerning the possibility of stopping the rebels.[42]

To the surprise of the palace defenders Trejo stopped his advance and turned toward the city of Los Teques, which lay in the mountains some thirty kilometers from Caracas and eighty kilometers from the rebel stronghold at Maracay. Evidently he believed there were not enough munitions to carry out the attack.[43] Instead his column captured Los Teques late in the evening of 1 January. The only military objective there was the national guard troops school.[44]

At about this time, late on 1 January and early the following day, government forces reached Maracay. The rebel forces dispersed, their leaders escaping to Colombia in an air force C-54. Sosa Ríos, informed of the surrender, ordered the naval ships that had sailed from La Guaira to return. The commander in chief of the navy, Captain Oscar Ghersi Gómez, asked why the ships had sailed from La Guaira without his authorization, to which Sosa Ríos responded that with an air force rebellion it was wise to disperse the ships. Captain Ghersi accepted this and did not inquire further.[45]

The rebellion collapsed, and in early January the government arrested numerous military, political, religious, and media personalities. However, neither the air force–led Maracay rebellion nor the one led by Lieutenant Colonel Trejo had had any contact with the Civilian-Military Committee, so most of its members escaped the arrests and continued to work for the downfall of Pérez Jiménez.

On 9 January the government ordered the arrest of numerous naval officers. It learned that a series of meetings had taken place in naval facilities, and that on 8 January there was an unauthorized fleet departure from La Guaira. In addition, by order of the chief of the General Staff, army brigade General Rómulo Fernández, ammunition was removed from the ships off La Guaira and deposited in the arsenal, under the direct control of the minister of defense.[46]

The next day the Civil-Military Committee contacted marine Ensign Haroldo Rodríguez Figueroa of marine Battalion No. 1 and won him over to the cause.[47]

During these tumultuous days Pérez Jiménez assumed direct control of the Defense Ministry and made various changes in key civil as well as military positions. Captain Oscar Ghersi Gómez, commander in chief of the navy, was made governor of Caracas, though in a few days he was replaced by Lieutenant Colonel Guillermo Pacanins of the Venezuelan air force. Rear Admiral Wolfgang Larrazábal became the new navy head on 16 January. Rear Admiral Carlos Larrazábal, Wolfgang's brother, was named the minister of industry and commerce, thus becoming a member of the emergency cabinet organized by Pérez Jiménez.[48]

On 14 January the Civil-Military Committee learned of a navy plan to rebel the following day under the leadership of Captain Miguel Rodríguez Olivares.[49] Air Force Lieutenant José Luis Fernández immediately contacted Commander José Vicente Azopardo, one of the dissidents, and the naval officers agreed to join forces with the civil-military movement.[50]

Two days later Captain Rodríguez Olivares asked Wolfgang Larrazábal to join the plot, which he did.[51] On 20 January the principal members of the Civilian-Military Committee met, and Commander Azopardo and Commander Carbonell Izquierdo proposed that Larrazábal be selected to head the ruling junta after the deposition of Pérez Jiménez.[52] This met with approval.[53]

Throughout the crisis the United States expressed concern for the stability of the Pérez Jiménez government, to which she had given substantial military aid. The destroyer *Allen M. Sumner* was dispatched to Venezuelan waters to watch over national interests. U.S. companies had invested heavily in the Venezuelan petroleum industry, and an estimated forty thousand U.S. citizens resided there, most of them oil industry workers and their families.

The Patriotic Junta proclaimed a general strike at 1200 on 21 January. Strikers and police clashed; people were killed and property destroyed. At 1800 the government imposed a curfew. For various reasons Captain Italo Brett Smith of the national guard failed to instigate a planned uprising at the various military schools. Civil disturbances continued the following day, ending in more street fighting and additional deaths.

According to plan, at 1600 on 22 January the frigate *General José de Austria* and marine Battalion No. 2 rebelled at Puerto Cabello Naval Base. The marines took over the base and the munitions in the arsenal. These were immediately conveyed to La Guaira, where the destroyer *Nueva Esparta* and the frigates *Almirante Brión* and *Almirante García* awaited them.[54] The transport *Dos de Diciembre*, also at La Guaira, joined the rebellion.[55]

Meanwhile, the destroyers *Aragua* and *Zulia* were steaming toward Puerto Cabello to find munitions.[56] After Pérez Jiménez ordered the air force to attack, aircraft intercepted the warships at sea but did not fire on them. At Puerto Cabello the destroyers received the munitions along with marine Battalion No. 1 and transported them to the vicinity of La Guaira. The marines waited to march on Caracas and unite there with national guard troops. This force would then reinforce the rebels at the military and armed forces academies.[57]

At 2200 Colonel Pedro J. Quevedo, director of the military academy, informed Pérez Jiménez that subversives had infiltrated the school system, whereupon the president threatened to attack with army Infantry Battalion No. 3. During the night he gave orders to Rear Admiral Larrazábal, who rather than comply presented the dictator with an ultimatum to resign. Pérez Jiménez now realized that it was impossible to suppress the insurrection. His naval aide negotiated his surrender through Commander José Vicente Azopardo, a member of the Civilian-Military Committee, and he was guaranteed safe passage from the country.[58] On 23 January the president boarded an air force C-54 with his family and flew to the Dominican Republic, where Generalísimo Rafael Leonidas Trujillo received him.[59]

On 23 January Rear Admiral Larrazábal met with the Civilian-Military Committee at the military academy and they formed a provisional government. Eventually a civilian-military junta was organized with Larrazábal at its head. The influence and prestige the navy had gained during recent events resulted in the award to naval personnel of important positions, including chief of aides-de-camp to the president and prefect of Petare, a suburb of Caracas. For the first time in Venezuelan history the presidential guard was composed of sailors.

The new junta promised a rapid return to popular rule, holding elections in December 1958. Larrazábal ran as the Democratic Republican Union and Communist Party candidate and won a substantial majority of the Caracas vote. However, the rural electorate gave victory to Rómulo Betancourt of the Social Democratic Party. The reins of government passed to the newly elected president without incident.[60]

The Venezuelan navy played an important military and political role in the removal of Pérez Jiménez. Militarily, its actions on 22 January were much more united than those of the other services, which undoubtedly gave confidence to those supporting the revolt in the army, air force, and national guard. The participation of the Venezuelan marine corps proved to be critical. Politically, the navy contributed to the junta an individual who did not threaten to become a military strongman like Pérez Jiménez, for as a naval officer he would have to rule by compromise, in absence of the military base to do otherwise. Rear Admiral Larrazábal led his nation at a most difficult time and helped to create a democracy that has endured for almost thirty years.

The democratic government that assumed power in Venezuela when Rómulo Betancourt became president on 13 February 1959 soon faced threats from political forces on both the extreme right and the extreme left. Some in the military wished to return to the privileged positions they had held under Pérez Jiménez and previous dictators. Some on the extreme left wished to gain power by emulating Fidel Castro in Cuba.

Between April 1960 and June 1961 four major political events occurred in which military personnel were implicated. On 19 April 1960 air force Brigadier General Jesús M. Castro León, former minister of defense, revolted and subverted the army garrison at San Cristóbal in the Andes. Without the hoped-for support of air force, army, and national guard units, however, his movement failed. The following day army troops supported by the national guard and air force Canberra bombers overpowered the rebels.

In May 1960 the majority of youth under the leadership of Domingo Alberto Rangel abandoned the Democratic Action Party and founded the Leftist Revolutionary Movement, of Marxist orientation. Rangel, waging "popular war," was responsible for incidents of urban terrorism and rural guerilla warfare that plagued Venezuela throughout the 1970s.

On 24 July 1960, as President Betancourt was motoring to a ceremony honoring the Venezuelan army, dynamite planted in a parked car exploded, wounding him and killing his chief of aides-de-camp. A Venezuelan investigation concluded that Rafael Leonídas Trujillo, president of the Dominican Republic, was behind the conspiracy. Among Venezuelans implicated in it was a naval officer, Captain Eduardo Morales Luengo, who was tried and sentenced. Venezuela placed her military on alert, denounced Trujillo, and asked the OAS to apply sanctions against the Dominican Republic. Eventually the OAS adopted some mild measures against the Trujillo regime.

On 26 June 1961 a group of officers from the army and national guard, supported by civilians, tried to capture the army garrison at Barcelona. A few hours and many deaths later forces loyal to the government suppressed the insurrection.

In 1962 three major rebellions against the Betancourt government occurred in which the navy, in particular the marine corps, played central roles and received active support from members of political parties from the extreme left. In the first incident, on 28 January 1962, hundreds of youths—many of them students of Central University—rampaged through the streets of La Guaira, ostensibly in support of a transportation strike. They confronted the barracks of marine corps Battalion No. 1 in hopes of arming themselves for an uprising. The action had been instigated by the Communist Party of Venezuela, which may have wanted a massacre to create an instant array of martyrs. The leader of the battalion, Lieutenant Commander Victor Hugo Morales Monasterios, exercised restraint and called the police, who detained more than two hundred youths. Two ensigns assigned to the battalion were implicated in the subversive action, but Morales Monasterios and later the commander of the navy, Vice Admiral Carlos Larrazábal, defended their activities.[61]

On 9 February President Betancourt summoned Rear Admiral Sosa Ríos, who had recently taken over command of the navy from Vice Admiral Larrazábal, to an urgent meeting at the Palacio de Miraflores with the minister of defense and the director of the armed forces intelligence service. The admiral was informed of a plot against the government instigated by the Communist Party and the Leftist Revolutionary Movement. Among the alleged conspirators was Morales Monasterios, as well as the commander of army Armored Battalion No. 8 in Caracas and the commander of national guard Detachment No. 99 in Maiquetía. President Betancourt ordered Sosa Ríos to replace Morales Monasterios immediately as commanding officer of the marine battalion. To expedite the order Sosa Ríos accompanied Commander Gómez Muñoz to the seat of marine corps Battalion No. 1 at Maiquetía, some fifteen miles north of Caracas. There the battalion was assembled and the command changed, after which the admiral returned to Caracas with Morales Monasterios in custody. With the other military services also replacing accused conspirators, this subversive movement, known as El Guairazo, failed. Left within the navy, however, and especially the marine corps, were those who did not support the new reign. Their continued efforts to conspire eventually came to a head in May.[62]

At 0500 on 4 May marine corps Infantry Battalion No. 3, stationed in the coastal city of Carúpano, some 367 miles east of Caracas, revolted. Lieutenant Commander Jesús Teodoro Molina Villegas, commanding officer of the battalion, was supported by the majority of his officers, a group of citizens, some army and national guard officers, and prominent members of the Communist Party and Leftist Revolutionary Movement.[63] After forming a revolutionary militia they discussed the possibility of advancing against the national guard in Caripito but decided against it because of a shortage of men, munitions, and transport.[64]

Within half an hour of the commencement of the revolt President Betancourt placed the armed services on alert. Admiral Sosa Ríos ordered the frigate *General Morán* to patrol off Carúpano and instructed Captain José C. Seijas Villalobos to establish a naval command post at Cumaná, a port about eighty-seven miles west of Carúpano.⁶⁵ At 0600 air force Canberras attacked rebel positions in Carúpano. The navy began laying plans for an amphibious assault in support of government forces that were to advance upon the city. Immediately available in Cumaná were the destroyer *Nueva Esparta*, the medium landing ships *Los Monjes* and *Los Roques*, plus marine corps Battalion No. 2. The minister of defense organized a three-thousand-man force made up of army, national guard, and marine corps personnel. Army Colonel Francisco J. Sánchez Olivares was made operational commander. Sosa Ríos petitioned the president and the operational commander to allow marine corps personnel in the land force so they would be in a position to accept the surrender of their rebellious colleagues and arrest those responsible. The request being granted, Company A of marine corps Battalion No. 1 joined the land force, and the naval task force under Seijas Villalobos became subordinate to Sánchez Olivares.⁶⁶

On 5 May, one day after the revolt, four motorized columns advanced on Carúpano. Meanwhile, constant harassment by air force aircraft forced Molina Villegas to transfer the seat of rebel command away from the marine barracks. At 1600 Company A of marine corps Battalion No. 1 was airlifted from Maiquetía to Cumaná by air force Fairchild C-123Bs and Douglas C-47s. The company joined the motorized column that was approaching Carúpano from the west.⁶⁷

At dawn the next day government and rebel forces clashed as the former approached Carúpano. Rebel mines planted along roads into the city did little to deter the advancing columns. At 1130 a company from Battalion No. 2, the last element of the amphibious task force, was airlifted from Puerto Cabello to Cumaná.⁶⁸ Throughout the day army field pieces and the battery of the *General Morán* joined air force aircraft in attacks against rebel positions.

Under cover of mortar fire the government column approached the Carúpano airport from the west. It was defended by thirty men under Lieutenant Octavio Acosta Bello. During the fighting a warrant officer in charge of a fifty-caliber machine-gun post retired from his rearguard position and informed Molina Villegas that he was not going to continue fighting because marines from Battalion No. 1 were leading the government's advance and he did not wish to kill fellow marines. Molina Villegas then ordered Acosta Bello to remain in front of the airport and make every shot count. After a token demonstration of force the rebels retired from the airport and government forces occupied the position. At this point Molina

226 POLITICAL INTERVENTION

Villegas began negotiations with Colonel Sánchez Olivares to surrender. On 6 May the rebel forces capitulated, and, as previously arranged, the loyal marines from Battalion No. 1 occupied the barracks of rebellious Battalion No. 3. Within forty-eight hours government forces had eliminated remaining pockets of resistance.

The third and most serious revolt led by the marines, known as El Porteñazo, occurred a month later.[69]

At 1500 on 1 June Sosa Ríos called Captain Jesús Carbonell Izquierdo, commander of the fleet, to headquarters in Caracas and informed him that marine corps and national guard units at La Guaira, Maiquetía, and Puerto Cabello might rebel.[70] Sosa Ríos ordered him to Puerto Cabello, the fleet's home port, to maintain the loyalty and readiness of his warships. That afternoon Carbonell Izquierdo, accompanied by the executive officer of marine corps Battalion No. 2, returned by air to Puerto Cabello. There military and civilian authorities met them, and a discussion of the possibility of a rebellion ensued.[71] Upon arrival at the naval base, Carbonell Izquierdo called together the commander of Puerto Cabello Naval Base and Captain Andrés Oswaldo Moreno Piña, commander of Destroyer Division No. 1, to inform them of his conversation with Sosa Ríos. As a result the warship at Puerto Cabello and the destroyer *Aragua*, then at La Guaira, were placed on alert. These ships were about the only units then operational.[72]

At 1850 Admiral Sosa Ríos ordered all naval personnel to their quarters and less than two hours later ordered the *Aragua* and the ships at Puerto Cabello to prepare themselves against air attack. Late that night Carbonell Izquierdo and Moreno Piña, inspecting the naval base and the marine barracks, found nothing out of the ordinary. Just before midnight Carbonell Izquierdo met with senior naval commanders and told them that he expected a rebellion at 0400 the next day, 2 June.[73]

At 0015 on the second Carbonell Izquierdo informed the naval command in Caracas that all was normal. At 0430 he and senior officials decided once again to tour the facility to see firsthand that nothing was irregular. At the same time a group of middle-grade officers and warrant officers numbering about a thousand subverted marine corps Battalion No. 2 and arrested those officers who would not join the rebellion, including the commanding and executive officers of the battalion. Members of the naval security police swelled the rebel ranks to about fifteen hundred.[74] They began attacks on the naval base and the adjacent military establishments, seizing Castle Liberator, which guarded the entrance to the port, and Fort Solano, located on a hill that overlooked the town. At 0540 the leaders of the rebellion—Captain Manuel Ponte Rodríguez, the commander; Commander Pedro Medina Silva, the chief of naval operations;

and Lieutenant Commander Victor Hugo Morales Monasterios, the chief of land operations—clandestinely entered the naval base.[75]

At 0615 the head of national guard Detachment No. 55 notified his command in Caracas that a rebellion had taken place at Puerto Cabello. Carbonell Izquierdo, asleep in the admiral's residence, was awakened by an escort of men, some naval police, armed with submachine guns. They arrested him in the name of a nationalist movement to correct social injustice. The other senior officers were arrested and escorted to the officers' quarters. Taking advantage of the confusion, Lieutenant (j.g.) Justo Pastor Fernández Márquez hid in a closet to avoid arrest, a fact that would later assist government forces recapturing the base.[76]

The rebel command began organizing its forces to capture Puerto Cabello and adjacent strategic sites such as the airport, railroad station, and radio station. Morales Monasterios freed a group of Marxist guerrillas being held by the government in Castle Liberator, who, along with militants from the Communist Party and the Leftist Revolutionary Movement, helped rebellious marines, naval security police, and sailors take the city.

At 0700 Lieutenant Colonel Juan Ramón Zerpa Tovar, commander of army Infantry Battalion No. 41 quartered in Valencia some thirty-five miles from Puerto Cabello, sent an advanced patrol supported by an M-8 armored car to reconnoiter the rebels. At the same time the air force began reconnaissance flights. At 0720 Zerpa Tovar started from Valencia with the main body of his battalion to attack the rebels.[77]

Back in Caracas the government of President Betancourt, seeing the magnitude of the insurrection, ordered a full military alert. The minister of defense appointed Colonel Alfredo Mönch Siegert, commander of the Fourth Army Division, to be chief of the Puerto Cabello operational theater and gave him a force of three thousand men drawn from diverse army, air force, and national guard units.[78] Betancourt rejected a plan of operation, presented by the armed forces chief of joint staff, which called for a seige of the city. The president ordered an immediate attack on the rebels, a decision to which the minister of defense agreed.[79]

The rebels took the center of Puerto Cabello in the morning (2 June) and overpowered the civilian police. But when the attacking force arrived at the airport it discovered that the advanced elements of army Battalion No. 41 were already there. In the meantime Zerpa Tovar, advancing along the highway with the main body of the battalion, established an advanced post in the railway station. There and at the airport rebel and government forces clashed, resulting in the death of a marine. Commander Medina Silva, after broadcasting a revolutionary proclamation over the city's captured radio station, ordered the rebellious forces to fall back from the air-

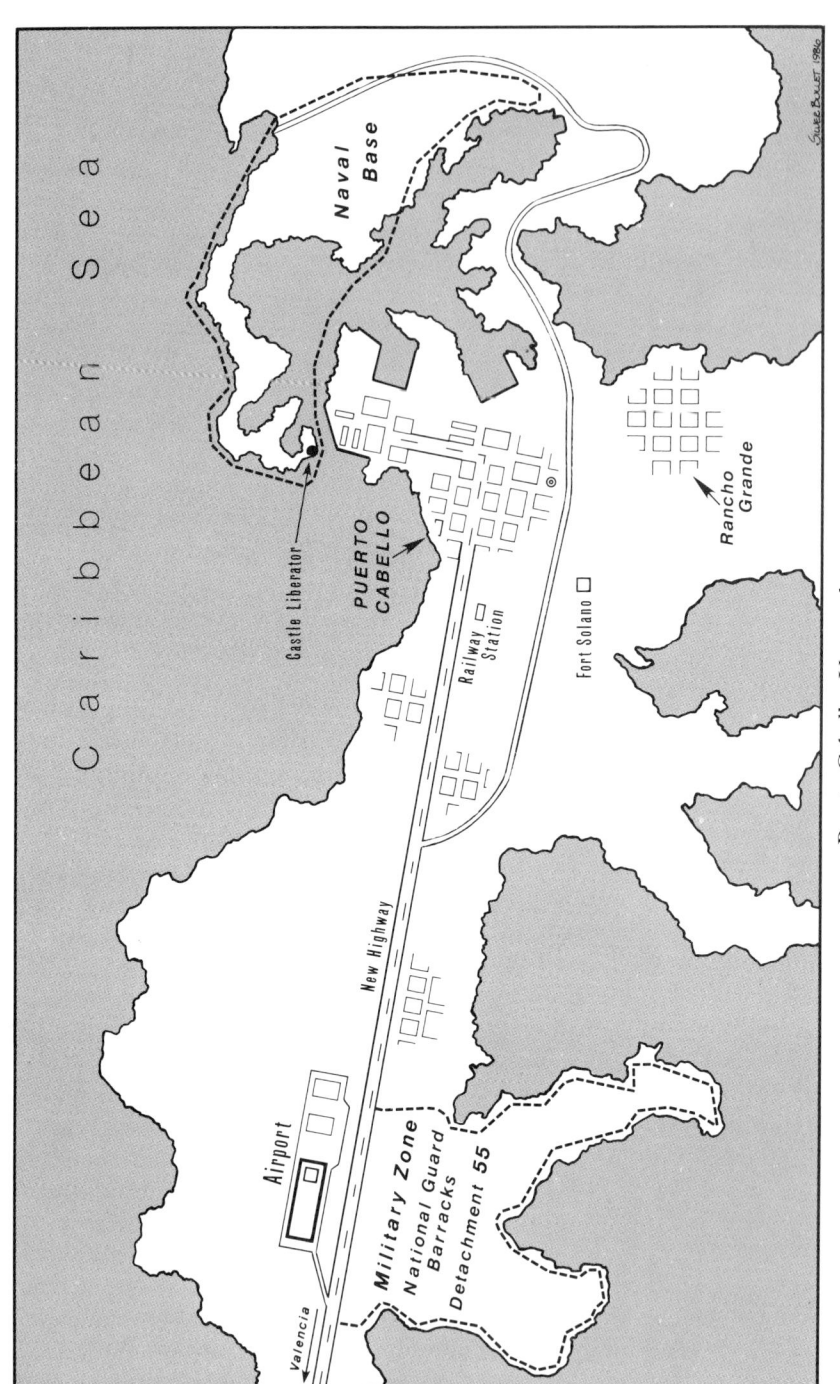

Puerto Cabello, Venezuela

port and rail station and establish defensive positions closer to the port. At 1000 Morales Monasterios asked Carbonell Izquierdo to join the movement. The latter refused, and also withheld orders to his warships not to bombard the rebels.

Meanwhile the fleet, lying in the naval base, remained quiet. At 1005 a task group made up of the frigate *General Morán* and a sister, the *Almirante Clemente*, took up position in front of the naval base while it was under fire from an air force Vampire. Ten minutes later the commanding officer of the destroyer *Zulia* ordered the gunners of a forty-mm mount to fire on a group of rebellious marines that had approached within 328 feet of the ship, which was docked inside the naval base. The gunners disobeyed the order and fired into the water. This action resulted in the arrest of the officer in charge of the gun. Within minutes a group of officers and chiefs from the crew took control of the *Zulia* and freed him.

At 1020 the government-controlled *Almirante Clemente* and *General Morán* began firing their forty-mm cannon into the marine corps barracks, destroying the building. Three marines were killed and ten injured, and the rebel leader, Captain Ponte Rodríguez, was wounded. At this point the insurgents decided to evacuate the barracks and move to Castle Liberator before any more bombardments took place.[80]

The only land communication between Puerto Cabello, on a strip of land bordered on the north by the Caribbean and on the south by coastal mountains, and the rest of the country was provided by a highway and rail line that entered the city from the west. To the east were some small towns, the port and its facilities, and the naval base. To confront the rebels at the naval base, government forces first had to pass through the port city.[81] There Medina Silva remained in charge of the rebel defenses.[82] At approximately 1100 army Battalion No. 41 began to advance on the rebels and came under fire. The loyalists were anchoring the medium landing ship *Los Roques* in front of the dry dock to protect the destroyer *Nueva Esparta*, which needed repairs, and about that time the destroyer *Zulia* and frigate *General Flores* were being moved to the outer roadstead with the aid of tugs. At noon government reinforcements began to arrive. A company from air force Parachute Battalion No. 1 appeared at the airport. On the northern outskirts, between the rebellious marines and Battalion No. 41, intense fighting broke out and continued for hours.

Fernández Márquez, the lieutenant who had hidden himself in a closet at the officers' residence, found a cassock in the chaplain's room and disguised himself as a priest. He went to the quarters of the sailors who worked at the base headquarters and convinced some twenty of them to help him recapture the quarters where Carbonell Izquierdo and the other loyal officers were being held.[83]

Fighting broke out at the naval base. In the patrol craft *Mejillon* an en-

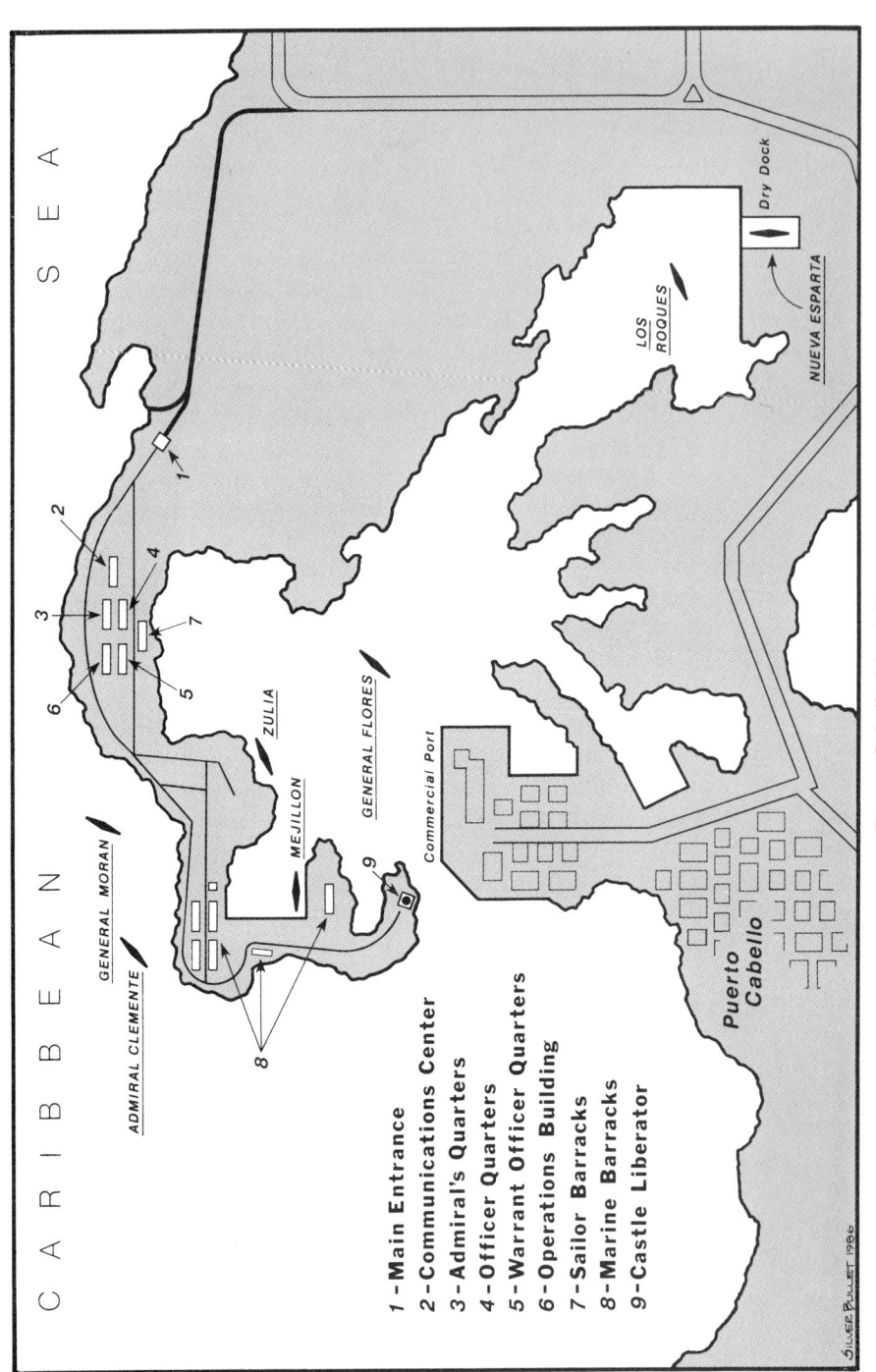

Puerto Cabello Naval Base

sign took control of a fifty-caliber machine gun and opened fire on a group of rebellious marines. They in turn attacked the craft with antitank grenades. After an hour of fighting those in the *Mejillon* surrendered and the craft fell to the rebels.

Heavy fighting continued throughout 2 June. At 1500 the First Company of army Battalion No. 41 tried to attack the city from the south. There insurgent marines turned them back, killing nine men. The rebels also captured a national guard patrol craft that had entered the naval base. At 1530 the frigate *Almirante Clemente* once again lashed the rebels in the naval base with her forty-mm cannon. Morales Monasterios, who had boarded the destroyer *Zulia*, radioed that if the frigate did not cease fire the *Zulia* would respond with her 4.5-inch guns. Within a few minutes the frigate's guns fell silent. Government reinforcements, including army Infantry Battalion No. 31 and national guard Detached Company No. 57, continued to arrive.

By 1700 Fernández Márquez and his group of loyal sailors had freed all of the senior officers at the naval base and gained control over the operations building. Carbonell Izquierdo telephoned Sosa Ríos in Caracas and solicited orders. Two rebel officers were arrested when they entered the operations building unaware that it had been recaptured.

At 1730 a patrol from army Battalion No. 41 supported by an M-8 armored car advanced into the city and took the fire station, capturing the ensign in charge of rebel forces there. Within half an hour army Infantry Battalion No. 32 arrived in Puerto Cabello. At 1815 Captain Moreno Piña and Fernández Márquez, accompanied by ten sailors, captured Morales Monasterios in the vicinity of the operations building. Army Artillery Company No. 41, with six 155-mm M-114 howitzers, arrived in Puerto Cabello at 1900 as the government's strength continued to swell.

In the evening rebels used the national guard patrol craft they had captured earlier in the day to harass government troops that had taken up positions along the beach. Ensign Jaime Penso Nebrús was in command of the craft, manned by twenty rebellious sailors and marines armed with two fifty-caliber machine guns, hand grenades, and FAL 7.62-mm automatic rifles. They attacked and dispersed the government forces. At 2000 a company from army Armored Battalion No. 4 arrived at Puerto Cabello with sixteen AMX-13 light tanks.

By 2030 Carbonell Izquierdo had assembled a force of some fifty loyal sailors at the operations building. He ordered the occupation of all adjacent buildings and sent patrols to determine rebel positions. The majority of insurgents had retired to Castle Liberator. They controlled the main gate of the naval base, which was protected by two fifty-caliber machine guns and one eighty-one-mm mortar.[84]

At 0200 on Sunday morning, 3 June, Carbonell Izquierdo sought permission from the commander of the navy for the frigates *Almirante Clemente* and *General Morán* to fire on Castle Liberator. Only two hours earlier the captain had learned that the rebels controlled the destroyer *Zulia*. At 0405 sailors loyal to the government captured Castle Liberator and arrested key leaders of the rebellion, specifically Captain Ponte Rodríguez and Ensigns Penso Nebrús and Sierra Acosta. During the fighting a lieutenant loyal to the government was killed.[85] By 0530 a group of loyal sailors recaptured the main gate to the naval base and minutes later another loyal force recaptured the *Mejillon*. Within half an hour Colonel Mönch Siegert's forces broke through the rebel defenses around Puerto Cabello. Street fighting between the some one thousand marines and government forces remained heavy throughout the day. Government troops employed artillery, light tanks, and aircraft, while the marines had to rely on bazookas, mortars, and heavy machine guns for support. The tactics Siegert used to retake the city were later criticized by many. He had soldiers position themselves behind each tank as it entered the disputed area, and as a result, about thirty soldiers from Infantry Battalion No. 31 were killed or wounded in what became known as the Butchery of the Sewer.

At 0630, while loyal army troops were making slow progress through the streets, air force aircraft attacked the rebels at Fort Solano with rockets and machine guns. At 0800 loyal sailors surrounded the *Zulia*, which was still docked, and Carbonell Izquierdo demanded the destroyer's unconditional surrender. An hour and a half later Lieutenant (j.g.) Antonio Piccardo, leader of the rebels in the destroyer, surrendered. After two hours of fighting the rebels defending the southern sector had almost depleted their ammunition, so they fell back to Rancho Grande. The *Almirante Clemente* was ordered at 0922 to bombard Fort Solano in support of the advancing army troops. In the northern sector the First Company of Battalion No. 41 and national guard Detachment No. 55 successfully attacked the rebels after an intense bombardment by 106-mm guns. A group of rebellious marines was captured. At 1100 Carbonell Izquierdo informed Admiral Sosa Ríos in Caracas that the naval base and insurgent ships had been captured. By noon government forces had resumed control of sixty percent of the city. Nevertheless, resistance continued throughout the day and well into Monday. Small pockets of marines fought in barrios in the city and in the mountains to the south. Resistance did not stop until the night of 4 June.

No one knows the total number of casualties resulting from the rebellion that has come to be called El Porteñazo. Among government forces, twenty were killed and seventy wounded. Sosa Ríos estimated that in all some two to three hundred men died. Sixteen naval officers, seven naval warrant officers, and thirty-four civilians were tried and condemned to prison for their participation in the rebellion.[86]

Haiti

In April 1970 the crews of the cutters *La Crête à Perrot* and *Vertieres* and the net-layer *Dessalines* rebelled against the government of François Duvalier, who after being elected in 1957 turned into an iron dictator. The ships shelled the presidential palace at Port-au-Prince, and the government countered by dropping fifty-five-gallon gasoline drums from air force planes whose bombs had been confiscated earlier for fear that the pilots themselves might rebel. Neither side scored any hits. The ships, apparently short on munitions and supplies, soon gave up their blockade and were given safe haven at the U.S. naval base at Guantánamo, Cuba.

Chile

In 1973 the Chilean navy, among other reasons fearful of increased communist activity in the government of Salvador Allende, acted in consort with sister services to oust him. In fact, the plan was initiated by Vice Admiral José Toribio Merino, chief of the First Naval Zone (Valparaíso), and General Gustavo Leigh, head of the air force, some three months prior to the coup. The chief of the army, General Augusto Pinochet Ugarte, was invited to take part less than one week before it took place.

In September the fleet sailed from Valparaíso, ostensibly to participate in the annual UNITAS exercises. It returned the following night to help the marines and other naval personnel capture Valparaíso, Talcahuano, and Concepción, their predetermined objectives. Particularly heavy fighting took place at the University of Concepción, where some 250 extreme leftists died. With the death of Allende in the presidential palace, opposition ceased and the military was in complete control. The Cuban merchant ship *Calle Larga*, which had been in Valparaíso, fled without sailing authorization. After being tracked by Chilean naval aircraft she was overtaken by the destroyer *Blanco Encalada* but permitted to proceed.[87]

The chiefs of the four armed services—army, navy, air force, and national police (*carabineros*)—became the ruling junta, presiding over a government almost all of whose important political posts were filled by military men.[88] As before, the navy was the principal power in Valparaíso and the southern part of the nation, the army the principal power in Santiago and elsewhere. Before long General Pinochet began to dominate the junta, and the other members were relegated to the role of an advisory board.

CHAPTER FOURTEEN

The Malvinas Crisis, March–April 1982

WHILE U.S. INFLUENCE in Latin America waned, territorial disputes resurfaced as the dominant issues for the region's navies. Argentina in particular went to great lengths to reclaim territory she believed was rightfully hers. The controversy over the sovereignty of the Malvinas had smoldered since colonial times.[1] On 2 April 1982 the South American nation recaptured the islands, escalating her conflict with the British over the South Georgia islands. Argentina's military junta assumed that despite its use of force, Great Britain would eventually accept the takeover, as other colonial powers had accepted the occupation of Goa by India, of western Timor and western New Guinea by Indonesia, of the Spanish Sahara by Morocco, and of Cyprus by Turkey. In its belief that there would be no fighting, the junta badly misjudged its opponent. Not until the British fleet sailed did Argentina's leaders partially realize their catastrophic mistake; then they had one short month to prepare for war.

That month turned out to be a woefully inadequate period in which to mobilize against such a formidable enemy. This was Argentina's first war in almost 120 years, and before it erupted, the country, unlike NATO nations, had thought herself immune to threats that materialized in a matter of days. The only danger to Argentina, so it seemed, came from her traditional rivals, and they were easily monitored. Thus she fell prey to the sophism that the Malvinas could be recovered because Great Britain wouldn't fight, and because Great Britain wouldn't fight, there was no reason to undertake costly preparations. This explains the contradiction between Argentina's textbook landing operation of 2 April and the uncoordinated defense that ensued. Argentine forces had to leave the initiative to the enemy and could only attempt to counteract his moves. Britain, by contrast, maintained a high state of readiness.

He who has the initiative has also the privilege of choosing the most favorable moment for his operations. Argentina had that privilege; she decided when to recapture the Malvinas. Instead of choosing wisely, she executed her landing at a time that now looks almost as if it had been picked by Britain—when a Royal Navy fleet was exercising near Gibraltar, in preparation for NATO maneuvers scheduled to take place a few months later. Had the landing been delayed just a few days, this fleet would have been back in Britain on Easter holidays, thus giving Argentina precious extra time to prepare.

Another advantage for Britain was the season, autumn in the South Atlantic. With a proportion of nine hours of daytime to fifteen hours of nighttime, the British had plenty of hours under cover of darkness to close in to the coast for gunnery bombardments and landing operations. Pilots and aircraft only had to operate forty percent of the time, giving them sixty percent for rest, recovery, and maintenance. If the operations had taken place in summer, when there are just four to five hours of darkness, British ships would not have conducted themselves with such impunity, and carrier-based aviation would have suffered under the burden of a heavier mission requirement.

The choice of autumn, moreover, placed unnecessary hardships on Argentine aviation. Although numerically superior in this area, Argentina had no all-weather aircraft. Flying time was severely restricted by both the darkness and the bad weather that autumn brings. British aircraft, on the other hand, conducted most of their landings and ground combat at night, in fog, and in low overcast.

To this was added the fact that British personnel were, on the whole, better trained. The Argentine army, which generally recruits at the beginning of the year, had at the outbreak of war a preponderance of soldiers with only two to three months' basic training; they were to fight against such elite British units as the Royal Marines and the Royal Paratroopers. While many in the lower command echelons of the Argentine army fought well and with courage, the lack of training and the fact that the army had not seen combat for over a century proved to be tremendous disadvantages. Bad timing also plagued the navy. At the beginning of the year come most of that service's personnel changes and ship overhauls, as well as a long summer vacation. Yearly combat training commences afterwards. By

April of 1982, combat units had just finished their basic training or were emerging from overhauls. Although conscripts in the navy's Fifth Marine Battalion showed that they could perform well, and the marines, who recruited quarterly, had some well-trained units, this could not mend the gaps in the overall fighting capacity of the Argentine army.

Recapturing the Malvinas

In late March 1982 Argentine naval units prepared for Operation Rosario, the recapture from the British of the Malvina islands.[2] The Argentines believed the force holding them consisted of eighty marines (a forty-man garrison that rotated). The British navy obviously had many potential eyes; the ice patrol ship *Endurance*, the civilian auxiliary ships *Bransfield* and *John Biscoe*, and two smaller craft, the *Forrest* and the *Monsunen*, operated in these waters and could warn of any approaching force. In mid-March an Argentine naval P-2 Neptune began a discreet long-range reconnaissance and tracked these units. The Argentines also knew that two Beaver, three Cessna, and one Islander aircraft operated from the islands and were available for reconnaissance, and they suspected, wrongly, that a Polish factory ship, normally anchored in Puerto Groussac and in communication with thirty to forty craft that generally fished the waters north of the islands, was providing early warning to the British as part of the price for anchorage and fresh water.

At Puerto Belgrano, the principal naval base, two Argentine task forces assembled: the Amphibious Task Force (Task Force 40), composed of the destroyers *Santísima Trinidad* (flagship) and *Hércules*, corvettes *Drummond* and *Granville*, submarine *Santa Fe*, tank landing ship *Cabo San Antonio*, icebreaker *Almirante Irizar*, and cargo transport *Isla de los Estados;* and the Supporting Task Force (Task Force 20), made up of the carrier *25 de Mayo*, four destroyers—*Bouchard*, *Piedrabuena*, *Py*, and *Seguí*—fleet tanker *Punta Médanos*, and tug *Alferez Sobral*. General Osvaldo García, commanding officer of the army's Fifth Corps in Patagonia, was the theatre of operations commander, Rear Admiral Gualter Allara was the Amphibious Force commander, and marine corps Rear Admiral Carlos Busser was the Landing Force commander.

The mission of Task Force 40 was to capture Port Stanley, soon to be renamed Puerto Argentino by the Argentines. Its objectives were to seize the British marine barracks, the airport, and Cape Pembroke (San Felipe) Lighthouse and gain control of the population (see the map on page 240). Admiral Busser instructed his marines to accomplish their goals without causing death or destruction if possible. The Argentines hoped to so overwhelm the British defenders with their 874-man landing force that no resistance would be offered. They were, in effect, trying to duplicate in reverse the events of 1832. In that year Great Britain sent an expedition to

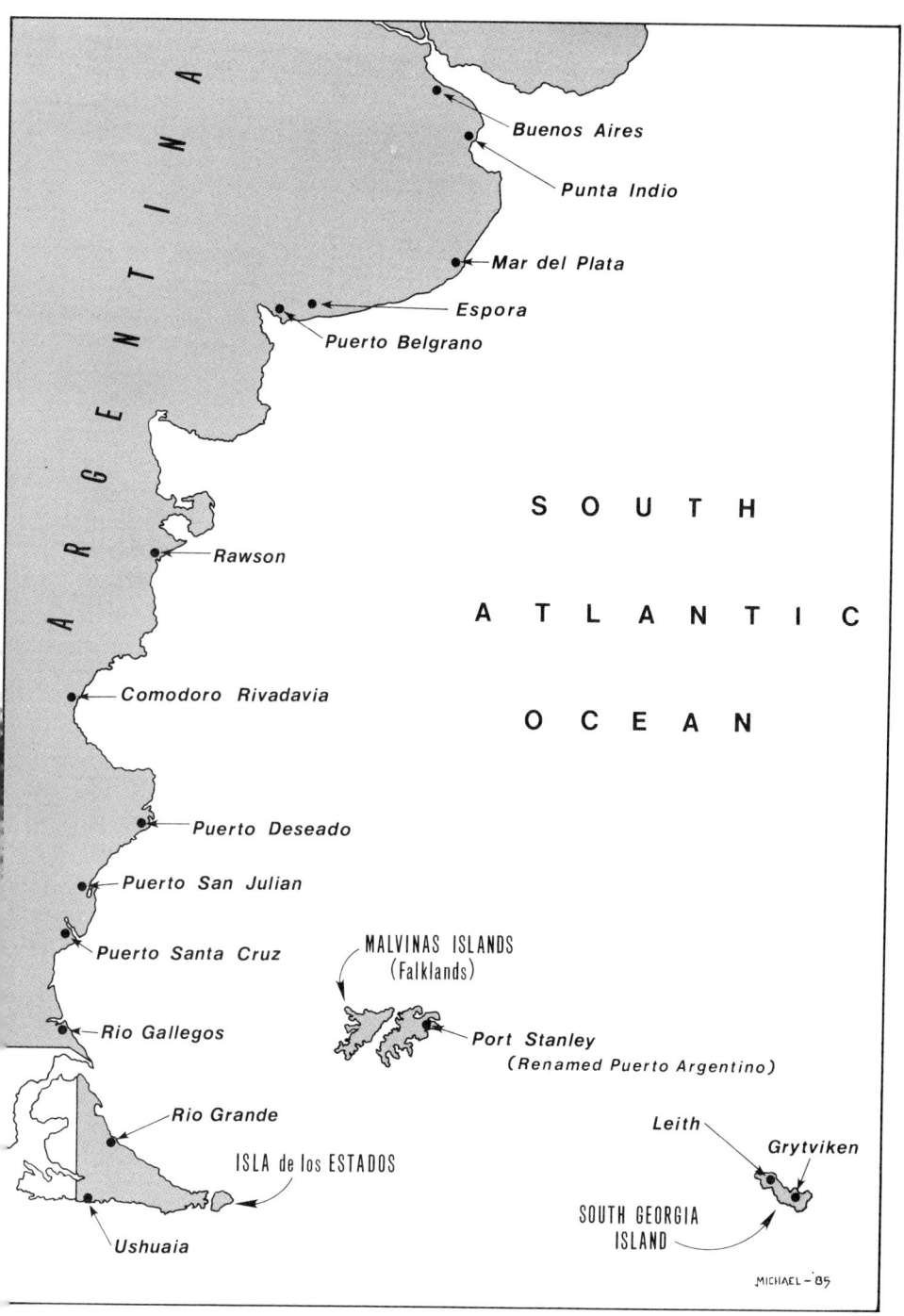

The Argentine Coast and the South Atlantic

occupy the islands, the title to which was disputed with Argentina. The British corvette *Clio* forced the weaker Argentine naval schooner *Sarandí* to retire, evicted the small Argentine population, and brought in British settlers.

Thus on 28 March 750 men from marine Battalion No. 2 and the Amphibious Vehicle Battalion, along with twenty-one amphibious vehicles (nineteen tracked landing craft to carry personnel, a tracked recovery vehicle, and a wheeled amphibious truck), four amphibious vehicles, and thirty marine and army vehicles, embarked in the hold and on the weather deck of the *Cabo San Antonio,* making a total combat load of some eight hundred tons. Integrated into the force was the vanguard (the command staff and twenty-five-mm antiaircraft guns) of the army's Twenty-fifth Infantry Regiment. The carrier *25 de Mayo* had on board four S-2E Trackers, eight A-4Q Skyhawks, and three Alouette and a few Sea King helicopters.

The majority of the units sailed separately on the twentieth, following their normal course to Ushuaia, the Argentine port at the tip of the continent, which brought them closer to the mainland than to the Malvinas. So as not to attract attention, the ships put to sea with the ammunition and stores they already had on board. Nonetheless, an Argentine newspaper discovered what was going on and published the news prior to the landing. The *Almirante Irizar* departed in the evening to avoid problems with the tide. The two corvettes, already at sea, joined the task force. Under cover of darkness the support force, Task Force 20, separated and took up position about 450 miles due north of the islands, around 43°40′ South latitude, 59°40′ West longitude.[3] The Trackers flew antisubmarine patrols to the south-southeast for 250 miles, while the invasion force continued south along the coast.

The original plan had been to sail below the islands to the west and then circle up counterclockwise from the southeast. But on the morning of the twenty-ninth the weather grew worse, and by midday the force was fighting fifty- to fifty-five-knot winds and heavy seas. By 1400 the icebreaker *Almirante Irizar* had caught up with the task force. Loaded with vehicles, cargo, and an extra helicopter, she had a difficult time maintaining station in the heavy seas. She rolled up to forty degrees, making life for the marines miserable. The task force reduced speed from fourteen knots to eight, and later to six. An army Puma helicopter broke its lashings during the storm and collided with a navy Sea King, thus reducing the task force's already small vertical-lift capability. Helicopter operations were becoming more and more dangerous, and as a result ships had to put their sterns into the wind to launch. On the thirtieth, during a conference in the *Santísima Trinidad,* task force commanders decided to reduce pounding on the ships by changing course to the north of the islands and to suspend helicopter operations. This required a change in the planned amphibious landing and postponed D-day until 2 April.

The only submarine used in the recapture of the Malvinas was the *Santa Fe*, which had departed Mar del Plata on 26 March with a small group of tactical divers on board. Her mission was to land the men off Cape Pembroke Lighthouse, whence they would mark the landing beach. If possible, the tactical divers were to capture the lighthouse, equipped as a lookout post with a direct telephone line to British police headquarters, without inflicting casualties. The *Santa Fe* was under orders to avoid attacks on shipping, to break contact with any ships that communicated with her, and to remain undetected.[4] Initially she traveled on the surface, but on her approach to the islands she dove and used her snorkel. On the night of the twenty-ninth, after arriving at her destination, she detected a ship leaving Port Stanley on a northern course. Its sound signature suggested that it might be the ice patrol ship *Endurance*.[5]

By midday on 31 March Task Force 40 learned that it had lost the element of surprise. The British governor on the islands was openly broadcasting instructions to his tiny military and civilian forces. The Argentines monitored the information and modified their plans accordingly. First, they delayed H-hour to 0630 so that the marines could hit the beach while it was still dark—thereby protecting the amphibious vehicles from antitank fire—and also reap the benefit of increasing daylight for their activities ashore. Second, plans to capture the lighthouse were canceled, since it was now fortified. Third, operations against Darwin, Goose Green, and Fox Bay were postponed to free up all forces for a concentrated attack against Port Stanley.

Task Force 40 arrived off the Malvinas after nightfall on 1 April. At 2115 the destroyer *Santísima Trinidad* anchored at Port Harriet (Puerto Enriqueta), south of Port Stanley. Eighty commandos of the marine corps amphibious landing company and navy tactical divers, technicians whose task it was to restore public services at Port Stanley should they be disrupted, paddled five hundred meters ashore in twenty rubber boats on a clear moonlit night, landing by 2300. Most in the landing party were to participate in the capture of the marine barracks, a smaller force in the seizure of the government house.[6]

On 1 April the commanding officer of the *Santa Fe*, having learned that the advantage of surprise was lost and the lighthouse fortified, and ten navy tactical divers picked another landing beach on the north shore of the bay, from which they would cross over to secure and mark Yorke Beach West for amphibious vehicles.[7] The submerged submarine moved to within 2,200 yards of the beach. At 2300 she surfaced off Kidney (Riñon) Island, and the commandos motored and paddled ashore in three Zodiac boats, carrying out their task without incident. Meanwhile, the *Santa Fe* submerged and proceeded to a position to the east of Port Stanley.

At approximately 0400 the destroyer *Hércules* and the corvette *Drummond* escorted the tank landing ship *Cabo San Antonio* as she approached

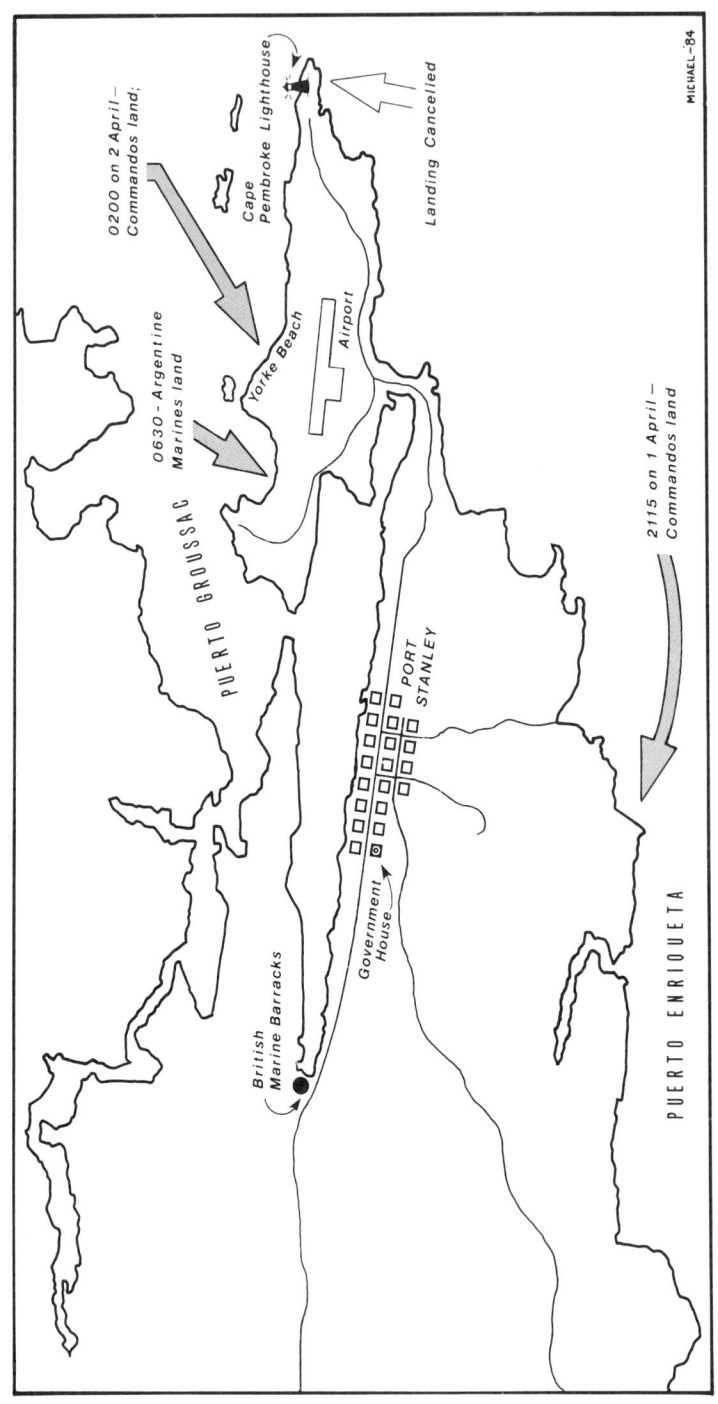

Argentine Landing at Port Stanley (Puerto Argentino), 1 April 1982

Port Stanley. The *Hércules* proceeded ahead to make sure there was no trap. At 0620 the *Cabo San Antonio* approached and disembarked the nineteen tracked landing vehicles at Yorke Beach. As they came ashore, unopposed, the *Santísima Trinidad* and the *Granville* moved to gunfire support position. The vanguard neared Port Stanley in the face of concentrated small-arms fire from buildings on the edge of town, but there were no casualties.[8] The on-site marine commander, Lieutenant Commander Hugo Santillán, successfully dislodged the British from the weather station without incurring casualties.[9] At about this time the *Drummond*, hearing the fire, requested permission to provide fire support with her hundred-mm gun. Permission was denied on the grounds that this would be an excessive response.

The *Almirante Irizar* and the *Granville* took up position to the south of Cape Pembroke Lighthouse. Argentine army troops, which had landed from the *Cabo San Antonio*, and a rifle platoon from E Company, marine Battalion No. 2, cleared the Port Stanley air strip of vehicles. A Sea King helicopter flying from the *Almirante Irizar* carried reserve marines from Battalion No. 1. At 0830, while the destroyer *Hércules* controlled air traffic, the first air force C-130 landed, bringing in the rest of the Twenty-fifth Infantry Regiment to take control of the islands from the marines. Immediately after the landing started, English broadcasts from the *Santísima Trinidad* asked the islanders to offer no resistance and avoid bloodshed. As the amphibious vehicles proceeded into the city, they were met by the commandos who had debarked from the *Santísima Trinidad*. The larger part of the landing force had found the Royal Marine barracks unoccupied and marched to the government house, where they could hear firing. One Argentine had been killed in the fight, Lieutenant Commander Pedro Giachino. Two were also severely wounded.

At 0915 the governor surrendered. The marine force departed in air force and navy transport aircraft on the third, leaving behind one company of Battalion No. 1 to protect harbor installations. Amphibious vehicles and supporting equipment departed in the *Cabo San Antonio* on 4 April. The army took over ground defenses and later requested a marine battalion for reinforcement. On 3 April the *Almirante Irizar, Isla de los Estados,* and *Drummond* transported army personnel who had been flown in on C-130s to Darwin, Goose Green, and Fox Bay.

The Georgias Operation

The Georgias operation, independent of Operation Rosario, was precipitated when an Argentine commercial work force went to the islands to disassemble an old whaling station and became embroiled in a controversy over its right to be there. As political tension escalated, the Argentine navy positioned its forces for any contingency. The recently completed polar supply ship *Bahía Paraíso*, a naval auxiliary, was conducting a scientific program around the Orkney islands in the Antarctic when on 23 March she was ordered to sail at flank speed to the Georgias and support the scrap workers at Leith. She arrived on the night of the twenty-fourth with two helicopters on board, a navy Alouette and an army Puma. In compliance with the Antarctic Treaty, neither ship nor helicopters were armed. The corvette *Guerrico*, undergoing repairs in a dry dock at Puerto Belgrano when the crisis broke, had to be ready within forty-eight hours. On 26 March, with the forty-man Alfa Company of marine Battalion No. 1, she sailed from Puerto Belgrano for the Georgias, where she joined the *Bahía Paraíso* and transferred her marines to that ship in the late afternoon of 2 April. Together the ships were designated Task Force 60.[10]

On the morning of 3 April the two Argentine ships approached Grytviken, capital of the South Georgias. The small port appeared tranquil. At 1100 the Alouette reconnoitered the landing site for the marines, and after an hour in which the crew saw nothing, not even people, which the pilot thought strange, they chose a landing site near the dock. The initial plan was to land while the *Guerrico* created a diversion by bombarding the mountains behind the port with her hundred-mm gun. The Argentines established radio contact with the town and were told that no resistance would be put up. The bombardment was canceled, even though, as the Argentines knew, there were British marines on the island. At 1200 the Puma airlifted to the island the first load of marines, numbering fifteen, about one-third of the occupation force. The Alouette flew nearby for protection; a crewman watched through an open door with a handheld machine gun. The Puma returned for the second load of marines, and when they were about to disembark, British marines opened fire from an ambush. The Puma, hit by small-arms ammunition, lifted off. Filling with smoke, it careened off to the other side of the bay and crashed. The Alouette followed it across the bay and landed at the crash site to rescue wounded marines and army personnel under heavy fire. Two marines died and the helicopter was destroyed.[11]

Meanwhile, British marines opened fire on the *Guerrico*, which had moved in close to the port of Grytviken. An antitank rocket hit the corvette just below the Exocet launcher on her port side. British small-arms fire scored hits as well, killing an Argentine sailor. The *Guerrico* responded with her one-hundred- and forty-mm guns, and after a few rounds the English surrendered.[12]

Following the recapture of the Malvinas, the invasion fleet withdrew with its amphibious vehicles. Air force and naval air transports flew marine Battalion No. 2 to Espora. Only the *Santísima Trinidad* and the *Granville* lingered behind to control air traffic while the Argentine air force set up its equipment. At 1330 on 3 April two Trackers flew from the *25 de Mayo* to Port Stanley, now Puerto Argentino, where they were stationed until the thirteenth, primarily to look for suitable sites for airfields. By 7 April the invasion and covering forces had returned to Puerto Belgrano. The submarine *Santa Fe* patrolled the Malvinas area for five days before being ordered to return to Mar de Plata around the eighth of the month. On the seventh Vice Admiral Juan José Lombardo, head of naval operations, was appointed commander of the South Atlantic operations theater, which put him in charge of all armed forces involved in the campaign. His newly created command, first headquartered at Puerto Belgrano, was later moved to Comodoro Rivadavia.

The Argentines figured that 9 April was the earliest date a British nuclear-powered submarine could arrive on the scene. On the ninth Great Britain announced a two-hundred-mile maritime exclusion zone of the islands to take effect at 0500 (GMT) on the twelfth.

Argentine strength on the islands increased slowly. The army had primary responsibility for ground defenses, of which naval forces were an integral part. Between the eighth and the twelfth of April naval aviation flew marine Battalion No. 5 from Río Grande to the Malvinas. Normally stationed in Tierra del Fuego, this force of six hundred strong—about one-twelfth of the troops defending Puerto Argentino—was well acclimated to the local weather and terrain. Among the first combat troops to arrive, they were assigned defensive positions to the west and south of Puerto Argentino on Mount Tumbledown, Mount Williams, and Sapper Hill. One thirty-mm battery of the marine corps Antiaircraft Battalion, whose principal task was the defense of the airfield, arrived at the island by ship. The marines dug in according to the defense plan issued by the army. On 24 April orders were given to establish permanent defensive positions, as a British counterattack was expected at any time. A few Argentine coast guard (*prefectura*) units also traveled to the islands.

Between the twelfth and the thirteenth two Skyvans had flown to the Malvinas and been stationed at the emergency airstrip on Borbon Island. A coast guard Puma helicopter was carried to the island via ship, and two eighty-five-foot patrol boats, the *Río Igauzú* and the *Islas Malvinas*, crossed to the islands, arriving on the thirteenth.[13] In mid-April the *Cabo San Antonio*, cargo transports *Bahía Buen Suceso* and *Isla de los Estados*, and merchant ships *Formosa* and *Río Carcarañá* carried troops and supplies to the islands. The *Bahía Paraíso* made a number of trips between Puerto Deseado and the Malvinas transporting helicopters. On 13 April she was converted into a hospital ship at Puerto Belgrano. The *Almirante Irizar* was assigned to the task and registered under international law as a hospital ship.

Preparing for the British

The decision to recapture the Malvinas had been known only to a few people at the highest level of the Argentine government. Most of the intelligence community learned of the operation only when it was announced on public radio on 2 April. Naval intelligence had been evaluating developments in the Georgias during March but was ignorant of the invasion plans. On 2 April the intelligence community was asked to project the British reaction to the operation. Intelligence personnel soon discovered that while technical and military data on Britain was solid, they had but poor information on her political, economic, and sociological makeup. Still, on 7 April they knew enough to issue a projection stating that Great Britain would have complete freedom of action, nationally and internationally. NATO and the United States would back her totally. Furthermore, any military action would be a stimulus for the British economy. Therefore they would come, and with their best troops, first to occupy the Georgias and then to land on the Malvinas, but not before 16 May. The enemy, some twenty-five hundred strong, would land on Soledad (East Falkland) Island, probably at San Carlos Bay but maybe at Puerto Argentino.[14]

On 4 April the Argentine naval intelligence arm began to gather tactical data by monitoring the movement of British forces with commercial aircraft, merchant ships, and fishing craft. Normally, commercial aircraft flying from Buenos Aires to Europe flew up the coastline of South America, but now they flew a more easterly course over the Atlantic, attempting to observe ship movements from thirty thousand feet. The government-owned merchant fleet reconnoitered the Gibraltar-Ascension-Malvinas route in a north-south or east-west direction, depending on their origin or destination. Merchant ships in foreign ports or already at sea sent reports in transit. Some intentionally went out of their way to pass close to concentration points such as Ascension Island and Gibraltar. The success of this collection effort may be judged from appendix 15. After receiving information from commercial aircraft and merchant ships, the navy asked the Argentine air force on 21 April to fly its Boeing 707 on a reconnaissance mission to the southwest of Ascension, carrying naval intelligence personnel. The Boeing 707 was the only Argentine aircraft with enough endurance to reach and explore at such a long range; naval P-2s could be used if an enemy force reached the latitude of Buenos Aires. An air force KC-130 was also employed, for mid-range patrol. On its first mission the Boeing discovered British carriers and escorts at 19°39′ South latitude and 21°35′ West longitude.[15]

Six fishing craft were used to reconnoiter the waters northeast of the Malvinas and the waters between those islands and the Georgias. The *Narwal*, *María Alejandra*, and *Constanza* initially patrolled the first area, the *Usurbil*, *María Luisa*, and *Mar Azul* the second, both groups ultimately making contact with the British. The Argentine craft, equipped with standard navigational radar and medium-frequency radios but unarmed, were crewed by civilians. Only one member of the navy, Lieutenant Commander Juan Carlos Gonzalez Llanos, was on board any of the fishing craft, and that was the *Narwal*. The craft had been ordered to surrender if challenged.

Two Argentine merchant ships successfully transited the maritime exclusion zone established by Britain. On 19 April the general cargo ship *Formosa* sailed for Puerto Argentino, probably from Puerto Deseado, passing through the zone under the escort of a Neptune aircraft. The *Río Carcaraña* sailed through the zone on the twenty-fifth, also with an escort, and safely reached Puerto Argentino. A third merchant ship, the *Córdoba*, had been scheduled to sail from Puerto Deseado to Puerto Argentino, but the trip was canceled when British forces attacked the Georgias on 25 April. In addition to their merchant crews, each of these vessels, which were unarmed, had a naval commanding officer and radio operator.[16] As they approached Puerto Argentino they were met by a coast guard cutter that escorted them around the mines planted by the *Isla de los Estados*.[17]

From 17 to 25 April the fleet conducted intensive target practice and ASW exercises in coastal waters. In addition to their primary roles, the ships served as mock targets for the Argentine air force, which had never conducted firing practice at sea before.[18] The *Guerrico*, slightly damaged in the Georgias, rejoined the fleet after three days in the yard. A number of Argentine naval auxiliaries were stationed along the seaboard for rescue duty. The fleet tug *Alférez Sobral* was northwest of the Malvinas, the fleet tug *Comodoro Somellera* southwest of the islands, and the ocean tug *Francisco de Gurruchaga* off Isla de los Estados.

The Argentine junta decided to reinforce the Georgias, which if attacked was told to offer only token resistance. The *Santa Fe*, scheduled for decommissioning in July, was now ordered to prepare for a sixty-day patrol. She took on fuel, food, and torpedoes—U.S.-made Mk 14s and Mk 37 Mod 3s, since she was not capable of handling newer German SST-4 wire-guided torpedoes. Her immediate task was to transport twenty men to the Georgias. Eleven were technicians needed to restore services there, and nine were marines who, unlike the complement in the *Bahía Paraíso* that had captured the islands on 3 April, had been trained in antitank weaponry. Communications equipment and Bantam antitank missiles also went to the islands in the *Santa Fe*. After the passengers embarked in the night at Mar del Plata, the submarine charted a direct route to the principal island, San Pedro, initially running on the surface. Shortly a winter storm of the sort typical in those waters, with winds between forty and fifty knots from the south-southwest, whipped up. The submarine continued her approach, alternately submerged and snorkeling. When the intensity of the storm increased and the height and force of the waves prevented her from snorkeling, she continued her transit on the surface. The same day, 21 April, an Argentine Boeing 707 located the British fleet at 19° 39' South latitude, 21°35' West longitude.

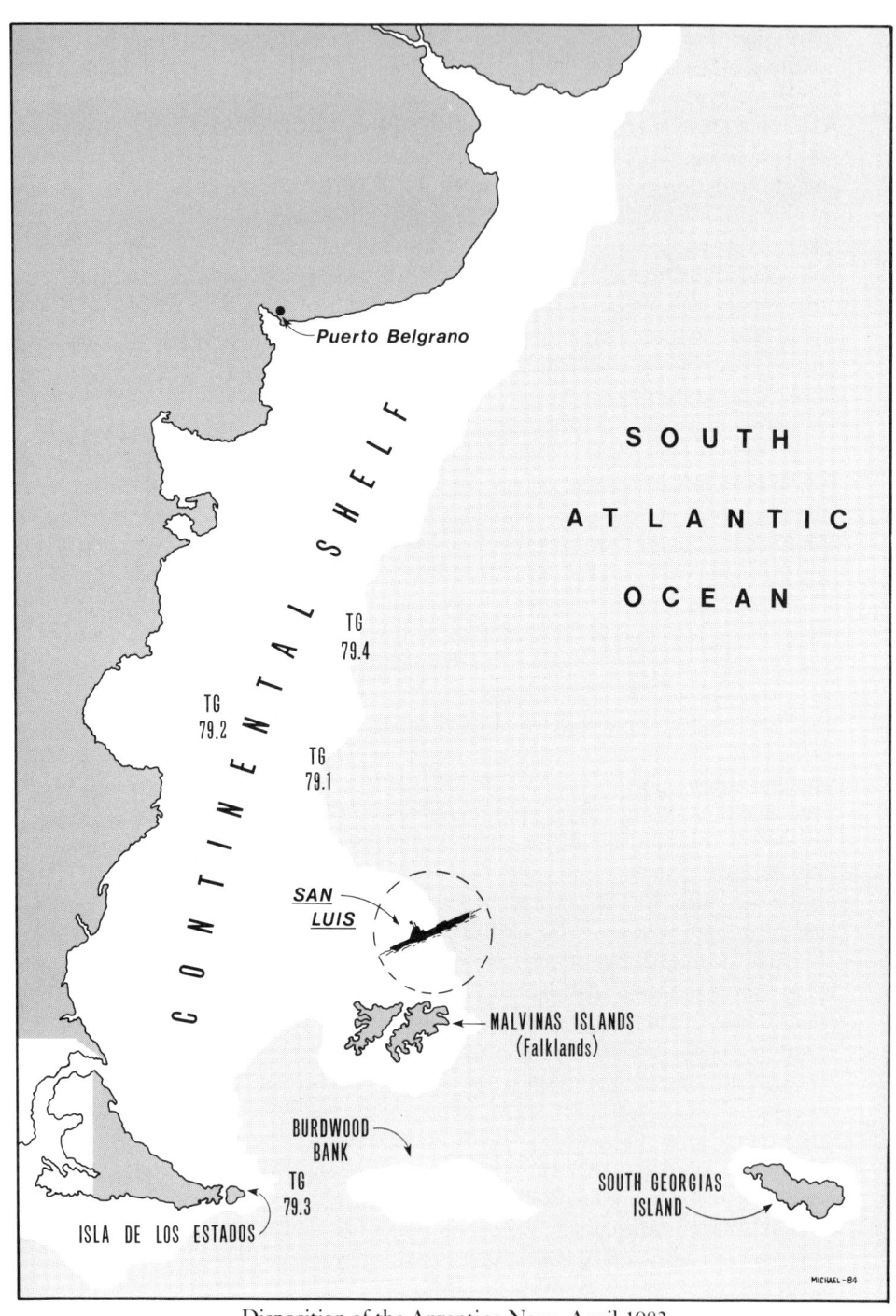

Disposition of the Argentine Navy, April 1982

On the twenty-third, when she was within one hundred nautical miles of San Pedro Island, the *Santa Fe* received a message from Mar del Plata saying that she could expect opposition from British surface units and submarines. (For their part, British units sailing toward the Georgias had been warned that the Argentine submarine might be in the area.) There were two possible approaches for her to take. The first was to run straight in, reducing the time in transit. The second was to circle the islands to the north and approach Grytviken from the south, greatly increasing transit time but possibly avoiding detection. Her commanding officer chose the direct route. The *Santa Fe* made her approach submerged, part of the time using the snorkel to conserve the battery. As she passed east of the islands to the more protected waters of the heavy seas, her sonar picked up a high-frequency transmission, about ten or twelve kilocycles. The skipper decided to continue the mission, and at about 2200 on the twenty-fourth she surfaced in front of Cumberland Bay. The night was dark, cloud covered, without a moon. The *Santa Fe* entered the bay and established VHF communications in front of Grytviken. Starting at about 0230 or 0300, launches from Grytviken transported the marines and supplies to the island. The transfer took about two hours.

The *Santa Fe* departed Grytviken, sailing along the shoreline of Cumberland Bay and looking for a favorable location to submerge. Suddenly a Wessex helicopter approached from the shore and attacked her. A second helicopter, a Wasp, joined the strike. Rifles in the submarine's armory—the only weapons on board except torpedoes—were passed up to the bridge and fired at the helicopters. The Wasp launched two AS.12 wire-guided missiles. One went through the sail and exploded coming out of the other side. The other, which the Argentines believed to be a depth charge, detonated near the stern and perforated the ballast tanks. The *Santa Fe*, now sinking, returned to Grytviken where the crew disembarked. British forces later seized her.

During the attack the mess steward was passing up rifles and ammunition from inside the submarine's sail when an AS.12 missile amputated his foot. Some days later, after the crew had been taken prisoner by the British, a sentry killed Chief Petty Officer Felix Artuso. These were the only casualties the Argentine submarine force suffered during the Georgias operation and the ensuing war in the Malvinas.[19]

By late April the Argentines believed that Great Britain was receiving satellite intelligence from the United States. To keep the British guessing, the *Santiago del Estero*, a "Guppy" submarine used as a training boat and unable to submerge, sailed to a hideout in Puerto Belgrano. The Argentines hoped that the British would learn of her absence from the submarine base and conclude that she was on a war patrol.

On 27 April the fleet deployed to counter a possible British attack against the Malvinas or the mainland. For the first time since the 1978 crisis with Chile the entire Argentine navy was at sea. Under the command of Rear Admiral Gualtar Allara, the fleet, designated Task Force 79, was divided into three task groups: 79.1, composed of the *25 de Mayo*, the destroyer *Santísima Trinidad*, three French type 69 corvettes, and an oiler; 79.2, made up of the ex–U.S. destroyers *Bouchard*, *Piedrabuena*, *Py*, and *Seguí*, the *Hércules*, and an oiler; and 79.3, consisting of the cruiser *General Belgrano* and an oiler. If the British attacked the islands or mainland, the mission of the Argentine force was to find and destroy the enemy fleet.

The one remaining operational submarine, the *San Luis*, had sailed from Mar del Plata in the second week of April to take up station, but she was not permitted to attack. She stayed in communication with the submarine base at Mar del Plata and patrolled north of the islands in a free-fire area inside the British exclusion zone (any ship entering the zone was assumed hostile). The area of operation was about eight hundred nautical miles from the submarine base. The *San Luis* snorkeled primarily at night, close to the islands.

Task Groups 79.1 and 79.2 positioned themselves to the east of Golfo de San Jorge, remaining in waters less than 262 feet—a depth at which, it was believed, a nuclear submarine would have to limit its speed to fifteen knots or greatly increase the possibility of detection. A number of Skyhawks were poised on the flight deck of the *25 de Mayo*, ready to serve as interceptors. Several times they were launched to investigate radar contacts, all of which proved to be friendly aircraft or false echoes. Task Group 79.3 operated in the proximity of Isla de los Estados, and in the meantime land- and carrier-based naval aircraft maintained a three-hundred-mile surveillance.

On 28 April Britain announced that a total exclusion zone would take effect in two days. Any ship or aircraft found inside it without British authorization would be subject to attack. On the Argentine side, Admiral Allara received a message cancelling the hold-fire order. On the twenty-ninth the *Bouchard* and the *Piedrabuena* were detached from Task Group 79.2 and assigned to 79.3. By the thirtieth, 79.1 and 79.2 had moved north-northwest of the Malvinas. Numerous Japanese, Polish, and Russian fishing craft frequented these waters, and the Argentines hoped that if the British discovered them, it would cause confusion.

The Argentine Fleet Tries to Attack

On 30 April the commander of the South Atlantic operational theater, Admiral Lombardo, reported to Admiral Allara that aircraft and helicopter activities indicating the presence of a carrier group had been sighted in 51° South latitude, 51° West longitude. Allara decided immediately to steam eastward to the southern tip of Golfo de San Jorge, at about 62° West longitude. For forty-eight hours he received no new intelligence. At 0059 on 1

May another message came from the South Atlantic theater: "It is not advisable to occupy positions outside the safety zone [probably referring to waters less than 262 feet in depth]."[20] Allara disregarded this and continued to steam toward the reported British position. Shortly after 0446 the Malvinas radioed the task force that the British had attacked the islands.

The submarine *San Luis* was the first vessel to counterattack. At approximately 0800 she made sonar contact with an enemy force northeast of the Malvinas. The enemy could not be seen by periscope, so the classification of the targets was incomplete; but apparently they were medium-size warships, probably type 42 destroyers and possibly type 21 or 22 frigates. The *San Luis* closed to about ten thousand yards and at 1005 fired one SST-4 wire-guided torpedo.[21] A few minutes later the wire broke and the submarine lost control of the weapon. She then came under attack by helicopters. They fired at her for twenty hours, using depth charges and at least one torpedo, but she made good her escape without receiving damage.

At 1515 Admiral Allara received a message saying, "Enemy tied-up [with amphibious operations]. You are free to attack." Fifteen minutes later an S2E Tracker flying from the *25 de Mayo* radioed, "One large, six medium-sized warships bearing 031, Puerto Argentino 120 miles." The Tracker had flown toward the reported location of the British force, scraping the tops of the waves, and honed in on electronic emissions. It rose once to sweep its radar and count the British ships, then escaped "on the deck" to avoid interception. The British task force was reported to be at 49°34′ South latitude, 57°10′ West longitude, some 250 to 300 miles from the Argentine carrier. Admiral Allara decided to attack this group and reported the information to Admiral Lombardo, who replied, "British group is not tied up and has superiority." Nonetheless, Allara continued to approach on course 140 degrees, for an attack scheduled for dawn on 2 May. During the night six A-4Q Skyhawks were armed with six five-hundred-pound bombs each. They were to attack from 240 miles away, Admiral Allara planning to take advantage of their range, which was longer than that of the Harrier. Two Skyhawks were to remain with the *25 de Mayo* for combat air patrol.

While it was still dark the wind ceased to blow—an unexpected turn of events in these breezy waters. Catapulting a bomb-laden Skyhawk from the aging carrier required a wind-over-the-deck of thirty-five knots. Regardless of this Admiral Allara pressed on, hoping for a gust of wind at dawn.

At 2213 he received the following message from Admiral Lombardo:

> A task group composed of aircraft carriers and 2 frigates attacked the islands in a sector southeast of Puerto Argentino. Effecting gunfire support and landings from helicopters. Radius of action: 90 miles.

A second task group is composed of 1 aircraft carrier, 6 destroyers, and 2 large ships.

I confirm necessity of early reconnaissance and massive attack on [these] units.[22]

If this information was true Admiral Allara would have a favorable opportunity to attack, for the British carriers would be tied to the beachhead. Allara ordered the three type 69 frigates supported by an oiler to form Task Group 79.4, an antisurface force.[23] The old destroyers and the three type 69 frigates were sent ahead to launch their Exocet missiles after the air attack.

During the night Task Force 79 closed to within two hundred miles of the British force. The Argentine carrier had to wait until almost dawn before launching, for although she could launch Skyhawks in the dark, her flight deck was too small for safe night landings. The attack aircraft, moreover, lacked radar, making a night attack almost impossible.

In early morning of 2 May the wind, less than ten knots, was too calm even to launch a bomb-laden Skyhawk with enough fuel for a radius of two hundred miles. Under existing conditions, a Skyhawk carrying six five-hundred-pound bombs would have had but a seventy- or eighty-mile radius. To reach the British force the load of each Skyhawk would have to be reduced to two five-hundred-pound bombs—much too inadequate for an effective attack.[24]

At 0135 radars in the Argentine ships detected a British aircraft, assumed to be a Harrier, some sixty to seventy miles from the Argentine task force. At 0400 a Tracker returning from a reconnaissance flight had to be diverted to elude the plane, but the Argentine advantage of surprise had already been lost. Further complicating matters, the unusually light wind condition was forecasted to continue throughout the day. At 0120 Admiral Allara received the following message from Admiral Lombardo: "There have been no [amphibious] landings; enemy carrier positions unknown; they constitute a strong menace for TF 79." Influenced by these events, at about 0200 Admiral Allara suspended the attack and ordered the task force to open distance with the British fleet after he had reached a position 250 miles north of the Malvinas.

During daylight the task force returned north-northeast, hoping not to miss the opportunity to strike should wind conditions improve. Such was not the case, so at about 2100 the task force withdrew to protected coastal waters. While it steamed north-northeast, a British submarine attacked and sank the cruiser *General Belgrano*.

The mission of Task Group 79.3—the *General Belgrano* and the destroyers *Bouchard* and *Piedrabuena*—was twofold. First, it was to provide early-warning defense for the southern mainland and to be in position to intercept any British reinforcements coming from the Pacific. Argentine naval intelligence suspected that a British type 42 destroyer and an oiler had passed through the Panama Canal and was circumnavigating the continent. This had not happened. Second, the task group was to show the flag in an area being closely watched by the Chileans. While on station, the *General Belgrano* plied the waters between Isla de los Estados and the Burdwood Bank, going out on a bearing 110° east-southeast and returning on 290° west-northwest. The patrol leg extended for about 250 nautical miles. Captain Héctor Elías Bonzo, commanding officer of both the *General Belgrano* and the task group, gave orders to maintain six thousand yards between the ships in the belief that if a submarine attack came, only one ship at a time could be targeted. The warships had been ordered to leave the scene if any of them were hit by a torpedo, for the *General Belgrano* had no sonar or ASW weapons and those on the destroyers were of 1950s vintage (SQS 29/30 sonars and Mk 32 ASW torpedo tubes).

At 1258 on 2 May Task Group 3 received an order from Admiral Lombardo to retire from "Luis" to "Miguel" (Luis was the code name for a position 250 miles due east of Isla de los Estados, Miguel for a position just off the island.[25] In fact, the *General Belgrano* had already turned west toward the continent at 0512 on the second, at the outer end of her patrol leg. At the time, with the watch just about to change, the cruiser was in a state of readiness—one-third of the crew was at battle stations, a third at work, and the remainder resting. Many sailors were relaxing in their quarters on the orlop deck; immediately forward of the blow sailors were crowded in the canteen buying personal items. At 1558, thirty-five miles outside the exclusion zone and 250 miles southwest of the British surface force, the *General Belgrano* was torpedoed twice while making ten knots in heavy seas.[26] One torpedo hit under her aft five-inch gun director, the second forward of the A turret on the port side. The first was a death blow; it raised the ship in the water, tore her emergency generators from their foundations, and sent a heat wave through her, which along with the explosion accounted for a lot of the casualties. Most of the people on the orlop deck and in the canteen were killed, which accounted for ninety-five percent of the casualties. The ship grew useless, and the crew, some three hundred of whom were conscripts, found their way up to the main deck and abandoned her in total darkness. They all maintained good discipline.

It was HMS *Conqueror*, a nuclear submarine, that had done the damage, firing the two torpedoes at the cruiser and a third that passed forward of her. The hits on the *General Belgrano* sent out shock waves that the destroyer *Bouchard* apparently mistook for a torpedo hit. The ship, which had run ahead of the other two, was in the process of doubling back to rejoin them when the impact was felt. At 1620—twenty minutes after the attack, a delay that can be attributed to confusion—her skipper radioed to Admiral Lombardo, "Attacked with torpedoes. Am beginning withdrawal."[27] Fifteen minutes later the *Bouchard* radioed another message: "*Belgrano* adrift. Latitude 55°18′18; longitude 61°67′. Without communication. Estimate lost. Do not observe explosions or smoke. Do not know if it was torpedoed. Request support to verify situation." And one minute later: "Confirm appreciation. Torpedoed without damage. Explosion outside hull. Simultaneously three white Bengal lights fired from *Belgrano*. Communications with the adrift cruiser interrupted. Separating to 20 miles, later return course to reestablish contact at 14 miles."[28]

As ordered, the two Argentine destroyers left the scene. Neither detected the attack submarine with its sonars, and neither fired or dropped ordnance.

The *General Belgrano* sank fifteen minutes after being abandoned at 55°24′ South latitude, 60°32′ West longitude.[29] Her commanding officer, Captain Bonzo, ordered the sixty-odd thirty-man life rafts to remain tied together so that the crew's chances of rescue would improve. But during the evening the weather deteriorated and the rafts had to be cut apart. Winds picked up to sixty mph, with seas running eighteen to twenty feet—so high that the canopy of at least one raft was pushed down and had to be supported by hand.

As soon as contact with the *General Belgrano* ceased, contingency plans went into effect and rescue vessels positioned along the coast started to search for survivors. The ocean tug *Francisco de Gurruchaga*, responsible for the southernmost search area off Isla de los Estados, was ordered to begin a search at 2338.[30] The last reported position of the *General Belgrano* was 150 nautical miles from the tug's location. At about 0800 on 3 May, as she approached to within fifty miles of the life rafts, the *Francisco de Gurruchaga* picked up distress calls but could not determine where precisely they were coming from. This was confirmation for the tug that the *General Belgrano* had sunk.

At 2200 on 2 May the first naval P-2 Neptune took off from Río Grande to look for survivors and flew to the limit of its range without finding anything. But when the second Neptune went out it discovered an oil slick. Using this as the starting point, the aircraft searched the direction in which the prevailing wind and current would have carried the life rafts. At about 1330 on 3 May it found the rafts fifty-seven miles from the slick and contacted the *Francisco de Gurruchaga*, giving her the location. Then the Neptune dropped Jezebel sonobuoys to search for enemy submarines in the immediate area. No contacts were made. The *Francisco de Gurruchaga* came upon the life rafts at about 1600 and worked nonstop from 1600 to 0500 of the following morning, 4 May. Picking up the survivors in worsening weather from rafts that did not show up on radar was an arduous task, for which a powerful searchlight and low freeboard aft turned out to be important assets. The tug would maneuver to place a life raft to her lee, pass a line to it, and struggle to take on shipwrecked sailors in fierce winds.

From nineteen life rafts the *Francisco de Gurruchaga* rescued 362 men, some seriously burned and injured, one of whom died from exposure while on the tug. The 205-foot vessel, crowded with survivors as well as her own crew of eighty, arrived at Ushuaia on 5 May.

There were additional survivors. The *Piedrabuena* rescued approximately 200, the *Bouchard* 150, and the *Bahía Paraíso*, which had been converted into a hospital ship, 80. The Chilean naval research ship *Piloto Pardo* sailed from the Beagle Channel to aid in the search but found no one. In all, 819 men were rescued, some three days after the cruiser sank. Three hundred and twenty-one died, 272 from the torpedo impact and 49 at sea or after rescue from wounds or exposure. Amazingly, ninety-four percent of those who abandoned ship survived in one of the world's most dangerous seas during a violent storm.[31]

The sinking of the cruiser outside the two-hundred-mile exclusion zone suggested that British submarines were engaging in unrestricted operations. This, and the belief that Great Britain possessed reconnaissance intelligence from U.S. satellites and aircraft, convinced the Argentine navy of the wisdom of retiring to secure coastal waters.[32] The carrier's aircraft deployed to southern naval bases where they could be used in the fighting for the Malvinas.

The Attack on the Alferez Sobral

Late on 2 May the oceangoing tug *Alférez Sobral*, stationed north of the Malvinas specifically to perform rescue missions, was ordered to search for the crew of an Argentine air force Canberra that had been downed. A large red cross on a white background was placed on the bridge of the tug and she travelled with her navigation lights on, but the Argentines did not register her as a hospital ship or disarm her. On 3 May a British Sea King helicopter came upon her making full speed to the reported ditching site. Both sides claimed the other fired first. The helicopter called for reinforcements, a pair of Sea Lynxes armed with Sea Skua missiles arrived, and two missiles were fired at approximately eight miles' distance. One hit, destroying the tug's launch and starting a fire on her deck that was quickly extinguished. Then the commanding officer, Lieutenant Commander Sergio Gómez Roca, ordered the entire crew except the bridge watch team to take cover below the main deck, whereupon the tug prepared to retire.

She was then attacked a second time. A Sea Skua hit the bridge, killing the commanding officer, the officer of the deck, and six noncommissioned personnel, and wounding several others. Only those below deck survived. The radio, compass, radar, and other navigational aids were destroyed—everything but a standard commercial radio, the property of a crew member. After restoring electricity, the remaining crew members set sail for the Argentine coast, judging their course with a boat compass and by the direction of the waves. On the fifth of May they reached the coast near San Julian, then sailed north, led by reconnaissance aircraft to Puerto Deseado.[33]

Lieutenant Commander Gómez was the first commanding officer of an Argentine warship killed in combat since 1827.

CHAPTER FIFTEEN

The Malvinas War, May–June 1982

The Navy's Island Defenders

THE BRUNT OF the navy's fight for the Malvinas fell upon its air arm, elements of the marine corps, sailors manning an assortment of support ships, a "do-it-yourself" Exocet antiship missile team, and the submarine *San Luis*.

The navy, which possessed the strongest air arm of any Latin American fleet, entered the conflict with three attack squadrons, one antisubmarine squadron, one reconnaissance squadron, two helicopter squadrons, two logistic squadrons, and one training squadron. The First Attack Squadron operated ten Aeromacchi (Macchi) MC-339s and seven Aeromacchi MC-326s that doubled as trainers and light-attack aircraft. The MC-326s had been obtained in the 1960s, and the MC-339s, updated versions, in 1981. Normally stationed at the naval aviation school in Punta Indio, the first four aircraft of this squadron were deployed to Río Grande on 2 April and the rest, in mid-April, elsewhere along the coast—four at Ushuaia, six at Río Grande, two at Trelew, and four at Bahía Blanca. One aircraft was cannibalized for spares. In addition, the First Attack Squadron had four naval T-34C trainers, gas-turbine-powered versions of the old T-34s. The Argentine navy received the T-34Cs in 1978, shortly after they entered service with the U.S. Navy.

Six aircraft of the First Attack Squadron—two MC-339s led by a Beechcraft B-200 and four T-34s led by a Beechcraft B-80—crossed to the Malvinas on 23 April in a flight, 435 miles, that took one hour and twenty minutes. The 339s, which during the fighting never numbered more than seven on the islands, had a superior brake system to that of the 326s, allowing them to operate from the short runway at Puerto Argentino; however, they could not take off from any of the auxiliary airfields on the island.[1] The number of 339s at Puerto Argentino was governed by the requirements of maintenance, which had to be done at Río Grande, and by congestion at the airfield. The Aeromacchis stationed at Puerto Argentino were armed with thirty-mm cannon and five-inch rockets, of which they carried two or four, depending on the mission. Prior to 1 May these aircraft completed three armed reconnaissance missions in the Malvinas. On 28 April they covered the landings of the T-34C trainers on Borbon Island and flew two reconnaissance flights over its northern area. The pilots inspected the airstrip on Borbon and determined that the T-34s could operate, with difficulty, from that location. The second pair of T-34s flew to the islands on the twenty-ninth, armed with two 7.62-mm machine-gun pods and, depending on the mission, two or four two-inch rocket pods (each pod containing four rockets). The T-34s also flew five reconnaissance sorties in the northern San Carlos area before 1 May.

The Second Attack Squadron was composed of five Super Etendards. Earlier, in 1981, fourteen Etendards and twenty air-to-surface Exocet missiles had been ordered to operate from the carrier *25 de Mayo;* they were to form a ten-plane squadron for shipboard deployment, with four planes in reserve.[2] However, this plan could not be carried out in May 1982 because the carrier had not yet been fitted with the necessary electronics. From November 1980 until August 1981 naval pilots and support personnel had trained for the Etendards in France, the pilots working from flight simulators and each receiving around forty-five hours of actual flight time. Between August and November 1981 the five aircraft and five missiles were shipped from France to Argentina, and five more of each were due to be shipped in April of 1982. In December 1981 the pilots began to fly the Etendards in-country. The following January and February the aircraft were test-flown to ensure the factory guarantees.

On 30 March 1982—two days before Argentine marines recaptured the Malvinas—the leader of the squadron, Commander Jorge Luis Colombo, received orders to make the AM-39 Exocet air-to-surface missiles operational. By now, the pilots had accumulated approximately eighty hours of flight time each; this would climb to one hundred hours by the time they went into action in May. But due to British pressure on France, the French technicians scheduled to make the missiles operational were not permitted to, so the Argentine pilots did not receive any doctrinal or tactical training at all, either in the use of the Exocet missile or in general attack and air combat procedures.[3] British pressure also resulted in the embargo of the remaining Etendards and missiles.

When he was ordered to prepare for war, Commander Colombo estimated that he would need one month, but his squadron was actually ready in two weeks. In this short time the men put into service the entire weaponry system, the Super Etendard-Exocet, from instruction manuals in French and without support from the builders. They also invented their Exocet attack tactics, trained with mock attacks against Argentine type 42 destroyers, rehearsed in-flight refueling (never before done by naval pilots) with air force KC-130 Hercules, and coordinated their flight patterns with Neptune search aircraft. Every time a flight carrying live missiles was aborted, the weapons had to be air-lifted to Espora for servicing.[4] On 15 April the Second Attack Squadron flew a dress rehearsal three hundred miles out from the coast, with Exocets on board and in-flight refueling, and declared itself ready to fight. With one aircraft set aside for cannibalization for spare parts, four operational Super Etendards were all the squadron could muster.[5] On 21 April the Etendards were moved to Río Grande Naval Air Station.

The Third Attack Squadron had twelve pilots and eight A-4Q Skyhawks, variants of the old A-4B.[6] The A-4Qs, purchased in 1972, lacked a detection system such as the Blue Fox radar found in the Harrier. On the eve of fighting the Argentines installed Omega radio navigation receiver systems in some of them. Before 8 May the Skyhawks operated from the carrier, but after the fleet pullback to protected waters they were moved to the mainland airfield at Río Grande, where they began operations on 12 May. Land-based and carrying four five-hundred-pound bombs, the Skyhawks had a four-hundred-mile radius—the exact distance between the Malvinas and Río Grande. They could not afford to loiter.

From Río Grande Naval Air Station the Reconnaissance Squadron operated two P-2 Neptunes, acquired in 1977 and nearing the end of their useful lives. They required a lot of maintenance and were much affected by the spare-parts embargo the United States had leveled in 1976. Due to their short remaining life and the improbability of success against a nuclear submarine, their job was to conduct surface reconnaissance. In the first two weeks of April they rehearsed with the Super Etendards, and in the early days of May they guided the attack aircraft to their potential targets. In the first practice attempt the Etendards, which required extremely accurate targeting information, could not locate their target with the information the Neptune supplied. This problem was corrected by improving the Neptune's navigational system so that the position of the Neptune, and thus of the target, could be more accurately fixed. To obtain a target's exact location, the Neptune would emit a short electronic signal that was received by three direction finders on the continent. This information was then fed into a navigational computer at Espora and verified by an Omega fix. However, the Neptunes were old, and this jury-rigged system provided only a temporary solution.[7]

The Antisubmarine Squadron was made up of five S-2E Trackers acquired in 1979. Until 2 May four of them had operated from the *25 de Mayo*. All five units were then based at Río Gallegos Naval Air Station, which, due to the crowding at the air force base, had been reactivated for naval aircraft.[8] Emergency repairs were needed to put the airfield in order.

The First Helicopter Squadron was composed of seven Alouette IIIs and two Sea Lynx WG-13s that were dispersed on various tasks throughout the war. Early in the conflict most of the Alouettes were on ships. One, operating from the *General Belgrano*, was lost when the cruiser was torpedoed. The two Argentine type 42 destroyers each carried a Sea Lynx.

The Second Helicopter Squadron was composed of five Sea Kings. One had been on the *Almirante Irizar* during the recapture of the Malvinas. In April and early May a few Sea Kings were on the *25 de Mayo*. When the carrier retired to protected waters, the Sea Kings operated from Viedma on ASW patrol, in collaboration with the type 42 destroyers.

The First Logistic Squadron comprised three L-188 Lockheed Electra turboprops and the second of three F-28 Fokker jets. From the second to the thirty-first of April some of these aircraft flew fifteen hundred persons and five hundred tons of supplies to and from the Malvinas. They carried the Second Marine Battalion back to Puerto Belgrano after the retaking of the islands on 2 April and the Fifth Marine Battalion to the Malvinas in mid-April. After the initial flights seats and carpets were removed so the payload could be increased. The squadron was also used to transfer the Second Marine Battalion from Puerto Belgrano to Río Grande in mid-April. On 30 April Great Britain declared an air blockade.

Two coast guard Skyvan aircraft and one Puma helicopter were also incorporated into the navy. The coast guard set up search and rescue centers in Río Gallegos, Río Grande, and Puerto Argentino, stationing a Skyvan and a helicopter in each location. A Puma helicopter arrived in the Malvinas on 12 April and initially operated from Puerto Argentino. The first Skyvan arrived in the islands on the nineteenth; it operated from Puerto Argentino and was later moved to Borbon Island. A second Skyvan flew in on the thirtieth to help ferry supplies. The two aircraft crossed the ocean very low, at 150 knots.[9]

The characteristics and tactics of the three naval attack squadrons made coordinated attacks difficult. The Macchis flew from the island airport and came under the operational control of the island commander. They could be armed with gravity bombs, but this option was not used during the war because the aircraft, being relatively slow, were not likely to penetrate the defenses of naval targets. The Macchis were frequently grounded by bad weather, and typically only three or fewer were operational at any time.

The Super Etendards flew from Río Grande and were controlled by the naval air command. They were armed with one Exocet missile each, a "fire and forget" missile. Attempting to achieve surprise, they flew in pairs at extremely low altitudes while maintaining radio silence, and each pair preferred to operate independently. The A-4Q Skyhawks were also stationed at Río Grande under the control of the naval air command. Carrying five-hundred-pound Mk 82 bombs fitted with Snakeye retarding tails for low-level delivery, they initially flew in sections of three; these were reduced to two following the losses of 21 May.

Naval fixed-wing aircraft could operate from two airfields in the islands, one at Puerto Argentino and the other in a pasture on Borbon Island. The runway at Puerto Argentino, made of asphalt, was 3,936 feet long and 98 feet wide. Its length could be extended another four hundred meters and the parking area could be increased with aluminum decking. But the runway, with water at one end, hills at the other, and a British sea blockade that made it difficult to import earth-moving machinery after mid-April, could not be quickly lengthened. A Super Etendard carrying a missile could take off from the runway in dry weather, but to do so in rainy weather was dangerous, and it was almost always wet. Navy and air force Skyhawk pilots inspected the runway at Puerto Argentino and came to the conclusion that, under anticipated weather conditions, it would be too dangerous to operate high-performance attack aircraft. The navy did install a wire arresting system so that hook-equipped aircraft like the Skyhawks and Etendards could use the runway in an emergency. This was similar to a system devised at Espora for practice landings: aircraft could land but could only take off with reduced weight.[10] To compensate for the lack of attack aircraft at Puerto Argentino, naval Macchis were stationed there.[11]

The remaining naval aircraft in the islands—T-34C trainers, Skyvans, and helicopters—were stationed at the Borbon Island airstrip. This grassy field, 3,280 feet long, had been discovered by a naval Tracker during its reconnaissance of the islands in mid-April. The T-34C proved too heavy for the turf field; its wheels sank, making it difficult to gather speed for takeoff. Air force Pucarás used the field, but navy Macchis could only land there in an emergency and would not be able to take off from the short runway with ordnance.

With the exception of the Trackers, all naval aircraft operating from the mainland against the British flew from Río Grande Naval Air Station. The Argentine navy, concerned about a British strike there and a reported buildup of Chilean forces in the south, took a number of precautions. First, the Second Marine Battalion flew to Río Grande in late May and set

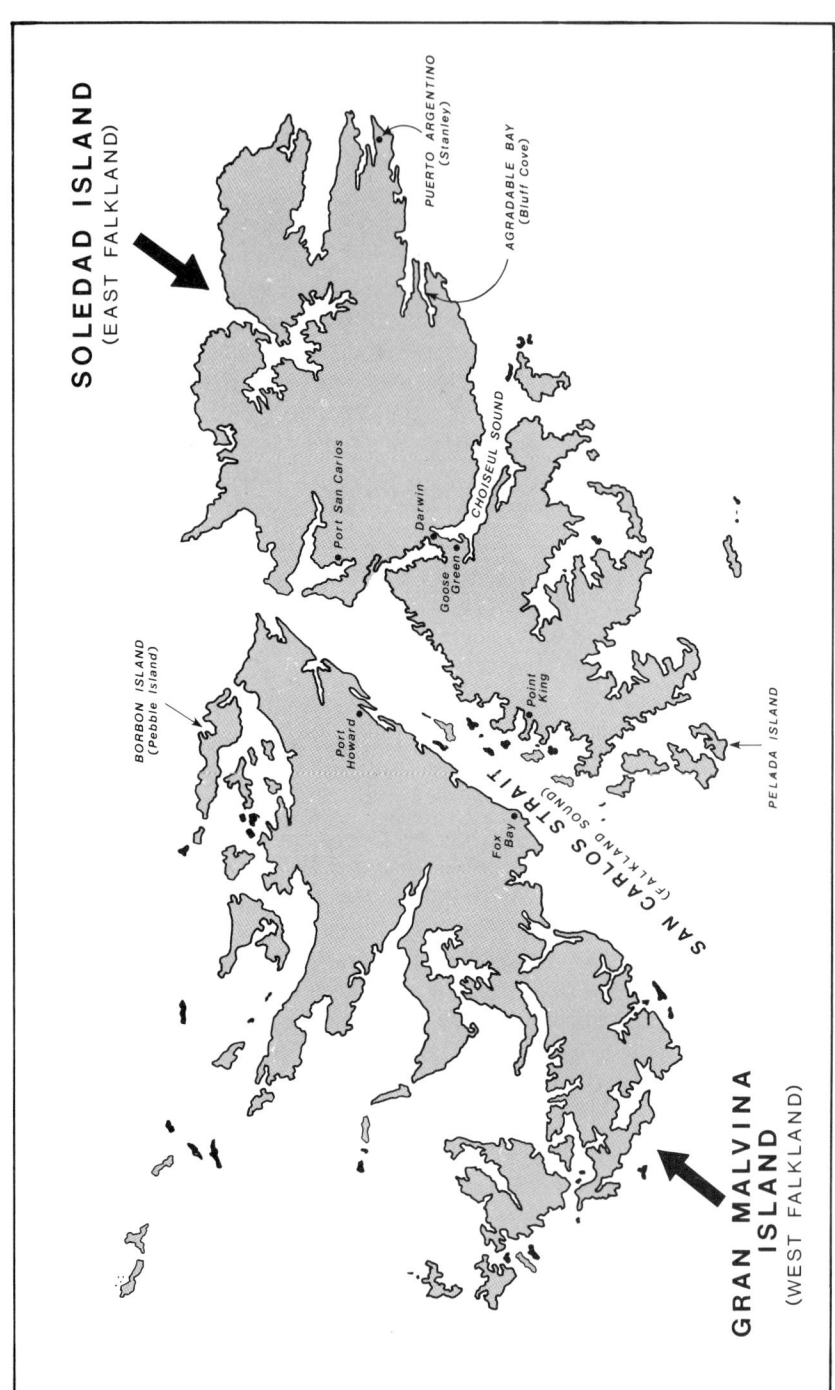

The Malvinas Islands (Falklands)

up a 360° perimeter defense. It was reinforced by Bravo and Charlie companies from the First Marine Battalion. Alouette helicopters from the First Helicopter Squadron were used to patrol the airfield's defenses. The destroyers *Bouchard* and *Piedrabuena*, which had been part of Task Group 79.3, remained along the Atlantic side of the Tierra del Fuego coast to provide early radar warning. At night the Super Etendards were parked on Highway 3 leading out to Río Grande, about a mile from the air station.

One reinforced marine corps battalion plus elements of the antiaircraft battalion were in the Malvinas. The overall commander of the army assigned the Fifth Marine Battalion, which had been there since early April, to a position in the defensive perimeter.[12] In addition to their small arms, the marines had 106-mm, 81-mm, and 60-mm mortars, antitank cannons and missiles, a field artillery battery of 105-mm guns, and a 50-caliber machine-gun platoon. Their greatest weakness was a lack of mobility: they had no helicopters, and at times wet weather made ground transportation impossible. Much of the terrain acted like a sponge, and when it rained people could sink up to their knees on what appeared to be solid ground. On 24 April the marines received orders to man defensive positions permanently, as British actions were expected at any time. These men ultimately bore the brunt of the British attack on Puerto Argentino.

The marine corps antiaircraft battalion was integrated into the airport's defenses, along with air force and army antiaircraft weapons. The battalion, which had arrived in the Malvinas between 6 and 8 April, had a battery of British Tigercat missiles (land-launched variants of the Sea Cat) and another of twelve Hispano Oerlikon thirty-mm guns. These weapons complemented air force and army twin-barrel forty-, thirty-five-, and twenty-mm guns and Roland missiles. An Argentine marine, Lieutenant Commander Héctor E. Silva, took charge of the airport's antiair defenses.

In April the Argentine navy established a support force in the Malvinas made up of a heterogeneous collection of ships, cutters, and boats, there by happenstance (see appendix 17) and crewed by naval personnel and volunteer merchant mariners. They operated both day and night, before 1 May without the support of arms.[13] Only the two coast guard cutters carried guns prior to that date. Three of the ships proved most useful because of their small size. They supplied the outposts—principally Darwin, Bahia Fox, Howard, and Borbon Island—and patrolled certain areas. The naval transport *Isla de los Estados* laid mines—a difficult task because she had not received any special outfitting for the work. Twenty-two were planted in the vicinity of Puerto Argentino.

None of the ships had secure communications, so Captain Antonio José Mozzarelli and his staff developed a code based on slang and colloquial expressions. Typical of their messages was one originating in the hands of the commanding officer of the *Forrest*, Lieutenant Rafael G. Molini, in mid-May. The cargo ship intercepted an enemy radio message stating that it, the *Forrest*, was painted red and white. Molini immediately had the red hull painted black and sent the following to his command: "I am no more from River [Club Atletico River Plate soccer team, whose colors are red and white]; I am dressed like a referee [referees wear black]."[14]

Previously, when Argentine naval commands were told to prepare for the seizure of the Malvinas, the commander of the Submarine Force (directly responsible to the commander of naval operations, who during the war would be appointed commander of South Atlantic theater operations) controlled four boats, two old U.S. Guppy units and two modern German type 209s. The Guppies were typical of submarines transferred to Latin American navies in the post–World War II period—large, slow, and old, built for the war against Japan nearly forty years earlier. The United States discarded its last Guppy in 1975. Modernization had increased the Argentine Guppies' underwater speed by six knots, but this still left them eight knots slower than modern conventional submarines and fifteen knots slower than nuclear boats. One, the *Santiago del Estero*, had been decommissioned in September 1981 and was stationed at the submarine base at Mar del Plata for training purposes. The operational capabilities of the other, the *Santa Fe* (ex-*Catfish* [SS-339]), had declined considerably. In particular, her sensors were unreliable and her batteries could take only a limited charge. Restrictions on her use were intended to extend the life of her batteries through 1982. But this measure didn't help much. The U.S. arms embargo, in effect since 1976, virtually thwarted Argentine efforts to keep these boats operational.

The two type 209 submarines formed the heart of the Argentine submarine force. The *Salta* and the *San Luis* were built in Germany and assembled in Argentina in the mid-1970s. Small, quiet boats, they operated well in the relatively shallow water around the Malvinas. They could manage twenty-two knots submerged for about an hour and could remain on station for about forty days, or until their large torpedo load was exhausted. At the commencement of hostilities in 1982 the *Salta* was undergoing major yard work. It may have been rushed, possibly because of events in the Georgias, for on 2 April she sailed ahead of schedule from Mar del Plata to Golfo Nuevo for trials. Excessive noise led to the conclusion that she was unfit for operation and could not be made ready before the end of the conflict. The *San Luis*, on the other hand, could operate without restriction. Her only drawback was a recently assembled crew. While in transit to the patrol area, her commander discovered that the main fire-control computer was inoperative, greatly reducing the potential of the boat. Now only one SST-4 wire-guided torpedo, the submarine's principal weapon, could be fired at a time since it had to be manually guided to its target. This seriously limited the strike capability of the boat and increased its exposure to counterattack.

Rear Admiral Eduardo Otero arrived in the Malvinas on 27 April to establish a naval command. The naval forces in the islands—naval aviators, marines, sailors manning the support ships, plus the Exocet team which came later—were responsible to the admiral who, in turn, answered to the island's commander, Brigadier General Mario Benjamín Menéndez. Later, looking back, Otero described the condition on the islands this way:

> The climate was terrible. . . . Freezing temperatures were very common, and we had particular problems where people lived in trenches and foxholes. It was difficult to live in those places because the water spilled over from the moss, and the rain was accompanied by subsurface water so that the soldiers' legs were often in water day and night. . . .[15]

Adverse conditions such as these did not hold up progress, though. Among Otero's accomplishments was the establishment of a joint air-plotting room in which several plotters evaluated data from the air force's island radar. It was this room that later had some success in pinpointing the positions of British carriers.

The First Air Attack on Puerto Argentino

At 0447 on 1 May a lone Vulcan bomber dropped twenty-one thousand-pound bombs on Puerto Argentino, and shortly after 0800 nine Sea Harriers attacked the airfield with six-hundred-pound cluster bombs and thousand-pound parachute-retarded bombs. Only one Harrier received damage, and that was slight.[16] The British air attack came as a surprise but caused only modest damage. Apparently both sides were skittish and missed their targets. It would take a few more days before marksmanship improved. The British did manage to bomb the runway, the only hit it would take during the entire conflict. Thirty fifty-five-gallon drums of aviation gasoline ignited, creating a lot of black smoke but not much damage.[17] Bomb splinters struck the control tower building and damaged it—not irreparably, for it served during the entire war—and the naval aviation shed burned down, destroying spare parts for the Macchis. This would hurt the operability of the aircraft in the days to follow.[18] A coast guard Skyvan, also damaged, was repaired in a few days and moved to the race track near Puerto Argentino. The ground there proved too soft and the nosewheel assembly collapsed. Eventually, when the island fell to the British, the aircraft was lost. (The remaining Skyvan was deemed no longer safe for the flight from Puerto Argentino because it created too large a radar blip and might attract attention.) After the attack flight operations were suspended so that the mess could be cleaned up and the damage assessed. The Argentines had suffered no casualties.

During the attack three T-34s stationed at the Borbon strip flew over Puerto Argentino and intercepted a helicopter. When they were preparing to attack, Harriers fired on them and they broke off contact.

When the air attack took place a number of Argentine ships were in Puerto Argentino, including the *Isla de los Estados*, *Río Carcarañá Bahía Buen Suceso*, *Formosa*, and other, smaller ships. Erroneously the Argentines thought they were not safe in the port, and so after the attack all of the larger ships were dispersed. The *Isla de los Estados* and the *Río Carcarañá* were sent to Port King. The *Bahía Buen Suceso* went to Fox Bay, where she could take on much-needed water. And the *Formosa* ran the British blockade to return to the mainland. In fact, these ships would have been safer under the antiaircraft umbrella at Puerto Argentino. They left this haven one by one, travelling to their ultimate destruction.

The *Formosa* had a complete merchant crew as well as a skipper, navy Lieutenant Commander Juan Carlos Ianuzzo, and a communication petty officer from the navy. She was anchored close to the airport when the Harriers struck on 1 May, and though she was not the object of the attack their bombs fell close to her. Between 1000 and 1100 she was ordered to sail south, hugging the coast until she reached Pelada Island, then travel on course 270° to a point northeast of Isla de los Estados, using a preset route that had been established for cargo ships. At about 0700 on 2 May she reached Pelada Island and turned west. Shortly afterward aircraft arrived to attack her. One bomb bounced off a derrick and exploded in the water. A second bomb, which landed in a hold but did not explode, was not discovered until 0900 on 3 May, many hours after the attack. Two navy tactical divers on board removed the firing pin and disarmed the bomb. The *Formosa* made it back to Argentina without further mishap, and the bomb was removed. As it turned out, the Argentine air force had erroneously carried out the attack.

At approximately 1100 on 1 May, in a small bay just north of Puerto Argentino, a helicopter attacked the *Forrest*. Under the command of Lieutenant Molini, she had just returned from delivering supplies to Borbon Island and was stationed north of the town to provide early warning against approaching warships. The crew had to defend the unarmed ship with rifles. The coast guard cutter *Islas Malvinas*, which was nearby, also came under attack from a helicopter. Armed with a twenty-mm cannon and two 7.62-mm machine guns, the ship returned the fire. The cannon, however, soon jammed, greatly reducing her firepower. One sailor was seriously wounded on the *Islas Malvinas*, and both ships received some superficial damage. After these attacks the supply ships traveled only by night, without using their radars or transmitting on their radios. They hugged the coastline, hoping to avoid detection and to improve the chances of rescue and salvage in case of attack.[19] The *Forrest* and another ship, the *Monsunen*, were fitted with machine guns.

From 1 May until mid-June British naval guns bombarded Argentine defensive positions almost nightly, concentrating on those held by the marine corps' Fifth Battalion to the east of Puerto Argentino. The battalion commander, Carlos Robacio, noted:

> Naval artillery had tremendous precision. Some may say otherwise, but I can assure you of this . . . because I was the first to have casualties on the first of May—one dead and seven injured. They fire at an impressive speed. You . . . must be well hidden to escape injury. We were hidden well enough, but if we so much as lifted our heads, we would be decapitated.[20]

The man killed was the only marine lost to naval gunfire. For the next five weeks, while waiting for the British, the marines continued to dig in and adjust fields of fire. At 1230 on 30 May they shot down one Harrier G.R.3 with a barrage of small-arms fire (the so-called Vietnamese barrier). The pilot ejected over the sea and was rescued by the British.[21]

The Macchis flew their first combat mission on 3 May after the air force radar at Puerto Argentino reported a possible landing ship in position bearing 160°, sixty miles from the town.[22] Two aircraft went out on an armed reconnaissance mission, flying in open formation ten feet above the water. The ceiling was very low and visibility was five miles, less where there were patches of fog. Going well beyond the reported landing-ship position, the Macchis found nothing. On their return they tried to make a very low approach so the British would not detect them and learn that the airport was operational. The second Macchi crashed against the runway at landing, killing the pilot, Lieutenant Carlos Benítez. This left but one Macchi on the island. Admiral Otero requested additional attack aircraft, and three more Macchis were sent from the mainland. Just flying to the Malvinas was a dangerous undertaking for them. To extend their range to four hundred nautical miles, the minimum necessary, they had to be fitted with auxiliary fuel tanks and they had to leave their armament behind. And once they were more than halfway to the islands, the unarmed aircraft did not have sufficient fuel to abort their mission and return to the mainland.[23]

Other aircraft were busy in the early days of May. The T-34s reconnoitered the northern part of the island looking for British raiders and potential landing strips.

The Super Etendards Attack

Two Super Etendards armed with Exocet missiles flew their first mission on 2 May, attempting to attack targets reported to the south of Puerto Argentino. When they encountered problems refueling in air, the mission had to be aborted.

Naval air had its first success on 4 May. At 0710 a Neptune detected a target, identified by its electronic emissions as a type 42 destroyer, at 52°48' South latitude and 57°40' West longitude. It was about 100 miles south of Puerto Argentino and approximately 380 miles to the east of Río Grande Naval Air Base. Two Super Etendards, each armed with an Exocet missile, took off at 0945. Twenty minutes later, they received fuel in flight from air force KC-130 tanker aircraft while some 250 miles from the target. The Etendards, piloted by Lieutenant Commander Augusto Bedacarratz and Lieutenant Armando Mayora, approached at high speed, flying about fifty feet above the water. The aircraft maintained visual contact with each other and kept radio and radar silence, relying on data from the Neptune. The weather deteriorated; they flew into rain and fog. Visibility shrank to thirty-three hundred feet and the ceiling to five hundred feet. At 1030 the Etendards received a target update from the Neptune. A short electronic emission helped the P-2 identify two medium-sized and one large ship 115 miles from the Etendards' position. The closest target was no longer emitting, so the Neptune periodically switched on its radar. When they were within estimated firing range, the two Etendards pulled up to about 120 feet and briefly switched on their radars to fix the location of the target. At 1104 the pilots fired their Exocet at a distance of twenty-seven nautical miles. One missile slammed into the side of the type 42 destroyer *Sheffield*. The other missile apparently missed.[24] Then at full speed the Etendards streaked away. Neither during nor after the attack did they encounter any electronic interference. The attack had been a complete surprise. It took two hours and twenty minutes from the time of target identification until the Etendards returned to their base. Shortly after 1500 the *Sheffield* was abandoned, and later she sank while under tow.[25]

The Neptune and the sister unit that relieved it maintained contact with the enemy off and on throughout the day. Because the Argentines monitored British plain-language transmissions, the Neptune knew the moment an enemy picket ship detected it on radar. It even heard the "red alert" and a flight of Harriers scrambling from the British carriers. To escape, the Argentine aircraft dropped below the radar coverage and then changed headings. Knowing the general direction from which the Harriers would approach, it traveled on an opposite track. Once well out of radar range of the picket, it returned to normal operating altitude and started up its two auxiliary jets to reach maximum speed.[26]

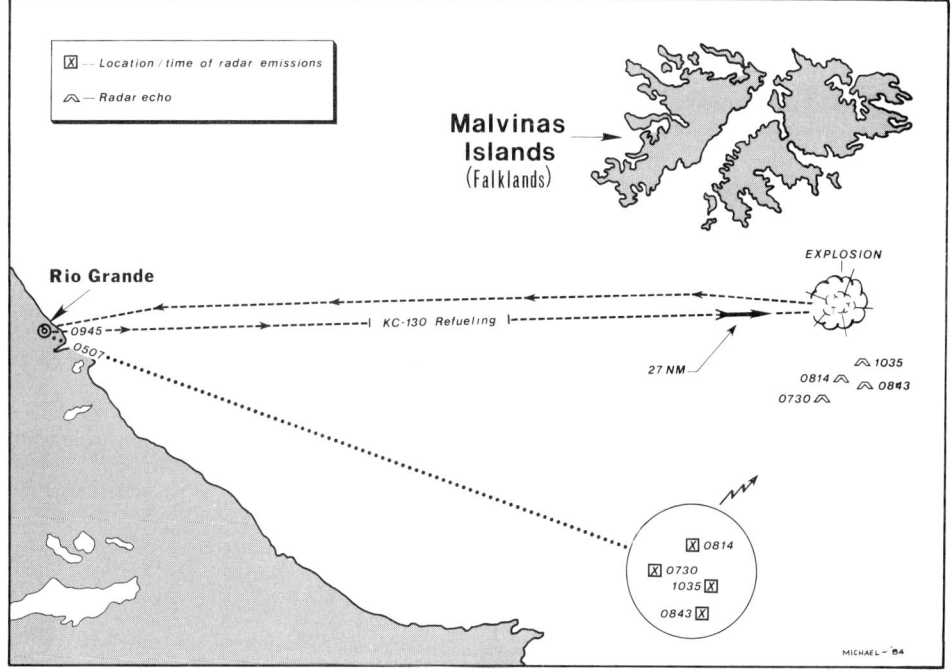

The Super Etendard Attack on the *Sheffield*, 4 May 1982

The following day, 5 May, while searching for the *Alférez Sobral*, a Tracker thought it might have a submarine contact north of the Golfo de San Jorge at 44°01′ South latitude and 64°00′ West longitude. It dropped depth charges and ASW torpedoes. There was a second possible contact in the same vicinity, and Trackers and Sea Kings attacked. Neither action was successful, and later it was reported that no British submarines were in the immediate area.

On 7 May Great Britain announced that any Argentine warship or military aircraft found more than twelve nautical miles from the Argentine coast would be considered hostile.

The San Luis *Attacks*

At 1900 on 8 May the Argentine submarine *San Luis*, lurking north of the Malvinas, attacked an underwater contact estimated to be three thousand yards away and moving at six or eight knots. The submarine fired a Mk 37 torpedo and after six minutes heard a small explosion—not the full charge of the warhead. The identity of the target and the amount of damage it sustained are still unknown. Three days later the *San Luis* saw further action. A British destroyer was coming northward out of the San Carlos

Strait; this was probably HMS *Alacrity*, which had just sunk the *Isla de los Estados*. Another destroyer was heading southward from a position north of the islands. The two joined up just north of the strait and proceeded east. The *San Luis*, with her computer limitation but good firing information, occupied a firing position in front of and between the destroyers and, at a close range of five thousand yards, attacked the target nearest the islands. The submarine had accurately calculated the course, speed, and distance of the target, but she had problems nonetheless. The SST-4 torpedo she fired broke its wire after two and a half minutes. By the time the submarine had positioned herself to fire the second torpedo, it was too late. The high speed of the target put it out of range. There was no counterattack. The *San Luis* terminated her patrol in part because of problems with the torpedoes, returning to Mar del Plata at the end of May.[27]

While the *San Luis* was still on patrol, the second type 209, the *Salta*, sailed to Golfo Nuevo to carry out tests on torpedoes. She fired two wire-guided torpedoes, both of which failed to respond to instructions. The *San Luis* broke radio silence three times, in each instance to report the failure of the torpedoes.

The Attack on the Narwal

The *Narwal*, the largest of the Argentine fishing vessels acting as naval surveillance craft, was assigned a new station some 260 miles southeast of the Malvinas. She arrived there at noon on 6 May after passing through the British exclusion zone and was scheduled to return to the mainland on the same day. But Lieutenant Commander Juan Carlos González Llanos, with plenty of fuel, decided to remain on station a couple of extra days. No contacts were made in the new patrol area, so González Llanos prepared to return to the mainland. He delayed a while because the weather was foggy and he could not fix his position with a sextant. Only with an accurate fix would any data obtained on the return trip have definite value. Planning to pass south of the Malvinas to take advantage of the local currents and, if necessary, obtain shelter in some small inlet of Isla de los Estados, he sailed at 1200 on 8 May for the ports on the Patagonian coast.

At 0905 on the ninth, at a point south of Beauchene Island (52°45′ South latitude and 58°02′ West longitude) and some sixty-five miles from Puerto Argentino, two Harriers dove on the *Narwal* and dropped four thousand-pound bombs.[28] Commander González Llanos took over control of the ship—she had been on autopilot—and tried to evade the attack. One bomb hit amidships on the port side and penetrated the crew's quarters, lodging there without exploding. The hull remained intact. González Llanos ordered the engines stopped, and a minute later the Harriers attacked with cannon. This time the craft was damaged, in the engine-room compartment below the waterline, and she began to take on water. The Harriers departed, leaving as their legacy a badly wounded fisherman who later died. There were no additional casualties.

This attack caught the *Narwal* by surprise. González Llanos, the only navy man on board, had been ordered to stop the engines in case of attack and obey the instructions of the attackers. The civilians on board, twenty-four in number, were not to risk their lives. But he did not have time to carry out his instructions.

He decided not to abandon the vessel. The weather was decent, and only one compartment, the engine room, was taking on water, so the ship was in no immediate danger of sinking. The crew would stay on board until their ship sank or was saved. The lifeboat and the only undamaged life raft on board were launched to make it easier to pack holes in the *Narwal*'s side with mattresses. Having them in the water anyway was a good precaution in case the *Narwal* went down. The crew was partially successful in stopping leaks, which enabled the craft to make a little headway. The injured crewman died at this time.

At about 1200 more Harriers appeared. The crew scattered—four to the lifeboat, three to the raft, the remainder to various places in the *Narwal*. Two enemy aircraft attacked starboard to port with rockets, cannon, and machineguns, hitting the ship, the lifeboat, and the life raft and injuring ten to twelve people, three seriously. The raft sank and the men on it scrambled back to the *Narwal*. Then the lifeboat broke loose from the ship and drifted away with four injured men who couldn't row. Back in the *Narwal*, the emergency generator was damaged so her pump could no longer be operated.

The *Narwal*'s crew gathered everything on the deck that would float and lashed it all together, waiting for the craft to sink. At about 1330 the Harriers reappeared, and men in the *Narwal* took cover for protection. But the aircraft did not attack. Two Sea King helicopters arrived, one hovering 150 feet to starboard, the other lowering some fifteen British marines along with a medic and an engineer. They searched the craft and attended to the wounded. After almost an hour the British began to evacuate the Argentines by helicopter. The four injured men in the lifeboat, now drifting about three thousand yards from the *Narwal*, were also rescued. Eventually everybody, including the casualty, was air-lifted to HMS *Invincible*. The dead sailor was later buried at sea with military honors. Next day the *Narwal* sank while under tow.[29]

Fighting in the Islands

In early morning of 9 May, during a British naval bombardment, a 114-mm shell destroyed the coast guard Puma helicopter parked on the race track outside Puerto Argentino. At the time the other coast guard aircraft were flying search and rescue missions from Río Grande and Río Gallegos to within fifty miles of the Malvinas.

On 10 May the *Isla de los Estados*, under the command of Lieutenant Commander Luis Payarola and with a mixed civilian-military crew, was ordered to transport the cargo remaining from the holds of the *Río Carcarañá* in Puerto Rey to Puerto Howard. The two ships had been together in Puerto Rey since 1 May, and the naval command feared that they would be easily discovered, particularly since the light-colored *Río Carcarañá* stood out from her surroundings. While transiting San Carlos Strait close to Isla del Cisne (Swan Island), the *Isla de los Estados* radioed at 2245 that she had come under artillery fire. At about the same time Argentine army forces at Puerto Howard reported firing on an unidentified ship. Not knowing of any British warships operating in the strait, they at first believed that the cargo ship had been sunk by friendly fire. In fact, it was the British frigate *Alacrity* that had caused her demise. The *Isla de los Estados* sank in only eight minutes after a tremendous detonation that made the British think she was carrying either mines or drummed volatile fuel.

Also on the tenth, the *Buen Suceso*, moored precariously at Puerto Zorro, began loading fresh water with the help of the army's Ninth Engineers Company. On the twelfth, a storm hit and she broke loose from the shaky pier and grounded. The small cargo vessel *Monsunen* tried but did not have enough power to free her. Expecting an air attack, the Argentines unloaded the cargo, which included fuel drums and food.

Meanwhile the island hoppers *Forrest* and *Penelope* started to search for the *Isla de los Estados*. On 11 May the *Forrest*, having discovered some abandoned English commando boats near San Carlos, was attacked by Harriers but escaped serious damage. Two days later she found the debris from the *Isla de los Estados*, and eventually two survivors, one of them Lieutenant Commander Payarola, were discovered on an island. Twenty-one men had gone down with the ship.[30]

The *Río Carcarañá* wasn't as lucky as the *Forrest*. Harriers attacked her on 16 May near Point King and she was abandoned. Her cargo had already been offloaded, and there were no casualties.

On 12 May four Trackers were transferred to Río Gallegos Naval Air Base, whence they would primarily perform reconnaissance flights north and south of the Malvinas, sometimes within thirty nautical miles of San Carlos Sound. Due to English air superiority and radar surveillance, the Trackers were forced to fly low and erratically, greatly reducing their effective range. But they did pick up intelligence, which was used to aid Argentine transport aircraft trying to break through the British aerial blockade to Puerto Argentino.

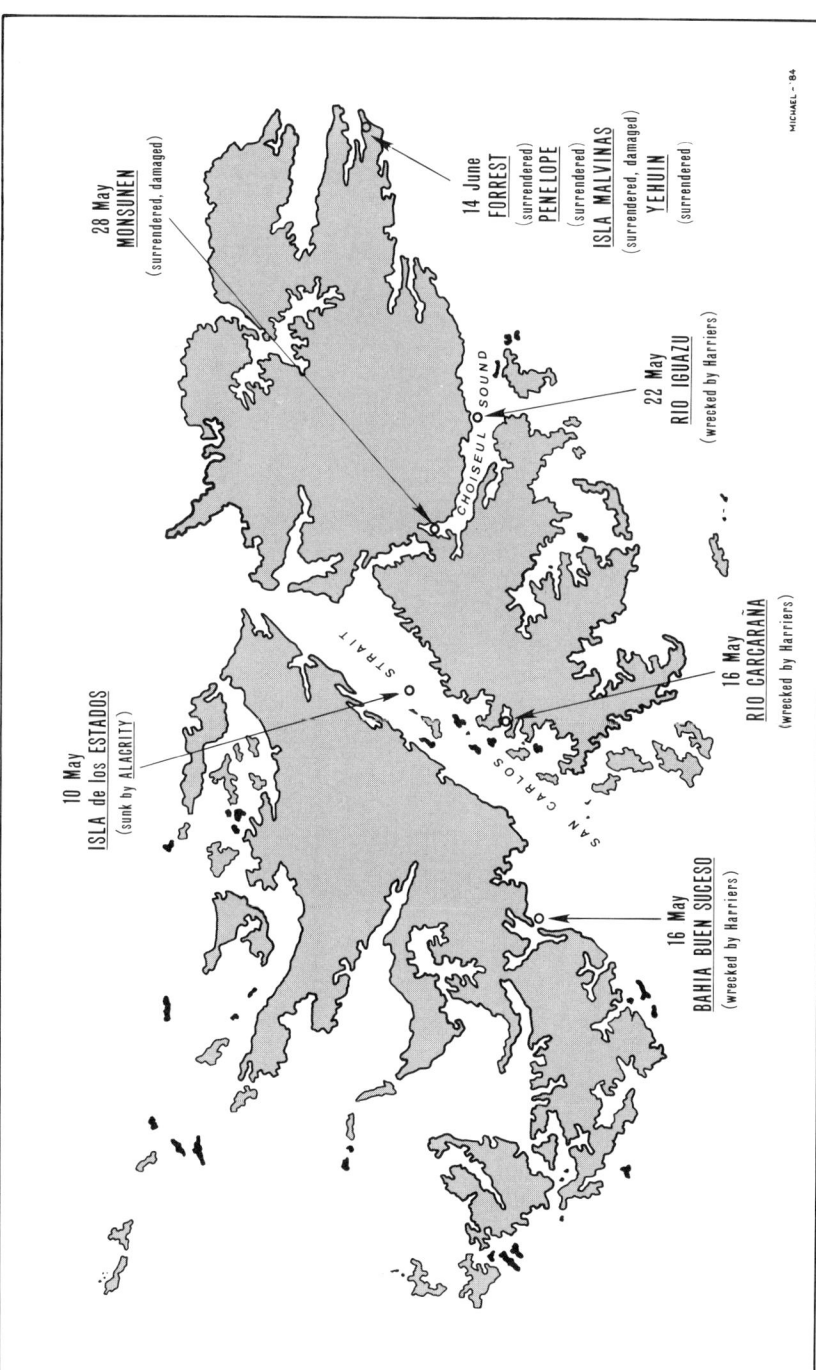

Argentine Supply Ships in the Malvinas

During the night of 15 May British commandos attacked the auxiliary landing strip on Borbon Island, at the time accommodating four navy T-34C trainers, one coast guard Skyvan, and the five air force Pucarás. The field was crowded with aircraft trying to escape the almost constant naval and air attacks on Darwin and Puerto Argentino. They were grounded because the weather was terrible for flying. The ceiling was low, visibility poor—at night nonexistent—and fog almost always obscured the runway in spite of strong prevailing winds. Rain, moreover, had turned the turf landing strip into mud. Aircraft trying to light down sank ten to twelve inches. By 9 May the airstrip was useless and the fixed-wing aircraft immobile.

The airstrip, which had been used for commercial purposes before the war, was well known to the British through aerial photographs and radar. At 0415 on 15 May, the first clear night in many, the British illuminated everything with red flares and the defenders couldn't move without being seen. A ship whose identity they did not know shelled their position nonstop. Forces destroyed the aircraft, still bogged down in mud, with phosphorous demolition charges that lit up the rocket pods on the Pucarás like an inferno. Only two British commandos were wounded.

After the land forces withdrew, the Royal Navy attacked from the air. On 1 June two Argentine naval Sea King helicopters from the continent evacuated some of the personnel. The Sea Kings had to carry the fuel needed for the return flight with them in fifty-five-gallon drums. It was a risky operation, conducted at night over a distance exceeding 350 miles one way. Argentine air force helicopters based in the islands rescued others, and some of the remaining personnel crossed to Gran Malvinas Island, a distance of eight miles, in inflatable rubber boats. A few soldiers stayed at Borbon until the end of the conflict.

Loss of the Neptunes

Naval air received a more serious setback later that day. The last Neptune went out of service because of a lack of spare parts. The Super Etendards, when attacking a target, needed to have its latitude and longitude pegged to within ten nautical miles, and up to this point they had used the Neptunes to perform the service. But from this date to the close of the conflict the navy had to rely on the shorter-legged Trackers and the air force radar at Puerto Argentino for long-range surveillance. The Trackers flying from Río Gallegos, whose sensors were much inferior to those of the larger Neptunes, were able to provide a limited amount of information only. The radar, a three-dimensional Westinghouse AN/TPS-43, was situated in the center of Puerto Argentino; the location was bad for performance, but provided protection since the British never intentionally bombed the town.

To reduce the possibility of the radar's antenna being destroyed by a Shrike antiradiation missile, a number of antennas were placed around Puerto Argentino. The data provided by air force radar operators was plotted by navy personnel, who were occasionally able to calculate the position of the British carriers by extrapolating the converging flight paths of their aircraft to the east. It was British practice to operate carriers from 90 to 120 miles east of the islands in a given area for a number of days. The ships would advance at 0830 and from 1200 until 1500 remain in a limited ellipsoid, approximately twelve by eight miles, to conduct air operations. Then at 1730 the fleet would retire to the east. The Argentines caught on to the fact that the British fleet was following some such pattern. With long-range reconnaissance gone, the question became how to catch a mathematician. Attacks conducted by the Super Etendards after 15 May were based on the hypothesis of repetition.[31]

On 17 May Puerto Argentino reported British units to be southeast of the town. Two Super Etendards took off from Río Grande, refueled in air from an air force KC-130, and tried to locate the targets. Their efforts fruitless, they returned to Río Grande without launching any missiles. The lack of tactical intelligence proved to be the navy's greatest handicap during the war.

The previous day, 16 May, Harriers had attacked Port King and sunk the *Río Carcarañá*, abandoned on the eleventh. At 1400 on the sixteenth, two Harriers strafed the stranded *Bahía Buen Suceso*, causing light damage. A communication and engineering watch remained on board, the rest of the crew went ashore. The *Penelope*, moored outboard of the old naval auxiliary, had apparently been overlooked. On 18 May two Harriers dropped bombs on the *Bahía Buen Suceso*. On the twenty-sixth and the thirtieth she was bombarded by British warships, causing additional damage.[32]

Naval Aircraft and Bomb Alley

Early on 21 May an army outpost reported numerous British units in the Straits of San Carlos. Two Macchis were to be sent from Puerto Argentino on an armed reconnaissance, but it turned out that two of the three had debilitating mechanical problems. Lieutenant Guillermo Owen Crippa took off in the lone operational Macchi. He flew northwest to the northern tip of Gran Malvina Island, then south down San Carlos Strait. There were a lot of British warships near Soledad Island. Next he turned due west toward Puerto Argentino, and as he was trying to observe enemy activity a helicopter appeared directly ahead of him. He aimed at it only to discover a frigate, the *Argonaut*, just below him in San Carlos Bay. Changing targets, he fired at the ship with two five-inch rockets and his thirty-mm cannon. Their effect, though he did not observe it, was to damage the superstructure. After exhausting his munitions, he broke off the action and returned to Puerto Argentino.[33] Air strikes were called in from the mainland.

Next the Third Attack Squadron—eight Skyhawks—was ordered to attack, in two groups of three. The squadron had twelve pilots, six of whom always remained on standby. Two aircraft were held in reserve. One, fitted with a "buddy-pack" refueling system, was to meet the returning Skyhawks in case any needed fuel. The mission was similar to an armed reconnaissance, each plane carrying four five-hundred-pound Mk 82 bombs fitted with Snakeye tails. The Skyhawk pilots had learned during mock attacks against the Argentine type 42 frigates, equipped with type 965 air-search radar, that they would have to approach at less than fifty feet once they were within 150 miles of the target.

The Skyhawks flew without any electronic transmissions. A few days earlier some had received a VHF Omega receiver that permitted them to navigate over the open water. They also had Trackers, which maintained radar contact with the area to be attacked and provided tactical information. The pilots did not know the exact position of the enemy units, nor were they aware of a landing at San Carlos that was taking place at the time.

On 21 May the first three naval Skyhawks flew up San Carlos Strait, and as they neared San Carlos Sound the flight leader, Lieutenant Commander Alberto Jorge Philippi, caught sight of the masts of a frigate. The aircraft hugged the coastline of Soledad Island and then wheeled around toward the west. They climbed to three hundred feet, and at 1515 they attacked, flying twenty seconds apart and dropping their bombs in sequence at an angle forty-five degrees to the ship's axis. The bombs from the first two A-4Qs impacted on or near the stern of the ship. The attackers did not observe where the bombs from the last hit. The frigate *Ardent*, which had been roughly treated shortly before by the Argentine air force, sank from accumulated damages.

As the planes were pulling out, Lieutenant (j.g.) Marcelo Márquez, in the last Skyhawk, spotted a Harrier, but before anything could be done about it the first A-4Q was hit by a Sidewinder missile. The pilot, Commander Philippi, lost control and ejected.[34] After landing in the water, he swam ashore and trekked across Soledad Island, where he was aided by kelpers and ultimately rescued by Argentine forces. Lieutenant Márquez was lost without a trace; a Harrier shot his plane down with cannons. The second A-4Q was hit by small-arms fire, probably from the *Ardent*, and by thirty-mm fire from the Harriers. Escaping at low altitude, the pilot, Lieutenant José Cesar Arca, made his way to Puerto Argentino, where he bailed out after determining that his plane could not make it back to the mainland or land on the islands. In the bay opposite the town an Argen-

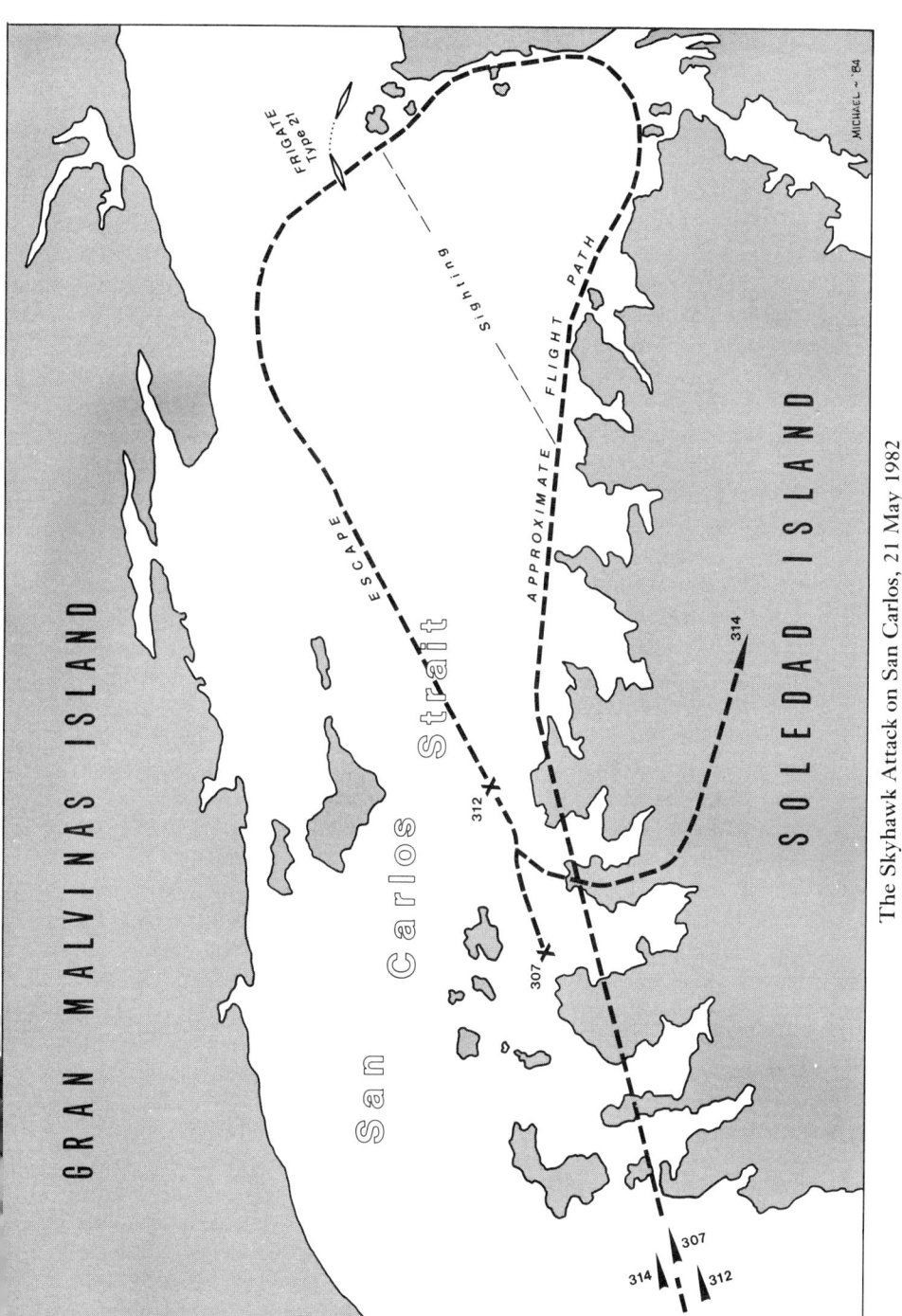

The Skyhawk Attack on San Carlos, 21 May 1982

tine army helicopter rescued him. The helicopter, not fitted to land on the water, submerged its skids so that Arca could grab on to one and cling to it while being flown to Puerto Argentino. Meanwhile, his Skyhawk circled overhead, refusing to fall until the antiaircraft gunners received orders to down it.

The second group of A-4Qs, which had been monitoring the fate of their comrades, attacked at 1530. They approached undetected and went after another type 21 frigate. Bombs from the first aircraft straddled the target, those from the second landed very near the hull, and those from the third were not observed by the attackers. The target ship has not yet been identified.[35] On the return flight very strong headwinds, blowing as much as one hundred knots, threatened the Skyhawks, and one returned with less than 450 pounds of fuel. For this reason all subsequent Skyhawk attacks had to be carried out with air-to-air refueling.

These were not the only events on 21 May. That day large numbers of Argentine air force planes, which included A-4Cs, also attacked the British. And the cutter *Río Iguazú* was ordered to transport replacement artillery parts for antiaircraft guns from Puerto Argentino to Darwin. British air superiority was making such transits more difficult, and the cutter was selected because her eighteen-knot capability allowed her to run full speed during the night, hugging the coast. But this did not avail her. At approximately 0830 on 22 May, in Choiseul Sound east of Darwin, Harriers attacked the *Río Iguazú*. Her twenty-mm cannon jammed, and while evading the strafing aircraft, she ran hard aground on a rock and was lost. One crew member was killed and two were wounded.[36] The rest made it to shore in a small boat and were rescued from Darwin. Later they returned to salvage artillery parts.

The weather was too poor for air operations on the twenty-second. That day the Argentines, thinking a British force was going to attack the airfields in Tierra del Fuego, positioned the destroyer *Seguí* off the coast to act as a radar picket. Nothing happened. It may have been that a large Russian fishing fleet operating off Tierra del Fuego was mistakenly identified as a British force.

On the twenty-third, with the improved weather, the A-4Qs renewed their attack on the British position at San Carlos, this time refueling from an air force KC-130 on their way to the islands. The commander on scene, Captain Héctor A. Martini, coordinated the naval air attack from Río Grande. It was made at low level in the face of a heavy antiair defense put up by both ships and land-based installations. At 1405 one aircraft attacked the destroyer *Antrim*, another a type 21 frigate, probably the *Antelope*.[37] The third failed to release its bombs. Despite its being extremely short on fuel because of a transfer problem, the leading aircraft made it back safely. The second returned without incident. As Lieutenant Commander Carlos Zubizarreta, in the third, was landing at Río Grande with a strong crosswind, his plane started to drift off the runway and he used his ejection seat. The procedure, though technically correct, resulted in Zubizarreta's death. His heavily damaged aircraft was salvageable.[38] This attack, plus those made by the air force, failed to dislodge the British.

At 1630 on 23 May three Harriers attacked the turf airstrip on Borbon. Although British special forces had destroyed ten Argentine aircraft on the fifteenth, the field was still operational and in Argentine hands. The Harriers caused no additional damage.[39]

At 0505 on 23 May helicopters attacked the *Monsunen*, commanded by Lieutenant (j.g.) Jorge Alberto Gopcevich, while she was transporting supplies from Port Fox to Darwin. Following orders, the cargo ship ran for the protection of the coast and accidentally grounded. The enemy broke off the attack, perhaps after losing radar contact (it was still dark). The *Forrest* towed the *Monsunen* to Darwin and salvaged the cargo.

Attack on the Atlantic·Conveyor

On 25 May the radar at Puerto Argentino again fixed the general location of the British fleet—approximately one hundred nautical miles to the east-northeast of the port and five hundred nautical miles from the Argentine naval air base at Río Grande. As part of their plan to attack, the Argentines positioned a refueling aircraft 160 to 180 nautical miles to the east of Puerto Deseado. By refueling in this location, the Super Etendards could fly more than one hundred nautical miles north of the Malvinas and thus avoid detection by British warships on radar picket duty close to the islands.

The two Etendards, piloted by Lieutenant Commander Roberto Curilovic and Lieutenant Julio Barraza, took off from Río Grande at 1428. They refueled without incident and commenced their final leg of 270 nautical miles. It took them due east, beyond the islands, and then south. When Curilovic picked up a radar emission on his receiving equipment, the two aircraft turned toward their targets and at 1632 launched a single Exocet missile apiece. Both missiles hit the *Atlantic Conveyor*, in position 50°38′ South latitude, 56°08′ West longitude.[40] Flying fifty feet above the water, the aircraft raced back toward Puerto Deseado. The air force KC-130s had been circling at the refueling site awaiting their return. After refueling for a second time, the Etendards returned to Río Grande. Their entire flight of 1,620 miles took four hours and ten minutes.[41]

Defenders in the Islands

Following the landing at San Carlos, British air and ground forces put increasing pressure on the Argentine defenders. On 28 May Argentine aircraft, air force and naval, supported ground forces at Darwin. The morning flight couldn't deliver an attack because visibility was zero, so they re-

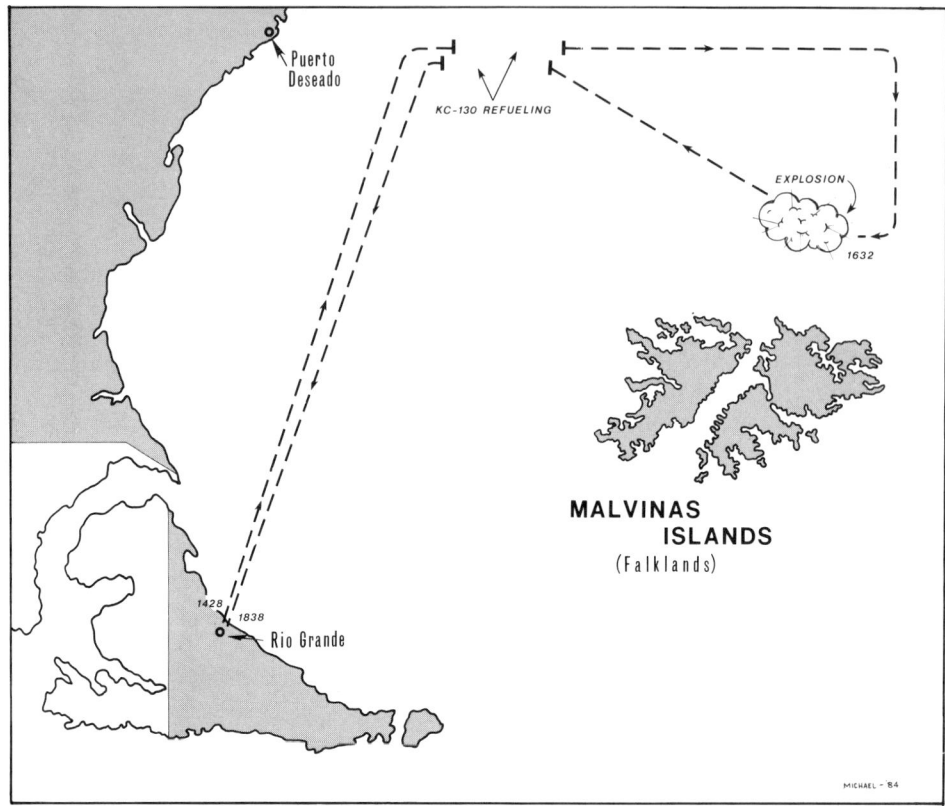

The Super Etendard Attack on the *Atlantic Conveyor*, 25 May 1982

turned to the Puerto Argentino landing field with a forty-knot wind blowing at a ninety-degree angle—conditions that were not unusual.

By 1530 the weather had cleared, and two Macchis took part in the afternoon air strike. (A few days earlier three Macchis had crossed from the mainland to Puerto Argentino, bringing the total there to six.) In the action one 339 was shot down, killing its pilot, Lieutenant Daniel E. Miguel. A British soldier fired a Blowpipe at what he believed to be a Pucará and struck its right wing. "It turned over and hit the ground in a tremendous ball of fire," he reported later.[42] This might well have been the naval Macchi. The pilot of the other Macchi, after delivering his ordnance—thirty-mm cannon fire and five-inch rockets—spotted an orange glow and assumed a missile had been fired at him. He cut his engine to idle and confronted the attack, losing altitude rapidly. The weapon missed the Macchi, and the aircraft escaped.[43]

On this day, the twenty-eighth, Darwin fell to the British. Next they would move against Puerto Argentino.

With the British in San Carlos, what was left of Argentina's small cargo ships could enter San Carlos Strait only from the south. They moved at night, hugging the shoreline, and continued to work almost up to the last week of the war. Apparently the supply fleet made forty sorties between 1 May and the fall of Puerto Argentino. In early June the *Penelope*, commanded by Lieutenant Horacio González Llanos, carried the ultimate cargo, thirty-mm ammunition, from Puerto Argentino to Fox Bay, tracing the southern route.[44] The naval command feared that she had been lost, because she was overdue and, by their calculations, out of fuel. But the resourceful crew did some successful foraging on Soledad Island, enabling their ship to return safely. Her only electronic navigational aid was an echo sounder, and her top speed was six knots.

The Final Super Etendard Attack

The fifth and last Etendard attack took place on 30 May. Puerto Argentino had reported British units in a general location about one hundred nautical miles to the southeast, and the Argentines had planned an attack sweeping in from the south in a counterclockwise motion. To reach the target, more than five hundred nautical miles from Río Grande Naval Air Base, by flying around the British picket line, the Etendards would have to refuel twice on the way to the target.

During the planning stage, the air force asked if it could send four A-4C Skyhawks along in the attack. This would bring both an advantage and a disadvantage. On the one hand, the more aircraft, the greater the potential to damage the enemy. On the other, the more the aircraft, the greater the possibility of detection. Until this attack the Etendards had relied on stealth. The A-4s, armed with two five-hundred-pound bombs each, would have to conform to the tactics of the Etendards. The benefit of having the air force planes along, it was decided, outweighed the disadvantages, and they joined the attack.

Two Etendards carried out the attack. One was armed with Argentina's last Exocet and accompanied by four A-4Cs; the other was a navigational backup in case the missile-carrying aircraft experienced electrical problems (the A-4s could not act as navigational aids so far over open ocean). The first refueling took place to the southeast of Isla de los Estados and the second south of Soledad Island. At about three hundred nautical miles from the British fleet, the aircraft swept up toward the northeast, searching for their enemy. Shortly afterward the Etendards detected radar emissions and turned toward the source. At about 1440 Lieutenant Commander Alejandro Francisco, flying the armed Etendard, launched his missile and then, with the other Etendard, retired. The A-4Cs followed the missile exhaust. Two were shot down on their approach, possibly, being inexperienced over water, because they flew too high; had they been on the deck, as naval pilots say, the Sea Dart missiles of the *Exeter* could not have got them. The other pair dropped their bombs. One of the pilots, Lieutenant Ernesto Ureta, described the attack as follows:

> The attack was made from about 30 degrees off the ship's stern. I released my bombs, and after flying directly over and away from the carrier, I made a turn and confirmed that my bombs had hit. I can confirm that the carrier was hit by the Exocet, because I saw the thick black column of smoke rising from it. So I am sure it did hit.[45]

Both pilots believed the ship they saw shrouded in black smoke at 51°42' South latitude, 55°50' West longitude, to be the *Invincible*, though in fact the ships attacked were the destroyer *Exeter* and the frigate *Avenger*. As it turned out, neither was damaged.[46] The missile flew up the middle of the task force and, when its fuel was exhausted, splashed harmlessly into the sea. Its homing guidance system evidently never acquired a target. On the flight back, the surviving aircraft refueled a third time.[47]

This attack by the Super Etendards has a lot of interesting features. Never before had Argentine naval and air force attack planes operated together. Because they had nothing to navigate with over the open sea, two A-4Cs had to fly formation with each Etendard. The double air refueling of six planes with two different consumption curves was a tricky logistics calculation. To extend range, the aircraft refueled first while flying with the KC-130 for over three hundred miles, taking successive "drinks" in a "merry-go-round" pattern. The four A-4C pilots were volunteers, since the chances of penetrating an antiair naval formation in open sea, without the opportunity to conceal themselves behind the radar shadow of land masses, were considered small. The flight was somewhat longer than the one against the *Atlantic Conveyor*, and unlike that, this one was conducted entirely over the sea, without alternate airfields, in an east-southeast direction to the rim of the Antarctic ice floes. It is understandable that, after such an aeronautical feat, the Argentine air force and navy pilots refuse to this day to believe that they hit nothing, even though that is indisputably the case.

With the last air-to-surface Exocet expended, the Super Etendards began training in bombing tactics. The conflict, however, ended before they could be used in this role.

By early June the constant operations of the Macchis in a hostile environment had taken its toll. Of the seven planes taken to the islands (the seventh had been brought after the 25 May flight), one had been lost on 3 May in an accident, one had been shot down over Darwin on 28 May, and

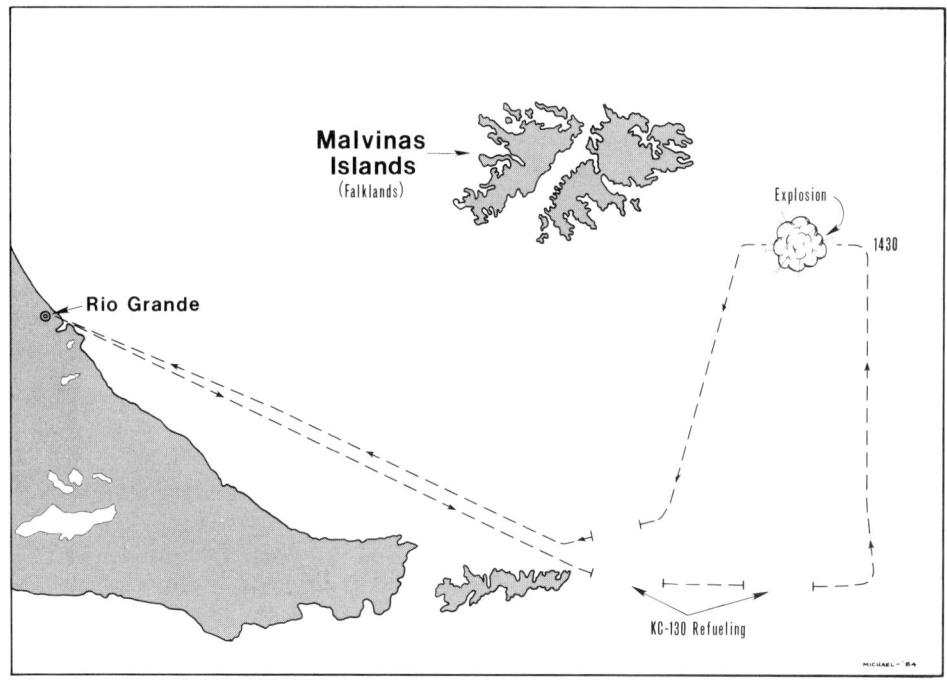

The Super Etendard Attack on the *Invincible*, 30 May 1982

three had developed mechanical problems. Only two were fully operational, and there were drop tanks for no more than two. On 9 June Admiral Otero ordered the two operational Macchis to return to the mainland. Plans were under way to fly drop tanks to the three serviceable Macchis, but Puerto Argentino fell to the British before they could be carried out. Before-hand, these three aircraft were disabled by the Argentines.[48]

Land-Based Exocets for the Malvinas

The first bombardment of Puerto Argentino by a British warship occurred on 1 May. Shortly afterward, the Argentine navy started to evaluate the possibility of putting an Exocet surface-to-surface system on the islands that would discourage British warships from approaching. They estimated that to transport a whole shipboard system—missile, radar, and supporting electronics—it would take forty-five days. That was too much time. A much simpler solution was needed, and to find it an ordnance engineering officer, Commander Julio Pérez, and two civilian technicians sequestered themselves. After a week they had the answer, and ten days later a makeshift system had been assembled. The technicians established a procedure for feeding information about the target's distance and bearing into the Exocet command system. To carry out the firing sequence they constructed a box with four switches, similar to an early telephone switchboard. Manual switches prevented the need for more circuiting, which would have required more time. They were thrown in a specific order while time was measured with a stopwatch. Success depended on the proper execution of this procedure and some luck. The entire system was mounted on two old trailers, the generator and supporting hardware on one, two ramps for the Exocet MM 38 box launchers on the other. This primitive system was christened the Do-It-Yourself Firing Installation.

On 24 May an attempt was made to fly Commander Pérez along with the entire installation into Puerto Argentino. British activity forced the transport aircraft, an air force C-130, to turn back on two separate days before it finally landed in the islands in early June. Once the weapons were there, the decision of where to install them was determined by their weight. The heavier trailer weighed over four tons, which meant that if it traveled on an unpaved road it would sink in the mud. The only paved road on Soledad Island was a short stretch between the airport and Puerto Argentino. Thus the town was chosen as the site. From there the Exocets could sweep a sixty-degree arc to the south. The air force's Westinghouse radar provided the long-range search, and an army artillery radar was used for fire control.

Each night the system was dragged out of a shed or from under netting, positioned behind a sixteen-foot mound, and made ready within two and a half hours, by 2030. Now all the Argentines needed was a British ship to enter the area. Almost a week went by before a ship entered the missile's field of fire. When one did arrive and the first missile was fired, it proved to be defective, possibly owing to damage received in transit. The second missile veered sharply to the right. By mistake the connection to the transformer had been reversed. The Argentines believed that the British had not detected these firings. In fact, one of the missiles may have passed directly over the helicopter pad on a type 21 frigate. Whatever the case, the British destroyers and frigates performing gunfire-support missions against Puerto Argentino had marked on the bridge plot a sector they should not enter due to missile threat.

More missiles were needed as quickly as possible. On 5 June a C-130 arrived carrying four. Again the Exocet crew waited for a target. Finally, at 0300 on 12 June, a ship entered the field of fire. When it came within thirty kilometers of Puerto Argentino the third Exocet was launched. The Argentines' patience was finally rewarded. They saw an orange glow coming from the target as the Exocet impacted. The target, the British destroyer *Glamorgan*, had fired a Sea Cat missile that missed the incoming weapon. The Exocet killed thirteen of the *Glamorgan*'s men. She had en-

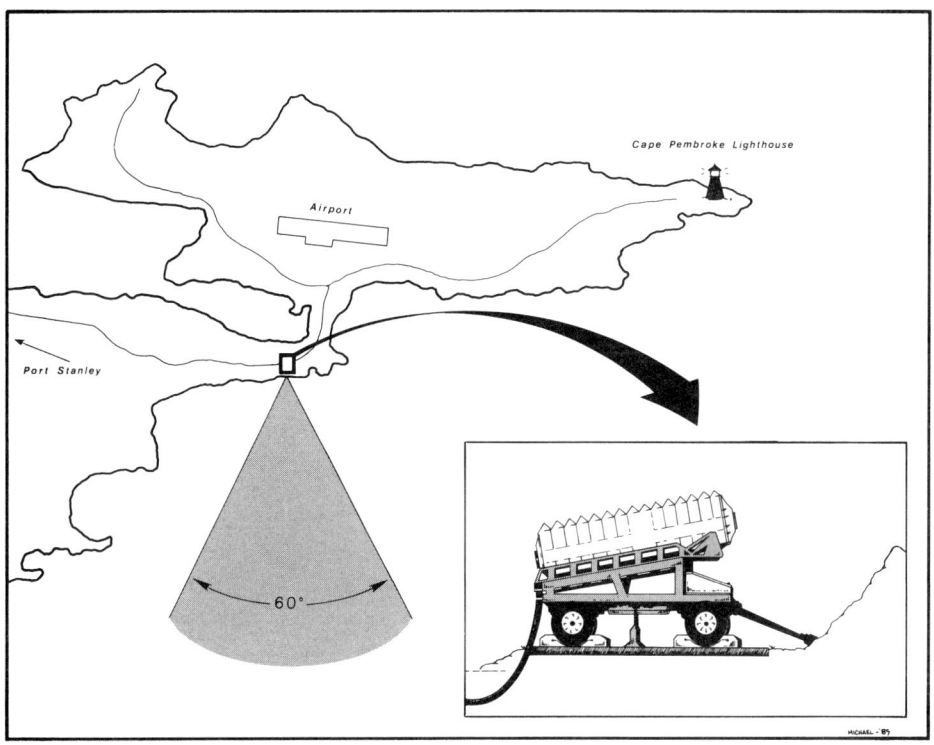

Land-Based Exocet, June 1982

tered the restricted sector by mistake, after bombarding Puerto Argentino, and was trying to get out when the missile hit.

The remaining three Exocet missiles were lost when Puerto Argentino was captured by the British.

Beginning of the End

From 1 May until 14 June navy logistics aircraft transported 304 persons and seventy tons of cargo to the Malvinas. The presence of English forces after the first of the month greatly altered their flying tactics. They approached at a fifty-foot altitude to within fifty miles, climbed slightly to cross over the islands, then dropped again after passing the east coast, turning north towards Puerto Argentino and then west to the runway there. In fact, to land they had to climb, for the runway was seventy-two feet above sea level. Later, transport aircraft flew counterclockwise around the southern and eastern rim of the islands, always at a fifty-foot altitude until they reached Puerto Argentino. They varied their routes as much as possible. Before the air blockade a direct flight took fifty-five minutes; afterwards it took ninety minutes. The C-130s came with an excess of fuel to build the supply on the islands.

Logistics aircraft, avoiding their radar during flight, used VHF and HF for communications. The procedure worked like this: a squadron member at Río Grande, in HF communication with the Malvinas would insert key words in the middle of a conversational sentence that would relay to an aircraft whether it was safe to approach Puerto Argentino; as the plane came within VHF range of the Malvinas—about thirty miles—it would receive transmissions on a frequency that changed each day. As we saw in the case of the Neptunes, the VHF Omega system was also used to aid in navigation. The accuracy of this system, however, left something to be desired; one aircraft directed by an Omega fix flew thirty miles east of Puerto Argentino—to within forty miles of an unknown British carrier.

As for the timing of the flights, many options were tried. Following 21 May, aircraft were scheduled to fly during Argentine air attacks against San Carlos in hopes of taking advantage of the confusion. And as June approached aircraft began night flights. Starting at about 1700 two planes would take off from Río Grande about a half hour apart—the minimum amount of time needed to land, unload, and take off again at Puerto Argentino. Getting into the airport became increasingly difficult, especially after 8 June, when the air force successfully attacked British amphibians at Agradable Bay (North Basin). As a result numerous British ships frequented the area. In this later period approximately thirty-five flights ran the blockade, their success depending partly on the weather, which out of the seventy days of war forced airport closure only on three. Those days the runway was wet and excessive winds blew at a ninety-degree angle.

The Final Defense of Puerto Argentino

After six weeks of air and sea bombardment, British ground forces closed in on the defenders of Puerto Argentino, approximately eight thousand combat troops holding the perimeters. Argentine General Menéndez had determined the defense strategy. Until the very end he expected a frontal amphibious assault coming from the east against Puerto Argentino. Therefore, his three best army regiments (of battalion strength) were looking eastward, towards the sea. Only two regiments, with the Fifth Marine Battalion—about three thousand men—covered the western front. As events unfolded, they had to face the attack of three British brigades. On 8 June a scout from the Fifth Marine Battalion detected an amphibious landing at Agradable Bay, an area Argentine forces had neglected to occupy. The British advanced from the beachhead, while Argentine forces advanced along two footpaths on either side of Challenger Mountain to block their progress. The attempt was futile; the Argentines were outflanked by British mobility.

The same day air force A-4Cs attacked the British beachhead through a cloud cover and much to their surprise encountered little antiaircraft fire. They hit the unescorted landing ships *Sir Tristram* and *Sir Galahad*, which were left with bad damage and many casualties.[49]

The setback did not deter the British, who pressed on with their land attack. At 2300 on 11 June three brigades totaling about nine thousand men—the Parachute Brigade, the Commando Brigade, and the Welsh Guards—attacked the defense perimeter of Puerto Argentino with fifty-four artillery pieces from the west. They were assisted by three to five ships from the north and south and constant Harrier attacks. The action commenced against Mount Harriet and Two Sisters, held by the Fourth Infantry Regiment, and Mount Longdon, held by the Seventh Infantry Regiment, all Argentine army units (see the map on page 287). By 0100 on 12 June the English carried Mount Harriet, Two Sisters, and half of Mount Longdon, thus controlling much of the highlands west of the town. The Fifth Battalion, supported by Argentine army units, held the remainder of the high ground, principally Tumbledown and Mount Williams. Some members of retreating army regiments joined the marines and fought under their command. The marine radio net directed all the shots of army artillery support fire. At the height of the action the British fired one thousand rounds an hour on the western front.

This was the last barrier to Puerto Argentino. By the twelfth the British had consolidated their position. For forty-eight hours they bombarded Argentine positions with fire from 114-mm naval guns, 105-mm land-based guns, and Harriers. Though no serious damage resulted, communications with the rear were interrupted. Next, at approximately 2100 on 13 June, the British attacked Mount Williams, using Mount Harriet as a jumping-off point. Supported by the army's adept handling of its artillery, the Argentine marines held their ground. The authors of *The Battle for the Falklands* note that "the Scots Guard could hear some of the Argentinians shouting and even singing as they fought. These were the best troops General Menéndez could put into the field, the 5th Marines. . . ."[50] At 2215 the British attacked Wireless Ridge, held by the Seventh Infantry Regiment, and Mount Williams for a second time. Fifteen minutes later they assaulted the marines on Tumbledown Ridge. The army's Seventh Regiment fell back, but once again the marines held their position, roughly repulsing their enemy with field artillery and mortars. The gap left by the retreat of the Argentine army regiment was filled by 0030 on the fourteenth.

Now the attack came along the entire front, and the fighting grew general. British forces flanked the Argentine marines to the north, at 0400

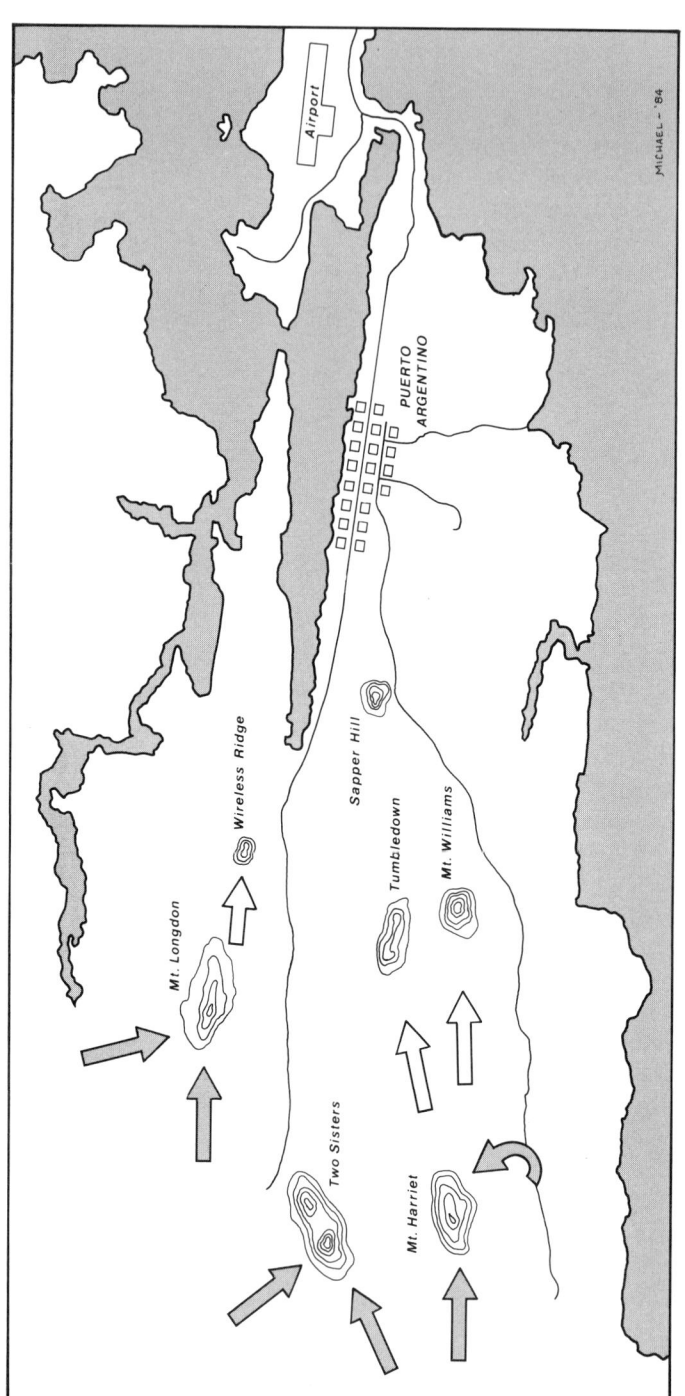

The Final Defense of Puerto Argentino, June 1982

pouring machine-gun fire into their position. The marines were forced back, but at 0600 they counterattacked with a platoon and regained some of their territory.

By 0700, with the front stabilized, the marines prepared to counterattack at the northern front. They requested artillery support, reinforcements for the northern flank, and ammunition—the battalion had about a four-hour supply remaining. At 0800 the British stormed Tumbledown Ridge. At 0900 the marines again requested reinforcements and ammunition. Instead of that they received orders to cancel the counterattack and fall back to prepared positions on Sapper Hill. There they were told to cease fire and assemble in Puerto Argentino. At 1300 a British helicopter-borne unit attacked M Company, which was protecting the withdrawal of the remainder of the battalion. Heavy fire forced the helicopter to withdraw and M Company disengaged, retreating in good order. By 1430 on 14 June the Fifth Marine Battalion arrived in the assembly area, bearing all of its light weapons. Before abandoning the area, they destroyed any artillery, vehicles, communication equipment, and supplies that could not be carried off. Then they marched back to Puerto Argentino and surrendered. Sixty-six days on the defensive left them with eighty casualties, including sixteen dead.[51]

On 14 June Argentine defenses collapsed and the fighting ended. When the British broke through and reached the town, three army regiments had to surrender, for they had no higher command, no artillery support, and no air support. The British rolled up the Argentine forces piecemeal from the town back toward the sea. The Fifth Marine Battalion was out of ammunition, and Argentine positions north and south of it had collapsed. By this time the Super Etendards had fired all of their Exocet missiles, and naval aviation in the Malvinas was nonexistent. Only two supply craft were fit for service, the *Forrest* and the *Penelope*. The *Monsunen* was at Darwin with hull and engine damage, and the cutter *Islas Malvinas* was at Puerto Argentino with propeller damage. Not one Argentine submarine was operating against the enemy when the town fell. The *San Luis* was rushing preparations for a second patrol, but she could not be on station for at least two weeks. The *Salta*'s problems had not yet been solved.

Toward the end of the war, the *Almirante Irizar* and the *Bahía Paraíso*, both converted into hospital ships, made numerous trips between the mainland and the islands caring for the wounded. A number of naval Sea King helicopters were assigned to these ships. On 5 June the *Bahía Paraíso* evacuated the crew of the *Bahía Buen Suceso* from Bahia Zorro to Puerto Argentino.

In Retrospect

The Argentine navy did not operate in a vacuum. It did not take or defend the Malvinas by itself. But it would be accurate to say the navy was primarily responsible for the capture of the islands and played an important role in the air, sea, and land war that followed. The navy sustained the greatest losses of the Argentine armed services. Approximately 375 naval personnel died, compared with 260 in the army and 55 in the air force.

Victory has no substitute, and the Argentines lost. Of the navy's disappointments, the biggest had to be its failure to hold the islands. Others were its inability to handle nuclear submarines, which accounted in large measure for the helplessness of its surface fleet against the British threat. The years of UNITAS exercises had come to nought. Nevertheless, fleet losses were minor. The submarine *Santa Fe* and a few small auxiliaries are gone, but the one was old and the others are easily replaced. The few units that were damaged have since been repaired. The only deeply felt loss is that of the *General Belgrano*. The cruiser, which provided firepower useful for support, will be missed.

The navy adopted an extremely conservative strategy during the war. A prime motivation for this was the belief that the Chileans might take advantage of the situation and attack. Thus numerous assets were hoarded and not used to their full potential. The high-speed torpedo boats *Intrépida* and *Indómita* stayed in the Beagle Channel instead of going to the Malvinas, an ideal operational area for them. When some suggested that an Argentine type 42 destroyer make a foray into the British line of communication flying the Union Jack, the idea was rejected. So was a proposal that the Super Etendards extend their radius by using Puerto Argentino as an emergency crashing site, regardless of the risk to the aircraft. The navy paid a heavy price for having constantly looked over its shoulder at Chile.

And it made costly tactical errors. It never gained positive control of tactical air operations, and three quarters of the aircraft it lost were destroyed on the ground by British forces. Naval aircraft losses, though, were moderate: three A-4Q Skyhawks, five MC-339 Macchis (three on the ground at Puerto Argentino), four T-34s (at Borbon on the ground), two Skyvans (on the ground), one Puma, and one Alouette (on board the *General Belgrano*). Four pilots died.

The navy's successes were less important. The service remained intact after confronting the third most powerful fleet in the world; this preserved the regional balance of power. Naval personnel who manned the "island hoppers" in the Malvinas and those who devised and operated the land-based Exocet were innovative in their defense of the islands. Naval intelligence worked smoothly and accurately and managed to predict enemy strategic and tactical actions, although these assessments were all too frequently lost in the collective voice of the intelligence community. The marine corps performed admirably. The Second Marine Battalion captured the islands in a classic and perfectly executed amphibious landing. Admittedly, it was opposed by only a handful of men, but they had over thirty-six hours of warning (from noon on 31 May until dawn on 2 April) to prepare a defense. And even in the midst of fire at the government house and on the outskirts of then Port Stanley, which resulted in casualties for them, the marines did as they had been ordered and inflicted none on the British. Their discipline in restraining themselves was outstanding. The Fifth Marine Battalion and the Marine Antiaircraft Battalion, though they lacked the air mobility that only helicopters could provide, fought stubbornly to defend the islands.

The navy should also be pleased with the performance of naval aviation. The Super Etendard pilots had accumulated less than one hundred flight hours in their aircraft prior to the conflict. At that time Argentina had five Exocet air-to-surface missiles, but none was operational. Argentine personnel got them ready without French assistance and later, after the capture of the islands, devised Exocet tactics during grueling hours of practice. This was all done without instruction from the French in the tactical use of the Etendard or the air-launched Exocet. That was the missile that sank the *Sheffield* and the *Atlantic Conveyor*, in the astonishingly long-range attacks of the Etendards. The Argentines also developed the capability for aerial refueling, which they had never practiced with the air force before; the process was conducted with French intakes and U.S.-type nozzles. The aging Skyhawk squadron, initially composed of eight aircraft, sank the type 21 frigate *Ardent* and contributed to the sinking of the *Antelope*. Naval support aircraft, Fokkers and Electras, completed seventy-five percent of their supply runs to the islands and operated up to the last day. Naval reconnaissance aircraft, Trackers and aging Neptunes, managed to locate British units and maintain contact in 150 of the 200 missions they carried out. Not one of these planes was lost.

Many of the reasons leading the Argentines into war are still being argued. However, considering how late they were getting their naval intelligence organized, their Super Etendard squadron and Exocet missiles operational, and their tactical planning finished, it can be said that this war was one more of the heart than the head for the Argentines.

Appendices

APPENDIX 1*

Latin American Naval Ranks

Naval ranks have been translated into English throughout the text. Listed below are U.S. ranks and their Spanish equivalents. Notable exceptions are footnoted in the text.

Mid-Nineteenth and Twentieth Century, U.S. Navy	Late Colonial Era, Spanish Navy	Early- and Mid-Nineteenth Century, Argentine Navy	Late-Nineteenth and Twentieth Century, Argentine Navy
Cadet	Guardiamarina	Aspirante Cadete	Cadete Guardiamarina
Midshipman	Alférez de Fragata	Subteniente de Marina	Teniente de Corbeta
Lieutenant Junior Grade	Alférez de Navío	Teniente de Marina	Teniente de Fragata
Lieutenant	Teniente de Fragata	Capitán de Marina	Teniente de Navío
Lieutenant Commander	Teniente de Navío	Sargento Mayor de Marina	Capitán de Corbeta
Commander	Capitán de Fragata	Teniente Coronel de Marina	Capitán de Fragata
Captain	Capitán de Navío	Coronel de Marina	Capitán de Navío
Rear Admiral	Brigadier de Marina	Coronel Mayor de Marina	Contraalmirante
—	Jefe de Escuadra	Comodoro	—
Vice Admiral	Teniente General	Brigadier de Marina	Vicealmirante
Admiral	Capitán General	—	Almirante

*Based on information in Destéfani, "Bases para los Estudios Marítimos Argentinos." For a comparison of officer ranks among Latin American armed forces during World War II, see Rogers, "Officer Ranks."

APPENDIX 2
Naval Participation in Political Revolts, 1890–1985

Year	Country	Revolt Against President	Degree of Naval Involvement	Outcome
1890	Argentina	Miguel Juárez Celman	Substantial: supported the revolt	Modestly successful: failed in broad goals but deposed the president
1891	Brazil	Manoel Deodoro da Fonseca	Substantial: led revolt, which was generally supported by army and populace	Successful: installed Marshal Floriano Vieira Peixoto as president
1891	Chile	José Manuel Balmaceda and the army	Dominant: supported the congress	Successful: restored congressional rule
1893	Argentina	Luis Sáenz Peña	Modest: only a few ships involved	Unsuccessful
1893	Brazil	Floriano Vieira Peixoto	Dominant	Unsuccessful
1924	México	Alvaro Obregón	Moderate: Gulf fleet supported Adolfo de la Huerta	Unsuccessful
1930	Argentina	Hipólito Irigoyen	Modest	Successful: overthrew the president and initiated an era of military interventions
1941	Paraguay	Higinio Morínigo	Modest: only a few officers involved	Unsuccessful

Year	Country	Revolt Against President	Degree of Naval Involvement	Outcome
1943	Argentina	Ramón Castillo	Modest: the naval warrant officers' school remained loyal to the president and fought army units	Successful
1945	Argentina	Juan Perón	Moderate	Unsuccessful
1947	Paraguay	Higinio Morínigo	Substantial	Unsuccessful
1948	Perú	José Luis Bustamente y Rivero	Moderate	Unsuccessful
1951	Argentina	Juan Perón	Modest: a small group of navy and army officers	Unsuccessful
1952	Cuba	Carlos Prío Socarrás	Modest: only a few officers	Successful: helped install Fulgentio Batista as president
1955	Brazil	Juscelino Kubitschek (president elect)	Moderate: acting President Carlos Luz commandeers cruiser	Unsuccessful
1955 (June)	Argentina	Juan Perón	Dominant: composed primarily of marine corps, naval aviation	Unsuccessful
1955 (Sep)	Argentina	Juan Perón	Dominant: led revolt, which was opposed by substantial elements of army and air force	Successful: installed General Eduardo Lonardi as president
1957	Colombia	Gustavo Rojas Pinilla	Modest	Successful
1957	Cuba	Fulgentio Batista	Dominant	Unsuccessful

Year	Country	Revolt Against President	Degree of Naval Involvement	Outcome
1958	Venezuela	Marcos Pérez Jiménez	Dominant	Successful: installed Rear Admiral Wolfgang Larrazabal as acting president
1962	Venezuela	Rómulo Betancourt	Dominant: elements of the navy, primarily marine corps personnel	Unsuccessful
1963	Argentina	Arturo Illia	Dominant	Unsuccessful: the Punta Indio naval air base fought against army and air force units and was captured
1964	Brazil	João Belchior Marques Goulart	Moderate	Successful: installed Marshall Humberto de Alencar Castello Branco as president
1970	Haití	François Duvalier	Dominant	Unsuccessful
1973	Chile	Salvador Allende	Moderate: cooperated with the other military services	Successful: installed a military junta
1976	Argentina	Isabel Perón	Moderate: cooperated with the other military services	Successful: installed a military junta

APPENDIX 3

Ships in the Argentine and Chilean Navies, 1890–1902

Argentina	Chile
Libertad (ex-*9 de Julio*) Coastal defense battleship, 2,330 tons 1890 laid down 1890 (11 Dec) launched 1892 (13 Dec) trials 1893 (25 Jan) arrived at Buenos Aires	*Capitán Prat* Second-class battleship, 6,901 tons 1887 funds appropriated 1890 (20 Dec) launched 1894 (13 Jun) arrived at Talcahuano
Independencia Coastal defense battleship, 2,330 tons 1890 laid down 1891 (26 Feb) launched 1892 (5 Mar) completed 1893 (7 Apr) accepted 1893 (29 Jun) sailed from Liverpool 1893 (31 Jul) arrived at Buenos Aires	*Presidente Errázuriz* Protected cruiser, 2,047 tons 1887 funds appropriated 1889 (Mar) ordered 1889 laid down 1890 (21 Jun) launched 1892 completed
25 de Mayo (ex-*Necochea*) Protected cruiser, 3,180 tons 1888 (18 Jun) laid down as a stock cruiser 1890 (5 May) launched; purchased by Argentina after this date 1890 (4 Nov) trials 1891 (18 May) accepted 1891 (27 Aug) arrived at Rio de la Plata 1891 (3 Sep) incorporated into fleet	*Presidente Pinto* Protected cruiser, 2,047 tons 1887 funds appropriated 1889 (Mar) ordered 1889 laid down 1890 (4 Sep) launched 1892 completed
	Blanco Encalada Protected cruiser, 4,568 tons 1892 (30 Sep) laid down 1892 (29 Nov) purchased 1893 (9 Sep) launched 1894 (Jul) completed 1895 (26 Jan) arrived in Chile
9 de Julio Protected cruiser, 3,600 tons 1891 (15 Oct) laid down 1892 (26 Jul) launched 1893 (24–25 Jan) ran trials 1893 (27 Jan) completed	*Esmeralda* Armored cruiser, 7,000 tons 1895 (15 May) ordered 1895 (4 Jul) laid down 1896 (14 Jun) launched 1896 (16 Dec) gun trials 1897 (22 Mar) sailed from Plymouth, England

Argentina	Chile
Buenos Aires Protected cruiser, 4,788 tons 1893 (2 Feb) laid down for the British navy 1894 (23 Nov) purchased by Argentina 1895 (10 May) launched 1895 (2 Nov) trials 1896 (Feb) co.npleted 1896 (29 Apr) arrived at La Plata *Garibaldi* (ex-*Giuseppe Garibaldi*) Armored cruiser, 6,773 tons 1895 (27 May) launched for the Italian navy 1895 (14 Jul) purchased by Argentina 1895 (12 Oct) accepted 1895 (10 Dec) arrived at Buenos Aires *San Martín* (ex-*Varese*) Armored cruiser, 6,773 tons 1896 (25 Apr) initial purchase agreement 1896 (25 May) launched 1896 (26 Oct) formally purchased 1898 (25 Apr) accepted 1898 (13 Jun) arrived in Argentina *Pueyrredón* (ex-*Giuseppe Garibaldi*) Armored cruiser, 6,773 tons 1897 purchased 1898 (25 Jul) launched 1898 (4 Aug) accepted 1898 (1 Sep) arrived in Argentina *General Belgrano* (ex-*Varese*) Armored cruiser, 7,069 tons 1897 (25 Jul) launched 1898 (8 Oct) accepted 1898 (6 Nov) arrived in Argentina	*Ministro Zenteno* Protected cruiser, 3,437 tons 1895 (6 May) laid down 1895 (Aug) purchased 1896 (1 Feb) launched 1896 (10 Jul) completed 1897 (22 Mar) sailed from Plymouth, England *O'Higgins* Armored cruiser, 8,500 tons 1896 (Mar) ordered 1896 (4 Apr) laid down 1897 (17 May) launched 1898 (2 Apr) completed 1898 (5 Jul) arrived in Chilean waters *Chacabuco* Protected cruiser, 4,160 tons 1896 (11 Aug) laid down as a stock cruiser 1898 (4 Jul) launched 1901 purchased by Chile 1902 completed *Constitución* Second-class battleship, 12,175 tons 1901 ordered 1902 (26 Feb) laid down 1903 (12 Jan) launched 1903 (12 Mar) purchased by Great Britain *Libertad* Second-class battleship, 12,175 tons 1901 ordered 1902 (26 Feb) laid down 1903 (15 Jan) launched 1903 (12 Mar) purchased by Great Britain

Argentina	Chile

Bernardino Rivadavia (ex-*General Mitre*)
  Armored cruiser 7,800 tons
  1901 ordered
  1902 (10 Mar) keel laid
  1902 (22 Oct) launched
  1903 (31 Dec) purchased by Japan
Mariano Moreno (ex-*General Roca*)
  Armored cruiser 7,800 tons
  1901 ordered
  1902 (May) keel laid
  1903 (9 Feb) launched
  1903 (31 Dec) purchased by Japan
Two first-class battleships
  15,000 tons
  1901 (May) letter of intent	

APPENDIX 4 *

The Chilean Congress's Request for Naval Intervention and Reply

To Captain Jorje Montt and the
commanders and officers of the Navy

Valparaíso, January 6, 1891

. . . the President of the Republic has placed himself outside of the constitutional regimen, he has renounced the lawful authority with which he was invested, and he has aspired to assume a personal and arbitrary power which has no other origin but his own will nor any other limits but those which circumstances may assign him.

In so grave an emergency it belongs to Congress to take upon itself the defense of the constitution and the adoption of such measures as circumstances may require for the reestablishment of its power. In the discharge of this august mission, Congress ought to count upon the efficacious assistance of the land and sea forces, because they exist only by virtue of the constitution, and it is not possible that they would care to forfeit their legal existence by placing themselves at the disposal of a dictatorial regimen springing from purely private desires of the President of the republic. Fifty-seven years of uninterrupted constitutional existence and a lengthened tradition of sacrifices made and glories reaped in the service of the nation point out to the army and navy of the Republic the path of duty, and compel them to resist, as opposed to their own honor, all attempts that may be projected or executed against the charta which is the foundation of the national institutions and from which the public powers derive their origin.

Congress, in fulfillment of duties imposed upon it by the actual situation, has adopted the resolutions which are to be found in the document annexed to this communication, and at the same time it has conferred upon the undersigned the necessary authority to present themselves to the navy and to order it to cooperate in its own sphere of action to the early reestablishment of the constitutional regimen.

In virtue whereof the undersigned have resolved that there be organized a naval division, to make the Republic comprehend that the navy obeys the

*From Sears and Wells, *The Chilean Revolution*, pp. 51–52.

constitution and, therefore, that it is indispensable that the annual law authorizing its existence be passed without delay.

The commander of this division will be Capt. Jorje Montt, and the undersigned will remain on board to attend to the development that this movement in defense of the constitution of the Republic may take.

>Waldo Silva
>Vice-President of the Senate
>
>Ramon Barros Luco
>President of the Chamber of Deputies

>Valparaíso, January 6, 1891

In view of the considerations stated in the preceding document, I accept the designation made for the organization of a naval division, which will be under my orders, to comply with the resolutions which may be adopted by the delegates of Congress.

Insert this resolution and the communication of the delegates in the order of the day, in order that they may come to the knowledge of the commanders, officers, and crews of the naval division.

>Jorge Montt

APPENDIX 5*
Manifestoes Issued by Rebellious Brazilian Naval Leaders, 1893–94

Rear Admiral Custódio José de Mello, 7 September 1893:

> In view of the openly dictatorial attitude assumed by the vice president of the Republic, who was instated in the name of the restored Republican Constitution of 24 February but who has stepped on it, without the least scruple, by offensively annulling the autonomy of the States, the federative principles, and the honesty of republican forms themselves; by denying to sanction the law that would have made him ineligible for presidential reelection; by dividing the country between winners and losers; by throwing away public monies at his will; and finally, by capriciously maintaining the fratricidal struggle that covers with blood the soil of the Rio Grande in spite of the desire for peace universally manifested in the nation, we, representing national sovereignty as members of the parliamentary opposition, believing we express the opinion of our colleagues, had only one way to go that would honor the Republic we represent—resistance, which is a sacred right of free people against oppression, when all constitutional and legal means have failed.

Rear Admiral Luis Philipe de Saldanha da Gama, 7 December 1893:

> Both logic and justice authorize the use of arms against the government, which on 15 November 1889 conquered Brazil at a time of national stupefaction in an act of military sedition that continues to this day.
>
> However, out of respect for the free manifestation of the national will, the nation should solemnly choose, on its own, which institutions it wishes its glorious destiny to be wrapped in.
>
> I offer my life and those of my brothers-at-arms on the altar of the country.

*The manifestoes were translated by Eduardo Italo Pesce. The Portuguese text may be found in Freire, *História da Revolta*, pp. 84–85, 88–89. See also Thompson, *Guerra Civil do Brasil*, pp. 89–95.

Rear Admiral Luis Philipe de Saldanha da Gama, 20 December 1893:

> The enlightened people, not only in this capital [Fortress of Ilha das Cobras] but in Brazil as a whole, know perfectly well that the manifesto and other documents attributed to me have been falsified in print (let the originals be presented), with the perfidious and despicable intent of dislodging the noble aims of the revolution against this dictatorial government, which is covered with shame before the world.
>
> These people also know that the idea of the plebiscite is precisely the same thing Rio Grande do Sul is fighting gloriously for—consulting the nation about which of the systems of republican government it wishes its glorious destiny to be wrapped in. Aware of all infamy employed against the revolution, the people of Rio de Janeiro, in spite of the regime of terror they live in, peacefully wait for the victory of the revolution, knowing that the constitution of a civil government will come with it and that the jacobinism plaguing the nation will be forever banished. For such desideratum the revolution fights victoriously, although those who are hired by the national treasury—now paid in counterfeit currency from the old monarchy, put back in circulation—say the opposite.
>
> > Long live the civilian Republic!
> > Long live the Revolution!
> > Death to jacobinism!

APPENDIX 6
Naval Activities in Latin America by Extraregional Nations

Year	Country	Action
ARGENTINA		
1831	United States	A party from the sloop *Lexington* landed in the Malvinas, destroyed a small fort, took private property, and removed six Argentines on 28 December.
1832	Great Britain	A landing party from the sloop *Clio* hoisted the British flag over the Malvinas on 3 January and evicted the remaining Argentines.
1833	United States	On 31 October a forty-three-man landing party of marines and sailors was sent ashore at Buenos Aires to protect U.S. interests. It was withdrawn on 15 November.
1838–40	France	Warships blockaded Río de la Plata from March 1838 until October 1840, for 949 days. In 1840 France dispatched Admiral Baron de Mackan with thirty-six ships and six thousand troops to La Plata. They forced the Argentine ruler, Manuel Rosas, who had drafted Frenchmen into his army, to give way to certain demands.
1843	United States	The frigate *Congress* captured the Argentine warships *9 de Julio*, *Americano*, and the *25 de Mayo* at Montevideo because an Argentine gunboat had fired a rifle shot at a U.S. merchant ship.
1845–48	France Great Britain	Warships blockaded Río de la Plata beginning in September. Great Britain withdrew in August 1847, after some seven hundred days, and France in June 1848, after some one thousand days. Naval actions took place at Vuelta de Obligado on 21 November 1845 and near Quebrado in June 1846.

Year	Country	Action
1852–53	France Great Britain United States	Marines from all three nations arrived to protect national interests following the defeat of Manuel Rosas by Justo José Urquiza. U.S. Marines were landed from the frigate *Congress* and sloop *Jamestown* with aid from the British navy on 3 February 1952. They remained ashore until 12 February 1952. Between 17 September and April 1853 marines were again landed to protect the U.S. consulate.
1890	Great Britain Spain United States	On 28 July warships halted a bombardment of Buenos Aires by rebellious naval forces, and U.S. Marines were landed from the *Tallapoosa* to protect the U.S. consulate. They were withdrawn on 30 July.
1914–18	Germany Great Britain	Both combatants on occasion violated Argentine neutrality. The most publicized event concerned the Argentine merchant ship *Presidente Mitre*, which was seized by the British auxiliary cruiser *Orama* some fifteen miles off Cape San Antonio on 27 November 1915 in water claimed by Argentina and taken to Montevideo, Uruguay. The British later released her.

BRAZIL

Year	Country	Action
1862	Great Britain	Warships seized five Brazilian merchant ships on 31 December as a reprisal for Brazil's refusal to pay reparations for the arrest of allegedly drunken British naval officers. Arbitration by the king of Belgium in 1863 favored Brazil.
1863	United States	The steam sloop *Wachusett* captured the Confederate navy's *Florida* in Bahia Harbor on 10 July. The United States later apologized to Brazil.
1893	France Italy Portugal United States	Naval commanders notified rebel naval forces on 1 October that they would oppose by force any further bombardment of Rio de Janeiro.
1894	Great Britain	Naval forces occupied Trinidade Island off the coast of Brazil on 1 January. The British flag was lowered on 25 August 1896.

Year	Country	Action
1914	Germany Great Britain	The German armed merchant cruiser *Cap Trafalgar* was fitted out and armed by the German gunboat *Eber* in Brazilian waters off Trinidade Island on 20 August. After engaging the British cruiser *Carmania* in these waters on 14 September, the *Cap Trafalgar* was sunk.
1939–42	Germany Great Britain	Both combatants violated Brazilian neutrality during the war. British warships stopped and searched a number of Brazilian ships. Ultimately, Brazil declared war on Germany because her U-boats were torpedoing ships off the Brazilian coast.
1963	France	The French destroyer *Tartu* patrolled off the northeast coast of Brazil, where three French lobster boats had been seized on 21 February. The destroyer was met by a superior Brazilian naval squadron.

THE CARIBBEAN (see also individual countries)

Year	Country	Action
1940	United States	U.S. troops were sent to guard air and naval bases at St. Lucia, the Bahamas, Jamaica, Antigua, Trinidad, and British Guiana. Great Britain had agreed to the occupation.

CHILE

Year	Country	Action
1812–14	Great Britain United States	The frigate *Essex* operated in Brazilian, Chilean, Ecuadorian (Galapagos Islands), and Peruvian waters during a wartime cruise. The *Essex* was trapped by the British frigates *Cherub* and *Phoebe* at Valparaíso on 28 March 1814 and destroyed.
1891	Germany	Germany sent the *Leipzig*, *Sophie*, and *Alexandre* to protect her interests following the attempt by the Balmaceda government to declare a blockade of the nitrate ports.
1891	United States	The Congresionalistas voluntarily handed over the Chilean merchant ship *Itata* to the cruiser *Charleston* in Chilean waters on 13 June in order to avoid provoking ill will. The Chilean ship had recently carried arms from the United States to Chile in the face of U.S. opposition.
1891	Germany Great Britain United States	Marines and sailors were landed to protect consulates at Valparaíso between 28 and 30 August, during the revolution.

Year	Country	Action
1891	United States	U.S. warships threatened to use force as a result of an incident in Valparaíso where on 16 October a mob killed two and injured sixteen from the USS *Baltimore*.
1914–18	Germany Great Britain	Both combatants violated Chilean neutrality during World War I. The most publicized events were the circumstances surrounding the German cruiser *Dresden*, which was sunk by British warships in Chilean waters while she too was violating Chilean neutrality.

COLOMBIA (see also PANAMÁ)

Year	Country	Action
1833	France	On 3 September the French consul was arrested for insulting the mayor, whereupon two French warships threatened a bombardment and blockade of Cartagena. The consul was released and an indemnity paid.
1836	Great Britain	When the local British consul was condemned to six years in prison following a fight with a district judge in which the latter was injured, two warships blockaded the coast of Panamá. The consul was released and a thousand-pound indemnity paid.
1856	United States	In April a North American voyager en route to the California gold fields refused to pay a local food vendor. The incident degenerated into a fight. Fifteen U.S. citizens and two locals died; seventeen U.S. citizens and thirteen locals were injured. Two warships landed marines in Panamá, and Colombia was forced to pay a $412,394 indemnity.
1856	United States	Marines landed on the Isthmus of Panamá on 19 September to protect U.S. interests. They were withdrawn three days later.
1860	United States	On 27 September marines landed on the Isthmus of Panamá to protect U.S. interests, including the trans-isthmus railroad. On the twenty-ninth an additional fifty sailors landed. The entire force was withdrawn on 8 October.

Year	Country	Action
1865	United States	Marines landed on the Isthmus of Panamá on 9 March to protect U.S. interests. They were withdrawn the next day.
1868	United States	Marines landed at Aspinwall on 7 April to protect U.S. interests. They were ordered out within a few days.
1873	United States	On 7 May 44 marines and about 160 sailors plus 4 artillery pieces landed on the Pacific coast to protect the consulate and railroad. They were withdrawn on 22 May.
1873	United States	On 23 September one hundred marines and sailors plus 2 howitzers landed on the Pacific coast. Additional troops were sent ashore in late September. They were withdrawn on 9 October.
1885	United States	Marines landed on 18 January to protect U.S. interests on the Isthmus of Panamá.
1885	United States	Marines landed on the Isthmus of Panamá on 18–19 January to protect U.S. interests. Again, on 16 March sixteen marines landed to protect the consulate and railway. Additional men were sent ashore on subsequent days. On 30 March revolutionaries tried to command the cargo of arms in the U.S. merchant ship *Colon*. The next day 126 marines and sailors landed. On 8 April a few hundred more troops arrived to occupy Colon and Panamá City. This force was withdrawn on 25 May after the collapse of the local revolution.
1895	United States	Between 8 and 9 March marines landed at Bocas del Toro, Panamá, to protect U.S. property.
1898	Italy	In 1885 the Italian consul became involved in a local rebellion. Some rebels who had taken refuge in his residence were arrested. The consul claimed damages. The arbitrator, President Grover Cleveland, awarded the consul sixty thousand pounds in 1896. Four Italian cruisers were sent to Cartagena on 22 July 1898 to extract an indemnity. After an ultimatum threatening a bombardment of Cartagena, the Italians obtained satisfaction on 15 August 1898.

Year	Country	Action
1901	United States	On November 21 marines landed at Colon to protect U.S. interests.
1901	United States	Marines landed on both sides of the Isthmus of Panamá. On 25 November a battalion was landed on the west coast and remained until 4 December. Marines and sailors who landed on 26 November on the east coast were also withdrawn on the fourth.
1902	United States	On 16 April thirty marines landed at Bocas del Toro to protect U.S. interests. They remained until the nineteenth, then returned three days later for a single day.
1902	United States	Troops landed on the east coast on 18 May and withdrew on the twenty-third.
1902	United States	Troops landed on 17 September and remained ashore during daylight hours until the twenty-first. On the twenty-second a marine battalion of 341 men landed at Aspinwall and remained until 18 November.

CUBA

Year	Country	Action
1814–25	United States	Numerous U.S. landings in Cuba were intended primarily to destroy bases used by pirates. Some of the "pirates" held letters of marque from new Latin American republics.
1825	Great Britain United States	A combined British and U.S. force landed at Sagua La Grande to capture pirates.
1898	United States	The U.S. Navy was critical to the defeat of Spain during the Spanish-American War. U.S. forces occupied Cuba until 1900.
1906–9	United States	Marines landed at Habana on 10 and 13 September to protect U.S. interests. At its peak, the force numbered more than three thousand. The troops were withdrawn on 1 February 1909.
1912	United States	Marines landed at Daiquiri on 30 May, and on 5 June marines assumed control of Guantánamo City. The force was withdrawn on 5 August.

Year	Country	Action
1917–22	United States	Marines landed at Guacanaybo Bay from the battleship *Maine* on 1 March 1917. Two companies remained until 6 February 1922. Four hundred marines also landed at Santiago.
1933	United States	Two warships with marines on board were stationed off Habana on 13 August to influence political developments ashore.
1933	United States	The U.S. Atlantic Fleet concentrated in Cuban waters following the overthrow of the Machado government, which had been arranged with the help of the United States in August. The naval force was withdrawn on 23 January 1934 after the creation of a new Cuban government.
1959–60	United States	A task force was deployed to the Caribbean with elements of the Second Marine Division on board to protect U.S. interests in Cuba.
1961	United States	A task force was stationed off the coast of Cuba to provide moral support to Cuban exiles attempting to overthrow the Castro government. The exiles landed and were captured at the Bay of Pigs on 15 April.
1962	United States	A Pan-American task force instituted a "quarantine" on the shipment of offensive missiles to Cuba from the Soviet Union.
1963	Great Britain	The frigate *Londonderry* cruised off the Bahamas after two Cuban warships landed there on 13 August to seize Cuban refugees.
1979	United States	An amphibious exercise was carried out in Guantánamo Bay on 17 October.

THE DOMINICAN REPUBLIC

Year	Country	Action
1903	United States	Between 30 March and 21 April twenty-six marines landed at Santo Domingo to protect U.S. interests.
1904	United States	Troops landed at Puerto Plata, Sosua, and Santo Domingo between 2 January and 11 February to protect U.S. interests.
1905	United States	The U.S. Navy took over the management of the customhouse on 18 January because the Dominican Republic was not paying her foreign debts.

Year	Country	Action
1914	United States	On 26 June a U.S. gunboat intervened at Puerto Plata to prevent warring factions from bombarding the city.
1916–24	United States	Marines landed on 4 and 15 May to prevent General Desiderio Arias from seizing the government. The occupation continued until 18 September 1924.
1962	United States	A task force including the carrier *Franklin D. Roosevelt*, the *Valley Forge*, and eighteen hundred marines was stationed off the Dominican Republic in November to secure the expulsion of the Trujillo family and to influence the establishment of a government acceptable to the United States.
1963	United States	The carrier *Boxer* was stationed off Santo Domingo in February as a show of force and to evacuate Vice President Lyndon Johnson, there on a diplomatic mission, in case of trouble.
1965	United States, and subsequently the OAS	On 28 April, during a civil war, four hundred marines landed from a task force. By 6 May twenty-two thousand U.S. troops were ashore and some nine thousand off shore. They were withdrawn on 20 September 1966.

EL SALVADOR

Year	Country	Action
1849	Great Britain	Great Britain blockaded La Unión on 12 November and forced El Salvador to accept financial claim demands.
1850	Great Britain	A blockade of La Unión on 16 October lasted until February 1851.

GRENADA

Year	Country	Action
1983	United States, supported by the island nations of Antigua, Dominica, St. Lucia, St. Kitts-Nevis, Montserrat, St. Vincent, Barbados, and Jamaica	U.S. marines and rangers landed on 25 October from a task force and bases in the Caribbean and overthrew a communist regime supported by Cuba.

Year	Country	Action
GUATEMALA		
1920	United States	Marines landed to protect U.S. interests between 9 and 27 April.
1948	Great Britain	The cruisers *Devonshire* and *Sheffield* were sent to Belize to support resistance against Guatemalan claims of annexation. They arrived in March.
1954	United States	A task force patrolled off the coast of Guatemala supporting the U.S. prohibition of the importation of Soviet arms. The patrols were carried out between 20 May and 7 June.
1972	Great Britain	In February the carrier *Ark Royal* arrived at Belize to defend against a Guatemalan invasion. Great Britain has kept a station ship in Belize almost continuously since the early 1970s to prevent such an invasion.
1975	Great Britain	The *Zulu* patrolled off Belize to fend off Guatemala in November.
1977	Great Britain	The *Achilles* patrolled off Belize to fend off Guatemala in July.
HAITÍ		
1865	Great Britain	British warships destroyed Haitian gunboats on 23 October after the latter had opened fire. HMS *Bulldog* was lost through stranding.
1872	Germany	Sailors from the screw frigates *Gazelle* and *Vineta* boarded and captured two Haitian corvettes on 11 June and forced Haití to pay a three-thousand-pound debt.
1876	Germany	The screw corvette *Victoria* intimidated the Haitian government.
1881	Spain	A squadron forced Haití to submit to various demands on 10 July 1881.
1888	United States	Warships were used on 20 December to persuade Haití to surrender a North American steamer that had been seized and charged with breech of blockade.
1891	Spain	A Spanish warship blockaded a North American gun runner, the *Hornet*, for eleven months at Port-au-Prince. The gun runner was finally escorted out of port by the U.S. Navy.

Year	Country	Action
1891	United States	Troops were landed on Navassa Island to protect U.S. interests. This island was claimed by both Haití and the United States.
1894	Germany	The warships *Charlotte* and *Stein* forced Haití to pay a twenty-thousand-dollar indemnity.
1897	Germany	The corvettes *Charlotte* and *Stein* forced the Haitian government to pay a thirty-thousand-dollar indemnity on 6 December.
1897	Germany	The cruiser *Geier* intimidated the Haitian government.
1902	France Italy	Two French cruisers and one Italian cruiser were used to intimidate Haití into paying seventy-five thousand and thirty thousand dollars, respectively, to their governments.
1911	United States	The cruiser *Des Moines* was stationed off Haití on 22 July to protect U.S. interests.
1914	France Germany Great Britain United States	Troops landed between 29 January and 9 February, 20 and 21 February, and 19 October to protect the interests of their respective countries.
1914	United States	Marines from the *Machias* landed at Port-au-Prince on 17 December and removed $500,000 from the National Bank, at the request of the bank, to prevent possible seizure.
1915–34	United States	Marines landed on 3 July. Eventually U.S. troops were stationed throughout the island and remained in control for almost two decades in an attempt to bring political and economic stability to the country. The last marines were withdrawn on 15 August 1934.
1963	Great Britain United States	A British destroyer and frigate and a U.S. task force, including the helicopter carrier *Boxer* and two thousand marines, cruised off Haití when tension between that unstable country and the Dominican Republic rose during April.

HONDURAS

1849	Great Britain	Marines landed at Trujillo on 4 October to enforce a claim of over $100,000.

Year	Country	Action
1873	Great Britain	A warship bombarded Omea on 19 August in retaliation for the looting of British property.
1903	United States	Troops were landed at Puerto Cortez to protect the U.S. consulate and the steamship wharf between 23 and 31 March.
1907	United States	Marines landed at Trujillo and at Ceiba on 18 March to protect U.S. interests. They were stationed in Trujillo, Ceiba, Puerto Cortez, San Pedro, Laguna, and Choloma. They were withdrawn on 8 June.
1911	United States	Troops landed on 26 January and remained in Honduras for a few weeks to protect U.S. interests.
1912	United States	A small force of marines landed on 9 January to prevent the seizure by Honduras of a U.S.-owned railroad at Puerto Cortez. Marines were withdrawn after the United States disapproved the action.
1919	United States	Marines landed at Puerto Cortez between 8 and 12 September to protect U.S. interests.
1924	United States	Marines landed at Ceiba between 28 February and 31 March and 10 and 15 September to protect U.S. interests.
1925	United States	Marines landed at Ceiba between 19 and 21 April to protect U.S. interests.
MÉXICO		
1829	Spain	Troops landed at Tampico on 18 August in an attempt to reconquer México. They were defeated on 11 September.
1838–39	France	A squadron blockaded Mexican ports beginning on 16 April to extract claims of about $600,000 for the damage of property belonging to French citizens. French warships bombarded the fortress of San Juan de Ulloa on 27 November, using shell guns for one of the first times. The French force retired on 7 April 1839.

Year	Country	Action
1842	United States	A U.S. squadron seized the Mexican ports of Monterey, California, on 19 October and San Diego, California, a week later, believing war had broken out between the United States and México. Discovering that this was not the case, the landing parties withdrew and saluted the Mexican flag.
1860	United States	A sloop supported by two Mexican vessels of the Juárez government captured Mexican warships belonging to the Miramon government on 6 March.
1861–67	France Great Britain Spain	The naval powers attempted to collect debts incurred largely during Mexico's bloody civil war. On 14 December the Spanish fleet seized Veracruz, and it was soon joined by British and French forces. On 22 April the Spanish and British withdrew, leaving the French, who remained until 1866. The French tried to establish Archduke Maximilian as the emperor of México but failed.
1870	United States	On 17–18 June troops landed to destroy the *Forward*, suspected of piracy, some forty miles up the Tecpan River.
1913	United States	On 10 December, during the Mexican Revolution, U.S. warships threatened to fire on combatants at Tampico if the siege were not raised. A few marines landed at Ciaris Estero between 5 and 7 September to protect U.S. interests.
1914	United States	Over six thousand sailors and marines landed at Veracruz on 21 April in part to prevent a German merchant ship from delivering guns to the Victoriano Huerta government. U.S. forces clashed with Mexican naval cadets and soldiers, resulting in approximately four hundred casualties, mostly Mexican. U.S. forces evacuated the city on 23 November.
1914	Holland	Marines landed at Tampico on 16 May to protect oil properties.
1920	United States	The destroyer *Thornton* stood off Manzanillo on 14 May to protect U.S. interests.

Year	Country	Action
1924	Great Britain	The cruiser *Capetown* was stationed off Minatitlan in January to protect a British refinery. A succession of warships relieved the cruiser.
1929	United States	The destroyer *Robert Smith* backed up diplomatic negotiations on 23 April, extracting a promise that the Mexican gunboat *Bravo* would not bombard Guayamas, which was in the hands of insurgents.

NICARAGUA

Year	Country	Action
1846	Great Britain	Warships blockaded Realejo in August to enforce financial claims.
1848	Great Britain	Warships occupied San Juan and ousted Nicaraguan officials in January. The argument was over financial arrangements.
1853	United States	Marines landed at San Juan del Sur on 11 March to protect the American Steamship Company's property and other U.S. interests. They were withdrawn on the thirteenth.
1854	United States	Warships bombarded and destroyed San Juan del Norte (Greytown) between 9 and 15 July to avenge an insult to the U.S. minister to Nicaragua.
1857	United States	Marines landed and forced the removal of the filibuster William Walker to the United States.
1867	United States	Marines occupied Managua and León to bring political stability.
1878	Germany	Naval force was used to intimidate the government into paying debts.
1894	United States	Troops landed at Bluefields between 6 July and 7 August to protect U.S. interests.
1895	Great Britain	Marines occupied Corinto and seized the customhouse on 27 April. They were withdrawn the next day.
1896	United States	Troops landed at Corinto between 2 and 4 May to protect U.S. interests.
1898	United States	Troops landed at San Juan del Sur between 7 and 8 February to protect U.S. interests.

Year	Country	Action
1899	United States	Troops landed at San Juan del Norte between 22 February and 5 March and at Bluefields a few weeks later to protect U.S. interests.
1909	United States	Gunboats were stationed off the coast following the execution of some North Americans on 18 November.
1909	United States	The cruiser *Des Moines* prevented fighting on 18 December between rivals at Bluefields, thus aiding the conservative cause.
1909	United States	Troops landed at Corinto on 20 December to restore political stability.
1910	United States	Troops landed at Corinto on 22 February and at Bluefields between 19 May and 4 September to protect U.S. interests.
1912	United States	Marines from the gunboat *Annapolis* landed near Managua on 4 August.
1912–25	United States	Some twenty-five hundred marines landed at Corinto on 14 August. On 4 September they took control of the railway. Most were withdrawn on 9 January 1913. A small force that served as a legation guard and to protect U.S. interests remained until 5 August 1925.
1914	United States	Five hundred marines landed at Bluefields on 14 August to restore political stability.
1922	United States	Thirty marines landed from the *Galveston* and the *Denver* on 25 January to reinforce the legation guard to Managua. They re-embarked on 11 February.
1926–33	United States	Marines landed from the cruiser *Cleveland* on 6 May to restore order. Other landings followed, and eventually the entire country was occupied. At its height, over five thousand marines and sailors were involved in the occupation. Troops were withdrawn on 3 January 1933.
1927	Great Britain	The cruiser *Colombo* was stationed off Corinto to intimidate the government, which had defaulted on debts.

Year	Country	Action

PANAMÁ (see also **COLOMBIA**)

1903–12	United States	To protect U.S. interests, marines and sailors landed on 4 November 1903 and remained ashore with only brief interruptions until 21 January 1914.
1918–20	United States	Additional marines were landed and used for policy duties at Chiriqui, in accordance with the provisions of the Hay-Bunau Varilla Treaty.
1921	United States	The battleship *Pennsylvania*, with four hundred marines on board, deployed off the coast in August to induce the Panamanian government to accept a decision concerning a border dispute with Costa Rica.
1925	United States	Some six hundred troops landed on 12 October to protect U.S. interests. They were withdrawn on the twenty-third.
1964	United States	Marines landed from warships during the Canal Zone riots.

PARAGUAY

1859	United States	A naval expedition of fifteen warships carrying seventy-seven guns, 1,448 sailors, and 291 marines entered Río de la Plata in January. The steamer *Fulton* went to Humaitá while the rest of the fleet remained in Montevideo. Paraguay was ordered to pay a ten thousand dollar indemnity for firing on the stranded USS *Water Witch* on 1 May 1855.
1869	Italy	The gunboat *Ardita* fired a shot and seized a boat belonging to the Asuncion harbor master in November. The Paraguayans had seized materials being sent to the Italian steamer *Venezia* by the Italian consul Lorenzo Chapperon, who was suspected of protecting contraband.

PERÚ

1835–36	United States	U.S. marines landed at Callao and were also employed in Lima to protect U.S. interests between 10 December 1835 and 24 January 1836, and 31 August and 7 December 1836.

Year	Country	Action
PUERTO RICO		
1824	United States	A landing party of two hundred men attacked Fajardo in November, which was believed to be sheltering pirates.
URUGUAY		
1846	Great Britain	Marines landed at Montevideo to protect British interests.
1855	France Great Britain United States	Landing parties occupied Montevideo between 25 and 30 November to protect the interests of their nations.
1858	United States	Marines landed at Montevideo to protect U.S. interests on 2 January. They were withdrawn on the twenty-seventh.
1868	United States	Marines landed at Montevideo between 7 and 8 February and 19 and 26 February to protect U.S. interests.
1939	Germany Great Britain	In December, action between a German pocket battleship and British cruisers continued in waters claimed by Uruguay.
VENEZUELA		
1856	Holland	Warships successfully supported an ultimatum on 5 March for a 100,000-peso indemnity.
1858	France Great Britain	The French *Cleopatra* and the British *Tartar* added a show of force to an ultimatum following an incident in which French citizens were attacked at the French legation.
1860	Spain	The warships *Blasco de Garay* and *Habanero* were sent to La Guaira to support claims of Spanish citizens.
1892	Germany	The cruiser *Arcona* forced the Venezuelans to salute the German flag at La Guaira.
1897	Germany	The cruiser *Geier* intimidated the Venezuelan government.
1899	United States	The U.S. Fleet, commanded by Admiral W. T. Sampson, made a visit from 4 to 7 April to show concern over Venezuela's debt situation.

Year	Country	Action
1902	Great Britain Germany Italy	The navies of these countries seized and scuttled the Venezuelan warships *Osún*, *Crespo*, and *Margarita* on 9 December, and on the eleventh German and British warships blockaded the coast. On the twelfth warships bombarded the forts at Puerto Cabello. On the nineteenth Italy joined in a "pacifist" blockade as President Theodore Roosevelt agreed to arbitrate claims. When the Argentine minister of foreign affairs, Luis M. Drago, objected to forcible collection of debts, German warships shelled Fort San Carlos, near the Gulf of Maracaibo, on 22–23 January 1903. The blockade ended on 17 February 1903. On the twenty-fourth Germany returned the gunboat *Restaurador* to Venezuela. She had been seized in October of the previous year.
1908	Holland	On 12 December a Dutch cruiser seized a Venezuelan coast guard vessel in reprisal for the seizure of Dutch property.

APPENDIX 7
Latin American Dreadnoughts

BRAZIL

Minas Gerais	*São Paulo*	*Rio de Janeiro*	*Riachuelo*
1906 ordered	1906 ordered	6 Aug 1910 construction announced	Oct 1913 design contracted; never laid down
17 Apr 1907 keel laid	30 Apr 1907 keel laid	14 Sep 1911 keel laid	
10 Sep 1908 launched	19 Apr 1909 launched	22 Jan 1913 launched	
6 Jan 1910 delivered	Jul 1910 completed	late 1913 sold	
17 Apr 1910 arrived Rio	25 Oct 1910 arrived Rio		
1923 refitted New York	1917–19 refitted New York		
1931–34 refitted Rio	1951 sold		
1939–43 refitted			
1953 sold			

ARGENTINA

Rivadavia	*Moreno*	*Unnamed*
19 Dec 1908 authorized	19 Dec 1908 authorized	Oct 1912 authorized; never laid down
25 May 1910 keel laid	9 Jul 1910 keel laid	
26 Aug 1911 launched	23 Sep 1911 launched	
Dec 1914 completed	Mar 1915 completed	
1924–26 refitted New York	1924–26 refitted New York	
8 Feb 1957 sold	8 Feb 1957 sold	

CHILE

*Almirante Latorre**		*Almirante Cochrane†*
1911 authorized	27 Nov 1920 sailed for Chile, arriving Feb 1921	1911 authorized
2 Nov 1911 ordered		29 Jul 1912 ordered
27 Nov 1911 keel laid	1 Aug 1920 commissioned	22 Jan 1913 keel laid
17 Nov 1913 launched	1929–31 refitted, Devonport, England	1917 purchased by Great Britain
9 Sep 1914 purchased by Great Britain	1950 refitted Talcahuano	
30 Sep 1915 completed as HMS *Canada*	Oct 1958 decommissioned	
Apr 1920 purchased by Chile	Feb 1959 sold	

*This dreadnought had the following sequence of names throughout her lifetime: *Valparaíso, Libertad, Almirante Latorre,* HMS *Canada, Almirante Latorre.*

† This dreadnought had the following sequence of names throughout her lifetime: *Santiago, Constitución, Almirante Cochrane,* HMS *Eagle.*

APPENDIX 8
Naval Assistance to Latin American Nations, 1810–1987

To	From	Period	Notes
Argentina	Great Britain	1810–20s (independence era)	A few officers and some sailors served under individual contracts.
Argentina	Great Britain	1860s–90s	Some instructors served under individual contracts.
Argentina	United States	1934–82	Initially instructors were at the Naval War College. In the 1960s they were reorganized under the U.S. military group, which was always very small. They asked to leave during the Malvinas War.
Bolivia	Argentina	1960s–87	This mission probably had substantial influence on Bolivia's naval expertise.
Brazil	Great Britain	early 1820s	Some officers and sailors served under individual contracts.
Brazil	United States	1914–18	A few instructors were individually contracted.
Brazil	Great Britain	1917–22	An official naval mission was in operation.
Brazil	United States	1918–30	An official naval mission was in operation.
Brazil	United States	1932–77	A naval mission was reorganized in the 1960s under the U.S. military group. In 1977 Brazil terminated the mission.
Chile	Great Britain	1816–24 (independence era)	Officers and sailors served under individual contracts.

To	From	Period	Notes
Chile	Great Britain	1839–1987	Numerous Chilean officers were trained in British warships. In the 1890s Chilean officers started training in British schools, a practice that continues to this day.
Chile	Great Britain	1911–32	An official naval mission was established. Its operation was interrupted from 1914 to 1922.
Chile	United States	1945–74	An official naval mission was reorganized under the U.S. military group in the 1960s. In 1974 the U.S. Congress terminated the mission.
Colombia	Chile	1907–10	A few instructors were individually contracted.
Colombia	United States	1932–34	An officer was sent "on loan."
Colombia	Great Britain	1936–38	A few instructors were individually contracted.
Colombia	United States	1938–87	An official naval mission was in operation.
Cuba	United States	1943–59	An official naval mission was in operation.
Cuba	U.S.S.R.	1959–87	The size of this mission is not known.
Dominican Republic	United States	1943–60s	An official naval mission was reorganized in the 1960s under the U.S. military group.
Ecuador	Chile	1896–1920	A few instructors served during these years.
Ecuador	United States	1936–?	A few advisors were individually contracted. Eventually an official mission was established.
Grenada	United States	1984–87	A security-assistance control team was sent.

To	From	Period	Notes
Haití	United States	1942?–49	An official naval mission was in operation.
México	Great Britain	1830s–40s	A few officers and some engineers served under individual contracts.
México	Great Britain	1890s	A few instructors were privately contracted.
Paraguay	Great Britain	Mid-19th century	A few officers and some engineers served under individual contracts.
Paraguay	Argentina	1926–?	A few Paraguayan officers and petty officers received training.
Paraguay	Chile	1931–?	A few instructors were sent.
Paraguay	Argentina	1943–87	This mission was interrupted briefly in 1952.
Perú	Great Britain	Mid-19th century	A few officers and some engineers served under individual contracts.
Perú	United States	1902	A few Peruvian cadets received training.
Perú	France	1904–12	An official naval mission was in operation.
Perú	United States	1920–60s	An official naval mission was in operation. It was interrupted from 1934 to 1937.
Uruguay	United States	1953–60s	An official naval mission was in operation.
Venezuela	United States	1940–60s	The naval mission was reorganized into a military group.

APPENDIX 9
Declarations of War by Latin American Nations During World War II

	Severance of Diplomatic Relations with			Declaration of War or State of Belligerency Against		
	Germany	Italy	Japan	Germany	Italy	Japan
Costa Rica				11 Dec 41	11 Dec 41	8 Dec 41
Dominican Republic				11 Dec 41	11 Dec 41	8 Dec 41
Guatemala				11 Dec 41	11 Dec 41	8 Dec 41
Nicaragua				11 Dec 41	11 Dec 41	8 Dec 41
El Salvador				12 Dec 41	12 Dec 41	8 Dec 41
Haití				12 Dec 41	12 Dec 41	8 Dec 41
Honduras				13 Dec 41	13 Dec 41	8 Dec 41
Cuba				11 Dec 41	11 Dec 41	9 Dec 41
Panamá				12 Dec 41	12 Dec 41	10 Dec 41 *
México	11 Dec 41	11 Dec 41	8 Dec 41	22 May 42	22 May 42	22 May 42
Brazil	28 Jan 42	28 Jan 42	28 Jan 42	22 Aug 42	22 Aug 42	6 Jun 45
Bolivia	28 Jan 42	28 Jan 42	28 Jan 42	7 Apr 43	7 Apr 43 †	7 Apr 43 †
Colombia	19 Dec 41	19 Dec 41	8 Dec 41	27 Nov 43		
Ecuador	29 Jan 42	29 Jan 42	29 Jan 42			2 Feb 45 ‡
Paraguay	28 Jan 42	28 Jan 42	28 Jan 42	7 Feb 45		7 Feb 45
Perú	24 Jan 42	24 Jan 42	24 Jan 42	11 Feb 45		11 Feb 45
Chile	20 Jan 43	20 Jan 43	20 Jan 43	12 Feb 45		12 Feb 45
Venezuela	31 Dec 41	31 Dec 41	31 Dec 41	14 Feb 45		14 Feb 45
Uruguay	25 Jan 42	25 Jan 42	25 Jan 42	22 Feb 45		22 Feb 45
Argentina	26 Jan 44		26 Jan 44	27 Mar 45		27 Mar 45

* Declaration was made retroactive to 7 December 1941.

† Sanctioned by the congress on 26 November 1943 and promulgated on 4 December 1943.

‡ Declaration was made retroactive to 7 December 1941.

APPENDIX 10
Brazilian Warships Under Construction in 1939

Class	No. of Units	Type	Builder	Fate
Juruena (British H class)	6	destroyers 1,400 tons (standard)	Vickers-Armstrong White Thornycroft (2 units each)	All launched in 1939; appropriated by British navy
Marcílio Dias (modified American *Mahan* class)	3	destroyers 1,500 tons (standard)	Ilha das Cobras (U.S. assistance)	All launched in 1940–41; completed in 1943–44
Carioca	6	minelayers/escorts 552 tons (standard)	Ilha das Cobras (British assistance)	All launched in 1939; completed in 1940–41

APPENDIX 11*
U.S. Warships Transferred to Brazil in World War II

Incorporated into Brazilian Navy	Brazilian Name	U.S. Name and Hull Number	Type	Place of Transfer
24 Sep 42	Guaporé	PC-544	Submarine chaser	Natal
24 Sep 42	Gurupi	PC-547	Submarine chaser	Natal
5 Jan 43	Javari	SC-763	Submarine chaser	Miami
5 Jan 43	Jutaí	SC-762	Submarine chaser	Miami
5 Jan 43	Juruá	SC-764	Submarine chaser	Miami
9 Mar 43	Jaguarão	SC-765	Submarine chaser	Miami
9 Mar 43	Jaguaribe	SC-767	Submarine chaser	Miami
29 May 43	Juruena	SC-766	Submarine chaser	Miami
29 May 43	Jacuí	SC-1288	Submarine chaser	Miami
29 May 43	Jundiaí	SC-1289	Submarine chaser	Miami
11 Jun 43	Guaíba	PC-604	Submarine chaser	Miami
11 Jun 43	Gurupá	PC-605	Submarine chaser	Miami
19 Oct 43	Guarajá	PC-607	Submarine chaser	Miami
29 Oct 43	Goiana	PC-554	Submarine chaser	Miami
15 Nov 43	Grajaú	PC-1236	Submarine chaser	Miami

*Compiled from da Gama, *Segunda Guerra Mundial*, pp. 67–77; and the U.S. *Dictionary of American Naval Fighting Ships* 4, appendix 1. The date on which these ships were transferred from the U.S. Navy is often a few days earlier than the date on which they were formally commissioned into the Brazilian navy.

Incorporated into Brazilian Navy	Brazilian Name	U.S. Name and Hull Number	Type	Place of Transfer
30 Nov 43	*Graúna*	PC-561	Submarine chaser	Miami
1 Aug 44	*Bertioga*	*Pennewill* DE-175	Destroyer escort	Miami
1 Aug 44	*Beberibe*	*Herzog* DE-178	Destroyer escort	Miami
15 Aug 44	*Bracuí*	*Reybold* DE-177	Destroyer escort	Miami
15 Aug 44	*Bauru*	*McAnn* DE-179	Destroyer escort	Miami
19 Dec 44	*Baependi*	*Cannon* DE-99	Destroyer escort	Miami
19 Dec 44	*Benevente*	*Christopher* DE-100	Destroyer escort	Miami
10 Mar 45	*Babitonga*	*Alger* DE-101	Destroyer escort	Miami
20 May 45	*Bocaina*	*Marts* DE-174	Destroyer escort	Miami
16 Jul 45	*Duque de Caxias*	*Orizaba* AP-24	Transport	Tampa

APPENDIX 12*
Italian Tankers Commandeered by México, 8 April 1941

Mexican Name	Former Name	Gross Tonnage	Barrel Capacity	Commanding Officer, Mexican Navy
Ebano	Stelvio	6,903	66,000	Lt. Miguel Manzárraga
Minatitlán	Tuscania	6,903	64,000	Lt. Enrique Altamirano Domínguez
Pozo Rica	Fede	7,884	96,000	Lt. Antonio Cortés Acosta
Amatlán	Vigor	6,511	55,000	Lt. Cdr. Adolfo Meza Burgos
Tuxpan	Americano	7,008	62,000	Lt. Cdr. Gonzalo Montalvo Salazar
Pánuco	Giorgio Fazzio	6,735	70,000	Lt. Armando Cañizares
Faja de Oro	Genoano	6,077	70,000	Lt. Pablo Escobio Ruiz
Potrero del Llano	Lucífero	4,000	37,000	Lt. Gabriel Cruz Díaz
Las Choapas	Atlas	2,005	17,000	Lt. Pedro Calderón Lozano
		54,030	537,000	

*Cárdena, *Semblanza Marítima* 1:258.

APPENDIX 13

Attack Aircraft Employed on Argentine Aircraft Carriers

Designator	Name	Manufacturer	Country of Origin	Number of Aircraft Acquired	In Service on Carrier
F4U	Corsair	Vought/Goodyear	United States	30	1959–66
F9F	Panther	Grumman	United States	28	1959–69
T-6	Texan	North American	United States	61	1959–69
TF-9J	Cougar	Grumman	United States	2	1962–68
T-28B	Trojan	North American	United States	65	1969–78
A-4Q	Skyhawk	McDonnell Douglas	United States	20	1972–present
SUE	Super Etendard	Dassault	France	14	1982–present

Notes: Panthers and Cougars did not operate from the *Independencia*. Texans, Cougars, and Trojans were designated as trainers but could serve in an attack capacity if necessary.

APPENDIX 14
The Service Lives of the Carriers *Independencia*, *25 de Mayo*, and *Minas Gerais*

ARGENTINA		BRAZIL
Independencia	*25 de Mayo*	*Minas Gerais*

As *Warrior*
  12 Dec 1942 keel laid
  20 May 1944 launched
  24 Jan 1946 completed
  1946–58 served in British and Canadian navies
  1952–53 modernized
  1955–56 modernized, receiving partial angled deck and improved arresting gear
As *Independencia*
  Jul 1958 purchased by Argentina
  1969 placed in reserve
  17 Mar 1971 sold for scrapping
  1974 scrapped

As *Venerable*
  5 Dec 1942 keel laid
  30 Dec 1943 launched
  17 Jan 1945 completed
As *Karel Doorman*
  1 Apr 1948 purchased by Holland
  1955–58 reconstructed in Holland, receiving angled deck, steam catapult, mirror landing system, and new antiaircraft battery
  29 Apr 1968 damaged by boiler-room fire
As *25 de Mayo*
  15 Oct 1968 purchased by Argentina
  12 Mar 1969 commissioned
  Aug 1969 refitted at Rotterdam
  1979 angle deck increased, computerized British Naval Tactical Data System installed
  1982–83 fitted to handle Super Etendard aircraft

As *Vengeance*
  16 Nov 1942 keel laid
  23 Feb 1944 launched
  15 Jan 1945 completed
  1945–56 served in British and Australian navies
As *Minas Gerais*
  14 Dec 1956 purchased
  1957–60 reconstructed at Rotterdam, receiving angled deck, steam catapult, mirror landing system, radar update; able to handle aircraft up to 15 tons
  6 Dec 1960 commissioned at Rotterdam
  1976–79 extensively overhauled at Rio de Janeiro Navy Yard
  1984–85 initially to be fitted with A-4 Skyhawks, plans abandoned

APPENDIX 15
Information Received by Argentine Naval Intelligence During the Malvinas War, 1982

Month (Buenos Aires Time)	Platform	Information Obtained
4 April	Aircraft	Discovered a naval force navigating on course 18° north of the Canarias islands
12 April (0740)	Merchant ship *Chubut*	Overflown by a twin-engine aircraft; detected a large ship, not considered to be an aircraft carrier, on course 235°, destination Ascension Island
12 April (1105)	Merchant ship *Chubut*	Discovered 5 destroyers and frigates patrolling 20 miles southwest of Ascension; discovered 4 destroyers and frigates 2 miles southwest of island; noted intensive movement between helicopters, ships, and land over the radio
15 April	Aircraft	Discovered 3 destroyers, 3 frigates, 1 submarine, 2 transports, and 3 tankers at Ascension
15 April	Aircraft	Discovered 2 aircraft carriers, 1 destroyer, 7 frigates, 2 amphibious landing tanks, 4 amphibious landing ships, 3 transports, and 2 oilers at 06°30'N, 14°30'W
15 April	Aircraft	At 27°10'N, 11°10'W discovered 2 transports, 1 oiler, and 1 frigate sailing toward Ascension
21 April	Aircraft	Discovered part of a task force made up of 2 aircraft carriers and 7 destroyers and frigates at 19°39'S, 21°35'W; discovered 1 destroyer and 1 oiler in the South Georgias

Month (Buenos Aires Time)	Platform	Information Obtained
21 April	Maritime platform (type unknown)	Discovered amphibious and logistics ships anchored at Ascension
22 April	Aircraft	Discovered a battle group of 2 aircraft carriers and 7 destroyers at 22°58'S, 22°45'W, sailing toward the Malvinas
23 April	KC-130 aircraft	Discovered 1 destroyer and 1 oiler refueling at 53°36'S, 36°25'W, in the proximity of the Georgias
23 April	Maritime platform (type unknown)	Again discovered a group composed of 2 aircraft carriers and 6 or 7 destroyers at 28°00'S, 24°50'W, in the area of operations
24 April	Aircraft	Discovered 1 transport with 2 helicopters on board transiting with HMS *Endurance* at 54°21'S, 36°12'W
24 April	Aircraft	Again discovered a group of 2 aircraft carriers, 1 destroyer, 7 frigates, 6 landing ships, 3 transports, and 2 oilers at 33°15'S, 27°55'W
24 April (0640)	Merchant ship *Río Olivia*	Navigating 15 miles east of Ascension, detected a minor unit; intercepted a VHF transmission regarding a munitions transfer to the *Sir Lancelot*
24 April (1835)	Merchant ship *Río de la Plata*	To the west of Ascension discovered a concentration of amphibious and logistics units identified as the *Fearless, Antelope, Sir Tristram, Sir Galahad, Elk*, 3 transports (cargo not identifiable), 2 oilers, *Stromness, Canberra, Pellew* (?), *Typhoon*, and *Irishman*
26 April	Maritime platform (type unknown)	At 39°56'S, 37°40'W discovered a warship whose type could not be identified

APPENDICES 335

Month (Buenos Aires Time)	Platform	Information Obtained
26 April	Maritime platform (type unknown)	At 40°00′S, 32°40′W discovered 2 aircraft carriers and supporting units
27 April (0918)	Merchant ship *Río de la Plata*	Discovered the following ships near Ascension: an oiler completing discharge, the *Elk* and *Canberra* using disembarking ladders, and a transport effecting repairs; the following radio traffic was intercepted: the *Stromness* hoped to load that day, the *Fearless* completed embarking landing pontoons the day before—they measured 20 × 8 × 5 feet and weighed 4 to 6 tons, a squall made work with helicopters and that of levy workers difficult, the *Sir Tristram* hoped to receive oxygen tanks, and the *Typhoon* was taking on water
27 April (1636)	Merchant ship *Río de la Plata*	Overflown by a British reconnaissance aircraft at 06°58′S, 28°08′W, course 220°
27 April (2233)	Merchant ship *Río de la Plata*	Discovered a frigate on a northeast course at 17°40′S, 26°05′W
28 April (1927)	Merchant ship *Río de la Plata*	Overflown by a commercial aircraft with an RAF insignia and a rear turbine
28 April	Maritime platform (type unknown)	Discovered HMS *Fort Grange* at 34°38′S, 31°26′W
29 April	Maritime platform (type unknown)	At 22°03′S, 37°15′W discovered an oiler on course 065°, navigating in VHF silence
29 April	Maritime platform (type unknown)	Discovered an aircraft, helicopters, 2 frigates, and part of an amphibious group at Ascension
30 April	Fishing craft *Narwal*	Discovered British warships; overflown by Harriers and Sea Kings

Month (Buenos Aires Time)	Platform	Information Obtained
1 May (0800)	Merchant ship *Río Olivia*	Passed by Gibraltar in poor visibility and saw what looked like 2 to 4 destroyers or frigates and 1 or 2 submarines
4 May (1050)	Merchant ship *Río Iguazú*	On radar observed 2 or 3 ships at Ascension
4 May (1958)	Merchant ship *Río Iguazú*	Navigated to within 12 miles of Ascension; discovered 2 frigates and CCB 501; overflown by an aircraft
5 May	Maritime platform (type unknown)	On radar detected 2 ships at Ascension
7 May (1502)	Merchant ship *Tucumán*	Around the Straits of Gibraltar detected 5 minor ships at anchor, presumably 2 or 3 merchant ships
14 May (1400)	Merchant ship *Glaciar Ameghino*	Reconnoitering as far as 100 miles north of Ascension, saw no British units
15 May (1925)	Merchant ship *Almirante Stewart*	Overflown by British aircraft 230 miles from Ascension; arrived at Ilha de Trinidade without sightings or electronic contacts
15 May (1355)	Merchant ship *Corrientes II*	Discovered 8 ships, position 24°30′S, 19°28′W, and a convoy of oilers, 2 frigates, and destroyers on a southern course; overflown repeatedly by a helicopter
17 May (1420)	Merchant ship *Santa Fe II*	Discovered what was probably the *Queen Elizabeth II* at 24°05′S, 18°43′W on a southern course at 25 knots without escort; 1 helicopter was on her stern and another circling
18 May (1440)	Merchant ship *Tucumán*	Made no radar contact; overflown 3 times by British aircraft
18 May (1645)	Merchant ship *Glaciar Ameghino*	Overflown by French reconnaissance aircraft

APPENDICES 337

Month (Buenos Aires Time)	Platform	Information Obtained
21 May (1600)	Merchant ship *Chubut*	Overflown three times by an oiler on course 182° at 15 knots
21 May (1740)	Merchant ship *Tucumán*	Approximately 330 miles southeast of Ilha de Trinidade, detected 2 aircraft with large wingspans possibly refueling in flight
21 May (2345)	Merchant ship *Chubut*	Detected a transport aircraft with large wingspan heading for Ascension
23 May (1740)	Merchant ship *Malvagni*	Discovered a military transport on a southern course at 09°10′S, 15°08′W; detected an eastbound transport aircraft
24 May (1917)	Merchant ship *Malvagni*	Discovered a military transport with a black hull and one stack on course 211°, estimated speed 19 knots; observed troops on board and combat aircraft providing air cover
24 May (1855)	Merchant ship *Chubut*	At 63°10′S, 17°40′W discovered a laden oiler with a white superstructure and dark hull on course 169° at an estimated speed of 15 knots

APPENDIX 16
Distances in Nautical Miles Between Strategic Sites During the Malvinas War

	Malvinas	Georgias	Ascension	Great Britain	Rio Grande	Buenos Aires
Malvinas	—	780	3,300	6,800	400	950
Georgias	780	—	3,000	6,600	1,200	1,400
Ascension	3,300	3,000	—	3,700	4,000	2,800
Great Britain	6,800	6,600	3,700	—	7,100	6,100
Rio Grande	400	1,200	4,000	7,100	—	1,100
Buenos Aires	950	1,400	2,800	6,100	1,100	—

APPENDIX 17
The Malvinas Naval Support Force

Name	Type	Year Built	Tonnage	Dimensions (in feet)	Owner
Río Carcarañá	Cargo	1962	8,482 gross	516 loa × 67 max b × 31 max d*	Empresa Líneas Marítimas Argentinas
Bahía Buen Suceso	Naval auxiliary	1951	5,255 fl displacement	312 loa × 47 max b × 26 max d	Argentine navy
Isla de los Estados	Cargo	1975	3,840 fl displacement	267 loa × 44 max b × 15 max d	Argentine navy
Río Iguazá	Cutter	1979	81 fl displacement	91 loa × 17 max b × 5 d	Argentine coast guard
Isla Malvinas	Cutter	1979	81 fl displacement	91 loa × 17 max b × 5 d	Argentine coast guard
Monsunen	Cargo	1957	230 gross	138 loa × 21 max b × 10 max d	Commandeered from British
Forrest	Cargo	1967	140 gross	86 loa × 23 max b × 11 max d	Commandeered from British
Penelope	Former pleasure craft	?	?	60 loa × 11 max d (estimated)	?
Yébuin	Oilfield supply tug	1967	495 gross	176 loa × 37 max b × 13 max d	Geomatter, Sociedad Anónima

*Loa = length overall, max b = maximum beam, max d = maximum draft, fl = full load.

APPENDIX 18

Operational Statistics for Argentine Naval Aviation During the Malvinas War

Units	Type of Aircraft	Flights	Total Hours
Exploration Squadron	P-2	87	437.4
	B-200	74	245.7
First Attack Squadron	MC 32/33	309	473.4
Second Attack Squadron	SUE	283	371.8
Third Fighter and Attack Squadron	A4Q	214	238.9
Reconnaissance Squadron	B-30	261	463.2
	B-200	101	184.4
First Logistics Squadron	L-188	404	1,355.1
Second Logistics Squadron	F-28	631	908.5
Antisubmarine Squadron	S-2E	203	734.4
	EMB-111	33	165.7
First Helicopter Squadron		330	419
	WG-3	106	132.7
Second Helicopter Squadron	H-3	211	290.7
Naval Aviation School	T-34C	36	43.6
Prefectura (coast guard)			417
Civil helicopters manned by naval aviators			42
TOTAL		3,289	6,923.5

Transport Flights			
Between continental bases	Tons		1,030
	Personnel		10,160
Between the continent and the Malvinas	Tons		500
	Personnel (2–31 April)		1,500
	Tons		70
	Personnel (1 May–14 June)		340
	TOTAL TONS		1,600
	TOTAL PERSONNEL		12,000

Losses			
Personnel	Officers		4
	Chief petty officers		2
Aircraft	Combat (3 A4Qs, 1 MC339)		4
	Operational accidents (1 MC339)		1
	Destroyed on the ground (3 MC339s, 4 T34Cs, 2 Skyvans, 1 Puma),		10
	on board (1 AI03 on *General Belgrano*)		1

Damage   Ships sunk   3 (*Sheffield, Ardent, Atlantic Conveyor*)
           Tons sunk   34,720
           Aircraft
             destroyed 11 helicopters (10 on *Atlantic Conveyor*, 1 on
                        Ardent)*

*Two more aircraft were destroyed by other navy units, one Harrier by marine small arms fire, and one helicopter (on the *Glamorgan*) by the impact of a shore-based Exocet.

APPENDIX 19

Weather Conditions in the South Atlantic, 1 May–14 June 1982

Place	Less Than Minimal*	Marginal†	Without Major Restrictions
Malvinas and proximity	14 days	6 days	24 days
Continent	3 days	2 days	39 days

*Days less than minimal: 4, 9, 10, 14, 22, and 27 May, and 2, 3, 4, 5, 9, 10, 12, and 13 June.

†Marginal days: 11, 12, 13, 15, and 29 May, and 7 June.

Source Notes

Chapter One

1. Spain, Ministerio de Marina, *Estado General de la Real Armada*: 3–10. The term *liner* was frequently used during the nineteenth century when referring to a ship of the line. The term is used this way throughout this book.
   For a brief treatise on the rise and decline of Spanish sea power during the colonial era, see Madariaga, *Spanish American Empire*, chapter 19. He concludes that "by 1700 Spain had really lost her sea sovereignty, an inevitable prelude to the loss of her empire" (317).

2. Fermin, "Samuel Guillermo Taber"; Destéfani, *Historia Naval Argentina*, 224–25.

3. The Spanish navy consisted of five ships of the line, ten frigates, and fifty lesser craft. See Spain, *Memoria leída en las Cortes, 1814*, 1–10, and Hasbrouck, *Foreign Legionaires*, 15–45.

4. Of the two hundred, more than forty were born in the Viceroyalty of Río de la Plata (Argentina), fifty in Cuba, more than twenty in Perú, more than twenty in Colombia, and the remainder in Venezuela, México, Puerto Rico, Chile, Ecuador, Guatemala, and the Dominica. Among the most prominent was Manuel Blanco Encalada. Born in Argentina, he trained in the Spanish navy, where he reached the rank of ensign (*alférez de marina*), and chose the patriot cause in 1812. Later he rose to the rank of admiral in the Chilean navy. See Guillen, "Independencia del Plata," 473–75.

5. The outfitting of these ships was partially paid for by the help of a North American businessman in Buenos Aires, Robert P. White.

6. Brown's force was composed of one frigate, three corvettes, one brigantine, and four minor craft. The Spanish fleet was composed of two frigates, two corvettes, two brigantines, and five lesser craft. Only the Spanish corvette *Mercurio* had been built as a warship from the keel up. The Spanish force was almost entirely destroyed or captured. To commemorate this victory, 17 May was instituted as Navy Day in Argentina.

7. Caillet-Bois, *Historia Naval Argentina*, 130–40.

8. Guillen, *História Marítima Española* 1:338–39. For example, there was the 10 August 1816 Treaty of Alcalá de Henares with Holland, which obligated Spain to maintain a squadron in the Mediterranean of one ship of the line, two frigates, one brigantine, and sixteen gunboats to suppress the Algerian pirates.

9. Initially, the plan had been to attack the Río de la Plata area; however, with the fall of Montevideo, the landing site had to be changed. See Carranza, *Campañas Navales* 2:19–21.

10. The liners were disposed of between 1821 and 1823. One of four frigates was captured by the Chileans in 1818. The last remained in service until 1828 (Guillen, *História Marítima* 1:338).

11. San Martín, who had been promoted in the field of battle against Napoleon, had resigned his commission as a Spanish lieutenant colonel and offered his services to his homeland, Argentina.

12. Carranza, *Campañas* 2:154–57.

13. Thomas Cochrane was renowned as a daring and intrepid frigate captain during the Napoleonic wars. In 1814 he was dismissed from the British navy as a result of the stock exchange scandal. During the wars of Latin American independence, Cochrane served in first the Chilean navy and then the Brazilian navy. He was pardoned and reinstated in the British navy in 1832.

14. During the wars of independence, smaller expeditions as well as those cited were escorted to the Costa Firme, Habana, Veracruz, Lima, and Montevideo. In all, more than forty-two thousand troops were escorted to the Americas.

15. *Memoria leída a las Cortes . . . 1822*, 1–10; Destéfani, "Real Armada Española," 60–74.

16. Simón Bolivar noted, "The Colombian and Peruvian navies cost us more than we are worth, because the officers and seamen are English, and the lowest in rank is paid eighteen to twenty *pesos*. They are maintained in the English manner, which costs three times as much as it would in England" (Lecuna and Bierck, *Selected Writings of Bolivar* 2:433).

17. Lecuna and Bierck, *Selected Writings of Bolivar* 2:581.

Chapter Two

1. Lecuna and Bierck, *Selecting Writings* 1:307.
2. Condell, "Defensa de nuestro litorial."
3. Bauer, "U.S. Navy and Texas Independence," 44–48.
4. Cárdenas, *Semblanza Marítima* 1:100–103; Wells, "Battle of Campeche," 217–20.
5. Scheina, "Forgotten Fleet," 46–50; Scheina, "Seapower Misused," 203–9.
6. Bancroft, *History of Mexico* 7:778–80.
7. Ferdinand Maximilian Joseph, the archduke of Austria, claimed the throne of México in 1864 with the support of France and some conservative Mexicans. In 1867 the forces of Benito Juárez defeated those of Maximilian, which no longer had the aid of French army, and Maximilian was executed.
8. Lecuna and Bierck, *Selected Writings of Bolivar* 2:533–36.
9. Bamio, "Guerra Contra Brasil," 57–59; *Manchester Guardian*, 15 September

1827, 1. See Wheelock, "American Commodore," for a description of the raiding tactics employed by the weaker Argentine navy.

10. Bauer, "Sancala Affair," 174–86.

11. Ynsfran, *Expedición contra Paraguay* 1:24.

12. The *Tacuari* was 488 tons. She had two 180-hp steam engines and was armed with two sixty-, two thirty-two-, and two eight-pounders. She sailed from Bordeaux, France, on 11 November 1854, carrying a cargo that included Francisco S. Lopez and his entourage and eight or ten steam engines for use in ships to be built at Asunción.

13. Santiago Canstatt apparently was a merchant who had contacts with the Paraguayan opposition then in exile in Buenos Aires. The British consul protested his arrest several times. On 8 January 1859 the British consul presented an ultimatum to the Paraguayan government. On the fifth, diplomatic relations were severed. This led to the incident between the *Tacuari* and the two British warships. In the meantime, Canstatt and four others were condemned to death, and nine more received four years of prison. Carlos A. Lopez had two executed and approximately twelve were pardoned, including Canstatt, who left the country. The British government insisted, nonetheless, on an apology and an indemnity and threatened to seize all Paraguayan ships. Apparently Canstatt, whose father was a Belgian, acquired British citizenship, or at least a British passport, under somewhat dubious circumstances.

14. Meister, "Flussoperationen," October and November.

15. A fourth steamer, the *Paraguari*, was also sunk at Riachuelo. She was later refloated and towed to Asunción. The Paraguayans were unable to repair the *Paraguari* before they had to evacuate their naval arsenal, so the hulk was scuttled to block part of the river.

16. Mendonça and Vasconcelos, *Repositório de Nomes Esquadra Brasileira*, 36, 122–23, 165, 177, 241; English, *Armed Forces of Latin America*, 107.

17. Somervell, "Anglo-Chilean Naval Relations," 6; López Urrutia, *Historia de la Marina de Chile*, 158–59; Fuenzalida Bade, *La Armada de Chile* 2:379.

18. Somervell, "Anglo-Chilean Naval Relations," 18–19.

19. Somervell, "Naval Relations," 6–7; Novoa de la Fuente, *Historia Naval de Chile*, 111; Fuenzalida Bade, *La Armada*, 532.

20. These two ships had originally been ordered from France by the Confederate states of America as the *Georgia* and the *Texas*. They were purchased by Perú from the builders.

21. The *Almirante Cochrane* arrived in Valparaíso on 26 December 1874. The ship had to be dry-docked for completion of the work, but there was no appropriate facility in Chile. This ultimately led to the construction of another ship at Talcahuano. (Rojas, *Administración Naval de Chile*, 75.) In 1877 the *Almirante Cochrane* returned to Great Britain for its lead sheathing. (Langlois, *Influencia del poder naval*, 164.)

22. The *Huáscar*, the principal Peruvian warship, was no more than a seagoing monitor with a ram. Built in the 1860s, the ship had a turret that was still trained by manpower. It would take a team of sixteen men and almost as many minutes to crank the turret to a broadside firing position and then to return it to the loading position. The muzzle-loading gun could only be withdrawn into the turret for loading when trained directly ahead. The *Huáscar* could only fire on the beams because a forecastle blocked the field of fire over the bow. It was easier to train the ship than the gun.

The *Huáscar* was faster than most reference books give her credit for being. Apparently on builders' trials, she made 12.3 knots with a maximum pressure of thirty pounds in four boilers. According to Samuel MacMahon, her chief engineer, the maximum speed that the *Huascar* was capable of at Angamos was sixty to sixty-three revolutions per minute with twenty-five to thirty pounds' pressure, giving her about eleven knots. If she had had a clean bottom, she might have made twelve or more knots. See Lopez, *Historia de la guerra* 2:138. Other Peruvian sources credit the *Huascar* with only nine knots.

23. The steam frigate *Apurimac*, built in London in 1854, sank together with a floating dry dock in which she was being repaired at San Lorenzo Island in 1860. She was refloated four years later and repaired. She took part in the Chilean-Peruvian naval action against Spain off Abtao on 7 February 1866. She suffered severe damage in a storm during June 1866, and her boilers and engine were in such bad condition that she was made a stationary school ship for recruits in 1873. The corvette *America*, sister ship to the *Union*, was destroyed at anchor off Arica on 13 August 1868 by a tidal wave. On 13 July 1876 the gunboat *Chanchamayo* was lost through stranding near *la punta falsa* of Aguja, between Payta and Eten (Melo, *Historia de la Marina del Peru* 1:282).

24. In many respects the Bolivian congress was right. Bolivia did not have the money, crews, know-how, ports, or shore installations to support these proposed warships.

25. See Carvajal, "¿Pudo haber escapado el *Huascar?*" 39–46. The author argues that the *Huascar* could have escaped.

26. There is some disagreement as to the exact number who died in defense of the *Huascar*. A plaque on board the ship lists officers Grau, Aguirre, Ferré, and Rodriguez, along with twenty-eight men, but overlooks Palacios, giving a total of thirty-three. Melo claims the number to be thirty-three including Palacios (*Historia de la Marina* 2:146). According to Vegas, seven more were killed, all from the Infantry Batallion No. 3, which formed part of the crew (*Historia de la Marina*, 321). This gives a total of forty killed out of a crew of two hundred. Twenty-six were wounded. The Chileans found thirty-one bodies on board the *Huascar* and took 165 prisoner, which leaves four men unaccounted for. They probably fell overboard.

27. Pisagua was defended by 1,095 allies (498 from the Bolivian Victoria Batallion, 397 from the Bolivian Independencia Batallion, about two hundred from the Peruvian Nacionales de Pisagua Batallion—mostly untrained volunteers) plus two 100-pound guns. The allies lost 941 to death or capture, the Chileans 231 men.

28. José Gálvez was the son of the Peruvian minister of war, who was killed in the Spanish bombardment of Callao on 2 May 1866.

29. Federico Blume Othon, born on Saint Thomas in the Lesser Antilles, was educated as an engineer in Germany and spent three decades constructing railroads in the United States, Chile, and Perú. Early in his career he was influenced by the work of Robert Fulton and developed an interest in building a ship that could navigate underwater. During the War with Spain he sent to General Juan Antonio Pezet, president of Perú, plans and specifications for an underseas craft, but nothing came of them and apparently the details were lost. His interest in submarine design lingered, and, using his own money and a railway workship, he built the boat known as the *Toro Submarino* in Paita, Perú.

30. Following the war, Blume continued to crusade for the creation of a submarine force for the Peruvian navy. He died in 1901 without succeeding. See Galvez, "Submarino, minas y brulotes," 23–26; Sapunar, "Precursores Submarinos Chileano-Peruanos," 176–80; and Valdizán, "Cincuentenario de Nuestra Fuerza Submarina," 437–39.

31. The Haitian warships were the *Dessalines* and the *Défense* and the Dominican *El Presidente*.

32. On 2 November U.S. marines had been ordered to seize the Panamá railroad, keep the Isthmus of Panamá clear, and prevent Colombian troops from landing within fifty miles of the isthmus if a revolution broke out.

33. Heinl, *Written in Blood*, 331.

34. Pulido Santana, *Diplomacia en Venezuela*, 116; Spector, "Roosevelt, the Navy, and the Venezuelan Controversy."

Chapter Three

1. Article 39, the Treaty of Friendship, Commerce, and Navigation between the Argentine Confederation and Chile, was signed at Santiago on 30 August 1855.

2. The discovery of coal, which held great promise since there are few deposits in all of Latin America, did not live up to expectations.

3. The minister in Buenos Aires was Thomas O. Osborn, in Santiago, Thomas A. Osborn.

4. The *Almirante Cochrane, Valparaíso, Magallanes*, and *Pilcomayo* (Burr, *By Reason or Force*, 204).

5. Caillet-Bois, *Historia Naval Argentina*, 496.

6. Burr, *By Reason or Force*, 134–35; Arguindeguy, *Apuntes Buques Argentina* 3:1202–6.

7. Caillet-Bois, *Historia Naval*, 498–501. See also González, *Armada en la Conquista del Desierto*, 161–62, and Destéfani, "Conquista del Desierto," 32–44.

8. The principal warships of the Argentine navy were the central battery corvette *Almirante Brown* (4,200 tons, built 1880), the coastal defense battleships *La Plata* and *Los Andes* (both 1,500 tons, built 1874), and the protected cruiser *Patagonia* (1,450 tons, built 1885). The principal warships of the Chilean navy were the central battery ironclads *Almirante Cochrane* and *Blanco Encalada* (both 3,370 tons, built 1874 and 1875), and the protected cruiser *Esmeralda* (2,950 tons, built 1883). The Chilean navy also had the seagoing monitor *Huáscar* (2,030 tons, built 1865), which had been captured from Perú in 1879. She was not a modern warship by 1889 standards.

In 1885 Chile did sell two spar torpedo boats to Great Britain. The Chilean navy was adopting the Whitehead torpedo, and these two boats were obsolete and too expensive to update. The funds were used to buy a new first-class torpedo boat. See Gouch, *Royal Navy*, 230.

9. Chile's financial position was weakened by the claims of Peruvian creditors, which Chile had inherited by conquering the nitrate territories and agreed to satisfy in the treaties ending the War of the Pacific.

10. The small, fast torpedo boat could approach the enemy under cover of darkness, select its target, run in and fire its torpedoes, then use its high speed to escape during the confusion that followed. Torpedo boats were acquired by Argentina, Brazil, Chile, and Perú, and by a few smaller Latin American navies. The challenge the torpedo boat posed to the battleship was short-lived. Battleships were soon armed with a battery of light, quick-firing guns to keep the torpedo-carrying pest beyond effective launching range, and a new, larger destroyer-torpedo boat, also armed with small quick-firing guns, was developed to accompany the battleship at sea. The destroyer-torpedo boat could intercept and destroy its smaller sisters. These developments increased the already serious difficulties torpedo boats encountered in finding their targets and in destroying them with the always temperamental torpedo. See Haberlein and Scheina, "Century of Naval Revolution," 16.

11. The *Capitán Prat* was the first warship in the world to use electricity to

power gun elevation and ammunition hoists. See Encina, *Historia de Chile* 19: 319–20.

12. See *Conway's, 1860–1905*, 401–4, 410–15; Brook, "Elswick Cruisers" 7: 154–76, 8:246–73, 9:237–53; Arguindeguy, *Apuntes Buques Argentina* 4: 1727–1944.

13. National Archives, Records of Foreign Service Posts, Dispatches from U.S. Ministers to Argentina, telegram from J. R. G. Pitkin, minister to Argentina, to James Blaine, secretary of state, 21 May 1892.

14. See *Conway's, 1860–1905*, 401–4, 410–15; Brook, "Elswick Cruisers" 7:154–76, 8:246–73; Arguindeguy, *Apuntes Buques Argentina* 4:1727–1944. Fuenzalida, *Armada de Chile* 4:1068–69.

15. Burr, *By Reason or Force*, 204.

16. Huber's submarine had a 15.5-ton displacement, was 26 feet 3 inches (8 meters) long, 8 feet 2 inches (2.5 meters) in beam, 11 feet 6 inches (3.5 meters) in overall height, and was shaped like a cigar. It had a conning tower 31.5 inches (80 centimeters) in diameter and 4 feet (1.2 meters) high. The boat was fitted with a periscope and six viewing ports. A tail which moved like that of a fish, driven by an 8-horsepower motor and powered by batteries that could hold a 10-hour charge, provided propulsion. Two other electric motors operated the ventilation system. See Sapunar, "Precursores Submarinos," 179.

17. Destéfani, *Historia Naval Argentina*, 227–28.

18. This 2,950-ton ship had been built in 1883, and she was outclassed by newer protected cruisers in the Argentine fleet. Japan was in the market for warships. Accordingly, a strange deal was negotiated whereby Chile sold the ship to Ecuador, which acted as a flag of convenience. Reportedly, the Ecuadorian consul in Valparaíso is said to have raised the Ecuadorian flag on the warship after it left Valparaíso without the authority of his government. The Chilean crew, commanded by Commander Emilio Garín under the Ecuadorian flag, delivered the ship to the Japanese in the Ecuadorian Galapagos Islands. A primary figure in the financial arrangements was the North American Charles R. Flint, who possibly bought and sold more military hardware for Latin American navies than any other individual (Barros, *Historia Diplomática de Chile*, 505–9; Flint, *Memories of an Active Life*, 180–82).

19. Brook, "Elswick Cruisers," 9:239; Fuenzalida, *Armada de Chile* 4:1067.

20. The complete names for the four Argentine armored cruisers were the *Garibaldi*, *San Martín*, *Pueyrredón*, and *General Belgrano*. Frequently references listed the surnames of all four units with the title *General* appended. This is correct only for the *General Belgrano*. See Arguindeguy, *Apuntes Buques Argentina*, 4:1764–1832.

The selection of the name *Garibaldi* by the Argentines for the first of their armored cruisers is interesting. Giuseppe Garibaldi fought in mid-century South American wars always on the side opposed to the established Argentine government. Perhaps the name was chosen to please the large number of Italian immigrants flocking to Argentina in the late nineteenth century.

21. Brook, "Elswick Cruisers" 9:242; Fuenzalida, *Armada de Chile* 4:1069.

22. Rauch, "Cruisers for Argentina" 15:297–98.

23. Burr, *By Reason or Force*, 224–25.

24. Rauch, "Cruisers for Argentina" 15:302–4.

25. Burr, *By Reason or Force*, 226–27.

26. Caillet-Bois, *Historia Naval Argentina*, 517; Destéfani, *Manual de Historia Naval Argentina*, 144; Fuenzalida, *Armada de Chile* 4:1077–78. Almost all of the

remaining Argentine and Chilean warships were in southern waters to support the advanced squadrons carrying their respective presidents.

27. These two ships were originally to have been named the *General Mitre* and the *General Roca*.

28. Brook, "Elswick Cruisers" 8:265; *Conway's, 1860–1905*, 413.

29. U.S. Department of the Navy, Records of the General Board, file 420-6. The United States had made inquiries in Chile prior to the Spanish-American War to see if the then-completing armored cruiser *O'Higgins* was for sale. Chile, engaged in her own arms race, told the North Americans no.

30. National Archives, Dispatches from U.S. ministers to Chile, telegram from the U.S. minister in Chile, Henry L. Wilson, to the secretary of state, John Hay, 11 July 1901.

31. *Conway's, 1860–1905*, 39.

32. Burr, *By Reason or Force*, 245.

33. According to Chilean sources, the Argentine negotiations to purchase the two 15,000-ton battleships failed on 5 May 1902. Whether the construction of these battleships was abandoned and then the decision to sign a naval limitation treaty made or vice versa is unclear. Chile, Archives of the Minister of Foreign Relations, telegram from the minister in Buenos Aires, Carlos Concha, to the minister of the navy.

34. Varela, *Defensa de pactos internationales*, 9.

35. *Times* (London), 27 May 1902, 1–3.

36. Perry, *Consolidated Treaty Series* 191:223–24.

37. Acta Aclaratoria de los Pactos Sobre Arbitraje y Limitación de Armamentos, documento no. 30, in Fraga, *Argentina y el Atlántico Sur*, p. 306.

38. The sale of the *Bernardino Rivadavia* and the *Mariano Moreno* to Japan helped create good relations between that country and Argentina, which resulted in an Argentine naval officer, Juan Pablo Sáenz Valiente, being invited to embark in the Japanese fleet to witness the Battle of Tsushima.

39. In fact, the Russians made an immediate cash offer for these two ships, but the British could ill afford to let them be purchased by Russia against the best interests of their ally Japan, so the Admiralty somewhat reluctantly took them over as the *Swiftsure* and the *Triumph*. They were originally to have been named *Constitución* and *Libertad*.

40. The disarmament of these three armored cruisers could not include their heavy ordnance because Argentina did not have cranes capable of lifting the guns from the turrets. Apparently, the *Capitán Prat* had been in bad condition since the mid-1890s.

Chapter Four

1. The constitutions of a few Latin American countries vaguely assign to the military the responsibility of interpreting the law of the land. For example, the Brazilian constitution of 1967 states, "It is the mission of the armed forces to defend the country and to guarantee the constituted powers and law and order" (chapter 7, section 6, paragraph 1). And the Peruvian Constitution of 1933: "The purpose of the armed forces is to assure the rights of the Republic, compliance with the Constitution and the preservation of public order" (title 12, article 213). And the Argentine, 1853: "Every Argentine citizen is obliged to bear arms in defense of his country and of this Constitution . . ." (part 1, article 21).

Prominent Latin American naval officers who were active in politics include the Argentine-born Chilean Manual Blanco Encalada, the Chilean president Jorge

Montt, and Irish-born William Brown, who for some time was governor of the province of Buenos Aires.

2. Ranges were beginning to open. At the Battle of Yalu (1894) the range declined from 6,000 to 3,000, and then to 2,500 yards. At the Battle of Santiago (1898) fighting took place at various ranges between 7,000 and 1,400 yards. At Tsushima (1905) distances varied from 7,000 to 1,000 yards. Ranges under 3,000 yards were obtained after the enemy had been severely damaged. Main artillery duels were fought between 6,000 and 4,000 yards. See Wilson, *Ironclads in Action* 2:82–125.

3. A few countries did acquire warships designed to carry a landing force. In 1902 México purchased the *Vera Cruz* and the *Tampico* from Cresent Shipyards in Elizabeth Port, New Jersey. In addition to their normal complement, these gunboat transports had facilities for 250 troops plus four- and six-pound carriage guns. The ships' longboats provided transportation ashore. In 1908 México bought another cruiser transport, the *General Guerrero*, built by Vickers in England. She could transport 550 troops, forty-five horses, and a few field pieces. Thirty years later the Mexican navy ordered five gunboat transports from Spain. Three—the *Potosí*, *Querétaro*, and *Guanajuato*—could accommodate 250 troops and twenty horses. The larger *Durango* and *Zacatecas* could carry 490 soldiers plus eighty mounts. The *Potosí*, *Querétaro*, *Guanajuato*, and *Durango* were delivered to México prior to the outbreak of the Spanish Civil War. The *Zacatecas*, still under construction, was seized by the Nationalists and became the *Calvo Sotelo*, thus was never delivered. This fanned Mexican hostility towards the Nationalists. Longboats again landed troops, and were used to deal with smuggling and bandits because their landing parties were too weak to confront regular troops. See "American-Built Mexican Gunboats," *Shipping World*; *Revista General de Marina* (Madrid) 62; *Conway's, 1906–21*, 418; "Mexico," *Proceedings*.

4. To cite an example of such an emergency, following the War of the Pacific Chile's newly acquired nitrate provinces in the north were a hotbed of labor unrest. The distant region lacked an adequate north-south rail line, and before the development of air transport the only way Chile could maintain order there was to have her fleet transport troops. Annual maneuvers were frequently interrupted by calls to the north. In the 1920s the Argentine navy carried army regiments to Patagonia to crush the bloody rampage of bandits. In July 1932 the Peruvian cruiser *Almirante Grau* transported troops from Callao to Trujillo to help put down an insurrection.

5. Sommi, *Revolución del 90*, 179–80; Mendía and Naón, *Revolución del 90*, 31–36; Ferre, "Armed Forces in Argentine Politics," 80–84.

6. Sommi, *Revolución*, 179–81, 261; Arguindeguy, *Apuntes Buques Argentina* 4:1585, 3:1280.

7. Sommi, *Revolución*, 263; "Síntesis Histórica de la Infantería de Marina," *Del Mar*, 63–64; Quartaruolo, "Armada y la Revolución de 1890," 57–64.

8. The foreign warships in Buenos Aires were Britain's *Beagle* (steel screw sloop, built 1889) and *Bramble* (composite gunboat, built 1886), Spain's *Infanta Isabel* (cruiser, built 1885), the United States' *Tallapoosa* (sidewheel gunboat, built 1864), and Uruguay's *General Rivera* (gunboat, built 1884).

9. National Archives, National Records Collection, log of the *Tallapoosa*, 28 July 1890.

10. Etchepareborda, *Revolución Argentina del 90*, 60.

11. U.S. Department of the Navy, Bureau of Navigation, *International Code of Signals*, 11.

12. Quartaruolo, "Armada," 63; National Archives, National Records Collection, log of the *Tallapoosa*, 29 July 1890.
13. Sommi, *Revolución*, 300–331.
14. Herring, *History of Latin America*, 625.
15. Quartaruolo, "Armada," 31–35.
16. Lieutenant Valotta is somewhat of a mystery. His name does not appear among those who graduated from the Argentine Naval Academy. Probably he belonged to the classes commissioned prior to the creation of the school in 1872. This could explain why he was still a lieutenant (j.g.) in 1893.
17. Quartaruolo, "Armada," 31–35; Arguindeguy, *Apuntes Buques Argentina* 3:1213.
18. Warships remaining loyal were the *Independencia* (coastal defense battleship, built 1891), *Libertad* (coastal defense battleship, built 1890), *Almirante Brown* (central battery corvette, built 1880), *Nueve de Julio* (protected cruiser, built 1892), *Patagonia* (protected cruiser, built 1885), *Espora* (torpedo boat, built 1890), and *Pinedo* (torpedo boat, 1890).
19. Burzio, *Historia del Torpedo*, 355–62; Quartaruolo, "Armada," 31–35.
20. The *Los Andes* was originally armed with two 7.5-inch guns which fired 200-pound shells at a maximum distance of some 1,300 to 1,650 yards. She and her sister, the *El Plata*, were rearmed in 1883 with two Armstrong 9.45-inch guns that fired a 198-pound shell a maximum distance of 2,700 yards.
21. Arguindeguy, *Apuntes Buques Argentina* 3:1213–14, 4:1746–47, 1935.
22. Iñiquez, *Golpe de estado y la revolución*, 50–51; Nabuco, *Balmaceda*, 129.
23. The *Huáscar* was out of commission. The Congresionalistas, unchallenged by the city's forts, boarded her and towed the ironclad to the fleet's anchorage. There she was placed in commission. The *Huáscar* was an aged but formidable warship. The ship's old muzzle-loading guns had been replaced by breech-loading 8-inch, 32-cal Elswick-Armstrong guns in 1882. She also had new boilers, two 4.7-inch guns, and two Maxim machine guns in 1891. In 1885 a steam-driven winch had been installed to turn the turrets. To train the guns on the beam it now took five minutes, as opposed to fifteen when the turret had been manually trained.
24. Clowes, *Four Modern Naval Campaigns*, 136.
25. *Journal of the American Society of Naval Engineers*.
26. In addition to those gunboats, the Gobiernista navy consisted of the steamer *Imperial*, the torpedo launch *Sargente*, and the eight Yarrow-type launches *Guale, Fresia, Lauca, Quindora, Glaura, Janequeo, Rucumilla,* and *Tegualda*. See Clowes, *Four Naval Campaigns*, 133–86; Novoa de la Fuente, *Historia Naval de Chile*, 137–47.
27. The U.S. Supreme Court ultimately ruled that the seizure of the *Itata* was illegal. See Clowes, *Four Naval Campaigns*, 150–52.
28. Emilio Körner was a German army captain contracted in 1886 to found an army war college. The German authorities objected to Körner's joining the Congresionalistas but pardoned and congratulated him after Körner helped win the civil war. He did not take an active part in the war until May 1891.
29. Clowes, *Four Naval Campaigns*, 154–55.
30. Sears and Wells, *Chilean Revolution of 1891*, 28–29.
31. Wilson, *Ironclads in Action* 2:32–33.
32. The only other large amphibious assaults in the western hemisphere handled with such planning and skill were the U.S. landing at Vera Cruz in 1847 and the Brazilian-Argentine river crossing near Paso de la Patria in 1866.
33. In fact, Manuel Blanco Encalada, Argentine born and a nationalized Chilean, briefly served as president of Chile in 1826. Blanco Encalada had been the

fleet commodore prior to and after Lord Cochrane's stay with the Chilean navy. Jorge Montt was a dominant figure in the Chilean navy until his death in 1922. Following his retirement from the navy in 1913, he was mayor of Valparaíso.

34. The uprising in Río Grande do Sul was sparked by the rebellion of General Silva Tavares against Governor Júlio de Castilhos. Numerous signs of unrest followed. The thirteen generals and admirals were retired on 7 April 1892. Five days later, additional army and naval officers who criticized the government were forced to retire. Professors were dismissed from universities in Recife (Pernambuco) and Río. A 17 December 1892 decree amalgamated the Bank of the Republic and the Bank of Brazil in order to facilitate the unregulated printing of paper money. See Freire, *História da Revolta*, 23–44; Thompson, *Guerra Civil do Brasil*, 13–25.

35. Freire, *História da Revolta*, 10, 52; Thompson, *Guerra Civil do Brasil*, 28–31.

36. The *Aquidabã* proved to be an unlucky ship. She was the first warship to be hit by an automotive torpedo while under way, this on 16 April 1894. On 21 January 1906 she was destroyed by an internal explosion.

37. Freire, *História da Revolta*, 52–53, 76–77; Wilson, *Ironclads in Action* 2:35.

38. The rebel fleet included the battleship *Aquidabã*; cruisers *República* and *Tamandaré*; corvettes *Trajano* and *Guanabara*; monitor *Javary*; large torpedo boats *Araguary* and *Marcílio Dias* and five smaller ones; merchantman *Júpiter, Sete de Setembro, Marajo, Amazonas, Madeira, Pallas, Venus, Corytiba, Alagoas, Laguna, Vitória*, and others; seven merchant-tugs; and the former imperial yacht (Thompson, *Guerra Civil do Brasil*, 33; Freire, *História da Revolta*, 91; Clowes, *Four Naval Campaigns*, 188).

39. Freire, *História da Revolta*, 92–94, 111–12, 115, 119, 130–32, 150–59; "La Guerra del Brazil y sus Ensenanzas Navales," *Revista General de Marina*; Gonçalves, "Almirante Gonçalves" 4:517.

40. Flint, *Memories of an Active Life*, 89–100.

41. John Ericsson was the most famous U.S. naval architect of his day. He had designed the USS *Princeton* and USS *Monitor* of Civil War fame. The *Destroyer* was an experimental "torpedo" craft built in the early 1880s. A non-self-propelled torpedo was fired from an underwater gun mounted in the bow. The craft had been evaluated by the U.S. Navy but not accepted.

42. Flint, *Memories of an Active Life*, 89–100.

43. Garrido, "Fortificações do Brasil," 278–459.

44. Thompson, *Guerra Civil do Brasil*, 155–61; Vivian, "United States Policy During the Brazilian Naval Revolt," 245–61.

45. The rebel fleet under Admiral Saldanha in Rio had been organized into three divisions in early December. The First Division under Rear Admiral Saldanha's personal command had the cruisers *Liberdade* (flagship), *Tamandaré, Guanabara*, and *Trajano*. The Second Division under Captain Eliezer Coutinho Tavares had the cruisers *Júpiter* (flagship), *Mercúrio, Pereira da Cunha, Parahyba*, and *Lagoa* (these were merchantmen armed as auxiliary cruisers). The Third Division under Lieutenant João da Silva Retumba had the auxiliary cruiser *Marte* (flagship); transports *Vitória* and *Aymore;* steamer *Itacolomy* (engine and artillery workshops); *Corytiba, União*, and *Oceano* (ammunition depots); *Itália* and *Itaúna* (coal and engine spares depots); *Industrial* (isolation ward for yellow fever patients); steamers *Olinda* and *Penedo*, and sailing vessels *Feliz Competidor* and two others (food depots); dispatch vessel *Adolpho de Barros;* and galliot *Quinze de Novembro*. In addition to these ships, there were three small torpedo boats as well as twelve steam tugs and seventeen steam launches at first attached to the divisions but later commanded by midshipmen employed on detached duty (Freire, *História da Revolta*, 207–9).

46. Present at Bahia on 25 January 1894 were the *Nictheroy* (ex-*El Cid*) from the

United States, *Gustavo Sampaio* from Great Britain, and minor Brazilian warships *Parnahyba, Primero de Março, Bracanot, Piraja,* and *Caravellas.* On the twenty-sixth, the *Andrade* (ex-*America*), *Piratinim* (ex-*Destroyer*), and torpedo boats *Tamborim* and *Greenhalg* arrived from the United States. A few days later five torpedo boats arrived from Europe (Freire, *História da Revolta,* 207–9).

47. Wilson, *Ironclads in Action* 2:41.

48. The fleet was split into three divisions. The First Division consisted of the *Nictheroy* (fleet flagship), torpedo boats *Sabino Vieira* and *Andrada,* cruiser *Parnahyba,* and steamer *Itaipú.* The Second Division commanded by Captain Gaspar de Silva Rodrigues, consisted of the steamer *São Salvador* (with the Ninth Infantry battalion) and torpedo boats *Pedro Ivo, Pedro Affonso, Silvado, Silva Jardim, Piratinim, Tamborim,* and *Greenhalg.* The Third Division, from Montevideo, commanded by Commander Jose Pedro Alves de Barros, consisted of the cruiser *Tiradentes,* coastal defense battleship *Bahia,* and steamer *Santos* (Freire, *História da Revolta,* 255–56).

49. Clowes, *Four Naval Campaigns,* 209.

50. Thompson, *Guerra Civil do Brasil,* 155–61.

51. The government squadron was made up of the armed merchantmen *Nictheroy, Andrada, São Salvador, Itaipú,* and *Santos,* torpedo gunboat *Tiradentes,* and torpedo boats *Gustavo Sampaio, Affonso Pedro, Pedro Ivo,* and *Silvado.*

52. Dulles, *Yesterday in Mexico,* 7, 76, 212, 246, 259–60.

53. "Brazil: Details of Recent Naval Mutiny," *Monthly Information Bulletin,* 58.

54. Ibid., 59.

55. Ibid., 58–60.

56. Levine, *Vargas Regime,* 66–67.

Chapter Five

1. Baron de Rio Branco, José Maria de Silva Paranhos, was the author of the "free birth" law of 1871, which stated that any child born to a slave mother would be free. The baron earned a name for himself with his brilliant presentations of Brazilian claims during boundary arbitrations at the end of the nineteenth century. He held the position of minister of foreign affairs under four presidents, from 1902 to 1912.

2. The 1904 naval program made provisions for the submarine, which finally took root in Brazil. Three boats, the *F-1, F-3,* and *F-5,* and the submarine tender *Ceara,* were acquired from Italy. They served from 1913 to 1933.

Like Argentina, Chile, and Perú, Brazil had shown an interest in the submarine during the nineteenth century. Luís Jacinto Gomes, an assistant naval machinist, and Luis de Melo Marques, a civil engineer, each designed models built by the Brazilian navy and used for testing between 1892 and the beginning of the twentieth century. Neither model evolved into a full-scale boat. Meanwhile, Lieutenant (later Admiral) Júlio Emilio Hess formulated plans for a submarine. After presenting his idea to the navy, he was sent abroad to study with some of the world's most noted submarine inventors. Although his plans did not lead to the construction of a boat, he did become the champion of the submarine during his service in the Brazilian navy.

On 19 June 1894 Captain João Justino de Proença commissioned the French inventor Claude Goubet to construct a submarine for the Brazilian navy. Like so many late–nineteenth century submarines, the *Goubet II* came equipped with all the latest inventions, including dispatch bottles for communications with the surface. Brazil never fully paid for the boat, and she remained in France. Finally, on 12 September 1902, she was sold at auction for forty-five thousand francs to a group of the inventor's friends. Technical details concerning Goubet's submarine may be found in *Shipping World and Herald of Commerce* (1 December 1895):278. (Statements concerning the number of boats built for and delivered to Brazil are in error.) See Scavarda, "Os Sumarinos no Brasil," 43–69; Le Masson, *Du Nautilus au Redoutable*, 85–89.

3. Gama, *Primeira Guerra Mundial*, 7–8.
4. *Navy League Annual, 1910–11*, 103.
5. *Navy League Annual, 1908–9*, 99. The third unit of the *Minas Gerais* class was never built. A Spanish naval periodical observed:

> Few ships in the last few years have attracted so much attention as the Brazilian *Dreadnought*. . . . That country undertook the construction of the three at the same time, when all of the great powers doubted the wisdom of constructing this type of ship. It is only natural that rumors began to circulate supporting the argument that Brazil acted as an intermediary for some great power which would acquire them before they terminate their construction (*Revista de General de Marina* 64).

6. President Rodrigues da Fonseca remarked:

> When I assumed office I found that my predecessor had signed a contract for the building of the battleship *Rio de Janeiro*, a vessel of 32,000 tons, with an armament of 14 in. guns. Considerations of every kind pointed to the inconvenience of acquiring such a vessel and to the revision of the contract in the sense of reducing the tonnage. This was done, and we shall possess a powerful unit which will not be built on exaggerated lines such as have not as yet stood the test of experience" (*Navy League Annual*, 1911–12, 53–54).

7. "Brazil," *Navy* 18:322.
8. In 1921 Great Britain offered the *Agincourt* (ex-Turkish *Sultan Osman I* and ex-Brazilian *Rio de Janeiro*) to Brazil for one million pounds. The offer was rejected. National Archives, Records of the Office of Naval Intelligence, U.S. naval attaché to Brazil to director of naval intelligence, "Purchase of ships by Brazil, British propaganda," 31 August 1921, box C101, file C14170.
9. González, *Historia del Centro Naval*, 128–32.
10. With the decision by Brazil not to construct a third dreadnought, Argentina decided not to obtain a third unit either. Chile, Congress, Senate, *Diario de Sesiones de la Cámara de Senadores*, 32nd session (10 September 1912), 2–3; (17 September 1912), 2–17.
11. The following were the most serious bidders: Blohm and Voss (Germany); Armstrong, Whitworth, and Co., and Vickers, Sons, and Maxim (Great Britain); Cramps Shipbuilding Co., Newport News Shipbuilding Co., Fore River Shipbuilding Co., and New York Shipbuilding Co. (United States).
12. *Navy* (London) 15.
13. "The Argentine project, though it will give comparatively small impetus to shipbuilders, is welcome to them [the British], and they are likely to make tenders on such a narrow margin of profit for the purpose of keeping the work going that American rivals to the British firms will be unable to compete" (*New York Herald*, 17 January 1909, 3). See also *Daily Mail* (London), 11 February 1910, 3.
14. U.S. Congress, *Battleships for the Argentine Republic*, letter from the secretary of the navy, 30 March 1911, 2.
15. *Revista General de Marina* 66. One dreadnought, the *Rivadavia*, was to be constructed by Fore River, while construction of the second, the *Moreno*, was sublet to New York Shipbuilding Corporation, Camden, New Jersey.

SOURCE NOTES 355

16. "Argentina," *Navy* (Washington) 4 (July 1910):30.
17. "Operational Histories of South American Battleships," *Warship International*.
18. National Archives, General Correspondence of the Secretary of the Navy, letter from U.S. secretary of state to U.S. secretary of the navy, 28 November 1911, enclosure 1 of 5 November 1911, p. 4.
19. In 1910 the Chilean navy ordered two Holland-type submarines from the Electric Boat Company, which subcontracted the work to Todd Shipbuilding in Seattle, Washington. The boats were to be named the *Iquique* and the *Antofagasta* and to be commanded by Edgardo von Schroeders and Luis A. Concha. However, the construction firm sold them to British Columbia on the eve of World War I. The boats were taken from the builder's yard in the dead of night. A history of the yard states that they were sold "after a disagreement over price." Pedro Sapunar, writing on the early Chilean submarines, states that the firm justified the sale by claiming that the ships "did not comply with the technical specifications" ("Precursores Submarinos," 180). The two boats became the Canadian *CC-1* and *CC-2*.

Chile obtained her first submarines in 1917. Her six Holland-type boats had been built for the British by the Fore River Company in the United States, where they were embargoed because of North American neutrality during the early years of World War I. After their release in 1917 the British government, with North American approval, gave five to Chile as partial payment for Chilean warships appropriated at the outbreak of the war. The Chileans purchased the sixth. After weathering a storm off Cape Hatteras, the boats, the *H-1* through the *H-6*, arrived off Valparaíso on 20 July 1918. The submarines remained in service until the late 1940s and early 1950s. See Mitchell, *Every Kind of Shipwork*, 24; *Jane's Fighting Ships, 1916*, 134; Fuenzalida, *Armada de Chile* 4:1125-27.

20. Public Record Office, FO 371/3679, letter of 8 November 1919 from T. W. S. Anderson, Admiralty, to the under secretary of state, foreign affairs; Somervell, "Naval Affairs in Chilean Politics," 389-90.
21. Beasley was attached to the cruiser *Exeter*, and Torres was a gunnery officer and commanding officer of the Las Salinas ammunition depot.
22. Public Record Office, ADM 116/3920.
23. *Navy* (Washington) 4 (June 1910). The comparison is continued in *Navy* (Washington) 4 (October 1910). "It is pointed out in *International Marine Engineering* that the two Argentine battleships [*Rivadavia* and *Moreno*] for which contracts were recently placed in America will be the most powerfully armed ships afloat, and that in other respects they will represent the highest development of modern Dreadnoughts" (*Navy* [Washington] 4 [July 1910]).
24. *Navy* (Washington) 2; *Navy* (Washington) 4 (July 1910); Breyer, *Schlachtschiffe*, 468-70.
25. "All this goes to show that three Latin American states are rapidly developing naval strength, and may, individually or collectively, become allies of importance to the United States" ("South American Sea Power," 29).

In 1913 the Russian navy tried to purchase the new Argentine and Chilean battleships being built in the United States and Great Britain. See Rohwer, "Admiral Gorshkov," 159.

Chapter Six

1. With the outbreak of war, the British government requisitioned Chilean and Brazilian warships under construction in Great Britain: two Chilean dreadnoughts, the *Almirante Cochrane* and the *Almirante Latorre;* four Chilean destroyers of the *Almirante Lynch* class; some minor Chilean vessels; and the Brazilian monitors *Javary*,

Madeira, and *Solimoes*. For characteristics of the monitors, see "Armored River Monitors for Brazil," *International Marine Review*. There were reports that Brazil in fact wanted to sell these ships "on account of their unsuitability for river navigation," and the outbreak of war might have provided a convenient opportunity. See *Navy* (London) 19.

2. See Smith, *Influence of the Great War Upon Shipping*, 3–78.

3. Eight Latin American nations declared war against the Central Powers: Brazil, Costa Rica, Cuba, Guatemala, Haití, Honduras, Nicaragua, and Panamá. Five broke diplomatic relations: Bolivia, the Dominican Republic, Ecuador, Perú, and Uruguay. Seven remained neutral: Argentina, Chile, Colombia, México, Paraguay, El Salvador, and Venezuela.

4. Brazil, Ministério das Relações Exteriores, *Relatório* 2: special appendix, 169.

5. "Latin American Trade," *Navy*.

6. *Statesman's Year-Book, 1918*, 723.

7. Brazil, Ministério das Relações Exteriores, *Relatório* 1:1.

8. Naval War College, *International Law Documents, 1917*, 64. See also Brazil, Ministério das Relações Exteriores, *Relatório* 1:23.

9. "Attitude of South America," *Proceedings*.

10. Wilgus, *Argentina, Brazil, and Chile*, 253.

11. Brazil had ratified the convention on 5 January 1914.

12. *Brazilian Green Book*, 42.

13. Forty-four ships are listed in da Gama, *Primeira Guerra Mundial*, 24–25. The *Belmonte* (ex-*Valesia*) is not entered because she was used by the Brazilian navy.

14. Brazil, Ministério das Relações Exteriores, *Relatório* 1:136–41, 2: special appendix, 165–81.

15. Argentina had a small merchant marine. Her first ship to be lost to war action was the sailing vessel *Monte Protegido*, which sank on 4 April 1917 ("River Plate News," *Fairplay* [7 June 1917]).

16. Healy, "Admiral William B. Caperton," 297–323.

17. Brazil, Ministério da Relações Exteriores, *Guerra da Europa*, 75.

18. Gama, *Primeira Guerra Mundial*, 38–39.

19. "Then, also, there are hundreds of thousands of Germans in South Brazil, and rumor has it that they are drilling and have found arms" ("River Plate News," *Fairplay* [31 May 1917]). In fact, many of these people were Brazilians of German descent. See *Correio de Manhã*, 1, concerning suspected U-boat activity.

20. Gama, *Primeira Guerra Mundial*, 75.

21. "German Plots Revealed," *Proceedings*.

22. Martin, *Latin America and the War*, 72–73; "South America," *Proceedings*.

23. The German gunboat *Eber* had been stationed in southwest Africa before the outbreak of war. On 31 August 1914 the gunboat handed over her two 105-mm guns, her six revolving cannons, and most of her crew to the auxiliary cruiser *Cap Trafalgar* (former liner) near the Brazilian island of Trinidade. With a skeleton crew and no weapons, the *Eber* reached Bahia, Brazil, where she was interned.

24. Brazil, Ministério das Relações Exteriores, *Relatório, 1917–18*, 116–17.

25. Robinson, "Brazilian Navy in the World War," 1717.

26. Gama, *Primeira Guerra Mundial*, 130–35; Almeida, *Memórias*, 113.

27. Duarte, *Dias de Guerra No Atlântico Sul*, 10–13.

28. Gama, *Primeira Guerra Mundial*, 146–54. A number of accounts credit the destroyer *Río Grande do Norte* with sinking a U-boat (Burns, "Brazilian Navy," 27). Writings concerning U-boat losses do not support this claim. See Grant, "Known Sunk: German Submarine War Losses," 66–77.

SOURCE NOTES   357

29. Furlong, *Class of 1905, United States Naval Academy*, 430–41. In late September 1919 beriberi broke out on board the *Minas Gerais* while she was at the New York Navy Yard. Ninety sailors were hospitalized, three died. See the surgeon general's report in U.S. Department of the Navy, *Annual Report of the Secretary of the Navy, 1921*, 107.

30. Gama, *Primeira Guerra Mundial*, 93–96. The Brazilian navy also sent pilots to serve in the British naval air service in 1918, and the Brazilian army sent a medical mission to France.

31. Initially forty-five ships were requisitioned from the Germans. Two, the *Acary* (ex-*Ebernburg*) and the *Maceio* (ex-*Santa Anna*), were torpedoed and lost.

32. Brazil, Ministério das Relações Exteriores, *Relatório, 1921*, ix–xxxv.

33. Gama, *Primeira Guerra Mundial*, 155–60.

34. *British Vessels Captured or Destroyed by the Enemy* 2: tables D and E. The seven do not include the *Taquary* which lost eight men in an attack, but the ship did not sink.

35. Martin, *Latin America and the War*, 2.

36. National Archives, Records of the Office of Naval Intelligence, U.S. naval attaché reports, Cuba, file 191, box 2.

37. National Archives, Naval Records Collection of the Office of Naval Records and Library, U.S. naval operational reports, "Campaign Order No. 1, August 10, 1917," *Army and Navy Journal*, 26 May 1917, file ICB.

38. Steamers turned over to the United States were the *Adelheid, Bavaria, Constantia*, and *Olivant*. The ship retained was the *Kadonia* (*Shipping Illustrated* 60).

39. National Archives, Naval Records Collection of the Office of Naval Records and Library, U.S. naval operational reports, "Campaign Order No. 2, June 19, 1918," file ICB.

40. Lagos, *Poder Naval*, 21–23.

41. Naval War College, *International Law Documents, 1917*, 22–23, 30–32.

42. The auxiliaries were the *Chaca, Guardia Nacional*, and *Pampa* (*Shipping Illustrated* 53, 59).

43. "Shipping Policy of South America," *Marine Journal*.

44. "Protest from Argentina," *Proceedings*. A public ceremony saluting the Argentine flag was carried out in Germany after the end of World War I.

45. *New York Times*, 24 August 1917, p. 1.

46. "German Secret Dispatches Through Sweden," *Proceedings*.

47. "Argentina," *Proceedings* (October, November); *New York Herald*, 30 September 1918, 1; *British Vessels Captured or Destroyed by the Enemy* 2: table E.

48. Chile, Ministerio, *Memoria*, 103. Belligerent warships would be provided enough coal to enable them to reach the nearest coaling port of a neighboring nation. Merchant ships would be limited to the capacity of their ordinary bunkers unless they sailed directly to Europe (*Shipping Illustrated*, 49).

49. Ireland, *Boundaries in South America*, 250–51. The Battle of Coronel had taken place on 1 November 1914. See Martin, *Latin America and the War*, 332–33.

50. "Breaches of Neutrality," *Shipping Gazette Weekly;* "Sinking of the *Valentine*," *Shipping Gazette Weekly;* Chile, Ministerio, *Memoria*, 194–97.

51. "British Apology to Chili"; Naval War College, "Convention Concerning the Rights and Duties of Neutral Powers in Naval War," *International Law Situations, 1908*, 213–21.

52. Again in 1917 Germany violated Chilean neutrality. The crew of the German auxiliary cruiser *Seeadler*, which had been stranded on Mepelia Island, seized the passing French trading schooner *Lutece* and sailed her to Easter Island, where

she sank. The German crew then boarded the Chilean sailing ship *Falcon* and reached Talcahuano, Chile. There their weapons were confiscated, but the fifty-eight men were treated as shipwrecked sailors and not interned.

In another odyssey, twenty-eight interned German merchant sailors boarded the Chilean barque *Tinto* (built ca. 1853, 460 tons) and sailed from Chile to Drontheim, Norway, arriving at the end of March 1917. It is unclear how much aid these sailors received from Chileans.

53. *Evening Star* (New York), 6 September 1918, 1; *New York Herald*, 28 September 1918, section 1, part 2, p. 6.

54. Lavalle y Garcia, *El Perú y la Gran Guerra*, 12; Basadre, *Historia de la Republica* 12:411–21; *New York Herald*, 1 October 1917, section 1, part 2, p. 10; *New York Times*, 15 June 1918, 1; U.S. Naval Institute *Proceedings* 44.

55. Akers, *History of South America*, 243; *British Vessels Captured or Destroyed by the Enemy* 2: table E; *New York Herald*, 24 November 1918, section 2, p. 2.

Chapter Seven

1. All navies have their mutinies, or breakdowns in discipline which they prefer to call by some other name. In this century the navies that have set the standards which others have strived to achieve—the fleets of Germany, Great Britain, and the United States—have experienced mutiny. The German navy revolted in 1918 and refused to sail into battle with the British navy. The British fleet mutinied in 1919 and in 1931 over cuts in pay. And in 1944 fifty black enlisted men of the U.S. Navy refused to load ammunition on ships bound for the Pacific theater after an explosion that killed more than three hundred people in Port Chicaco, California. The mutineers were sentenced to fifteen years at hard labor and given dishonorable discharges. In 1946 these sentences were overturned, and the men were allowed to return to active duty and subsequently given honorable discharges. In 1972, "work stoppages" took place on the carriers *Constellation* and *Kitty Hawk* and the oiler *Hassayampa*. See Zumwalt, *On Watch*, 217–20.

2. Caddick, "Brazilian Navy," 146; "Iconoclast Abroad," *Shipping Illustrated*.

3. "Operational Histories of South American Battleships," *Warship International*.

4. "Iconoclast Abroad," *Shipping Illustrated*.

5. Caddick, "Brazilian Navy," 146; "Iconoclast Abroad," *Shipping Illustrated*.

6. National Archives, Records of the Office of Naval Intelligence, "Political Conditions in Brazil," letter from naval attaché, Rio de Janeiro, to the director of naval intelligence, 17 September 1919, file E9D, pp. 63–64.

7. Ibid.

8. Fuenzalida, *Armada de Chile* 4:1175.

9. National Archives, Records of the Office of Naval Intelligence, naval attaché, Santiago, letters to director of naval intelligence, 2 September 1931–29 May 1933, file 901-100. These letters formed the basis of the article "The Chilean Naval Mutiny."

10. In 1930 the government had reduced the overseas bonus by fifty percent and the salaries of the fleet by ten percent (Von Schroeders, *Delegado del Gobierno*, 9–10).

11. National Archives, Records of the Office of Naval Intelligence, American embassy, Santiago, enclosure 1 to dispatch 958 to the secretary of state, 9 September 1931, file 901-100.

12. Vio, *Manual de Historia de Chile*, 181; Sater, "Chilean Naval Mutiny of 1931," 239–48; Fuenzalida, *Armada de Chile* 4:1176–77.

13. *Mercurio* (Valparaíso), 11 September 1931, 1.

SOURCE NOTES 359

14. Fuenzalida, *Armada de Chile* 4:1179.
15. The submarine tender *Araucano;* submarines *Capitán Thompson, Almirante Simpson, H-1, H-2, H-4;* protected cruiser *Blanco Encalada;* coast guard craft *Orompello, Leucoton, Elicura, Micalvi,* and *Colo-Colo.*
16. The Maipo Regiment was suspected of being in sympathy with the mutineers and supplying them with munitions (Fuenzalida, *Armada de Chile* 4:1179; "Chilean Naval Mutiny," 14).
17. Sater, "Chilean Naval Mutiny of 1931," 244–45.
18. Fuenzalida, *Armada de Chile* 4:1178.
19. The new finance minister was Arturo Prat Carvajal (Fuenzalida, *Armada de Chile* 4:1178).
20. Von Schroeders, *Delegado del Gobierno,* 17–26, 58–60, 98–99.
21. "Chilean Naval Mutiny," *Monthly Information Bulletin,* 16.
22. Sater, "Chilean Naval Mutiny of 1931," 247.
23. Fuenzalida, *Armada de Chile,* 4:1180.
24. "Chilean Naval Mutiny," *Monthly Information Bulletin,* 14, 17; Fuenzalida, *Armada de Chile* 4:1180.
25. National Archives, General Records of the Department of State, U.S. ambassador to Chile, telegram to the secretary of state, 6 September 1931.
26. National Archives, General Records of the Department of State, State Department, telegram to the U.S. ambassador to Chile, 6 September 1931.
27. Martínez, *Historia de la Fuerza Aérea de Chile* 1:159–65.
28. National Archives, Records of the Office of Naval Intelligence, naval attaché, Santiago, letters to director of naval intelligence, 2 September–29 May 1933, file 901-100. Fuenzalida states that there were only fourteen aircraft: two Junkers, two Wibaults, three Vickers, and seven Curtisses (*Armada de Chile* 4:1180).
29. These four-inch, forty-five-caliber guns were similar to the Mk V on board British battleships of the period. They replaced the three-inch guns installed by the British in 1915. During her 1929–31 modernization, the *Almirante Latorre* also received two high-angle director control towers, one on either side of the foremast on the former searchlight platforms. This necessitated the rearrangement of the six-inch directors.
30. See Vergara, *Por rutas extraviadas,* 38–61. Fuenzalida states that one aircraft was damaged and had to make an emergency landing between Coquimbo and Ovalle (*Armada de Chile* 4:1180).
31. Sater, "Chilean Naval Mutiny of 1931," 253.
32. Ibid., 250–58.
33. National Archives, Records of the Office of Naval Intelligence, naval attaché, Santiago, letters to the director of naval intelligence, 2 September–29 May 1933, file 901-100.
34. Sater, "Chilean Navy Mutiny of 1931," 258–59; *Mercurio* (Santiago), 12 October 1931, 18.
35. One of the ringleaders was ultimately given a consular post in São Paulo, Brazil. Another became the director of Chilean prisons.
36. *Mercurio* (Valaparaíso), 17 February 1932, 1; 10 October 1931, 1.
37. For a discussion of the political implications of the mutiny, see Sater, "Chilean Naval Mutiny of 1931," 251–68. The *Almirante Latorre* was in reserve through at least 1935 and possibly until her 1937 refit at Talcahuano. At that time the catapult was probably removed and a few light antiaircraft guns were added.
38. Apristas was the popular name for the political party Alianza Popular Revolucionaria Americana (Popular Revolutionary Alliance for America).
39. "Mutiny in the Peruvian Navy," *Monthly Information Bulletin,* 19.

40. Ibid.; Ugarteche, *Sánchez Cerro* 3:86. Ugarteche states that the sailor, a third-class helmsman by the name of Casapía, warned Callao. He makes no mention of Casapía's having first warned the submarines.

41. Ugarteche, *Sánchez Cerro* 3:92–93.

42. Ibid.

43. According to "Mutiny in the Peruvian Navy," *Monthly Information Bulletin*, a submarine fired a torpedo across the bow of the *Almirante Grau* and a white flag was immediately hoisted (19–20). Then the cruiser *Coronel Bolognesi* fired several three-inch shells at the submarine without effect. Reportedly, at this point the submarine returned the fire. It is unlikely that the Peruvians would have endeavored to induce the surrender by firing an expensive and not always predictable torpedo as a warning shot.

44. "Mutiny in the Peruvian Navy," 20.

45. Basadre, *Historia de la Republica del Perú* 14:225; "Mutiny in the Peruvian Navy," 20. Years later, during the presidency of José Luis Bustamante y Rivero (1945–48), the remains of the eight executed mutineers were disinterred from San Lorenzo Island and given a public funeral in the Lima cemetery (Ugarteche, *Sánchez Cerro* 3:88–89).

Chapter Eight

1. Pimental Winz, "Plácido de Castroe a Integração do Acre," 45–59.

2. Romero, *Marina Fluvial de Guerra*, 89; Ireland, *Boundaries in South America*, 219–29.

3. Romero, *Marina Fluvial de Guerra*, 115–16; Ireland, *Boundaries in South America*, 185–95.

4. The most important Colombian riverine units were the *Barranquilla* (gunboat, built 1932); *Cartagena* (gunboat, built 1932); *Santa Maria* (gunboat, built 1932); *Pichincha* (coast guard cutter, built 1925); *Bogota* (gunboat, built 1918); *Cordova* (gunboat, built 1918); *General Nariño* (gunboat, built 1897); *Boyaca* (transport, built 1920); and *Presidente Mosquera* (sternwheel steamer, date of construction unknown). The principal riverine craft of the Peruvian navy were the *America* (gunboat, built 1904); *Napo* (gunboat, built 1925); *Iquitos* (launch, built 1875); *Cahuapanas* (launch, built circa 1880); and *Portillo* (launch, built circa 1880).

5. The *Coronel Bolognesi* had been sent to Balboa, Panamá, to get new boilers. With hostilities looming, she carried the boilers as part of her deck cargo to Callao, where they were eventually installed (English, *Armed Forces of Latin America*, 382).

6. *Jane's Fighting Ships*, 1931, 135.

7. The new president was a friend of Colombian diplomat Alfonso López. Their relationship played an important role in subsequent diplomatic interactions. (Ireland, *Boundaries in South America*, 202).

8. Garaycochea, *Legislación Naval* 8:204; Ireland, *Boundaries in South America*, 202–03.

9. English, "Chaco War," *Army Quarterly*, 351.

10. Vargas, *Tradición Naval del Pueblo Bolivia*, 88–89; González, *Preparación del Paraguay para la Guerra del Chaco* 1:5–6.

11. The Paraguayan navy was made up of the *Paraguay* (armored gunboat, built 1931); *Humaitá* (armored gunboat, built 1931); *Tacuary* (gunboat, built 1910); *Capitán Cabral* (patrol boat, built 1907); *Coronel Martinez* (patrol boat, built 1908); and *Teniente Herreros* (patrol boat, date of construction unknown). The following merchant craft were taken into the navy: the cargo types *Holanda, San Francisco, Chaco, Pollux*, and *Daymán*; cattle boat *Pingo*; passenger boats *Posadas* and *Cuyabá*; tugs

Parapití, Toro, and *Rodolfo B;* eighteen small tugs, eight barges of one hundred tons or more; twelve smaller barges; and eleven motor launches.

12. See Speratti, *Historia de la Armada,* 69–76; English, *Armed Forces in Latin America,* 355–56.

13. Speratti, *Historia de la Armada,* 77–84; English, "Chaco War," *An Consantóir* 4 (September 1974): 308.

14. Among the officers serving in the Paraguayan army and navy were a number of Russian exiles. In fact, five were regiment commanders and six of these officers lost their lives fighting for Paraguay.

15. Apparently, R-2(?) saw little service (Bozzano, *Reminisencias,* 65–69).

16. English, "Chaco War," *Army Quarterly,* 357–58.

Chapter Nine

1. Military missions from more developed nations to less developed ones have been a recognized tool of statecraft since ancient times. The objective of missions is to improve the military capability of an active or potential ally in exchange for influence within that country, particularly political, economic, and military. For the recipient, the foreign military mission has been essentially a stopgap. As the military capability of a developing nation improves, the nation becomes less dependent on foreign aid. The objective of the foreign mission is therefore a paradox.

2. Spears continued, "For the first time it is our [U.S.] policy to employ our military establishments for competition in the development and expansion of our trade and political relations in world affairs. It is merely an instrument that our competitors for South American trade have used for years" ("U.S. Naval Missions," 5–6).

3. Epstein, "European Military Influence," 254. A U.S. naval intelligence publication noted:

> [I]t is common knowledge that Argentine naval officers who have been in the United States Navy or in the naval commission in the United States have succeeded in preventing the purchase of Italian and British submarines, aeroplanes, and munitions by using arguments that it is ridiculous to train officers in one Navy (the United States Navy) and then buy other apparatuses, ships, etc., than those used by those officers during the training. These officers [U.S. trained] have been successful in preventing purchase at attractive prices of English and Italian material on the argument of "buy only material of a kind that our aviators have been brought up with" (*Monthly Information Bulletin* 4).

On occasion a mission failed to win the contract for home industries, for example in the mid-1920s when Brazil contracted an Italian firm to build a submarine, even though the members of the U.S. mission lobbied strongly for U.S. firms. The winning Italian bid cost less than half of the one submitted by Electric Boat Company and a third of that proposed by Bethlehem Shipbuilding. In spite of the huge difference in price, the issue was in doubt for some time, primarily because of the influence of the North American mission ("Brazil: Additional Submarines Proposed," *Monthly Information Bulletin*).

4. W. O. Spears wrote, "It would be greatly to the interest of the country to replace all European missions in South America by missions from our own. . . ." "U.S. Naval Missions," 31). David Caddick, a naval analyst, observed, "It is greatly to be regretted that Great Britain . . . was not chosen for this important task [naval mission to Peru]" ("Peruvian Navy," 29).

5. "It is reported that much satisfaction has been expressed in naval circles at

Santiago de Chile at the greatly improved results of target practice in the Chilean Navy. It is acknowledged that this is due to the British officers who have been lent to Chile for instructional purposes" (*Navy* [London] 16). Such opportunities for evaluation are few. In peacetime one must cautiously rely on the opinions of professional observers. The success of military missions can only be considered on a case-by-case basis, but for the most part, professional observation supports the conclusion that Latin American navies have been helped by foreign missions.

6. Epstein, "European Military Influence," 273.

7. Chisholm, *Independence of Chile*, 286; Cubitt, "Lord Cochrane and the Chilean Navy," 189–92.

8. Curtis, "South American Yankee," 566.

9. Akers, *History of South America*, 497.

10. Perú, *Boletín*, 1905 8:1.

11. Garaycochea, *Legislación naval* 2:227.

12. *Conway's, 1860–1905*, 303.

13. La Roerie, "Una misión naval en el Perú," 885–909.

14. Aubry, after resigning from his commission, became the Electric Boat Company's sales agent in South America. He attempted to interest Argentina and Brazil in submarines built by his company. Later he was reinstated in the Peruvian navy and served as the Peruvian naval attaché to France. Following this, he worked again for the Electric Boat Company (U.S. Congress [73rd], Senate, *Munitions Industry* 1, 74–75, 85).

15. Law no. S.4435. This made it necessary for the U.S. Congress to pass public law no. 272 of 5 June 1920. See U.S. Department of State, *Statutes at Large*, 1056, part 1; Herring, *History of Latin America*, 544.

16. Contract of Captain Frank B. Freyer, USN, 1 July 1920. See Garaycochea, *Legislación naval* 1:366–69. Numerous contracts with mission personnel are published in this work.

17. National Archives, Records of the Office of Naval Intelligence, Charles Davy, senior member of the U.S. naval mission to Perú, to the director of naval intelligence, Lima, 1 September 1924, box E-9-D, file 12524.

18. National Archives, Records of the Office of Naval Intelligence, U.S. naval attaché reports, summary, U.S. naval mission to Perú, pp. 3–4.

19. U.S. Congress (37th), Senate, *Munitions Industry*, 311; Garaycochea, *Legislación naval* 4:672–73.

20. The submarine has evolved into the principal weapon of the Peruvian navy. The four *R*-class boats returned to New London, Connecticut, in 1950 and were modernized by Electric Boat Company. In 1953 Perú ordered four new *Tiburón*-class submarines from the same company; the design was based on that of the pre–World War II U.S. *Mackerel* class. Two boats arrived in Perú in 1954, the two others in 1957. The first pair were fitted with deck guns, but the second were not. All four boats served until the 1960s.

In 1962 a U.S. intelligence publication rated Perú as having the best submarine force in Latin America. In 1974 Perú purchased two second-hand Guppy boats from the United States. The present premier submarine of the Peruvian navy is the German type 209; six of these boats have been built for Perú. The country's current submarine force is larger than ever before and the biggest in Latin America, which explains why submariners hold influential positions in and out of the navy. Unless Peruvians are given cause to change their minds, the submarine will probably continue to be a dominant weapon in the arsenal of their navy (Garaycochea, *Legislación naval* 3:631–32, and 4:24, 713–14, 844–45; "Combatant Ships Potential of the Latin American Navies," ONI Review, 543).

SOURCE NOTES 363

21. U.S. Congress (37th), Senate, *Munitions Industry*, 155–56.
22. National Archives, Records of the Office of Naval Intelligence, U.S. naval attaché reports, "Correspondence and Reports of U.S. Naval Mission to Perú, 1929–33," file 194, box 1.
23. National Archives, Records of the Office of Naval Intelligence, U.S. naval attaché reports, "U.S. Naval Mission to Perú, 1929–33," 2 February 1932, pp. 1–3.
24. Copies of the contracts are in National Archives, Records of the Office of Naval Intelligence, box C-10-G, file 19517.
25. U.S. Department of State, *Foreign Relations*, 889.
26. U.S. Congress (63rd), Senate, "Naval War College of Brazil," 16255.
27. Captain C. T. Vogelgesang, USN, Commander W. O. Spears, USN, Lieutenant P. A. Cusocks, USNR, and Ensign Oliver James, USNR. See Spears, *U.S. Naval Missions*, 20–21.
28. President Pessôa observed, "I am pleased to state that the battleship *São Paulo* on March 13 last returned from the United States, where she received . . . important repairs and underwent radical improvements, among other things the installation of fire control, establishing her as a war vessel of the first order" (*Monthly Information Bulletin* 3:32).
29. U.S. Department of Commerce, *Experimental Firing of the Brazilian Battleship São Paulo*, 1–15.
30. *Monthly Information Bulletin* 5 (May 1922).
31. For a list of American and British officers and their assignments, see National Archives, Records of the Office of Naval Intelligence, William O. Spears to the director of naval intelligence, New York, 1 March 1921, box C-10-1, file 14171.
32. "Brazilian Navy: Long-Range Target Practice."
33. National Archives, Records of the Office of Naval Intelligence, "Purchase of Ships by Brazil: British Propaganda," from Brazilian naval attaché to director of naval intelligence, 31 August 1921, box C-10-G, file 19519.
34. This was probably the largest naval mission sent to Latin America (*Jornal do Brasil*, 1).
35. The *São Paulo* went to Guantánamo ostensibly to have her guns calibrated and to conduct target practice. While she was there, her tripod mast was measured for gunfire vibrations. The mast was an integral part of the fire-control system. All U.S. units at the time were equipped with cage (as opposed to tripod) masts. ("Measurement of Mast Vibration on the Tripod Mast During Gun Trials of the Brazilian Battleship *São Paulo.*")
36. *Monthly Information Bulletin* (6 April 1923).
37. Epstein, "European Military Influence," 254–56.
38. National Archives, Records of the Bureau of Construction and Repair, letter from chief of the bureau to Commander L. M. Atkins, U.S. naval mission to Brazil, 31 March 1928.
39. The *Humaitá* was not a complete success. In 1935 she was in such poor condition that she had to be withdrawn from the annual maneuvers. On 16 April 1937 a serious engine-room explosion injured twenty of her crew. See "Brazil: Additional Submarines Proposed," *Monthly Information Bulletin;* "Trials of Brazilian Submarine *Humayta,*" *Monthly Information Bulletin;* Hilton, "Military Influences on Brazilian Economic Policy," 77.
40. Da Gama, *Segunda Guerra Mundial*, 6–7; Smith, "American Diplomacy and the Naval Mission to Brazil," 89–91.
41. Levine, *Vargas Regime*, 157.
42. Wood, "External Restraints," 4–5.
43. Epstein, "European Military Influence," 258.

44. *New York Times*, 12 August 1937, 6; National Archives, Records of the Office of Naval Intelligence, box C-10-J, file 12269E.

Senator Arthur Vandenberg summed up the opposition: "When we go into the business of arming South American countries on the theory that we are arming them against some foreign foe in some other land we are nevertheless arming them against each other; and that was the precise result which flowed from the American traffic which the Munitions Committee explored and exploded" (Epstein, *European Military Influence*, chapter X).

45. Da Gama, *Segunda Guerra Mundial*, 1–3, 22, 64–65, 70.

46. Except those countries linked by alliance with Great Britain.

47. Somervell, "Anglo-Chilean Naval Relations," 381–402; "Visits to the Navies of South America," *Brassey Naval Annual*, 101; Caddick, "Chilian Navy," 148–50.

48. Somervell, "Anglo-Chilean Naval Relations," 21–22.

49. U.S. Navy Department, General Correspondence of the Secretary of the Navy, letter of 28 November 1911 from the American minister to Chile to the secretary of state, enclosure 1 of 15 November 1911, 3.

50. "Withdrawal of English Officials from Chile," 21–22.

51. The 1924 contract between Archibald Domville and the Chilean government appears in *Monthly Information Bulletin* 8 (August 1924).

52. *Monthly Information Bulletin* 9 (October 1926).

53. "Competition for New Destroyers," 19–20.

54. Britain did suspend the training of foreigners between 1897 and 1906 and between 1914 and 1920. Following the overthrow of Allende in 1973, the British navy again suspended the training of Chilean naval personnel, but it was resumed after a few years. Chile has had a permanent purchasing mission attached to its London legation since the closing decades of the nineteenth century. Although most Chilean warships were purchased from Great Britain, this commission ordered three ships from France in 1889 and military hardware from other European countries.

55. Epstein, "European Military Influence," 251; *Army and Navy Journal* 13.

56. Destéfani, *Historia Naval Argentina*, 226, 228; "Notes on Argentine Navy," *Monthly Information Bulletin*, 52; "Effects of Prohibiting Training of South American Officers," *Army and Navy Journal*, 35–36; Epstein, "European Military Influence," 250; *Revista General de Marina* 42. Copies of the contract may be found in the National Archives, Records of the Office of Naval Intelligence, box C-10-A, files 21643 and 21643A.

57. A copy of the contract is in the National Archives, Records of the Office of Naval Intelligence, file C-10-F.

58. Buck, "Role of the Naval Mission," 14; U.S. Naval Institute *Proceedings* 68: 1489; Conn and Fairchild, *Western Hemisphere*, 173–74.

59. "Argentine Naval Scholarships in Paraguay," *Monthly Information Bulletin*, 3; *Patria*, 17 January 1972, 3; Garaycochea, *Legislación naval* 10:116–17 and 124–25, 11:310.

60. National Archives, Records of the Office of Naval Intelligence, memorandum from the U.S. naval mission in Perú to the Office of Naval Intelligence, 25 October 1920, box E-9-D, file 12524.

61. In fact, the Ecuadorian government was greatly embarrassed by the arrangement because the diplomat signed the papers without authorization from his government concerning the sale of the *Esmeralda*. See Zanabria, *Luchas y Victorias*, 101–261; U.S. Naval Institute *Proceedings* 68:1489.

Chapter Ten

1. Campoamor and Fernandez Castillejo, *Heroismo Criollo*, 1–20.
2. Connell-Smith, *Inter-American System*, 112–13.
3. For example, Argentina patrolled the outer limits of the Río de la Plata, beyond the pilots' pontoon anchorage, alternating with the obsolete coastal defense battleships *Independencia* and *Libertad*.
4. Connell-Smith, *Inter-American System*, 113.
5. Obviously, Argentina was concerned over the longstanding issue of the Malvina islands.
6. Furer, *Administration of the Navy Department*, 688.
7. Argentina has been much maligned for her pro-Axis position during the war. In fact, although the June 1943 coup brought to power a number of influential individuals who were admirers of the Axis, in 1940 and 1941 neutralism was an attitude shared by most Argentines as well as most citizens of the United States. Until mid-1943 the Argentine policy of neutrality was supported by a democratically elected civilian government.
8. National Archives, Records of the Office of Naval Intelligence, records of the division of pan-American affairs and U.S. naval missions, summary of naval staff conversations and agreements with American representatives, August–October 1942, entry 49, box 1.
9. Gunther, *Inside Latin America*, 347–49.
10. The meeting took place at Petrópolis, a summer resort in the mountains near Rio de Janeiro.
11. U.S. Department of State, *Foreign Relations of the United States, 1942*, xxiii.
12. Connell-Smith, *Inter-American System*, 120–21.
13. Ibid., 122–23.
14. U.S. Naval Institute *Proceedings* 73; Hilton, "Military Influence on Brazilian Economic Policy," 83; U.S. Congress (89th), Senate, *Hearings Before the Committee on Foreign Relations*, 632.
15. Classified by the Uruguayans as a cruiser. With a 1,150-ton displacement, 278-foot length, and 23-knot speed, she was similar to the smaller gunboats of major navies. Built at Stettin, Germany, in 1910, the *Uruguay* was obsolete by 1939.
16. Uruguay, Ministerio de relaciónes exteriores, *Uruguayan Blue Book*, report no. 65-14, p. 39. The British only recognized a three-mile limit. Argentina and Uruguay claim that between Punta del Este, Uruguay, and Cape San Antonio, Argentina, there are internal waters over which they hold sovereignty.
17. Ibid. Fuentes' remarks concerning the battle taking place in Uruguayan territorial waters obviously apply to the last phase of the action only. Great Britain does not share the Argentine or Uruguayan interpretations of territorial limits in the La Plata estuary.
18. Bidlingmaier, "K. M. *Admiral Graf Spee*," 92. The British were probably pleased with the extension to seventy-two hours, because it gave them additional time to concentrate forces to oppose the *Admiral Graf Spee*.
19. For the text of the Declaration of Panamá (9 October 1939), the American republics' statement on the *Admiral Graf Spee*, and subsequent British, French, and German responses, see Naval War College, *International Law Situations, 1939*, 66–78.
20. Rohwer and Hümmelchen, *Chronology of the War at Sea* 1:3, 6, 19, 41.
21. The new battleship *Richelieu* had been immobilized by a British attack on 8 July 1940. See Dulin and Garzke, *Allied Battleships*, 83–93.
22. Morison, *Naval Operations* 1:37; Rohwer, "Operações Navais," 5–6.

23. Gama, *Segunda Guerra Mundial*, 10–11; Rohwer and Hümmelchen, *Chronology of the War at Sea* 1:68. German warships also stopped Brazilian merchantmen, during the early years of the war near the three-hundred-mile limit of the Pan American security zone. Illustrative of German activity is the inspection of the *Siqueira Campos* by a U-boat three hundred miles off Cape Verde on 1 July 1941.

24. Gama, *Segunda Guerra Mundial*, 10–11.

25. Samuel E. Morison states that a Brazilian squadron was ordered to patrol the coast from Belem, Para, to Santos, São Paulo, and to stop any activities, whether in port or in territorial waters, that were "contrary to the interests of the United States" (*Naval Operations* 1:378). Admiral Saldanha da Gama, in a letter to the author dated 2 April 1984, states that no order referenced the United States at that time.

26. The *U-432* torpedoed the *Buarque* on 14 February; the *U-432* the *Olinda* on 18 February; the *U-155* the *Arabutã* on 7 March; the *U-94* the *Cayrú* on 9 March. The *Cabedelo* sank for unknown reasons around 25 February. See Gama, *Segunda Guerra Mundial*, 19, 276; Rohwer, *Axis Submarine Successes*, 69–124.

27. Dönitz, *Memoirs*, 239.

28. *New York Times*, 29 May 1942, 1. The Ministry of Aeronautics and Brazil's air force were formally established on 20 January 1941.

29. Morison, *Naval Operations* 1:376; U.S. Department of the Navy, *Commander, South Atlantic Force*, 28 April 1942, A12/serial 0025.

30. Rohwer, "Operações Navais," 14–15; Dönitz, *Memoirs*, 239.

31. Rohwer, *Axis Submarine Successes*, 69–124; Gama, *Segunda Guerra Mundial*, 276–77; Dulles, *Vargas of Brazil*, 234.

32. Dönitz, *Memoirs*, 252–53.

33. Aircraft flying from Brazilian bases sank eleven U-boats during the war. U.S. Department of the Navy, "U.S. Naval Administration" 1:xviii, U.S. Department of the Navy, *Naval Chronology*, 10.

34. U.S. Department of the Navy, "U.S. Naval Administration" 1:248.

35. "Brazil," *Proceedings* 68:1337–38.

36. The *Minas Gerais* was refitted between 1934 and 1938, when eighteen coal-firing Babcock boilers were exchanged for oil-firing Thornycroft ones and modern auxiliary machinery was installed. Turrets B and Y were each fitted with Zeiss rangefinders. An eighteen-magnification range finder, brought to Brazil for demonstration, was placed in the foretop.

37. U.S. Naval Institute *Proceedings* 65.

38. See "Brazil," *Proceedings* 65:1658.

39. Lourival Coutinho, *O General Góes depõe*, 340–41, 348–49.

40. Gama, *Segunda Guerra Mundial*, 141–285; Morison, *Naval Operations* 1:389.

41. The U.S. administrative history series states that it was also to increase his prestige. U.S. Department of the Navy, "U.S. Naval Administration" 1:333.

42. English, *Armed Forces in Latin America*, 112.

43. Rohwer, *Axis Submarine Successes*, 69–124.

44. Rohwer, "Operações Navais," 16–17; Morison, *Naval Operations* 1:387; Rohwer, *Axis Submarine Successes*, 158, 183. A number of sources state that the *William Gaston* was torpedoed by *U-861* while part of convoy JT-39 and under escort of Brazilian warships. In fact, she was traveling alone from Buenos Aires to Rio de Janeiro to join JT-39. The *William Gaston* was torpedoed off the coast of Santa Catarina (26°24′S 46°12′W), which is to the south of where the convoy began (*Subsídios para a História Marítima do Brasil* 12:229).

45. Gama, *Segunda Guerra Mundial*, 98–99 (Doc. 6, Pasta 2, Gaveta 3.104,

Arquivo de Marinha—Of. 398, de 8-7-943, do Comando da Força Naval do Nordeste ao Chefe do Estado-Maior de Armada).
46. Gama, *Segunda Guerra Mundial*, 99-100 (Arquivo MRF—Presidente da Republica—Secreto—JBC/CMF 14-7-943).
47. Gama, *Segunda Guerra Mundial*, 100 (Ofício No 11, de 5-1-945, do *Rio Grande Do Sul*—Doc. I, Pasta 266, Gaveta 3.111).
48. Gama, *Segunda Guerra Mundial*, 198.
49. The *U-164* was sunk off Fortaleza by aircraft from the U.S. patrol squadron VP-83 flying from Natal on 4 January 1943; the *U-507*, off Parnaíba by a U.S. Catalina aircraft on 13 January 1943; the *Arquimede*, off Cape São Roque by U.S. VP-83 and VP-84 aircraft flying from Natal on 15 April 1943; the *U-128*, off Alagoas by U.S. VP-74 aircraft operating from a tender at Largo de Florianopólis, and by the U.S. destroyers *Moffett* and *Jouett*, on 17 May 1943; the *U-590*, off Amapá by U.S. VP-94 aircraft flying from Bélem on 7 September 1943; the *U-513*, off Santa Catarina by U.S. VP-74 aircraft operating from a tender at Largo de Florianopólis on 19 July 1943; the *U-662*, off Amapá by U.S. VP-94 aircraft flying from Bélem on 21 July 1943; the *U-598*, off Cape São Roque by U.S. VB-107 aircraft flying from Natal on 23 July 1943; the *U-161*, off Salvador by U.S. VP-74 aircraft flying from Aratu on 27 September 1943; the *U-591*, off Recife by U.S. VP-127 aircraft flying from Natal on 30 July 1943; and the *U-199*, off Rio de Janeiro by U.S. VP-74 and Brazilian air force Third Squadron aircraft flying from Aratu on 31 July 1943. See Gama, *Segunda Guerra Mundial*, 164-73; Duarte, *Dias de Guerra No Atlântico Sul*, 293-94.
50. Gama, *Segunda Guerra Mundial*, 197, 276-77.
51. Langer and Gleason, *Undeclared War*, 619.
52. Humphreys, *Latin America and the Second World War* 1:162-63.
53. Gama, *Segunda Guerra Mundial*, 98-100; Langer and Gleason, *Undeclared War*, 621; Naval War College, *International Law Situations, 1940*, 44-53.
54. Caillet-Bois, *Historia Naval Argentina*, 532. Following the war, seven of these ships were repurchased by Italy. This had been an option in the original sale. See U.S. Naval Institute *Proceedings* 72.
55. Argentina lost three merchant ships to U-boats during the war. The steamer *Uruguay* was sunk by the *U-37* in the North Atlantic on 27 May 1940. The tanker *Victoria* was torpedoed by the *U-201* off the northeast coast of the United States on 18 April 1942. The steamer *Río Tercero* was torpedoed by the *U-202*, also off the northeast coast of the United States, on 22 June 1942. See Rohwer, *Axis Submarine Successes*, 18, 90, 105.
56. U.S. Naval Institute *Proceedings* 69.
57. Arguindeguy, *Aviación Naval Argentina* 2:601-2; Gonzáles, "Actividades Marítimas en la Antártida," 242-43.
58. Schaeffer, *U-boat 977*, 141.
59. No evidence to support this conjecture has ever been discovered. From time to time, the fact that these U-boats chose to surrender to Argentina is used to help "prove" that Hitler escaped and is alive and well in Argentina. See Schaeffer, *U-boat 977*, 140-48.
60. U.S. Naval Institute *Proceedings* 63.
61. National Archives, Records of the Office of Naval Intelligence, records of the division of pan-American affairs and U.S. naval missions, correspondence with U.S. naval missions in Latin America, 1922-42, entry 49, box 1.
62. The one tanker was the *18 de Marzo* (ex-*San Ricardo*), 6,438 gross tons (Cárdenas, *Gesta en el Golfo*, 22).

63. The school was founded on 27 November 1918 with an initial class of thirty-six students. In January 1937 it closed for financial reasons. See Cárdenas, *Educación Naval in México* 1:249.

64. Renamed the *Cerro Azul* and the *Tampico*, they went into service on 21 January 1940 and 6 March 1940.

65. Cárdenas, *Semblanza Marítima* 1:257.

66. Sources vary widely on the exact value and composition of her cargo.

67. Steps were taken to hide the identity of merchant ships carrying war materials to Spain. The following ships were used, and possibly others as well:

Arno-Mendi (5,754 gross tons, built 1920, Spanish flag throughout the war)

Cabo Quilates (6,629 gross tons, built 1927, Spanish flag throughout the war, also used the name *Ibai* late in the war)

Carmen (350 gross tons, built 1889, Panamanian flag throughout the war, name changed to *Clifford* in 1938 and later to *Storm*)

Magallanes (9,688 gross tons, built 1928, Spanish flag throughout the war)

Manuel Arnus (7,578 gross tons, built 1923, Spanish flag throughout the war)

Mar Cantabrico (6,632 gross tons, built 1930, Spanish flag, captured by Nationalists on 8 March 1936)

Motomar (5,724 gross tons, built 1921, Spanish flag throughout the war)

Santi (2,958 gross tons, built 1918, Spanish flag 1936, Panamanian flag 1936–38, name changed to *Vera Cruz*, *America*, and *Cocle*)

Sebastian (3,024 gross tons, built 1920, Spanish flag throughout the war)

Sil (2,522 gross tons, built 1928, Spanish flag throughout the war)

Silvia (3,175 gross tons, built 1898, Greek flag, captured in 1937 by Nationalists)

Yolande (3,859 gross tons, built 1912, French flag, sunk in port by aircraft January 1939)

68. Two Mexicans became Republican generals, Juan Bautista Gomez and Alfaro Siqueiros (also known as David Alfaro Xiqueiros). Some twenty Mexicans fought on the side of the Nationalists.

69. Cárdenas, *Gesta en el Golfo*, 167–72.

70. Conn and Fairchild, *Framework of Hemisphere Defense*, 336.

71. Cárdenas, *Semblanza Marítima* 1:259.

72. The *Cuauhtémoc*, *Tampico*, *Cerro Azul*, *Juan Casiano*, *Toteco*, *Veracruz* and *Tamaulipas* (Cárdenas, *Semblanza Marítima* 1:257, and 2:258–60, document no. 72).

73. The *Orinoco* (renamed *Puebla*), *Hameln* (renamed *Oaxaca*), and *Marina O* (renamed *Tabasco*) (Cárdenas, *Semblanza Marítima* 1:258).

74. Hull, *Memoirs* 2:1142.

75. Cárdenas, *Gesta en el Golfo*, 56–91; Cárdenas, *Semblanza Marítima* 1:259–63, and 2: document 73; Conn and Fairchild, *Framework of Hemisphere Defense*, 348–49; Rohwer, *Axis Submarine Successes*, 76–112.

76. Cárdenas, *Gesta en el Golfo*, 189; Cárdenas, *Semblanza Marítima* 1:261–62.

77. Conn and Fairchild, *Framework of Hemisphere Defense*, 349.

78. A squadron of the Mexican air force participated in the Pacific theater operations. On 24 July 1944 Squadron 201 proceeded to Greenville, Texas, for training. It departed for the Pacific theater on 22 February 1945 (Cárdenas, *Gesta en el Golfo*, 198, 202; *Semblanza Marítima* 1:262).

79. Cárdenas, *Semblanza Marítima* 1:263; Cárdenas, *Gesta en el Golfo*, 129.

80. *Conway's, 1922–1946*, 424.

81. This was composed of eleven forty-three-foot and one fifty-two-foot former pleasure craft that had been taken into the service due to a shortage of patrol craft.
82. These craft had been designed for the U.S. Coast Guard as fast patrol craft. Nicknamed "sub busters" during the war, none of the 242 units built was ever credited with sinking a submarine. See Scheina, *Coast Guard Cutters*, 222–34.
83. Reynolds, *Gulf Sea Frontier*, 292–301.
84. Rohwer, *Axis Submarine Successes*, 175; Reynolds, *Gulf Sea Frontier*, 245, 292–301.
85. Román Bazurto, *Proas en Tres Mares*, 82–93.
86. *Historia Grafica* 2:60–62; Nweihed, *La Vigencia del Mar* 2:325–26.

Chapter Eleven

1. In 1968 Admiral Benigno Varela, commander in chief of the Argentine navy, denounced the dependence of the fleet on the United States. He complained that the only modern units in the fleet, three destroyers and a submarine, were on loan from the United States for five years with strings attached. They could not be used against an ally of the United States, and they could not be employed against U.S. fishing vessels. See Olive, "U.S. Tries to Improve Military Relations."
2. In discussing military hardware, obsolescence is determined by competition, not age, a fact underscored by the impact of revolutionary warships such as the USS *Monitor* and HMS *Dreadnought*. A number of predreadnoughts completed after the battleship *Dreadnought* were outclassed by this revolutionary warship.
3. Argentina acquired four disarmed frigates, ten tank landing ships, numerous small amphibians, three small tankers, and a number of tugs and miscellaneous yard craft; Brazil, two small tankers and three reserve tugs; Chile, two cargo ships, three ocean tugs, and forty-one minor amphibians; Colombia, one frigate; Cuba, three frigates, two rescue tugs, and seven minor warships; Ecuador, a frigate; México, four frigates and five submarine chasers; Perú, a frigate, two rescue tugs, four minor amphibians, two tugs, and two minesweepers; Venezuela, one tank landing ship and two tugs.
4. "Venezuela," *Proceedings*. In June 1946 seven ex-Canadian *Flower*-class corvettes were commissioned: *Carabobo* (ex-HMCS *Kamsak*), *Constitucion* (ex-HMCS *Algoma*), *Federacion* (ex-HMCS *Amherst*), *Independencia* (ex-HMCS *Dunvegan*), *Libertad* (ex-HMCS *Batleford*), *Patria* (ex-HMCS *Oakville*), and *Victoria* (ex-HMCS *Westaskawin*).
5. U.S. Congress (81st), House, *First Semiannual Report on the Mutual Defense Assistance Program*, 46.
6. U.S. Department of State, *United States Treaties*, TIAS 2442–44. Perú was also to have received two cruisers, but she never did. Eventually she acquired two British light cruisers, replacing them in the late 1970s with two Dutch cruisers.
7. Admiral Segundo R. Storni expressed the need for a "one-power standard." But, in fact, the Argentine navy reached a two-power standard that lasted for years.
8. U.S. Congress (86th), Senate, *United States–Latin American Relations*, 38; Buck, *Role of the Naval Mission*, 28–29. In 1964 the U.S. instructors at the Argentine Naval War College became part of the U.S. military group in Argentina; they continued to be known as advisors, not as a mission.
9. U.S. Department of the Navy, "Importance of U.S. Naval Missions in Latin America."
10. "Brazil," *ONI Review*.
11. "Peru," *ONI Review*.

12. The first multinational exercise with the U.S. and Latin American navies took place between 29 February and 1 May 1959. The exercise had no name. UNITAS I took place in 1960. See Vinock, "UNITAS: A South American Perennial."

13. Letter of 21 March 1985 from Commander Alfredo Luzuriaga, Argentine navy, to the author.

14. ASROC is a rocket that can deliver an ASW torpedo or depth charge to a preprogrammed target area. The target's location is supplied by the ship's sensors (*World's Missile Systems:* 119–20).

15. Hereford, *U.S. Military Assistance*, 31.

16. Letter of 3 August 1984 from Captain José María Cohen, Argentina navy, retired, to the author. Captain Cohen served in the Argentina navy from 1945 to 1976. His assignments included command of the destroyer *Espora*, chief of staff of the fleet, and lecturer at the naval war college.

17. Middendorf, "USN's Latin American Partners," 35. In recent years increasing numbers of Latin American naval officers have received training in European schools. Since 1960 Argentina has sent at least ten officers to school in France. One became commander in chief and another, Admiral Jorge Anaya, head of state. The current commander in chief of the Venezuelan navy, Vice Admiral Justo Pastor Fernandez Marquez, also attended French naval schools.

18. Arguindeguy, *Apuntes Buques Argentina* 5:2201.

19. Buck, "Role of the Naval Mission," 28; Mecham, *Survey*, 336; Barber and Ronning, *Internal Security*, 218.

20. "Colombian Frigates in the Korean War," *ONI Review*, 548–50; *History of the United Nations Forces* 3:175–76.

21. *History of the United Nations Forces* 3:175–76.

22. "Colombian Frigates in the Korean War," *ONI Review*, 548–50.

23. *History of the United Nations Forces* 3:176–77; Román, *Proas en Tres Mares*, 104–7.

24. "Colombian Frigates in the Korean War," *ONI Review*, 548–50; *History of the United Nations Forces* 3:178–79; Román, *Proas en Tres Mares*, 106–8.

25. Douds, "Role of the Brazilian Military."

26. Jose, *Inter-American Peace Force*, 42.

27. Dennison, "Reminiscences," 461.

28. Countries offering assistance were Argentina, Colombia, Costa Rica, Dominican Republic, Ecuador, El Salvador, Guatemala, Haití, Honduras, Nicaragua, Panamá, and Venezuela.

29. Johns, "United We Stood," 84.

30. Ibid.

31. Ibid.

32. Dennison, "Reminiscences," 431.

33. The Argentine *Espora* and *Rosales*, Dominican *Gregorio Luperon* and *Capitan Pedro Santana*, Guatemalan *Jose Francisco Burrunda*, a Uruguayan destroyer escort, and the Venezuelan *Nueva Esparta*, *Zulia*, and *Carite*.

34. At the heart of the dispute was whether the lobster swam or walked to propel itself through the water. The French claimed it swam and therefore could be fished. The Brazilians held that it walked and was therefore a resource of the continental shelf.

35. Argentina, Australia, Chile, France, Great Britain, New Zealand, and Norway claim sovereignty over various sectors. Belgium, Japan, South Africa, the Soviet Union, and the United States, along with the seven claiming sovereignty rights, were the signatories to the 1959 Antarctic Treaty. Poland and West Ger-

many became treaty members in 1982, and Brazil, China, and India have shown interest in doing so.

36. Gonzáles Lonziéme, "Actividades Marítimas en la Antártida, 244–54.
37. Hormazabal, *El Canal de Beagle*, 144.
38. Argentina argued that the subjects of arbitration were only the Beagle Channel and Picton, Nueva, and Lenox islands. The court had awarded to Chile not only these but also the islands in an area east of Cape Horn. Argentina also complained that Chile had acted upon the terms of arbitration before the nine-month moratorium to allow for challenges had expired. See Fraga, *La Argentina y el Atlántico Sur*, 180.
39. Joint Publications Research Service, "Communiqué Confirms Solidarity."
40. Details concerning the military operations that took place during the 1977 crisis have been well guarded by both sides. This account has been pieced together from a multitude of sources and probably represents an accurate overall picture; however, specific details may be erroneous.

Chapter Twelve

1. Sarmiento's program called for modern warships, a naval academy (which was founded in 1872), a naval arsenal, and the establishment of a regular officer corps (Ratto, *Sarmiento y la Marina de Guerra*, 37).
2. Most Latin American marine corps are currently known by traditional Iberian nomenclature, either as *infantería de marina* or, as in the case of Brazil, *corpo de fuzileiros navais*. The following Latin American countries have marine corps, listed with the dates of their establishment or most recent reestablishment: Argentina (1810), Brazil (1822), Chile (1818), Colombia (1937), Cuba (late 1970s), Ecuador (1943), México (1910), Paraguay (1865), Perú (1943), El Salvador (1985), and Venezuela (1943).
3. "Argentina's Infantería de Marina," *ONI Review*, 232.
4. Urutu is a snake native to Brazil. The vehicle has been well received by arms experts. After an inspection of the Urutu armored amphibious vehicle, General Hac Shi, armed forces chief of staff of South Korea, stated, "I was taken by surprise when I found here that very advanced stage of technology, primarily in military equipment. I admire the progress of your country in that field, which is usually concentrated in the hands of the big powers" (*Jornal do Brasil* 6 April 1973, p. 3).
5. The Portuguese marine corps was created in 1797.
6. Monteiro, "Comandantes do Corpo de Fuzileiros Navais," 9–12; *ONI Review* 7.
7. *ONI Review* 7.
8. During the war with Brazil (1825–27) a marine battalion was formed, and in 1830 a company of naval artillery. Authorization for a coastal artillery battalion came in 1879, and in 1880 a marine infantry battalion was created. The marine infantry, outlawed in 1893, disbanded in 1898. See English, *Armed Forces*, 39–41.
9. *Monthly Information Bulletin* 5 (March 1922); "Síntesis Histórica," *Del Mar*.
10. "Argentina's Infanteria de Marina," *ONI Review*, 232; *ONI Review* 5:31, and 6:34; Arguindeguy, *Apuntes Buques Argentina* 6:3058.
11. *ONI Review* 5:32; Vio Valdivieso, *Manual de Historia Naval*, 115–17. "British and German influence, strong in the Navy and the Army, is almost nonexistent [in the marine corps]" (*ONI Review* 5:33).
12. English, *Armed Forces of Latin America*, 386, 390; Garaycochea, *Legislación naval* 1:171–74, 6:648; "Latin American Navies," *ONI Review*, 34–35.
13. "Latin American Navies," *ONI Review*, 33.

14. Fortini, "Sobre la Fundación Aviación Naval," 40–46; *Jane's Aircraft, 1926*, 3–4a.

15. One aircraft did not complete the trip because of engine trouble (*Monthly Information Bulletin* 6 [August 1923]).

16. For a listing of aircraft used by Argentine naval aviation, see Andrade, *Latin-American Military Aviation*, 32–41, and Sequeira, *Aviación Naval Argentina*, 1–126.

17. ". . . [A]viation . . . will weigh equally with algebra, trigonometry, history, and geography in the final examinations which determine classifications according to the officers of the fleet. We already know that seniority also constitutes one grade. Further, the marine guards [midshipmen], the ensigns, in order to receive promotion, must first complete a certain number of hours of flight, whereas up until now they have been required to spend . . . much time in loading ships, . . . the discharge of various commissions, and the completion of a series of exercises destined to test their aptitude and condition for the hard life of a mariner.

The higher authorities [no longer] consider aviation . . . a voluntary service of the marines to acquire a knowledge necessary to a sea career" (*Monthly Information Bulletin* 9 [February 1926]). In 1983 the second-highest-ranking man in the Argentine navy, the chief of the general naval staff, was an aviator.

18. English, "Latin American Naval Aviation," 338; U.S. Naval Institute *Proceedings* 66.

19. Arguindeguy, *Apuntes Buques Argentina* 4:3064.

20. *ONI Review* 12.

21. *Jane's Ships, 1972–73*, 4. The propulsion plant was virtually replaced with new components taken from HMS *Leviathan*. That ship, a *Majestic*-class unit, had been maintained in an incomplete state by the Royal Navy since the close of World War II and was about to be scrapped. Fire damage and financial considerations had forced the early retirement of *Karel Doorman* from the Dutch navy.

22. Selser, "¿Argentina, para que sirven las misiones militares?", 16–17.

23. English, "Latin American Naval Aviation," 339, 342; *Monthly Information Bulletin* 5 (September 1922).

24. *Monthly Information Bulletin* 8 (January 1925): 16.

25. *Monthly Information Bulletin* 8 (December 1925).

26. National Archives, Records of the Office of Naval Intelligence, memorandum from William Sackville, military attaché to Brazil, to Office of the Chief of Staff, Military Intelligence, 9 November 1932, box C-10-K, file 15445-AB.

27. English, "Latin American Naval Aviation," 339. The Brazilian navy did not have a Williams Moffett to campaign for the development of naval aviation as a weapon for achieving victory at sea.

28. *ONI Review* 9.

29. National Archives, Records of the Office of Naval Intelligence, memorandum from W. B. Fletcher, senior member, U.S. naval commission to Brazil, to director of naval intelligence, Rio de Janeiro, 15 December 1922, box C-10-1, file 14794-A.

30. The *Minas Gerais* received a steam catapult, a mirror landing system, and new fire control and radar equipment. The flight deck was reinforced to handle aircraft weighing twenty thousand pounds, this being an increase of six thousand pounds over the original design. A new steam catapult was installed, capable of launching a twenty-thousand-pound aircraft at sixty knots. The increase in flight-deck strength and the capabilities of the new catapult would allow the ship to operate modern aircraft. She also received the largest angled flight deck installed in any of the ships of her class.

SOURCE NOTES   373

31. The Dutch had supplied three surplus TBM-3 Avengers, which were used by the Brazilian navy for familiarization training in the North Sea during 1960. See Andrade, *Latin-American Military Aviation*, 88.
32. For a listing of the aircraft flown by the Brazilian navy, see Andrade, *Latin-American Military Aviation*, 87–93.
33. Olive, "Brazil's Naval Air Force," 481.
34. They were Ernesto de Mello Baptista, minister of the navy, Zilmar de Araripe, commander in chief of the fleet and commanding officer of the *Minas Gerais*, and Augusto Hamann Rademaker, director of naval personnel.
35. "Brazil: Belle Antonio," *Newsweek;* Pesce, "A Case for a V/STOL Brazilian Naval Air Arm."
36. López, *Historia de la Marina de Chile*, 348; Vio Valdivieso, *Manual*, 130–33.
37. *Monthly Information Bulletin* 6 (April 1923): 56; *Monthly Information Bulletin* 9 (October 1926).
38. Rodriguez, *Crónicas nacionales*, 258–60, 355–57.
39. Rodriguez, "Portaaviones *Roosevelt*," 49–50.
40. "Navy International Interviews Chile Navy's Chief of Naval Staff," *Navy International*.
41. Garaycochea, *Legislación naval* 1:162–65; *Jane's Aircraft, 1926*, 71a.
42. Garaycochea, *Legislación naval* 1:183, 141–42; English, "Latin American Naval Aviation," 339.
43. English, "Latin American Naval Aviation," 340.
44. Cárdenas, *Gesta en el Golfo*, 191.
45. English, "Latin American Naval Aviation," 338–43.

Chapter Thirteen

1. Volta Gaona, *Revolucion de 1947*, 15–285.
2. Thomas, *Pursuit of Freedom*, 659, 668.
3. "Case History of a Revolution," *ONI Review*, 280–83.
4. Key Cuban naval officers arrested following the 5 September 1957 coup attempt were Captain Guillermo Driggs Guerra, director of the naval academy; Commander Augusto N. Juarrero Erdman, commanding officer of the *Antonio Maceo;* Commander Alberto Juarrero Erdman, chief of flight, naval air arm; Lieutenant Commander Andres Gonzalez Lines, assigned to the naval academy; and Lieutenant Miguel Pons Goizueta, commanding officer of the *Baire*.
5. Thomas, *Pursuit of Freedom*, 961–65.
6. "Epitaph for the Cuban Navy," *ONI Review*.
7. Skidmore, *Politics in Brazil*, 149–58; Dos Pasos, *Brazil on the Move*, 159–60; Alexander, "Army in Politics," 161.
8. The admiral's appointment as head of the marine corps had been opposed by many senior naval officers (*New York Times*, 5 December 1963, p. 26). See also Skidmore, *Politics in Brazil*, 296–97.
9. Skidmore, *Politics in Brazil*, 296–97.
10. The following officers, who were not involved in the 28 September 1951 attempt at a coup, were retired because of the positions they held: Minister of the Navy Admiral Enrique B. Garcia; Chief of Naval Operations Admiral Ismael I. Pérez del Cerro; Undersecretary of the Navy Rear Admiral Victorio Malatesta; and Subsecretary of National Defense Rear Admiral Carlos A. Machiavelli.
11. Olivieri, *Dos veces rebelde*, 105–40; Cavallo, *Puerto Belgrano*, 36–46; Plater, *Una gran lección*, 27–35.

12. "Masacraron al Pueblo Indefenso," *Democracia*.
13. Rouquié, *Poder militar* 2:110; Cavallo, *Puerto Belgrano*, 21, 41; "Comando conjunto de las Fuerzas Armadas," *Nación*.
14. Among those retired as a result of the 16 June 1955 coup attempt were Admiral Ramon A. Brunet, chief of naval operations; Vice Admiral Pedro Insussarry, director general; Vice Admiral Miguel Angel Pedrozo, assistant director general; Rear Admiral Anibal O. Olivieri, secretary of the navy; Rear Admiral Gaston D. Lestrade, subsecretary of the navy; Rear Admiral Adolfo B. Piva, chief of naval general staff; Rear Admiral Rolando O. Esteverena, commandant of La Plata Naval Base; and Rear Admiral Samuel Toranzo Calderón, commandant of marines.
15. *Democracia* (Buenos Aires), 18 August 1955, 2; Rouquié, *Poder militar* 2:108–9.
16. *Nación* (Buenos Aires), 20 June 1955, 3.
17. Cavallo, *Puerto Belgrano*, 55.
18. Rouquié, *Poder militar* 2:117.
19. "Señor general Ferrazzano: usted se hará cargo, seguramente, de este Escuela Naval y de la Base Naval contigua. Recuerde que ambos establecimientos son propiedad de Nación Argentina y que no deberá repetirse el bochornoso hecho ocurrido el 16 de Junio último cuando fuerzas del Ejército ocuparon el Ministerio de Marina tomándolo como si fuera botín de guerra" (text of note provided courtesy of Admiral Isaac F. Rojas).
20. Rouquié, *Poder militar* 2:117.
21. "Argentine Navy's Role," *ONI Review*.
22. The original commanding officer had been relieved when he refused to open fire on the storage tanks.
23. Rouquié, *Poder militar* 2:119.
24. "Su invitación para transladarnos a Buenos Aires impongo: La reunión tendrá lugar a bordo de la nave insignia de la Marina de Guerra en Operaciones, crucero *17 de Octubre* el martes 20 a 1700 hs. Estaré fondeado en Rada la Plata" (text of message provided courtesy of Admiral Isaac F. Rojas).
25. Text of conditions provided by Admiral Rojas.
26. "Le ruego permita la entrada a Buenos Aires de uno o dos buques tanques porque la ciudad se está quedando sin combustible" (text of message provided courtesy of Admiral Rojas).
27. "En cuanto acepte los términos del Acta No 1 firmada ayer se levantará el bloqueo y podrán entrar todos los buques que sean necesarios" (text of message provided courtesy of Admiral Rojas).
28. Rouquié, *Poder militar* 2:121.
29. According to Arguindeguy, "she was assigned the name *17 de Octubre*, which had no significance at all to the Argentine Navy . . . and includes the later falsification of the Argentine commissioning date [which was actually 12 April 1951]. . . . This is an opportune place to correct the historical record . . ." (*Apuntes Buques Argentinos* 5:2633).
30. Admiral Rojas also held the position of chief of naval operations as a rear admiral. Rear Admiral Teodoro Hartung became the navy minister. In May 1958 Congress elevated Rojas to full admiral over his own objections. The decision passed both houses by unanimous vote.
31. "Argentine Navy's Role," *ONI Review*.
32. Venezuela has four military forces. Traditionally, in order of size, they are the army, national guard, navy, and air force. The national guard is a regular force responsible for protecting the borders, airports, harbors, industrial areas, for en-

SOURCE NOTES 375

gaging in antismuggling operations, and for patrolling the coast. It is not a component of the army, as in the United States.

33. The Venezuelan military academy trains officers for the army. It has a long history and has undergone numerous changes of name. It traces its roots to the military academy of mathematics, established in 1760 by the Spanish colonial government. In its capacity as the official officer's school of the Venezuelan army, it began to function on 5 July 1910.

The armed forces academy came into being on 8 August 1954 as part of the organization of the military academy. Its purpose was to unify the first two years of study for students in the military academy, naval school, school of aviation, and national guard academy. After completing two years of basic studies at the armed forces academy, students transferred to the service academy of their choice to complete two years of specialized training. Upon graduation, they were commissioned as second lieutenants in the army, air force, or national guard, or as ensigns in the navy.

In January 1958 the armed forces academy moved to a new site and began to function separately from the military academy. For various reasons, including rivalry among the armed forces, the school closed within seven months. The majority of Venezuelan generals, colonels, admirals, and naval captains today are graduates of the armed forces academy.

34. Based on conversations between Rear Admiral Tulio Márquez Planas, Venezuelan navy, retired, and Mr. Carlos Hernández-González. Andrés Brito Martínez, who graduated from the Venezuelan naval academy in July 1955, became the Venezuelan minister of defense as a vice admiral in July 1984.

35. Muñoz, *Conspiración* 1:197.

36. Air force leaders were Major Martín Parada, Major Luis Evencio Carrillo, and Major Edgar Suaréz Mier y Terán; Army leaders included Major Homero Leal Torres, Captain Juan Luis Massó Perdomo, Captain Luis Enrique Sucre, Lieutenant Santiago F. Testamark, and Lieutenant José M. Cordova Montaner.

37. Blanco Muñoz, *Conspiración* 1:51–52. One Venom jet flown by air force Second Lieutenant Luis L. Viana Lama was damaged by antiaircraft fire and forced to land at the Maíquetia International Airport.

38. The naval education center had been established on 14 July 1949 with the name Centro de Entrenamiento Naval. In the early 1960s it received its correct name, the Naval Education Center "Captain Felipe Santiago Esteves" (CANES). Today, CANES is composed of a warrant officers school, a technical school, and a conscript school.

The officers present at the meeting called by Sosa Ríos were Captain Miguel Rodriguez Olivares, Captain Armando López Conde, Captain Eduardo Morales Luengo, Commander Miguel Hernández Saucier, Commander Juan J. Molina Villegas, and Commander Manuel Ponte Rodriguez.

39. Sosa Ríos, *Mar de Leva*, 21–29.

40. Major Venezuelan military units bear both a name and a number. For example, the Urdaneta Marine Battalion is Battalion No. 2.

41. Blanco Muñoz, *Conspiración* 1:97–99.

42. Trejo, *Revolución no ha terminado*, 81–116.

43. Ibid.

44. The national guard troop school, founded in August 1937, educated the nucleus of professional troops belonging to the national guard. This school should not be confused with the national guard academy, located near Caracas.

45. Sosa Ríos, *Mar de Leva*, 21–29.

46. Blanco Muñoz, *Conspiración* 1:53, 58; Sosa Ríos, *Mar de Leva*, 21–29.
47. Haroldo Rodríguez Figueroa graduated from the Venezuelan naval academy in 1955. In the rank of vice admiral he served as commander of the navy between June 1983 and June 1984.
48. Blanco Muñoz, *Conspiración* 1:188–92.
49. Miguel J. Rodríguez Olivares, who graduated from the Venezuelan naval academy, became commander of the fleet in 1958. In October 1958 he became a member of the governing junta, representing the navy, after Rear Admiral Wolfgang Larrazabal's resignation as president; Dr. Edgar Sanabria was designated the new president. Rodríguez Olivares died of cancer in 1960, a few days before being designated chief of naval staff, a position he never held. Promoted to rear admiral post-mortem, he was buried with ex-president's honors.
50. "23 de enero: 25 años," 7–12.
51. Rodríguez Olivares had approached Wolfgang Larrazábal with the knowledge of the other naval conspirators—Commander Andrés de la Rosa, Commander José Vicente Azopardo, and Commander Miguel Hernández Saucier.
52. Dr. Oscar Centeno Lusinchi represented the civilians; Commander José Vicente Azopardo was coordinator for military officers of the army, navy, air force, and national guard; Commander Andrés de la Rosa, Commander José Manuel Hernández, and Commander Jesús Carbonell Izquierdo represented the navy; Captain Felipe Párraga Núñez, Captain J. Leal Morales, Captain Angel Rodriguez Corro, and Lieutenant Rafael Marín Granadillo represented the army; Lieutenant José Luis Fernández represented the air force and the armed forces academy; and Captain Italo Brett Smith represented the national guard.
53. Blanco Muñoz, *Conspiración* 1:35.
54. Captain Rafael Rosales Alvarez, commanding officer of the *Nueva Esparta*, was the senior rebel leader at La Guaira.
55. Blanco Muñoz, *Conspiración* 1:376–77; Sosa Ríos, *Mar de Leva*, 21–29.
56. Captain Pablo Cohén Guerrero and Captain Armando Medina were the senior rebel officers when these ships were at sea.
57. "23 de enero: 25 años," 7–12.
58. Ibid.; Blanco Muñoz, *Conspiración* 1:14, 65.
59. Muñoz, *Conspiración* 1:330.
60. Alexander, *Venezuelan Democratic Revolution*, 51–52, 106, 114.
61. Blanco Muñoz, *Conspiración* 4: 18–21, 56–57, 201–2.
62. Sosa Ríos, *Mar de Leva*, 85–87; Blanco Muñoz, *Conspiración* 4: 285–87.
63. With the exception of Commander Molina Villegas and perhaps one other officer, the officers of Marine Battalion No. 3 apparently did not have any links with the Marxist movement but rebelled out of loyalty to their chief. Mid-level officers in the other rebellious services had connections with the Communist Party and the Leftist Revolutionary Movement.
64. Apparently the size of Marine Battalion No. 3, normally 1,000 strong, was between 250 and 400 men at the time of the rebellion (Blanco Muñoz, *Conspiración* 4: 92–118).
65. José Constantino Seijas Villalobos graduated from the U.S. Naval Academy in 1945, was promoted to rear admiral in July 1967, and in 1969 became commander of the navy. In July 1971 he became a vice admiral, in 1972 chief of joint staff of the armed forces, and in 1974 inspector general of the armed forces and vice minister of defense.
66. Sosa Ríos, *Mar de Leva*, 65–68.
67. Sosa Ríos, *Mar de Leva*, 65.

68. Blanco Muñoz, *Conspiración* 4: 120–50; Sosa Ríos, *Mar de Leva*, 67.
69. Blanco Muñoz, *Conspiración* 4: 113–65; Sosa Ríos, *Mar de Leva*, 65.
70. Jesús Carbonell Izquierdo graduated from the Venezuelan Naval Academy in January 1943. In 1967 he became commander of the navy with the rank of rear admiral; in 1969, armed forces chief of the joint staff; in 1970, inspector general of the armed forces (vice minister of defense) as vice admiral; in 1971, minister of defense. He was the second naval officer to hold this last position. The other was Vice Admiral Lino de Clemente y Palacios, who on 19 April 1810 was designated secretary of war and navy for the junta.
71. Sosa Ríos, *Mar de Leva*, 71; Morales Monasterios, *Del Porteñazo*, 54–55.
72. The destroyer *Nueva Esparta* was in dry dock in Puerto Cabello, and the destroyer *Zulia* was undergoing maintenance. In the United States the submarine *Carite* was being overhauled. The frigates *Almirante Clemente*, *General Flores*, and *General Moran* were operational at Puerto Cabello. The frigates *General de Austria*, *Almirante Garcia*, and *Almirante Brion* were in Livorno, Italy, being modernized. The medium landing ships *Los Frailes* and *Los Roques* were capable of navigating only in an emergency. The medium landing ship *Los Testigos* was operational at Margarita Island, the medium landing ship *Los Monjes* at Orchila Island. The transport *Las Aves* navigated between Los Roques Island and La Guaira. The survey ship *Puerto Santo* was at sea, and the patrol craft *Mejillon* was operational at Puerto Cabello. See Sosa Ríos, *Mar de Leva*, 71–72; Morales Monasterios, *Del Porteñazo*, 55; and *Jane's Fighting Ships, 1964–65*, 446–47.
73. Sosa Ríos, *Mar de Leva*, 71–72; Morales Monasterios, *Del Porteñazo*, 55–56.
74. The Venezuelan naval police, about the size of an army regiment, is equivalent to the Venezuelan army's military police. In 1964 the naval police became part of the marine corps and served as its security force.
75. Captain Ponte Rodríguez, removed as chief of the second section in the naval chief of staff a few weeks prior to the rebellion, was awaiting assignment. Commander Medina Silva was second in command of the Puerto Cabello Naval Base. Lieutenant Morales Monasterios had been the commanding officer of Marine Battalion No. 1 since 9 January 1962 and under direct orders from the commander of the navy. A few days before the rebellion, the lieutenant had been designated assistant naval attaché in London, a position he never filled.
76. Vice Admiral Justo Pastor Fernández Márquez, who graduated from the Venezuelan Naval Academy in July 1956, became commander of the navy in June 1984. Those arrested by the rebels included Captain Guillermo Ginari Tronconis, commander of the Puerto Cabello Naval Base, and Captain Andrés Oswaldo Moreno Piña, commander of the First Destroyer Division. See Morales Monasterios, *Del Porteñazo*, 56–57, and Sosa Ríos, *Mar de Leva*, 73.
77. Morales Monasterios states that the origin of the defeat was the rapid intervention of army Infantry Battalion No. 41. According to him, the rebels calculated that it would be at least six hours before the government's forces could begin to react. The loyal military units that were sent from Caracas, Maracay, and Valencia to fight the rebels in Puerto Cabello used an old narrow road known as the Ditch, since by June 1962 the new highway had not been finished. This delayed their arrival to Puerto Cabello (*Del Porteñazo*, 56–58).
78. The force was composed of army Infantry Battalion No. 41, 600 men; a company from army Infantry Battalion No. 3, 150 men; a company from army Infantry Battalion No. 31, 150 men; a company from army Infantry Battalion No. 32, 150 men; a company from army Armored Battalion No. 4, with sixteen AMX-13 light tanks; a battery from army field artillery Group No. 41, with six

M-114 155-mm howitzers; a company from army Military Police Battalion No. 1, 150 men; a company of air force Parachute Battalion No. 1; national guard Detachment No. 55, 600 men; and a company from national guard Detachment No. 57, 150 men. (See Morales Monasterios, *Del Porteñazo*, 76.) In addition to these land forces, Colonel Monch Siegert was supported by Sabre, Venom, and Vampire aircraft from air force Fighter Group 12; Canberra aircraft from air force Bomber Squadron No. 39, and Sikorsky S-55/UH-19 and Bell 47/OH-13 helicopters from air force Reconnaissance Squadron No. 1.

79. Márquez, *Vida de Cuartel*, 297–98.

80. Morales, *Del Porteñazo*, 57–60, 63–65; Sosa Ríos, *Mar de Leva*, 75–76; Blanco Muñoz, *Conspiración* 4: 37–38.

81. An amphibious landing and a vertical assault were not possible. The only marine battalion available for an amphibious landing was No. 1, No. 3 being reorganized, following the rebellion in May, and No. 2 in revolt. Only four medium landing ships were available to the government. The topography of the region made a parachute drop almost impossible, and the air force only had ten Sikorsky S-55/UH-19 and a few small Bell 47/OH-13 helicopters for a "heli-assault."

82. The northern sector was commanded by Ensign Freddy Figueroa Bastardo; the central sector by Ensign Andrés Leal Romero, supported by Master Chief Petty Officer Oswaldo Becerra; and the southern sector by Master Chief Petty Officer Manuel de Jesús Poyer.

83. Morales Monasterios, *Del Porteñazo*, 66–68, 77; Sosa Ríos, *Mar de Leva*, 74–77.

84. Blanco Muñoz, *Conspiración*, 38; Morales Monasterios, *Del Porteñazo*, 68–69, 71–83; Sosa Ríos, *Mar de Leva*, 75–78.

85. Fabio Galliapoli was promoted to the rank of lieutenant commander postmortem, and on 9 March 1971, the Venezuelan navy renamed the former USS *Wannalancet* (YTM-385) the *Favio Galliapoli*.

86. Captain Ponte Rodríguez died in prison of a heart attack on 24 July 1964. Commander Medina Silva escaped from prison after a short incarceration and lived in exile until 1970, at which time he was permitted to return. Commander Morales Monasterios was held in prison until 1968, when he was deported to West Germany. He lived there for five years, then was permitted to return to Venezuela. None of the condemned naval officers served a full sentence. The punishment for the majority was dismissal from the service.

87. *El Mercurio* (Valparaíso), 13 September 1973, p. 1.

88. Naval officers who held important positions following the overthrow of the Allende government were Admiral José Toribio Merino, member of ruling junta; Rear Admiral Ismael Huerta Díaz, minister of foreign relations; Rear Admiral Lorenzo Gotusso Borlando, minister of the treasury; Vice Admiral Patricio Carvajal Prado, minister of defense; and Captain Matías Valenzuela Labra, mayor of Valparaíso.

Chapter Fourteen *

1. Numerous publications have stated that in December 1981 Admiral Jorge Issac Anaya, commander in chief of the navy and a member of the ruling junta, supported General Leopoldo Galtieri for the leadership of the junta and therefore

---

*For the list of interviews from which much of the information in this chapter is derived, see the Bibliography.

the presidency on the condition that he back the admiral's actions in the Malvinas. But people who are knowledgeable about Argentine interforce relations tend to disregard this assumption on the ground that no Argentine armed force would allow another force to meddle in its internal politics for the selection of a new commander in chief. In December the Argentine navy made plans to recapture the Malvinas, probably in late 1982. The plans were to be ready by May or June of 1982. It is unlikely that the navy would have planned a winter landing. In all probability, the junta did not have a fixed invasion date but rather was preparing a military option of readiness for the time it would demand serious negotiations of the British. That the Argentines considered the recapture only as a political move in a negotiations game is indicated by the planning for the landing, conducted secretly by a small, select group; neither the rest of the navy nor the other armed forces were given the slightest hint about stepping up military preparedness for a possible war.

Events occurred during March 1982 in the Georgias that sparked the invasion of those islands and the Malvinas. In mid-March a private Argentine company, acting in accordance with a contract signed with a British firm and known to the British government, landed forty-one Argentine civilians and eighty tons of equipment on the island of South Georgia in order to disassemble whaling facilities for the purpose of scraping them. These civilians were transported to South Georgia by the Argentine naval auxiliary *Bahía Buen Suceso*, which departed after the men and equipment were landed. The use of naval ships to support commercial enterprises is a common practice in developing areas of South America. The owner of the scrap company, Constantino Davidoff, had visited Argentine naval headquarters in late 1981 to obtain navy support for the undertaking.

The British embassy in Buenos Aires had been informed and approved of the scrap workers' trip prior to their departure, and the Argentines believed that they had obtained permission for the job. According to Hastings and Jenkins, "The British embassy agreed to the expedition and merely told Davidoff that his men would need formal authorization on arrival from the British Antarctic Survey base 20 miles down the coast of Grytviken. Whether through lethargy, bravado or instructions from a naval officer, the party of thirty-nine workmen failed to comply with this request" (*Battle of the Falklands*, 55). Argentine sources indicate that the workers were issued a "white card" by the Argentine foreign office, a document Argentina and Great Britain, by mutual agreement, used to identify all persons traveling in the disputed area. The British disregarded the card and demanded that the workers have their passports stamped by the Grytviken authorities, which could have been construed as a factual recognition by the Argentines of British sovereignty. The workers refused and the conflict started. Once on the islands, in March, a worker raised the Argentine flag. The British ordered the Argentines to leave the islands. Both sides scrambled to support their people militarily, and the political crisis escalated. This was the catalyst for the Argentine invasions of the Georgias and Malvinas.

Political events in March motivated Argentina to choose a military solution. Events in February and March provoked the ruling junta into shortening the invasion plan, then executing it in April.

See Cardoso, Kirschbaum, and van der Kooy, *Malvinas La Trama Secreta*, 17–38, and Rice and Gavshon, *Sinking of the* Belgrano, 23.

2. The Argentine claim to the islands is based in large part on Spanish activities during the colonial era. There are many documents indicating Spanish discovery of the islands at the beginning of the sixteenth century, starting with Magellan's

voyage around the world in 1520. The islands were registered on several Spanish charts in approximate positions in 1529, or sixty-three years before the first British claim of discovery, by John Davis, who deserted the expedition of Sir Francis Drake. Davis allegedly saw the islands in 1592 on his return voyage to England, a claim made by a shipmate eight years later, when the Dutch discovery by Sebald de Weert became known.

More than 160 years afterwards, French mariners from Saint Malo named the islands Malouines, the origin of Malvinas, and became the first settlers of the west island in 1764. After Spanish protests and long negotiations, France peacefully accepted Spain's sovereignty and handed over the colony in April 1767. Meanwhile, in January 1766, the British had founded a settlement on the east island from which they were driven by a Spanish expedition in June 1770. Diplomacy prevented a war between Spain and England. The British, allowed to return in September 1771, abandoned the islands in May 1774. The English had occupied them for a period, first of four and a half, then of two and a half years.

Spain ruled the Malvinas for forty-four years, withdrawing in 1811 because of the Argentine independence movement. Argentina, as heir to the former Spanish territory, raised her flag over the deserted islands in 1820, colonized them, established a garrison and a population, and held them until 1832. In that year the U.S. sloop *Lexington* imprisoned some Argentines as punishment for their detaining, rough handling, and fining of American sealers hunting on the islands without Argentine permission.

One year later the British, who had recognized Argentine independence in 1825, sent an expedition to occupy the islands. They forced a weaker Argentine ship to retire, evicted the remaining Argentine population, and brought in British settlers.

Great Britain's claim to the Malvinas has long been questioned by the British themselves. In July 1829 the Duke of Wellington, then British prime minister, wrote, "I have perused the papers respecting the Falkland Islands. It is not clear to me that we have ever possessed the sovereignty of these islands." In August 1829 the British Foreign Office sent an official note to its chargé d'affaires in Buenos Aires stating, among other things, that "having realized the growing importance of the islands, regarding relations with South American states and its extensive trade in the Pacific Ocean, the government of the United Kingdom considered highly desirable the possession of a safe port, as a supply base for its vessels, and, if necessary, for its careen." This does not read like a statement from a foreign office that believed the islands to be British. On 25 July 1848, at a session of the House of Commons, Sir William Molesworth said, ". . . there are the wretched [Malvinas] islands, no good for wheat growing, the trees do not grow, are humbled by almost perpetual winds. The islands that since 1841 have cost us 45,000 pounds sterling, with no benefits whatsoever. I am determined that this worthless possession be given back to the government of Buenos Aires who, with justice, claims them." On 12 December 1910 Gerald Spicer, head of the British Foreign Office's American department, wrote, "From a perusal of this memo [prepared by the office's assistant librarian, Gaston de Bernhardt, concerning the historical background] it is difficult to avoid the conclusion that the Argentine Government's attitude is not altogether unjustified, and that our action has been somewhat high-handed." John Troutbeck, Spicer's successor, stated in 1936, "The difficulty of our position is that our seizure of the Falkland Islands in 1833 was so arbitrary a procedure. . . ." He added that it would not be "easy to explain our position without showing ourselves up as international bandits." See Beck, "The Anglo-Argentine Dispute." Many

English-language works present the British claims to the islands. Among the more recent is Hastings and Jenkins, *Battle for the Falklands*, chapters 1 and 2.

3. The British had calculated that the Argentine carrier force was between eight and nine hundred miles north of the Malvinas. No source is available explaining how they reached this reasonably accurate tactical estimate. Committee of Privy Counsellors, *Falkland Islands Review*, par. 224.

4. The British were aware that an Argentine submarine was sailing to South Georgia. Committee of Privy Counsellors, *Falkland Islands Review*, par. 223.

5. They were wrong. The *Endurance* had sailed on 21 March for South Georgia. Those on board the *Santa Fe* might have detected a civilian survey ship carrying forty Royal Marines from Montevideo for the routine relief of the detachment on the Malvinas.

6. From an interview with Commander José Luis Tejo, commanding officer of the *Santisima Trinidad*, at Puerto Belgrano on 13 September 1982.

7. This decision proved to be very sound. The original landing site was flanked on both ends with machine-gun nests.

8. The British opened fire at four hundred meters. An LVT was hit numerous times but sustained only superficial damage.

9. From a conversation with Lieutenant Commander Hugo Santillán at Baterías, 16 September 1982. Altogether, three seventy-five-mm shells and a few mortar rounds were fired.

10. Captain N. J. Barker, commanding officer of the *Endurance*, stated that "in his view the operation must have been planned for some time, as the *Bahia Paraiso* had arrived from Antarctica, not from Argentina" (Committee of Privy Counsellors, *Falkland Islands Review*, par. 201). See Trombetta, "Ocupación de las Islas Georgias." Captain Baker was correct; the *Bahía Paraíso* had come from other than Argentina and was carrying troops, but these personnel did not have as their purpose the takeover of the Georgias.

The Argentine navy probably intended to establish a weather station on South Georgia in the summer of 1981–82, similar to the one it had built on the South Shetlands in 1977. For this purpose a landing party of naval personnel, mostly technicians, embarked in the supply ship *Bahía Paraíso* for the Antarctic summer campaign. When the Davidoff project evolved, the navy decided to postpone this plan. After the British sent the survey vessel *Endurance* with a platoon of marines to South Georgia to evict the scrap workers, the closest thing the Argentines had on hand to counter them was the landing party on board the *Bahía Paraíso*, by then still operating in Antarctica. The *Bahía Paraíso* was ordered to proceed at full speed to Leith and land the party. It was a bold bluff; the *Bahía Paraíso* was completely unarmed, and the twelve or so technicians of the landing party, although clad as marines and armed with hand-carried weapons, would be no match for the more than twenty marines in the *Endurance*. But apparently the trick worked, for the British abstained for the moment from using force. When Grytviken was taken by Argentine marines transported in the corvette *Guerrico* on 3 April, their British counterparts were taken prisoner.

11. From a briefing given by the Argentine Naval Aviation Command at Espora on 15 September 1982 and an interview with Lieutenant Omar Bousson, pilot of the Alouette, at Espora on the same date.

12. From an interview with the commanding officer of the *Guerrico*, Commander Carlos Luis Alfonso, at Puerto Belgrano on 15 September 1982.

13. From an interview with members of the Prefectura at Buenos Aires on 7 September 1982.

14. Hastings and Jenkins are in error when they state that "a prewar [Argentine] naval study had concluded that San Carlos was an 'impossible' site for a successful landing" (*Battle for the Falklands*, 200).

15. Ethell and Price cited the crew report as follows: "British fleet at 19 deg 29 min south and 21 deg west, 2,300 km [1,430 miles] ENE of Rio de Janeiro. Fleet split into three groups, with eight ships in each of the two forward groups and an unknown number in the third group" (*Air War South Atlantic*, 41). In fact, the British fleet totaled eleven ships.

16. From interviews with Commander Luis C. Vázquez, commanding officer of naval air Squadron No. 2, at Espora on 15 September 1982, and Lieutenant Commander Juan Carlos Ianusso, naval commanding officer of the *Formosa*, at Buenos Aires on 30 September 1983.

17. The cargo ship *Isla de los Estados* had arrived in the islands before 8 April, and the naval auxiliary *Bahia Buen Suceso* arrived on the eleventh.

18. HMS *Splendid* sighted these ships on 26 April and shadowed them for a while. Eventually she was ordered to break off and search for the carrier and cruiser (Hastings and Jenkins, *Battle for the Falklands*, 147).

19. Had the *Santa Fe* escaped the attack in Cumberland Bay, it seems likely that she would have been used against the British supply lines between Ascension and the Georgias. Argentine naval intelligence had predicted that, should negotiations fail, the British would first move against the Georgias, and that they would do so in late April. The *Santa Fe* was obsolete and would have been at a disadvantage against a British carrier task force. She would have had a better chance of success against British supply lines, where she could have been a headache for the enemy's naval planners.

Those on board the submarine believe that at least one torpedo, which failed to explode, was dropped. Hastings and Jenkins write that the *Santa Fe* was "attacked with depth charges and torpedoes" (*Battle for the Falklands*, 129). In this author's opinion, no torpedoes were used.

20. Cardoso, *Malvinas La Trama Secreta*, 339.

21. As the *San Luis* proceeded to station in mid-April, her crew discovered that the fire control computer was not operating properly. This meant that all firing data had to be calculated manually and only one torpedo at a time could be guided in the manual mode.

22. Cardoso, *Malvinas La Trama Secreta*, 339.

23. The Argentine navy had been very impressed with the performance of the French-built corvettes during antisurface exercises.

24. According to war game statistics, only one out of six aircraft could be expected to penetrate the British defenses. If accurate, the entire air group would have to be sacrificed in order to deliver two bombs, which still had to hit the target.

25. Cardoso, *Malvinas La Trama Secreta*, 340.

26. The British submarine, HMS *Conqueror*, had detected the *General Belgrano* at least thirty hours earlier and had been shadowing the cruiser. See Dalyell, *Thatcher's Torpedo*, 10; Rice and Gavshon, *Sinking of the* Belgrano, 101; Hastings and Jenkins, *Battle for the Falklands*, 147.

27. Apparently all three torpedoes were intended for the *General Belgrano*. According to Rice and Gavshon, the message of 1620 read, "*Bouchard* attacked. Torpedo struck but did not explode. Am beginning withdrawal" (*Sinking of the Belgrano*, 104). See Cardoso, *Malvinas La Trama Secreta*, 340.

28. Cardoso, *Malvinas La Trama Secreta*, 340.

29. There is confusion over exactly where the *General Belgrano* sank. On 3 May the Argentine United Nations representative gave the position as 55°24'S, 60°32'W.

In an announcement the *Conqueror* claimed that it was 55°30'S, 60°40'W. Dalyell locates the position at 55°27'S, 61°25'W (*Thatcher's Torpedo*, 14, 36). Rice and Gavshon place the *General Belgrano* at 55°24'S, 61°32'W (*Sinking of the Belgrano*, 102).

30. Evidence suggests that the tug had been stationed around Isla de los Estados to support the high-speed patrol boats *Intrepida* and *Indomita*, which apparently were operating in this area. Contingency plans may have existed to move the two craft to the Malvinas if an opportune moment arose.

31. Bonzo, "Crucero A.R.A. *General Belgrano*."

32. One of the most serious political mistakes made by the junta during these early days was not accurately projecting the actions of the United States. Argentine and U.S. relations had been improving, and the junta apparently believed that the United States would remain neutral. Far from neutral, the United States contributed significantly to the potential for a British victory, permitting Great Britain to use facilities on Ascension Island, a critical halfway point between England and the Malvinas. The list of military hardware supplied by the United States is extensive. According to an Australian newspaper, it included eight Stinger antiaircraft missiles, Vulcan-Phalanx air-defense gun systems, Harpoon antiship missiles, Shrike air-to-ground radar-seeking missiles, four hundred tons of airfield matting, 12.5 million gallons of aviation fuel, 60-mm illuminating mortar rounds, 40-mm high-explosive ammunition, two hundred Sidewinder AIM-9L air-to-air missiles, and much more. Some systems had no influence on the fight, such as the Vulcan-Phalanx and the Harpoons, but the Sidewinder Ls and the logistical support greatly contributed to the British victory (*Focus* [*The Weekend Australia*], 10–11 March 1984, 17).

Ethell and Price state that the British fired twenty-six AIM-9L Sidewinders, which accounted for the destruction of eighteen Argentine aircraft and contributed to the loss of one more. The Argentines lost a total of 102 aircraft, of which 32 were captured on the ground. Therefore the Sidewinder L accounted for more than one-fourth of the Argentine aircraft shot down (*Air War South Atlantic*, 215, appendix 5).

Great Britain also received valuable intelligence from the United States. In the words of Hastings and Jenkins, "Although British intelligence improved markedly as the Falklands conflict escalated—with critical assistance from American Sigint—information about enemy formations, their condition and tactics, remained sketchy in the extreme. Contrary to public belief at home, the British commanders in the South Atlantic never received a single satellite photograph of the battlefield, from American or any other sources." They also add, however, that "in the first days of the operation, the Chief of Defence Staff submitted personal requests for help and information to his counterparts in both Paris and Washington, and was rewarded with thick books of information from each" (*Battle for the Falklands*, 90, 132).

33. Numerous authors have supported the claim of the British that they sank a second patrol boat on the same night in the proximity of the *Alferez Sobral*. The name frequently attached to the second boat is the *Comodoro Somellera*. I saw, boarded, and photographed this tug at Ushuaia in September 1983. She had not undergone any structural work, confirming that she had not received any damage. I believe the British attacked one tug, the *Alferez Sobral*, more than once, and believed that they had attacked two different ships.

Ethell and Price state that four Sea Skua missiles were fired, and that, in all likelihood, one hit on each of two attacks (*Air War South Atlantic*, 77). I inspected and photographed the damaged bridge after it had been removed from the deck. It had only been hit once, on the second attack. Perhaps the tug was hit more than twice but sustained only superficial damage.

Chapter Fifteen*

1. The braking capabilities of the aircraft had been tested at Punta Indio in April.

2. Ironically, they were not the Argentine navy's first choice. The navy had wanted to buy A-4M Skyhawks from the United States, but the Carter administration refused to sell them. So Argentina chose the only other attack aircraft available that could operate from her light carrier, the *25 de Mayo*. This proved to be a mixed blessing during the war. The Super Etendards with their fire-and-forget Exocets were much more advanced than the Skyhawks, but the latter could have operated from the carrier and many more of them could have been purchased for the price of fourteen Etendards.

3. Rice and Gavshon write that "the French played a key role in arming these lethal aircraft [with Exocet missiles]" (*Sinking of the* Belgrano, 45). The source cited is an interview with Captain Raúl Galmarini, former commanding officer of the Espora Naval Air Base, home of the Super Etendard Squadron. Galmarini retired more than fifteen years before the war. The author was told in the numerous interviews conducted with Argentina naval aviators including Captain Carmelo I. Astesiano Agote, chief of staff, naval aviation command at the time of the war, and Commander Jorge Colombo, commander of the Super Etendard Squadron during the war, that the French withdrew their help in mid-April.

The confusion can possibly be attributed to the fact that Argentine sources claim the French technicians had been recalled to France. This is inaccurate. They remained in Argentina but did not work with the missiles.

4. The Super Etendard could also be armed with Magic 550 air-to-air missiles and bombs. However, due to limited preparation time, all effort was expended on making the air-to-surface Exocets operational.

5. Colombo, "Operaciones de aviones Super Etendard."

6. The Argentine air force and navy have developed the capability to rebuild A4s completely. Two or three aircraft, being overhauled at the beginning of hostilities, would have been available in a few months.

7. From an interview with Commander Luis C. Vázquez, commanding officer of Naval Air Wing No. 2, at Espora on 15 September 1982.

8. Late in the war two Embraer (Baudeirante) aircraft provided by Brazil were incorporated into the squadron based at Río Gallegos.

9. From an interview in Buenos Aires on 7 September 1982 with coast guard (prefectura) pilot Pedro Ernesto Gómez, Skyvan pilot in the Malvinas.

10. The air force Daggers and Mirage required a concrete runway of 2,200 meters. The C-130, which normally requires 550 meters for landing and 1,050 meters for takeoff, experienced no major problem flying from Puerto Argentino.

11. There were a number of charted grass strips in the islands. One of the most important was at Darwin (Goose Green). It was a pasture 410 meters long and 400 meters wide with a useable diagonal of 620 meters. The Argentines covered two-thirds of this strip with aluminum decking. The field was too short for several aircraft, and it was built on a muddy hill, severely hampering operations. Many Pucarás broke their nose-wheels using the field.

12. A typical marine corps battalion comprises seventy percent conscripts, twenty-five percent noncommissioned officers, and five percent officers. The conscripts serve a fourteen-month enlistment, while most of the noncoms, volunteers under four-year contracts, make a career out of the service. The officers are all

---

*For the list of interviews from which much of the information in this chapter is derived, see the Bibliography.

graduates of the five-year naval academy. The marines incorporate their conscripts quarterly in equal shares, so that they have a trained cadre all year round. The Argentine army incorporates all conscripts in January and February.

13. From an interview with Captain Antonio José Mozzarelli, commanding officer of the Malvinas Support Force, at Buenos Aires on 30 September 1983.

14. "Yo no soy más de River; me vestí de árbitro." From an interview with Captain Antonio Mozzarelli at Buenos Aires on 30 September 1983.

15. From an interview with Rear Admiral Eduardo Otero, commander of naval forces, Malvinas, at Buenos Aires on 8 September 1982.

16. Ethell and Price, *Air War South Atlantic*, 60–62.

17. Some of the defenders speculated that the smoke gave the British reason to believe they had done significant damage, thus influencing their decision to end the attack.

18. Molteni, "Malvinas . . . Así lo viví yo."

19. From an interview with Captain Antonio Mozzarelli at Buenos Aires on 30 September 1983.

20. From an interview with Commander Carlos Robacio, commanding officer of the Fifth Marine Battalion, at Buenos Aires on 9 September 1982.

21. Ethell and Price, *Air War South Atlantic*, 167.

22. Molteni, "Malvinas . . . Así lo viví yo."

23. From an interview with Lieutenant Commander Carlos Molteni at Buenos Aires on 10 September 1982 and his article, "Malvinas . . . Así lo viví yo," 223–42.

24. "The *Yarmouth* reported seeing a missile fly past her" (Hastings and Jenkins, *Battle for the Falklands*, 151).

25. From an interview with Commander Jorge Colombo at Espora on 15 September 1982; Colombo, "Operaciones de aviones Super Etendard."

26. The jets had not been started earlier because the Neptune pilots believed that the piston engines were much less likely to attract a heat-seeking missile.

27. From an interview with Commander Fernando Azcueta, commanding officer of the *San Luis*, at Mar del Plata on 22 September 1983.

28. These bombs were to have been dropped on Puerto Argentino, but the mission was canceled due to bad weather, and the Harriers used them while returning to their carrier. See Ethell and Price, *Air War South Atlantic*, 86.

29. The crew members of the *Narwal* were eventually set free at Montevideo, Uruguay.

30. From an interview with Captain Antonio José Mozzarelli at Buenos Aires on 30 September 1983.

31. "A mathematician and chess player, he [Rear Admiral John Woodward] had risen through the ranks by sheer brains . . ." (Hastings and Jenkins, *Battle for the Falklands*, 115).

32. On 5 and 6 June British warships again bombarded the *Bahia Buen Suceso*. Upon surrender on 15 June, the ship's watch destroyed and threw overboard all important material and flooded the tanks. The hulk of the *Bahia Buen Suceso* was later used as a torpedo target and sunk by the British.

33. From an interview with Commander Carlos Molteni at Buenos Aires on 10 September 1982. See Ethell and Price, *Air War South Atlantic*, 102.

34. Ethell and Price, *Air War South Atlantic*, 122–24.

35. According to Ethell and Price, no hits were scored in this attack (*Air War South Atlantic*, 124).

36. From an interview with coast guard (prefectura) officer Jorge Carlos Carrega, commander of the *Río Iguazu* at Buenos Aires on 7 September 1982.

37. The *Antelope* sank on 23 May when an undetonated bomb exploded while

being defused. It is not clear whether this was a one-thousand-pound bomb, the type dropped by the air force, or a five-hundred-pound bomb, the type dropped by the navy.

38. As soon as the Argentines occupied the Malvinas, the United States embargoed military cargo to Argentina. This included ejection cannisters from the Argentine navy's A-4Qs, which had been sent to the United States to be rebuilt. Some naval A-4Qs were being flown with expired cannisters, others with cannisters borrowed from the air force. Whether this contributed to the pilot's death, as many Argentines believe, is unclear.

39. Ethell and Price, *Air War South Atlantic*, 132–33.

40. The *Atlantic Conveyor* sank on 27 May, taking with her cargo that included one Sea Lynx, six Wessex, and three Chinook helicopters. See Ethell and Price, *Air War South Atlantic*, 150–56. They state, incorrectly, that the *Atlantic Conveyor* sank on the thirtieth.

41. Colombo, "Operaciones de aviones Super Etendard."

42. Eddy, *Falklands War*, 227. Seldom do English eyewitness accounts mention Macchis; it appears that they were being mistaken for Pucarás.

43. Ethell and Price, *Air War South Atlantic*, 169.

44. Lieutenant Horacio González Llanos was a member of Captain Mozzarelli's staff and doubled as the commanding officer of the *Forrest* and *Penelope* whenever needed. His brother, Lieutenant Commander Juan Carlos González Llanos, was the commanding officer of the *Narwal*.

45. From an interview with Lieutenant Commander Carlos Molteni at Buenos Aires on 10 September 1982.

46. Ethell and Price, *Air War South Atlantic*, 169.

47. From an interview with Commander Jorge Colombo at Espora on 15 September 1982.

48. From an interview with Lieutenant Commander Carlos Molteni at Buenos Aires on 10 September 1982.

49. The *Sir Galahad* was eventually scuttled and the *Sir Tristram* transported on board a float on/float off lift ship to Great Britain for repair.

50. Hastings and Jenkins, *Battle for the Falklands*, 303.

51. From an interview with Commander Carlos Robacio at Buenos Aires on 9 September 1982.

Bibliography

Written Sources

Akers, Charles Edmond. *A History of South America*. New York: E. P. Dutton and Co., 1930.
Alcofar Nassaes, J. L. *Las fuerzas navales en la guerra civil española*. Barcelona: DOPESA, 1971.
———. *La marina italiana en la guerra de España*. Barcelona: EUROS, S.A., 1975.
———. *SPANSKY: Los extranjeros que lucharon en la guerra civil española*. Barcelona: DOPESA, 1973.
Alexander, Robert J. "The Army in Politics." In *Government and Politics in Latin America*, edited by Harold E. Davis. New York: Ronald Press, Co., 1958.
———. *The Venezuelan Democratic Revolution*. New Brunswick: Rutgers University Press, 1964.
Almeida Guillobel, Renato de. *Memórias*. Serviço Gráfico da Fundação, 1973.
Alzogaray, Alvaro de. *Diario de Operaciones de la escuadra republicana, campaña del Brasil (1826–28), lo publica el Archivo general de la nacion*. Montevideo: Taller Tipografico de la Marina, 1934.
"American-Built Mexican Gunboats." *Shipping World and Herald of Commerce* (London) 27 (19 November 1902): 502.
Andrada, B. H. *Guerra aérea en las Malvinas*. Buenos Aires: Emecé Editores, 1983.
Andrade, John M. *Latin-American Military Aviation*, Leicester: Midland Counties Publications (Aerophile), 1982.
Anselmi, Luis Félix. "La Aviación Naval en las Malvinas." *Boletin del Centro Naval* 735 (April–June 1983): 117–38.
Argentina. Armada. *Historia Marítima Argentina*. 4 vols. Buenos Aires: Cuántica Editora, S.A., 1983–.
———. *Infantería de Marina: Tres Siglos de Historia y Cien años de vida orgánica, 1879–19 de noviembre 1979*. Buenos Aires: Apus, 1979.
"Argentina." *Navy* (Washington) 4 (July 1910).
"Argentina." U.S. Naval Institute *Proceedings* 43 (October 1917): 2295, (November 1917): 2593–94.
"Argentina's Infantería de Marina." *ONI Review* (Washington) 17 (May 1962): 231–35.

"Argentina Seizes Nine Soviet and Bulgarian Trawlers." *Marine Fisheries Review* 40 (April 1978): 37–40.
"Argentine Naval Scholarships in Paraguay." *Monthly Information Bulletin* 9 (January 1927): 3.
"The Argentine Navy." *Shipping Illustrated* 48 (19 September 1914): 278–80.
"The Argentine Navy's Role in the Overthrow of the Peron Regime." *ONI Review* (Washington) 10 (December 1955): 624–29.
Arguindeguy, Pablo E. *Apuntes Sobre Los Buques de la Armada Argentina (1810–1970)*. 7 vols. Buenos Aires: Secretaría General Naval, 1972.
———. *Historia de la Aviación Naval Argentina*. 2 vols. Buenos Aires: Secretaría General Naval, 1980.
"Armored River Monitors for Brazil." *International Marine Review* 18 (November 1913): 471–72.
Army and Navy Journal 13 (18 March 1876): 522; 14 (13 January 1877): 366–67.
Aston, G. G. *Letters on Amphibious Wars*. London: John Murray, 1910.
"Attitude of South America." U.S. Naval Institute *Proceedings* 43 (May 1917): 1094.
Bamio, Jose R. "La Guerra Contra el Imperio del Brasil, Primeras Acciones Navales." *Del Mar* 112 (September–December 1979): 57–59.
Bancroft, Hubert H. *The Works of Hubert Howe Bancroft: History of Mexico*. 6 vols. San Francisco: A. L. Bancroft and Co., 1883–88.
Bañados Espinosa, Julio. *Balmaceda: Su Gobierno y la Revolución de 1891*. París: Librería de Gernier Hermanos, 1894.
Barandiarán, José F. "Nuestro Servicio de Aviación." *Revista de Marina* (Callao) 8 (November–December 1923): 717–22.
Barber, Willard F., and C. Neale Ronning. *Internal Security and Military Power*. Ohio: Ohio State University Press, 1966.
Barros Arana, Diego. *Historia General de Chile*. 16 vols. Santiago: Rafael Jover Editor, 1884–1902.
Barros Franco, José Miguel. *Apuntes para la Historia Diplomática de Chile: El caso del Baltimore*. Santiago: Talleres Gráficos Casa Nacional del Niño, 1950.
Basadre, Jorge. *Historia de la Republica del Perú*. 20 vols. Lima: Ediciones Historia, 1961–64.
Bauer, K. Jack. "The *Sancala* Affair: Captain Voorhees Seizes an Argentine Squadron." *American Neptune* 29 (July 1969): 174–86.
———. *Surfboats and Horse Marines: U.S. Naval Operations in the Mexican War, 1846–48*. Annapolis: Naval Institute Press, 1969.
———. "The United States Navy and Texas Independence: A Study in Jacksonian Integrity." *Military Affairs* 34 (April 1970): 44–48.
Baumann, G. G. *Extranjeros en la guerra civil española: Los Peruanos*. Lima: private edition, 1979.
Bazo C., Alfredo. "El Perú y la Proxima Guerra." *Revista de Marina* (Callao) 10 (March–April 1925): 218–34.
Beaver, Paul. "The Air Lesson Post Falklands." *Navy International* 88 (April 1983): 216–23.
Beck, Peter J. "The Anglo-Argentine Dispute over Title to the Falkland Islands: Changing British Perceptions on Sovereignty Since 1910." *Millennium Journal of International Studies* 12 (Spring 1983): 12–21.
Bemis, Samuel F. *The Latin American Policy of the United States: An Historical Interpretation*. New York: Harcourt, Brace, and Co., 1943.
Bidlingmaier, Gerhard. "K. M. *Admiral Graf Spee*." In *Warships in Profile*, edited by John Wingate, vol. 1. New York: Doubleday and Co., 1972.

Bidwell, Robert. "The First Mexican Navy, 1821–1830." Ph.D. diss., University of Virginia, 1960.
Black, E. F. "The ASW Role of the Latin American Navies." U.S. Naval Institute *Proceedings* 92 (December 1966): 127–30.
Blanco Muñoz, Agustín. *La Conspiración Civico Militar: Guairazo, Barcelonazo, Carupanazo y Porteñazo.* Colección Testimonios violentos. 4 vols. Caracas: Universidad Central de Venezuela, 1981.
Bonzo, Héctor E. "Crucero A.R.A. *General Belgrano.* ¡A ellos y sus seres!" *Boletín del Centro Naval* 737 (October–December 1983): 299–33.
Bozzano, José A. *Reminiscencias.* Asunción: Casa Editórial Toledo, 1962.
"Brazil: Additional Submarines Proposed." *Monthly Information Bulletin* 8 (August 1925): 5–6.
"Brazil: Bello Antonio." *Newsweek* (25 January 1965), 46.
"Brazil: Details of Recent Naval Mutiny." *Monthly Information Bulletin* 7 (December 1924): 58–61.
Brazil. Ministério da Marinha. *Subsidios para a História Marítima do Brasil.* 25 vols. Rio de Janeiro: Governo Federal, 1938–72.
Brazil. Ministério das Relações Esteriores. *Brazilian Green Book, Consisting of Diplomatic Documents Relating to Brazil's Attitude with Regard to the European War.* London: G. Allen and Unwin, 1918.
———. *Guerra da Europa: Documentos Diplomáticos: Attitude do Brasil, 1914–1917.* Rio de Janeiro: Imprensa nacional, 1917–18.
———. *Relatório, 1917–18.* Rio de Janeiro: Imprensa nacional, 1918.
———. *Relatório, 1921.* Rio de Janeiro: Imprensa nacional, 1921.
"Brazil." *Navy* (London) 15 (February 1910): 35; 18 (November 1913): 322.
"Brazil." *ONI Review* (Washington) 5 (June 1950): 249.
"Brazil." U.S. Naval Institute *Proceedings* 65 (November 1939): 1658.
———. U.S. Naval Institute *Proceedings* 68 (September 1942): 1337–38.
"Brazilian Navy: Long-Range Target Practice." *Monthly Information Bulletin* 5 (15 May 1922): 4–8.
"Breaches of Neutrality." *Shipping Gazette Weekly Summary* 59 (27 November 1914): 758.
Breyer, Siegfried. *Schlachtschiffe und Schlachtkreuzer, 1905.* Munich: J. F. Lehmanns Verlag, 1970.
"British Apology to Chili." U.S. Naval Institute *Proceedings* 41 (May–June 1915): 991–92.
"British Naval Visit to South America." *International Defense Review* (Geneva) 2 (January 1969): 14.
British Vessels Captured or Destroyed by the Enemy. 3 vols. N.p. 1918–19.
Brook, Peter. "The Elswick Cruisers." *Warship International* (Toledo) 7 (Spring 1970): 154–76; 8 (Fall 1971): 246–73; 9 (Fall 1972): 237–53.
Buck, Roger L. "The Role of the Naval Mission in United States–Latin American Relations." Master's thesis, U.S. Naval War College, 1967.
Burns, R. C. "The Brazilian Navy." *Armed Forces Journal International* 113 (December 1975): 27.
Burr, Robert N. *By Reason or Force: Chile and Balance of Power in South America, 1830–1905.* Berkeley: University of California Press, 1967.
Burzio, Humberto F. *Historia del Torpedo y sus Buques en la Armada Argentina, 1874–1900.* Buenos Aires: Departamento de Estudios Históricos Navales, 1968.
Caddick, David. "The Brazilian Navy." *Navy* (London) 26 (May 1921): 144–46.
———. "The Chilian Navy." *Navy* (London) 25 (October 1920): 148–50.
———. "The Peruvian Navy." *Navy* (London) 26 (January 1921): 27–33.

Caillet-Bois, Teodoro. *Historia Naval Argentina.* Buenos Aires: Emecé Editores, 1944.
Campoamor, Clara, and Federico Fernandez Castillejo. *Heroismo Criollo: La Marina Argentina en el Drama Español.* Buenos Aires: Centro Naval, Instituto de Publicaciones Navales, 1983.
Carballo, Pablo Marcos. *Dio y los Halcones.* Buenos Aires: Editorial Abril, 1983.
Cárdenas de la Peña, Enrique. *Educación Naval en México.* 2 vols. México: Talleres Gráficos de la Nación, 1967.
———. *Gesta en el Golfo: La Segunda Guerra Mundial y México.* México: Editorial Primicias, 1966.
———. *Semblanza Marítima de México Independiente y Revolucionario.* 2 vols. México: Secretaria de Marina, 1970.
Cardoso, O. R., R. Kirschbaum, and E. van der Kooy. *Malvinas La Trama Secreta.* Buenos Aires: Sudamericana/Planeta, 1983.
Carranza, Anjel Justiniano. *Campañas Navales de la Republica Argentina.* 2d ed. 4th vol. Buenos Aires: Departamento de Estudios Históricos Navales, 1962.
Carvajal Prado, Patricio. "¿Pudo haber escapado el *Huáscar* el 8 de Octubre de 1879?" *Revista de Marina* (Valparaíso) 76 (1960): 39–46.
"The Case History of a Revolution: The Batista Coup d'État in Cuba." *ONI Review* (Washington) 7 (July 1952): 280–83.
Castro Fox, Robolfo Alberto. "La Tercera Escuadrilla Aeronaval de Caza y Ataque durnate el conflicto del Atlántico Sur, 1982." *Boletin del Centro Naval* 734 (January–March 1983): 1–9.
Cavallo, Miguel Angel. *Puerto Belgrano, hora cero: La marina se subleva.* 4th ed. Buenos Aires: Edit Americana, 1956.
Chile. Archives of the Minister of Foreign Affairs, Santiago. Argentina Catalogue, chamber 3, volume 7.
Chile. Armada. *El Poder Naval Chileno.* 2 vols. Santiago: Alfabeta Impresores, 1985.
Chile. Congreso. Cámara de diputados. *Sesiones.* Santiago: n.p., 19-.
Chile. Congreso. Senado. *Diario de sesiones legislatura.* Santiago: La Nación, n.d.
Chile. Ministerio de relaciónes exteriores. *Memoria.* Santiago: n.d.
"The Chilean Naval Mutiny." *Monthly Information Bulletin* 14 (July–October 1931): 11–20.
"Chilian Battleship for Sale." *Shipping World* 28 (4 March 1903): 215.
Chisholm, Adam. *The Independence of Chile.* Boston: Sherman, French and Co., 1911.
Clowes, William L. *Four Modern Naval Campaigns.* London: Unit Library, 1902.
"Colombian Frigates in the Korean War." *ONI Review* (Washington) 18 (December 1953): 525–50.
Colombo, Jorge Luis. "Operaciones de aviones Super Etendard en la guerra de las Malvinas." *Boletin del Centra Naval* 733 (October–December 1982): 319–30.
"Comando conjunto de las Fuerzas Armadas." *Nación* (Buenos Aires) (20 June 1955): 1.
"Combatant Ship Potential of the Latin American Navies." *ONI Review* (Washington) 17 (December 1962): 543–48.
The Committee of Privy Counsellors. *Falkland Islands Review.* London: Her Majesty's Stationery, 1983.
"Competition for New Destroyers." *Monthly Information Bulletin* 10 (August 1927): 19–29.
Condell, Carlos. "Defensa de nuestro litorial." *Revista de Marina* (Valparaíso) 1 (1885): 134–38.

Conn, Stetson, and Byron Fairchild. *The Framework of Hemispheric Defense.* Vol. 1, *The Western Hemisphere, U.S. Army in World War II.* Washington: Government Printing Office, 1960.
Connell-Smith, Gordon. *The Inter-American System.* London: Oxford University Press, 1966.
Conway's All the World's Fighting Ships. Edited by Robert Gardiner. *1860–1905. 1906–21. 1922–46. 1947–82,* 2 vols. London: Conway Maritime Press.
Correio da Manhã (Rio de Janeiro), 17 July 1917.
Coutinho, Lourival. *O General Góes depõe.* 3d ed. Rio de Janeiro: Coelho Branco, 1956.
Crespo, Jorge. *Brasil: El Ejercito y Marina.* 2 vols. Buenos Aires: Juan Perrotti, 1919.
Cubitt, D. J. "Lord Cochrane and the Chilean Navy (1818–1823), with an Inventory of the Dundonald Papers Relating to His Service with the Chilean Navy." Ph.D. diss., University of Edinburgh, 1974.
Currier, Theodore S. *Los corarios del Río de la Plata.* Faultad de Filosofia y Letras, no. 45. Buenos Aires: Publicaciones del Instituto de Investigaciones Historicas, 1929.
Curtis, William Eleroy. "The South American Yankee." *Harper's New Monthly Magazine* 75 (September 1887): 566.
Dallett, Francis James. "The Creation of the Venezuelan Naval Squadron." *American Neptune* 30 (October 1970): 260–78.
Dalyell, Tam. *Thatcher's Torpedo.* London: Cecil Woolf, 1983.
Davy, Charles Gordon. "La Guerra Quimica." *Revista de Marina* (Callao) 8 (May–June 1923): 293–99.
Dellepiane, Carlos. *Historia militar del Perú.* 2 vols. 4th ed. Lima: Biblioteca del oficial, 1943.
Destéfani, Laurio H. "Bases para los Estudios Marítimos Argentinos." *Del Mar* 111 (May–August 1979): 65–75.
———. "La Conquista del Desierto y la Armada Argentina." *Del Mar* 110 (January–April 1979): 32–44.
———. *Manual de Historia Naval Argentina.* 3d ed. Buenos Aires: Tall. Gráf. de la DIAB, 1980.
———. "La Real Armada Española y la Guerra Naval de la Emancipación Hispanoamericana." *Del Mar* 115 (September–December 1980): 60–74.
Dickens, Paul D. "The Falkland Islands Dispute Between the United States and Argentina." *Hispanic American Historical Review* 9 (November 1929): 471–87.
Dictamen de la Comisión de Marina de la H. Camara de Diputados relativo al estado de las unidades tácticas de la Escuadra Nacional y dependencias de la Marina de Guerra 1915. Lima: Empresa Tipografica, 1915.
Dönitz, Karl. *Memoirs Ten Years and Twenty Days.* London: Weidenfeld and Nicolson, 1958.
Dos Passos, John. *Brazil on the Move.* New York: Doubleday and Co., 1963.
Douds, Andrew J. "The Role of the Brazilian Military, 1954–1965." Seminar report, American University, 14 December 1970.
Duarte, Paulo de Q. *Dias de Guerra no Atlântico Sul.* Rio de Janeiro: Biblioteca do Exército, 1968.
Dulin, Robert O., and William H. Garzke. *Allied Battleships in World War II.* Annapolis: U.S. Naval Institute Press, 1980.
Dulles, John W. F. *Vargas of Brazil.* Austin: University of Texas Press, 1967.
———. *Yesterday in Mexico.* Austin: University of Texas Press, 1972.

Dundonald, Thomas (Lord Cochrane). *Narrative of Services in the Liberation of Chile, Peru, and Brazil.* 2 vols. London: James Ridgeway, 1859.
Eddy, Paul, and Magnus Linklater. *The Falklands War.* London: Sphere Books, 1982.
"Effect of Order of Navy Department, Argentina, in Prohibiting Training of More South American Officers in the U.S. Navy." *Monthly Information Bulletin* 4 (15 July 1921): 35–36.
"Effect of Torpedoes on *Aquidabā.*" *Army and Navy Journal* 31 (11 August 1894): 878.
Eljuri-Yunez S., Antonio R. *La Batalla Naval del Lago de Maracaibo.* 2d ed. Caracas: Impreso en la Oficina Técnica del Ministerio de la Defensa, 1973.
Encina, Francisco Antonio. *Historia de Chile desde la prehistoria hasta, 1891.* 20 vols. Santiago: Editorial Nascimento, 1940–52.
English, Adrian J. *Armed Forces in Latin America.* London: Jane's Publishing Co., 1984.
———. "Chaco War." *War Monthly* 15 (April 1975): 42–48.
———. "The Chaco War." *An Cosantóir* (May 1974): 135–40, (July 1974): 231–34, (August 1974): 281–84, (September 1974): 306–9.
———. "The Chaco War." *Army Quarterly and Defence Journal* 109 (July 1979): 350–58.
———. "Latin American Naval Aviation." *Navy International* 90 (June 1983): 338–43.
"Epitaph for the Cuban Navy." *ONI Review* (Washington) 15 (December 1960): 503–7.
Epstein, Fritz T. "European Military Influence in Latin America," 1941. Unpublished manuscript. Library of Congress.
Etchepareborda, Roberto. *La Revolución Argentina del 90.* Buenos Aires: Edit Eudeba, 1966.
———. *Tres Revoluciones: 1890, 1893, 1905.* Buenos Aires, 1968.
Ethell, Jeffrey, and Alfred Price. *Air War South Atlantic.* London: Sidgwick and Jackson, 1983.
Evening Star (New York), 6 September 1918.
Fermin Pensotti, Mario. "Samuel Guillermo Taber." *Del Mar* 111 (May–August 1979): 29–42.
Ferre, José. "The Armed Forces in Argentine Politics to 1930." Ph.D. diss., University of New Mexico, 1965.
Flint, Charles R. *Memories of an Active Life.* New York: G. P. Putnam's Sons, 1923.
Fortini, Enrique L. "Sobre la Fundación de la Aviación Naval." *Del Mar* 112 (September–December 1979): 40–46.
Fraga, Jorge A. *La Argentina y el Atlántico Sur.* Buenos Aires: Instituto de Publicaciones Navales, 1983.
Freire, Felisbelo. *História da Revolta de 6 de Setembro de 1893.* Brasília: Editora Universidade de Brasilia, 1982.
Froehlick, Richard C. "The United States Navy and Diplomatic Relations with Brazil, 1822–1871." Ph.D. diss., Kent State University, 1971.
Fuenzalida Bade, Rodrigo. *La Armada de Chile.* 2d ed. 4 vols. Santiago: Talleres Empresa Periodística, 1978.
Furer, Julius A. *Administration of the Navy Department in World War II.* Washington: Naval History Division, 1959.
Furlong, William Rea. *Class of 1905, United States Naval Academy.* Annapolis: U.S. Naval Academy, 1930.

Galvez Velarde, Pedro J. "Submarino, minas y brulotes en la Guerra del 79 y sus autores." *Revista de Instituto del Estudios Histórico–Marítimos del Perú* 1 (January–June 1978): 23–36.
Gama, Arthur Oscar Saldanha da. *A Marinha do Brasil na Primeira Guerra Mundial.* Rio de Janeiro: CAPEMI Editora e Gráfica Ltda, 1982.
———. *A Marinha do Brasil na Secunda Guerra Mundial.* Rio de Janeiro: CAPAMI Editora e Gráfica Ltda, 1982.
Garaycochea, León, ed. *Legislación naval.* 18 vols. Lima: Imprenta Segrestan, 1928–45; Imprenta H. C. Rozas, 1946.
García Arroyo, Raziel. "La invasión de Veracruz en 1914." *Revista General de la Armada de México* (April 1964): 5–27.
Garrido, Carlos Miguez. "Fortificações do Brasil." In *Subsidios para a História Marítima do Brasil*, issued by Ministério da Marinha, Divisão de História Marítima. Vol. 3. Rio de Janeiro: Governo Federal, 1940.
"German Plots Revealed." U.S. Naval Institute *Proceedings* 43 (December 1917): 3082.
"German Secret Dispatches Through Sweden." U.S. Naval Institute *Proceedings* 43 (October 1917): 2436–37.
Goebel, Julius. *The Struggle for the Falkland Islands: A Study in Legal and Diplomatic History.* New Haven: Yale University Press, 1927.
Gonçalves, Alberto. "Almirante Jerônimo Francisco Gonçalves." In *Subsidios para a História Marítima do Brasil*, issued by Ministério de Marinha, Divisão de História Marítima. Vol. 4. Rio de Janeiro: Governo Federal, 1942.
González, Antonio E. *La Rebelion de Concepción.* Buenos Aires, 1947.
González Echegaray, R. *La marina mercante y el tráfico marítimo en la guerra civil.* Madrid: Editorial San Martín, 1977.
González Lonzième, Enrique. "Actividades Marítimas en la Antártida." In *Temas de Historia Marítima Argentina.* Buenos Aires: Fundación Argentina de Estudios Marítimos, 1970.
———. *La Armada en la Conquista del Desierto.* Buenos Aires: Editorial Universitaria de Buenos Aires, 1977.
———. *Historia del Centro Naval en su Centenario.* Buenos Aires: Instituto de Publicaciones Navales, 1983.
Gouch, Barry M. *The Royal Navy and the Northwest Coast of North America, 1810–1914.* Vancouver: University of British Columbia, 1971.
Grant, Robert M. "Known Sunk: German Submarine War Losses, 1914–1918." U.S. Naval Institute *Proceedings* 64 (January 1938): 66–77.
"The Great Arms Race." *Time* 88 (11 November 1966): 43.
Greenhalgh, Juvenal. "A Missão Naval *Norte Americana.*" *Diario de Notícias* (Rio de Janeiro) (13 July 1892): 15–16.
"La Guerra del Brazil y sus Ensenanzas Navales." *Revista General de Marina* (Madrid) 35 (1894): 160–64.
Guillen y Tato, Julio F. "La Independencia del Plata en los papeles del Archivo de Marina." *Boletín de Centro Naval* 645 (October–December 1960): 450–75.
Gunther, John. *Inside Latin America.* New York: Harper and Brothers, 1941.
Guzmán Cortés, Leonardo. *Un episodio olvidado de la historia nacional, Julio–Noviembre de 1931.* Santiago: Editorial Bello, 1966.
Haberlein, Jr., Charles R., and Robert L. Scheina. "The Century of Naval Revolution." *Navy International* (January 1980): 14–23.
Haring, Clarence H. *Argentina and the United States.* Boston: World Peace Foundation, 1941.

Hasbrouck, Alfred. *Foreign Legionnaires in the Liberation of South America.* New York: Octagon Books, 1969.
Hastings, Max, and Simon Jenkins. *The Battle for the Falklands.* London: Michael Joseph, 1983.
"A Haytian Naval Engagement." *Army and Navy Journal* 21 (2 February 1884): 553.
Healy, David. "Admiral William B. Caperton and United States Naval Diplomacy in South America, 1917–1919." *Journal of Latin American Studies* 8, part 1 (November 1976): 297–323.
Heinl, Robert D. *Written in Blood.* New York: Houghton Mifflin, 1978.
Hereford, J. D., et al. *United States Military Assistance to Latin America.* Newport: U.S. Naval War College, 1969.
Herring, Hubert. *A History of Latin America.* 3d ed. New York: Alfred A. Knopf, 1968.
Hilton, Stanley E. "Military Influences on Brazilian Economic Policy, 1930–1945: A Different View." *Hispanic American Historical Review* 53 (February 1973): 71–94.
Historia Gráfica de Venezuela. 2 vols. Caracas: Centro Editor, 1977.
Historia Marítima del Perú. Vol. 1. Lima: Editorial Ansonia, 1972.
The History of the United Nations Forces in the Korean War. 5 vols. Seoul: The Ministry of National Defense, n.d.
"En Honor a la Verdad." *Revista de Marina* (Callao) 49 (May–June 1963): 207–26.
Hormazabal, Manuel. *El Canal de Beagle es Territorio Chileno.* Santiago: Editorial del Pacifico, 1970.
Hull, Cordell. *The Memoirs of Cordell Hull.* 2 vols. New York: Macmillan, 1948.
Humphreys, R. A. *Latin America and the Second World War.* 2 vols. London: The Athlone Press, 1981–82.
"The Iconoclast Abroad." *Shipping Illustrated* 33 (31 December 1910): 290.
Iñiquez Vicuña, Antonio. *El golpe de estado y la revolución, primero y siete de enero 1891.* Santiago: Imprenta Victoria, 1891.
Ireland, Gordon. *Boundaries, Possessions, and Conflicts in South America.* Cambridge: Harvard University Press, 1938.
Jane's All the World's Aircraft, 1926. Edited by C. G. Grey and Leonard Bridgman. London: Sampson Low, Marston.
Jane's Fighting Ships, 1916. Edited by Fred T. Jane. London: Sampson Low, Marston. *1931*, edited by Oscar Parks. London: Sampson Low. *1964–65, 1966–67*, and *1972–73*, edited by Raymond Blackman. New York: McGraw-Hill.
Johns, Forrest R. "United We Stood." U.S. Naval Institute *Proceedings* 111 (January 1985): 78–84.
Joint Publications Research Service. "Communiqué Confirms Solidarity." *Translations on Law of the Sea* 88 (22 November 1978): 54.
Jornal do Brasil (Rio de Janeiro), 23 December 1922.
Jose, James R. *An Inter-American Peace Force Within the Framework of the Organization of American States.* Metuchen, N.J.: Scarecrow Press, 1970.
Journal of the American Society of Naval Engineers 4 (1892): 528–29.
Komorowski, Raymond. "Latin America: An Assessment of U.S. Strategic Interest." U.S. Naval Institute *Proceedings* 99 (May 1973): 148–71.
Lagos Trindade, Maria J. *El Poder Naval.* Buenos Aires: L. J. Rosso y Cia, 1921.
Laing, E. A. M. "The Royal Navy on the River Paraná During the Allied Intervention, 1845–1846." *American Neptune* 36 (April 1976): 125–43.
Langer, William L., and S. Everett Gleason. *The Undeclared War, 1940–1941.* New York: Harper and Brothers, 1953.

Langlois Vidal, Luis. *Influencia del poder naval en la historia de Chile, desde 1810 a 1910*. Valparaíso: Imprenta de la Armada, 1911.
La Roerie, Guilleux. "Una misión naval en el Perú, 1905–1914." *Revista de Marina* (Callao) 42 (November–December 1957): 885–909.
"Latin American Navies." *ONI Review* (Washington) 5 (January 1950): 33–35.
"Latin American Trade." *Navy* (Washington) 8 (November 1914): 451–55.
Lavalle y García, Juan Bautista de. *El Perú y la Gran Guerra*. Lima: Imprenta america, 1919.
Lecuna, Vicente, comp., and Harold A. Bierck, Jr., ed. *Selected Writings of Bolivar*. 2 vols. New York: Colonial Press, 1951.
Leigh, Gustavo. "No tolerar el cáncer marxista." *Ercilla* 1991 (26 September–2 October 1973): 17.
Le Masson, Henri. *Du Nautilus (1800) au Redoutable*. Paris: Presses de la Cité, 1969.
Levine, Robert M. *The Vargas Regime: The Critical Years, 1934–38*. New York: Columbia University Press, 1970.
Livermore, Seward W. "Battleship Diplomacy in South America, 1905–1925." *Journal of Modern History* 16 (1944): 31–48.
López, Jacinto. *Historia de la guerra del guano y del salitre; o guerra del Pacífico entre Chile, Bolivia y Perú*. 2 vols. New York: De Laisne and Rossboro, 1931.
López Urrutia, Carlos. *Historia de la Marina de Chile*. Santiago: Editorial Andres Bello, 1969.
McCann, Jr., Frank D. *The Brazilian-American Alliance, 1937–1945*. Princeton: Princeton University Press, 1973.
McClintock, Robert. "Latin America and Naval Power." U.S. Naval Institute *Proceedings* 91 (October 1965): 31–37.
McCloskey, Michael B. "The United States and the Brazilian Naval Revolt, 1893–1894." *Americas* 2 (January 1946): 296–321.
Machuca, Francisco A. *Las Cuatro Compañas de la Guerra del Pacífico*. 4 vols. Valparaíso: Imprenta Victoria, 1927.
McKanna, Clare V. "The *Water Witch* Incident." *American Neptune* 31 (January 1971): 7–18.
Madariaga, Salvador de. *The Rise of the Spanish American Empire*. New York: Macmillan Co., 1947.
Mahan, David. "La Marina de Chile: Proyecto de Ensayo Bibliografico." 2d ed. Valparaíso, 1974.
Manchester Guardian, 15 September 1827.
Manning, William R. *Diplomatic Correspondence of the United States: Inter-American Affairs, 1831–1860*. 12 vols. Washington: Carnegie Endowment for International Peace, 1932–39.
"Marino: Un Portaaviones para la Flota." *Revista de Marina* (Chile) 62 (January–February 1948): 3–12.
Márquez, Alípio. *Vida de Cuartel*. Caracas: Ediciones Garrado, 1977.
Martin, Percy Alvin. *Latin America and the War*. Baltimore: The Johns Hopkins Press, 1925.
Martinez-Hidalgo y Teran, José Maria, ed. *Enciclopedia General del Mar*. 2d ed. 8 vols. Barcelona: Ediciones Garriga, 1968.
Martínez Montero, Homero. *Armada Nacional-Estudio Histórico Biográfico*. Montevideo: Club Naval, 1977.
Martínez V., Rodolfo. *Historia de la Fuerza Aérea de Chile*. 2 vols. N.p., n.d.
"Masacraron al Pueblo Indefenso y Huyeron Cobardemente al Uruguay." *Democracia* (Buenos Aires) (19 August 1955): 3.

Masterson, Daniel. "Soldiers, Sailors, and Apristes: Conspiracy and Power Politics in Peru, 1932–48." In *The Underside of Latin American History*, edited by John F. Bratzel and David Masterson. East Lansing: Michigan State University Press, 1977.
"The Measurement of Mast Vibration on the Tripod Mast During Gun Trials of the Brazilian Battleship *São Paulo*." U.S. Experimental Model Basin, report 10, March 1920. Navy Department Library, Rare Book Room.
Mecham, J. Lloyd. *A Survey of United States–Latin American Relations*. Boston: Houghton Mifflin, 1965.
Meister, Jürg. "Die Flußoperationen der Triple-Allianz gegen Paraguay, 1864–1870." *Marine Rundschau* 69 (October 1972): 594–616; 69 (November 1972): 660–75.
Melo, Rosendo. *Historia de la Marina de Perú*. 3 vols. Lima: El Auxiliar del Comercio, 1907–15.
Mendía, José M., and L. O. Naón. *La revolución del 90*. Buenos Aires: Editorial Artes y Letras, 1927.
Mendonça, Mário F., and Vasconcelos, Alberto. *Repositório de Nomes dos Navios da Esquadra Brasileira*. 3d ed. Rio de Janeiro: Serviço de Documentação, Geral da Marinha, 1959.
Mendoza, Cesar. "Restablecer el orden jurídico." *Ercilla* 1991 (26 September–2 October 1973): 17.
Mercurio (Santiago), 12 October 1931.
Mercurio (Valparaíso), 11 September 1931; 10 October 1931; 17 February 1932; 13 September 1973.
Merino, José Tobibio. "Chile sabrá entender nuestro sacifico." *Ercilla* 1991 (26 September–2 October 1973): 16–17.
"Mexico." U.S. Naval Institute *Proceedings* 59 (December 1933): 1808.
Middendorf, J. William. "The USN's Latin American Partners." *Jane's Naval Review, 1983–84*. Edited by John Moore. London: Jane's Publishing Co., 1983.
Miller, John, ed. *Memoirs of General Miller, in the Service of the Republic of Peru*. 2 vols. London: Longman, Rees, Orme, Brown and Green, 1828–29.
Mitchell, C. Bradford. *Every Kind of Shipwork, A History of Todd Shipyards Corporation, 1916–1981*. New York: Todd Shipyards Corporation, 1981.
Molinari, Nicanor. *Asalto y toma de Pisagua, 2 de Noviembre de 1879*. Santiago: Imprenta Cervantes, 1912.
Molteni, Carlos Alberto. "Malvinas . . . Así lo viví yo." *Boletin del Centro Naval* 736 (July–September 1983): 223–42.
Monteiro Filho, Clemente José. "Comandantes do Corpo de Fuzileiros Navais, Dados Biograficos." In *Subsidios para a História do Brasil*, issued by Ministerío de Marinha, Divisão de História Marítima. Vol. 22. Rio de Janeiro: Imprensa Naval, 1966.
Monthly Information Bulletin 3 (August 1920): 32–34; 4 (May 1921): 90–91; 5 (March 1922): 6–7; 5 (May 1922): 5; 5 (September 1922): 5–13; 6 (March 1923): 42; 6 (April 1923): 47–50, 56; 6 (August 1923): 46; 7 (August 1924): 37–38; 8 (January 1925): 2–3, 16; 8 (August 1924): 37–38; 8 (December 1925): 2–3; 9 (February 1926): 1; 9 (October 1926): 3; 14 (February–March 1931): 6.
Morales Monasterios, Victor Hugo. *Del Porteñazo al Perú*. Caracas: Editorial Domingo Fuentes, 1971.
Morison, Samuel E. History of United States Naval Operations in World War II. 15 vols. Boston: Little, Brown, 1947–62.
"Mutiny in the Peruvian Navy." *Monthly Information Bulletin* 15 (July–October 1932): 19–21.

Nabuco, Jaoquin. *Balmaceda*. Rio de Janeiro: Levzinger, 1895.
Nación (Buenos Aires), 18 May 1968, "Día de la Armada."
National Archives. Dispatches from U.S. Ministers to Chile, 1826–1906. Record Group 48.
———. General Correspondence of the Secretary of the Navy. Record Group 80.
———. General Records of the Department of State. Record Group 59.
———. Naval Records Collection of the Office of Naval Records and Library. Record Group 45.
———. Records of Foreign Service Posts. Record Group 84.
———. Records of the Bureau of Construction and Repair. Record Group 19. Suitland Federal Records Center.
———. Records of the Office of Naval Intelligence. Record Group 38.
Naval War College. *International Law Situations with Solutions and Notes*. Washington: Government Printing Office, 1901–.
Navy (London) 15 (February 1910): 35; 16 (November 1911): 291; 17 (August 1912): 207; 19 (May 1914): 137.
Navy (Washington) 2 (September 1908): 88; 4 (June 1910): 10; 4 (July 1910): 30; 4 (October 1910): 264.
"Navy International Interviews Chile Navy's Chief of Naval Staff." *Navy International* 88 (April 1983): 198.
The Navy League Annual. London: Navy League of Great Britain, 1906–20.
"The Navy Lost." *Newsweek* 61 (15 April 1966): 54.
Nikol, John, and Francis X. Holbrook. "Naval Operations in the Panama Revolution, 1903." *American Neptune* 37 (October 1977): 253–61.
"Notes on Argentine Navy." *Monthly Information Bulletin* 4 (15 February 1921): 52.
Novoa de la Fuenté, *Historia Naval de Chile*. Valparaíso: Imprenta de la Armada, 1944.
Nweihed, Kaldone G. *La Vigencia del Mar.* 2 vols. Caracas: Ediciones de la Universidad Simón Bolívar, 1974.
Olive, Ronaldo S. "Brazil's Naval Air Force." *Jane's Defence Review* 4 (May 1983): 479–89.
———. "U.S. Tries to Improve Military Relations with Brazil." *Jane's Defence Weekly* 1 (3 March 1984): 311.
Olivieri, Anibal O. *Dos veces rebelde*. Buenos Aires, Siglo, 1958.
ONI Review (Washington) 5 (January 1950): 31–33; 6 (January 1951): 34; 7 (December 1952): 492–94; 9 (August 1954): 332; 12 (February 1957): 67.
Operación Rosario. Buenos Aires: Editorial Atlantida, 1984.
"Operational Histories of South American Dreadnought Battleships." *Warship International* 9, no. 4 (1972): 438–39.
Pan American Union, General Secretariat, OAS (Washington, D.C.). *Constitution of Argentina, 1853*. 1968.
———. *Constitution of Brazil, 1967*. 1967.
———. *Constitution of the Republic of Perú, 1933*. 1962.
Paulette A., Miguel. "Aviación para la Marina." *Revista de Marina* (Callao) 33 (January–February 1948): 3–6.
Paz, Armano. *Los servicios de espionaje en la guerra civil de España, 1936–39*. Madrid: Editorial San Martín, 1976.
Perry, Clive, ed. *The Consolidated Treaty Series*. Dobbs Ferry, New York: Oceana Publications, 1969–.
Perú. Ministerio de Relaciones Exteriores. *Boletín*. Lima: 1903–.
"Peru." *ONI Review* (Washington) 8 (June 1953): 300.

Pesce, Eduardo Italo. "A Case for a V/STOL Brazilian Naval Air Arm." U.S. Naval Institute *Proceedings* 109 (March 1983): 127–31.

Pimentel Winz, Antônio. "Plácido de Castroe a Integração do Acre." *Navigator Subsídios para a Historia Marítima do Brasil* 10 (December 1974): 45–66.

Pinochet, Augusto. "Construir una nación de hermanos." *Ercilla* 1991 (26 September–2 October 1973): 16.

Plater, Guillermo D. *Una gran lección*. Buenos Aires: Almafuerte, 1956.

"Political Conditions in Brazil." *Monthly Information Bulletin* 1 (14 November 1919): 63–64.

Pomer, Leon. *Os Conflictos da Bacia do Prata*. São Paulo: Editora Brasiliense, 1979.

Portella Roca, Jorge. "Acción de la Marina de Guerra en el Progresso y Desarrollo en la Selva Peruana." *Revista de Marina* (Callao) 50 (November–December 1964): 670–86.

Posner, Walter H. "American Marines in Haiti, 1915–1922." *Americas* 20 (January 1964): 231–66.

Prizes of War: War Casualties and Vessels and Cargoes Detained. London: Lloyd's, 1916.

"Protest from Argentina." U.S. Naval Institute *Proceedings* 43 (June 1917): 1356.

Pulido Santana, Mariá Trinidad. *La Diplomacia en Venezuela*. Doctoral thesis, Universidad Central de Venezuela, Caracas, 1963.

Quartaruolo, V. Mario. "La Armada y la Revolución de 1890." *Del Mar* 118 (January–June 1982): 57–64.

———. "La Armada y la Revolución de 1893." *Del Mar* 117 (May–December 1981): 31–35.

"Quién es Quién." *Ercilla* 1991 (26 September–2 October 1973): 44–46.

Ratto, Hector Raul, et al. *Sarmiento y la Marina de Guerra*. Buenos Aires: Departamento de Estudios Históricos Navales, 1963.

Rauch, Georg von. "Cruisers for Argentina." *Warship International* 15, no. 4 (1978): 297–317.

"The Recent Engagement Between Peruvian ship *Huscar* and the Two British Ships, *Shah* and *Amethyst*. . . ." *Army and Navy Journal* 14 (21 July 1877): 807.

Revista General de Marina (Madrid) 42 (1898): 820; 62 (1908): 417; 64 (1908): 724; 66 (1910): 309–10.

Reynolds, J. A. *History of the Gulf Sea Frontier*. Miami: Headquarters of the Gulf Sea Frontier, 1946.

Rice, Desmond, and Arthur Gavshon. *The Sinking of the* Belgrano. London: Secker and Warburg, 1984.

"River Plate News." *Fairplay* 68 (31 May 1917): 915, (7 June 1917): 947.

Robacio, Carlos Hugo. "El Batallón de Infantería de Marina N°5 en las Malvinas." *Boletín del Centro Naval* 735 (April–June 1983): 139–62.

Robinson, Walton L. "The Brazilian Navy in the World War." U.S. Naval Institute *Proceedings* 62 (December 1936): 1712–20.

Rodriguez Sepúlveda, Juan Agustín. *Crónicas Nacionales y Navales*. Valparaíso: Imprenta de la Armada, 1953.

———. "El Portaaviones *Roosevelt* y la aviación naval." *Revista de Marina* (Chile) 73 (January–February 1957): 49–50.

———. "Relaciones Navales con Gran Britaña." *Revista de Marina* (Chile) 75 (March–April 1959): 135–37.

Rogers, Francis Millet. "Officer Ranks of the Armed Forces of the Western Hemisphere." *Bulletin of the Pan American Union* (January 1945): 16–22.

Rohwer, Jürgen. "Admiral Gorshkov and the Influence of History upon Sea Power." U.S. Naval Institute *Proceedings* 107 (May 1981): 150–73.

———. *Axis Submarine Successes, 1939–45*. Annapolis: Naval Institute Press, 1983.

———. "Der Falkland-Malvinas Konflikt." *Marine-Rundschau* 79 (July 1982): 382–87.
———. "Operações Navais da Alemanha no Litoral do Brasil durante a Segunda Guerra Mundial." *Navigator Subsidios para a Historia Maritima do Brasil* 18 (January–December 1982): 3–38.
Rohwer, Jürgen, and Gerhard Hümmelchen. *Chronology of the War at Sea, 1939–1945*. 2 vols. New York: Arco Publishing Co., 1973.
Rojas M., Francisco E. *Administración naval de Chile comparada: Su desarrollo, evolución y organización: 1817–1932*. Santiago: Imprenta Chile, 1934.
Román Bazurto, Enrique. *Proas en Tres Mares*. Bogotá: Imprenta de las Fuerzas Militares, n.d.
Romero P., Fernando. *Notas para una Historia de la Marina Fluvial de Guerra*. Lima: La Punta, 1959.
Rouquié, Alain. *Poder Militar y Sociedad Política en la Argentina*. 2 vols. Buenos Aires: EMECE Editores, 1982–83.
Ruge, Friedrich. *Der Seekrieg: The German Navy's Story, 1939–1945*. Annapolis: Naval Institute Press, 1957.
Salas, Ramon. *Historia del ejército popular de la República*. 2 vols. Madrid: Editora Nacional, 1973.
Salles Oliveira, Armando de. *Diagrama da una situação política manifestos políticos do exílio*. São Paulo: Editora Renasçenca, 1945.
Sanchez Lamego, Miguel A. *La invasión española de 1829*. México: Editorial Jus, 1971.
Sandoval Hernández, Ariel. "Las acciones de corso en aguas chilenas durante la Primera Guerra Mundial." *Revista de Marina* (Valparaíso) 87 (1970): 731–33.
Sapunar Peric, Pedro. "Los Precursores Submarinos Chileno: Peruanos del Siglo XIX." *Revista de Marina* (Valparaíso) 87 (675): 176–80.
Sater, William F. "The Abortive Kronstadt: The Chilean Naval Mutiny of 1931." *Hispanic American Historic Review* 60 (May 1980): 239–68.
Scavarda, Levy. "Os Submarinos no Brasil: Notas para a História." *Navigator* 7 (June 1973): 43–69.
Schaeffer, Heinz. *U-boat 977*. New York: Ballantine Books, 1952.
Scheina, Robert L. "The Forgotten Fleet: The Mexican Navy on the Eve of War, 1845." *American Neptune* 30 (January 1970): 46–55.
———. "Indigenous Latin American Sea Power, 1890–1974." Ph.D. diss., Catholic University of America, 1976.
———. "Latin American Naval Purpose." *U.S. Naval Institute Proceedings* 103 (September 1977): 116–19.
———. "Latin American Navies." *U.S. Naval Institute Proceedings* 107 (March 1981): 22–27; 108 (March 1982): 30–34; 109 (March 1983): 30–34; 110 (March 1984): 30–35; 111 (March 1985): 32–37; 112 (March 1986): 32–36.
———. "Latin American Navies: Their Future." *Navy International* 86 (September 1981): 516–20.
———. "Seapower Misused: Mexico at War, 1846–48." *Mariner's Mirror* 57 (no. 2, 1971): 203–14.
———. "South American Navies: Who Needs Them?" *U.S. Naval Institute Proceedings* 104 (February 1978): 61–66.
———. *U.S. Coast Guard Cutters and Craft of World War II*. Annapolis: Naval Institute Press, 1982.
Scroggs, William O. "William Walker and the Steamship Corporation in Nicaragua." *American Historical Review* 10 (July 1905): 797–811.
Sears, John H., and B. W. Wells. *U.S. Office of Naval Intelligence: The Chilean Revolu-*

tion of 1891. Information from Abroad War Series, no. 4. Washington, D.C.: Government Printing Office, 1893.
Selser, Gregorio. "¿Argentina, para qué sirven las misiones militares?" *Marcha* (Montevideo) 35 (11 January 1974): 16–17.
Sequeira, Sebastián, Carlos Cal, and Cecilia Calatayud. *Aviación Naval Argentina.* Buenos Aires: SS and CC Ediciones, 1984.
Shipping Illustrated 49 (26 December 1914): 238; 53 (18 December 1915): 284; 59 (26 May 1917): 212; 60 (25 August 1917): 189.
"Shipping Policy of South America." *Marine Journal* 39 (7 April 1917): 3.
Simpson, Lloyd P. "The German-Haitian Naval Clash of 1902." *Warship International* (Toledo) 3 (Summer 1966): 216.
"Sinking of the Valentine." *Shipping Gazette Weekly Summary* 59 (4 December 1914): 768.
"Síntesis Histórica de la Infantería de Marina." *Del Mar* 112 (September–December 1979): 61–64.
Skidmore, Thomas E. *Politics in Brazil, 1930–1964.* New York: Oxford University Press, 1967.
Smith, J. Russell. *Influence of the Great War upon Shipping.* New York: Oxford University Press, 1919.
Smith, Joseph. "American Diplomacy and the Naval Mission to Brazil, 1917–1930." *Inter-American Economic Affairs* 35 (Summer 1981): 73–91.
Somervell, Philip D. "Anglo-Chilean Naval Relations from Independence to 1932: An Exploratory Essay." Master's thesis, University of London, 1980.
———. "Naval Affairs in Chilean Politics, 1910–1932." *Journal of Latin American Studies* 16, part 2 (November 1984): 381–402.
Sommi, Luis V. *La revolución del 90.* 2d ed. Buenos Aires: Ediciones Pueblos de América, 1957.
Sosa Ríos, Ricardo. *Mar de Leva.* Caracas: Edreca Editores, 1979.
"South America." U.S. Naval Institute *Proceedings* 43 (December 1917): 3082.
"South American Naval Possibilities." *Shipping Illustrated* 15 (7 April 1906): 17.
"South American Sea Power." *Navy* (Washington) 5 (June 1911): 29.
Souza e Silva, Augusto de. *O Almirante Saldanha, Comandante en chefe na revolta de Armada: Reminiscencias de um revoltoso.* Rio de Janeiro: Editora A. Norte, 1940.
Spain. Ministerio de Marina. *Estado General de la Real Armada.* Isla de León: Oficina de Franciscio de Paula Perín, 1811.
———. *Memoria leída a las Cortes el 5 de mayo de 1822.* Madrid: Imprenta Nacional, 1822.
———. *Memoria leída a las Cortes por el Secretario del Destacho de Marina en 4 de mayo de 1814.* Madrid: Imprenta Naciónal, 1814.
Spears, W. O. "U.S. Naval Missions." N.d. Navy Department Library. Typescript.
Spector, Ronald. "Roosevelt, the Navy and the Venezuela Controversy: 1902–3." *American Neptune* 32 (October 1972): 257–63.
Speratti, Juan. *Historia de la armada nacional en le período 1925–1937.* Asunción: Tall. Gráf. de la Escuela Técnica Salesiana, 1972.
The Statesman's Year-Book: Statistical and Historical Annual of the States of the World. New York: St. Martin's Press, 1864–1919.
Storni, Segundo R. *Intereses Argentinos en el Mar.* Buenos Aires: A. Moen y hermanos, 1916.
Taibo, X. I. "Brazil's Navy Proceeds Independently." *Defence* 14 (July 1983): 409–15.

Theberge, James D., ed. *Soviet Seapower in the Caribbean: Political and Strategic Implications.* New York: Praeger Publishers, 1972.
Thomas, Hugh. *Cuba: The Pursuit of Freedom.* New York: Harper and Row, 1971.
Thompson, Arthur. *Guerra Civil do Brasil: Vida e Morte do Alm: Saldanha da Gama.* Rio de Janeiro: Editora Ravaro, 1934.
Thursfield, H. G., ed. *Brassey's Naval Annual, 1948.* New York: Macmillan, 1948.
Times (London), 27 May 1902.
Torwil [pseud.]. "La Rebusca del *Dresden.*" *Revista de Marina* (Valparaíso) 76 (1960): 376–89.
Trejo, Hugo. *La Revolución no ha terminado.* Valencia, Venezuela: Vadell Hermanos Editores, 1977.
"Trials of Brazilian Submarine *Humayta* [sic] Being Built in Italy." *Monthly Information Bulletin* 10 (September 1928): 895.
Trombetta, César. "Ocupación de las Islas Georgias durante el Conflicto del Atlántico Sur en 1982." *Boletín del Centro Naval* 735 (April–June 1983): 107–15.
Túrolo, Carlos M. *Malvinas Testimonio de su Gobernador.* Buenos Aires: Editorial Sudamericana, 1983.
Ugarteche, Pedro. "Para la historia marítima del Perú: Adquisición de los cruceros [sic] *Guisse* y *Villar.*" *El Comercio* (Lima), 21 March 1968, 3–4.
―――. *Sánchez Cerro papeles y recuerdos de un presidente de Perú.* 3 vols. Lima: Editorial Universitaria, 1969.
Unwin, P. J. "Brazil: A Maritime Role in the South Atlantic." *Navy International* 81 (December 1976): 4–6.
Uruguay. Ministerio de Relaciones Exteriores. *Uruguayan Blue Book.* London: Hutchinson, 1940.
U.S. Congress. House. Committee on Foreign Affairs. *First Semiannual Report on the Mutual Assistance Program.* 81st Congress, 1950. Document 613.
U.S. Congress. Senate. *Battleships for the Argentine Republic.* 62nd Cong., 1st sess., 1911. Document 2.
U.S. Congress. Senate. Committee on Appropriations. *United States–Latin American Relations.* 86th Cong., 1960. Document 125.
―――. *Hearings Before the Committee on Foreign Relations on the Foreign Assistance Program.* 89th Cong., 1st sess., 1965.
―――. *Hearings Before the Special Committee to Investigate the Munitions Industry.* 73rd Cong., 1934. S. res. 206, pt. 1.
―――. "Naval War College of Brazil." In *Congressional Record.* 63rd Cong., 1914.
U.S. Department of Commerce. *Report of the Bureau of Standards to the Bureau of Ordnance, Navy Department, on the Experimental Firing of the Brazilian Battleship São Paulo, February 1920.* Washington, 1921.
U.S. Department of State. *Battleships for Argentine Republic.* A message from the president of the United States, transmitting the answer of the secretary of state to a Senate resolution concerning the construction of battleships for Argentina. Washington: Government Printing Office, 1911.
―――. *Foreign Relations of the United States, 1938.* Vol. 5. Washington: Government Printing Office, 1938. *1942.* Government Printing Office, 1942.
―――. *The Statutes at Large of the United States of America.* Vol. 41, *May 1919–March 1921.* Washington: Government Printing Office, 1921.
―――. *United States Treaties.* Vol. 3, pt. 2. Washington: Government Printing Office, 1952.
U.S. Department of the Navy. *Annual Report of the Secretary of the Navy, 1921.* Washington: Government Printing Office, 1921.

———. Bureau of Navigation. *The International Code of Signals*. American ed. Washington: Government Printing Office, 1889.

———. Commander in Chief, U.S. Atlantic Fleet. Vol. 1, "Commander in Chief, U.S. Atlantic Fleet." Typescript. N.d. Vol. 11, "Commander, South Atlantic Force." Typescript. N.d. Navy Department Library, Washington, D.C.

———. Historical section. *Dictionary of American Naval Fighting Ships*. 8 vols. Washington: Government Printing Office, 1959–86.

———. Historical section. *Naval Chronology, World War II*. Washington: Government Printing Office, 1955.

———. Historical section. "U.S. Naval Administration in World War II." 2 vols. Unpublished manuscript. N.d.

———. "Importance of U.S. Naval Missions in Latin America, March 17 1959." Memorandum from chief of naval operations for distribution. Vertical file, Navy Department Library, Washington, D.C.

———. Office of Naval Intelligence. *Information from Abroad*. Washington: Government Printing Office, 1890–1902.

U.S. Naval Institute *Proceedings* 44 (October 1918): 2376–77; 63 (April 1937): 587; 65 (February 1939): 265; 66 (November 1940): 1952; 68 (October 1942): 1486, 1489; 69 (October 1943): 1391; 72 (September 1946): 1261; 73 (November 1947): 1406–7; 74 (June 1948): 781.

Valdizán Gamio, José. "El Cincuentenario de Nuestra Fuerza Submarina." *Revista de Marina* (Callao) 47 (July–August 1961): 437–45.

———. "El *Huáscar* de Nuestra Amazonía (1911)." *Revista de Marina* (Callao) 52 (July–August 1966): 547–53.

———. "La Operación Unitas VIII." *Revista de Marina* (Callao) 56 (January–February 1970): 34–55.

———. *Tradiciones Navales Peruanas*. 2 vols. Lima: Marina de Guerra, 1969.

Vanterpool, Alan. "The *Riachuelo*." *Warship International* (Toledo) 6 (Spring 1969): 140–41.

Varela, Luis Vicente. *Defensa de los últimos pactos internacionales*. Buenos Aires: Imp. de Prodel, Carranza and cia, 1902.

Vargas, Francisco Alejandro. *Historia naval de Venezuela*. Caracas: Publicaciones de las Fuerzas Navales de la República de Venezuela, 1964.

———. *Nuestros Próceres Navales*. Caracas: Editorial Grafolít, 1948.

Vargas Valenzuela, José. *Tradición Naval del Pueblo Bolivia*. La Paz: Editorial Los Amigos del Libro, 1974.

Vegas G., Manuel I. *Historia de la Marina del Perú, 1821–1924*. Lima: Impreso en los Talleres Gráficos de la Imprenta de la Marina, 1973.

"23 de enero: 25 años." *El Diario de Caracas*. Special edition, 23 January 1983.

"Venezuela." U.S. Naval Institute *Proceedings* 72 (February 1946): 331.

Vergara Montero, Ramón. *Por rutas extraviadas*. Santiago: Imprenta Universitaria, 1933.

Vidigal, Armando Amorim Ferreira. *A Evolução do Pensamento Estratégico Naval Brasileiro*. Rio de Janeiro: Biblioteca do Exército Editora, 1985.

Vinock, Eli. "UNITAS: A South American Perennial." U.S. Naval Institute *Proceedings* 110 (July 1984): 124–26.

Vio Valdivieso, Horacio. *Manual de Historia Naval de Chile*. Valparaíso: Imprenta de la Armada, 1972.

"Visits to the Navies of South America." In *Brassey Naval Annual, 1939*. Edited by H. G. Thursfield. London: William Clowes and Sons, 1939.

Vivian, James F. "United States Policy During the Brazilian Naval Revolt, 1893–

94: The Case for American Neutrality." *American Neptune* 41 (October 1981): 245-61.
Volta Gaona, Enrique. *La Revolución del 47*. Asuncion: Editora Litocolor, 1982.
Von Schroeders, Edgardo. *El delegado del Gobierno y el motín de la escuadra*. Santiago: Sociedad Imprenta y Litografía Universo, 1933.
Warren, Harris G. *The Sword Was Their Passport: A History of American Filibustering in the Mexican Revolution*. Baton Rouge: Louisiana State University Press, 1943.
"We Cannot Fight the Chilian Navy." *Army and Navy Journal* 23 (1 August 1885): 16.
Wells, Tom Henderson. "The Battle of Campeche." *American Neptune* 21 (July 1961): 216-21.
Wheelock, Phyllis DeKay. "An American Commodore in the Argentine Navy." *The American Neptune* 6 (January 1946): 5-18.
Wilgus, A. Curtis, ed. *Argentina, Brazil, and Chile Since Independence*. Washington, D.C.: The George Washington University Press, 1935.
Wilson, Herbert W. *Ironclads in Action: A Sketch of Naval Warfare from 1855 to 1895*. 2 vols. Boston: Little, Brown and Co., 1896.
"Withdrawal of English Officials from Chile." *Monthly Information Bulletin* 4 (15 July 1922): 21-22.
Wood, Bryce. "External Restraints on the Good Neighbor Policy." *Inter-American Economic Affairs* 16 (Autumn 1962): 3-24.
―――. *The United States and Latin American Wars, 1932-1942*. New York: Columbia University Press, 1966.
Worcester, Donald. *Sea Power and Chilean Independence*. Gainesville: University of Florida Press, 1962.
The World's Missile Systems. 2d ed. General Dynamics, Pomona Division, 1975.
Ynsfrán, Edgar L. *La irrupción moscovita en la Marina Paraguaya*. Asunción, 1947.
Ynsfran, Pablo M. *La expedición norteamericana contra el Paraguay, 1858-1859*. 2 vols. Mexico and Buenos Aires, 1954-58.
Young, Jordan M. *The Brazilian Revolution of 1930 and the Aftermath*. New Brunswick: Rutgers University Press, 1967.
Zanabria Zamudio, Rómulo. *Luchas y Victorias por la Definición de una Frontera*. Lima: Impreso en Editorial Jurídica, 1969.
Zar, Marcos. "Aviación de Nuestra Marina y para Nuestra Marina." *Revista de Marina* (Callao) 16 (September–October 1931): 543-60; 16 (November–December 1931): 703-25.
Zig Zag (Santiago), 10 August 1957.
Zumwalt, Elmo R. *On Watch: A Memoir*. New York: Quadrangle/New York Times Co., 1976.

Interviews

The following members of the Argentine navy were interviewed by the author during trips to Argentina. Ranks and positions listed were those held during the Malvinas War.

Agote, Captain Carmelo, Commander Jorge Czsar, and Commander Luis Vasquez. Espora, 13 September 1982. The captain and commanders presented an overview of naval air operations during the Malvinas War.
Alfonso, Commander Carlos Luis, commanding officer of the corvette *Guerrico*. Puerto Belgrano, 15 September 1982.
Allara, Rear Admiral Gualter, commander, Task Force 79. Buenos Aires, 30 Sep-

tember 1983. The rear admiral provided information concerning the chronology of the movements of the *25 de Mayo*.
Azcueta, Commander Fernando María, commanding officer of the submarine *San Luis*. Mar del Plata, 22 September 1983.
Bonzo, Captain Héctor, commanding officer of the cruiser *General Belgrano*. Buenos Aires, 8 September 1982. The captain supplied information on the events in his ship.
Bousson, Lieutenant Omar, pilot of the Alouette helicopter used in the capture of the South Georgias. Espora, 15 September 1982.
Büsser, Rear Admiral Carlos, commandant of the Argentine marine corps. Baterías, 14 September 1982. The rear admiral provided information on marine corps activities in the recapture of the Malvinas.
Carrega, Lieutenant Jorge Carlos, commanding officer of the coast guard cutter *Rio Iguazu*. Buenos Aires, 7 September 1982.
Castro Fox, Lieutenant Commander Rodolfo, commanding officer of the Third Attack Squadron. Espora, 13 September 1982. The lieutenant commander gave information on the operations of his squadron.
Coli, Captain Carlos, and Commander Jorge Acosta. Puerto Belgrano, 15 September 1982. The captain and commander presented an overview of fleet operations.
Colombo, Commander Jorge, commanding officer of the First Attack Squadron. Espora, 15 September 1982. The commander provided information on the composition and operations of his squadron.
Fernandez Osuna, Lieutenant Oscar Cesar, operations officer of the submarine *Santa Fe*. Mar del Plata, 21 September 1983. The lieutenant provided information on the operations of his submarine.
Gómez, Lieutenant Pedro Ernesto, a coast guard Skyvan pilot. Buenos Aires on 7 September 1982.
González Llanos, Lieutenant Commander Juan Carlos, naval officer on board the *Narwal*. Buenos Aires, 30 September 1983. The lieutenant commander provided most of the account of the attack on the *Narwal*.
Ianusso, Lieutenant Commander Juan Carlos, commanding officer of the *Formosa*. Buenos Aires, 30 September 1983. The lieutenant commander gave details concerning the attack on the *Formosa*.
Molteni, Lieutenant Commander Carlos, commanding officer of the Second Attack Squadron. Buenos Aires, 10 September 1982. The lieutenant commander supplied information on the composition and operations of his squadron.
Mozzarelli, Captain Antonio José, commanding officer of the Malvinas Support Force. Buenos Aires, 30 September 1983.
Otero, Rear Admiral Eduardo, commander of naval forces in the Malvinas. Buenos Aires, 8 September 1982.
Pereiro, Commander Norberto, commanding officer of the First Logistics Squadron. Buenos Aires, 10 September 1982. The commander gave information on the composition and operations of his squadron.
Pérez, Commander Julio, in charge of the preparation and operation of the Exocet MM38 missiles placed in the Malvinas. Buenos Aires, 9 September 1982. The commander supplied information on the operations of the Exocet.
Robacio, Commander Carlos, commanding officer of the Fifth Marine Battalion. Buenos Aires, 9 September 1982.
Santillán, Lieutenant Commander Hugo, second in command of Second Marine Battalion. Baterías, 16 September 1982.

Tejo, Commander José Luis, commanding officer of the destroyer *Santísima Trinidad*. Puerto Belgrano, 13 September 1982.

Vázquez, Álvaro, commanding officer of the *Francisco de Gurruchaga* during the rescue of survivors from the *General Belgrano*. In the *Santísima Trinidad*, 20 September 1983.

Vázquez, Commander Luis C., commanding officer of Naval Air Squadron No. 2. Espora, 15 September 1982. The commander provided background on Neptune operations.

Index

THIS BOOK is organized by topic, and thus not always chronologically. To aid those interested in the history of a particular navy, the index entry for each navy is arranged chronologically.

Small navies have different concerns from those of large ones. The subjects of special interest to Latin American navies, such as blockades, force in being, and interpreting the national political will, have been given special emphasis in the index.

This work covers a period of more than 175 years; much territory and many ships have changed hands within this time. Thus, when citing a city or province, I have also cited the country to which it belonged *at the time*. If it was held or ownership was actively disputed by more than one nation, each nation is cited. For example, "Monterey (Mexico/United States)" means that at least the first time it is cited, Monterey is a Mexican possession, the last time, a U.S. possession. I have used a similar method when listing ships. For example, "*Huascar* (Peruvian/Chilean navy seagoing monitor)" means that the ship first served in the Peruvian navy, then in that of Chile.

Many Latin American warships are named for dates commemorating special events. In a few cases, the navy in question spells out the numeral, but more frequently it uses an Arabic numeral. Ships whose names begin with Arabic numerals have been placed at the end of the index. In some instances, I have assigned ships of the same name and type a Roman numeral in a bracket to distinguish them. For example, *Marcilio Dias* [I] and [II] are two different ships.

Abtao, Battle of, 30, 345
Abtao (Chilean navy warship), 33
Acapulco, México, 3, 167
Acary (Brazilian merchant ship), 95, 356
Achilles (British navy frigate), 312; (British navy light cruiser), 148
Acosta Bello, Octavio (Venezuelan navy), 225
Acre (Brazilian navy river gunboat), 92
Acre Province (Bolivia/Perú), 118
Actée (French navy destroyer), 131
Acul, Haití, 39
Adelheid (German merchant ship), 357
Admiral Graf Spee (German navy pocket battleship), 147–48, 163, 365
Adolpho de Barros (Brazilian navy dispatch boat), 352
Aeritalia-type aircraft, 198
Aeromacchi-type aircraft, 198
Aerospatiale-type aircraft, 198
Africa, 95–96, 148, 152, 356
Agincourt (British navy dreadnought), 135, 354
Agote, Carmelo I. Astesiano (Argentine navy), 383
Agradable Bay, 284
Aguarico River, 119
Águila (Chilean navy brigantine), 5; (Mexican navy warship), 15
Aguilar Ruiz, José (Cuban navy), 206
Aguiles (Chilean navy brigantine), 28
Aguirre, Elias (Peruvian navy), 346
Aguja, Perú, 345
Airport Development Project, 151
Ajax (British navy light cruiser), 147–48
Alacrity (British navy frigate), 268
Alagoas, Brazil, 366
Alagoas (Brazilian merchant ship), 351; (Brazilian navy monitor), 25–26; (Brazilian navy destroyer), 92
Alcalá de Henares, treaty, 343
Aldea (Chilean navy destroyer), 107, 110–11, 113
Aldea, Juan de Dios (Chilean navy), 33
Alejandro I (Spanish navy ship of the line), 6
Alejandro Acosta, Juan (Dominican navy), 38
Alejandro Palma, Jorge Julio (Argentine navy), 212
Alencar, Alexandrino Faria de (Brazilian navy), 80, 92
Alessandri Palma, Arturo (president of Chile), 199
Alessandri Rodriguez, Jorge (president of Chile), 200
Alexandre (German navy warship), 306

Alferez Sobral (Argentine navy tug), 236, 245, 253–54, 267, 383
Alfonso, Carlos Luis (Argentine navy), 381
Alger (U.S. Navy destroyer), 329
Algeria, 343
Algoma (Canadian navy corvette), 369
Allara, Gualter (Argentine navy), 236, 248–50
Allende, Salvador (president of Chile), 193, 233, 296, 364, 378
Allen M. Sumner (U.S. Navy destroyer), 221
Allies: World War I, 89–90, 92, 94, 96–98, 135; World War II, 144–45, 148, 151–53, 155, 160–62, 168, 170
Almirante Brión (Colombian navy frigate), 198; (Venezuelan navy frigate), 222, 376
Almirante Brown (Argentine navy central battery corvette), 57, 191, 347, 350; (Argentine navy heavy cruiser), 143, 183, 194
Almirante Clemente (Venezuelan navy frigate), 230–32, 376; class, 218
Almirante Cochrane (Chilean navy ironclad), 31–36, 59, 61, 345–47; (Chilean navy dreadnought), 322, 355
Almirante Condell (Chilean navy torpedo gunboat), 61–62, 142; (Chilean navy destroyer), 103
Almirante García (Venezuelan navy frigate), 222, 376
Almirante Grau (Peruvian navy scout cruiser), 104, 115–16, 122, 130, 350, 359
Almirante Guise (Peruvian navy destroyer), 122
Almirante Irizar (Argentine navy icebreaker), 190, 236, 238, 241, 243, 258, 287
Almirante Latorre (Chilean navy dreadnought), 85–86, 107–08, 110, 112–14, 139, 164, 199, 322, 355, 359
Almirante Lezo (Colombian navy gunboat), 40
Almirante Lynch (Chilean navy torpedo gunboat), 61–62, 64–65, 142; class (Chilean navy destroyers), 355
Almirante Padilla (Colombian navy frigate), 177–78
Almirante Simpson (Chilean navy submarine), 358; (Chilean navy torpedo boat), 142
Almirante Stewart (Argentine merchant ship), 336
Almirante Storni (Argentine navy destroyer), 184
Almirante Tamandaré (Brazilian navy protected cruiser), 68, 74

INDEX   409

Almirante Villar (Peruvian navy destroyer), 122
Alonso (Bolivian merchant launch), 118
Alouette-type helicopter, 201, 238, 258, 261, 288, 381
Altagarcia Modesto, José (Dominican navy), 179
Altamirano Domínguez, Enrique (Mexican navy), 330
Althaus, Juan (Peruvian navy), 115
Alvena (? merchant ship), 40
Amapá (Brazilian navy river gunboat), 92
Amatlán (Mexican merchant tanker), 168, 330
Amazonas (Brazilian merchant ship), 351; (Brazilian navy destroyer), 92; (Brazilian navy sail frigate), 22
Amazonas State (Brazil), 67, 92, 118
Amazon River, 77, 117–18, 121–22, 124, 140, 155
America (Norwegian merchant ship), 352
América (Panamanian merchant ship), 768; (Peruvian navy river gunboat), 121, 360; (Peruvian navy steam corvette), 30, 345
Americano (Argentine navy warship), 304; (Italian merchant tanker), 330
Amethyst (British navy warship), 31
Amherst (Canadian navy corvette), 369
Amphibious warfare: Nineteenth-century developments in, 54, 188; during Mexican–American War (1846–48), 15, 351; at Paysandú (1865), 20, 188, 351; during Chilean Civil War (1891), 62, 64–66, 188, 351; lack of during Brazilian Civil War (1893–94), 76; developments in (1942–45), 189–90; used against Perón's forces (1955), 216; first UNITAS exercise (1981), 176; in recapture of the Malvinas (1982), 236–41; landing at San Carlos (1982), 273–74
Anaya, Jorge (Argentine navy), 183, 369, 378
Ancón, 28, 36; Treaty of, 37
Andean War, 28–29
Andes Mountains, 5, 44, 61, 117, 123, 126, 185, 223
Andrade (British navy auxiliary cruiser), 352
Anegada Passage, 180
Angamos, Battle of, 34–35, 129, 345
Angamos (Chilean navy armed merchant ship), 35; (Chilean transport), 49
Angostura, Paraguay, 26
Angoteros (Ecuador/Perú), 119–20
Angulo, Pedro (Chilean navy), 28
Aníbal Benécolo (Brazilian merchant ship), 152

Anjambaby (Brazilian/Paraguayan navy gunboat), 20, 24–25
Annapolis (U.S. Navy gunboat), 317
Ansaldo, Italy, 49–51, 136, 164, 218
Antarctic, 6, 52, 162, 183–84, 187, 242, 280, 380–81
Antarctic Treaty, 183–84, 242, 370
Antelope (British navy frigate), 276, 289, 334, 385
Antigua Island, 306
Antiquois (Colombian navy destroyer), 122
Antisubmarine rocket, 175, 369
Antisubmarine warfare, 95, 98, 155, 160, 168, 170, 172, 174–75, 198, 200, 245, 251
Antofagasta (Bolivia/Chile), 32–33, 64, 103, 354
Antonio João (Brazilian navy gunboat), 25
Antonio Maceo (Cuban navy gunboat), 206–7, 373
Antrim (British navy destroyer), 276
Apristas (Peruvian political party), 115–16, 359
Apure River, 4
Apurimac (Peruvian navy school ship), 37, 345
Aquidabã (Brazilian navy battleship), 67–69, 72–76, 80, 351
Aquin, Haití, 38
Arabutá (Brazilian merchant ship), 365
Aracaju (Brazilian merchant ship), 197
Aragao, Candido de Costa (Brazilian navy), 208
Aragua (Venezuelan navy destroyer), 222
Araguary (Brazilian navy torpedo boat), 351
Aranha, Oswaldo (Brazilian ambassador to the United States), 137
Arara (Brazilian merchant ship), 222
Araraquara (Brazilian merchant ship), 152
Araripe, Zilmar de (Brazilian navy), 372
Aratu, Brazil, 366–67
Araucano (Chilean navy tender), 109, 112–13
Arauco (Chilean merchant steamer), 29
Araujo, Oavo de (Brazilian navy), 160
Arca, José Cesar (Argentine navy), 274
Arcona (German navy cruiser), 319
Ardent (British navy frigate), 274, 289, 341
Ardita (Italian navy gunboat), 318
Arecutacua, Paraguay, 205
Aréthusa (French navy cruiser), 69
Argentina, 2–3, 17–27, 42–52, 54–59, 72, 74, 76, 82–89, 92, 100–102, 120, 128, 137–48, 151–52, 158–59, 161–63, 173–80, 183–95, 203, 205,

Argentina (*continued*)
209–17, 234–89, 294–99, 304–5, 323, 325, 343–44, 354, 364–65
Argentine air force, 179, 187, 195, 210–17, 244–45, 253, 259, 263–64, 273, 276–77, 279–80, 282, 284, 288, 384
Argentine army, 22–27, 54–59, 82–84, 179, 187, 194, 209–17, 235–36, 238, 243, 284–88, 350
Argentine coast guard, 243, 245, 258–61, 381
Argentine fishing fleet, 244–45
Argentine marine corps, 179, 185–87, 189, 191–92, 209–17, 236–43, 255, 258, 265, 284–89, 371, 384
Argentine merchant marine, 100–101, 158–59, 162, 244–45, 356
Argentine navy: ranks (nineteenth and twentieth centuries), 293; wars of independence (1814–16), 2–3, 191, 343; war with Brazil (1825–27), 17–18, 344; seized by U.S. Navy (1844), 18; seizes Uruguayan warship (1863), 19; warships captured at Corrientes (1865), 20; as a riverine force (1870s), 45; sails for Patagonia (1878), 45; interest in torpedoes (1870s), 46; foreigners in fleet (1876), 140; gains experience in Patagonia (1880s), 46; acquisition race with Chile (1880s–90s), 46–52; units rebel (1890), 55–57, 294; foreign navies intervene (1890), 56; units rebel (1893), 57–59, 294; and the submarine (1890s), 47–48; rendezvous with Chilean fleet (1899), 49; limits acquisitions (1902), 51–52; acquires dreadnoughts (1908–15), 82–86, 354; acquires torpedo tubes from United States (1910), 83; early problems with dreadnoughts (1912), 84; attempts to enforce neutrality (1914–18), 100–102; receives submarine training in United States (1917), 140; dreadnoughts inactive (1920s), 86; attitude toward missions (1920s), 139–40; receives first submarines (1920s), 145; significantly increases (1920s), 145; develops aviation (1920–80s), 190, 193–95; fights bandits (1921), 191, 350; removal of Irigoyen (1930), 294; protects interests off Spain (1936–37), 145–46; attempts to enforce neutrality (1939), 148; flies to Malvinas (1942), 162; sends expedition to Antarctic (1942–43), 162; removal of Castillo (1943), 295; joins Allies (1945), 162–63; influence of World War II (1945), 146; develops amphibious capability (1950s), 192; aids Paraguayan navy (1950s–80s), 141–42; acquires cruisers from United States (1951), 173; attempts to oust Juan Perón (1945, 1951, 1955), 202, 209–17, 295; holds exercises with Paraguay (1950s–80s), 193; acquires aircraft carrier (1958), 194–95; influence of UNITAS (1959–80s), 175–76; aids Bolivian navy (1960s–80s), 142; aviators aid Perú (1960s), 200; participates in Cuban quarantine (1962), 178–80; units rebel (1963), 296; seizes Russian trawlers (1966), 182; exercises with French (1968), 195; Antarctic operations (1971), 184; removal of Isabel Perón (1976), 296; seizes Russian and Bulgarian trawlers (1977), 182–83; prepares for possible war (1978), 185–87; increases logistic support (1978), 187; chooses wrong time to fight (1982), 235; recaptures Malvinas (1982), 236–41; captures the Georgias (1982), 241–43; prepares for British (1982), 243–48; intelligence at work (1982), 244–45; locates British fleet (1982), 244–45; tries to attack (1982), 248–53; *Alferez Sobral* is attacked (1982), 253–54; as island defenders (1982), 255–63; Malvinas are attacked (1982), 263–66; Super Etendards attack (1982), 266–67; *San Luis* attacks (1982), 267–68; *Narwal* is attacked (1982), 268–69; fighting in islands (1982), 269–72; loss of Neptunes (1982), 272–73; Bomb Alley (1982), 273–77; *Atlantic Conveyor* is attacked (1982), 277; defense of islands (1982), 277–79; final Super Etendard attack (1982), 279–81; land-based Exocet operations (1982), 281–83; end of fighting (1982), 283–84; final defense (1982), 284–87; contributes to war (1982), 288
Argentine revolutions (1890, 1893), 53, 55–59
Argerich, Juan C. (Argentine navy), 209
Argonaut (British navy frigate), 273
Arias, Desiderio (Dominican army), 311
Arkansas (U.S. Navy dreadnought), 86
Ark Royal (British navy aircraft carrier), 312
Armaçáo, Brazil, 69, 73
Armstrong, Whitworth and Company (England), 81–82, 354. *See also* Vickers, Armstrong
Arno-Mendi (Spanish merchant ship), 367

INDEX   411

Arquimeda (Brazilian merchant ship), 366
Artuso, Felix (Argentine navy), 247
Ascension Island, 244, 333–37, 382
Asmussen, Alberto (Chilean navy), 142
Aspinwall, Colombia, 40, 308–9
ASROC. *See* Antisubmarine rocket
Astica, Manuel (Chilean navy), 108, 113
Asturias (British navy auxiliary cruiser), 150
Asunción, Paraguay, 19–20, 22–23, 25–26, 124, 126, 129, 203–5, 217, 344–45, 318, 381
ASW. *See* Antisubmarine warfare
Atacama Desert, 31–32, 61
Atahualpa (Peruvian navy monitor), 35, 37
Atkins, L. M. (U.S. Navy), 136
Atlanta (U.S. Navy ironclad), 39
Atlantic Conveyor (British merchant ship), 277, 280, 289, 341, 385
Atlantic Ocean, 1–3, 7–8, 17–20, 45, 52, 121, 148, 162, 168, 184–85, 244
Atlas (Italian merchant tanker), 330
Aubry, Lûis (Peruvian navy), 131, 361
Audaz (Brazilian navy tug), 73
Austin (Texas navy sloop), 14–15
Australia, 198, 370
Austria, 128
Avant-Garde (Haitian navy schooner), 38
Avay, Battle of, 26
Avenger (British navy frigate), 280
Avenger-type aircraft, 201
Aviation, development of in: Argentina, 140, 193–95, 254–59, 265–69, 272–81; Bolivia, 201; Brazil, 195–98; Chile, 112–13, 198–200; Ecuador, 201; Mexico, 201; Paraguay, 126, 201; Perú, 116, 132–33, 200–201; Uruguay, 201; Venezuela, 201. *See also* individual air forces and aircraft types
Avila Camacho, Manuel (president of México), 166–67
Aviocar-type aircraft, 186
Avro-type aircraft, 212
Axis Powers, 144–46, 148
Ayacucho, Battle of, 7
Avacucho (Colombian navy patrol craft), 170
Aymore (Brazilian transport), 352
Azcueta, Fernando (Argentine navy), 385
Azopardo, José Vicente (Venezuelan navy), 221–22, 375
Azopardo, Juan Bautista (Argentine navy), 2
Azua, Haití, 38

B. D. I (Argentine navy landing ship), 213
B. D. II (Argentine navy landing ship), 213

Babitonga (Brazilian navy destroyer escort), 329
Baependi (Brazilian merchant ship), 152; (Brazilian navy destroyer escort), 329
Bahamas, 306, 310
Bahia, Brazil, 8, 73, 152–53, 155, 158, 305, 356
Bahia (Brazilian navy armored corvette), 25–26; (Brazilian navy coastal defense battleship), 71, 352; (Brazilian navy scout cruiser), 92–95, 97, 105, 153, 160–61
Bahía Blanca, Argentina, 215, 255
Bahia Blanca (German merchant ship), 102
Bahía Buen Suceso (Argentine navy auxiliary), 243, 264, 270, 273, 287, 339, 378, 381, 385
Bahía Catalina, Chile, 199
Bahia Negra (Bolivia/Paraguay), 124, 126
Bahía Paraíso (Argentine navy polar supply ship), 190, 242–43, 245, 253, 287, 378, 380–81
Bahia State, Brazil, 92
Baire (Cuban navy gunboat), 98–100, 206, 373
Baja California, 40
Baker, N. J. (British navy), 380–81
Balboa, Panamá, 116, 360
Balmaceda, José Manuel (president of Chile), 59, 61–66, 294
Baltic, 122
Baltimore (U.S. Navy cruiser), 47, 307
Baptista, Ernesto de Mello (Brazilian navy), 160, 372
Baquedano (Chilean navy training ship), 103
Baquedano, Manuel (Chilean army), 59
Barbados, 311
Barbarigo (Italian navy submarine), 151
Barbosa, Ruy (Brazilian senator), 67, 72
Barbuzzi, Humberto (Argentine navy), 185
Barcelona, Venezuela, 223
Barilari, Atilio S. (Argentine navy), 47
Baroja, Vicente M. V. (Argentine navy), 209
Barranquilla (Colombia navy gunboat), 121, 360
Barraza, Julio (Argentine navy), 277
Barros, Jose Pedro Alves de (Brazilian navy), 352
Barroso (Brazilian navy armored corvette), 25–27; (Brazilian navy cruiser), 79, 93
Basque, 29
Basso, Juan B. (Argentine navy), 213
Batista y Zaldívar, Fulgencio (president of Cuba), 201, 206–8, 295

412 INDEX

Batleford (Canadian navy corvette), 369
Bauru (Brazilian navy destroyer escort), 329
Bavaria (German merchant ship), 357
Bay of Pigs, Cuba, 310
Beagle (British navy steam sloop), 56, 350
Beagle Channel, 49, 184–85, 187, 253, 288, 370
Beasley, F. M. (British navy), 85, 355
Beauchene Island, 268
Beaver-type aircraft, 236
Beberibe (Brazilian navy destroyer escort), 328
Becerra, Oswaldo (Venezuelan navy), 377
Bedacarratz, Augusto (Argentine navy), 266
Beechcraft-type aircraft, 256
"Bel-Antonio," 197
Belen, Brazil, 47, 118, 152–53, 365–66
Belgium, 128, 305, 370
Belize, 312
Bell-type helicopters, 196, 201
Belmonte (Brazilian navy tender), 95, 97, 356
Benatuil, Guastini (Venezuelan navy), 180
Benavides, Alfredo (Peruvian navy), 115
Benavides, Oscar R. (president of Perú), 122
Benesch, Bernardo F. (Argentine navy), 212
Benevente (Brazilian navy destroyer escort), 329
Benham, Andrew (U.S. Navy), 73
Benítez, Carlos (Argentine navy), 265
Benjamin Constant (Brazilian navy training ship), 68
Berenguela (Spanish navy warship), 31
Berlin, Germany, 49, 173
Barnardes, Arthur da Silva (president of Brazil), 77
Bernardino Rivadavia (Argentine navy armored cruiser), 49, 299, 349
Beron Victoria, Hernando (Colombian navy), 178
Betancourt, Rómulo (president of Venezuela), 222–34, 296
Betbeder, Onofre (Argentine navy), 82
Bethlehem Shipbuilding (United States), 361
Betiroga (Brazilian navy destroyer escort), 328
Beuret, J. D. (U.S. Navy), 136
Beytiá, Ramón (Chilean navy), 114
Bienvenido Lara, Augusto (Dominican navy), 179
Binta (Norwegian merchant tanker), 164
Bisbee (U.S. navy frigate), 178
Bisca (Norwegian merchant tanker), 164

Blanco Encalada, Manuel (Chilean navy), 5, 28, 349, 351
Blanco Encalada (Chilean navy destroyer), 233; (Chilean navy ironclad), 31–36, 59, 64, 347; (Chilean navy protected cruiser), 47, 113, 297, 358
Blasco de Garay (Spanish navy warship), 319
Blockade: of Arica (1879–80), 34; of Bahia (1823), 8; of Buenos Aires (1826), 17; of Callao (1820), 6, (1880), 35; of Chile (1864), 29, (1891), 61–62; of Cuba (1962), 172, 178–80; of Dominican Republic (1844), 38; of Germany (1939–45), 150, 161; of Great Britain, (1939–45), 161; of Guayaquil (1829), 27–28; of Haití (1883), 40; of Iquique (1879), 32; of Malvinas (1982), 243–87; of Mexican coast (1838), 13, (1842), 14, (1846–47), 15–16; of Montevideo, (1814), 3, (1844), 18, (1864), 19–20; of New York (1942–45), 162; of Perú (1937), 28–29; of Port-au-Prince (1970), 233; of Rio de Janeiro (1893–94), 76; of Río de la Plata (1839–40), 18, 304, (1866), 22–23, 27, (1955), 213–17; of Spain (1936–37), 165–66; of Texas coast (1837), 13–14, (1839–40), 14; of Uruguay River (1863), 19; of Valparaíso (1818), 5, (1865–66), 30; of Venezuela (1902), 41; of Veracruz (1858), 16
Blowpipe missile, 278
Bluefields, Nicaragua, 316–17
Blume Othon, Federico (Peruvian inventor), 36–37, 346
Blyth and Company, Great Britain, 19
Boca del Riachuelo, 55
Boca del Toro, Panama, 308–09
Bocaina (Brazilian navy destroyer escort), 329
Boeing-type aircraft, 240–43
Bogotá, Colombia, 121
Bogotá (Colombian navy river gunboat), 360
Bois de Chêne (Haitian transport), 40
Bolivar, Simón, 4, 7, 11, 17, 344
Bolivia, 27–32, 44, 46, 118–26, 145, 165, 185, 201, 323, 346, 355
Bolivian-Peruvian Confederation, 29
Bolivian air force, 124
Bolivian army, 32, 119, 346
Bolivian navy: no need for (1879), 32; during Chaco War (1932–35), receives aid from Argentina (1960s–80s), 142; develops aviation (1980s), 201
Bolognesi, Francisco (Peruvian army), 34
Bolsheviks. *See* Communists
Bom Destino (Bolivia/Brazil), 119

INDEX 413

Bonnemaison, Manuel Elías (Peruvian navy), 36
Bonzo, Hector Elias (Argentine navy), 251–52
Borbon Island, 243, 253, 258–59, 261, 264, 277, 288
Bouchard (Argentine navy destroyer), 236, 248, 250–53, 261
Bouchard, Hipólito (Argentine navy), 3
Bousson, Omar (Argentine navy), 381
Boyacá, Battle of, 4
Bozzano, José A. (Uruguayan navy), 204
Bracuí (Brazilian navy destroyer escort), 329
Braga, Euclides de Souza (Brazilian navy), 150
Bramble (British navy gunboat), 56, 350
Branco, Humberto Castello (president of Brazil), 197, 296
Bransfield (British merchant ship), 236
Bravo, Enrique (Chilean army), 109
Bravo (Mexican navy gunboat), 316
Brazil, 7–8, 12, 17–27, 45, 47, 66–82, 85–98, 100, 117–19, 129, 131, 133–38, 144–61, 171–73, 175, 180, 188, 190–91, 195–98, 208, 294–96, 304–6, 323, 355, 369–70
Brazilian air force: 151, 196–98, 365, 367
Brazilian army, 18, 22–27, 77, 150, 178, 208, 356
Brazilian expeditionary force, 160
Brazilian marine corps, 67, 189–91, 208, 371
Brazilian merchant marine, 88, 90, 92, 94–95, 97–98, 152–53, 160–61
Brazilian navy: during wars of independence (1822–25), 7–8; in war with Argentina (1825–27), 17–18; expedition to Paraguay (1855), 19; blockade of Montevideo (1865), 19–20; engagement with *Villa del Salto* (1865), 20; captures Corrientes (1865), 22; victory at Riachuelo (1865), 22; controls the Paraguay River (1865–70), 23–27; confronts the *Shamokin* (1866), 23; attacks Humaitá (1868), 25–26; attacked from *camalotes* (1868), 26; defeats Paraguayan navy (1870), 27; rebels (1891), 66–67, 294, (1893–94), 67, 294, 302–3; gathers its forces (1893), 68; bombards Rio and Nictheroy (1893), 69; seizes Desterro (1893), 69–70; tries to extend rebellion (1893–94), 72–73; challenged by U.S. squadron (1893), 73; government pulls together a navy (1893–94), 73–74; rebellion fails (1894), 74–76; *Aquadabã* torpedoed (1894), 74–76; cruiser bought by Chile (1895), 47; major building program (1904), 81, 92, 353; among first to acquire dreadnoughts (1906–13), 80–82, 86, 353–54; dreadnoughts mutiny (1910), 81, 86, 105–6; dreadnoughts inactive (1910s), 86; warships commandeered (1914), 88, 355; develops aviation (1916–80s), 190, 195–98; condition (1917), 92, 94; acquires aircraft (1917), 94; patrols South Atlantic (1917–18), 92–93; receives British mission (1917–22), 134; sends pilots to Europe (1918), 356; squadron sent to fight off Africa (1918), 95–98; squadron ravaged by influenza (1918), 97; debate between U.S. and British supporters (1918), 96; contributes to World War I (1918), 98, 128; receives U.S. mission (1918–41), 133–38, 150; potential mutiny (1919), 106–7, 358; Peruvian cadets sail in school ship (1920), 142; isolated units support rebellion (1924), 77; the *São Paulo* rebels (1924), 77–79; advised to buy battleships and submarines (1927), 135–36; remains loyal to central government (1930s), 79; seeks cruisers and destroyers from U.S. (1930s), 137; condition of (1930s–40s), 128, 136–37, 144, 151; warships commandeered (1939), 15ff, 153; patrols shipping lanes (1942), 152; establishes convoy system (1942–45), 155–58; receives lend-lease ships (1943–45), 155; problems with neutral ships (1943–45), 158–59; receives ASW training (1943–45), 160; escorts troops to Europe (1944), 160; mans rescue sites (1945), 160; contributes to war (1945), 161; influence of World War II upon (1945), 146; acquires cruisers (1951), 173; attempts to influence government (1955, 1964), 202, 208, 294–95; holds ASW exercises (1950s–80s), 174–76; participates in Suez peace force (1956–57), 178; seizes French fishing vessel (1963), 182
Brazilian revolution (1893–94), 53, 66–76
Brazilóide (Brazilian merchant ship), 158
Brazoria, México, 13
Brest, France, 90
Brett Smith, Italo (Venezuelan national guard), 221, 376
Breyer, Siegfried (German analyst), 86
Brión, Luis (Venezuelan navy), 4
British Columbia, 354
British Guiana, 306
British marines, 236–42, 284–86, 305, 380
British merchant marine, 14, 18, 31, 89

414   INDEX

British navy: during wars of independence (1810–24), 4–5, 7; officers serve in Latin American navies (1800s), 129–30; arrests Chilean warships (1839), 29; *Guadalupe* built for (1842), 15; blockades Rio de la Plata (1845), 18; arrests Chilean ships (1851), 29; fires at *Tacuari* (1859), 19; attacks México (1861), 16; sinks Haitian warship (1865), 39; intervenes against Argentine navy (1890), 56; Chile tries to buy Pacific fleet flagship (1891), 61; cruiser being built for (1893), 47; purchases Chilean battleships (1902), 52, 349; seizes Venezuelan warships (1902), 41; influence of dreadnought design (1912), 84–85; sends mission to Chile (1911–32), 84, 127, 138–39, 361; commandeers Latin American warships (1914), 85, 88; fights off west coast of South America (1914–15), 102–4; seizes Argentine merchant ship (1915), 100; sends mission to Brazil (1917–22), 134; patrols South Atlantic (1917–18), 91–92; Brazilian squadron operates under (1918), 95; battles *Admiral Graf Spee* (1939), 147–48; fights off Brazil (1939–40), 148–50; sells aircraft carrier to Brazil (1956), 197; sells aircraft carrier to Argentina (1958), 194; during Malvinas War (1982), 235–89; exercises near Gibraltar (1982), 235; recaptures Georgias (1982), 247; attacks Puerto Argentino (1982), 263–64; captures *Narwal* (1982), 268–69; attacks Borbon (1982), 272; lands at San Carlos (1982), 273–74. *See also* Great Britain

Brito Martínez, Andrés (Venezuelan navy), 218, 375
Brown, Michael (Argentine navy), 3
Brown, William "Guillermo" (Argentine navy), 3, 8, 17–18, 191, 349
Brunet, Ramon A. (Argentine navy), 373
Brutus (Texas navy warship), 14
Bruzzone, Carlos M. (Argentine navy), 212
Buarque (Brazilian merchant ship), 150, 365
Buenaventura (Dominican navy schooner), 38
Buenos Aires, Argentina, 2–3, 5–6, 17–20, 22, 42, 44–45, 54–56, 76, 101–2, 137, 141, 148, 162, 165, 194, 203–4, 209–10, 213–17, 244, 304–5, 344, 346, 350, 381, 384, 386
Buenos Aires (Argentine navy protected cruiser), 47, 298; (Argentine navy sail frigate), 17

Buenos Aires class (Argentine navy destroyers), 162
Bulldog (British navy warship), 38, 312
Bulnes, Manuel (president of Chile), 28
Burdwood Bank, 185, 251
Burlington (U.S. Navy frigate), 178
Burne, Charles (British navy), 138–39
Busser, Carlos (Argentine navy), 236
Bustamente y Rivero, José Luis (president of Perú), 295, 359
Buzzard (British navy warship), 19

C3-S-A1 (cargo vessel), 194
Cabedelo (Brazilian merchant ship), 365
Cabimas (Colombian navy tanker), 169
Cabo de Hornos (Argentine navy school ship), 45
Cabo Frio, 73, 196
Cabo San Antonio (Argentine navy landing ship), 189, 236–41, 243
Cahuapanas (Peruvian navy armed launch), 119, 360
Cainas Sriva, Jorge (Cuban navy), 208
Caldas (Colombian navy destroyer), 122, 169
Caldera, Chile, 33, 61, 64
Calderón Lozano, Pedro (Mexican navy), 330
Callao, Perú, 2, 5–8, 28, 30–36, 104, 115–16, 122, 130, 174, 201, 318, 346, 350, 359–60
Calle Larga (Cuban merchant ship), 233
Calvo Sotelo (Spanish navy gunboat), 350
Camalotes, 26
Camaquã (Brazilian navy minelayer), 151, 158
Camaquey, Cuba, 169
Campeche, México, 14, 77
Campecheano (Yucatecan/Mexican navy gunboat), 15
Campo Colombia, Cuba, 206
Campos, Abel (Chilean navy), 107, 113–14
Campos, Manuel J. (Argentine army), 54
Camus, Hermógenes (Chilean army), 64
Canada, 12, 144, 173
Canada (British navy dreadnought), 139, 322
Canarias (Spanish navy heavy cruiser), 165
Canave, Arsenio (Chilean navy), 33
Canberra (British passenger ship), 334–35
Canberra-type aircraft, 253
Cândido, João (Brazilian navy), 106
Cañizares, Armando (Mexican navy), 330
Cannon (U.S. Navy destroyer escort), 329
Canopus (Brazilian navy survey ship), 196
Canseco, Diez (Peruvian navy), 33
Cant-type aircraft, 126

INDEX 415

Capaz, Dionisio (Spanish navy), 6
Cape Dos Bahias, 182
Cape Dungeness, 45
Cape Frio, 150
Cape Hatteras, 39, 167, 355
Cape Horn, 17, 31, 163, 184–85, 187, 370
Cape Pembroke, 236, 239
Caperton, William B. (U.S. Navy), 91–92, 97, 131
Cape San Antonio, 100, 305, 365
Cape São Roque, 151, 366
Capetown (British navy cruiser), 316
Cape Verde islands, 96, 122, 151, 365
Capitán Cabral (Paraguayan navy tug), 178, 360
Capitán Pedro Santana (Dominican navy frigate), 179, 370
Capitán Prat (Chilean navy battleship), 46, 72, 297, 347, 349
Capitán Thompson (Chilean navy submarine), 358
Capitán Tono (Colombian navy frigate), 178
Cap Trafalgar (German navy auxiliary cruiser), 306, 356
Carabobo (Colombian navy corvette), 369; (Colombian navy submarine chaser), 169–70
Caracas, Venezuela, 207, 218–22, 224, 226–27, 231–32, 375, 377
Caravelas (Brazilian navy dispatch boat), 352; (Brazilian navy minelayer), 158
Carbonell Izquierdo, Jesús (Venezuelan navy), 221, 226, 230–32, 375
Cárdenas, Lázaro (president of México), 164, 166
Caribbean, 3–5, 37–41, 122, 144–45, 168–69, 178–80, 193, 230, 306–7. *See also* Gulf of Mexico
Caribe (Cuban navy gunboat), 206
Caridad (Dominican merchant schooner), 38
Carioca: Brazilian navy minelayer, 158; class, 153, 155, 327
Caripito, Venezuela, 224
Carite (Venezuelan navy submarine), 179, 370, 276
Carl Fritzen (German merchant ship), 148
Carmania (British navy auxiliary cruiser), 306
Carmelo, Uruguay, 204
Carmen (Dominican merchant schooner), 170
Carmen (Spanish merchant ship), 367
Carnavon Castle (British navy auxiliary cruiser), 162

Carrega, José Carlos (Argentine coast guard), 385
Carrillo, Luis Evencio (Venezuelan air force), 375
Carrizal, Chile, 33
Cartagena (de Indias), Colombia, 2, 4–5, 169, 177, 307–8, 360
Cartagena (Colombian navy river gunboat), 121
Carúpano, Venezuela, 224–25
Carvajal Prado, Patricio (Chilean navy), 378
Casa-type aircraft, 186
Casablanca, Cuba, 206
Casa Rosada, Buenos Aires, 55–56
Cascardo, Herolino (Brazilian navy), 77, 79
Cascavel armored car, 190
Casma (Chilean navy destroyer), 142
Castilho, Júlio de (Brazilian politician), 351
Castillo, Ramón S. (president of Argentina), 148, 295
Castro, Fidel (premier of Cuba), 180, 193, 201, 206–8, 223, 310
Castro, Raul (Cuban army), 207–8
Castro León, Jesús M. (Venezuelan air force), 223
Catalina-type aircraft, 199
Catia La Mar, Venezuela, 218
Cayes, Haití, 39
Cayo Frances, Cuba, 169
Cayrú (Brazilian merchant ship), 365
CC-1 (Canadian navy submarine), 365
CC-2 (Canadian navy submarine), 354
Ceará (Brazilian merchant ship), 95
Ceará (Brazilian navy tender), 92, 353
Celman, Miguel Juárez (president of Argentina), 54, 57, 294
Centeno Lusinchi, Oscar (Venezuelan politician), 375
Central America, 13, 39–41, 145, 193. *See also* individual nations
Central Powers, 88–89, 92–93, 355
Ceres (Argentine merchant steamship), 57
Cerrito Island, 204
Cerro Azul (Mexican merchant tanker), 367–68
Cervantes (Argentine navy destroyer), 213
Cessna-type aircraft, 201, 236
Chaca (Argentine navy auxiliary), 357
Chacabuco, Battle of, 5
Chacabuco (Argentine navy warship), 17; (Chilean navy protected cruiser), 49, 298; (Chilean navy sail corvette), 5–6; (Chilean navy steam corvette), 31
Chaco (Paraguayan merchant craft), 360
Chaco Boreal, 26, 118, 122–26, 203

416   INDEX

Chaco War, 118, 122–25, 136, 185, 201
Chagres River, 2
Chaguaramas, Trinidad, 179
Chalaco (Peruvian transport), 37
Chamezor, Chile, 199
Chamorro, Ignacio C. (Argentine navy), 213
Chañaral, Chile, 33
Chancay, Perú, 35–36
Chanchamayo (Peruvian navy gunboat), 345
Channel O'Brien, 185
Chapuseaux, Roberto (Chilean navy), 109, 114
Charleston (U.S. Navy protected cruiser), 64, 73, 306
Charlotte (German navy warship), 313
Cherub (British navy sail frigate), 306
Chiapas State, México, 77
Chichester (British navy frigate), 184
Chilca, Perú, 28
Chile, 5–7, 11–12, 17, 27–37, 42–52, 59, 82, 84–89, 100, 102–4, 128–29, 138–39, 144–46, 151–52, 161–64, 173–75, 183–87, 189, 192–93, 198–200, 233, 248, 251, 294, 296–99, 306–7, 323–25, 345–49, 354, 368, 370
Chilean air force, 111–14, 199–200, 233, 359
Chilean army, 28–29, 32–37, 46, 59–66, 111–14, 127, 199, 233, 346
Chilean marine corps, 64, 189, 192–93, 233, 370
Chilean merchant marine, 31, 104
Chilean national police, 233
Chilean navy: during wars of independence (1813–24), 5–7, 192; foreigners in the fleet (1816), 129–30, 138; captures Peruvian warships (1836), 28; blockades Perú (1837), 28; lands troops at Chila and Ancon (1838), 28; blockades Perú (1839), 29; attacked by Peruvian navy (1839), 29; warships arrested by British navy (1839), 29; only one ship prepared (1851), 29; war with Spain (1864–66), 30; superior to that of Argentina (1870s), 44–45; operates off Patagonia (1870s), 45; prepares for war with Argentina (1878), 45; contemporary evaluation (1879), 31–32; seizes Antofagasta (1879), 32; blockades Iquique (1879), 32; seeks decisive action (1879), 32; battle of Iquique (1879), 32–33; searches for *Huáscar* (1879), 33; overhauls ships (1879), 33; captures *Huáscar* (1879), 34, 346; expedition against Pisagua (1879), 34; blockades Arica (1879–80), 34; blockades Callao (1880–81), 34–37; attacks Callao (1880), 36–37; interest in the torpedo (1880s), 46; superior to U.S. Navy (1880s), 11; dominates west coast of South America (late 1800s), 142; maintains order in the north (late 1800s), 350; acquisition race with Argentina (1880s-90s), 46–52; rebels (1891), 59–66, 294, 300–301; gathers strength (1891), 62, 64; attacked by torpedo boats (1891), 64; develops amphibious capability (1891), 54, 64–66, 188; among the most experienced in the world (1890s), 46; and the submarine (1890s), 47; aid to Ecuador (1896–1920), 142; rendezvous with Argentine navy (1899), 49; seeks to buy U.S. warships (1901), 50; aid to Colombia (1902–10), 142; limits acquisitions (1902), 51–52; acquires dreadnoughts (1911–37), 84–86; British mission to (1912–32), 84, 127, 361; Great Britain commandeers warships (1914), 85, 88, 355; tries to enforce neutrality (1914–18), 102–104; develops aviation (1916–80s), 190, 198–200; acquires submarine (1917), 85, 354–55; mutinies (1931), 107–15; attacked by air force (1931), 112–18; *Almirante Latorre* inactive (1930s), 86; aviators train in United States (1930s), 163; aid to Paraguay (1932), 142; seeks cruisers (1930s), 85, 163; condition of (1930s), 144; influence of World War II upon (1945), 146; acquires cruisers (1951), 173; holds ASW exercises with United States (1950s–80s), 174–76; influence of UNITAS on (1959–80s), 175–76; overthrow of Allende (1973), 200, 233, 296; prepares for war (1978), 185–87; sends fleet south (1982), 259
Chilean revolution (1891), 46–47, 53, 76, 115, 217, 351
Chiloé, 28, 30
Chimbote, Perú, 12
Chimbote (Peruvian navy landing ship), 200
Chincha islands, 29
Chinook-type helicopter, 385
Chipamanu River, 119–20
Chiriqui, Panamá, 318
Choiseul Sound, 276
Choloma, Honduras, 314
Chonos Archipelago, 103
Chorrillos, Battle of, 37
Chorillos, Perú, 36
Christobal del Tren, Perú, 36
Christopher (U.S. Navy destroyer), 329

INDEX 417

Chubut (Argentine merchant ship), 333, 337
Ciaris Estero, México, 315
Cibao (Dominican navy frigate), 38
Cienfuegos, Cuba, 207–8
Cincinnati (U.S. Navy protected cruiser), 97
Clavero, Manuel (Peruvian navy), 121
Clemenceau (French navy aircraft carrier), 195
Clement (British merchant ship), 148
Clemente y Palacios, Lino de (Venezuelan navy), 376
Cleopatra (French navy warship), 319
Cleveland (U.S. Navy cruiser), 317
Clifford (Spanish merchant ship), 367
Climax (U.S. sail merchant ship), 14
Clio (British navy sail corvette), 238, 304
Coal, 44, 88, 95, 100, 102–3, 346, 357
Cobija, Bolivia, 124
Cobra islands, 105
Cochrane, Thomas (Chilean/Brazilian navy), 6–8, 129, 138, 344, 351
Cocle (Panamanian merchant ship), 368
Cohen, José María (Argentine navy), 176, 369
Colo-Colo (Chilean coast guard cutter), 358
Colocolo (Chilean navy warship), 28
Colombia, 3, 12, 40–41, 89, 121–22, 133, 142, 145, 177–78, 201, 220, 295, 306–8, 324, 355, 369–70
Colombian air force, 201
Colombian army, 40, 346
Colombian marine corps, 370
Colombian navy: expense of (1820s), 344; foreigners in the fleet (1820s), 344; offered alliance (1825), 17; receives aid from Chile (1902–10), 142; attempts to hold Panamá (1903), 40; develops aviation (1920–80s), 201; riverine war with Perú (1932), 121–22; missions (1932–41), 140–41; fights in World War II (1943–45), 169–70; serves in Korean war (1950–53), 177–78; involved in rebellion (1957), 295
Colombo (British navy cruiser), 317
Colombo, Jorge Luis (Argentine navy), 256–57, 383, 385–86
Colon, Colombia/Panamá, 40, 269, 308–9
Colon (U.S. merchant ship), 308
Colossus class (British navy aircraft carriers), 194–95, 197
Colusa (British merchant steamer), 102
Communists: incite potential Brazilian mutiny (1919), 107; and involvement in Chilean mutiny (1931), 108, 111, 115; and involvement in Peruvian mutiny (1932), 116; overrun eastern Europe (1945–50), 173; China falls (1945–48), 173; role in Paraguayan rebellion (1947), 203; victory in Cuba (1960), 180–82, 206–8; role in Venezuela (1958–70s), 222–32, 376; role in Brazilian rebellion (1964), 208; and presence in Chilean government (1973), 233; and role in Grenada (1983), 311. *See also* Soviet Union
Comandante Aguirre (Peruvian navy armored cruiser), 131
Comandante Espora, Argentina, 212–15, 217, 259
Comodoro Murature (Argentine navy torpedo boat), 57
Comodoro Somellera (Argentine navy tug), 245, 383
Concepción, Chile, 29, 233
Concepción, Paraguay, 203–5
Concha, Carlos (Chilean diplomat), 49, 349
Concha, Luis A. (Chilean navy), 354
Condell, Carlos (Chilean navy), 12
Condell (Chilean navy torpedo boat), 46; (Chilean navy destroyer), 111
Confederate States of America, 345. *See also* Ex-Confederates
Congresionalistas. See Chilean revolution
Congress (U.S. Navy sail frigate), 304–5
Conqueror (British navy submarine), 251, 282
Consolidated-type aircraft, 162, 165
Constantia (German merchant ship), 357
Constanza (Argentine fishing vessel), 244
Constellation (U.S. Navy aircraft carrier), 358
Constitución (Argentine navy gunboat), 45; (Chilean navy battleship), 298, 349; (Chilean navy dreadnought), 322; (Venezuelan navy corvette), 369
Copacabana, Fort, 77–78
Coquimbo, Chile, 29, 62, 64, 107–8, 110, 112–13, 199, 359
Coquimbo (Chilean navy warship), 17
Córdoba, Argentina, 212, 215
Córdoba (Argentine merchant ship), 245
Córdova (Colombia navy river gunboat), 360
Córdova Montaner, José M. (Venezuelan air force), 375
Corinto, Nicaragua, 316–17
Cornes, Luis J. (Argentine navy), 212
Coro Cora, Battle of, 27
Coronel, Battle of, 103
Coronel Bolognesi (Peruvian navy scout cruiser), 104, 115–16, 130, 359–60

Coronel Martínez (Paraguayan navy gunboat), 204–5, 360
Corral, Chile, 103
Corrêa, Serzedello (Brazilian minister of finance), 67
Correo de Méjico (Mexican customs ship), 13
Corrientes, Argentina, 20, 23, 57, 193
Corrientes (Argentine navy destroyer), 102; (Argentine navy landing ship), 141
Corrientes II (Argentine merchant ship), 336
Corsairs. *See* Privateers
Corsair-type aircraft, 179, 331
Corso, Operation, 192
Cortés Acosta, Antonio (Mexican navy), 330
Corumbá, Paraguay, 24–25
Corytiba (Brazilian merchant ship), 351–52
Costa Firme, 3–4, 344
Costa Rica, 145, 180, 318, 355, 370
Coups. *See* National political will
Covadonga (Spanish/Chilean navy gunboat), 29–30, 32–33, 35
Cozumel, México, 167–68
Crespo (Venezuelan navy warship), 41
Crête à Pierro (Haitian navy gunboat), 41
Crippa, Guillermo Owen (Argentine navy), 273
Cruz Díaz, Gabriel (Mexican navy), 330
Cuauhtémoc (Mexican merchant tanker), 368
Cuba, 8, 12, 37, 98–100, 133, 145, 168–70, 172, 177–82, 193, 201, 206–8, 223, 233, 295, 309–10, 324, 355, 369
Cuba (Cuban navy gunboat), 100, 206, 208
Cuban air force, 210
Cuban marine corps, 193, 371
Cuban merchant marine, 169, 182, 208
Cuban Missile Crisis, 178–80
Cuban navy: seeks U.S. mission (1916), 98; during World War I (1917–18), 98–100; suppresses rebellion (1933), 206; develops aviation (1937–59), 201; no ASW capability (1941), 168; United States mans flotilla (1942–43), 168–69; receives lend-lease ships (1943–45), 169; helps sink a U-boat (1943), 169; contributes to war (1945), 169; helps instate Batista (1952), 202, 206, 295; attempts to change government (1957), 202, 206–8, 295; attaches defect (1960), 207; old discarded and new created (1962–80s), 180–82

Culbertson, William S. (U.S. ambassador to Chile), 111–12
Cumaná, Venezuela, 5, 225
Cumberland Bay, 247, 381
Curaçao, 41
Curato Mojones, Paraguay, 205
Curilovic, Roberto (Argentine navy), 277
Curitiba, Brazil, 74
Curtiss-type aircraft, 112, 165, 194–95, 359
Curupaití, Battle of, 23
Curuzu, Paraguay, 23
Custodio de Melo (Brazilian navy transport), 178
Custodio Lira, Angel (Chilean navy), 200
Customhouses, 16, 31, 310. *See also* economic influences
Cuyabá (Brazilian merchant ship), 95; (Paraguayan merchant craft), 360
Cydonia (British merchant ship), 165

Dagger-type aircraft, 384
Daiquiri, Cuba, 309
Dakar, Senegal, 95–97, 150
Danuzzio, Santiago (Argentine navy), 57
Darwin (Great Britain/Argentina), 239, 241, 261, 272, 276–80, 287, 387
Dassault-type aircraft, 331
Daymán (Paraguayan merchant craft), 360
Decepción Island, 162, 182
Defense (Haitian navy warship), 346
Democracia (Buenos Aires), 210
Democratic Action Party (Venezuela), 223
Democratic Republican Union (Venezuela), 222
Dennison, Robert (U.S. Navy), 179–80
Denver (U.S. Navy cruiser), 317
Deodoro (Brazilian navy coastal battleship), 92, 105, 136
Des Moines (U.S. Navy cruiser), 313, 317
Desolación (Dominican rebel corvette), 38
DeSoto class (U.S. Navy landing ships), 189
Dessalines (Haitian navy gunboat), 40, 346
Desterro, Brazil, 68–70, 74
Detroit (U.S. Navy protected cruiser), 73
Destroyer (U.S. experimental craft), 71, 352
Devonshire (British navy cruiser), 312; (U.S. merchant ship), 45
De Zeven Provincien (Dutch navy cruiser), 201
Díaz, Antonio (Venezuelan navy), 4
Dichato, Chile, 109
Dieu Protège (Haitian navy schooner), 38
Divisão Naval em Operações de Guerra (DNOG), 95–98
Dolores, Battle of, 34

INDEX 419

Dominica, 180, 311
Dominican merchant marine, 170
Dominican navy: wars with Haití (1844–93), 38–39; serves in World War II (1941–45), 170; participates in Cuban quarantine (1962), 179–80
Dominican Republic, 38–39, 89, 133, 145, 170, 177–80, 222–23, 310–11, 324, 355, 370. *See also* Santo Domingo
Dönitz, Karl (German navy), 152
Dorsetshire (British navy cruiser), 150
Dos de Diciembre (Venezuelan navy transport), 220, 222
Douglas type aircraft, 210, 225
Douhet, Giulio (Italian army), 196
Douro (Portuguese navy destroyer), 122
Drago, Luis M. (Argentine minister to Venezuela), 41, 320
Drake, Millington (British ambassador to Uruguay), 147
Drake Passage, 162, 185
Dreadnought (British navy dreadnought), 369
Dreadnought-type battleship, 80–87, 321–22
Dresden (German navy cruiser), 307
Driggs Guerra, Guillermo (Cuban navy), 373
Drontheim, Norway, 357
Drummond (Argentine navy corvette), 236, 239, 241
Duguay-Trouin (French navy training ship), 130
Dunvegan (Canadian navy corvette), 369
Duprat Shipyard, Chile, 30
Dupuy de Lôme (French navy armored cruiser), 131
Duque de Caxias (Brazilian navy transport), 329
Durango (Mexican navy gunboat), 165, 350
Dutch navy, 197
Dutra, Alfredo Soares (Brazilian navy), 153, 159
Duvalier, François (president of Haití), 233, 296
Dynamite gun, 71–74, 76

Eagle (British navy aircraft carrier), 85, 322
Easter Island, 357
Ebano (Mexican merchant tanker), 330
Eber (German navy gunboat), 95, 306, 356
Echeverría, Lino (Bolivian army), 120
Economic influences, 9, 29, 41–42, 46–47, 50–51, 61, 85–86, 88–89, 104, 106, 114, 139, 161, 217, 347
Ecuador, 28–30, 89, 119–20, 142, 145, 179, 187, 201, 324, 348, 355, 369–70
Ecuadoran marine corps, 371
Ecuadoran navy: war with Perú (1829), 27–28; receives aid from Chile (1896–1920), 142; receives mission from United States (1940), 141; develops aviation (1967–80s), 201; seizes fishing craft (1971), 183
Eider (British mail steamer), 40
El Barcelonazo rebellion, 223
El Carúpanazo rebellion, 224–26
El Cid (U.S. merchant steamship), 71, 352
Electra-type aircraft, 165, 258
Electric Boat Company (United States), 128, 132, 354, 361–62
El Guarirazo rebellion, 223–24
El Plata (Argentine navy seagoing monitor), 351
El Porteñazo rebellion, 224–26
El Presidente (Dominican navy warship), 346
El Pumerillo, Argentina, 212
El Salvador, 145, 355, 370
Elicura (Chilean coast guard cutter), 358
Elk (British merchant ship), 334–35
Embraer-type aircraft, 198, 384
Empresa (Bolivia/Brazil), 118–19
Encina, Alberto (Argentine navy), 55, 57
Endurance (British ice patrol ship), 236, 239, 334, 380
England. *See* Great Britain
Entre Ríos (Argentine navy destroyer), 175, 183
Entre Ríos Province, Argentina, 57
Errázuriz, Federico (president of Chile), 49
Escobio Ruiz, Pablo (Mexican navy), 330
Esmeralda (Chilean navy armored cruiser), 12, 48, 129, 297; (Chilean navy protected cruiser), 48, 142, 347, 364; (Chilean navy steam corvette), 32–33; (Spanish navy sail frigate), 6
Esperança (Brazilian transport), 72, 74
Espina, Mariano (Argentine navy), 57
Espinillo Island, 58
Espora, Argentina, 381, 385–86
Espora (Argentine navy destroyer), 179–80, 369–70; (Argentine navy torpedo gunboat), 57, 350
Essex (U.S. Navy sail frigate), 306
Essex David (British merchant ship), 165
Estero Bellaco, Paraguay, 63
Esteverena, Rolando O. (Argentine navy), 373
Estigarribia, José Felix (president of Paraguay), 203
Estonia, 122

Ex-Confederates, 22, 46
Exeter (British navy heavy cruiser), 148, 355; (British navy destroyer), 280
Exocet missiles: air to surface, 256–57, 266, 277, 279–80, 287, 289, 383–84; surface to surface, 255, 281–83
Ezeiza, Argentina, 210, 212

F-1 (Brazilian navy submarine), 353
F-3 (Brazilian navy submarine), 353
F-5 (Brazilian navy submarine), 353
Fairchild-type aircraft, 197, 225
Fairey-type aircraft, 199
Faja de Oro (Mexican merchant tanker), 167, 330
Fajardo, Puerto Rico, 319
Falcon (Chilean merchant schooner), 357
Falcon-type aircraft, 112
Falkland islands. *See* Malvina islands
Falklands, Battle of the, 100, 113
Faustin I (emperor of Haiti), 38
Favio Galliapoli (Venezuelan navy tug), 378
F class (Brazilian navy submarines), 92
Fearless (British navy landing ship), 334–35
Fede (Italian merchant tanker), 330
Federación (Venezuelan navy corvette), 369
Felipe Larrazabal (Venezuelan navy tug), 220
Felix Competidor (British merchant ship), 352
Ferero Gonalez, Dario (Colombian navy), 178
Fernández, José Luis (Venezuelan air force), 221, 376
Fernández, Rómulo (Venezuelan army), 221
Fernández Márquez, Justo Pastor (Venezuelan navy), 227, 230–31, 369, 377
Fernando VII (king of Spain), 3–4
Fernando Siliceo Merchant Marine Academy, 164
Ferrazzano, Heraclio (Argentine army), 213, 373
Ferré, Diego (Peruvian navy), 346
Ferré (Peruvian navy submarine), 130–31
Fidanza, Hector W. (Argentine navy), 213
Fierro-Sarratea Treaty, 45
Figueroa Bastardo, Feddy (Venezuelan navy), 377
Filibusters, 9, 37, 39, 40
Fire-control systems, 83, 147
Firefly (Chilean merchant steamer), 29
Fisher, S. Rhodes (secretary of the Texas navy), 14
Fitz-John Porter (U.S. merchant ship), 158, 160

Fletcher class (U.S. Navy destroyers), 179
Flint, Charles (U.S. citizen), 71, 79, 348
Flora (Chilean merchant ship), 110
Flores, Ramón (Argentine navy), 57
Floriano (Brazilian navy coastal battleship), 92
Florianópolis, Brazil, 68–69, 366
Florida (Confederate navy warship), 305
Florida Maru (Japanese merchant ship), 165
Flower class (British navy escorts), 173, 369
Fonseca, Hermes Rodrigues da (president of Brazil), 81–82, 106, 353–54
Fonseca, Manoel Deodoro da (president of Brazil), 66–67, 294
Force in being: definition, 12; torpedo boat, 46, 347; dreadnought, 86–87
Fore River Company (United States), 83–84, 354
Formosa (Argentine merchant ship), 243, 245, 264, 381
Forrest (British merchant ship/Argentine naval auxiliary), 236, 261–62, 264–65, 270, 287, 339
Fortaleza, Brazil, 151, 153, 366
Fort Grange (British navy auxiliary), 335
Fossil Bluff, Antarctica, 184
Fox Bay (Great Britain/Argentina), 239, 241
"Foxtrot" class (Soviet navy submarines), 182
France, 4, 12–14, 16–18, 61, 68–69, 83, 89–91, 97–98, 128–31, 140, 144, 146, 148, 150–51, 166, 172, 189, 256, 304–7, 313–15, 319, 325, 345, 362, 364–65, 369–70, 383–84
Francia, Rodriguez de (president of Paraguay), 20
Francisco, Alejandro (Argentine navy), 279
Francisco de Gurruchaga (Argentine navy tug), 245, 252–53
Franklin D. Roosevelt (U.S. Navy aircraft carrier), 311
Frederick (U.S. Navy armored cruiser), 91
Freetown, Sierra Leone, 95
French army, 130, 344
French marine corps, 305
French navy: attacks México (1838), 13–14; blockades Río de la Plata (1845), 18; attacks México (1861), 16–17; sends mission to Perú (1904–14), 130–31; patrols South Atlantic (1917–18), 92; sends warship to Brazil (1963), 182; exercises with Argentina (1968), 195
Fresia (Chilean navy torpedo launch), 36, 351

INDEX   421

Frödden, Carlos (Chilean navy), 139
Frontin, Pedro Max Fernando de (Brazilian navy), 93, 95
Fuentes, Fernando J. (Uruguayan navy), 147
Fuentes, Hugo (Venezuelan army), 218
Fuerto Olimpio, Brazil, 19
Fulton, Robert (U.S. inventor), 346
Fulton (U.S. Navy steamer), 318

G-28 (Mexican navy patrol boat), 168
Gabrielli, Nester P. (Argentine navy), 213
Galapagos islands, 348
Galliapoli, Fabio (Venezuelan navy), 378
Galmarini, Raúl (Argentine navy), 383
Galtieri, Leopoldo (president of Argentina), 378
Galveston (U.S. Navy cruiser), 317
Galvez, Enrique B. (Argentine navy), 373
Galvez, Jose (Peruvian navy), 35, 346
Gaña, Jorge (Chilean air force), 200
Garayo, Paraguay, 27
García, Osvaldo (Argentine army), 236
García Castelblanco, Alejandro (Chilean navy), 109
Gargiulo, Benjamín (Argentine navy), 211
Garibaldi (Argentine navy armored cruiser), 48, 52
Garin, Emilio (Chilean navy), 348
Garrido, Victorino (Chilean navy), 28
Gaspard, Augustin (Haitian navy), 4
Gazelle (German navy warship), 41, 312
Geier (German navy warship), 313, 319
General Artigas (Uruguayan navy warship), 19
General Belgrano (Argentine navy armored cruiser), 49, 298, 348; (Argentine navy light cruiser), 183, 217, 248, 250–52, 258, 288, 340, 382
General Bravo (Mexican navy brig), 14
General de Austria (Venezuelan navy frigate), 376
General Flores (Venezuelan navy frigate), 230, 376
General Guerrero (Mexican navy gunboat), 349
General José de Austria (Venezuelan navy frigate), 222
General Miramon (Mexican navy steamer), 16
General Mitre (Argentine navy armored cruiser), 299, 348
General Morán (Venezuelan navy frigate), 225, 230, 232
General Nariño (Colombian navy gunboat), 360
General Rivera (Uruguayan navy gunboat), 56, 350

General Roca (Argentine navy armored cruiser), 299, 348
General Santana (Dominican navy schooner), 38
General Terán (Mexican navy brig), 14
General Urbaneta (Venezuelan navy gunboat), 170
General Urrea (Mexican navy brig), 14
General W. H. Mann (U.S. Navy transport), 160
Genoano (Italian merchant tanker), 330
Georgia (Confederate navy steamer), 345
Georgias. *See* South Georgias
Gergerac, Fort, 38
German air force, 196
German merchant marine, 90–91, 95, 97, 99–100, 102–4, 159, 167
German navy: battles Haitian warships (1872), 41; captures Venezuelan warships (1902), 41; fights off west coast of South America (1914–15), 102–4; seizes Brazilian steamer (1916), 90; uses unrestricted submarine warfare (1917–18), 90, 94–95, 101–2, 104; believed to have secret bases (1917–18), 94, 99; mutiny (1918), 357–58; *Admiral Graf Spee* fights British (1939), 147; violates Pan American zone (1939–41), 365; U-boats operate off Brazil (1941), 151; attacks Brazilian shipping (1942), 152, 155; attacks Mexican shipping (1942–44), 167–68; submarines lost to Brazilian bases (1943–45), 366–67
Germany, 18, 41, 89–91, 94, 100, 102–4, 124, 128, 134, 140–41, 143–44, 146–48, 150–52, 161–62, 166–68, 172, 262, 305–7, 312–13, 319–20, 346, 365, 370–71, 378. *See also* Axis Powers, Central Powers
Ghersi Gómez, Oscar (Venezuelan navy), 220–21
Giachino, Pedro (Argentine navy), 241
Gibraltar, 336
Gill, Sindulfo (Paraguayan navy), 203
Ginari Tronconis, Guillermo (Venezuelan navy), 377
Giorgio Fazzio (Italian merchant tanker), 230
Giuseppe Garibaldi [I] (Italian navy armored cruiser), 48, 298; [II] (Italian navy armored cruiser), 48–49, 298
Glaciar Ameghino (Argentine merchant ship), 336
Glamorgan (British navy destroyer), 282–83, 341
Glasgow (British navy cruiser), 103
Glaura (Chilean navy torpedo launch), 351

Gloster-type aircraft, 212–13
Goa, 234
Gobiernistas. *See* Chilean revolution (1891)
Goiana (Brazilian navy submarine chaser), 328
Goiás (Brazilian navy torpedo boat), 78
Golfo de San Jorge, 246, 267
Golfo Nuevo, 100, 262, 268
Gômes, Eduardo (Brazilian air force), 152, 198
Gômes, Luís Jacinto (Brazilian inventor), 353
Gômes, Wenceslau Braz Pereira (president of Brazil), 91, 97
Gómez, Juan Bautista (Mexican soldier), 368
Gómez, Pedro Ernesto (Argentine coast guard), 384
Gómez Roca, Sergio (Argentine navy), 253–54
Gonaires, Haití, 41
Gonçalves, Jeronimo (Brazilian navy), 71, 73
Gonçalves Dias (Brazilian merchant ship), 152
Goñi, L. A. (Chilean navy), 138
González, Ernesto (Chilean navy), 108, 113
González Lines, Andres (Cuban navy), 373
González Llanos, Horacio (Argentine navy), 279, 385
González Llanos, Juan Carlos (Argentine navy), 244, 268–69, 385
Good Hope (British navy cruiser), 103
Goose Green (Great Britain/Argentina), 239, 241, 384
Gopcevich, Alberto (Argentine navy), 277
Gotusso Borlando, Lorenzo (Chilean navy), 378
Goubet II (private submarine), 352
Goulart, João Belchior Marques (president of Brazil), 197, 208, 296
Grain, 46
Grajaú (Brazilian navy submarine chaser), 328
Granadillo, Rafael Marín (Venezuelan army), 376
Gran Colombia, 27
Gran Malvina Island, 272
Granville (Argentine navy corvette), 236, 241–42
Grappler (British navy warship), 19
Grau, Miguel (Peruvian navy), 32–34
Graúna (Brazilian navy submarine chaser), 328
Great Britain, 3–5, 7, 12, 14–15, 18–19, 30–31, 41, 44, 47–49, 51, 61, 64, 68–69, 83, 88–91, 95, 98, 100, 102–6, 112, 121–22, 127–29, 137–41, 146–48, 150, 153, 161–62, 164, 166, 172–73, 182–84, 192, 194, 196, 199–200, 234–89, 304–7, 309–17, 319–20, 323–25, 345, 349, 352, 355, 361, 364–65, 370–71. *See also* British navy
Greece, 165
Greenhalgh (Brazilian navy torpedo boat), 352
Gregorio Luperon (Dominican navy frigate), 179, 370
Grenada, 180, 311, 324
Greytown, Nicaragua, 314. *See* San Juan del Norte
Grow, H. B. (U.S. Navy), 133, 136
Grumman-type aircraft, 197–98, 201, 331
Grytviken, South Georgias, 242, 247, 379, 381
Guacanaybo Bay, 134
Guadaloupe, 180
Guadalupe (Mexican navy steamer), 15
Guaíba (Brazilian navy submarine chaser), 328
Guajira, Colombia, 169
Guale (Chilean navy torpedo boat), 351
Gualeguay (Argentine navy warship), 20
Guanabara (Brazilian navy cruiser), 69; (Brazilian navy steam corvette), 351–52
Guanabara Bay, 191, 197
Guanajuato (Mexican navy gunboat), 349–50
Guano. *See* Nitrates
Guantánamo, Cuba, 99, 233, 309–10, 363
Guaporé (Brazilian navy submarine chaser), 328
Guarajá (Brazilian navy submarine chaser), 328
Guardia Nacional (Argentine navy auxiliary), 357
Guatemala, 145, 179, 312
Guatemalan navy, 179
Guayamas, México, 77, 316
Guayaquil, Ecuador, 3, 27
Guazu Canal, 204
Guedes, Duarte Huet de Bacellar Pinto (Brazilian navy), 81
Güepi (Perú/Colombia), 122
Guerrero (Mexican navy gunboat), 77; (Argentine navy corvette), 242, 243, 381
Guerrière (Haitian navy schooner), 38
Guerrilla warfare, 27, 37
Guise, Martín (Peruvian navy), 7, 27
Gulf of México, 15–16, 168. *See also* Caribbean
"Guppy" class (U.S. Navy submarines), 262, 362

INDEX 423

Gurupá (Brazilian navy submarine chaser), 328
Gurupi (Brazilian navy submarine chaser), 328
Gustavo Sampaio (Brazilian navy torpedo boat), 74–75, 352

H-1 (Chilean navy submarine), 358
H-2 (Chilean navy submarine), 358
H-4 (Chilean navy submarine), 112–13, 358
H class (Brazilian navy destroyers), 137; (Chilean navy submarines), 107, 355
Habana, Cuba, 2–3, 16, 99–100, 144, 165, 168–69, 206–8, 309–10, 344
Habanero (Spanish navy warship), 319
Hague Convention of 1907, 91, 103
Haití, 4, 38–41, 91, 133, 145, 233, 296, 312–33, 325, 355, 370
Haitian air force, 233
Haitian navy: during wars of independence (1812), 4; rebels (1970), 233, 296, (1973), 202, 233
Hameln (German merchant tanker), 368
Harpoon missile, 382
Harrier-type aircraft, 250, 263–64, 268–70, 273–74, 277, 285, 335, 385
Hartung, Teodoro (Argentine navy), 374
Hassayampa (U.S. Navy tanker), 358
Hayitian Republic (U.S. merchant ship), 40
Hay-Bunau Varilla Treaty, 318
Health, Fortín, 120
Heitor Perdigão (Brazilian navy tug), 151
Heli Nuñez, C. B. (Ecuadoran navy), 142
Helibras-type helicopter, 198
Hellen Gunther (Paraguayan river craft), 204
Hércules (Argentine navy destroyer), 236, 239, 241, 248
Hercules-type aircraft, 257, 266, 277, 279–80, 282, 284, 384
Herey (Russian fishing factory ship), 183
Hermes (British navy aircraft carrier), 200
Hernández-Gonzáles, Carlos (Venezuelan analyst), 375
Hernández, José Manuel (Venezuelan navy), 375
Hernández Saucier, Miguel (Venezuelan navy), 375
Herreshoff torpedo boats, 35
Herval (Brazilian navy warship), 27
Herzog (U.S. Navy destroyer escort), 328
Hess, Júlio Emilio (Brazilian navy), 353
Heureaux, Ulises (president of the Dominican Republic), 39
Heureuse Réunion (Haitian navy warship), 4
Hip-type aircraft, 187

Hispaniola, 37–38
Hitler, Adolf, 152, 163, 367
Holanda (Paraguayan merchant craft), 360
Holger (German merchant ship), 100
Holland, 18, 90, 140, 166, 195, 315, 319–20, 343. *See also* Dutch navy
Holland-type submarine, 354–55
Honduras, 145, 180, 313–14, 355, 370
Hornet (U.S. merchant ship), 312
Howard (Great Britain/Argentina), 261
Hozven, Alberto (Chilean navy), 107, 113–14
Huáscar (Peruvian/Chilean navy seagoing monitor), 30–36, 59, 129, 345–47, 351
Huasco, Chile, 33
Huber, José (Chilean inventor), 47, 347
Huerta, Adolfo de la (Mexican secretary of the treasury), 77, 294
Huerta, Victoriano (president of México), 77, 315
Huerta Díaz, Ismael (Chilean navy), 378
Humaitá, Paraguay, 23, 25–26, 318; (Brazilian navy submarine), 136, 153, 363; (Paraguayan navy river gunboat), 124, 141–42, 203–5, 360
Hyatt (Chilean navy destroyer), 107, 113
Hyppolite, Florville (president of Haití), 39

Ianuzzo, Juan Carlos (Argentine navy), 264, 381
Ibai (Spanish merchant ship), 165, 367
Ibáñez del Campo, Carlos (president of Chile), 108, 199
Ibarborde, Jorge P. (Argentine navy), 215
Ibarra, Hilario A. (Argentine navy), 57
I class (British navy battle cruiser), 85
Idaho (U.S. Navy dreadnought), 135
Idarwall (German merchant ship), 167
Ignacio, Joaquin José (Brazilian navy), 25
Igurey (Paraguayan navy warship), 25
Ihaguay River, 27
Ihu, Paraguay, 27
Ilha do Governador, 190–91
Ilha Grande, 107
Illia, Arturo (president of Argentina), 296
Illustrious class (British navy aircraft carrier), 194
Ilo (Perú/Chile), 34
Iman (Yucatecan/Mexican navy brig), 15
Imperial (Chilean navy steamer), 351
Indefatigable (British navy aircraft carrier), 194
Independence (Texas navy warship), 14
Independencia (Argentine navy aircraft carrier), 176, 179, 194–95, 332, 350; (Argentine navy coastal battleship), 46, 57–59, 148, 364; (Brazilian navy armed

424 INDEX

Independencia (continued)
launch), 119; (Chilean/Argentine navy sail corvette), 6, 17; (Mexican navy warship), 14; (Peruvian navy armored warship), 30–33; (Venezuelan navy corvette), 369
Indiana (U.S. Navy battleship), 50
Indianola (Mexican navy steamer), 16
Indómita (Argentine navy patrol boat), 288, 382
Indonesia, 234
Industrial (Brazilian navy hospital ship), 352
Infanta Isabel (Spanish navy cruiser), 56, 350
Ingavi, Battle of, 29
Ingram, Jonas H. (U.S. Navy), 151–52, 155
Integralist Party (Brazilian political party), 79
Inter-American Defense Board, 146
Inter-American Reciprocal Assistance Treaty, 171–74
International Brigade (Spanish Civil War), 166
Intervention, Latin American concerns, 11, 33, appendix 6
Intrépida (Argentine navy patrol boat), 288, 382
Invincible (British navy aircraft carrier), 269, 280; (British navy battle cruiser), 138; (Texas navy warship), 14
Iquique (Perú/Chile), 32–34, 62, 64
Iquique (Chilean navy submarine), 354
Iquitos, Perú, 119, 122
Iquitos (Peruvian navy river launch), 360; (Peruvian navy training ship), 130
Irigoyen, Hipólito (president of Argentina), 92, 294
Íris (Brazilian navy armed merchant ship), 74
Irishman (British merchant ship), 334
Iron Duke (British navy dreadnought), 86
Isla de los Estados, 163, 245, 248, 251–52, 268, 382
Isla de los Estados (Argentine navy auxiliary), 236, 241, 243, 245, 261, 264, 268, 270, 339, 381
Islander-type aircraft, 236
Islas Malvinas (Argentine coast guard cutter), 243, 264, 287, 339
Itacolomy (Brazilian navy steamer), 352
Itagiba (Brazilian merchant ship), 152
Itaipú (Brazilian merchant steamer), 352
Itália (Brazilian merchant ship), 352
Italian air force, 196, 199
Italian merchant marine, 162, 166–67

Italian navy: blockades Venezuela (1902), 41; sells armored cruisers to Argentina (1895), 48; submarine attacks Brazilian coast (1942), 152
Italy, 12, 41, 69, 128, 133, 136–37, 140–41, 146, 152–53, 162, 164, 166–68, 172, 198, 305, 308, 313, 318, 320, 353, 361, 366
Itape (Brazilian merchant ship), 150
Itapiru, Fort, 18
Itata (Chilean navy steamship), 64, 306, 351
Itaúna (Brazilian merchant ship), 352
Ita-Ybaté, Paraguay, 26, 205
Ituzaingo, Paraguay, 17, 204

Jacabina (Argentine merchant steamer), 20
Jacira (Brazilian merchant ship), 152
Jackson (U.S. revenue cutter), 14
Jacmel, Haití, 40
Jacuí (Brazilian navy submarine chaser), 328
Jaguarão (Brazilian navy submarine chaser), 328
Jaquaribe (Brazilian navy submarine chaser), 328
Jamaica, 306, 311
Jamaica Packet (British mail steamer), 38–39
Jamestown (U.S. Navy sailing sloop), 305
Janequeo (Chilean navy torpedo launch), 35, 351
Japan, 142, 145, 160–63, 166–67, 182, 189, 262, 348–49, 370
Japanese fishing fleet, 248
Jaura (Brazilian navy gunboat), 25
Javari (Brazilian navy submarine chaser), 158, 328
Javary [I] (Brazilian navy monitor), 69, 351; [II] (Brazilian navy monitor), 355
Jeanne Amélie (French merchant ship), 45
Jérémie, Haití, 39
João VI (king of Portugal and Brazil), 7
John Biscoe (British merchant ship), 236
John I. Stephens (U.S. merchant steamer), 16
Jorge I (Paraguayan merchant steamer), 124
José Bonifacio (Brazilian navy armed yacht), 93
José Francisco Burrunda (Guatemalan navy corvette), 179, 370
José Martí (Cuban navy gunboat), 206
Jouett (U.S. Navy destroyer), 366
Juan Casiano (Mexican merchant tanker), 164, 168, 368
Juan Fernández islands, 103

INDEX 425

Juárez, Benito (president of México), 16, 315, 344
Juarrero Erdman, Alberto (Cuban navy), 373
Juarrero Erdman, Augusto (Cuban navy), 373
Juncal (Argentine merchant tanker), 160
Jundiaí (Brazilian navy submarine chaser), 328
Junin (Perú/Chile), 34
Junker-type aircraft, 112, 359
Junta de Mayo (Argentine congress), 2
Júpiter (Brazilian merchant ship), 67, 351–52
Juruá (Brazilian navy river gunboat), 92
Juruena class (Brazilian navy submarine chaser), 327
Jutaby (Brazilian navy river gunboat), 92
Jutaí (Brazilian navy submarine chaser), 328

Kadonia (German merchant ship), 357
Kamsak (Canadian navy corvette), 369
Kangaroo (? merchant ship), 131
Karl Doorman (Dutch navy aircraft carrier), 175, 332, 372
Kear, Carlton R. (U.S. Navy), 98
Killick, Hamerton (Haitian navy), 41
Kindey Island, 239
King (Argentine navy frigate), 213
Kitty Hawk (U.S. Navy aircraft carrier), 358
"Komar" class (Soviet navy missile craft), 182
"Koni" class (Soviet navy frigates), 182
Korean War, 177–78
Körner, Emilio (German army), 64, 351
Kronprinz Wilhelm (German navy auxiliary cruiser), 100
Kubitschek, Juscelino (president of Brazil), 197, 208, 295

La Argentina (Argentine navy light cruiser), 143, 148, 194, 215; (Argentine navy sail frigate), 3
La Constitución (Dominican navy schooner), 38
La Crête à Perrot (Haitian navy cutter), 233
La Maria Chica (Dominican navy schooner), 38
La Patrie (Haitian rebel steamer), 40
La Plata (Argentine navy seagoing monitor), 140, 347
La Rioja (Argentine navy destroyer), 213
Larrazábal, Carlos (Venezuelan navy), 221, 224

Larrazábal, Wolfgang (Venezuelan navy), 221–23, 296, 375
Las Aves (Venezuelan naval transport), 376
Las Carrera (Dominican navy warship), 38
Las Choapas (Mexican merchant tanker), 167, 330
Lauca (Chilean navy torpedo launch), 351
Laura (U.S. steam tug), 13
Laurindo Pitta (Brazilian navy tug), 95
Lautaro (Chilean navy sail frigate), 5–6
Laveriero-Wanderley, Nelson Freire (Brazilian air force), 197
League of Nations, 122
Leal Morales, J. (Venezuelan army), 375
Leal Romero, Andrés (Venezuelan navy), 377
Leal Torres, Homero (Venezuelan air force), 375
Lebel rifles, 165
Leftist Revolutionary Movement (Venezuelan political party), 223–24, 277, 376
Leipzig (German navy warship), 306
Lemaire Strait, 163
Lend-Lease Act, 155, 173
Lenox Island, 184, 370
León, Nicaragua, 316
Lestrade, Gaston (Argentine navy), 373
Leticia, Colombia, 121, 133
Leucoton (Chilean coast guard cutter), 358
Leviathan (British navy aircraft carrier), 372
Lexington (U.S. Navy sloop), 304, 379
Liberation Expedition (La Expedición Libertadora), 6, 8
Liberdade (Brazilian navy gunboat), 352
Libertad (Argentine navy coastal battleship), 46, 57, 297, 350, 364; (Chilean navy battleship), 298, 349; (Chilean navy dreadnought), 322; (Cuban navy auxiliary), 169; (Venezuelan navy corvette), 369
Libertador (Mexican navy brig), 14
Libertador Bolivar (Ecuadoran navy warship), 142
Libertador Castle, Puerto Cabello, 226–27, 230–32
Liberté (Haitian navy warship), 39
Lima, Perú, 5–8, 28–29, 35–37, 121, 131–33, 318, 344, 359
Lima (Peruvian navy gunboat), 122, 131, 200
Lima Barros (Brazilian navy warship), 26–27
Lincoln-type aircraft, 212
Lira, Ramón (Argentine navy), 55
Lisbon, Portugal, 106, 150

Loa (Chilean transport), 35
Loayza, A. (Peruvian navy), 132, 193
Lockheed-type aircraft, 258
Lombardo, Juan José (Argentine navy), 243, 248–52
Lonardi, Eduardo A. (president of Argentina), 213–17, 295
London Declaration of 1909, 98
Londonderry (British navy frigate), 310
London Naval Treaty of 1936, 137
López, Alfonso (Colombian diplomat), 360
López, Carlos (president of Paraguay), 20, 344
López, Francisco (Mexican navy), 14
López, Francisco Solano (president of Paraguay), 19–20, 22–27, 129, 344
López, Raúl (Chilean navy), 185
López Conde, Armando (Venezuelan navy), 375
Lorena, Frederico (Brazilian navy), 70
Loreto (Peruvian navy transport launch), 121
Lorondo, Bay of, 3
Los Andes (Argentine navy seagoing monitor), 45, 55–59, 140, 347, 350
Los Frailes (Venezuelan navy landing ship), 376
Los Monjes (Venezuelan navy landing ship), 225, 376
Los Roques (Venezuelan navy landing ship), 225, 230, 376
Los Teques, Venezuela, 220
Lott, Henrique (Brazilian army), 208
Louisiana (U.S. sail merchant ship), 14
Lower-Deck Committee, 108, 110, 113
Lowther, Gerardo (British minister to Chile), 51
Lucero, Franklin (Argentine army), 210, 216
Lucífero (Italian merchant tanker), 330
Lutece (French merchant schooner), 357
Luxburg, Count (German Ambassador to Argentina), 101–2
Luxor (German merchant ship), 104
Luz, Carlos (president of Brazil), 208, 295
Luzuriaga, Alfredo (Argentine navy), 369
Lynch, Patrico (Chilean navy), 36, 138
Lynch (Chilean navy destroyer), 107; (Chilean navy torpedo boat), 46

Macao (Brazilian merchant steamer), 94
Macchi-type aircraft, 126, 255–56, 258, 265, 273, 280–82, 288
Maceio, Brazil, 153
Maceio (Brazilian merchant ship), 356
Machado y Morales, Gerado (president of Cuba), 310
Machias (U.S. Navy gunboat), 313
Maciavelli, Carlos (Argentine navy), 373
MacIver, Enrique (Chilean deputy), 12
Mackau, Baron de (French navy), 304
Mackerel class (U.S. Navy submarines), 362
MacMahon, Samuel (Peruvian navy), 345
Madeira (Brazilian merchant ship), 351; (Brazilian navy monitor), 355
Madeira River, 124
Magallanes (Chilean navy gunboat), 31, 33, 45, 59, 346; (Spanish merchant ship), 165, 367
Magdalena River, 2
Magellan Strait, 161, 163
Magic missile, 384
Magnificent (British navy aircraft carrier), 194
Maine (U.S. Navy battleship), 310
Maipo (Chilean navy steamship), 62
Maipú (Argentine navy warship), 56
Maiquetía, Venezuela, 224–26, 375
Majestic class (British navy aircraft carriers), 194, 372
Malatesta, Victorio (Argentine navy), 373
Maldonado Harbor, 149
Mallea, Luis (Argentine navy), 212
Malvagni (Argentine merchant ship), 337
Malvina islands, 148, 162, 183–85, 189, 234–89, 304, 364, 378–86
Malvinas War, 41, 140, 176, 183, 187, 190, 195, 234–89, 333–42, 378–86
Managua, Nicaragua, 316–17
Manaos, Brazil, 121
Manco Capac (Peruvian navy monitor), 34–35
Manduvira River, 27
Mannlicher rifles, 62
Manuel II (king of Portugal), 106
Manuel Arñus (Spanish merchant ship), 165, 367
Manuripe. *See* Chipamanu
Manzanillo, México, 39, 165, 315
Manzárraga, Miguel (Mexican navy), 330
Mar Azul (Argentine fishing vessel), 244
Mar Cantabrico (Spanish merchant ship), 165, 367
Maracaibo, Venezuela, 5, 320
Maracana (Brazilian navy gunboat), 19
Maracay, Venezuela, 218–20, 377
Marajo (Brazilian merchant ship), 351
Maranhão, Brazil, 8
Maranhão (Brazilian navy destroyer), 153
Maranhão State, Brazil, 67
Marañón (Ecuadorian navy warship), 142
Marañón (Peruvian navy school ship), 37
Marchant, Hipólito (Chilean navy), 109
Marcílio Dias [I] (Brazilian navy destroyer), 160; [II] (Brazilian navy destroyer), 175;

INDEX   427

(Brazilian navy torpedo boat), 70, 351
Marcílio Dias class (Brazilian navy destroyers), 153, 327
Mar del Plata, Argentina, 182, 194, 211, 216, 239, 243, 245, 247–48, 262
Margarita (Venezuelan navy warship), 41, 320
Margarita Island, 3–4, 376
Marguerye, Paúl de (French navy), 130
María Alejandra (Argentine fishing vessel), 244
María Isabel (Spanish navy sail frigate), 5–6
María Luisa (Argentine fishing vessel), 244
Mariano Moreno (Argentine navy armored cruiser), 49, 299, 349
Mari-Baru, Haití, 38
Mariel, Cuba, 182
Marín, Tomás (Mexican navy), 15–16
Mariner-type aircraft, 201
Marino O (German merchant ship), 368
Mariscal Estigarribia (Paraguayan merchant tanker), 203–4
Mariz e Barros (Brazilian navy destroyer), 175; (Brazilian navy warship), 27
Marotte, Alberto de (Argentine navy), 216
Marqués, Luis de Melo (Brazilian inventor), 353
Marqués de la Habana (Mexican navy steamer), 16
Marqués de Olinda (Brazilian mail steamer), 20
Márquez, Marcelo (Argentine navy), 274
Márquez Planas, Tulio (Venezuelan navy), 218, 374
Marte (Brazilian navy auxiliary cruiser), 352
Martin-type aircraft, 201, 210
Martínez Fretes, Nestor (Paraguayan navy), 204–5
Martínez Quintano, Enrique (Argentine navy), 55
Martín García Island, 3, 18, 58, 191
Martini, Hector A. (Argentine navy), 276
Martinique, 122
Martins, Jorge Dodsworth (Brazilian navy), 152
Marts (U.S. Navy destroyer escort), 328
Mas Afuera Island, 103
Massó Perdomo, Juan Luis (Venezuelan air force), 375
Matagorda, Texas, 167
Matamoros, México, 14, 16
Matanzas, Dominican Republic, 38
Mata Tapera, Argentina, 191
Matias Cousiño (Chilean navy warship), 35
Mato Grosso (Brazilian navy destroyer), 92, 95

Mato Grosso State, Brazil, 20, 67
Mattos, Francisco de (Brazilian navy), 95
Mavila, Oscar (Peruvian navy), 119–20
Maximilian (Emperor of México), 17, 315, 344
Mayora, Armando (Argentine navy), 266
Mbutum (Bolivia/Paraguay), 126
McAnn (U.S. Navy destroyer escort), 126
McDonnell-Douglas–type aircraft, 198, 331
McDowell, L. R. (U.S. Navy), 164
McNeely, R. W. (U.S. Navy), 84
Medina Silva, Pedro (Venezuelan navy), 226–27, 230, 377–78
Mediterranean Sea, 97, 343
Mejahuira River, 120
Mejillon (Venezuelan navy patrol craft), 230–32, 376
Melchior Island, 162, 183
Mello, Custodio José de (Brazilian navy), 67–74, 76, 302–3
Méndez Nuñez, Casto (Spanish navy), 30–31
Mendoza Province, Argentina, 5
Mendoza (Argentine navy destroyer), 183; (French merchant ship), 150
Menéndez, Benjamín (Argentine army), 209
Menéndez, Mario Benjamín (Argentine army), 263, 284
Mepelia Island, 357
Merced (Dominican navy schooner), 38
Mercúrio (Brazilian merchant ship), 352; (Spanish navy sail corvette), 343
Merino, José Toribio (Chilean navy), 233, 378
Merino Benítez, Julio (Chilean navy), 109
Merino Bielich, Vicente (Chilean navy), 138
Merope (French merchant tanker), 168
Meteor-type aircraft, 212–13
Meteoro (Brazilian navy armed merchant ship), 74; (Peruvian navy school ship), 37
Mexican air force, 368
Mexican army, 13, 16
Mexican marine corps, 371
Mexican merchant marine, 164–68
Mexican navy: too weak to oppose Spanish (1829) and French (1838), 13; war with Texas (1835–43), 13–15; war with Yucatan (1842–43), 14–15; war with United States (1846–48), 15; conservative warships captured (1858), 16; foreigners in the fleet (1891), 129–30; transport capability (early twentieth century), 349–50; cadets defend Veracruz (1914), 315; rebels (1924),

428   INDEX

Mexican navy (*continued*)
  76–77, 294; significantly increases (1930s), 144; aids Republican Spain (1936–37), 165; develops aviation (1940–80s), 168, 201; officers man merchant ships (1942–45), 167–68; no ASW capability (1942–45), 168; contributes to war (1945), 168
Mexicano (Mexican navy brigantine), 15
México, 5, 12–17, 39–40, 76–77, 89, 136, 145–46, 164–68, 177, 179, 201, 294, 314–16, 325, 349–50, 355, 369
México City, 16, 206
Mexique (French merchant ship), 166
Meyer, Pedro (Paraguayan navy), 205
Meza Burgos, Adolfo (Mexican navy), 330
Miami, 179, 328–29
Midnight Sun (Norwegian merchant ship), 71
Miguel, Daniel F. (Argentine navy), 278
Minas Gerais (Brazilian navy aircraft carrier), 190, 194, 197–98, 332, 372; (Brazilian navy dreadnought), 77–79, 81–82, 86, 92, 94, 96–97, 105–7, 134, 153, 195, 321, 353, 356, 366
Minas Gerais State, Brazil, 67
Minatitlán (Mexican merchant tanker), 330
Minatitlán, México, 316
Mindello (Portuguese navy gunboat), 69
Mines: lack mobility and target discrimination, 12; used in the War of the Triple Alliance (1866), 23, 27; used in defense of Callao (1880), 35; used in Rio (1893), 69; used to defend Aquidabá (1894), 75; used on Amazon River by Colombia (1911), 121; planted during Malvinas War (1982), 245, 261
Ministro Zenteno (Chilean navy protected cruiser), 47, 49, 298
Miraflores, Battle of, 37
Mirage-type aircraft, 384
Miragoâne, Haití, 39
Misiones (Argentine navy destroyer), 183
Misiones, Argentina, 20, 22
Missões (Brazilian navy river gunboat), 92
Moffett (U.S. Navy destroyer), 366
Moffett, William (U.S. Navy), 196, 372
Molina, Juan J. (Venezuelan navy), 375
Molina Villegas, Jesús Teodoro (Venezuelan navy), 224–25, 376
Molini, Rafael G. (Argentine navy), 261–62
Molteni, Carlos (Argentine navy), 384–86
Monagas (Venezuelan merchant tanker), 170
Mönch Siegert, Alfredo (Venezuelan army), 227, 232, 377

Monitor (U.S. Navy monitor), 352, 369
Monmouth (British navy cruiser), 103
Monserrat Island, 180
Monsumen (British merchant ship/Argentine naval auxiliary), 236, 265, 270, 277, 287, 399
Montezuma (Mexican navy steamer), 15
Montalvo Salazar, Gonzalo (Mexican navy), 330
Montaña, Carlos (Argentine navy), 57
Monteagudo (Peruvian merchant ship), 28
Monte Penedo (German merchant ship), 197
Monte Protegido (Argentine merchant ship), 101, 356
Monterey (México/United States), 3, 315
Montevideo, Uruguay, 2–3, 8, 19–20, 67, 71, 73, 79, 100, 147–48, 213, 305, 318–19, 343–44, 380, 385
Mont Organisé (Haitian navy warship), 39, 41
Montserrat, 311
Montt, Jorge (Chilean navy), 47, 49, 59, 66, 300–301, 349, 351
Moore, Edwin (Texas navy), 14–15
Morales Luengo, Eduardo (Venezuelan navy), 223, 375
Morales Monasterios, Victor Hugo (Venezuelan navy), 220, 224, 227, 230–31, 377–78
Moreno (Argentine navy dreadnought), 84, 140, 143, 185, 194, 321, 354–55
Moreno Piña, Andrés Oswaldo (Venezuelan navy), 226, 231, 377
Morice, George Francis (Paraguayan navy), 129
Morinigo, Higinio (president of Paraguay), 203, 294–95
Morla Vicuña, Carlos (Chilean minister to the United States), 50
Moron, Argentina, 210
Morris, Raimundo (Chilean navy), 5
Motomar (Spanish merchant ship), 165, 368
Motta, Sylvio Borges de Souza (Brazilian navy), 208
Mozzarelli, Antonio José (Argentine navy), 261, 384
Mujeres Island, 14
Mullinix (U.S. Navy destroyer), 180
Muñoz, Gómez (Venezuelan navy), 224
Muñoz Artigas, Luis (Chilean navy), 109
Muñoz Valdés, Luis (Chilean navy), 111
Murature (Argentine navy frigate), 213
Mutiny: causes, 105; in Spanish navy *Trinidad* (1818), 6; in Chilean navy *Aguiles* (1828), 28; in merchant ship *Monteagudo* (1835), 28; in Texas navy's

San Antonio (1842), 14; in Brazilian dreadnoughts (1910), 81, 86, 105–6; German navy (1918), 357–58; Brazilian navy (1919), 106–7; British navy (1919, 1931), 357–58; Chilean navy (1931), 107–15; Peruvian navy (1932), 115–16; U.S. Navy (1944), 357–58; U.S. Navy work stoppage (1972), 357–58
Mutual Defense Assistance Act, 173
Mutual Security Act, 173–74, 177

Napoleon I, 2, 7
Napoleonic wars, 1–2, 6–7
Napo River, 119
Narwal (Argentine fishing vessel), 244–45, 268–69
Nashville (U.S. Navy cruiser), 40
Natal, Brazil, 153
Natchez (U.S. Navy sloop), 14
National Liberation Alliance (Brazilian political party), 79
National political will: background, 53, 349; Argentina (1890), 54–57, 294; (1893), 57–59, 294; (1930), 294, (1943), 295; (1945, 1951, 1955), 209–17, 295; (1963), 296; (1976), 296; Brazil (1891), 66, 294; (1893–94), 66–77, 294; (1924), 77–79; (1955, 1964), 208, 295–96; Chile (1891), 59–66, 294; (1973), 233, 296; Colombia (1957), 295; Cuba (1933, 1952, 1957), 206–8, 295; Haití (1970), 233, 296; México (1924), 77–78, 294; Paraguay (1941), 294; (1947), 203–5; Peru (1948), 294; Venezuela (1957, 1962), 217–32, 296
NATO. *See* North Atlantic Treaty Organization
Nautilus (Spanish navy training ship), 130
Nebraska (U.S. Navy battleship), 97
Neembucu (Paraguayan navy tug), 204–5
Negro River, 124
Nemesis (U.S. coast guard cutter), 167
Neptune-type aircraft, 179
Neri, Silverio (Brazilian governor), 118
Netherlands. *See* Holland
Neto, Coelho (Brazilian minister of the navy), 73
Neutrality Zone of 1939–41, 144, 147–48, 150
Newark (U.S. Navy protected cruiser), 73
New Guinea, 234
New York (U.S. Navy armored cruiser), 73
Nicaragua, 40, 89, 145, 180, 316–17, 355, 370
Nickels, J. Federick (Haitian navy), 39
Nictheroy, Brazil, 68–69, 73, 78
Nictheroy (Brazilian navy armed merchant ship), 73, 352

Nigeria (British navy cruiser), 183
Nitrates, 31, 42, 44–45, 61–62, 88, 104
Noronha, Julio Cesa de (Brazilian navy), 80
North American–type aircraft, 197, 331
North Atlantic Treaty Organization, 173, 234–35, 244
North Dakota (U.S. Navy dreadnought), 135
North Sea, 372
Novoa, Guillermo (Chilean army), 111
Nueva Altaoracia (Dominican merchant schooner), 170
Nueva Esparta (Venezuelan navy destroyer), 179–80, 222, 225, 230, 370, 376
Nueva Esparta class (Venezuelan navy destroyers), 218, 367
Nueva Island, 184, 370
Numero 7 (Argentine navy torpedo boat), 57
Numero 8 (Argentine navy torpedo boat), 57

Oakville (Canadian navy corvette), 369
Oaxaca (Mexican merchant steamer), 167, 368
Obregón, Alvaro (president of México), 77, 294
Obregoso (Peruvian merchant ship), 28
O'Brien (Chilean navy destroyer), 107
Oceano (Brazilian merchant ship), 352
O'Connor, Eduardo (Argentine navy), 55–56
O'Higgins (Chilean navy armored cruiser), 48–49, 107–8, 113, 298, 348; (Chilean navy sail frigate), 6; (Chilean navy steam corvette), 31–32
Olimpo, Fortin, 124
Olimpo (Paraguayan navy gunboat), 25
Olinda (Brazilian merchant ship), 25; (German merchant ship), 148
Oliva (Dominican navy corvette), 38
Olivant (German merchant ship), 357
Oliveira, Pedro Ferreira de (Brazilian navy), 19
Olivieri, Anibal Osvaldo (Argentine navy), 211, 217, 373
Omaha (U.S. Navy cruiser), 151
Omea, Honduras, 314
Opium War, 138
Orama (British navy auxiliary cruiser), 100, 305
Orchila Island, 376
Ordnance, 53–54
Orella (Chilean navy destroyer), 107, 113
Organization of American States, 178–80, 223, 311

Oriana (Argentine merchant ship), 101
Orinoco (German merchant ship), 167; (German merchant tanker), 368
Orinoco River, 155
Orion-type aircraft, 165
Orizaba (U.S. Navy transport), 329
Orompello (Chilean coast guard cutter), 358
Orton River, 119
Osborn, Thomas A. (U.S. minister to Chile), 346
Osborn, Thomas O. (U.S. minister to Argentina), 346
Osún (Venezuelan navy warship), 41, 320
Otero, Eduardo (Argentine navy), 263, 265, 281, 384
Ovalle, Chile, 112, 359

Pacanins, Guillermo (Venezuelan air force), 221
Pacific Ocean, 3, 5–7, 12, 15–16, 27–37, 44, 52, 148, 162, 184, 251
Pacocha (Perú/Chile), 31, 34
Pacts of May, 51–52
Padilla, José Prudencio (Venezuelan navy), 5
Páez, José Antonio (Venezuelan army), 4
Paita, Perú, 6, 36, 345–46
Palacios, Enrique (Peruvian navy), 346
Palacios (Peruvian navy submarine), 130–31
Pallas (Brazilian merchant ship), 70, 351
Palma de Mallorca, Spain, 165
Pampa (Argentine naval auxiliary), 357
Panamá, 11–12, 16–17, 40–41, 112, 144–45, 174, 177, 307–9, 318, 355, 370
Panamá Canal, 104, 122, 131–32, 142, 145, 161, 180, 251, 318
Panamá City, 40, 308
Panamá Railroad, 40, 308, 346
Panamanian merchant marine, 153
Pan American (? merchant ship), 135
Pando, José Manuel (president of Bolivia), 119
Panther (German navy gunboat), 41
Panther-type aircraft, 195, 331
Pánuco (Mexican merchant tanker), 330
Pará, Brazil, 122, 365
Pará (Brazilian navy destroyer), 92, 94; (Brazilian navy warship), 26
Pará class (Brazilian navy destroyers), 153
Parada, Martín (Venezuelan air force), 375
Paraguari (Paraguayan navy steamer), 345
Paraguay, 18–27, 118, 122–26, 142, 172, 193, 202–5, 217, 294–95, 325, 355
Paraguay (Paraguayan navy river gunboat), 124, 141–42, 203–5, 217, 360

Paraguayan air force, 204–5
Paraguayan army, 20, 22–27, 124, 126, 203–5
Paraguayan marine corps, 126, 193, 371
Paraguayan merchant marine, 124
Paraguayan navy: foreigners in the fleet (1854), 129; and *Water Witch* affair (1855), 18–19; confronts British navy (1859), 19; captures *Marques de Olinda* (1864), 20; captures Corrientes (1865), 20–22; defeated at Riachuelo (1865), 22; employs *camalotes* (1868), 26; final battles against Brazilian navy (1869), 27; receives aid from Chile (1932), 142; during Chaco War (1932–35), 124, 126; develops naval aviation (1929–35), 126, 201; involvement in rebellion (1941), 294; attempts to change government (1947), 202–6, 294; receives aid from Argentina (1950–80s), 141–42, 193
Paraguay class (Paraguayan navy river gunboats), 124
Paraguay River, 19–20, 23–27, 45, 122–24, 126, 193
Parahyba (Brazilian merchant ship), 352; (Brazilian navy destroyer), 92, 95; (Brazilian navy gunboat), 352
Paraná (Argentine navy gunboat), 55; (Brazilian merchant steamer), 90; (Brazilian navy destroyer), 92
Parana River, 18–27, 45, 57–59, 193, 204–5
Parapití (Paraguayan tug), 360
Pardo, Mariano Ignacio (president of Perú), 32
Paredes López, Oscar (Venezuelan navy), 220
Pareja, José Manuel (Spanish navy), 29–30
Paris Declaration of 1856, 98
Parnaíba, Brazil, 366
Parque de Artillería, Buenos Aires, 54
Párraga Núñez, Felipe (Venezuelan army), 375
Paso de la Patria, Paraguay, 23, 188, 204, 351
Pastry War, 13–14
Patagonia, 42–45, 184, 192, 236, 268
Patagonia (Argentine navy protected cruiser), 55–57, 347, 350; (German merchant steamer), 100
Patria (Argentine navy gunboat), 49; (Cuban navy gunboat), 99–100, 206; (Peruvian navy landing ship), 200; (Venezuelan navy corvette), 369
Paucarpata, Treaty of, 28
Paunero, Wenceslao (Argentine army), 22

INDEX 431

Payarola, Luis (Argentine navy), 270
Paysandú, Uruguay, 20
PC 536 (U.S. Navy submarine chaser), 167
PC 544 (U.S. Navy submarine chaser), 328
PC 547 (U.S. Navy submarine chaser), 328
PC 554 (U.S. Navy submarine chaser), 328
PC 561 (U.S. Navy submarine chaser), 328
PC 604 (U.S. Navy submarine chaser), 328
PC 605 (U.S. Navy submarine chaser), 328
PC 607 (U.S. Navy submarine chaser), 328
PC 1236 (U.S. Navy submarine chaser), 328
Pearl Harbor attack, 144–45, 151, 166–67
Pebble Island. *See* Borbon Island
Pedro I (emperor of Brazil), 7
Pedro Afonso (Brazilian navy torpedo boat), 74–75, 352
Pedro Ivo (Brazilian navy torpedo boat), 74–75, 352
Pedrozo, Miguel Angel (Argentine navy), 373
Peixoto, Floriano Vieira (president of Brazil), 67–74, 76, 294
Pelada Island, 264
Pellew (British ? merchant ship), 334
Pelotaslóide (Brazilian merchant ship), 160
Penelope (British/Argentine craft), 270, 273, 279, 287, 339
Penido, José María (Brazilian navy), 77
Pennewill (U.S. Navy destroyer escort), 328
Pennsylvania (U.S. Navy dreadnought), 318
Pensacola, Florida, 140, 194, 199
Penso Nebrús, Jaime (Venezuelan navy), 231–32
Pequot (U.S. Navy gunboat), 39
Peralta, Carlos F. (Argentine navy), 180
Pereia da Cunha (Brazilian merchant ship), 352
Pérez, Antonio (Argentine navy), 55
Pérez, Julio (Argentine navy), 281
Pérez del Cerro, Ismael (Argentine navy), 373
Pérez Jiménez, Marcos (president of Venezuela), 218, 220–23, 296
Perla (Chilean/Spanish navy sail frigate), 5
Pernambuco, Brazil, 148, 351
Perón, Evita (Argentine citizen), 216
Perón, Isabel (president of Argentina), 296
Perón, Juan (president of Argentina), 177, 192, 195, 209–17, 295
Persia (German merchant ship), 197
Perú, 5–7, 32–37, 42, 44, 46, 104, 119–26, 128, 130–33, 140, 142, 144–45, 188, 191, 295, 318, 325, 345–46, 355, 369
Peruvian air force, 133, 200
Peruvian army, 28, 32–37, 119–26, 350
Peruvian marine corps, 189, 191, 371
Peruvian merchant marine, 104
Peruvian navy: expense of fleet (1820s), 344; foreigners in fleet (1820s), 244; during wars of independence (1825), 7; captures Guayaquil (1829), 27; warships captured (1836), 28; attacks Chilean navy (1839), 29; increases strength (1865), 30; during war with Spain (1865–66), 30–31; awaits *Huáscar* (1866), 31; *Huáscar* surrenders to (1876), 31; contemporary evaluation of (1879), 32; not prepared for war (1879), 32; battle of Iquique (1879), 32–33; attacks Chilean coast (1879), 33; *Huáscar* captured (1879), 34, 346; foreigners in fleet (1879), 129–30; defense of Callao (1880), 35–36; innovative defense (1880), 35; attempts to use submarine (1880), 36–37, 346; destroys its ships (1880), 37; operations in La Selva (1903), 119–20; interest in submarines (1905–present), 130–33, 362; academy established at Callao (1905), 130–31; fights with Colombia (1911), 121; tries to enforce neutrality (1914–18), 104; receives U.S. naval mission (1920–40), 127, 131–33; develops naval aviation (1920–80s), 132–33, 200–201; cadets on Brazilian school ship (1920), 142; mutinies (1932), 115–16; transports army (1932), 350; submarines remain loyal (1932), 115–16; riverine war with Colombia (1933), 121–22; involvement in rebellion (1948), 295; holds ASW exercises with United States (1953–80s), 174–76; seizes whalers (1954), 182; conducts amphibious landing (1981), 187
Peruvier (Belgium merchant ship), 131
Pessôa, Epitacio da Silva (president of Brazil), 97–98, 135, 362
Petare, Venezuela, 222
Petion (Haitian navy warship), 38
Petite Rivière, 38
Petit Goave, Haití, 39
Petróleos Mexicanos, 167
Petroleum, 153, 164, 166, 170, 218, 221
Petropolis, Brazil, 365
Petropolis, Treaty of, 119
Pezet, Juan Antonio (president of Perú), 346
Philippi, Alberto Jorge (Argentine navy), 274

Phoebe (British navy sail frigate), 306
Phrigia (German merchant ship), 167
Piauby (Brazilian navy destroyer), 92, 95
Piccardo, Antonio (Venezuelan navy), 232
Pichincha (Colombian coast guard cutter), 360
Picolet (Haitian navy schooner), 38
Picton Island, 184, 370
Piedra Buena, Argentina, 183
Piedrabuena (Argentine navy destroyer), 183, 236, 248, 250, 253, 261
Piérola, Nicolás de (president of Perú), 36
Pilatus-type aircraft, 197
Pilcomayo (Peruvian/Chilean navy steam corvette), 34–35, 61, 346
Pilcomayo River, 122, 126, 203
Piloto Pardo (Chilean navy research ship), 253
Pinedo (Argentine navy torpedo boat), 350
Pingo (Paraguayan cattle boat), 360
Pinochet, Augusto Ugarte (president of Chile), 233
Pinzón, Luis H. (Spanish navy), 29
Piraja (Brazilian navy gunboat), 352
Piratinim (Brazilian navy torpedo boat), 352
Pires, Christóvão Nuñes (governor of Santa Catharina), 70
Pisagua, Perú/Chile, 34, 346
Pisco, Perú, 6, 36
Pittsburgh (U.S. Navy armored cruiser), 91
Piva, Adolfo (Argentine navy), 373
Pizarro, Manuel D. (Argentine senator), 57
Placido de Castro, José (Brazilian citizen), 118–19
Plate River. *See* Río de la Plata
Plaza de Mayo, Buenos Aires, 55
Poi Island, 26
Poisson, Maurice (Chilean navy), 200
Poland, 98, 144, 370
Polish fishing fleet, 248
Pollux (Paraguayan merchant craft), 360
Pons Goizueta, Miguel (Cuban navy), 206, 373
Ponte Rodríguez, Manuel (Venezuelan navy), 226, 230, 232, 375, 377–78
Pontón, Argentina, 215
Port-au-Prince, Haití, 39, 41, 233, 312
Port de Paix, Haití, 39
Port Fox. *See* Puerto Zorro
Port Harriet (Great Britain/Argentina), 239
Portillo (Peruvian navy launch), 360
Port King, Malvinas, 264. *See* Puerto Rey
Porto Acre. *See* Puerto Alonso
Porto Alegre, Brazil, 197
Portobello, (Colombia/Panamá), 2
Port of Spain, Trinidad, 122
Port Stanley, Malvinas, 184, 236–42. *See also* Puerto Argentino
Portugal, 7–9, 17, 69, 122, 305
Portuguese marine corps, 7, 190, 371
Portuguese navy, during wars of independence (1823), 7–8
Posadas (Paraguayan merchant craft), 350
Potosí (Mexican navy gunboat), 349–50
Potrero del Llano [I] (Mexican merchant tanker), 167, 330; [II] (Mexican merchant tanker), 168
Potrillo (Chilean/Spanish navy brigantine), 5
Poyer, Manuel de Jesús (Venezuelan navy), 377
Pozo Rica (Mexican merchant tanker), 330
Prat, Arturo (Chilean navy), 33
Prat Carvajal, Arturo (Chilean finance minister), 358
Pratt Gill (Paraguayan navy steamer), 203
Prefectura. *See* Argentine coast guard
Presidente Errázuriz (Chilean navy protected cruiser), 46, 297
Presidente Mitre (Argentine merchant ship), 100, 305
Presidente Mosquera (Colombian navy river transport), 122, 360
Presidente Pinto (Chilean navy protected cruiser), 46, 61, 297
Presidente Saavedra (Bolivian navy armed steamer), 124
Presidente Siles (Bolivian navy armed steamer), 124
Presidente Trulillo (Dominican merchant ship), 170
Prieto Silva, Carlos (Colombian navy), 178
Primero de Março (Brazilian navy gunboat), 352
Princeton (U.S. Navy steam frigate), 352
Prio Socarras, Carlos (president of Cuba), 295
Privateers, authorized by Spain during wars of independence (1816), 4; used by México during wars of independence (1820), 5; as offensive weapon against Spain (1824), 7; used against México (1835), 13; Perú tries to hire (1839), 29; during Haitian Dominican wars (1844–93), 38–40; México does not employ (1846), 15; ex-Confederates propose their use to Paraguay (1866), 22
Proenca, João Justino de (Brazilian navy), 353
Providence (Haitian rebel steamer), 38

INDEX   433

Prueba (Spanish navy sail frigate), 6
Pucará-type aircraft, 272, 384–85
Pueblo (Mexican merchant tanker), 368
Pueblo (U.S. Navy armored cruiser), 91
Puerto Aldea, Chile, 139
Puerto Alonso (Bolivia/Brazil), 118–19
Puerto Argentino, Malvinas, 236, 242, 244–45, 256, 258–59, 261, 263–68, 270–83, 385
Puerto Belgrano, Argentina, 100, 148, 179, 185, 194, 211–15, 236, 242–43, 247, 381
Puerto Bello, Venezuela, 41
Puerto Cabello, Venezuela, 3, 5, 179, 220, 222, 225–32, 320, 376–78
Puerto Casado, Paraguay, 124
Puerto Copacar, Paraguay, 205
Puerto Cortez, Honduras, 314
Puerto Deseado, Argentina, 243, 245, 264, 277
Puerto Groussac, Malvinas, 236
Puerto Howard, Malvinas, 270
Puerto Leda, Paraguay, 124
Puerto Madryn, Argentina, 100, 182
Puerto Milagro, Paraguay, 204–5
Puerto Militar. *See* Puerto Belgrano
Puerto Montt, Chile, 199
Puerto Plata, Dominican Republic, 38, 310–11
Puerto Rey, Malvinas, 270, 273
Puerto Rico, 8, 37
Puerto Santo (Venezuelan navy survey ship), 376
Puerto Suarez, Paraguay, 124
Puerto Zorro, Malvinas, 270, 277
Pueyrredón (Argentine navy armored cruiser), 49, 52, 100, 194, 298, 348
Puma (British navy frigate), 184
Punta Arenas, Chile, 45, 49, 103, 199
Punta de Atacama, 49
Punta del Este, Uruguay, 79, 147, 365
Punta Indio, Argentina, 209–10, 255, 383
Punta Jacquet Island, 205
Punta Medanos (Argentine navy tanker), 187, 236
Purus River, 118
Putumayo River, 122
Py (Argentine navy destroyer), 182–83, 236, 248
Py, Luis (Argentine navy), 45

Quadros, Jânio (president of Brazil), 197
Quebrado, Battle of, 18, 304
Querétaro (Mexican navy gunboat), 349–50
Quevedo, Pedro J. (Venezuelan army), 222
Quindora (Chilean navy torpedo launch), 351
Quintero, Chile, 61, 109–11, 199
Quinto Misiones (Argentine merchant steamship), 57
Quinze de Novembro (Brazilian merchant ship), 352

R 4 (Peruvian navy submarine), 116
Radar, 147
Rademaker, Augusto Hamann (Brazilian navy), 370
Radical Party (Argentina), 57
Railroads, 40, 42, 62, 86, 124, 151, 314
Raleigh (U.S. Navy protected cruiser), 97
Ramirez, Luis J. (Venezuelan navy), 180
Ramirez Delgado, Mario (Cuban navy), 169
Rancho Grande, Venezuela, 232
Rangel, Domingo Alberto (Venezuelan citizen), 223
R class (Peruvian navy submarines), 122, 132, 362
Realejo, Nicaragua, 316
Recife, Brazil, 152–53, 155, 158, 160, 179, 351, 366
Regenerador (Mexican navy tug), 15
Regina Margherita (Italian navy battleship), 50
Remington rifles, 57
República (Argentine navy gunboat), 45; (Brazilian navy cruiser), 67–68, 70, 73–74, 92, 351
République (Haitian rebel ship), 39
Resolución (Spanish navy steam frigate), 29
Restaurador (Venezuelan navy gunboat), 320
Retiro, Buenos Aires, 55
Returmba, João da Silva (Brazilian navy), 352
Revista de Marina (Valparaíso), 199
Reybold (U.S. Navy destroyer escort), 329
Reyes Canal, Julio Cesar (Colombian navy), 177
Rhein (German merchant ship), 167
Riacho Guyacuru, Paraguay, 26
Riachuelo, Battle of, 22, 25, 193, 345
Riachuelo (Brazilian navy battleship), 68; (Brazilian navy dreadnought), 82, 321
Rial, Arturo H. (Argentine navy), 212
Ricaldoni, Tebaldo (Argentine citizen), 48
Richelieu (French navy dreadnought), 365
Riesco, Germán (president of Chile), 50–51
Rimac (Chilean/Peruvian transport), 33, 37
Río Afua (Bolivian armed launch), 118–19
Río Apa (Paraguayan navy warship), 24–25

434 INDEX

Rio Branco, Baron de (Brazilian minister of foreign affairs), 80, 353
Rio Branco (Brazilian merchant steamer), 90; (Brazilian navy hydrographic ship), 158
Río de Carapañá [I] (Argentine merchant ship), 158–59
Río Carcarañá [II] (Argentine merchant ship), 243, 245, 264, 270, 339
Rio de Janeiro, 67–74, 77–79, 92, 94, 96–98, 106–107, 135, 145–46, 150, 152, 155, 160, 179, 195–98, 208, 305, 352, 366–67
Rio de Janeiro (Brazilian merchant ship), 95; (Brazilian navy dreadnought), 81–82, 135, 321, 353–54; (Brazilian navy ironclad), 23, 27
Rio de Janeiro Protocol of 1935, 122
Rio de Janeiro State, Brazil, 67, 69, 92
Rio de la Plata, 2, 18–23, 100, 117–18, 124, 148, 318, 304, 343, 364–65
Río de la Plata (Argentine merchant ship), 334–35
Río Gallegos, Argentina, 258, 270
Río Grande, Argentina, 185, 243, 253, 255–59, 261, 266, 270, 273, 276–79, 284
Rio Grande do Norte (Brazilian navy destroyer), 93, 95–97, 356
Rio Grande do Sul, Brazil, 20, 67
Rio Grande do Sul (Brazilian navy monitor), 25–26; (Brazilian navy scout cruiser), 92–95, 97, 153, 158–60
Rio Grande do Sul State, Brazil, 66–67, 72, 74, 93, 148, 351
Río Igauzú (Argentine coast guard cutter), 243, 276, 339, 385; (Argentine merchant ship), 336
Rio Manduvira, 26
Río Olivia (Argentine merchant ship), 334, 336
Rio Ozama, 38
Rio Pact. *See* Inter-American Reciprocal Assistance Treaty
Rio Pardo (Brazilian merchant steamer), 90
Rio Real, 152
Río San Lorenzo, Paraguay, 25
Río Santiago, Argentina, 211, 213
Río Tercero (Argentine merchant ship), 162, 367
Riquelme (Chilean navy destroyer), 107, 113
Rivadavia (Argentine navy dreadnought), 84, 86, 140, 143, 177, 185, 194, 321, 354–55
River class (Canadian navy escorts), 173
Riverine wars, 19–27, 57–59, 117–26, 203–5

Riveros (Chilean navy destroyer), 111
Riveros, Galvarino (Chilean navy), 33, 35
River Plate, Battle of, 147–48
Rivolta, Antonio H. (Argentine navy), 209
Roamar (Colombian merchant ship), 169
Robacio, Carlos (Argentine navy), 265, 384, 386
Robbio Pacheco, Mario (Argentine navy), 212
Robert Smith (U.S. Navy destroyer), 316
Robles Osses, Orlando (Chilean navy), 110
Roca, Julio A. (president of Argentina), 45, 48–49
Rodolfo B (Paraguayan tug), 360
Rodrigues, Gaspar de Silva (Brazilian navy), 352
Rodrigues, Paulo Mario da Cunha (Brazilian navy), 208
Rodríguez, José Melitón (Peruvian navy), 346
Rodríguez Calderón, José (Cuban navy), 206
Rodríguez Corro, Angel (Venezuelan army), 375–76
Rodríguez Figueroa, Haroldo (Venezuelan navy), 221, 375
Rodríguez Oliveres, Miguel (Venezuelan navy), 221, 375
Rodríguez Sepulveda, Juan Agustín (Chilean navy), 200–201
Rogers, Calixto (Chilean navy), 108–109
Rojas, Isaac F. (Argentine navy), 211–17, 373–74
Rojas, Rosendo (Bolivian army), 119
Rojas Pinilla, Gustavo (president of Colombia), 295
Romarate, Jacinto (Spanish navy), 2
Roper (U.S. Navy destroyer), 177
Rosa, Andrés de la (Venezuelan navy), 375
Rosalba (U.S. merchant ship), 18
Rosales (Argentine merchant ship), 45; (Argentine navy destroyer), 179–80, 182, 370
Rosales Alvarez, Rafael (Venezuelan navy), 376
Rosario, Argentina, 57–59
Rosario, Paraguay, 205
Rosario (Uruguayan merchant ship), 104
Rosario Operation, 236–41
Rosas, Manuel (president of Argentina), 18, 304–5
Ross, Charles Baynes Hodgon (British navy), 29
Rotalbe, Carlos (Peruvian navy), 115–16
Ruby (Colombian merchant ship), 169

INDEX   435

Rucumilla (Chilean navy torpedo launch), 351
Rui Barbosa (Brazilian armed river craft), 118
Russia, 4–5, 122, 349, 360. *See also* Soviet Union
Russian fishing fleet, 182–83, 248
Russian navy: tries to buy dreadnoughts (1913), 355

Sabara (Brazilian merchant ship), 197
Sabine River, 12
Sabino Vieira (Brazilian navy torpedo boat), 352
Sabre-type aircraft, 218
Sáenz Peña, Luis (president of Argentina), 57, 294
Sáenz Valiente, Juan Pablo (Argentine navy), 349
Sagua la Grande, Cuba, 309
Saint Marc, Haití, 38
Saldanha da Gama, Luis Philipe de (Brazilian navy), 68, 72–74, 76, 302–3, 352
Sale Trou, Haití, 38
Salinas, Brazil, 19
Salm-type aircraft, 126
Salnave (Haitian navy warship), 39
Salta (Argentine navy submarine), 262, 268, 287
Salto (Argentine merchant steamer), 19
Salto de Guairaa (Paraguayan navy warship), 25
Salvador, Brazil, 91, 366
Salvajes islands, 162
Sampson, W. T. (U.S. Navy), 319
San Antonio (Texas navy warship), 14
San Bernard (Texas navy warship), 14
San Carlos, Fort, 41, 320
San Carlos, Malvinas, 244, 256, 267, 270, 273–77, 284
San Carlos de Ancud, Chile, 28
Sánchez Cerro, Luis (president of Perú), 116, 122
Sánchez Olivares, Francisco J. (Venezuelan navy), 225–26
Sánchez Sañudo, Alberto (Argentine navy), 212
San Cristóbal, Venezuela, 223
San Diego (México/United States), 64, 174, 177, 315
San Felipe, Chile, 113–14
San Felipe, Uruguay, 2
San Felipe (U.S. sail merchant ship), 17
San Francisco (Paraguayan merchant craft), 360
San Francisco (U.S. Navy protected cruiser), 73
San Jacinto, Battle of, 13

San Juan, Puerto Rico, 179
San Juan Bautista, México, 14
San Juan del Norte, Nicaragua, 316–17
San Juan del Sur, Nicaragua, 316
San Juan de Ulúa, México, 2
San Julian, Argentina, 254
San Julian, Cuba, 169
San Lorenzo (Colombia/Panamá), 2
San Lorenzo, Perú, 115–16, 345, 359
San Lorenzo River, 20
San Luis (Argentine navy destroyer), 183
San Luis (Argentine navy submarine), 248–49, 255, 262, 268, 287, 382
San Luis Province, Argentina, 57, 215
San Martín (Argentine navy armored cruiser), 48, 298, 348; (Chilean navy sail frigate), 5–6
San Martín, José de (Patriarch), 5, 7–8, 188, 210, 343
San Miguel (Spanish merchant ship), 5
San Nicolás, Battle of, 2
San Pedro, Honduras, 314
San Pedro, Paraguay, 205
San Pedro, South Georgias, 245, 247
San Pedro de Alcántara (Spanish navy ship of the line), 4
Santa Anna, Antonio López de (president of México), 13–14
Santa Anna (German merchant ship), 365
Santa Catharina, 68–70, 74
Santa Catharina (Brazilian navy destroyer), 92, 95
Santa Cruz, Andrés (president of Peruvian-Bolivian confederation), 28–29
Santa Cruz (Argentine navy destroyer), 182–83
Santa Cruz, Brazil, 79, 198
Santa Cruz, Fort, 67, 78–79
Santa Cruz Province, Argentina, 183
Santa Cruz River, 45
Santa Fe, Argentina, 57
Santa Fe (Argentine navy submarine), 236, 239, 243, 245, 247, 262, 288, 380–82
Santa Fe II (Argentine merchant ship), 336
Santa Maria (Colombian navy river gunboat), 121, 360
Santander, Spain, 165
Santa Rosa, Argentina, 217
Santa Rosa (Bolivia/Brazil), 119
San Telmo (Spanish navy ship of the line), 6
Santi (Spanish merchant ship), 368
Santiago, Battle of, 349
Santiago, Chile, 5, 30, 42, 44, 47, 51–52, 61–62, 64, 109–10, 113, 346, 361
Santiago (Chilean navy dreadnought), 322
Santiago, Cuba, 206, 310
Santiago del Estero (Argentine navy submarine), 247, 262

436   INDEX

Santillán, Hugo (Argentine navy), 241, 380
Santísima Trinidad (Argentine navy sail frigate), 3; (Argentine navy destroyer), 236–42, 248
Santo Domingo, 38, 310–11. *See also* Dominican Republic
Santos, Brazil, 79, 208, 365
Santos (Brazilian merchant steamer), 352
Santos, João Carlos Mourao dos (Brazilian navy), 92
São Bento Hill, Rio de Janeiro, 69
São Diego (Brazilian merchant steamer), 69
São Paulo, Brazil, 152, 359, 365
São Paulo (Brazilian navy dreadnought), 77–79, 81–82, 86, 92, 94, 96–97, 105–6, 134, 153, 321, 362–63
São Paulo State, Brazil, 67, 77, 79, 93
São Pedro d'Aldeia, Brazil, 197–98
São Salvador (Brazilian navy armed merchant ship), 74–75, 352
São Tomé, Brazil, 150
São Vicente, Cape Verde, 122
Sapper Hill, Malvinas, 243, 287
Sarandí (Argentine naval schooner), 238
Saratoga (U.S. Navy sail sloop), 16
Sargente (Chilean navy torpedo launch), 351
Sarmiento (Argentine navy school ship), 49, 142
Sarmiento, Domingo F. (president of Argentina), 45, 188, 370
Sasebo, Japan, 177
Savoia-type aircraft, 126
SC-13 (Cuban navy submarine chaser), 169
SC-762 (U.S. Navy submarine chaser), 328
SC-763 (U.S. Navy submarine chaser), 328
SC-764 (U.S. Navy submarine chaser), 328
SC-765 (U.S. Navy submarine chaser), 328
SC-766 (U.S. Navy submarine chaser), 328
SC-767 (U.S. Navy submarine chaser), 328
SC-1288 (U.S. Navy submarine chaser), 328
SC-1289 (U.S. Navy submarine chaser), 328
Scasso, León L. (Argentine navy), 148
Schafer, Heinz (German navy), 163
Schichau of Germany, 74
Schiff 10 (German navy warship), 150
Schroedors, Edgardo von (Chilean navy), 109–10, 354

Seabat-type helicopter, 197–98
Seabra, J. J. (Brazilian congressman), 67
Sea Cat missile, 282
Sea Dart missile, 280
Sea King–type helicopter, 198, 238, 253, 258, 269, 272, 287
Sea Lynx–type helicopter, 253, 385
Sea Skua missile, 253, 383
Sebastian (Spanish merchant ship), 368
Second Air Group (Chilean air force), 110, 112
Second Paraguayan Horse Artillery Regiment, 22
Seeadler (German navy auxiliary), 357
Seguí (Argentine navy destroyer), 82–83, 236, 248, 276
Seijas Villalobos, José C. (Venezuelan navy), 225, 376
Selva region, Amazon, 200
Sergipe (Brazilian navy destroyer), 93
Sergipe State, Brazil, 92
Serrano (Chilean navy destroyer), 107, 113
Serrano, Ignacio (Chilean navy), 33
Sete de Setembro (Brazilian merchant ship), 351
Seydlitz (German merchant ship), 100
Shah (British navy warship), 31
Shakleton (British research ship), 184
Shamokin (U.S. Navy gunboat), 23
Sheffield (British navy cruiser), 312
Sheffield (British navy destroyer), 266, 289, 341
Sheppard, Thomas D. L. (British navy), 95
Short-type aircraft, 199
Shrike missile, 273, 382
Siboney (Cuban navy gunboat), 206
Sidewinder missile, 186, 274, 382–83
Sikorsky-type helicopters, 197–99, 205
Sil (Spanish merchant ship), 165, 368
Silva, Héctor E. (Argentine navy), 261
Silvado (Brazilian navy monitor), 27
Silvado (Brazilian navy torpedo boat), 74–75, 352
Silva Jardim (Brazilian navy torpedo boat), 352
Silvia (Greek merchant ship), 368
Simpson (Chilean navy destroyer), 107
Simpson (Chilean navy submarine), 185
Sims-Edison torpedo, 78
Singapore, 198
Sino-Japanese War, 44
Siqueira Campos (Brazilian merchant ship), 150, 365
Siqueiros, Alfaro (Mexican soldier), 368
Sir Galahad (British landing ship), 334, 384, 386
Sirius (British navy cruiser), 69

INDEX 437

Sirius (Brazilian navy survey ship), 196
Sir Lancelot (British landing ship), 334
Sir Tristram (British landing ship), 334–35, 384, 386
Sisaleno (Yucatecan navy gunboat), 15
Skyhawk-type aircraft, 186, 198, 238, 248–50, 257–58, 274–76, 279–80, 285, 288–89, 331, 383, 385
Smith, Federico W. (Paraguayan army), 203
Snipe (British navy frigate), 183
Snipe Island, 184
Social Democratic Party (Venezuela), 222
Solano, Fort, 226, 232
Soledad Island, 244, 273–74, 279, 282
Solimoes (Brazilian merchant ship), 118; (Brazilian navy monitor), 355
Sonar, 147, 155
Songjin, Korea, 177
Sophie (German navy warship), 306
Sopwith-type aircraft, 199
Sosa Ríos, Ricardo (Venezuelan navy), 218, 220, 224–32, 375
Sosua, Dominican Republic, 310
Source Salée, Haití, 40
Southampton (British navy sail frigate), 4
South Dakota (U.S. Navy armored cruiser), 91
South Georgia islands, 184, 241–45, 262, 333–34, 378–82
South Orkney islands, 184
South Sandwich islands, 184
South Shetland islands, 162, 183
Souza e Mello, Mario de (Brazilian air force), 197
Soviet Union, 163, 172, 178–80, 182, 310, 312, 324, 370. *See also* Russia
Spain, 1–9, 13, 17, 27, 29–31, 37–38, 94, 98, 104, 128, 140, 143–44, 158–59, 162, 164–66, 188, 217, 305, 312–14, 319, 345
Spanish American War, 98, 309, 348
Spanish Civil War, 143, 164–66, 367–68
Spanish navy: during colonial era, 343; ranks (early nineteenth century), 293; during wars of independence (1810–26), 1–8, 343–44; attempts to recapture Tampico (1829), 13; attacks México (1861), 16; sent to Perú (1864), 29; bombards Valparaíso and Callao (1866), 30–31, 346; intervenes against rebellious Argentine navy (1890), 56
Spartacus (Rio de Janeiro), 106
Spartan-type aircraft, 165
Spear, W. O. (U.S. Navy), 127, 134
Spee, Maximilian Johannes (German navy), 103–4
Splendid (British navy submarine), 381

Spoerer, Enrique (Chilean navy), 109
Steembecker, Guillermo (Chilean navy), 109–10
Stein (German navy warship), 313
Stelvio (Italian merchant tanker), 330
Stinger missiles, 382
Stori, Segundo R. (Argentine navy), 369
Storm (Spanish merchant ship), 367
Stromness (British navy auxiliary), 334–35
Suaréz Mier y Terán, Edgar (Venezuelan air force), 375
Submarines. *See* names of individual navies
Sucre, Luis Enrique (Venezuelan air force), 375
Sultan Osman I (Turkish navy dreadnought), 354
Super Etendards, 256–57, 259, 266–67, 272–73, 277, 279–80, 289, 331, 383–85
Swan Island. *See* Isla del Cisne
Swiftsure (British navy battleship), 349
Sylvain (Haitian navy warship), 39
Sylvia (Spanish merchant ship), 165

Tabasco (Mexican merchant ship), 368
Tabasco, México, 77
Tabasco River, 14
Taber, William (North American), 2
Tacna, Battle of, 35
Tacna, Perú, 32, 36
Tacuari (Paraguayan navy steamer), 19–20, 22, 25–26, 129, 344
Tacuary (Paraguayan navy river gunboat), 124, 360
Taffinder, Sherwoode (U.S. Navy), 132
TAG II Society, 205
Tahuamanu (Bolivian navy river warcraft), 124
Talara, Perú, 187
Talcahuano, Chile, 5–6, 47, 109–11, 114, 199, 233, 345, 357, 359
Talisman (Peruvian transport), 37
Tallapoosa (U.S. Navy gunboat), 305, 350
Taltal, Chile, 33
Tamandaré (Brazilian navy ironclad), 27; (Brazilian navy light cruiser), 208; (Brazilian navy protected cruiser), 351
Tamandaré, Joaquim (Brazilian navy), 20, 22–23, 25
Tamaulipas (U.S. merchant tanker), 167, 368
Tamborim (Brazilian navy torpedo boat), 352
Tamoio (Brazilian navy submarine), 136–37, 153, 174
Tampa, Florida, 329
Tampico, México, 13, 168, 314–15

438   INDEX

Tampico (Mexican merchant tanker), 367–68; (Mexican navy gunboat), 77, 349
Taquari (Brazilian merchant ship), 95, 356
Taranto, Battle of, 196
Tarapacá (Perú/Chile), 34
Tarapacá (Perú/Colombia), 122
Tarqui, Battle of, 27
Tartar (British navy warship), 319
Tartu (French navy destroyer), 182, 306
Tauamanu River, 119
Taubaté (Brazilian merchant ship), 150
Taua Suarez, Jorge (Colombian navy), 178
Tavares, Eliezer Coutinho (Brazilian navy), 352
Tavares, Silva (Brazilian army), 351
Tayi, Paraguay, 25
Taylorcraft-type aircraft, 197
Technology, 11, 42, 53–54, 94, 146–47, 172, 175–76, 188–90, 369, 371. *See also* Antisubmarine warfare, *Dreadnought*, Dynamite gun, Fire control systems, Mines, Radar, Sonar, and Torpedo
Tecolutla, México, 167
Tecpan River, 315
Teffé (Brazilian navy river gunboat), 92
Tegualda (Chilean navy torpedo launch), 351
Tehuantepec, México, 168
Tejo, José Luis (Argentine navy), 380
Tejo (Portuguese navy destroyer), 122
Telémaque, Fort, 39
Teniente Herreros (Paraguayan navy patrol boat), 360
Teniente Rodríguez (Peruvian navy torpedo boat destroyer), 122, 131
Tenth Infantry Regiment (Argentine army), 54
Terreur (Haitian navy gunboat), 39
Terry, José Antonio (Argentine minister to Chile), 51
Testamark, Santiago F. (Venezuelan air force), 375
Texan Navy, war with México (1835–43), 13–15
Texas (Confederate navy steamer), 345
Texas-type aircraft, 331
Thames (British merchant ship), 71
Therón, José A. (French navy), 130
Thetis (British navy frigate), 28
Thor. See *Schiff 10*
Thorne (Argentine torpedo gunboat), 57
Thornton (U.S. Navy destroyer), 315
Thornycroft, 153
Thrush (U.S. Navy minesweeper), 151
Tiburón class (Peruvian navy submarines), 362

Tierra del Fuego, 44, 62, 185, 243, 261, 276
Tigre, Argentina, 57
Tijuca (Brazilian merchant ship), 90
Timbira (Brazilian navy submarine), 136–37, 153
Timbó, Paraguay, 26
Timor, 234
Tine Asmussen (German merchant tanker), 164
Tinto (Chilean merchant barque), 357
Tiradentes (Brazilian navy cruiser), 68, 71, 92, 352
Tirador (Paraguayan river craft), 204
Tocopilla, Chile, 33
Tolten (Chilean navy steamer), 31
Tomlin, George N. (British navy), 139
Tongoi, Bay of, 113
Toranzo Calderon, Samuel (Argentine navy), 211, 217, 373
Torata (Perú/Chile), 35
Toro (Argentine merchant ship), 101; (Paraguayan tug), 360
Toro Submarino (Peruvian navy submarine), 36–37, 346
Torpedo: possesses minimal range, 12; spar type planned (1866), 30; Lay type fired by *Huáscar* (1879), 33; Lay type torpedo brigade at Callao (1880), 35; Lay type fitted to *Toro Submarino* (1880), 36; automobile type appears (1880s), 46; Chile adopts Whiteheads (1880s), 347; *Blanco Enclada* torpedoed (1891), 64–66; Argentine torpedo base rebels (1893), 57; Brazilian navy takes warheads out of storage (1893), 68; Sims-Edison type on dynamite fleet (1893), 73; *Aquidabã* torpedoed (1894), 74–76; U.S. torpedo tubes provided for Argentine dreadnoughts (1910), 83; torpedoes armed following *São Paulo* rebellion (1924), 79; used during Malvinas War (1982), 245, 249, 251, 262–63, 267–68
Torpedo boats, 46, 48, 64, 72–76, 347
Torres, Carlos (Chilean navy), 85, 355
Torres Causano (Ecuador/Perú), 120
Tortuguera, Battle of, 38
Toteco (Mexican merchant tanker), 368
Tracker-type aircraft, 179, 197–98, 238, 242, 249–50, 268–69
Trajano (Brazilian navy steam corvette), 351–52
Trejo, Hugo (Venezuelan army), 218, 220
Trelew, Argentina, 255
Tres Bocas, Argentina, 19, 23
Trinidad (Spanish sail transport), 6
Trinidade Island, 305–6, 336–37, 356

INDEX 439

Trinidad Island, 122, 151, 155, 306
Triumph (British navy destroyer), 349
Triunfo (Spanish navy warship), 29
Trojan-type aircraft, 331
Trucco, Manuel (president of Chile), 109, 114
Trujillo, Honduras, 313–14
Trujillo, Peru, 350
Trujillo, Rafael Leonidas (president of the Dominican Republic), 222–23, 311
Tucumán (Argentine merchant ship), 336–37; (Argentine navy destroyer), 143
Tucumán Province, Argentina, 57
Tumbledown, 285–87
Tupi (Brazilian navy submarine), 136–37, 153, 160
Tuquí Air Field, Chile, 112
Turiamo, Venezuela, 220
Tuscania (Italian merchant tanker), 330
Tuxpan (Mexican merchant tanker), 167, 330
Tuxpan, México, 167
Tuyuty, Battle of, 23
Type 209 submarine, 262, 268, 362
Typhoon (British navy tug), 334–35
Tyree, John A. (U.S. Navy), 129

U-37 (German navy submarine), 367
U-94 (German navy submarine), 365
U-106 (German navy submarine), 167
U-124 (German navy submarine), 155
U-126 (German navy submarine), 170
U-128 (German navy submarine), 366
U-129 (German navy submarine), 167, 169
U-154 (German navy submarine), 155, 169
U-155 (German navy submarine), 365
U-161 (German navy submarine), 366
U-164 (German navy submarine), 366
U-166 (German navy submarine), 170
U-171 (German navy submarine), 167–68
U-176 (German navy submarine), 169
U-185 (German navy submarine), 158
U-199 (German navy submarine), 366
U-201 (German navy submarine), 367
U-202 (German navy submarine), 367
U-432 (German navy submarine), 365
U-502 (German navy submarine), 152
U-505 (German navy submarine), 169
U-507 (German navy submarine), 152, 366
U-510 (German navy submarine), 155, 158
U-513 (German navy submarine), 366
U-516 (German navy submarine), 169
U-518 (German navy submarine), 158
U-530 (German navy submarine), 163
U-552 (German navy submarine), 167
U-564 (German navy submarine), 167
U-590 (German navy submarine), 366
U-591 (German navy submarine), 366
U-598 (German navy submarine), 366
U-662 (German navy submarine), 366
U-861 (German navy submarine), 158, 366
U-977 (German navy submarine), 163
União (Brazilian merchant ship), 352
Unión (Haitian navy schooner), 38, 41
Unión (Peruvian navy steam corvette), 30, 34, 36–37, 345
Unión Cívica (Argentina), 54, 57
UNITAS, 174–76, 197, 233, 288, 369
United Nations, 177–78, 217, 382
United States, 4–5, 9, 11–18, 27, 31, 36, 39–41, 44, 46, 47, 49–50, 69, 71, 83, 88–92, 94, 96–102, 111–12, 128–29, 131–41, 144–46, 150–51, 160–64, 166–83, 189–91, 194, 197–98, 221, 234, 244, 247, 253, 262, 304–19, 324–26, 346, 352, 368, 370, 382, 385
Uranus (Brazilian armed merchant ship), 74
Urdaneta, Venezuela, 220
Ureta, Ernesto (Argentine air force), 280
Uribe, Luis (Chilean navy), 47
Urquiza, Justo José (president of Argentina), 18, 305
Uruguay, 17–22, 79, 82, 92, 104, 142, 144–45, 147–48, 161, 179, 188, 201, 319, 325, 355, 365
Uruguay (Argentine merchant ship), 367; (Argentine navy school ship), 45; (Uruguayan navy training ship), 147, 365
Uruguayan merchant marine, 104
Uruguayan navy: warship seized by Argentine navy (1863), 19; intervenes against rebellious Argentine navy (1890), 56; establishes aviation (1925–80s), 201; attempts to enforce neutrality (1939), 147; holds ASW exercises with United States (1950s–80s), 174–76; offers ship for Cuban quarantine (1962), 179
Uruguay River, 3, 19–20, 22
"Urutu" armored car, 190, 371
U.S. Army, 15, 164
U.S. coast guard, 368
U.S. Congress, 171–72, 175
U.S. Department of State, 135–37
U.S. Marine Corps, 40, 189, 191–93, 346, 305–19
U.S. merchant marine, 75

U.S. Naval War College, 176
U.S. Navy: ranks (mid-nineteenth and twentieth centuries), 293; seizes Argentine warships (1844), 18; war with México (1846–48), 15–16; expedition against Paraguay (1859), 18–19; seizes Mexican warships (1860), 16; transports Haitian rebel (1865), 39; confronts Brazilian warships (1866), 23; peace talks held on *Lackawanna* (1880), 36; inferior to Chilean navy (1880s), 11; takes possession of the *Itata* (1891), 47, 64; challenges rebellious Brazilian navy (1893), 73; *Baltimore* crew attacked (1893), 47; defeats Spanish fleet (1898), 8; Chile seeks to buy warships (1901), 50; guarantees success of Panamanian revolution (1903), 40; supplies torpedo tubes to Argentina (1910), 83; approves instructors for Cuba (1916), 98; Pacific Fleet visits Brazil (1917), 91; trains Argentine in submarines (1917), 140; patrols South Atlantic (1917–18), 92; sends mission to Brazil (1917–18), 127; uses Cuban ports (1917–18), 78; sends mission to Perú (1920–40), 127, 131–33; trains Chilean aviators (1930s), 163; sends advisor to Colombia (1932), 140–41; sends mission to Ecuador (1940), 141; sends mission to Venezuela (1940), 141; meets with most Latin American navies (1940–41), 145; seeks Chilean warships (1941), 164; warships go to Brazil (1941), 151–52; patrols shipping lanes off Brazil (1942), 152; convoying established off Brazil (1942–45), 155–58; aids Cuban navy (1942–45), 168–69; trains Brazilian navy in ASW (1943–45), 160; escorts Brazilian troops to Europe (1944), 160; mutiny (1944), 357–58; emphasizes ASW (1950s–80), 174–76; trains Brazilians in carrier operations (1960s), 197; operations during Cuban quarantine (1962), 178–80; work stoppage (1972), 358; mission asked to leave Brazil (1977), 172
U.S. Navy Bureau of Construction and Repair, 136
U.S. Navy Bureau of Navigation, 50
U.S. Navy Bureau of Ordnance, 83
U.S. Navy General Board, 50
U.S. Navy Office of Naval Intelligence, 50, 64–66

V-105 (German navy torpedo boat), 98
V-106 (German navy torpedo boat), 98

Valdes Peninsula, 192
Valdivia-Corral, Chile, 2, 6
Vale, Edmundo Jordão Amorim do (Brazilian navy), 159
Valencia, Venezuela, 227, 377
Valentine (French merchant ship), 103
Valenzuela Labra, Matías (Chilean navy), 378
Valesia (German merchant ship), 355
Valle, Roberto (Chilean navy), 114
Valley Forge (U.S. Navy aircraft carrier), 311
Valotta, Gerardo (Argentine navy), 57, 350
Valparaíso, Chile, 5–6, 12, 17, 28, 30, 47, 59, 62, 64–66, 76, 85, 102–3, 107, 109, 111, 114, 199, 233, 306–7, 345, 348, 351, 378
Valparaíso (Chilean navy dreadnought), 322; (Chilean navy ironclad), 31, 346
Vampire-type aircraft, 218, 230
Van Voorhis (U.S. Navy destroyer), 175
Varela, Benigno (Argentine navy), 368
Varese (Italian navy armored cruiser), 48–49, 298
Vargara Donoso, José Francisco (Chilean foreign minister), 51
Vargas, Getulio (president of Brazil), 79, 151–52, 159
Vargas Prada, Félix (Peruvian navy), 116
Vázquez, Julio A. O. (Argentine navy), 180
Vázquez, Luis C. (Argentine navy), 381, 384
Vegara Montero, Carlos (Chilean army), 109, 111–12
Vegara Montero, Ramón (Chilean air force), 109
Velarde, Jorge (Peruvian navy), 33
Velasco (Spanish navy destroyer), 165
Veloz (Peruvian navy armed launch), 120
Vencedor del Alamo (Mexican navy brig), 14
Venerable (British navy aircraft carrier), 332
Venezia (Italian merchant steamer), 318
Venezuela, 3, 41, 89, 145, 170, 174, 177–80, 193, 201, 217–32, 296, 319, 325, 355, 369–70
Venezuelan air force, 201, 217–32
Venezuelan army, 217–32, 374
Venezuelan marine corps, 189, 193, 217–32, 371, 374
Venezuelan national guard, 217–32, 374–75
Venezuelan navy: during wars of independence (1812–23), 3–5; warships seized (1902), 41, 320; develops aviation

(1922–80s), 201; receives U.S. mission (1940), 141; during World War II, 170; holds ASW exercises with United States (1950s–80s), 174–76; attempts to change government (1958 and 1962), 202, 217–32, 296; participates in Cuban quarantine (1962), 178–80
Vengeance (British navy aircraft carrier), 197, 332
Venom-type aircraft, 218
Venus (Brazilian merchant ship), 351
Veracruz (Mexican merchant tanker), 368
Vera Cruz (Mexican navy gunboat), 349
Veracruz, México, 2–4, 13–16, 164–65, 168, 315, 344
Vera Cruz (Panamanian merchant ship), 368
Verde River, 124
Versailles Peace Conference of 1919, 97–98
Vertieres (Haitian navy cutter), 233
Viana Lama, Luis L. (Venezuelan air force), 375
Viceroyalties, 27, 44
Vichy government, 150
Vickers-type aircraft, 112, 199, 359
Vickers (Armstrong, England), 85, 130, 139, 349
Victoria (Argentine merchant tanker), 162, 367; (German navy steam corvette), 312; (Venezuelan navy corvette), 369
Victoria R (Argentine rebel tug), 58–59
Vicuña, Ramón (president of Chile), 28
Videla (Chilean navy destroyer), 107, 113
Vigor (Italian merchant tanker), 330
Villa, Francisco "Pancho" (Mexican revolutionary), 164
Villa del Salto (Uruguayan navy warship), 20
Villa Montes (Bolivia/Paraguay), 126
Villarino (Argentine transport), 55
Villegaignon, Fort, 68
Vineta (German navy warship), 41, 312
Vita (Spanish yacht), 167
Vital de Oliveira (Brazilian navy auxiliary), 158, 160
Vitória (Brazilian transport), 351–52
Vitriones (Bolivia/Paraguay), 126
Vixen-type aircraft, 112
Volgelgesang, C. T. (U.S. Navy), 134–35
Voorchees, Philip F. (U.S. Navy), 18
Vought-type aircraft, 199, 331
Vuelta de Obligado, Battle of, 18, 304
Vultee-type aircraft, 165

Wachusett (U.S. Navy steam sloop), 305
Wakama (German merchant ship), 150

Walker, William (U.S. filibuster), 40, 316
Wandenkolk, Eduardo (Brazilian navy), 67
Wannalancet (U.S. Navy tug), 378
War of the Pacific, 11, 31–37, 42, 44, 46, 59, 61–62, 129–30, 142, 185, 192–93, 345–47, 350
War of the Triple Alliance, 19–27, 129, 188, 193
Warrior (British navy aircraft carrier), 194, 332
Wars of independence, 1–8, 17, 192
Warspite (British navy armored cruiser), 61
War with Spain, 29, 31, 192
Washburn, Charles A. (U.S. ambassador to Paraguay), 23
Washington Naval Armament Limitation Treaty of 1922, 112, 137
Wasp-type helicopter, 247
Water Witch (U.S. Navy steamer), 18, 318
Wave (Mexican navy steamer), 16
Wessex-type helicopter, 247, 385
Westaskawin (Canadian navy corvette), 369
Westland-type aircraft, 196
Wharton (Texas navy warship), 15
Whitehead torpedo. *See* Torpedo
Wibault-type aircraft, 112, 359
Widgeon-type helicopter, 196
Willemstad, Curaçao, 122
William Gaston (U.S. merchant ship), 366
Williams, Phillip (U.S. Navy), 133
Williams Rebolledo, Juan (Chilean navy), 30, 32–33
Wilson, Henry L. (U.S. minister to Chile), 50, 348
Winchester rifles, 119
Wireless Ridge, 285
Woodward, John (British navy), 385
World War I: 86, 88–104, 128–29, 131, 134–35, 138–40, 150–53, 354–57
World War II: 128–29, 133, 137, 141–70, 172–74, 180, 183, 188–89, 191, 193–95, 199, 201–2, 208, 326

Xiqueiros, David Alfaro (Mexican soldier), 368

Yalu Battle, 349
Ybapobo, Paraguay, 204–5
Yehuin (Argentine merchant ship), 339
Ygurey (Paraguayan navy gunboat), 26
Yolande (French merchant ship), 165, 368
Yorke Beach West, Malvinas, 239
Ytororó, Battle of, 26
Yucatán, 13–15, 77, 168
Yucatecan navy: war with México (1842–43), 14–15

Yucateco (Yucatecan navy brigantine), 15
Yungai, Battle of, 29

Zacatecas (Mexican navy gunboat), 350
Zavala (Texas navy steamer), 14
Zerpa Tovar, Juan Ramón (Venezuelan army), 227
Zulia (Venezuelan navy destroyer), 179–80, 222, 230–32, 370, 376
Zuloaga, Félix (president of México), 16
Zulu (British navy frigate), 312

1 de Mayo (Argentine navy transport), 162
9 de Julio (Argentine navy coastal battleship), 297
9 de Julio (Argentine navy protected cruiser), 46, 57, 297, 350
9 de Julio (Argentine navy light cruiser), 212–17
9 de Julio (Argentine navy schooner), 304
17 de Octubre (Argentine navy light cruiser), 212–17, 374
18 de Marzo (Mexican merchant tanker), 367
22 de Decembre (Haitian navy corvette), 39
25 de Mayo (Argentine/Paraguayan navy gunboat), 20, 25
25 de Mayo (Argentine navy gunboat), 304
25 de Mayo (Argentine navy protected cruiser), 46, 297
25 de Mayo (Argentine navy heavy cruiser), 143, 183, 194
25 de Mayo (Argentine navy aircraft carrier), 185–86, 195, 236, 238, 242, 248–49, 256, 258, 332, 383
27 de Febrero (Dominican privateer/navy brigantine), 38